# Contemporary Literature, 1970 to Present

# Research Guide
## to American Literature

RESEARCH GUIDE
TO AMERICAN LITERATURE

# Contemporary Literature, 1970 to Present

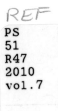

Linda Trinh Moser
*Missouri State University*
*and*
Kathryn West
*Bellarmine University*

A BRUCCOLI CLARK LAYMAN BOOK

Facts On File
*An imprint of Infobase Publishing*

**Research Guide to American Literature: Contemporary Literature, 1970 to Present**
Copyright © 2010 by Kathryn West and Linda Trinh Moser

Facts On File, Inc.
An imprint of Infobase Publishing
132 West 31st Street
New York NY 10001

**Library of Congress Cataloging-in-Publication Data**
Research guide to American literature. — New ed.
    p. cm.
"A Bruccoli Clark Layman book."
Includes bibliographical references and index.
ISBN 978-0-8160-7861-5 (v. 1 : acid-free paper)—ISBN 978-0-8160-7862-2 (v. 2 : acid-free paper)—ISBN 978-0-8160-7863-9 (v. 3 : acid-free paper)—ISBN 978-0-8160-7864-6 (v. 4 : acid-free paper)—ISBN 978-0-8160-7865-3 (v. 5 : acid-free paper)—ISBN 978-0-8160-7866-0 (v. 6 : acid-free paper)—ISBN 978-0-8160-7867-7 (v. 7 : acid-free paper) 1. American literature—Research—Methodology—Handbooks, manuals, etc. 2. American literature—History and criticism. 3. Canon (Literature) I. Franklin, Benjamin, 1939– II. Vietto, Angela III. Habich, Robert D., 1951– IV. Quirk, Tom, 1946– V. Scharnhorst, Gary. VI. Anderson, George Parker, 1957– VII. Cusatis, John. VIII. Moser, Linda Trinh, 1964– IX. West, Kathryn, 1962– X. Facts on File, Inc.
PS51.R47 2010
810.7'2—dc22
                              2009047815

Text design by Erika K. Arroyo
Composition by Bruccoli Clark Layman
Cover printed by Art Print, Taylor, PA
Book printed and bound by Maple Press, York, PA
Date printed: June 2010
Printed in the United States of America

10 9 8 7 6 5 4 3 2 1

This book is printed on acid-free paper.

*For Adam*
*For Miles Trieu and Ryan Trinh*

# Contents

# Acknowledgments

We are indebted to many colleagues and friends who provided us with inspiration, support and helpful feedback throughout the writing process.

Thanks to John Boyd of Bellarmine University Library for generous and invaluable assistance with Interlibrary loan. John Gatton and Annette Powell have offered the kind of moral support, inspirational conversation, and critical insight of the best possible colleagues. Chris Chism, Pat Holt, and Michelle Trotta have sustained me with support, conversation, and insight, as well as friendship and love beyond measure. Thanks to Sally West for more than I can express, and to Jack West for long-distance moral support and never-swerving faith in me.

Much appreciation to colleagues in the English Department of Missouri State University, especially Keri Franklin, whose friendship I could never do without. Thanks to WD Blackmon and Kris Sutliff for not noticing my absence at meetings and to Barb Gressel and Wilma Catlin for their constant support and friendship. For their perspectives on American poets, thanks also to Jane Hoogestraat and Marcus Cafagña. It is an honor to work with MSU graduate students, who are always enthusiastic about learning and reading; many thanks to Jaimie Young, Isaiah Vianese, Steve Rucker, D. Gilson, Magi Smith, Jake Helton, and students in ENG 700. Melanie Cox's administrative help and biographical research are also much appreciated. Love and gratitude to my family, especially Patrick who brings me joy every day.

# Contributors

# Series Introduction

*Research Guide to American Literature* is a series of handbooks for students and teachers that recommends strategies for studying literary topics and frequently taught literary works and authors. The rationale for the series is that successful study is predicated on asking the right questions and then devising a logical strategy for addressing them. The process of responsible literary investigation begins with facts and usually ends with opinions. The value of those opinions depends on the ability of the reader to gather useful information, to consider it in context, to interpret it logically, and finally to decide what the interpretation means outside the confines of the literary work. Often the answers to questions a sophisticated reader asks about a literary topic are subjective, involving a reader's perception of an author's or a character's motive; always the search for the answer to a meaningful question involves a process of self-education and, in the best of circumstances, self-awareness.

*RGAL* is intended as a resource to assist readers in identifying questions to ask about literature. The seven volumes in this series are organized chronologically, corresponding to generally accepted literary periods. Each volume follows this general pattern:

Part I provides the social and historical context for a literary period, explaining its historical boundaries, describing the nature of the literary output of the time, placing the literature in its social and historical contexts, identifying literary influences, and tracing the evolution of critical approaches.

Part II comprises ten study guides on general themes or topics related to the period, organized alphabetically. Each guide first provides necessary background information, then suggests questions or research topics that might be fruitfully considered, along with specific primary and secondary works that students will find useful. Each guide also includes an annotated checklist of recommended secondary works and capsule identifications of people mentioned.

Part III comprises some thirty study guides for particular literary works or authors, organized alphabetically by the author's name. Each guide begins with a brief overview of the author's career to provide context, and then suggests some half a dozen topics for discussion and research, with advice about how to begin investigating the topic. These topics are meant to facilitate classroom discussion as well as to suggest interesting ideas for research papers. Each guide includes an annotated checklist of recommended secondary works.

Part IV is an annotated general bibliography recommending the most useful general works of literary history, literary criticism, and literary reference pertinent to the period.

Part V is a glossary of terms used in the volume.

A keyword index is included in each volume.

The purpose of *RGAL* is not to tell students what literature means but to help them determine the meaning for themselves by asking significant questions and seeking answers diligently and thoughtfully. That is how learning that matters takes place. The method is as old as Socrates.

—*Richard Layman*

# Part I
# Overview

# Boundaries of the Period

To differentiate them from the forms, modes, sensibilities, and concerns of earlier periods, many of the literary works published from 1970 through the first decade of the twenty-first century have been described with labels such as *postconfessional, postfeminist, postracial, postcolonial, poststructural, Postmodernist,* and even *post-Postmodernist.* The common prefix, however, can be misleading. Attached to *feminist* and *racial,* for example, it gives the impression that gender and racial equality have been achieved. *Postcolonial,* too, is misleading: although a nation may be legally independent, it may still be subordinated culturally and economically to another. The writings of many American Indians and Native Hawaiians particularly challenge the idea that colonialism has ended. Even the terms that refer to form suggest a discontinuity of style and theme that is not always helpful or accurate. Postconfessional poets, for example, employ the self-revelatory and personal mode of their predecessors, and Postmodernist and post-Postmodernist writers, like Modernists, emphasize self-consciousness, fragmentation of narrative structures, ambiguity, and dehumanized and decentered subjects. Rather than making a definitive break with the styles and concerns of the previous eras, literature of this period continues to explore themes and ideas related to identity and reality. The nature of that identity and reality have changed, however, leading writers to explore representational modes that include both traditional and innovative elements.

"The world is here," Ishmael Reed declares in the essay "America: The Multinational Society" in his *Writin' Is Fightin': Thirty-Seven Years of Boxing on Paper* (1988). Contemporary American literature, he says, is "a place where the cultures of the world crisscross." The essay argues for a broader meaning of American identity and reflects on the "blurring of cultural styles" that marks everyday life in the United States. This multicultural environment, along with technological advances, philosophical and scientific developments, and changes in the social order, have transformed the ways Americans view and engage with the world at home and abroad. This transformation is reflected in literature, where previous notions about reality and how to represent it are changing. Accordingly, contemporary literature is characterized by diversity, proliferation, and fluidity. Works published from 1970 onward represent many styles, themes, forms, and modes of delivery. Voices from across the spectrum of American experience offer perspectives not often—or ever—heard in earlier eras of American literature. Writers of various races, ethnicities, social classes, sexual orientations, and geographic regions have reenergized and expanded American writing.

The proliferation and diversity of cultural perspectives are accompanied by the use of literary forms in new and imaginative ways. Writers continue to work within the traditional forms of poetry, short story, novel, drama, essay, and memoir but also develop and experiment with new and combined forms, including the short-story cycle, the composite novel, New Journalism, creative nonfiction, the graphic novel, and the comic book. As genre and identity have come to be understood in more fluid terms, distinctions between high, or elite, and popular, or mass, culture have disintegrated. Popular culture has become a subject of serious study for academics and a model for writers such as Michael Chabon, Joyce Carol Oates, Robert Pinsky, Don DeLillo, and David Foster Wallace, all of whom incorporate themes, images, and structures from genre fiction into literary fiction. The contemporary era is one of innovative, ethnically diverse writing that offers new insights into previously underrepresented populations. The age-old pleasure of storytelling is strong in this era, perhaps more so than in those immediately preceding it, as writers meet the challenge of representing "the world" that is America.

While any period demarcation is somewhat arbitrary, several events in 1970 heralded the concerns that have preoccupied much of the era. The publication of Studs Terkel's nonfiction *Hard Times: An Oral History of the Great Depression* helped to inspire awareness of class as it shapes people's lives. *Essence* magazine, aimed at an African American readership, was founded in 1970. Novels published by African American women in 1970 include Toni Morrison's *The Bluest Eye,* Alice Walker's *The Third Life of Grange Copeland,* and Maya Angelou's *I Know Why the Caged Bird Sings.* African American women were also well represented in poetry, with Nikki Giovanni, Audre Lorde, and Sonia Sanchez all publishing collections in 1970. Along with the founding of the Feminist Press, 1970 brought several key works of the feminist movement: Shulamith Firestone's *The Dialectic of Sex: The Case for Feminist Revolution,* Germaine Greer's *The Female Eunuch,* and Robin Morgan's anthology *Sisterhood Is Powerful.* The prolific Oates received the 1970 National Book Award for her fourth novel, *them* (1969). *One Hundred Years of Solitude,* the English translation of the Colombian author Gabriel García Márquez's *Cien años de soledad* (1967), appeared in 1970; in the following decades elements of García Márquez's magical realism, intertwining the supernatural with the mundane, showed up in the works of many North American authors.

# Dominant Genres and Literary Forms

The contemporary period offers such diversity in genres and forms that is difficult to identify any as "dominant." The novel continues to be popular, with writers such as John Barth, Joyce Carol Oates, Philip Roth, and John Updike, who were working in previous decades, still making important contributions after 1970. Postmodernist novelists experiment with narrative form, challenging traditional fiction genres; Richard Brautigan's *The Hawkline Monster: A Gothic Western* (1974), for example, combines elements of Southern Gothic with tropes of the Western. Other novelists play with the boundaries between fiction and nonfiction. In *My Life As a Man* (1974) Roth creates the autobiographical Jewish writer Peter Tarnopol, who recounts his life in the second part of the novel, "My True Story." Tarnopol's short stories, two of which make up the first part of the novel, "Useful Fictions," feature Nathan Zuckerman, a name Roth uses for a character in later novels, and parody Roth's novel *Portnoy's Complaint* (1969). E. L. Doctorow's *The Book of Daniel* (1971), *Ragtime* (1975), *Billy Bathgate* (1989), and *Homer & Langley* (2009) combine facts from twentieth-century history with fictional details. On the basis of a brief account of Margaret Garner's failed 1856 attempt to escape from slavery, Morrison imagines Garner's life in *Beloved* (1987).

Other writers, shaped by different cultures and experiences, have transformed the contemporary novel in other ways. Maxine Hong Kingston's *Tripmaster Monkey: His Fake Book* (1989), Oscar Hijuelos's *Mambo Kings Play Songs of Love* (1989), and Chang-rae Lee's *A Gesture Life* (1999) draw on the immigrant experience to depict the ways in which individuals lose, maintain, or transform their cultural identities. Some novelists address the ways identity is complicated by sexuality. As homosexuality becomes more visible in mainstream society, writers such as Michael Cunningham find more recognition and readers; his *The Hours* (1998) won the Pulitzer Prize. Other important writers on gay and lesbian themes include Rita Mae Brown, Paula Gunn Allen, Sarah Schulman, Armistead Maupin, and Edmund White.

The short story has enjoyed a resurgence in this period. Following a slide in status that accompanied the rising popularity of television and a decline in magazines featuring short fiction that had begun in the 1950s, short-story collections began again to appear on best-seller lists. Academic literary journals such as the *Sewanee Review, Kenyon Review,* and *Southern Review,* along with mass-market magazines such as *The New Yorker, Esquire,* and *Harper's,* helped to bring about the change. Fostered by Gordon Lish, fiction editor at *Esquire* and then at Alfred A. Knopf, Inc., Raymond Carver paved the way for writers of stories about working-class lives; many of these writers were labeled "Dirty Realists" or "minimalists." Important collections include Andre Dubus's *Adultery and Other Choices* (1977), Russell Banks's *Trailerpark* (1981), Ann Beattie's *The Burning House* (1982), Richard Ford's *Rock Springs* (1987), and Bobbie Ann Mason's *Shiloh and Other Stories* (1982). Other writers known for their short stories include Oates, Dorothy Allison, Annie Proulx, and Pam Houston. A recent development is the emergence of the extremely short story. Generally consisting of no more than a thousand words, they are called "sudden" or "flash" fiction; the latter term is the title of a 1992 anthology of such works edited by James Thomas, Denise Thomas, and Tom Hazuka. The abbreviated nature of these stories makes them particularly well suited for the Internet.

American poetry in this period is produced by a more diverse group of poets in terms of class, gender, race, ethnicity, and sexuality than in earlier times. Thematically it has been described as "postconfessional"—that is, nonautobiographical—but it continues the emphasis on individual experience and expression of the confessional poetry of previous decades. Major figures, including Lorde, Mark Doty, Louise Glück, Jorie Graham, Robert Pinsky, Sharon Olds, Cathy Song, and Natasha Trethewey, employ the personal in poems that exhibit varying degrees of movement toward larger themes and various levels of accessibility and difficulty. Their styles resist traditional classifications: Agha Shahid Ali uses the *ghazal,* an ancient Persian form; Reed, Michael S. Harper, and Yusef Komunyakaa echo the rhythms of jazz and blues; and American Indian oratory can be heard in the work of Joy Harjo, Simon J. Ortiz, and Louise Erdrich.

Like the short story, poetry has enjoyed a resurgence in popularity in the contemporary period as poets have attempted to make their work more accessible and relevant and to promote social and environmental justice. Poets have protested U.S. military actions and advocated peace during the Vietnam War and the wars in Iraq and Afghanistan; and they have expressed hope and patriotism in poems commissioned for presidential inaugurations—Angelou's "On the Pulse of Morning" for Bill Clinton in 1993, Miller Williams's "Of History and Hope" for Clinton in 1997, and Elizabeth Alexander's "Praise Song for the Day" for Barack Obama in 2009. Several poets laureate have worked to "promote poetry"—a responsibility of the position—by making it an everyday presence and pleasure in American life. The anthology *Poetry 180: A Turning Back to Poetry* (2003), edited by Billy Collins, provides a poem for each day of the school year. Pinsky, another poet laureate, founded the "Favorite Poem Project," in which eighteen thousand Americans of all ages submitted their favorite poems. Other efforts to make poetry more available to the general public include audio and video recordings and a proliferation of websites maintained by professional organizations. Open readings, poetry "slams," and community writing groups and workshops organized by bookstores, coffee shops, and public libraries have also helped to move poetry out of academic institutions and into everyday life.

Drama since 1970 has benefited from the birth of Off Broadway in the 1950s and Off Off Broadway and the expansion of regional theaters in the 1960s. Freed from the expense of production on Broadway and the pressure it exacts to produce commercially successful plays, these venues allowed for more experimentation in both form and content, including fuller representation of previously marginalized groups, and led to greater breadth in American theatrical offerings. Broadway veterans from the previous era continued to see new works into production after 1970. Neil Simon, who had a string of commercially successful plays in the 1960s such as *Barefoot in the Park* (1963) and *The Odd Couple* (1965), made a comeback in the 1980s with his autobiographical trilogy *Brighton Beach Memoirs* (1983), *Biloxi Blues* (1985), and *Broadway Bound* (1986). Edward Albee, whose Broadway career began in 1960 with *The Zoo Story* and included *Who's Afraid of Virginia Woolf?* (1962), received Pulitzer Prizes for *Seascape* (1975) and *Three Tall Women* (1994). One of the most important dramatists of the contemporary period, Sam Shepard, has premiered his experimental plays in Off Broadway, Off Off Broadway, and regional theaters. Realism has not disappeared from American drama; David Mamet's *American Buffalo* (1976) and *Glengarry Glen Ross* (1982) employ realistic settings and mundane characters whose speech mimics everyday conversation. Their use of language that is fragmented and sprinkled with clichés, however, calls attention to the superficiality of defining the American Dream and masculinity in terms of money. Elements that break the realism of David Henry Hwang's *M Butterfly* (1988)—the main character directly addressing the audience and the use of flashbacks—nevertheless convey psychological realism and problems related to racism and imperialism. The presence of a ghost in August Wilson's *The Piano Lesson* (1987) is not mere fancy but suggests an African-centered cultural perspective that challenges that of mainstream America. Since 1970 playwrights such as Reed, Frank Chin, María Irene Fornés, Tony Kushner, Marsha Norman, Ntozake Shange, Anna Deavere Smith, Paula Vogel, Wendy Wasserstein, and Lanford Wilson have expanded American theater to include representations of identities previously excluded on the basis of class, race, gender, and sexual orientation.

Truman Capote's "nonfiction novel" *In Cold Blood* (1965), the "New Journalism" pioneered in the 1960s by Tom Wolfe, and Hunter S. Thompson's "Gonzo Journalism"—a term he coined in 1970—led to the development of "creative nonfiction." Combining factual reporting with narrative techniques borrowed from fiction, creative nonfiction features multiple points of view, including first-person, scene-by-scene construction; an emphasis on "color" details to draw out the character of people and places; close observation; and extensive use of dialogue. Writers who employ these techniques in their journalistic works include Joan Didion, Norman Mailer, Barbara Ehrenreich, John McPhee, and Gail Sheehy, while Susan Cheever, Adam Gopnik, Andrew X. Pham, and Tobias Wolff use them to shape their memoirs. As Lee Gutkind explains on the website of the literary journal *Creative Nonfiction*, these "writers do not make things up; they make ideas and information that already exist more interesting and, often, more accessible."

The use of creative elements in nonfiction has called attention to the ethics of mixing fiction and fact. Delivering a talk at Goucher College in 2003, Vivian Gornick shocked her audience when she admitted inventing scenes and using composite characters in *Fierce Attachments* (1987), an account of her relationship with her mother. Her former *Village Voice* editor admonished her, as did other writers and readers. The criticism she has received, however, does not compare to that aimed at James Frey after it was revealed that he had embellished and even invented aspects of *A Million Little Pieces* (2003), his "memoir" of drug addiction. His failure to emphasize what he remembered rather than what he imagined led to the loss of his literary agent; a televised face-to-face rebuke by Oprah Winfrey, whose promotion of the book on her show had led to its best-seller status; and a legal settlement entitling a refund to readers who felt defrauded by the book's claim to be nonfiction. Writers and readers will continue to engage in discussions related to accuracy, creative expression, responsibility, and genre distinctions as creative nonfiction continues to be studied and developed in the twenty-first century.

# Historical and Social Context

In the wake of the counter-culture movement of the 1960s many Americans became increasingly distrustful of the federal government. Investigative reporting in print and on television, along with photojournalism, contributed to the public's lack of confidence in official reports and rhetoric about government actions at home and abroad. An economic downturn and rising inflation in the 1970s ended a period of growth and prosperity that had begun after World War II, further threatening the confidence and sense of well-being of many Americans. The increasingly unpopular war in Vietnam led to protest marches and sit-ins, many on college campuses, across the nation. President Richard M. Nixon had promised to end U.S. involvement in Vietnam when running for office in 1968, but his decision to invade Cambodia, announced on 30 April 1970, led to the public perception that the war was escalating. On 4 May 1970 Ohio National Guard troops fired on a group of unarmed students at Kent State University in Ohio; four died, and nine others were wounded. Nixon issued a statement describing the deaths at Kent State as "tragic and unfortunate" but also placed blame on the antiwar demonstrators. Through his press secretary the president announced that "This should remind us all once again that when dissent turns to violence, it invites tragedy." Ten days after the Kent State shootings, police fired on students demonstrating at Jackson State University in Mississippi, killing two and wounding twelve. Photographs of dead and wounded students galvanized public sentiment against the war, and more than nine hundred colleges and universities were shut down by student strikes. The last American ground troops departed on 29 March 1973, and the war ended with the fall of Saigon to North Vietnamese troops on 30 April 1975.

Nixon had become a symbol of political corruption in 1973 when details of his involvement in covering up the break-in at the Democratic National Committee headquarters in the Watergate hotel and office complex in Washington, D.C., came to light. To avoid impeachment, Nixon resigned in 1974—the first U.S. president to do so. Carl Bernstein and Bob Woodward described the events that led to the Watergate cover-up and Nixon's resignation in *All the President's Men* (1974). Vice President Gerald R. Ford assumed the presidency and later pardoned Nixon of all charges related to the Watergate case. James Earl "Jimmy" Carter, the relatively unknown governor of Georgia, was elected in the 1976 over Ford largely because he seemed untainted by Washington, D.C., politics. During his single term the nation suffered shortages and rising prices for fuel; inflation; high interest rates; a growing national deficit; and the Iran hostage crisis. These events further eroded many Americans' faith in government and eclipsed Carter's accomplishments: his promotion of international human rights; his key role in the Camp David Accords, which led to a peace treaty between Egypt and Israel; and his efforts to secure the release of the fifty-two American hostages held by Iranian militants at the American embassy in Tehran, who returned home the day Carter's successor, Ronald Reagan, took office.

In response to problems at home and abroad, many Americans turned inward and became preoccupied with self-awareness, a trend that inspired Tom Wolfe's description of the 1970s as the "me decade." In contrast to the activism of the 1960s, Americans focused on improving themselves as individuals rather than as a society. But while therapy, self-help, fitness, and diet books and programs become extremely popular in the 1970s, Americans did not abandon their efforts to secure environmental, social, and political justice. The first Earth Day was celebrated, and the Clean Air Act was passed, in 1970; the Endangered Species Act became law in 1973. Civil-rights groups continued to fight for racial equality, supporting affirmative-action programs to help minorities gain greater access to education, jobs, and professions. In 1973 members of the American Indian Movement (AIM) occupied the town of Wounded Knee, South Dakota, for seventy-one days to protest poverty on the Pine Ridge Reservation. The gay-liberation movement gained momentum in the 1970s, as well, challenging stereotypes of gays and lesbians while calling for equity. In 1970 about five thousand gay men and lesbians marched in New York City on the first anniversary of the Stonewall Riots, when the patrons of a Greenwich Village gay bar had fought back against a police raid. Women also continued to push for equal rights. In 1972 Title IX was added to the Civil Rights Act of 1964, forbidding discrimination on the basis of sex by institutions receiving federal funds; the principal effect was to ensure equal funding and opportunity for female athletes at colleges and universities. The following year the U.S. Supreme Court's *Roe v. Wade* decision made it legal nationwide for women to choose abortion for any reason in the first trimester of pregnancy, although states could impose restrictions in later stages. In 1972 the U.S. Senate and House of Representatives passed the Equal Rights Amendment (ERA), a proposed twenty-seventh amendment to the Constitution that would guarantee that equal rights under federal, state, and local law could not be denied on account of sex. ERA opponents claimed that the amendment would send women into combat, deny them the right to be financially supported by their husbands, eliminate separate public restrooms for men and women, grant more power to the federal government at the expense of states and individuals, and legalize homosexual marriages. By the 30 June 1982 deadline it remained three states short of the thirty-eight needed for ratification. Nevertheless, Americans in the 1980s witnessed several "firsts" for women: the appointment of Sandra Day O'Connor to the U.S. Supreme Court in 1981, astronaut Sally Ride's 1983 trip into space, and Democrat Geraldine Ferraro's vice presidential nomination on a major party national ticket in 1984.

The backlash against feminism was accompanied by antigay and antilesbian movements. Although activists had transformed what had been an underground subculture to a more open community by successfully challenging discriminatory laws and practices, well-organized conservative groups such as the Moral Majority, a conservative Christian-oriented political movement founded by minister Jerry Falwell, worked to turn back those gains. AIDS (acquired immune deficiency syndrome) was officially identified in the United States in 1982. The majority of victims early in the AIDS epidemic were gay men, and antigay rhetoric played on the widespread fear of the disease. On the other hand, the epidemic called forth increased activism on the part of gays. Gay communities rallied for the victims, creating organizations to provide assistance and services, to fund research and prevention programs, and to protect those who were infected from discrimination. In 1987 more than six hundred thousand people marched in Washington, D.C., to promote "gay power" and equal rights for gays. While some Christian groups continued to fight against gay rights, other religious bodies supported them. Reform Judaism, Unitarian Universalists, and some Episcopalian dioceses began to accept openly gay and lesbian rabbis and ministers.

During its two terms, from 1981 to 1989, the Reagan administration cut back on social-welfare programs, introduced tax cuts, and increased military spending, especially in areas related to technology. In addition to a rise of social conservatism with "the war on drugs," a call for "family values," and the emergence of religious fundamentalism, the decade of the 1980s is characterized by a faith in free markets and the pursuit of material wealth. Decreased federal regulation of business led to corporate mergers and takeovers, creating a new wealthy class epitomized by figures such as the real-estate mogul Donald Trump. As taxes fell and incomes rose, "baby boomers"—the generation born during the post–World War II "baby boom" from 1946 to 1964—experienced unprecedented prosperity and buying power, leading Wolfe to call them the "splurge generation."

The United States also continued to be an international presence. Cautious about military involvement overseas because of its experience in Vietnam, the United States nevertheless intervened in political situations abroad. In contrast to the lengthy involvement in Southeast Asia, military actions in the 1980s and early 1990s were precisely identified and executed relatively quickly with the use of highly advanced technology. In October 1983 Reagan ordered the invasion of the Caribbean island nation of Grenada after its prime minister was executed during a military coup by a group allied to Fidel Castro's Cuba; the war was over by December. Reagan's successor, George H. W. Bush, ordered the invasion of Panama in 1989 to depose its dictator, Manuel Noriega, who was brought to the United States, tried and convicted of cocaine smuggling, and sentenced to forty years in prison. In August 1990 Iraqi president Saddam Hussein ordered his troops to invade neighboring oil-rich Kuwait; on 17 January 1991 a United States–led coalition began air strikes on Iraqi targets, followed on 24 February by a ground assault. By 28 February the Iraqi troops had been driven out of Kuwait, and Operation Desert Storm was over.

More than American military might, however, the triumph of global capitalism contributed to the end of the Cold War. The Berlin Wall, erected in 1961 to separate Communist East Germany from West Germany, came down following East Germany's decision in November 1989 to allow its citizens to visit West Germany. Unable to compete economically with the West, the Soviet Union disintegrated in 1991. Events in the Balkans and the Middle East occupied the administration of William Jefferson "Bill" Clinton, whose two terms began in 1993. To stop the practice of Serbian "ethnic cleansing" of Muslims in the Kosovo region of Yugoslavia, Clinton authorized the use of American troops in 1999. The United States also launched Operation Desert Fox, a four-day bombing campaign against Iraq in December 1998. From 1991 to 2001 American military planes routinely attacked Iraqi antiaircraft installations inside "no-fly zones" where Iraqi planes were forbidden to operate.

Important scientific and technological advances occurred during Clinton's presidency. The Hubble Space Telescope was launched in 1990; the World Wide Web was introduced in 1991, and by 2000 more than one hundred million people were online in North America. Clinton also contended with issues related to gay rights. In 1993 the "Don't Ask, Don't Tell" policy was instituted, under which gays and lesbians could serve in the military as long as their sexual orientations remained secret. In 1996 Clinton signed into law the Defense of Marriage Act, defining marriage as the union of one man and one woman. A signal failure of the Clinton administration was its attempt to reform the health-care system. Clinton's presidency coincided with America's longest peacetime period of economic expansion, during which the federal budget went from deficit to record surpluses; some of this prosperity was, however, based on a "bubble" in prices of stocks of Internet-related companies and on unsustainable increases in home values. Clinton was impeached by the U.S. House of Representatives on 19 December 1998 for perjury and obstruction of justice in the investigation of his sexual relationship with White House intern Monica Lewinsky; he was acquitted of the charges by the U.S. Senate on 12 February 1999 and left office with the highest approval rating of any president since the end of World War II.

Advances in communications and transportation, along with the rise of multinational corporations and the spread of open markets, furthered globalization, changing social structures around the world. Although many Americans embraced the diversity and fluidity characterized by globalization, others regarded them as an assault on traditional ways of life. The terrorists who carried out bombings during the 1990s had little in common in terms of religious faith and cultural upbringing; but they did share an opposition to the U.S. government, which they envisioned as a threat to their values. In 1993 an Islamic fundamentalist group detonated a car bomb in a parking garage below the World Trade Center in New York City, claiming the lives of 6 people and injuring more than 1,000; the group had intended to harm many more. Two years later, a homemade bomb destroyed a federal building in downtown Oklahoma City, killing 168 people and injuring nearly 700 others in the largest terrorist attack on U.S. soil to that time. Timothy McVeigh had organized the bombing in protest of gun-control legislation and the fifty-one-day standoff between federal agents and the Branch Davidian religious cult in Waco, Texas, in 1993 that had ended in the burning of the cult's compound and the deaths of 82 men, women, and children.

The threat of international and domestic terrorism in the United States continued throughout the administration of George W. Bush, who became president in 2001 even though the Democratic candidate, Vice President Al Gore, had received a majority of the popular vote in the 2000 election. The 11 September 2001 attacks that destroyed the World Trade Center, damaged the Pentagon, and brought down an airliner in a Pennsylvania field claimed the lives of nearly three thousand victims, including not just Americans but also nationals from more than ninety countries. In response, the United States departed from the quick and localized military interventions of the previous two decades by instituting the "war on terror" against al-Qaeda, the Taliban, and other Islamist militant groups. Afghanistan and Iraq were invaded and occupied, ending the

Taliban regime in the former country and the presidency of Hussein, who was captured and ultimately hanged, in the latter. The quick victories were succeeded in Afghanistan by attacks on U.S. troops by Taliban guerrillas and in Iraq by an anti-Western insurgency and sectarian fighting between Sunni and Shiite Muslims. The wars, combined with tax cuts by the Bush administration, contributed to a growing national debt that reached $11.3 trillion dollars in 2008. In his second term Bush began to lose the confidence of Americans and the international community. The war on terror met with disapproval around the world, with many doubting the justice of America's actions. Photographs of American soldiers abusing prisoners in the Abu Ghraib prison in Baghdad caused widespread outrage, as did the long-term detention, without charges or trials, of "enemy combatants" at the American military base at Guantánamo Bay, Cuba. In November 2009 a court in Milan tried twenty-three Central Intelligence Agency (CIA) operatives in absentia for unlaw-fully kidnapping a Muslim imam in Italy and transporting him to Egypt for inter-rogation and torture. All were convicted and are considered fugitives. Domestically, the administration was faulted for not acting promptly and effectively on behalf of the victims of Hurricane Katrina, which made much of New Orleans uninhabitable in 2005. Economic problems added to the unpopularity of the Bush administration. Toward the end of his term in 2007 the country entered a recession characterized by increasing fuel prices, crises in the mortgage and housing industries, rising unem-ployment, and the failure of global financial firms.

A turning point in American politics and social life came in 2008 with the election of Illinois senator Barack Obama as the first African American president of the United States. Although African Americans had previously made bids for the office (most notably Shirley Chisholm in 1972 and Jesse Jackson in 1984 and 1988), Obama was the first African American to be nominated by a major party. Alaska governor Sarah Palin, the running mate of Obama's opponent, Arizona senator John McCain, was the first woman on the Republican presidential ticket. Obama inherited many of the problems that had plagued earlier administrations, including the war on terror in Iraq and Afghanistan, growing nuclear threats by North Korea and Iran, failing domestic and international economies, declining Social Security revenues, and issues with health care. Early in his presidency he began to develop plans to withdraw troops from Iraq, close the Guantánamo Bay detention camp, end the "Don't Ask, Don't Tell" policy to allow gays and lesbians to serve openly in the military, shore up the American economy with a massive stimulus, reduce the emission of "greenhouse gases" believed to cause global warming by the institution of a "cap-and-trade" system, and improve the availability and affordability of health care; by early 2010 most of these plans remained unfulfilled. In November 2009 the Obama administration settled a thirteen-year-old civil suit claiming that the federal government had misman-aged trust funds and cheated Native American tribes out of royalties for lands it had leased on their behalf for more than a century. While less than the highest estimated losses, the $3.4 billion sum exceeds all previous settlements received by Native Americans. The decision to award Obama the 2009 Nobel Peace Prize, which he accepted with "deep gratitude and great humility," led to both positive and negative responses at home and abroad. Obama's administration has met with opposition and criticism, Many liberals are disappointed that he has not pushed his programs more vigorously, while conservatives fear that he will push them too far.

In his 1961 essay "Writing American Fiction" Philip Roth declared: "The American writer in the middle of the twentieth century has his hands full in trying to understand, and then describe, and then make credible much of the American reality. It stupefies, it sickens, it infuriates, and finally it is even a kind of embarrassment to one's own meager imagination. The actuality is continually outdoing our talents and the culture tosses up figures almost daily that are the envy of any novelist." Actual events have often been so outrageous as to seem more likely fictional than real. The Polish American author Jerzy Kosinski, for example, plays on the absurdity of media culture in his novel *Being There* (1971). Despite lacking any noteworthy characteristics or ideas, an illiterate gardener is propelled to fame by the media and becomes a political adviser and heir to a fortune. Joyce Carol Oates chronicles two specific media events in her young-adult novels *Freaky Green Eyes* (2003) and *My Sister, My Love* (2008). The first takes its cue from the 1995 case in which the former football star O. J. Simpson was charged with murdering his former wife and her friend. Televised for 134 days, it was the most publicized criminal trial in U.S. history. The second novel revisits the murder of six-year-old beauty-pageant contestant JonBenét Ramsey and the extensive media coverage it generated. By presenting the perspectives of the victims' family members, Oates critiques the sensationalized coverage of these crimes.

In addition to attempting to capture the unreality of media culture, writers also tried to make sense of war. Early in the contemporary period the Vietnam War was addressed by novelists Tim O'Brien, Lan Cao, and Bobbie Ann Mason, poets Kevin Bowen, Michael S. Herr, and Yusef Komunyakaa, and playwrights David Rabe and Stephen Metcalfe, who described combat experiences, antiwar protests, and the effects of war on soldiers, veterans, and those left at home. More recently, writers have used fragmented and multiple perspectives in an attempt to capture the confusion, fear, anger, and sadness experienced by Americans during and after the attacks of 11 September 2001. Novels that deal with those events include William Gibson's *Pattern Recognition* (2003), Art Spiegelman's *In the Shadow of No Towers* (2004), Jonathan Safran Foer's *Extremely Loud and Incredibly Close* (2005), Julia Glass's *The Whole World Over* (2006), Jay McInerney's *The Good Life* (2006), Don DeLillo's *Falling Man* (2007), and Paul Auster's *Man in the Dark* (2008). Poets also address 11 September, mostly to commemorate those who were lost and to promote personal and national healing. Martin Espada's "Alabanza" ("praise" in Spanish) remembers the people from many nations who worked at the World Trade Center. Robert Pinksy's "9/11" and Billy Collins's "The Names" were commissioned to memorialize the victims one year after the attacks. Works by Tess Gallagher, Joy Harjo, Lucille Clifton, and other poets are included in *September 11, 2001: American Writers Respond* (2002). The victims of more-localized acts of violence that captured the attention of Americans were also remembered in literature. Events in Francine Prose's *After* (2004) and Jodi Picoult's *Nineteen Minutes* (2007) echo the 1999 Columbine High School shootings. Nikki Giovanni honored the thirty-two people killed in a 2007 mass shooting at the institution where she teaches with a chant poem beginning "We Are Virginia Tech."

Writers in the contemporary period also try to capture the tones of presidential administrations—usually to point out their limitations and highlight their more absurd characteristics. Robert Coover's *The Public Burning* (1976) is narrated by Nixon; although focused on events before 1970, it also satirizes the Watergate era. Joan Didion's *Political Fictions* (2001) plays on Reagan's previous occupation as a Hollywood actor when she describes his "performances" in office as "almost always flawless." Thomas Pynchon's *Vineland* (1990) takes place in 1984, the year of Reagan's reelection, and shows how policies such as the war on drugs curtail American civil liberties. Other works criticize the material consumption associated with Reagan's presidency; David Mamet's play *Glengarry Glen Ross* (1982) and Bret Easton Ellis's novels *Less than Zero* (1985) and *American Psycho* (1991) take up darker aspects of American entrepreneurship. Clinton's rise to the presidency is addressed in Joe Klein's *Primary Colors: A Novel of Politics* (1996), originally published anonymously while Klein was a columnist for *Newsweek*. Philip Roth's *The Human Stain* (2000) begins in 1998 with the Clinton-Lewinsky affair, setting the context for an exploration of the boundaries between truth and fiction.

Literature of this period also reflects the activism of the times and the social changes it brought about. Attention to, and new perspectives on, issues of race, ethnicity, gender, and the environment were key elements in both American politics and the American consciousness. These issues also formed some of the most significant concerns of writers; discussions of them can be found in Part II of this volume in the essays "Feminism and Women's Writing," "Multiculturalism and Globalization," "Literature and the Environment," "African American Literature," and "The Native American Renaissance."

The gay and lesbian literary movement included a proliferation of newspapers, magazines, journals, and bookshops; SeaHorse Press, New York's first gay publishing house, was founded in 1977. Gay experience was not a new phenomenon in literature, but its expression had been limited, muted, or coded in earlier works. Writers have tried to document the reflections and attitudes of earlier eras. Sarah Schulman's *Shimmer* (1998) imagines the life of a white lesbian in the McCarthy era of the 1950s. Early "out" writers in the contemporary era were located on the two coasts, with large gay and lesbian communities in New York and San Francisco. Several New York gay writers formed the Violet (or Lavender) Quill, which included Edmund White, Andrew Holleran, and Robert Ferro. On the West Coast, Armistead Maupin's multivolume series, which takes its name from the first installment, *Tales of the City* (1978), began as a series of daily columns in the *San Francisco Chronicle* and focuses on the gay and lesbian community around 28 Barbary Lane. Other writers depicted gay experience in other parts of the country. Lanford Wilson's play *5th of July* (1979), for example, features a gay couple at the center of a family in Lebanon, Missouri. Lesbian works such as Rita Mae Brown's *Rubyfruit Jungle* (1974) and poetry by Adrienne Rich found a large readership.

The AIDS epidemic and the ways gay communities faced the crisis have been documented in novels such as Paula Martinac's *Home Movies* (1993) and Michael Cunningham's Pulitzer Prize–winning *The Hours* (1998) and in plays including Larry Kramer's *The Normal Heart* (1985), Tony Kushner's *Angels in America: A Gay Fantasia on National Themes* (1993), and Paul Rudnick's *Jeffrey* (1994). Other important works trace characters' double marginalization based on race and sexuality; they include Audre Lorde's *Zami: A New Spelling of My Name* (1982), Paula Gunn Allen's *Woman Who Owned the Shadows* (1983), and Randall Kenan's *Let the Dead Bury Their Dead* (1992).

After decades of growth, publishers, booksellers, and writers faced more competition in the 1970s and subsequent decades. A rise in the cost of hardcover books, industry responses to these costs, and the development of the Internet, as well as technology in general, have transformed publishing methods and reading habits. The era experienced an explosion in the number of books being published and in the mega-bookstores, such as Barnes & Noble and Borders, and chains, such as B. Dalton and Waldenbooks, in which they were sold, accompanied by a shrinking number of independent bookstores. To survive, the latter started to engage in specialized marketing practices directed at local communities. Book clubs and reading groups have also grown, a trend strikingly similar to one that occurred in the 1890s. The local groups were inspired by Oprah's Book Club, created by the popular talk-show host Oprah Winfrey in 1996; it quickly developed the power to catapult Winfrey's selections to best-seller status in what has come to be known as the "Oprah effect." To readers these changes brought lower prices and more-convenient access to books; to publishers they brought increased profits and more-sophisticated tracking of reader tastes; and to writers they brought larger numbers of readers and, in some cases, enormous royalties. Some critics, however, have complained about an emphasis on formulaic writing and best sellers.

The trend toward mass-market and trade paperback books that had begun before 1970 continued, but with some innovations. Publishers more frequently released literary fiction as paperback originals instead of bringing them out first in hardcover. Some of these paperbacks even feature ragged-edge pages and cover flaps in imitation of hardback books and their dust jackets. McInerney's novel *Bright Lights, Big City* (1984) and Jhumpa Lahiri's short-story collection *Interpreter of Maladies* (1999) are examples of books that were published first in paperback. Since trade-size paperbacks sell for about a third less than their hardcover counterparts, they earn smaller profits for publishers and lower royalties for writers. But since they sell twice as fast as hardcover books, paperbacks can help writers build audiences. In addition, the lower production and royalty costs may encourage publishers to take a chance on new writers.

By the late 1990s hardcover sales were flat, with returns of unsold books reaching almost half. Booksellers found more-efficient distribution methods, using sophisticated scanning technologies and fewer employees to track sales. Amazon.com, which went online in 1995, is the largest Internet bookseller worldwide. Distributing and selling books are not the only aspects of book consumption that have relocated to the digital realm. Amazon also allows buyers to write reviews, fostering online communities where readers can share opinions about books. Reader reviews are taking the place of those in newspapers and magazines as these print media shrink in size or disappear. Professional critics and scholars have joined the move to the Internet; the poet Robert Pinsky, for example, serves as poetry editor for online magazine *Slate*.

Readers also discuss books in online venues such as blogs, podcasts, and fan sites in addition to the traditional settings of libraries, schools, bookstores, and homes. Writers also use weblogs, personal websites, and networking sites to market and share their works with readers. Less-established writers increasingly self-publish their work as computers and the Internet make it easier and less expensive to offer books online or to print them on demand. Writers with large readerships and best sellers in traditional print format have also embraced new technologies. In 2000 horror-fiction writer Stephen King began publishing his novel *The Plant* in five-thousand-word installments available for download on his website, asking readers to pay a dollar for each. Although he ended the experiment after four installments when the rate of paying readers fell below 75 percent, it suggested that writers did not need publishers, booksellers, or even physical books to attract readers.

In 2003 the Internet search-engine firm Google announced plans to digitize twenty million books, creating a searchable online library that would allow readers to preview, scan, and purchase books. Despite a legion of legal actions brought against the firm by publishers, writers, and other copyright holders, its plans are moving forward. An October 2008 settlement, amended in November 2009, limits Google to out-of-print books from English-speaking countries, restricts the ways in which the company can earn revenue from scanning and digitizing books, and requires a "Book Rights Registry" to seek out copyright holders. The latter can choose to make their entire books available for free or to restrict the number of pages readers can view.

More-recent inventions make it no longer necessary to have a computer to read electronic works, known as "eBooks." With portable electronic devices, such as Amazon's Kindle, Sony's Reader, and Barnes & Noble's nook, that are roughly the size of a trade paperback and lighter than the average one, consumers can download and read hundreds of books; a virtual library can be carried in a backpack, briefcase, or purse. At the end of the first decade of the 2000s eBooks represent the fastest-growing category in publishing. Their popularity may affect the pricing of traditional books, because many eBooks cost less than half the price of their paper counterparts. Pressured by customers to lower prices and worried about their profits, publishers delayed the release of digital versions of anticipated best sellers.

# Literary Influences

Although distinctions can be drawn between works published since 1970 and those of the previous period, much continuity exists. The minimalist impulse, emphasis on inarticulateness, and focus on the structure of language can be traced back to Modernist American writers such as Gertrude Stein, William Carlos Williams, and Ernest Hemingway. The confessional mode of Sylvia Plath and Anne Sexton continues in the work of poets such as Louise Glück, Sharon Olds, and Simon J. Ortiz, who use aspects of their own lives to draw attention to larger issues.

Other literary influences come from beyond the borders of the United States. American writers have always drawn from elsewhere, but in this period they are drawing from more extensive cultural and narrative sources than ever before. The "magical realism" of Latin American and Caribbean authors such as the Colombian Gabriel García Márquez, the Argentines Jorge Luis Borges and Julio Cortázar, the Chilean Isabel Allende, and the Cuban Alejo Carpentier is an important element. The term is also applied to the writing of Europeans such as the Czech Milan Kundera and the German Günter Grass and British immigrants Salman Rushdie from India and Kazuo Ishiguro from Japan. These authors incorporate fantastic or mythical elements in otherwise realistic fiction to illuminate the absurd nature of reality. The post–World War II influence of the Irish dramatist Samuel Beckett, the Prague-born Austrian fiction writer Franz Kafka, the French poet André Breton, and the French novelist and filmmaker Alain Robbe-Grillet can be seen in the fiction of the American Postmodernists Thomas Pynchon, Donald Barthelme, and John Barth and the dramas of Edward Albee and Sam Shepard. The blurring of fiction genres in the work of the Italian writers Italo Calvino and Umberto Eco is also evident in American writing of the period. Eco's *Il nome della rosa* (1980; translated as *The Name of the Rose*, 1983), for example, combines the historical novel—it is set in a fourteenth-century monastery—and the detective story. The arrival in the United States of British author J. K. Rowling's Harry Potter series transformed children's and young-adult fiction into a cultural phenomenon. The seven novels began with *Harry Potter and the Philosopher's Stone* (1997), which was published in the United States in 1998 as *Harry Potter and the Sorcerer's Stone*. Its success led *The New York Times* to create a separate best-seller list for children's literature in 2000 and has fostered a huge growth in popularity of this category of fiction.

# Evolution of Critical Opinion

The formalist methods and close reading practices of New Criticism, which dominated American critical approaches to literature from the mid 1930s until 1970, remain important in secondary schools and introductory college literature courses. Among scholars, however, New Criticism has largely been replaced by approaches derived from the European theories of structuralism and poststructuralism. Critics still ask what a work means, but this question is now accompanied and complicated by others: "What does it mean and to whom?" and "Why does it mean what it does?" Some readers have complained that these new critical approaches make literature less important. In terms of maintaining its elite and separate status as "art," this objection may be valid. One could argue, however, that these approaches make literature more relevant to everyday life.

In contrast to New Criticism, structuralism does not focus on literary value, and it makes no distinction between high and low art forms. Structuralism relies on linguistic analysis and seeks to uncover the organizing patterns and oppositions in the structure and meaning of "texts"—a word that replaced traditional terms such as "poem," "story," and "novel" in the 1970s and 1980s to allow comparison to other representative forms such as billboards and advertisements. Indeed, part of the innovation of structuralism is that it offers a way to think about culture in general, not just about literature.

Although poststructuralists criticize structuralism for being simplistic and ahistorical, they, too, emphasize the relational quality of language. Both movements regard culture as a system of "signs" in which words do not reflect or refer to an objective world but have meaning only in relation to each other. Both also focus on the way human thought and behavior are conditioned by social institutions. The French poststructuralist theorist Michel Foucault has influenced American literary criticism since 1970. In *Folie et déraison: Histoire de la folie à l'âge classique* (1961; abridged and translated as *Madness and Civilization,* 1965) Foucault investigates forms of knowing (which he calls "*epistemes*") as expressed by language, examining how these expressions affect society through the establishment of hierarchies and controlling institutions such as prisons. Most important for literary studies is Foucault's demonstration of the ways language masks the socially constructed aspects of important concepts and values. Later critics use these ideas to explore how markers of identity such as class, race, gender, and sexuality are socially constructed rather than biologically determined.

The dominant schools of criticism today have arisen from or responded to poststructuralist concepts; they include deconstruction, reader response, New Historicism, feminism, African American studies, Asian American studies, Native American studies, Latino/Latina studies, postcolonialism, and ecocriticism. Writers are aware of and affected by these shifts; John Barth, for example, integrates commentary on them into his works.

Jacques Derrida introduced deconstruction with his 1966 lecture at Johns Hopkins University, "La structure, le signe et le jeu dans le discours des sciences humaines" (translated as "Structure, Sign and Play in the Discourse of the Human Sciences" in his *Writing and Difference,* 1970) and three books published in 1967:

*La Voix et le phénomène: Introduction au problème du signe dans la phénoménologie de Husserl* (translated as *Speech and Phenomena, and Other Essays on Husserl's Theory of Signs,* 1973), *De la grammatologie* (translated as *Of Grammatology,* 1976), and *L'écriture et la différence* (translated as *Writing and Difference,* 1978). Derrida's notion of reading a text challenges its surface or intended meaning by uncovering its latent, hidden, or "accidental" features. Like New Criticism, deconstruction calls for line-by-line examination of the text, but it rejects New Critical notions about literature's aesthetic unity, universal meaning, and the primacy of the author. These ideas contributed to the "death of the author" movement initiated by Roland Barthes's landmark essay "The Death of the Author" (1967), in which he argues that an "author" is not a biological person but a socially and historically constructed subject who does not exist outside of language. In other words, writing creates the author and not the other way around.

Questioning the primacy of the author led to reader-response criticism. In "Is There a Text in This Class?" (1980) Stanley Fish argues that a text does not have an objective meaning; instead, the reader collaborates with the writer to create the meaning in the process of interpretation. New Historicism, represented by Stephen Greenblatt, Catherine Gallagher, Joel Feinman, and Louis Montrose, takes its cue from poststructuralism in its breaking down of the distinction between literary and nonliterary texts. New Historicists examine novels, poems, and plays alongside previously marginalized materials such as maps, letters, diaries, advertisements, and unofficial versions of historical events. They also argue that categories previously deemed "natural," such as the superiority of a William Wordsworth poem or racial or sexual identity, are socially and historically constructed.

The French feminist critics Hélène Cixous, Julia Kristeva, and Luce Irigaray, whose ideas profoundly influenced their American counterparts in the 1970s and 1980s, argued that female experience could not be adequately represented by male-formulated discourses marked by linear and rational thought processes. Cixous's formulation *écriture féminine* (feminine writing) refers to writing that emerges from the female body and its biological rhythms and is distinct from male writing in its nonlinearity.

Similar arguments have emerged in African American studies, Asian American studies, Native American studies, Latino/Latina studies, and postcolonial studies, all of which are grouped under the umbrella "cultural studies" or "cultural criticism." These critics analyze power relationships, share a commitment to social justice, and challenge a literary canon composed mostly of the works of white male writers. Those who are interested in race and sexuality focus on the ways these categories have been shaped socially and historically rather than biologically; those who study minority literature investigate images and ways of reading that are specific to the cultures from which they emerge, as opposed to Western or Anglo perspectives. In postcolonial studies Edward Said's groundbreaking *Orientalism* (1978) demonstrates the ways in which Western writers represent the Middle East as antithetical to European progress and values—as "other." All of these critics share a desire for literary and social pluralism and the elimination of borders between groups defined by class, race, gender, and sexuality. Green cultural studies, or "ecocriticism"—a term coined in the 1970s to describe literary criticism sensitive to environmental themes—desires to break down the separation of humanity and the natural world. An interdisciplinary strategy, ecocriticism considers history, ethics, philosophy, science, and psychology in addition to literary analysis as it attempts to uncover explicit and implicit attitudes toward the environment and to effect change in environmental practices.

# Part II
# Study Guides
# on General Topics

# African American Literature

African American writers have led the way in the explosion of ethnic literature since 1970 and have produced some of the most significant works of the era. The Civil Rights Movement was instrumental in giving voice to African American writers whose works raised awareness of the history and culture of black people in the United States. Debates about the black underclass, the ghettoization of many African Americans, and what the 1965 Moynihan Report called the deterioration of the black family, became part of the national discourse. A new recognition of the multiplicity of identities represented within African American culture was born.

The Black Arts Movement, led by the Harlem-based literary and political activist Amiri Baraka (born LeRoi Jones), was fueled by the assassinations of the civil-rights leaders Malcolm X in 1965 and Dr. Martin Luther King Jr. in 1968. It was often militant in tone, unapologetically political in promoting "Black Power" and black nationalist ideals, and insistent on the inherent goodness and beauty of blackness. Its primary focus, however, was the articulation of a distinctive aesthetic derived solely from black culture and the black experience. Often simultaneously populist and confrontational in tone, the Black Arts Movement emphasized vernacular traditions and public performance. Most of the key figures, including Baraka, Nikki Giovanni, June Jordan, Haki Madhubuti (born Don L. Lee), and Sonia Sanchez, were poets or dramatists. Their work continued into the 1970s, and several remain active in the twenty-first century. In a 1995 interview Ishmael Reed pointed to the continuing importance of the Black Arts Movement: "I think what Black Arts did was inspire a whole lot of Black people to write. Moreover, there would be no multiculturalism movement without Black Arts. Latinos, Asian Americans, and others all say they began writing as a result of the example of the 1960s. Blacks gave the example that you don't have to assimilate. You could do your own thing, get into your own background, your own history, your own tradition and your own culture." Many writers inspired by Black Arts, however, found it overly prescriptive, and by the mid 1970s they began to shape their art in different ways.

As the Black Arts Movement receded in the mid 1970s, African American women fiction writers began to appear; among them were Toni Morrison, Alice Walker, Paule Marshall, Gloria Naylor, Toni Cade Bambara, Sherley Anne Williams, and Gayl Jones. Their work signaled a significant shift in African American literature. Whereas writers who came to prominence in the 1940s and 1950s, such as Richard Wright, Ralph Ellison, and James Baldwin, had made African American oppression by white society a central focus, the female writers who came on the scene in the 1970s and continued to flourish in the 1980s and 1990s shifted their attention to the inner workings of African American communities. While these authors did not regard white oppression as a problem of the past with which they need not concern themselves, their primary interest was in African American culture and its concerns: they offered personal narratives of community, and they gave voice to women and children.

For example, in Morrison's first novel, *The Bluest Eye* (1970), such issues as the "color aesthetic" (the valuing by blacks, at some points in African American history, of light skin over dark), the beauty myth, poverty, and abuse are dramatized through main characters, who are children. Morrison's second novel, *Sula* (1973), portrays the friendship of two African American women growing up in the 1920s and 1930s. Her National Book Critics Circle Award–winning *Song of Solomon* (1977) has a male protagonist, but female experiences and perspectives play a significant role in the story.

Morrison's novel *Beloved* (1987) is the subject of a Study Guide on Works and Writers in this volume, as is Walker's *The Color Purple* (1982), another landmark work. Sterling Lecater Bland Jr. notes that Walker's later works maintain a focus on black women "in environments characterized by oppression, desperation, and transcendent faith," while they "illuminate human experience beyond limits traditionally defined by class and race."

Marshall, who was born of Barbadian parents and raised in a mixed West Indian-African American community in New York City, did not receive critical attention for her first novel, *Brown Girl, Brownstones* (1959), which explores American gender and racial stereotypes against the background of materialist culture, until it was republished by the Feminist Press in 1981. Marshall was among the first writers to focus on the subjectivity of the ethnic immigrant; *Praisesong for the Widow* (1983), her most popular novel, takes up the return motif as the middle-aged African American protagonist, Avey Johnson, journeys to the Caribbean and reclaims her national and personal identity. Marshall's narratives emphasize the centrality of women's voices and provide important evidence of the interconnectedness of African, Caribbean, and African American cultures.

Naylor's *The Women of Brewster Place* (1982) focuses on class issues and female bonding, while her *Mama Day* (1988) highlights family history, magic, and folklore in a love story. Bambara's short-story collection *Gorilla, My Love* (1972) celebrates African American culture and community. One of the most frequently anthologized stories in the collection, "The Lesson," presents language and literacy as central themes, using ethnic dialect to clear a space for alternative voices, as well as providing social commentary. Students interested in spirituality, powerful ancestor figures, and the relationship between individual and community fragmentation will also want to explore Bambara's *The Salt Eaters* (1980). Other important fiction by African American women from the 1970s and 1980s centering on the black female experience include Williams's *Dessa Rose* (1986) and Jones's *Corregidora* (1975). While some have criticized these works for displacing strictly racial paradigms in favor of a focus on communal issues and on romantic and familial relations, as well as for their sometimes strong critiques of black men, others argue that putting community and family at center stage "normalizes" minority life for an often racially prejudiced reading public and, thus, ultimately serves to overcome racial and ethnic stereotypes.

Important African American voices who emerged in the first two decades of the contemporary period were not, of course, limited to female writers. In addition to his novels, poetry, and essays, which are consistently satiric and parodic, Ishmael Reed has compiled the important anthologies *From Totems to Hip-Hop:*

*A Multicultural Anthology of Poetry across the Americas, 1900–2002* (2002) and *Pow-Wow: Charting the Fault Lines in the American Experience—Short Fiction from Then to Now* (2009), which present the American experience as truly pancultural by including works by people of all colors. Alex Haley wrote *Roots* (1976), a novel that blends history and fiction in telling the story of slavery in the Americas. The adaptation of the latter work as a highly successful television miniseries just two years after publication raised American awareness of the realities of slavery. John Edgar Wideman began publishing in the late 1960s; his early works show a strong Modernist influence. From 1973 to 1981 he avoided publishing to immerse himself in black history and culture. His Homewood trilogy, which consists of the short-story collection *Damballah* (1981) and the novels *Hiding Place* (1981) and *Sent for You Yesterday* (1983), reflects his experiences growing up in the Homewood neighborhood of the East End of Philadelphia. Wideman is also noted for the novel *Philadelphia Fire* (1990) and for *Brothers and Keepers* (1984), a memoir he wrote with his brother Robbie, who went to prison for life while Wideman was achieving success in the academic and publishing worlds. Other African American male fiction writers of the 1970s and 1980s include Ernest J. Gaines, who is the subject of a Study Guide on Works and Writers in this volume; and Charles Johnson, who is especially known for his National Book Award–winning *Middle Passage* (1990), relating the experiences of a free black man traveling on a slave ship in the 1830s.

In poetry, major figures include Michael S. Harper and Rita Dove (Dove is the subject of a Study Guides on Works and Writers in Part III of this volume), Lucille Clifton, and Audre Lorde; the careers of the Black Arts figures Giovanni and Sanchez have continued into the contemporary era, as well. While their individual expressions and personal visions vary, they have all experimented with the adaptation of musical forms into poetry and explored African American history. Clifton and Lorde write about experiences particular to women; Giovanni and Lorde have both written about suffering from cancer. (Giovanni is a survivor of the lung cancer that was diagnosed in 1995; Lorde died of breast cancer in 1992.)

In the 1980s and 1990s these poets were joined by Yusef Komunyakaa, who has written about his experiences as a soldier in Vietnam and about African American life in the rural South. For even more-recent noted African American poets, students might look to the work of Natasha Trethewey and Kevin Young. Trethewey's first collection, *Domestic Work* (2000), was chosen by Dove for the first Cave Canem Poetry Prize; her *Native Guard* (2006) won the Pulitzer Prize. Young's *Jelly Roll* (2005) is a collection of poetry that is inspired by the blues and by black vernacular and grows out of the oral tradition. Sapphire (pseudonym of Ramona Lofton) became known for her prowess at slam poetry and published three volumes of verse. Sapphire is also the author of *Push*, a haunting 1996 novel about an obese, illiterate African American teenager who is abused by her parents; the pursuit of literacy helps to free her from these circumstances but not without costs. The film adaptation, *Precious*, was released to critical acclaim in 2009. The novel and the movie raise questions about the potentially troubling political implications of such representations of blackness in contemporary literature.

Several black writers of the 1980s and 1990s attracted a general audience, including Terry McMillan, author of *Disappearing Acts* (1989), *Waiting to Exhale* (1992), and *How Stella Got Her Groove Back* (1996), all featuring African American women and their relationships. McMillan also edited the influential *Breaking Ice: An Anthology of Contemporary African American Fiction* (1990). Bebe Moore Campbell's 1994 novel, *Brothers and Sisters*, initiated discussions of race, sex, and class. Ten novels about gay black life by E. Lynn Harris, a gay black male, reached *The New York Times* best-seller list. Harris's work presents homosexual issues with a warmth and humor that make the historically taboo subject accessible. Randall Kenan, a writer and professor, has published several books that address gay black identity in the South and that feature the magical realism that often appears in the works of such popular female writers as Morrison, Walker, and Naylor. His first novel, *A Visitation of Spirits* (1989), is set in the fictional Tims Creek, North Carolina, as is his nationally acclaimed collection of stories *Let the Dead Bury Their Dead* (1992). His nonfiction work *The Fire This Time* (2007), part memoir and part homage to James Baldwin, looks at where America is now with regard to the issues Baldwin raised forty-four years earlier in *The Fire Next Time*.

Students interested in Postmodernism and African American literature will find several recent black authors who have taken up explicitly Postmodernist projects. Trey Ellis received critical attention for his metafictional first novel, *Platitudes* (1988). The following year he published the influential essay "The New Black Aesthetic," in which he describes middle- and upper-class African American males as "cultural mulattos" who feel as much connection to the late white rock icon Jim Morrison as they do to the black novelist Toni Morrison. Colson Whitehead has garnered both critical and popular success writing for publications such as the *Village Voice* and *Salon.com*. He received a MacArthur Foundation "genius" grant in 2002. His most noteworthy works include *The Intuitionist* (1999), *John Henry Days* (2001), and *Apex Hides the Hurt* (2006). Influenced by Thomas Pynchon and Ralph Ellison, Whitehead is attracted to popular-culture forms and inflects his work with references to the media and new technologies. Danzy Senna also looks to past African American masters while employing contemporary—often Postmodernist—techniques. Her debut novel, *Caucasia* (1998), offers a case study of race in America. Her first-person narrator extends the conversation begun in Nella Larsen's *Passing* (1929) and Ellison's *Invisible Man* (1952) by questioning the privilege and normative status of whiteness in America.

African American drama is discussed in the Study Guide on General Topics "Contemporary American Drama" in this volume, and a Study Guide on Works and Writers is devoted to the most prominent contemporary African American playwright, August Wilson. Students interested in innovations in drama early in the period might consider the work of Ntozake Shange, who created a new theatrical form, the "choreopoem"—a merging of poetry, prose, music, song, and dance—in *for colored girls who have considered suicide/when the rainbow is enuf* (1975). Anna Deavere Smith, a playwright, actress, and recipient of a MacArthur grant, is well known for her documentary-style dramas exploring race and community. Her one-woman plays *Fires in the Mirror* (1992) and *Twilight: Los Angeles 1992* (1993) won Obie (Off Broadway) Awards, and her 2008 solo show, *Let*

*Me Down Easy*, deals with the American health-care system. Suzan-Lori Parks is a prolific and important playwright and screenwriter whose bold, audacious, experimental, and idiosyncratic works defy easy categorization and have garnered much critical acclaim. Parks, the recipient of a MacArthur grant, a Pulitzer Prize, and two Obies, has an extensive body of work that has been widely produced. Her best-known plays include *Topdog/Underdog* (2001), for which she was the first black woman to win the Pulitzer in drama, and *The America Play* (1995). Students interested in Parks's work might examine the volume *Suzan Lori-Parks: A Casebook* (2007) in the Michigan Modern Dramatists series.

In the field of mystery and detective fiction, Walter Mosley introduced his character Ezekiel "Easy" Rawlins in *Devil in a Blue Dress* in 1990. Rawlins returns from World War II, settles in Los Angeles, and attempts to find a peaceful life but is forced to accept investigative jobs that take him into the seedy and violent areas of the city. Mosley, who was one of former president Bill Clinton's favorite writers, has also written two other mystery series, as well as science fiction, erotica, and nongenre novels. Barbara Neely initiated one of the first mystery series with a female African American protagonist in *Blanche on the Lam* (1992); the ironically named Blanche White is a cleaning woman who finds herself investigating a murder. Octavia Butler (treated in a Study Guide on Works and Writers in this volume) and Samuel Delany explore issues of race in science fiction. Finally, students interested in African American memoir might start with Maya Angelou's *I Know Why the Caged Bird Sings* (1970), which is the subject of a Study Guide on Works and Writers. By the 1990s several African American authors were using the memoir to explore issues of biracial identity: Shirlee Taylor Haizlip's *The Sweeter the Juice: A Family Memoir in Black and White* (1994), the first memoir that openly discusses the practice of passing as white; James McBride's *The Color of Water: A Black Man's Tribute to His White Mother* (1996); Gregory Williams's *Life on the Color Line* (1996); and *Black, White, and Jewish: Autobiography of a Shifting Self* (2001), by Rebecca Walker, the daughter of Alice Walker.

In works in all of these genres, readers will find African American voices reaching back to the past and forward to the future: working within long-standing oral traditions and experimenting with Postmodernist techniques and attitudes as they investigate the intersections of race, class, gender, and sexual orientation in challenging and stimulating writing.

## TOPICS FOR DISCUSSION AND RESEARCH

1. African American literature has strong roots in oral tradition. Field songs and folktales were handed down through the generations, along with the forms and structures that characterized them: call and response, African polyrhythmic beats, trickster figures, improvisation, vernacular language, ritual, and—as John Edgar Wideman puts it in the preface to *Breaking Ice*—the "incantatory power of the word to name, blame, shame, and summon power." Many folklorists maintain that oral traditions cannot exist in writing—that the two forms are, by definition, opposed. Yet, scholars have made compelling demonstrations of the integration of oral strategies in written forms: see, for instance, Gayl Jones's

*Liberating Voices: Oral Tradition in African American Literature* (1991) and Karla F. C. Holloway's *Moorings and Metaphors: Figures of Culture and Gender in Black Women's Literature* (1992). Students might find it interesting to look for traces of oral tradition in the prose or poetry of some of the writers mentioned in the essay above, examining such features in one work or comparatively across texts.

2. Many contemporary African American texts—especially prose works—feature ancestral figures: older people who serve as culture bearers, carrying forward the stories and traditions of the past and acting as teachers of the younger generations. Such characters include Pilate in Toni Morrison's *Song of Solomon*, Minnie Ransom in Toni Cade Bambara's *The Salt Eaters*, and Miranda Day in Gloria Naylor's *Mama Day*, as well as many instances in Wideman's novels and stories and the poetry of Lucille Clifton, Rita Dove, and Michael S. Harper. Ernest J. Gaines's novel *A Gathering of Old Men* (1983) also offers interesting examples. Using any of these works or other available possibilities, ask what strengths and flaws tend to characterize these figures. How do they stand in for the past, and what do they say about it? How can ancestral figures help those who are struggling with issues of identity or how to accomplish their goals? Might it be important to move past them in some ways? The works by Holloway, Trudier Harris, and Houston Baker cited in "Resources" offer starting places for such an investigation.

3. During the Harlem Renaissance, which began after World War I and lasted until the mid 1930s, authors such as Langston Hughes and Sterling Brown became noted for adapting jazz rhythms and blues music into their poetry. In an interview Dove explored the intricacies of this connection: "there's a way of incorporating into a poem the rhythms of speech, which are a source for both music and poetry. I'm thinking in particular of Langston Hughes, who could pull out the flavor of bebop and render it linguistically. You know: 'Good morning, Daddy! / Ain't you heard / The boogie-woogie rumble / Of a dream deferred?' He didn't try to make the poem into music; rather, he took the rhythms of a particular musical style, found the equivalent rhythms in the language spoken in his neighborhood, and made it into poetry" (Robb St. Lawrence, "'Taking the Cards You're Dealt and Building a House': An Interview with Rita Dove," *Bellingham Review*, 29 [Fall 2006]: 77–84; also available at <http://people.virginia.edu/~rfd4b/Bellingham%20Review.pdf> [accessed 7 January 2010]). This tradition continues in contemporary African American literature in work by such authors as Dove, Nikki Giovanni, Harper, and Kevin Young. Students might find it fruitful to compare an earlier African American poet's use of forms and strategies from music to that of a contemporary poet—for instance, Hughes to Harper or Young, or Claude McKay's "The Harlem Dancer" (1917) to Dove's poems about ballroom dancing. How do hip-hop and rap factor into this equation?

4. African American cultural and political expression, especially during the Civil Rights Movement, has had significant impact on the national consciousness. Earlier civil-rights leaders such as Malcolm X and Martin Luther King Jr. used songs, speeches, and pamphlets for rhetorical and persuasive purposes. The black rhetoric of the 1960s was aggressive, employing specific strategies to "move the

masses." Orators addressed themes such as the common enemy, American hypocrisy, threatened black manhood, and black unity as a prerequisite for black liberation. Students interested in researching this topic might consult *The Voice of Black Rhetoric,* edited by Arthur Smith and Stephen Robb (Boston: Allyn & Bacon, 1971), and Peniel E. Joseph's *Dark Days, Bright Nights: From Black Power to Barack Obama* (New York: BasicCivitas, 2010). Consider the ways in which contemporary African American orators such as Jesse Jackson, Al Sharpton, and President Barack Obama echo their predecessors. How have the themes evolved? What new strategies do they employ? Who is the contemporary audience, and how has it effected changes in strategy and message?

5. In recent years America has begun to acknowledge and celebrate the multiplicity of mixed-race identities in the country. Multiraciality has come to the forefront in popular discussions of race, and most notably in the media, with the recent election of the nation's first biracial president. This trend is also evident in literature of the mid to late 1990s such as James McBride's *The Color of Water,* Gregory Williams's *Life on the Color Line,* and Danzy Senna's *Caucasia.* How do these narratives deconstruct existing notions of race? Do they change your ideas about the fluidity of race? How does multiraciality complicate and/or potentially depoliticize cultural perceptions of race in America?

## RESOURCES

### Primary Works

Terry McMillan, ed., *Breaking Ice: An Anthology of Contemporary African American Fiction* (New York: Penguin, 1990).
Excellent anthology with strong coverage of important contemporary black writers, a valuable preface by John Edgar Wideman, and a useful introduction by McMillan.

Arnold Rampersad, ed., *The Oxford Anthology of African-American Poetry* (New York: Oxford University Press, 2006).
Excellent anthology with strong representation of the contemporary era and useful introductions.

### Criticism

William L. Andrews, Frances Smith Foster, and Trudier Harris, eds., *The Oxford Companion to African American Literature* (New York: Oxford University Press, 1997).
Invaluable volume of short essays on various movements and individual writers.

Houston A. Baker Jr., *Workings of the Spirit: The Poetics of Afro-American Women's Writing* (Chicago: University of Chicago Press, 1991).
Focuses on Zora Neale Hurston, Toni Morrison, and Ntozake Shange but extends beyond those authors to offer useful frameworks for understanding the

explosion of writing by African American women in the last three decades of the twentieth century.

Sterling Lecater Bland Jr., "Fire and Romance: African American Literature," in *A Concise Companion to Postwar American Literature and Culture*, edited by Josephine G. Hendin (Malden, Mass.: Blackwell, 2004), pp. 263–289.
A useful overview of contemporary African American literature, mainly fiction.

Madhu Dubey, *Signs and Cities: Black Literary Postmodernism* (Chicago: University of Chicago Press, 2003).
Discusses works by Octavia Butler, Samuel Delaney, Trey Ellis, Charles Johnson, Toni Morrison, Gloria Naylor, Ishmael Reed, Sapphire, and John Edgar Wideman in the context of Postmodernism and urbanity.

Richard Dyer, *White* (New York: Routledge, 1997).
Examines why whiteness goes unexamined as the norm and demonstrates how it is presented as the aesthetic ideal in film, painting, photography, and other visual media.

Henry Louis Gates Jr., *The Signifying Monkey: A Theory of African-American Literary Criticism* (New York: Oxford University Press, 1988).
A landmark of African American criticism that provides insight into how past African traditions and tropes are reflected in African American literature. With the exceptions of Alice Walker and Ishmael Reed, the authors discussed predate the period treated in the present volume.

Trudier Harris, *Saints, Sinners, and Saviors: Strong Black Women in African American Literature* (New York: Palgrave Macmillan, 2001).
Focuses on the positive and negative aspects of the figure of the strong black woman that appears in much contemporary African American literature. Authors whose works are discussed include Ishmael Reed, Toni Morrison, Toni Cade Bambara, J. California Cooper, Ernest J. Gaines, Octavia Butler, and Pearl Cleage.

Karla F. C. Holloway, *Moorings and Metaphors: Figures of Culture and Gender in Black Women's Literature* (New Brunswick, N.J.: Rutgers University Press, 1992).
Focuses on ancestral figures, oral traditions, and figurative metaphors from Africa as they are reimagined in works by such writers as Gloria Naylor, Alice Walker, Ntozake Shange, Octavia Butler, Gayl Jones, and Toni Morrison. The book is challenging but highly useful.

Noel Ignatiev and John Garvey, eds., *Race Traitor* (New York: Routledge, 1996).
Eclectic collection of pieces from *Race Traitor*, a polemical journal devoted to critiquing "whiteness" and demonstrating that it is a historical, not a natural, classification.

Gayl Jones, *Liberating Voices: Oral Tradition in African American Literature* (New York: Penguin, 1991).

Examines the oral tradition in African American poetry, short fiction, and novels. Jones offers readings of works by Michael S. Harper, Amiri Baraka, Alice Walker, Ernest J. Gaines, and Toni Morrison, as well as earlier authors.

Angelyn Mitchell, ed., *Within the Circle: An Anthology of African American Literary Criticism from the Harlem Renaissance to the Present* (Durham, N.C.: Duke University Press, 1994).
Includes two sections that are most relevant to those interested in contemporary literature: "Structuralism, Post-Structuralism, and the African American Critic" and "Gender, Theory, and African American Feminist Criticism."

David Roediger, *Working toward Whiteness: How America's Immigrants Became White: The Strange Journey from Ellis Island to the Suburbs* (New York: Basic Books, 2005).
Examines the intersections between race and class through an exploration of how Italian, Jewish, Polish, and other immigrants to America who were not considered "white" in the nineteenth century melded into the mass of "white people" over the course of the twentieth century.

Valerie Smith, Lea Baechler, and A. Walton Litz, eds., *African American Writers: Profiles of Their Lives and Works—From the 1700s to the Present* (New York: Collier, 1993).
Twenty-seven biographical/critical essays on African American writers. Figures from the contemporary period include Amiri Baraka, Ernest J. Gaines, Audre Lorde, Paule Marshall, Toni Morrison, Gloria Naylor, Ishmael Reed, Ntozake Shange, Alice Walker, and John Edgar Wideman.

Kevin J. Wetmore and Alycia Smith-Howard, eds., *Suzan-Lori Parks: A Casebook* (New York: Routledge, 2007).
Offers a chronology, an introduction surveying Parks's career, eight essays on various plays and on such topics as gender, language, and metatheater, as well as an interview by Wetmore.

## PEOPLE OF INTEREST

### Toni Cade Bambara (1939–1995)
Considered one of the best of African American short-story writers for her collections *Gorilla, My Love* (1972) and *The Seabirds Are Still Alive* (1977). She is also noted for her novels *The Salt Eaters* (1980) and the posthumously published *Those Bones Are Not My Child* (1999), based on the murders of forty black children in Atlanta between 1979 and 1981. Her essays and interviews were edited by Toni Morrison as *Deep Sightings and Rescue Missions: Fiction, Essays, and Conversations* (1996).

### Amiri Baraka (1934–   )
Poet, playwright, dramatist, essayist, music critic, literary theorist, activist, and founder of the Black Arts Movement; born LeRoi Jones. His play *Dutchman* (1963) is considered a landmark of African American theater. Collections of his

work include *The Selected Poetry of Amiri Baraka/LeRoi Jones* (1979) and the volume of essays *The Essence of Reparations* (2003).

### Lucille Clifton (1936–2010)

Poet known especially for her female-centered verse, collected in more than a dozen volumes. Her *Blessing the Boats: New and Selected Poems, 1988–2000*, appeared in 2000. In 2007 Clifton won the Ruth Lilly Poetry Prize, a $100,000 award honoring a living U.S. poet whose "lifetime accomplishments warrant extraordinary recognition."

### Samuel Delany (1942–   )

Novelist, critic, and memoirist. Most of his novels are in the science-fiction and fantasy genres; among the most popular are *Dhalgren* (1975) and the four-volume *Return to Nevèrÿon series* (1979–1987). His autobiography, *The Motion of Light in Water* (1988), recounts his life as a gay, black, dyslexic writer and received the Hugo Award.

### Trey Ellis (1962–   )

Novelist, essayist, memoirist, and blogger. His novel *Right Here, Right Now* (1999) received an American Book Award. *Bedtime Stories: Adventures in the Land of Single-Fatherhood* (2008) is a memoir of his life as a divorced father of two children.

### Nikki Giovanni (1943–   )

Poet, essayist, children's author, and activist who began her career with the Black Arts Movement. *The Collected Poetry of Nikki Giovanni* was published in 2003.

### Shirlee Taylor Haizlip (1937–   )

Author of *The Sweeter the Juice: A Family Memoir in Black and White* (1994).

### Alex Haley (1921–1992)

Novelist best known for *Roots: The Saga of an American Family* (1976), loosely based on the history of his own family. It was made into one of the most successful miniseries in television history. He also collaborated on *The Autobiography of Malcolm X* (1965), completing the work after Malcolm's assassination.

### E. Lynn Harris (1955–2009)

Best-selling novelist known for his works about closeted gay black men. His *If This World Were Mine* (1998) won the James Baldwin Award for Literary Excellence.

### Charles Johnson (1948–   )

Writer who began his career as a journalist and cartoonist before turning to fiction. His novels include *Faith and the Good Thing* (1974), *Oxherding* (1982), *Middle Passage* (1990), and *Dreamer* (1998). He is also the author of *The Sorcerer's Apprentice: Tales of Conjurations* (1985) and *Being and Race: Black Writing since 1970* (1988).

### Gayl Jones (1949–   )

Novelist and literary critic whose best-known novels are *Corregidora* (1975), *Eva's Man* (1976), and *The Healing* (1998).

**June Jordan** (1936–2002)
Poet, novelist, dramatist, and activist of Caribbean heritage who began her career as part of the Black Arts Movement. She published twenty-seven books, including *Some of Us Did Not Die* (2002), a collection of her highly acclaimed political journalism. *Directed by Desire: The Collected Poems of June Jordan* appeared posthumously in 2005.

**Randall Kenan** (1963–   )
Writer who focuses on black gay life in the South. He is best known for the novel *A Visitation of Spirits* (1989), the short-story collection *Let the Dead Bury Their Dead* (1992), and *The Fire This Time* (2007), a nonfiction tribute to James Baldwin.

**Yusef Komunyakaa** (pseudonym of James Willie Brown Jr., 1947–   )
Poet who served in Vietnam with the United States Army from 1965 to 1967 and was awarded a Bronze Star. He received the Pulitzer Prize in 1994 for *Neon Vernacular: New & Selected Poems, 1977–1989* (1993). His other works include *Copacetic* (1983), *I Apologize for the Eyes in My Head* (1986), *Dien Cai Dau* (1988), *Talking Dirty to the Gods* (2001), and *Pleasure Dome: New & Collected Poems, 1975–1999* (2001).

**Audre Lorde** (1934–1992)
Poet and essayist whose works of poetry include *The First Cities* (1968), *Cables to Rage* (1970), *From a Land Where Other People Live* (1972), *New York Head Shop and Museum* (1974), *The Black Unicorn* (1978), *The Cancer Journals* (1980), *Chosen Poems, Old and New* (1982), *Our Dead behind Us* (1986), and the National Book Award–winning *A Burst of Light* (1988).

**James McBride** (1957–   )
Memoirist and musician whose *The Color of Water: A Black Man's Tribute to His White Mother* (1996) was a best seller.

**Terry McMillan** (1951–   )
Novelist and anthologist known especially for her exploration of black women's friendships and romantic relationships. Her major works include *Disappearing Acts* (1989), *Waiting to Exhale* (1992), *How Stella Got Her Groove Back* (1996), and *Breaking Ice: An Anthology of Contemporary African American Fiction* (1990).

**Paule Marshall** (1929–   )
Poet, novelist, and recipient of a MacArthur grant. Her novels include *Brown Girl, Brownstones* (1959), *The Chosen Place, the Timeless People* (1969), *Praisesong for the Widow* (1983), and *Daughters* (1991); her memoir *Triangular Road* appeared in 2009.

**Bebe Campbell Moore** (1950–2006)
Novelist, journalist, and author of children's books, known for the best sellers *Brothers and Sisters* (1994), *Singing in the Comeback Choir* (1998), and *Your Blues Ain't Like Mine* (1993), which was a *New York Times* Notable Book of the Year.

**Walter Mosley** (1952–  )
Best known for his Easy Rawlins crime series, which comprises nine novels and two short-story collections; the series began with *Devil in a Blue Dress* in 1990 and ended with *Blonde Faith* in 2007. His three Fearless Jones novels are also crime fiction, while the three Socrates Fortlow books combine crime with literary fiction. Notable among his other works are the novels *RL's Dream* (1995) and *The Man in the Basement* (2004)—an homage to Ralph Ellison's novel *Invisible Man* (1952)—and nonfiction pieces on topics ranging from writing to peace.

**Gloria Naylor** (1950–  )
Novelist whose first book, *The Women of Brewster Place* (1982), brought her immediate acclaim and was made into a film in 1987. Her other works include *Linden Hills* (1985), *Mama Day* (1988), *Bailey's Café* (1992), and the anthology *Children of the Night: The Best Short Stories by Black Writers, 1967 to the Present* (1995).

**Barbara Neely** (1941–  )
Novelist and short-story writer, author of the four-novel Blanche White series of mysteries. *Blanche on the Lam* (1992) won the Agatha, Macavity, and Anthony Awards, three of the four major prizes that recognize a first mystery novel.

**Suzan-Lori Parks** (1963–  )
Playwright, screenwriter, and essayist whose dramas include *Devotees in the Garden of Love* (1991), *The America Play* (1995), and *Father Comes Home from the Wars (Parts 1, 8 & 9)* (2009). In 2001 she received a MacArthur Foundation "genius" grant.

**Ishmael Reed** (1938–  )
Prolific fiction writer, poet, anthologist, and recipient of a MacArthur grant. He is noted for his satire and unrelenting critique of contemporary intellectual life in such novels as *Yellow Back Radio Broke-Down* (1969), *Mumbo Jumbo* (1972), and *The Last Days of Louisiana Red* (1974).

**Sonia Sanchez** (1934–  )
Poet, playwright, children's author, and member of the Black Arts Movement. Her most notable poetry collections include *We a Baddddd People* (1970); *Love Poems* (1973); *Homegirls and Handgrenades* (1985), winner of the American Book Award; and *I've Been a Woman: New and Selected Poems* (1995).

**Sapphire** (pseudonym of Ramona Lofton, 1950–  )
Author of three volumes of poetry and the novel *Push* (1996), adapted as the film *Precious* in 2009.

**Danzy Senna** (1970–  )
Multiracial author of the novels *Caucasia* (1998) and *Symptomatic* (2003) and the memoir *Where Did You Sleep Last Night: A Personal History* (2009).

**Ntozake Shange** (1948–   )
Playwright, poet, novelist, children's writer, and feminist whose plays include *A Photograph: A Study of Cruelty* (1977), *Spell #7* (1979), *The Love Space Demands* (1992), and *Hydraulics Phat Like Mean* (1998).

**Anna Deavere Smith** (1950–   )
Playwright and actress known for her one-woman shows *Fires in the Mirror* (1991) and *Twilight: Los Angeles, 1992* (1993), both of which deal with race riots.

**Natasha Trethewey** (1966–   )
Poet who was awarded the Pulitzer Prize in 2007 for *Native Guard* (2006). Her other books are *Domestic Work* (2000) and *Bellocq's Ophelia* (2002).

**Rebecca Walker** (1969–   )
Feminist author of *Black, White, and Jewish: Autobiography of a Shifting Self* (2000) and *Baby Love: On Choosing Motherhood after a Lifetime of Ambivalence* (2007).

**Colson Whitehead** (1969–   )
Novelist and MacArthur fellow known for such Postmodernist works as *The Intuitionist* (1999), *John Henry Days* (2001), and *Apex Hides the Hurt* (2006).

**John Edgar Wideman** (1941–   )
Novelist and memoirist who received PEN/Faulkner Awards for *Sent for You Yesterday* (1983) and *Philadelphia Fire* (1990). His other notable works include the novel *Reuben* (1987); the short-story collections *Damballah* (1981), *Fever* (1989), and *The Stories of John Edgar Wideman* (1992); and the memoirs *Brothers and Keepers* (1984) and *Fatheralong: A Meditation on Fathers and Sons, Race and Society* (1994).

**Gregory Howard Williams** (1944–   )
Author of *Life on the Color Line: The True Story of a White Boy Who Discovered He Was Black* (1996).

**Sherley Anne Williams** (1944–1999)
Novelist, poet, and literary critic best known for the novel *Dessa Rose* (1986) and the collection *The Peacock Poems* (1975).

**Kevin Young** (1970–   )
Poet whose *Jelly Roll* (2005) was nominated for a National Book Award. He was strongly influenced by the work of Langston Hughes.

*—Kathryn West and Annette Harris Powell*

# Contemporary American Drama

Since 1970 American theater has variously entertained, challenged, offended, and edified audiences with productions that might uphold, question, or reject popular tastes, traditions, taboos, and mores. Veteran Broadway playwrights such as Neil Simon and Edward Albee continued to produce popular plays. They were joined by a profusion of new artists fostered and encouraged by the emergence of Off Broadway and the expansion of regional professional theater that had begun in the 1950s and 1960s. As had been true in the turbulent 1960s, a wealth of dramatists, composers, and lyricists in subsequent decades drew particular inspiration from political movements and protests opposing war (in Vietnam and the Middle East) and discrimination based on race, gender, and sexual orientation.

## VIETNAM, THE MIDDLE EAST, AND AMERICAN DRAMA

The Vietnam War and its aftermath, when Americans did not always cheer their returning troops, elicited an array of thought-provoking plays. Between 1969 and 1976 David Rabe, a Vietnam veteran, crafted four disturbing and, at times, surreal dramas on this contentious era in the nation's history. In *Sticks and Bones, The Basic Training of Pavlo Hummel, The Orphan* (based on Aeschylus's trilogy *Oresteia*), and *Streamers* he depicted the debilitating, dehumanizing, and desensitizing effects of war on new soldiers, seasoned combatants, their families, and American society. Stephen Metcalfe's characters struggle to comprehend the deaths of their sons and friends in Vietnam in his one-act plays *Sorrows and Sons* and *Spittin' Image* (both 1986). From their wartime experiences eight veterans crafted *Tracers* (1980), a theatrical collage of explicit and arresting stories and scenes about such realities as boot camp, search-and-destroy missions, drug and alcohol abuse, rats, Saigon brothels, and body bags; sound effects and rock music complemented these vignettes.

Returned veterans and their readjustment (societal, psychological, emotional) to stateside life received sensitive, compelling, even humorous portrayals in many dramas. Among them are *Medal of Honor Rag* (1975), by Tom Cole; *An Evening with Dead Essex* (1978), by Adrienne Kennedy; James McLure's *Lone Star* and *Pvt. Wars* (both 1979) and *Laundry and Bourbon* (1980); *Strange Snow* (1983), by Stephen Metcalfe; *The Speed of Darkness* (1991), by Steve Tesich; and Lanford Wilson's *Fifth of July* (1978) and *The Rosewood Curtain* (1993).

Later U.S. military involvements in the Middle East similarly evoked stage works from prominent playwrights. *Two Rooms* (1998) by Lee Blessing focuses on an American hostage in Lebanon. Tony Kushner's *Homebody/Kabul* (1999; revised, 2004) explores the beauty and devastation of Afghanistan. The Iraq wars shadow *States of Shock* (1991), by Sam Shepard, Charles L. Mee's *Iphigenia 2.0* (2007), and *Beast* (2008), by Michael Weller (author of the 1970 Vietnam play *Moonchildren*).

# AFRICAN AMERICAN DRAMA

August Wilson is an African American playwright and one of this country's greatest dramatists. His magnum opus is "The 'Century' or 'Pittsburgh' Cycle," a collection of ten engrossing plays (see the Study Guide on Wilson in Part III of this volume). Paving the way for Wilson and others was Charles Gordone, who in 1970 became the first African American playwright to win the Pulitzer Prize in drama for *No Place to Be Somebody* (1969). In succeeding years black dramatists considerably enhanced the repertoire of the American theater, with several garnering Pulitzers.

*A Soldier's Play*, by Charles Fuller (1982 Pulitzer), exposes racial assumptions and hatreds on a segregated military base in 1944. The eleven playlets, or "exhibits," in *The Colored Museum* (1986), by George C. Wolfe, satirize black stereotypes, history, and culture. He also wrote the book (that is, the script) for and directed *Jelly's Last Jam* (1992), a "warts-and-all" musical biography of jazz pioneer Jelly Roll Morton. Suzan-Lori Parks writes provocatively, poetically, and often allegorically about stereotypes, discrimination, the United States' racial history, and the resilience of black America in the four-part *Imperceptible Mutabilities in the Third Kingdom* (1989), *The Death of the Last Black Man in the Whole Entire World* (1990), and *Venus* (1996). *Topdog/Underdog* (2002 Pulitzer) follows the long-standing rivalry between African American brothers named Lincoln and Booth to its violent conclusion.

Musicals and revues either celebrating African American composers and themes or with African American casts or creators delighted diverse audiences. Successful productions include *Purlie* (1970), *Don't Bother Me, I Can't Cope* (1972), *The Wiz* (1975), *Ain't Misbehavin'* (1978), *Dreamgirls* (1981), *Sophisticated Ladies* (1981), *The Tap Dance Kid* (1983), *Bring in 'Da Noise, Bring in 'Da Funk* (1996), *The Lion King* (1997), *Caroline, or Change* (2002), and *The Color Purple* (2005).

# FEMINIST DRAMA

Prize-winning dramas and comedies by women about their gender's repression, victimization, rejection of rules imposed by a patriarchal society, and quest for selfhood enlivened contemporary American theater. Ntozake Shange presents such themes in African American culture in her "choreopoem" *for colored girls who have considered suicide/when the rainbow is enuf* (1975). María Irene Fornés, a native of Cuba who writes on familiar feminist issues, regularly experiments with the forms of her theatrical pieces by combining modernism, magical realism, film techniques, humor, and nonrealistic staging. These traits distinguish *Fefu and Her Friends* (1977), *Mud* (1983), and *The Conduct of Life* (1985).

Mississippi native Beth Henley peoples her plays with Southern women, often eccentrics and grotesques, whose lives are marked by violence, ostracism, disease, and heartache; they are also fighters, whose struggles earn them a measure of hope for a better future. In her first play, the Southern Gothic comedy *Crimes of the Heart* (1979), three quirky sisters reunite and commiserate about their unsatisfactory love lives, including the abusive husband shot by the youngest sibling; two of them succumb to guilty but liberating laughter at their domineering grandfather's coma, and they all bond over birthday cake. The promiscuous protagonist in *The Miss Firecracker Contest* (1984) determines to gain her town's respect by winning its annual Fourth of July beauty and talent competition.

Marsha Norman creates female characters who take stock of their troubled pasts to decide how—or whether—to carry on. In her gritty debut drama, *Getting Out* (1977), a young woman just released from prison after serving eight years for homicide rejects her original, violent self, "Arlie," by insisting that she be called "Arlene." To reinforce her new identity, she rebuffs job offers from her former pimp, fights off sexual advances by her longtime guard, and accepts friendship and guidance from her new neighbor, a female ex-convict. In *'night, Mother* (1982; Pulitzer, 1983), a middle-aged daughter, who judges her life a failure, calmly announces to her mother that she will commit suicide that evening; she views this act as a personal victory, since she will choose what to do with her life.

Wendy Wasserstein is the premier female American dramatist of her time. The protagonists in her humorous, insightful plays such as *The Sisters Rosensweig* (1993) are educated, independent, professional women of means, who nevertheless feel unfulfilled as they confront careers and motherhood in a sexist world. Her comedy-drama *The Heidi Chronicles* (1988), spanning the years 1965 to 1989, charts the development of the modern women's movement in America and the changing roles of women through the experiences of the title character, a successful professor of art history, and her friends.

Paula Vogel writes imaginatively about pedophilia, AIDS, gender issues, and similar controversial subjects. The memory play *How I Learned to Drive* (1997) blends humor and horror as a woman recalls her sexual abuse by an uncle, starting when she was eleven, and how she survived.

*The Vagina Monologues* (1999), by Eve Ensler, celebrates female sexual anatomy through hilarious, explicit, angry, and moving real-life narratives. Since 1998, Ensler has sponsored "V-Day" from February 1 to March 31 each year, allowing the play to be staged on college campuses and other venues without paying royalties, provided the proceeds are donated to nonprofits working to end violence against women. As of 2008 the benefit performances and surrounding activities had raised more than $50 million to fight violence against women. Some performances have been met with controversy owing to the explicit content of some of the monologues.

## GAY AND LESBIAN DRAMA

Mart Crowley's 1968 play *The Boys in the Band*, in which eight (and possibly all nine) of the characters are homosexuals, proved popular with mainstream audiences, running for one thousand performances and bringing gay culture to the forefront of American theater. One year later, riots sparked by a New York City police raid on a Greenwich Village gay bar, the Stonewall Inn, launched the gay-rights movement. An abundance of notable plays subsequently explored gay and lesbian subjects. A college student in Albert Innaurato's comedy *Gemini* (1977) wrestles with his sexual identity. *Bent*, by Martin Sherman (1979), centers on gay victims of the Holocaust. A lesbian with terminal cancer discovers true love in *Last Summer at Bluefish Cove* (1980), by Jane Chambers. David Mamet's comedy *Boston Marriage* (1999) depicts love between "women of fashion" in the early twentieth century. In pioneering presentations of homosexuality in Chicano/a theater, Cherríe Moraga dramatizes lesbian desire in *Giving up the Ghost: Teatro in Two Acts* (1986); in *Heroes and Saints* (1989), with a subplot about a gay character who contracts AIDS; and in *The Hungry Woman* (2001). Homophobia, homosexuality, and racism in a baseball team help fuel Richard Greenberg's complex play *Take Me Out* (2002).

For more than thirty years Terrence McNally has treated with humor, honesty, and eloquence such gay-related concerns as AIDS, homophobia, and relationships. His works include *The Ritz* (1971), *André's Mother* (1988), *Lips Together, Teeth Apart* (1991), *Love! Valour! Compassion!* (1994), and *Corpus Christi* (1998). McNally also wrote the books for the musicals *Kiss of the Spider Woman* (1993) and *A Man of No Importance* (2002), which feature gay protagonists.

Harvey Fierstein drew on aspects of his life to create the three one-act plays tracing the loves, losses, and triumphs of a Jewish drag queen in *Torch Song Trilogy* (1983). He wrote the script for *La Cage aux Folles* (1983), notably featuring gay characters in the principal roles of a French nightclub owner and his longtime love, a female impersonator.

From more than two hundred interviews Moisés Kaufman and the members of Tectonic Theater Project assembled *The Laramie Project* (2000). Through the reactions and stories of the town's residents, this moving docudrama presents the events surrounding the brutal assault on and death of Matthew Shepard, a gay twenty-one-year-old university student, in Laramie, Wyoming.

Provocative dramas, comedies, and musicals about AIDS and this country's responses to it proliferated after the disease was first diagnosed in the 1980s and labeled "the gay plague." Representative plays include *As Is* (1985), by William M. Hoffman; *The Normal Heart* (1985), by Larry Kramer; *Before It Hits Home* (1989), by Cheryl L. West; *Angels in America, Part One: Millennium Approaches* (1991; Pulitzer, 1993), and *Part Two: Perestroika* (1992), by Tony Kushner; *The Baltimore Waltz* (1992), by Paula Vogel; *Jeffrey* (1993), by Paul Rudnick; *Patient A* (1993), by Lee Blessing; and *Lonely Planet* (1993), by Steven Dietz; and the popular musicals *Falsettos* (1992), by William Finn and James Lapine; and *Rent* (1996), by Jonathan Larson.

Homosexuality also figured in productions that were not specifically AIDS, gay, or lesbian works. They included *Six Degrees of Separation* (1990), by John Guare; *The Young Man from Atlanta* (1995), by Horton Foote; *As Bees in Honey Drown* (1997), by Douglas Carter Beane; and the long-running musical *A Chorus Line* (1975), by Michael Bennett, James Kirkwood Jr., Nicholas Dante, Marvin Hamlisch, and Edward Kleban.

In these and other plays and musicals created in the four decades from 1970, American theater addressed transformative societal and moral concerns. However, the breadth of this nation's contemporary theatrical offerings reflect the breadth of audience tastes. Thus, attractions also embraced plays on religious themes—*Agnes of God* (1982), by John Pielmeier, and *Doubt: A Parable* (2005), by John Patrick Shanley; more hit musicals, among them *Grease* (1972), and *Chicago* (1975); Disney spectacles based on animated films (and one opera), such as *Beauty and the Beast* (1994); performance art by Laurie Anderson and Karen Finley; and contemporary comedies and dramas, including those by Broadway veterans and by newer voices Margaret Edson, Donald Margulies, David Auburn, Nilo Cruz, Tracy Letts, and Lynn Nottage. In addition to their entertainment value, the best of these examples of contemporary American theater, regardless of genre, articulated profound truths, positive and otherwise, about the country and the human spirit.

## TOPICS FOR DISCUSSION AND RESEARCH

1. The Pulitzer Prize in drama has been awarded in most years since its creation in 1917. Students could research the history of this most prestigious of American drama awards, attentive to newspaper publisher Joseph Pulitzer's intentions in establishing and endowing it, as well as to additional standards guiding the selection process. Students might then choose and analyze one Pulitzer Prize–winning play or musical since 1970 to determine why it merited the award. Alternatively, students could research and analyze a major play (or plays) staged in a year since 1970 in which no Pulitzer Prize in drama was awarded to determine why it (or they) did not win. Dramas were not honored in 1972, 1974, 1986, 1997, or 2006. Search the Internet Broadway Database by "Season" for productions in specific years. Helpful sources for such an undertaking are John L. Toohey, *A History of the Pulitzer Prize Plays* (New York: Citadel, 1967) and the website <www.pulitzer.org>.

2. The essay above refers to prominent performance artists Laurie Anderson and Karen Finley. Students could research the development of performance art (with emphasis on post-1970 examples). Areas for larger exploration, discussion, and analysis might include genres and styles of performance art, the range of its themes and goals, women as performance artists, performance art as "theater" and/or "art," and its place in popular culture. See A. A. Bronson and Peggy Gale, *Performance by Artists* (Toronto: Art Metropole, 1988); RoseLee Goldberg, *Performance Art: Futurism to the Present* (New York: Abrams, 1988); Moira Roth, *The Amazing Decade: Women and Performance Art in America, 1970-1980* (Los Angeles: Astro Artz, 1983); and Mariella R. Sandford, ed., *Happenings and Other Acts* (New York: Routledge, 1985).

3. Spanish-language theater in North America dates to the late 1500s. Today, Latino/a theater in the United States exists in three forms, representing major ethnic populations: Chicano/a theater, Cuban-American theater, and Puerto Rican theater, which is often called *Nuyorican*. María Irene Fornés, Cherríe Moraga, and Nilo Cruz are prominent figures in Latino/a theater. Students could trace the development of one or more branches of Latino/a theater and analyze (or compare and contrast) themes, acting styles, and languages in representative plays since 1970. In addition to the writings in

RESOURCES by Vera V. Chernysheva, Lynda Hart, Jon D. Rossini, and Stephen Watt, see Nicolás Kanellos, ed., *Hispanic Theatre in the United States* (Houston: Arte Público, 1984); Kanellos, *Mexican American Theatre: Then and Now* (Houston: Arte Público, 1984); John V. Antush, ed., *Recent Puerto Rican Theatre: Five Plays from New York* (Houston: Arte Público, 1991); Antush, ed., *Nuestro New York: An Anthology of Puerto Rican Plays* (New York: Mentor, 1994); and topical entries in Bordman and Hischak and in Wilmeth and Miller.

4. Throughout the history of American drama, African Americans, homosexuals, Jews, and Asians have often been represented with demeaning stereotypes and caricatures. Students could analyze one such portrayal from an older American play and a depiction from a post-1970 work. Some possible pairings include *The Children's Hour* (1934), by Lillian Hellman, and *Last Summer at Bluefish Cove* (1980), by Jane Chambers, which deal with lesbianism; *Abie's Irish Rose* (1922), by Anne Nichols, and *The Sisters Rosensweig* (1992), by Wendy Wasserstein, featuring Jewish characters; and John Luther Long's *Madame Butterfly* (1900) or Richard Rodgers and Oscar Hammerstein III's *Flower Drum Song* (1958) and Velina Hasu Houston's *Tea* (1987) or Hwang's *M. Butterfly* (1988). How does each piece reflect its time? What cultural forces and intervening dramatic texts led to changes in that group's representation on the stage? What stereotypes remain? Where? Why? To what extent does the use of stereotypes versus more fully realized characterizations affect the quality of the play?

5. Since 1970 many revues and musicals have celebrated the lives of noted African American musicians, among them, Jelly Roll Morton, Eubie Blake, Bessie Smith, and Fats Waller. Students could research the life and career of one such musician, then, discuss the extent to which the stage biography accurately presents that personality. They should analyze omissions and fabrications, relative to the facts, to determine their effects (positive and negative) on the stage work's picture of the individual.

# RESOURCES

## Criticism

Gerald Bordman and Thomas S. Hischak, *The Oxford Companion to the American Theatre,* third edition (New York: Oxford University Press, 2004).
Extensive entries on people, plays, musicals, and special topics in theater history.

Vera V. Chernysheva, "Latino Drama," in *Critical Survey of Drama,* second revised edition, 8 volumes (Pasadena, Cal.: Salem, 2003), VII: 3787–3791.
Concise history, discussions of playwrights and dramatic themes, and an annotated bibliography.

John M. Clum, *Still Acting Gay: Male Homosexuality in Modern Drama,* revised edition (New York: Palgrave Macmillan, 2000).
Critical analyses of gay plays by American and British writers.

David J. DeRose, "*The Speed of Darkness* and 'Crazed Vets on the Doorstep' Drama," *Viet Nam Generation Journal & Newsletter*, 3 (November 1991) <http://www2. iath.virginia.edu/sixties/HTML_docs/Texts/Reviews/DeRose_Crazed_Vets. html> [accessed 15 March 2010].
Discusses thematically related plays by Steve Tesich, Stephen Metcalfe, and others.

DeRose, "*States of Shock*," *Vietnam Generation Journal*, 4 (November 1992) <http:// www2.iath.virginia.edu/sixties/HTML_docs/Texts/Reviews/DeRose_States_ Shock.html> [accessed 15 March 2010].
Lengthy analysis of Sam Shepard's play *States of Shock*, which condemns both America's military invasion of Iraq in 1991 and the American public's complacent reaction to it.

Lynda Hart, ed., *Making a Spectacle: Feminist Essays on Contemporary Women's Theatre* (Ann Arbor: University of Michigan Press, 1984).
Includes discussions of playwrights such as María Irene Fornés, Ntozake Shange, Tina Howe, Marsha Norman, and Beth Henley.

Errol G. Hill and James V. Hatch, *A History of African American Theatre* (Cambridge, England: Cambridge University Press, 2006).
Definitive study of its subject, discussing such topics as African American writers, performers, theatrical genres, and acting companies.

Thomas Hischak, *The Oxford Companion to the American Musical: Theatre, Film, and Television* (New York: Oxford University Press, 2008).
First authoritative volume on this broad topic, with biographies of performers, writers, composers, and lyricists; plots; production histories; and guides to recordings.

*Internet Broadway Database* <www.ibdb.com>.
Allows searches by the categories Shows, People, Theatres, Characters, Awards, Songs, and Media.

*Lortel Archives—The Internet Off-Broadway Database* <www.lortel. org/LLA_archives>.
Allows searches by the categories Show Title, Theatre, People, Awards, Company Name, and All.

Carol P. Marsh-Lockett, ed., *Black Women Playwrights: Visions on the American Stage* (New York: Routledge, 1998).
Critical essays on themes and issues in plays from the later nineteenth century into the 1990s.

Brenda Murphy, ed., *The Cambridge Companion to American Women Playwrights* (Cambridge, England: Cambridge University Press, 1999).
Includes discussions of contemporary dramatists in later chapters.

Frank Rich, *Hot Seat: Theater Criticism for* The New York Times, *1980–1993* (New York: Random House, 1998).
Collection of more than three hundred reviews and essays by the former Broadway critic.

Jon D. Rossini, *Contemporary Latina/o Theater: Wrighting Ethnicity* (Carbondale: Southern Illinois University Press, 2008).
Discusses plays by Miguel Piñero, Luis Valdez, Guillermo Reyes, Octavio Solis, José Rivera, and Cherríe Moraga, among others.

June Schlueter, ed., *Modern American Drama: The Female Canon* (Rutherford, N.J.: Fairleigh Dickinson University Press, 1990).
Twenty essays on twentieth-century plays by women.

Sanford Sternlicht, *A Reader's Guide to Modern American Drama* (Syracuse, N.Y.: Syracuse University Press, 2002).
Historical contexts, theater trends, biographies, discussions of works by some eighty playwrights.

Jeffrey Ullom, *The Humana Festival: The History of New Plays at Actors Theatre of Louisville* (Carbondale: Southern Illinois University Press, 2008).
Historical-critical account of the play festival in which many major contemporary dramatists and dramas have debuted.

Stephen Watt, *Postmodern/Drama: Reading the Contemporary Stage* (Ann Arbor: University of Michigan Press, 1998).
Analyses of works by David Rabe, Cherríe Moraga, Karen Finley, and others.

Don B. Wilmeth and Tice L. Miller, eds., *Cambridge Guide to American Theatre,* updated edition (Cambridge, England: Cambridge University Press, 1996).
Encyclopedic source with more than 2,300 entries.

## PEOPLE OF INTEREST

**Edward Albee** (1928–   )
One of America's most celebrated and controversial dramatists. His masterpiece is *Who's Afraid of Virginia Woolf?* (1962). He won the Pulitzer Prize in drama for *A Delicate Balance* (1967), *Seascape* (1975), and *Three Tall Women* (1994).

**Laurie Anderson** (1947–   )
Performance artist, composer, and musician whose albums include *United States Live* (1984) and *Talk Normal: The Laurie Anderson Anthology* (2000) as well as the films *Home of the Brave* (1986) and *Hidden Inside Mountains* (2006).

**David Auburn** (1969–   )
Playwright, screenwriter, and film director who won the 2001 Pulitzer Prize in drama for *Proof.* Other plays include *What Do You Believe about the Future?* (1996) and *Skyscraper* (1997).

**Douglas Carter Beane** (1959–   )
Playwright and screenwriter. His plays include *Advice from a Caterpillar* (1990), *The Little Dog Laughed* (2006), and the book for the musical *Xanadu* (2007).

**Michael Bennett** (1943–1987)
Choreographer and director of *Company* (1970), *Follies* (1971), and *Dreamgirls* (1981). He also created the concept for *A Chorus Line* (1975).

**Lee Blessing** (1949– )
Playwright whose works include *Eleemosynary* (1986), *A Walk in the Woods* (1987), *Down the Road* (1989), and *Cobb* (2000).

**Jane Chambers** (1937–1983)
Lesbian playwright, novelist, poet, and television writer. Her plays include *A Little Snow* (1974), *My Blue Heaven* (1981), *Kudzu* (1981), and *The Quintessential Image* (1983).

**Tom Cole** (1933–2009)
Playwright, screenwriter, and educator. Among his plays are *An End to Chivalry* (1965), *Fighting Bob* (1979), and *About Time* (1990).

**Mart Crowley** (1935– )
Playwright and television executive. His plays include *Remote Asylum* (1970), *A Breeze from the Gulf* (1975), *Avec Schmaltz* (1984), and *The Men from the Boys* (2002), the sequel to *The Boys in the Band* (1968).

**Nilo Cruz** (1960– )
Cuban-born playwright, who, at age ten, immigrated with his family to the Little Havana section of Miami. He won the 2003 Pulitzer Prize for his play *Anna in the Tropics*. His other plays include *Dancing on Her Knees* (1994), *A Park in Our House* (1995), and *Beauty of the Father* (2006).

**Nicholas Dante** (1942–1991)
Playwright who wrote the book with James Kirkwood Jr. for the musical *A Chorus Line* (1975).

**Steven Dietz** (1958– )
Playwright and educator. His plays include *God's Country* (1988), *Halcyon Days* (1991), *Private Eyes* (1996), and *Shooting Star* (2008).

**Margaret Edson** (1961– )
Playwright and kindergarten teacher in Atlanta. Her first work, *Wit* (1995), won the 1999 Pulitzer Prize in drama.

**Eve Ensler** (1953– )
Playwright, performer, author, feminist, and activist. Her plays include *Necessary Targets* (1996), *The Good Body* (2005), and *The Treatment* (2006).

**Harvey Fierstein** (1954– )
Playwright, actor, and gay activist. His stage pieces include *Safe Sex* (1987) and the libretto for *Legs Diamond* (1988). He memorably appeared as Baltimore housewife Edna Turnblad in the Broadway musical *Hairspray* (2002).

**Karen Finley** (1956– )
Controversial visual and performance artist and writer whose recordings and theatrical pieces have often been labeled "obscene." Her solo performances include *The Constant State of Desire* (1987), *We Keep Our Victims Ready* (1989), *A Certain Level of Denial* (1992). She also put out the album *The Truth Is Hard to Swallow* (1998) and the DVD *Karen Finley Live* (2004).

**William Finn** (1952–  )
Playwright, composer, and lyricist. His musicals include *A New Brain* (1998, book coauthored with James Lapine), *The 25th Annual Putnam County Spelling Bee* (2004, with Rachel Sheinkin, libretto).

**Horton Foote** (1916–2009)
Actor, playwright, screenwriter, and television dramatist. His notable plays include *The Trip to Bountiful* (1953), *Lily Dale* (1986), and *The Last of the Thorntons* (2000). His autobiography is titled *Beginnings* (2002).

**María Irene Fornés** (1930–  )
Playwright and director. Her later plays include *Enter the Night* (1993), *Summer in Gossensass* (1999), and *Letters from Cuba* (2000).

**Charles Fuller** (1939–  )
African American playwright and screenwriter. His plays include *The Brownsville Raid* (1976), *Zooman and the Sign* (1979), and a series of six plays written in the 1990s about blacks' fight for rights after the Civil War.

**Charles Gordone** (1925–1995)
African American playwright, director, actor, and educator whose plays include *Baba Chops* (1974), *The Last Chord* (1976), and *Roan Brown and Cherry* (1985).

**Richard Greenberg** (1958–  )
Playwright whose works include *Eastern Standard* (1988), *Hurrah at Last* (1999), and *The Violet Room* (2003).

**John Guare** (1938–  )
Playwright and librettist whose first major success was *The House of Blue Leaves* (1971). His later works include the plays *Lydie Breeze* (1982), *Four Baboons Adoring the Sun* (1992), and *Chaucer in Rome* (2001), and the book and lyrics for the musical *Two Gentlemen of Verona* (1971) and the book for *Sweet Smell of Success* (2002).

**Marvin Hamlisch** (1944–  )
Composer of the Broadway musicals *They're Playing Our Song* (1979), *The Goodbye Girl* (1993), and *Sweet Smell of Success* (2002). His autobiography, *The Way I Was*, was published in 1992.

**Beth Henley** (1952–  )
Playwright and actress. Her works include *The Wake of Jamie Foster* (1982), *The Lucky Spot* (1986), and *Impossible Marriage* (1998).

**William M. Hoffman** (1939–  )
Playwright, opera librettist, television writer, and editor. His works include the plays *A Book of Etiquette* (1978) and *The Cherry Orchard, Part II* (1983) and the opera libretto *The Ghosts of Versailles* (1991), with score by John Corigliano.

**Velina Hasu Houston** (1957–  )
Playwright, essayist, and poet of Japanese, Blackfoot Pikuni and African American heritage, best known for her play *Tea* (produced, 1987; published, 2000).

**David Henry Hwang** (1957–   )
Considered one of the premier Asian American playwrights in the contemporary theater. He is best known for *FOB* (1980, Obie award) and *M. Butterfly* (1988, Tony Award), as well as his work in opera, musical theater, and film.

**Albert Innaurato** (1948–   )
Playwright, director, and television-film writer. His plays include *Ulysses in Traction* (1977), *Passione* (1980), and *Coming of Age in Soho* (1985).

**Moisés Kaufman** (1963–   )
Playwright, director, founder of Tectonic Theatre Project, and author of the docudrama *Gross Indecency: The Three Trials of Oscar Wilde* (1997).

**Adrienne Kennedy** (1931–   )
African American playwright and author. Her plays include *Funnyhouse of a Negro* (1962), *A Rat's Mass* (1967), *A Movie Star Has to Star in Black and White* (1976), *Ohio State Murders* (1992), and *Mom, How Did You Meet the Beatles?* (with Adam Kennedy, 2008).

**James Kirkwood Jr.** (1925–1989)
Playwright and author who wrote the book with Nicholas Dante for the musical *A Chorus Line* (1975). His plays include *P.S. Your Cat Is Dead* (1975) and *Legends!* (1987).

**Edward Kleban** (1939–1987)
Lyricist for *A Chorus Line* (1975).

**Larry Kramer** (1935–   )
Playwright, screenwriter, novelist, and AIDS- and LGBT (Lesbian, Gay, Bisexual, Transgender)-rights activist. His plays include *The Normal Heart* (1985); *Just Say No: A Play about a Farce* (1988); and *The Destiny of Me* (1992), the sequel to *The Normal Heart*.

**James Lapine** (1949–   )
Playwright and director. In addition to collaborations with William Finn, he wrote the books for Stephen Sondheim's musicals *Sunday in the Park with George* (1984), *Into the Woods* (1987), and *Passion* (1994).

**Jonathan Larson** (1960–1996)
Playwright, composer, and lyricist of the popular rock musical *Rent* (1996). He died of an aneurysm the day before the show's first preview performance. An earlier musical, *Tick, Tick . . . Boom!* (revised by David Auburn), was an Off-Broadway success in 2001.

**Tracy Letts** (1965–   )
Playwright, author, and actor who won the 2008 Pulitzer for his play *August: Osage County*. His other plays include *Killer Joe* (1993), *Bug* (2004), and *Superior Donuts* (2008).

**Donald Margulies** (1954–   )
Playwright and educator who won the 2000 Pulitzer Prize for *Dinner with Friends*. His other plays include *Found a Peanut* (1984), *Sight Unseen* (1991), *What's Wrong with This Picture?* (1994), *The Model Apartment* (1995), *Collected Stories* (1996), *Two Days* (2003), *Brooklyn Boy* (2004), and *Time Stands Still* (2009).

**James McLure** (1939–2006)
Playwright and screen and television writer. His plays include *Max and Maxie* (1992), *Ghost World* (1993), *Southern Christmas* (1995), and *Iago* (2003).

**Terrence McNally** (1939–   )
Playwright on gay themes.

**Charles L. Mee** (1938–   )
Playwright, political historian, and author. His plays include *Big Love* (2000), *bobrauschenbergamerica* (2001), *Hotel Cassiopeia* (2006), and *Cardenio* (2008, with Stephen Greenblatt). His memoir, *A Nearly Normal Life* (1999) discusses the effects of polio (contracted at age 14) on his life. Complete texts of Mee's plays are available free of charge on his website, *the (re)making project* <www.charles-mee.org>.

**Stephen Metcalfe** (1953–   )
Writer for stage, screen, and television and film director. His plays include *Vikings* (1981), *Pilgrims* (1985), *White Men Dancing* (1987), *Write Me Letters* (1992, companion to *Pilgrims*), and *Loves & Hours* (1993).

**Cherríe Moraga** (1952–   )
Chicana playwright, poet, and essayist whose writings include *The Last Generation: Poetry and Prose* (1993) and *Heroes and Saints and Other Plays* (1994).

**Marsha Norman** (1947–   )
Playwright and educator. Her works include the plays *Traveler in the Dark* (1984), *Loving Daniel Boone* (1993), and *The Last Dance* (2003), as well as the book and lyrics for musical *The Secret Garden* (1991) and the libretto for *The Color Purple* (2005).

**Lynn Nottage** (1964–   )
African American playwright who won the 2009 Pulitzer for *Ruined*. Her other plays include *Poof* (1993), *Crumbs from the Table of Joy* (1995), *Mud, River, Stone* (1998), *Las Meninas* (2002), *Intimate Apparel* (2003), and *Fabulation, or the Re-Education of Undine* (2004). She received a MacArthur Foundation ("Genius") Grant in 2007.

**Suzan-Lori Parks** (1964–   )
African American playwright, screenwriter, and essayist. Her dramas include *Devotees in the Garden of Love* (1991), *The America Play* (1990–1993), and *Father Comes Home from the Wars (Parts 1, 8 & 9)* (2009). In 2001, she received a MacArthur Foundation ("Genius") Grant.

**John Pielmeier** (1949–   )
Playwright, screen and television-film writer, actor, and director. His Broadway dramas include *The Boys of Winter* (1985) and *Voices in the Dark* (1999).

**David Rabe** (1940–   )
Playwright, screenwriter, and novelist. His later dramas include *Hurlyburly* (1984), *Those the River Keeps* (1994), and *The Dog Problem* (2001).

**Paul Rudnick** (1957–   )
Playwright, screenwriter, novelist, and magazine columnist. His plays include *Cosmetic Surgery* (1983), *Raving* (1984), *I Hate Hamlet* (1991), *The Naked Eye* (1996), *The Most Fabulous Story Ever Told* (1998), and *The New Century* (2008).

**Ntozake Shange** (1948–   )
African American playwright, poet, novelist, children's writer, and feminist. Her plays include *A Photograph: A Study of Cruelty* (1977), *Spell #7* (1979), *The Love Space Demands* (1992), and *Hydraulics Phat* [sic] *Like Mean* (1998).

**John Patrick Shanley** (1950–   )
Playwright, screenwriter, and director. His plays include *Danny and the Deep Blue Sea* (1984), *Italian-American Reconciliation* (1988), and *Psychopathia Sexualis* (1996). He won the Academy Award for best original screenplay for *Moonstruck* (1987).

**Martin Sherman** (1938–   )
Playwright, screenwriter. His plays include *Messiah* (1984), *When She Danced* (1989), *Some Sunny Day* (1996), and *Rose* (1999).

**Neil Simon** (1927–   )
Since the 1960s America's premier writer of stage comedy; also a screen and television writer and librettist. He won the 1991 Pulitzer Prize for *Lost in Yonkers*. His other plays include *Barefoot in the Park* (1963), *The Odd Couple* (1965), and the autobiographical trilogy *Brighton Beach Memoirs* (1983), *Biloxi Blues* (1985), and *Broadway Bound* (1986). He wrote the librettos for *Little Me* (1962), *Sweet Charity* (1966), *Promises, Promises* (1969), *They're Playing Our Song* (1979), and *The Goodbye Girl* (1993) and the autobiographies *Rewrites* (1996) and *The Play Goes On* (1999).

**Steve Tesich** (1942–1996)
Stage, screen, and television writer and novelist born in Yugoslavia. His plays include *Division Street* (1980), *Baptismal* (1990), and *Arts & Leisure* (1996). He won the Academy Award for best original screenplay for *Breaking Away* (1979).

**Paula Vogel** (1951–   )
Feminist/lesbian playwright and educator. Her plays include *The Oldest Profession* (1981), *And Baby Makes Seven* (1984), *Desdemona—A Play about a Handkerchief* (1993), *Hot 'n' Throbbing* (1994), *The Mineola Twins* (1996), *The Long Christmas Ride Home* (2003), and *A Civil War Christmas: An American Musical Celebration* (2004). In 2008 Vogel became chair of the playwriting department at the Yale School of Drama.

**Wendy Wasserstein** (1950–2006)
Playwright, television and screen writer, essayist, and children's author. Her plays include *Uncommon Women and Others* (1977), *Isn't It Romantic?* (1981), *An American Daughter* (1997), *Old Money* (2000), and *Third* (2005).

**Michael Weller** (1942–  )
Playwright, screenwriter, and educator. His most noteworthy plays are *Loose Ends* (1979), *The Ballad of Soapy Smith* (1984), *Spoils of War* (1988), *Lake No Bottom* (1990), *What the Night Is For* (2002), *Approaching Moomtaj* (2004), and *Side Effects, Zero* (2007/2008).

**Cheryl L. West** (1957–  )
African American playwright whose works include the plays *Jar the Floor* (1991), *Puddin 'n' Pete* (1993), *Holiday Heart* (1994), and the book for the musical *Play On!* (1997).

**Lanford Wilson** (1937–  )
Playwright, opera librettist, and a founder of the Off Broadway theater the Circle Repertory Company (1969). His most notable plays are *The Hot l Baltimore* (1973), *The Mound Builders* (1975), *Talley's Folly* (1979), *Burn This* (1987), *Talley & Son* (1981; revised, 1985, 1986), *Book of Days* (2000), and *Rain Dance* (2001), as well as the opera librettos *Summer and Smoke* (1971) and *This Is the Rill Speaking* (1992), both with composer Lee Hoiby.

**George C. Wolfe** (1954–  )
African American playwright, librettist, director, producer, and artistic director of the New York Shakespeare Festival/Public Theatre (1993–2004). He was the lyricist for *Bring in 'Da Noise, Bring in 'Da Funk* (1996) and coauthored the book for the musical *The Wild Party* (2000).

—*John Spalding Gatton*

# Feminism and Women's Writing

Women's social movements in the United States can be divided into three "waves" (although these divisions are not strictly chronological or oppositional). First-wave feminism emerged from the involvement of women activists in the antislavery, temperance, and women's-suffrage movements in the nineteenth and early twentieth centuries. Second-wave feminism, associated with the women's-liberation movement, began in the 1960s and developed through the 1970s as women challenged traditional roles and agitated for equal rights and protection under the law. A rallying cry of 1970s feminism was "The personal is political!" During this decade—the peak of second-wave feminism—women began examining, undermining, and revising the cultural values associated with sex and gender. Third-wave feminism emerged in the 1990s as a response to the "backlash" (a term popularized by Susan Faludi) against the political and social changes initiated by the women's movement and the failure of the second wave to incorporate broader definitions of women's identity. As feminism moves into the twenty-first century, it continues to evolve and to explore the meaning of "difference." Some feminists believe that gender distinctions are innate; others see them as socially constructed and alterable.

Just as feminisms focus on gender-based social discrimination, feminist literary critics challenged women's literary misinterpretation, subordination, and exclusion. Early efforts uncovered sexual stereotypes in literature by men. A more central occupation became the recovery of women writers who had been "lost." In 1973 the Feminist Press republished Charlotte Perkins Gilman's *The Yellow Wallpaper* (1899) and Susan Glaspell's "A Jury of Her Peers" (1917); and in 1979 a volume of Zora Neale Hurston's works, edited by Alice Walker, appeared. In *A Literature of Their Own* (1977) Elaine Showalter uses the term "gynocriticism" to describe literary criticism that focuses on ways in which women are portrayed in texts, how the literary canon is formed and revised, and how women's literary forms and writing techniques are defined.

The influence of second-wave feminism on women's writing of the 1970s emerges in its challenges to traditional female roles. In *The Feminine Mystique* (1963) Betty Friedan (who in 1966 founded the National Organization for Women [NOW]) had examined the roots of the dissatisfaction experienced by women who were expected to be fulfilled by being wives and mothers, and in *Sexual Politics* (1969) Kate Millett had analyzed how negative female images and patriarchal attitudes permeated literature, philosophy, psychology, and politics. In 1972 Gloria Steinem founded *Ms.* magazine to highlight women's social issues, feminist politics, and news about women. In fiction, too, women sought definition beyond the post–World War II image of the nuclear family consisting of a male provider and a housewife raising the children. Alix Kates Shulman's novel *Memoirs of an Ex-Prom Queen* (1972) relates Sasha Davis's coming of age and attempt to be a proper 1950s wife. The protagonist's sexual activity shocked audiences, while her emotional and intellectual turmoil dramatized the dilemmas uncovered in *The Feminine Mystique* and *Sexual Politics*. In Erica Jong's *Fear of Flying* (1973) a poet leaves her husband to overcome her "fear of flying"—a metaphor for independence in both creative and sexual expression. Gail Godwin also creates women who define themselves outside the home. She signals the anomalous situation of her protagonist in the title of *The Odd Woman* (1974), about a female professor who teaches a course on "Women and Literature." Eleven of the seventeen stories in Grace Paley's *Enormous Changes at the Last Minute* (1974) feature women without husbands. Paley's depictions of close friendships between female characters challenge the notion that women need men in order to have fulfilling lives.

As early as 1970 women of color challenged the notion that all women share the same experience and began to frame feminism to reflect concerns related to racism as well as patriarchy. Works by three important African American women writers appeared that year: Toni Morrison's *The Bluest Eye,* Alice Walker's *The Third Life of Grange Copeland,* and Maya Angelou's *I Know Why the Caged Bird Sings;* all three writers continue to publish significant works in the twenty-first century. Also in 1970 an anthology, *The Black Woman,* gathered a selection of stories by black female writers that suggested a tradition separate from that of white women; the editor, Toni Cade Bambara, published a collection of her own of stories, *Gorilla, My Love,* in 1972. Black women expressed themselves in other forms, as well. Lucille Clifton, Rita Dove, Nikki Giovanni, June Jordan, and Audre Lorde published important poetry collections in the 1970s, and Ntozake Shange's "choreopoem" *for colored girls who have considered suicide/when the rainbow is enuf* was the second play by an African American woman to be performed on Broadway when it was produced in 1976. All of these writers reject hierarchies based not only on gender but also on race—the latter of which they found present in the women's movement—while celebrating traditions rooted in the African American experience.

Since the 1980s there has been an explosion of creative works by women engaging in and contributing to feminist efforts and debates begun in the 1970s. Women writers continue to challenge traditional domestic roles assigned to women; but leaving the literal and metaphorical confinements of the home no longer means entering the nine-to-five working world, as it did in women's fiction of the 1970s. In *Housekeeping* (1980), for example, Marilynne Robinson merges realism and fantasy to fashion a modern fairy tale about two orphan sisters: Ruth, who embraces the outdoors and a vagabond life, and her younger sister, Lucille, who adheres to a traditional role. The female wilderness fantasy later informed works as diverse as Ursula K. Le Guin's "She Unnames Them" (1985) and Morrison's *Jazz* (1992) and eventually found its way into realist fiction such as Pam Houston's *Cowboys Are My Weakness* (1993) and *Waltzing the Cat* (1999). Dorothy Allison's *Bastard out of Carolina* (1992) targets the intersection of gender, poverty, and the abuse of female children. The depiction of women in occupations traditionally occupied by men also challenged traditional roles. Sara Paretsky's Victoria Iphigenia "V. I." Warshawski and Sue Grafton's Kinsey Millhone offered female versions of the hard-boiled detective and ushered in a new golden age of mystery fiction. Female writers also began to take on violent and disturbing subject matter in a more graphic manner. Joyce Carol Oates claims for herself a tradition embodied by male writers such as Ernest Hemingway and Norman Mailer in *On Boxing* (1987), as does Annie Proulx with the Western in *Close Range: Wyoming Stories* (1999), which includes the acclaimed "Brokeback Mountain."

The efforts of women of color to expand definitions of American literature to include black, white, Native American, and Latina experience continue. Louise Erdrich, Leslie Marmon Silko, Joy Harjo, Paula Gunn Allen, Linda Hogan, and Wendy Rose explore intersections of Native American life and mainstream culture in their works. *This Bridge Called My Back: Writings by Radical Women of Color* (1981), edited by Gloria Anzaldúa and Cherríe Moraga, and Anzaldúa's *Borderlands/La Frontera* (1987) directed attention to Latina writers such as Julia Alvarez, Ana Castillo, Denise Chávez, Sandra Cisneros, Judith Ortiz Cofer, and Cristina García. The works of these writers, like those of their Asian American counterparts Maxine Hong Kingston, Amy Tan, Bharati Mukherjee, Theresa Hak Kyung Cha, and Gish Jen and the poets Cathy Song and Janice Mirikitani, depict the confusions, conflicts, and contradictions of female identity within hybrid cultures.

In the 1990s women emerged as a powerful influence on literary markets both as writers and as readers; by the end of the decade women had become the majority buyers of both fiction and nonfiction. Empowered by female support and the creativity of women writers, concerns once relegated primarily to women—motherhood, romance, body image, the difficulty of balancing family life and work, female rivalry, rape, and sexual abuse—have become part of mainstream literature and culture. Several writers have deliberately corrected the absence of these themes in canonical texts. In *A Thousand Acres* (1991) Jane Smiley retells William Shakespeare's *King Lear* (circa 1606) through Ginny, who is based on Goneril, and in *Ahab's Wife; or, The Star-Gazer* (1999) Sena Jeter Naslund expands on a detail in Herman Melville's *Moby-Dick* (1851). Additionally, women writers refuse to be limited by "female" themes and the narrative structures associated with them. Rather than focusing on the conflicts created by differences in gender, class, race, or sexuality, these writers are now more inclined to celebrate such differences. They are also more likely to explore simultaneously two sides of an issue that earlier writers felt were mutually exclusive: female identity as innate and as socially constructed. As feminists work toward broader definitions of women's identity, activities, and desires, so do women writers. No longer required to justify themselves in the literary marketplace, women are free to write what and how they wish. This statement should not, however, be taken to suggest that feminism or the ideas associated with its various "waves" are no longer useful. A more productive approach is to understand the multiple and innovative ways in which women writers seek to revise the conventions and themes of American literature.

## TOPICS FOR DISCUSSION AND RESEARCH

1. In *A Jury of Her Peers: American Women Writers from Anne Bradstreet to Annie Proulx* (2009) Elaine Showalter, drawing on her earlier study of British women

writers, *A Literature of Their Own* (1977), traces the development of American women's writing through four stages. The first, which she calls "feminine," consists of "a prolonged phase of imitation of the prevailing modes of the dominant tradition." In the second, "feminist" stage, "there is a phase of 'protest' against these modes, and 'advocacy' of independent rights and values." The third stage, "female," is one "of self-discovery, a search for identity and a specific aesthetic." In the last, or "free," stage, female writers "can take on any subject they want, in any form they choose." Students might use Showalter's categories to analyze two or more works by American women writers published from the early 1970s to the present. Do the works support or undermine Showalter's divisions? Do particular works fit neatly into separate categories, or do you see evidence of a combination of categories? Do you find, as Showalter does, that works published in the twenty-first century belong to the fourth category? What does it mean for women to be "free" to write on any subject? Chapters 18 through 20 of Showalter's *Sister's Choice: Tradition and Change in American Women's Writing* (1991) offer excellent starting points and suggest primary works to study. Also useful is Katherine B. Payant's *Becoming and Bonding: Contemporary Feminism and Popular Fiction by American Women Writers* (1993).

2. In *Of Woman Born: Motherhood as Experience and Institution* (1977) Adrienne Rich examines how motherhood in a patriarchal culture can, on the one hand, limit a woman's growth, while, on the other hand, it can be a source of pleasure or power. Various writers have depicted the paradoxical nature of motherhood and the various ways it can affect the relationship between mothers and daughters. Mothers in literature can be a source of encouragement and nurture but can also be unsuitable role models who, as representatives of patriarchy, socialize their daughters into accepting their inferiority to men. Students might analyze portrayals of mothers and/or mother-daughter relationships in one or more works. There are many works from which to choose, including Maxine Hong Kingston's *The Woman Warrior* (1975), Marilynne Robinson's *Housekeeping* (1980), Gail Godwin's *A Mother and Two Daughters* (1982), Marsha Norman's play *'night, Mother* (1983), Denise Chávez's *The Last of the Menu Girls* (1986), Sue Miller's *The Good Mother* (1986), Vivian Gornick's *Fierce Attachments: A Memoir* (1987*)*, Amy Tan's *The Joy Luck Club* (1989), Esmeralda Santiago's *When I Was Puerto Rican* (1994), Edwidge Danticat's *Breath, Eyes, Memory* (1994), Nora Okja Keller's *Comfort Woman* (1997), Chitra Banerjee Divakaruni's *Queen of Dreams* (2004), and poems by Rita Dove and Louise Glück that rework the myth of Demeter and Persephone. The collection edited by Mickey Pearlman (1989) and chapter 3 of Payant's book offer excellent starting points for this topic.

3. Speculative fiction, which includes science fiction, fantasy, and utopian works, has long been written by women—for example, Mary Shelley's *Frankenstein* (1818) and Charlotte Perkins Gilman's *Herland* (1915). In the late 1960s women began to explore overt feminist themes in works such as Ursula K. Le Guin's *The Left Hand of Darkness* (1969), Joanna Russ's *The Female Man* (1975), and Marge Piercy's *Woman on the Edge of Time* (1976). These works

use alternate worlds to explore and challenge social boundaries and definitions related to gender. Among African American writers, Octavia Butler's
Earthseed series and Nnedi Okorafor's *Zahrah the Windseeker* (2005) and
*The Shadow Speaker* (2007) will lend themselves well to discussions related to
race and culture, as well as to gender. Students interested in exploring gender
should pay particular attention to the ways women writers reformulate the
narrative structures of genre fiction. Helpful secondary sources include Anne
Cranny-Francis's *Feminist Fiction: Feminist Uses of Generic Fiction* (1990),
Merja Makinen's *Feminist Popular Fiction* (2001), and Payant's chapter on
Marge Piercy. The first two studies include useful discussions of the structural
features and conventions of genres. They also consider women's reformulations
of detective novels, another genre women writers appropriate for feminist concerns. Showalter also addresses female detectives in chapter 19 of *A Jury of Her
Peers*.

4. A more recent female genre to emerge in American fiction is "chick lit,"
which was initiated by the publication in 1996 of *Bridget Jones's Diary*,
by the English writer Helen Fielding. These wildly popular works feature
single women—usually white—in their twenties and thirties who struggle
with insecurities about their looks and in relationships with men, while also
trying to succeed professionally. Buoyed by warm friendships and often
the comfort of material goods, they eventually find the self-acceptance
that allows them to succeed both in love and work. The genre, however, is
not without its detractors. For example, in her *New York Times* column "Of
Divas and Ditzes: Gone with the Diary" (28 April 2001) Maureen Dowd
criticized chick lit as vacuous, apolitical, and consumerist. Suzanne Ferriss
and Mallory Young, however, argue for the legitimacy of chick-lit studies because it focuses on concerns "dear to cultural critics' hearts" such as
the relationship between identity and sexuality; consumer capitalism; and
race, ethnicity, and class. Even more to the point, chick lit deals with issues
essential to feminism, such as the pressures on women to balance work with
intimate relationships." Students may wish to weigh in on this debate or
simply examine a work's treatment of one or more issues related to feminism. Students may also be interested in variations by ethnic writers, such as
Alisa Valdes-Rodriguez's "chica lit" novel *The Dirty Girls Social Club* (2003),
Erica Kennedy's "sistah lit" novel *Bling* (2004), or Sonia Singh's *Goddess for
Hire* (2004). In addition to gender, these works express the concerns of the
specific cultural communities in which they take place. Students may also
wish to compare the treatment of an issue—body image, relationships, family, or work—depicted in an example of chick lit to that of an earlier work
such as Erica Jong's *Fear of Flying*. How do works from different decades
treat similar issues? What concerns remain the same for feminists? How do
they reflect differences between second- and third-wave feminisms?

5. Women writers have revised the traditional bildungsroman to highlight the
social construction of female identity. In the classic bildungsroman the male
protagonist's identity is at first shaped by the social environment, but he
eventually becomes aware of its pressure and rebels against it. The traditional

bildungsroman ends with the protagonist's adjustment to society as a sign of his full development. Students interested in exploring the female bildungsroman should pay close attention to the way women writers use the form. What aspects of society are identified as shaping the female protagonist? What form does rebellion take for the heroine? In addition, students should be aware of aspects of the anti-bildungsroman, especially in the denouement of a work. If the protagonist adjusts to society, is this resolution presented as a positive one? If the protagonist does not adjust, does the work propose an alternative to social conformity? Students might also consider memoirs and autobiographies, as these works also allow writers to explore the way society shapes female identity and agency. Possible works to examine include Maya Angelou's *I Know Why the Caged Bird Sings* (1970), Vivian Gornick's *Fierce Attachments: A Memoir* (1987), Susanna Kaysen's *Girl, Interrupted* (1993), Elizabeth Wurtzel's *Prozac Nation* (1994), Mary Karr's *The Liars' Club* (1995), and Alice Sebold's *Lucky* (1999). *Writing Women's Lives: An Anthology of Autobiographical Narratives by Twentieth-Century American Women Writers* (1994), edited by Susan Cahill, also identifies relevant sources.

## RESOURCES

### Primary Works

Susan Cahill, ed., *Writing Women's Lives: An Anthology of Autobiographical Narratives by Twentieth-Century American Women Writers* (New York: Harper, 1994).
Collection of fifty autobiographical narratives that depict an array of women's experiences by women writers including Louise Bogan, Annie Dillard, Sandra Cisneros, Dorothy Allison, Kate Millett, Denise Levertov, Jeanne Wakatsuki Houston, and Maya Angelou.

Barbara A. Crow, ed., *Radical Feminism: A Documentary Reader* (New York: New York University Press, 2000).
Collection of primary documents written in the 1960s and 1970s by American feminists, including manifestos, meeting minutes, newsletters, and essays essential to understanding the emergence and development of radical feminist thought in the United States.

Elisabeth A. Frost and Cynthia Hogue, eds., *Innovative Women Poets: An Anthology of Contemporary Poetry and Interviews* (Iowa City: University of Iowa Press, 2006).
Brings together the work of a group of poets diverse in terms of movements, ethnicity, and craft, with interviews and introductions that provide biographical and literary contexts.

Sandra M. Gilbert and Susan D. Gubar, eds., *The Norton Anthology of Literature by Women*, third edition (New York: Norton, 2007).
Essential collection of works in English in which contemporary American writers are well represented. The biographical information and introduction are useful in providing historical and social contexts for reading the works.

Lisa Maria Hogeland and Shay Brawn, eds., *The Aunt Lute Anthology of U.S. Women Writers*, volume 2: *The 20th Century* (San Francisco: Aunt Lute Books, 2007).
Comprehensive collection of works by twentieth-century American women, including fiction, poetry, drama, nonfiction, lyrics, stand-up comedy routines, and librettos.

Wendy Martin, ed., *The Beacon Book of Essays by Contemporary American Women* (Boston: Beacon, 1996).
Excellent examples of contemporary American women writing in the essay form, divided into topical sections on the family, identity, oppression and violence, bodies, and nature.

George Plimpton, ed., *Women Writers at Work: The* Paris Review *Interviews* (New York: Modern Library, 1998).
Interviews originally published between 1960 and 1994 with sixteen women writers, including Maya Angelou, Joan Didion, Toni Morrison, Joyce Carol Oates, and Susan Sontag.

Claudia Rankine and Juliana Spahr, eds., *American Women Poets in the 21st Century: Where Lyric Meets Language* (Middletown, Conn.: Wesleyan University Press, 2002).
Collection of works by the poets Rae Armantrout, Mei-mei Berssenbrugge, Lucie Brock-Broido, Jorie Graham, Barbara Guest, Lyn Hejinian, Brenda Hillman, Susan Howe, Ann Lauterbach, and Harryette Mullen, with short introductions.

Linda Wagner-Martin and Cathy N. Davidson, *Women's Writing in the United States* (New York: Oxford University Press, 1995).
Collection of short stories, poems, essays, plays, speeches, performance pieces, erotica, diaries, correspondence, and recipes by nearly one hundred American women writers. The introduction and notes are quite informative.

## Criticism

Pamela Butler and Jigna Desai, "Manolos, Marriage, and Mantras: Chick-Lit Criticism and Transnational Feminism," *Meridians: feminism, race, transnationalism*, 8, 2 (2008): 1–31.
Interprets the chick-lit genre within the context of critical race and transnational feminist theories, considering questions of race, class, and nation in the work of South Asian American women writers; for advanced students.

Anne Cranny-Francis, *Feminist Fiction: Feminist Uses of Generic Fiction* (New York: St. Martin's Press, 1990).
Analyzes how women writers adapt popular genres (science fiction, fantasy, utopian, detective, and romance) to feminist concerns.

*Critical Inquiry*, special issue, "Writing and Sexual Difference," edited by Elizabeth Abel, 8 (Winter 1981).

Useful essays examining the "notion of difference" in early feminist criticism and identifying issues that remain current. Judith Kegan Gardiner's "On Female Identity and Writing by Women" addresses problems in theoretical discussions of what makes women's writing different from men's. Also useful is Elaine Showalter's "Feminist Criticism in the Wilderness," which identifies varied feminist methodologies and ideologies and calls for their unification.

Cathy N. Davidson and Linda Wagner-Martin, eds., *The Oxford Companion to Women's Writing in the United States* (New York: Oxford University Press, 1995).
Essential resource of more than eight hundred entries that provide biographical and bibliographical information about women writers and about literary styles, genres, and institutions important to women's writing. Also useful are the time line of important activities and advances by women and the general bibliography.

Cynthia J. Davis and Kathryn West, *Women Writers in the United States: A Timeline of Literary, Cultural, and Social History* (New York: Oxford University Press, 1996).
An account of American women's literature in an accessible time-line format that treats a variety of types of women's writing (fiction, poetry, biography, essay, advice columns, and cookbooks) alongside a chronology of developments in social and cultural history significant to women's lives.

Josephine Donovan, *Feminist Theory: The Intellectual Traditions of American Feminism* (New York: Ungar, 1992).
Survey and analysis of the development of American feminist theory until 1982, discussing feminism, poststructuralism, multiculturalism.

Rita Felski, *Literature after Feminism* (Chicago: University of Chicago Press, 2003).
Although not focused entirely on contemporary American literature, offers an excellent assessment of feminist approaches to writing while dismantling the notion that the literary and political values of a work are mutually exclusive. The discussion in chapter 3 of various forms of plot is particularly useful.

Suzanne Ferriss and Mallory Young, "A Generational Divide over Chick Lit," *Chronicle of Higher Education*, 52 (26 May 2006): 13–14; <http://chronicle.com/article/A-Generational-Divide-Over-/1668/> [accessed 14 January 2010].
Short essay discussing the interest of younger scholars in a popular literary genre, which is dismissed by those who are more established.

Ferriss and Young, eds., *Chick Lit: The New Woman's Fiction* (New York: Routledge, 2005).
Useful collection of essays treating themes and variations of the genre. Essays included in part 3 examine manifestations of feminism and postfeminism in works.

Lisa Maria Hogeland, *Feminism and Its Fictions: The Consciousness-Raising Novel and the Women's Liberation Movement* (Philadelphia: University of Pennsylvania Press, 1998).
Traces the influence of the women's movement on novels of the 1970s that focus on feminist themes. Writers discussed are Erica Jong, Marilyn French, Marge Piercy, Alix Kates Shulman, Alison Lurie, Joanna Russ, and Joan Didion.

Merja Makinen, *Feminist Popular Fiction* (New York: Palgrave, 2001).
Argues that feminists have successfully appropriated genre fiction and provides useful overviews of several literary genres—detective fiction, science fiction, romance, and fairy tale—and a summary of critical feminist debates.

Katherine B. Payant, *Becoming and Bonding: Contemporary Feminism and Popular Fiction by American Women Writers* (Westport, Conn.: Greenwood Press, 1993).
Discusses how popular fiction written by women from the late 1960s through the early 1990s reflects feminist ideas, rather than applying feminist literary theory to the works. Individual chapters are devoted to Marge Piercy, Mary Gordon, and Toni Morrison.

Mickey Pearlman, ed., *Mother Puzzles: Daughters and Mothers in Contemporary American Literature* (Westport, Conn.: Greenwood Press, 1989).
Collection of essays analyzing why depictions of mothers in current literature by American women "has moved from sainted marginality (as icon), to vicious caricature (as destroyer), to the puzzling figure" and why many works feature sexual abuse and incest.

Alvina E. Quintana, ed., *Reading U.S. Latina Writers: Remapping American Literature* (New York: Palgrave Macmillan, 2003).
Essential collection of essays about important American Latina writers. The introduction situates the works historically, while the essays treat individual authors.

Elaine Showalter, *A Jury of Her Peers: American Women Writers from Anne Bradstreet to Annie Proulx* (New York: Knopf, 2009).
Offers the first comprehensive history of American women writers from 1650 to 2000. Chapters 18 through 20 treat the 1970s, 1980s, and 1990s, respectively.

Showalter, *Sister's Choice: Tradition and Change in American Women's Writing* (New York: Oxford University Press, 1991).
Collection of essays, based on Showalter's 1989 Clarendon lectures at Oxford University, exploring the contributions of women writers to American letters while also tracing a "literary history of mastery and growth."

Showalter, Lea Baechler, and A. Walton Litz, eds., *Modern American Women Writers* (New York: Scribners, 1993).
Essays examining the contributions of women to American letters. Each essay combines biographical information with analysis of literary works.

Cheryl A. Wall, ed., Changing Our Own Words: Essays on Criticism, Theory, and Writing by Black Women (New Brunswick, N.J.: Rutgers University Press, 1989).

Proceedings of a conference held at Rutgers University in October 1987.

## PEOPLE OF INTEREST

**Ai** (1947–2010)
Multiracial poet of Japanese, black, and Native American descent. Her works are *Cruelty* (1973); *Killing Floor* (1979), which won the Lamont Poetry Award; *Sin* (1986), which won the American Book Award; *Greed* (1993); *Vice* (1999), which received the National Book Award for Poetry; and *Dread* (2003). She was born Florence Anthony; her adopted name means "love" in Japanese.

**Meena Alexander** (1951– )
Poet and fiction writer, born Mary Elizabeth Alexander in India and raised there and in Sudan. Her first books of poems were published in Arabic translation when she was still a teenager. She has written *The Bird's Bright Ring* (1976), *Without Place* (1977), *Stone Roots* (1980), *Fault Lines: A Memoir* (1993), *Manhattan Music* (1997), and *Raw Silk* (2004).

**Paula Gunn Allen** (1939–2008)
Poet, novelist, and literary critic of Laguna, Sioux, and Lebanese-American descent who grew up in the Laguna Pueblo in New Mexico. Her works of criticism include *The Sacred Hoop: Recovering the Feminine in American Indian Traditions* (1986) and *Off the Reservation: Reflections on Boundary-Busting Border-Crossing Loose Canons* (1998). Among her other works are the novel *The Woman Who Owned the Shadows* (1983) and *Skins and Bones: Poems 1979–1987* (1988).

**Dorothy Allison** (1949– )
Self-described "working class storyteller" whose novel *Bastard out of Carolina* (1992) brought her recognition. Her other works include the novel *Cavedweller* (1998) and the short-story collection *Trash* (2002).

**Julia Alvarez** (1950– )
Novelist and poet who grew up in New York after spending the first ten years of her life in the Dominican Republic, which her family fled because of her father's involvement in a political rebellion. She is best known for her novels *How the Garcia Girls Lost Their Accents* (1991), *In the Time of the Butterflies* (1994), and *¡Yo!* (1997). Her poetry has been collected as *Homecoming: New and Selected Poems* (1984).

**Gloria Anzaldúa** (1942–2004)
Feminist and cultural theorist best known for *This Bridge Called My Back: Writings by Radical Women of Color* (1981), coedited with Cherríe Moraga, and the autobiographical *Borderlands/La Frontera: The New Mestiza* (1987), which she described as "autohistoria-teoría."

**Toni Cade Bambara** (1939–1995)
Feminist activist and writer whose collection of stories *Gorilla, My Love* (1972) helped to establish an African American female voice in fiction. Her short stories, essays, and interviews have been collected as *Deep Sightings & Rescue Missions: Fiction, Essays, and Conversations* (1999).

**Mei-mei Berssenbrugge** (1947–   )
Poet born in Beijing and raised in Massachusetts. Her works include *The Heat Bird* (1983), *Empathy* (1989), *Sphericity* (1993), *Endocrinology* (1997), *Four Year Old Girl* (1998), *Nest* (2003), and *I Love Artists: New and Selected Poems* (2006).

**Gwendolyn Brooks** (1917–2000)
Poet whose 1950 Pulitzer Prize for the collection *Annie Allen* (1949) was the first won by an African American. Her other works include *A Street in Bronzeville* (1945), *Selected Poems* (1963), *Riot* (1969), *The Near Johannesburg Boy and Other Poems* (1986), and *Blacks* (1987).

**Rita Mae Brown** (1944–   )
Writer whose first novel, *Rubyfruit Jungle* (1973), explicitly addressed lesbian themes. She has "coauthored" with her cat, Sneaky Pie Brown, a series of mystery novels, beginning with *Wish You Were Here* (1990), featuring the feline protagonist Mrs. Murphy.

**Dorothy Bryant** (1930–   )
Novelist whose first book, *Ella Price's Journal* (1972), features a stock character from the 1970s: a woman who begins to question her suburban-housewife role. Her second book, the speculative utopian novel *The Kin of Ata Are Waiting for You* (1976), is regarded as a foundational feminist novel.

**Ana Castillo** (1953–   )
Chicana poet, essayist, and fiction writer. Her works include the novels *The Mixquiahuala Letters* (1986), *Sapogonia* (1990), *So Far from God* (1993), *Peel My Love Like an Onion* (1999), and *The Guardians* (2007); the short-story collection *Loverboys* (1996); and *My Father Was a Toltec and Selected Poems, 1973–1988* (1995).

**Lorna Dee Cervantes** (1954–   )
Chicana–Native American poet who is the author of *Emplumada* (1981)—winner of the American Book Award—and *Cables of Genocide: Poems on Love and Hunger* (1991).

**Theresa Hak Kyung Cha** (1951–1982)
Korea-born writer who was raised in California and is known for her experimental novel *Dictee* (1982).

**Denise Chávez** (1948–   )
Chicana author who began her career as a writer of one-act plays but found recognition for *The Last of the Menu Girls* (1986), a collection of interrelated stories that was published as a novel. Her other works include *Face of an Angel* (1994) and *Loving Pedro Infante (2001)*.

**Marilyn Chin** (1955–  )
Poet and codirector of the MFA program at San Diego State University who was born in Hong Kong and raised in Portland, Oregon. Her collections are *Dwarf Bamboo* (1987), *The Phoenix Gone, the Terrace Empty* (1994), and *Rhapsody in Plain Yellow* (2002).

**Amy Clampitt** (1920–1994)
Poet who did not publish her first poem until she was sixty-three. Her first collection, *The Kingfisher* (1983), was followed by *What the Light Was Like* (1985), *Archaic Figure* (1987), *Westward* (1990), and *A Silence Opens* (1994).

**Michelle Cliff** (1946–  )
Jamaican American writer whose first two novels, *Abeng* (1984) and *No Telephone to Heaven* (1987) and prose poem *Claiming an Identity They Taught Me to Despise* (1980) discuss race-consciousness as a legacy of colonial racism. Her other works include the novel *Free Enterprise* (1993) and the short-story collections *Bodies of Water* (1990) and *The Store of a Million Items* (1998).

**Lucille Clifton** (1936–2010)
Poet whose collections include *Good Times,* which *The New York Times* called one of the best books published in 1969. Her other works include *Good Woman: Poems and a Memoir, 1969–1980* (1987), *Next: New Poems* (1987), *Quilting: Poems, 1987–1990* (1991), *The Book of Light* (1993), *The Terrible Stories* (1995), and *Blessing the Boats: New and Selected Poems, 1988–2000* (2000), which won the National Book Award. She also wrote children's books.

**Judith Ortiz Cofer** (1952–  )
Writer of poetry, fiction, and nonfiction who was born in Puerto Rico and raised there and in New Jersey and Georgia. Her poems have been collected in *Latin Women Pray* (1980), *Reaching for the Mainland* (1987), *Terms of Survival* (1989), *The Latin Deli: Prose & Poetry* (1993), and *The Year of Our Revolution: New and Selected Stories and Poems* (1998). She is also the author of the young-adult book *An Island Like You: Stories of the Barrio* (1996).

**Edwidge Danticat** (1969–  )
Writer born in Port-au-Prince, Haiti, and raised from the age of twelve in New York who is known primarily for her novel *Breath, Eyes, Memory* (1994). Her other works include the novels *The Farming of Bones* (1998) and *The Dew Breaker* (2004); a collection of stories, *Krik? Krak!* (1996); and a memoir, *Brother, I'm Dying* (2007), which won the National Book Critics Circle Award.

**Annie Dillard** (1945–  )
Pulitzer Prize–winning novelist, poet, and literary critic who is best known for her narrative nonfiction, including *Pilgrim at Tinker Creek* (1974) and her memoir, *An American Childhood* (1987).

**Chitra Banerjee Divakaruni** (1957–  )
Poet and fiction writer who was born in India and moved to the United States in 1976. Her works include the poetry collection *Leaving Yuba City* (1997); the

short-story collection *Arranged Marriage* (1995); and the novels *The Mistress of Spices* (1997), *Sister of My Heart* (1999), and *Queen of Dreams* (2004).

**Susan Faludi** (1959–  )
Journalist whose works include *Backlash: The Undeclared War against American Women* (1991), which won the National Book Critics Circle Award for nonfiction; *Stiffed: The Betrayal of the American Man* (1999); and *The Terror Dream: Myth and Misogyny in an Insecure America* (2007).

**Betty Friedan** (1921–2006)
Became a leading figure of the women's movement in the United States with the publication of *The Feminine Mystique* (1963) and as cofounder and president of the National Organization for Women in 1966. *Life So Far: A Memoir* (2000) is her autobiography.

**Sandra M. Gilbert** (1936–  )
Poet and critic best known for her collaborative works with Susan D. Gubar, especially *The Madwoman in the Attic: The Woman Writer and the Nineteenth-Century Literary Imagination* (1979), a foundational work of feminist literary criticism. Her poetry volumes include *In the Fourth World* (1978), *The Summer Kitchen* (1983), *Blood Pressure* (1988), *Kissing the Bread: New and Selected Poems* (2000), and *Inventions of Farewell: A Book of Elegies* (2001).

**Nikki Giovanni** (1943–  )
Poet, social activist, and teacher whose early works, including *Black Feeling, Black Talk* (1967) and *Black Judgment* (1968) are associated with the Black Arts Movement. Her other poetry collections include *My House* (1972), *Cotton Candy on a Rainy Day* (1978), *Love Poems* (1997), and *Acolytes* (2007). She has also published books of poetry for children, including *The Genie in the Jar* (1996) and *The Sun Is So Quiet* (1996). She received a Grammy nomination for her spoken-word CD *The Nikki Giovanni Poetry Collection* (2002).

**Gail Godwin** (1937–  )
Fiction writer who has had five novels on *The New York Times* best-seller list: *A Mother and Two Daughters* (1982), *The Finishing School* (1984), *A Southern Family* (1987), *Father Melancholy's Daughter* (1991), and *Evensong* (1999).

**Vivian Gornick** (1935–  )
Former staff writer for the *Village Voice* who described her relationship with her mother in *Fierce Attachments: A Memoir* (1987*)*.

**Sue Grafton** (1940–  )
Author of a series of detective novels featuring the female private eye Kinsey Millhone, published in alphabetical order starting with *A Is for Alibi* (1982). In 2009 she published *U is for Undertow*.

**Jorie Graham** (1951–  )
Poet whose collection *The Dream of the Unified Field: Selected Poems, 1974–1994* (1995) received the Pulitzer Prize in 1996. She is also the author of *Hybrids of*

*Plants and of Ghosts* (1980), *Erosion* (1983), *The End of Beauty* (1987), *Region of Unlikeness* (1991), *Materialism* (1993), *The Errancy* (1997), *Swarm* (2000), *Never* (2002), and *Sea Change* (2008).

**Susan D. Gubar** (1944–   )
Literary critic and professor of English and women's studies at Indiana University who is best known for her collaborative work with Sandra Gilbert.

**Joy Harjo** (1951–   )
Native American poet, playwright, and musician whose books include *The Last Song* (1975), *In Mad Love and War* (1990), *The Woman Who Fell from the Sky* (1994), *The Spiral of Memory: Interviews* (1996), *A Map to the Next World: Poems and Tales* (2000), *The Good Luck Cat* (2000), and *How We Became Human: New and Selected Poems, 1975–2001* (2002).

**Beth Henley** (1952–   )
Actress and playwright who was awarded the Pulitzer Prize in drama for *Crimes of the Heart* (1978). Her other works include *The Wake of Jamie Foster* (1982), *The Miss Firecracker Contest* (1984), *The Lucky Spot* (1986), and *Impossible Marriage* (1998).

**Linda Hogan** (1947–   )
Native American writer whose works include the novels *Mean Spirit* (1990) and *Power* (1998); the essay collection *Dwellings: Reflections on the Natural World* (1995); the play *A Piece of Moon* (1981); and *The Woman Who Watches over the World: A Native Memoir* (2001).

**Pam Houston** (1962–   )
Short-story writer, novelist, and essayist whose works include the best-selling *Cowboys Are My Weakness* (1992); *Waltzing the Cat* (1999); *A Little More about Me* (2000); and *Sight Hound* (2006).

**Gish Jen** (1956–   )
Asian American fiction writer whose works include the novel *Typical American* (1991); its sequel, *Mona in the Promised Land* (1996); and the short-story collection *Who's Irish?* (1999).

**Gayl Jones** (1949–   )
African American writer best known for her novel *Corregidora* (1985), published when she was a graduate student at Brown University.

**Erica Jong** (1942–   )
Novelist best known for works about women who seek lives outside of traditional female roles, including *Fear of Flying* (1973); *How to Save Your Own Life* (1977); and *Serenissima: A Novel of Venice* (1987), republished as *Shylock's Daughter: A Novel of Love in Venice* (1995).

**Mary Karr** (1955–   )
Poet and professor of English at Syracuse University who is best known for her memoir *The Liars' Club* (1995). She followed it with two more: *Cherry* (2000) and *Lit* (2009).

**Susanna Kaysen** (1945–   )
Writer best known for her memoir, *Girl, Interrupted* (1993), which describes her experience of being committed to a psychiatric hospital in 1967.

**Nora Okja Keller** (1965–   )
Novelist born in Korea to a Korean mother and a German father. Her *Comfort Woman* (1997) and *Fox Girl* (2002) are the first two works in a planned trilogy. She is also the coeditor of *Intersecting Circles: The Voices of Hapa Women in Poetry and Prose* (1999).

**Erica Kennedy** (? –   )
African American novelist who writes about the fashion and entertainment industries. Her novel *Bling* (2004) features a hip-hop mogul, while *Feminista* (2009) revised the "chick lit" genre as "sistah lit."

**Maxine Kumin** (1925–   )
Poet and fiction writer whose poetry collections include *Up Country* (1972), for which she won the Pulitzer Prize, and *Looking for Luck* (1992). She also coauthored three children's books with the poet Anne Sexton.

**Ursula K. Le Guin** (1929–   )
Science-fiction writer who received both the Hugo and Nebula Awards for *The Left Hand of Darkness* (1969) and *The Dispossessed: An Ambiguous Utopia* (1974). She won the National Book Award for *The Farthest Shore* (1972), part of her Earthsea Trilogy.

**Denise Levertov** (1923–1997)
Politically active poet and essayist who was born in England and immigrated to the United States in 1948. Her poetry collections include *Relearning the Alphabet* (1970), *Footprints* (1972), and *A Door in the Hive* (1989).

**Audre Lorde** (1934–1992)
African American poet and essayist whose works of poetry include *The First Cities* (1968), *Cables to Rage* (1970), *From a Land Where Other People Live* (1972), *New York Head Shop and Museum* (1974), *The Black Unicorn* (1978), *The Cancer Journals* (1980), *Chosen Poems, Old and New* (1982), *Our Dead behind Us* (1986), and *A Burst of Light* (1988), the last of which won a National Book Award.

**Paule Marshall** (1929–   )
Daughter of immigrants from Barbados who infuses her fiction with African and Caribbean backgrounds. She is the author of *Brown Girl, Brownstones* (1959), *Soul Clap Hands and Sing* (1961), *The Chosen Place, the Timeless People* (1969), *Praisesong for the Widow* (1983), *Reema and Other Short Stories* (1983), and *Daughters* (1991).

**Bobbie Ann Mason** (1940–   )
Fiction writer and literary scholar best known for her fiction, including *Shiloh and Other Stories* (1982), *In Country* (1986), *Spence + Lila* (1989), *Love Life: Stories* (1989), and *Feather Crowns* (1993).

**Kate Millett** (1934–   )
Activist and feminist writer best known for *Sexual Politics* (1970).

**Cherríe Moraga** (1952–   )
Chicana playwright, poet, and essayist whose writings include *The Last Generation: Poetry and Prose* (1993) and *Heroes and Saints and Other Plays* (1994).

**Bharati Mukherjee** (1940–   )
Fiction writer born into a Bengali Brahmin family in Calcutta who moved to the United States to do graduate work at the Iowa Writers' Workshop. Her novels include *The Tiger's Daughter* (1972), *Wife* (1975), *Jasmine* (1989), *The Holder of the World* (1993), *Leave It to Me* (1997), *Desirable Daughters* (2002), and *The Tree Bride* (2004). Other works include the nonfiction *Days and Nights in Calcutta* (1977; revised, 1986), written with her husband, Clark Blaise, and *The Haunting Legacy of the Air India Tragedy* (1987). Her short stories are collected in *Darkness* (1985) and *The Middleman* (1988).

**Gloria Naylor** (1950–   )
African American novelist whose works include the National Book Award–winning *The Women of Brewster Place* (1982); *Linden Hills* (1985); *Mama Day* (1988); *Bailey's Café* (1992); *The Men of Brewster Place* (1998); and the semiautobiographical *1996* (2005).

**Marsha Norman** (1947–   )
Playwright whose works include the dramas *Traveler in the Dark* (1984), *Loving Daniel Boone* (1993), and *The Last Dance* (2003) and the musicals *The Secret Garden* (1991) and *The Color Purple* (2005). She won the Pulitzer Prize for *'night, Mother* (1983).

**Sharon Olds** (1942–   )
Poet whose works include *Satan Says* (1980), *The One Girl at the Boys' Party* (1983), *The Dead and the Living* (1984), *The Gold Cell* (1987), *The Father* (1993), *The Wellspring* (1996), *Blood, Tin, Straw* (1999), *The Unswept Room* (2002), *Strike Sparks: Selected Poems* (2004) and *One Secret Thing* (2008).

**Mary Oliver** (1935–   )
Prolific poet who received the Pulitzer Prize in 1984 for *American Primitive* (1983). Since 2000 she has published *The Leaf and the Cloud* (2000), *What Do We Know* (2002), *Owls and Other Fantasies: Poems and Essays* (2003), *Why I Wake Early: New Poems* (2004), *Blue Iris: Poems and Essays* (2004), *Long Life: Essays and Other Writings* (2004), *New and Selected Poems, Volume Two* (2005), *Thirst: Poems* (2006), *Our World* (2007), *Red Bird* (2008), and *Evidence* (2009).

**Cynthia Ozick** (1928–   )
Fiction writer who explores the theme of Jewish identity in her novels *The Cannibal Galaxy* (1983) and *The Messiah of Stockholm* (1987) and her short-story collections *The Pagan Rabbi and Other Stories* (1972), *Bloodshed and Three Novellas* (1976), and *Levitation: Five Fictions* (1982).

**Grace Paley** (1922–2007)
Social activist and writer whose three volumes of short stories were published together as *The Collected Stories* (1994).

**Sara Paretsky** (1947–   )
Author of a series of novels featuring the female detective "V. I." Warshawski, beginning with *Indemnity Only* (1982). *Hardball* was published in 2009.

**Marge Piercy** (1936–   )
Activist, poet, and novelist whose early works are considered feminist classics. They include the speculative novel *Woman on the Edge of Time* (1976) and the poetry collection *The Moon Is Always Female* (1980).

**Marilynne Robinson** (1947–   )
Began writing *Housekeeping* (1980) while working on her dissertation at the University of Washington. She did not publish another novel until *Gilead* (2004), winner of the Pulitzer Prize, the National Book Critics Circle Award, and the Ambassador Book Award; in the interim she wrote nonfiction works including *Mother Country: Britain, the Welfare State and Nuclear Pollution* (1989) and *The Death of Adam: Essays on Modern Thought* (1998). *Home* (2008), the sequel to *Gilead*, won the Orange Prize for fiction and was a finalist for the National Book Award.

**Joanna Russ** (1937–   )
Teacher and writer best known for her groundbreaking works of speculative fiction, including *The Female Man* (1975), *We Who Are about to . . .* (1977), *The Two of Them* (1978), *Kittatinny: A Tale of Magic* (1978), *On Strike against God* (1980), and *Extra (Ordinary) People* (1984).

**Esmeralda Santiago** (1948–   )
Puerto Rico–born author of the memoirs *When I Was Puerto Rican* (1994), *Almost a Woman* (1999), and *The Turkish Lover* (2004) and the novel *América's Dream* (1997).

**Alice Sebold** (1963–   )
Author of the novels *The Lovely Bones* (2002) and *The Almost Moon* (2007). *Lucky* (1999) is a memoir describing her survival after being raped as a college freshman.

**Ntozake Shange** (1948–   )
African American playwright, poet, novelist, children's writer, and feminist. Her plays are *for colored girls who have considered suicide/when the rainbow is enuf* (1976), *A Photograph: A Study of Cruelty* (1977), *Spell #7* (1979), *The Love Space Demands* (1992), and *Hydraulics Phat Like Mean* (1998).

**Alix Kates Shulman** (1932–   )
Activist and author of novels, memoirs, books for children, two books on the anarchist Emma Goldman, and many short stories and essays. *The Oxford Companion to Women's Writing in the United States* (1995) calls her *Memoirs of an Ex-Prom Queen* (1972) "the first important novel to emerge from the Women's Liberation Movement." Her other most notable publications are the memoirs *Drinking the*

*Rain* (2004), which relates her retreat to an island with no electricity or telephone while experiencing midlife changes, and *To Love What Is* (2008), about caring for her husband after a life-altering brain injury.

**Sonia Singh** (? –   )
Daughter of immigrants from India who is the author of the popular novels *Goddess For Hire* (2004), *Bollywood Confidential* (2005), and *Ghost, Interrupted* (2007).

**Jane Smiley** (1949–   )
Fiction writer whose novel *A Thousand Acres* (1991) won the Pulitzer Prize. Her other works include *The Age of Grief* (1987), *The Greenlanders* (1988), *Ordinary Love and Good Will* (1989), *Moo* (1995), *The All-True Travels and Adventures of Lidie Newton* (1998), *Horse Heaven* (2000), *Good Faith* (2003), *Thirteen Ways of Looking at the Novel* (2005), *Ten Days in the Hills* (2007), and *The Georges and the Jewels* (2009).

**Cathy Song** (1955–   )
Poet whose first collection, *Picture Bride* (1983), was selected for the Yale Series of Younger Poets. Her other works include *Frameless Windows, Squares of Light* (1988), *School Figures* (1994), *The Land of Bliss* (2001), and *Cloud Moving Hands* (2007).

**Susan Sontag** (1933–2004)
Human-rights activist and writer whose works include the novels *The Volcano Lover* (1992) and *In America* (2001), the collection of short stories *I, Etcetera* (1978), the play *Alice in Bed* (1993), and the nonfiction collections *On Photography* (1977), *Illness As Metaphor* (1978), *AIDS and Its Metaphors* (1989), *Where the Stress Falls* (2001), *Regarding the Pain of Others* (2003), and *At the Same Time: Essays and Speeches* (2007).

**Gayatri Chakravorty Spivak** (1942–   )
Indian American translator, literary critic, and theorist best known for her essay "Can the Subaltern Speak?" (1988), a foundational text in postcolonial studies.

**Gloria Steinem** (1934–   )
Feminist activist, writer, and founder of *Ms.* magazine. Her books include *Outrageous Acts and Everyday Rebellions* (1983), *Marilyn: Norma Jean* (1986), *Revolution from Within: A Book of Self-Esteem* (1992), and *Moving beyond Words* (1994).

**Amy Tan** (1952–   )
Chinese American writer whose novel *The Joy Luck Club* (1989) spent eight months on *The New York Times* best-seller list. She has also published the novels *The Kitchen God's Wife* (1991), *The Hundred Secret Senses* (1995), and *The Bonesetter's Daughter* (2001); the children's books *The Moon Lady* (1992) and *Sagwa: The Chinese Siamese Cat* (2001); and the essay collection *The Opposite of Fate: A Book of Musings* (2003).

**Luci Tapahonso** (1953–   )
Diné (Navajo) poet and professor of American Indian Studies and English at the University of Arizona. Her works include *The Seasonal Woman* (1982), *A Breeze*

*Swept Through* (1987), *Sáani Dahataał: The Women Are Singing* (1993), *Blue Horses Rush In: Poems and Stories* (1997), and *Songs of Shiprock Fair* (1999).

### Anne Tyler (1941– )

Novelist whose *Breathing Lessons* (1988) was awarded the Pulitzer Prize. Her other works include *Dinner at the Homesick Restaurant* (1982), *The Accidental Tourist* (1985), *Ladder of Years* (1995), *Back When We Were Grownups* (2001), and *Noah's Compass* (2010).

### Alisa Valdes-Rodriguez (1969– )

Novelist who has also written music reviews. Although she claims not to read "chick lit," her first novel, *The Dirty Girls Social Club* (2003), established her as "the godmother of 'chica lit.'" She has since published *Playing with Boys* (2004), *Make Him Look Good* (2006), *Haters* (2006), *Dirty Girls on Top* (2008, a sequel to her first), and *The Husband Habit* (2009).

### Wendy Wasserstein (1950–2006)

Playwright, screenwriter, essayist, and children's author whose plays include *Uncommon Women and Others* (1977), *Isn't It Romantic?* (1981), *An American Daughter* (1997), *Old Money* (2000), and *Third* (2005).

### Sherley Anne Williams (1944–1999)

African American writer best known for *The Peacock Poems* (1975) and the novel *Dessa Rose* (1986), about a runaway slave and the white woman who helps her.

### Terry Tempest Williams (1955– )

Author, naturalist, and environmental activist who writes poetry and nonfiction. Her best-known work is *Refuge: An Unnatural History of Family and Place* (1991).

### Elizabeth Wurtzel (1967– )

Best known for her confessional memoirs *Prozac Nation* (1994) and *More, Now, Again: A Memoir of Addiction* (2002).

*—Linda Trinh Moser*

# Genre Fiction and Popular Reading

The term *genre fiction* generally refers to works for a general audience that are easily categorized by subject matter and usually by form and that follow conventions related to theme, plot, and character. Indeed, established patterns are expected by readers of these works. Romance, the largest and most popular of fiction genres in the United States, features the amorous attraction between a woman and man. The plot revolves around the attempts of lovers, one often reluctant, to be together despite—usually—seemingly impossible odds. Mystery fiction includes crime and detective novels, police procedurals, and thrillers, each of which can be divided further into subgenres such as hard-boiled detective fiction, cozies, and techno-thrillers. The genre features an attempt to solve a crime, normally murder, by a protagonist who may or may not be a professional detective. Through "detection," observation, and deduction, the protagonist eventually exposes the criminal or antagonist, usually in the plot's denouement. Speculative fiction includes science fiction, fantasy, utopian novels, and cyberpunk; all of these "speculate" about science, the future, and evolving social organizations. Science fiction usually features unusual settings—in alternative versions of Earth or on other planets, and posits theoretical developments extrapolated from current knowledge. Fantasy, a broader term, may include science-fiction elements. Works with this label feature newly imagined worlds or alternative versions of the past or present which can have utopian/dystopian characteristics. Fantasy fiction is often peopled by creatures and characters with mystical, supernatural, or magical abilities. Gothic works include horror fiction featuring supernatural violence, grotesque characterizations, and eerie settings, all of which inspire fascination, fear and revulsion. Westerns are set in the frontier American West and concern the conflict between civilization and lawlessness. They feature the lives and exploits of cowboys, Indians, lawmen, and scouts who tend to be loners and typically involve the pursuit of a personal sense of justice, not to be confused with the law.

Because of their popularity and formulaic plots, works of genre fiction are often regarded as low-quality literature chiefly produced for profit but may include distinguished work thought to be more skillfully written with a more serious purpose. Despite its large numbers of readers, genre fiction has a history of being ignored by academics. Indeed, literature and creative-writing classes do not usually focus on genre fiction because of the assumption of its inferiority. Many contemporary writers, however, embrace genre fiction, finding the categories adaptable and flexible enough to meet a variety of subject matter and concerns, including those of social and political importance.

In their resistance of simplified plotlines and themes, contemporary writers blur the lines between genre and literary fiction. E. L. Doctorow's *Welcome to Hard Times* (1975), Cormac McCarthy's Border Trilogy novels, and Annie Proulx's short stories all challenge earlier Westerns that romanticize frontier justice, rugged individualism, the destruction of natural habitats, and the conquest of Indian territories. Michael Chabon's *The Final Solution: A Story of Detection* (2004) encourages readers to reexamine the notion that evil can be easily conquered. In it, an elderly (and unnamed) Sherlock Holmes attempts to "solve" the mystery of a missing parrot belonging to a mute Jewish boy during World War II, while the greater crime—the Holocaust—eludes him. Women writers have reformulated the romance to address the problems arising from a preoccupation with relationships related to romantic love, or its perversion. Plus-sized characters in Jennifer Weiner's novels highlight the injustice of being measured against imposed standards of physical beauty. Jodi Picoult's work deals with rape and teen suicide.

Writers also acknowledge that genre fiction's ability to entertain and enlighten does not negate its capacity to comment upon social and political issues. African American writers Octavia Butler, Samuel Delany, and Nnedi Okorafor use the tradition of science fiction to address issues related to racial difference. While Okorafor concentrates on Africa and Africans in her work, Delany and Butler challenge gender and racial categories by creating characters with unstable and shifting racial and gender identities. Walter Mosley also writes science fiction, but he is better known for his series featuring black private detective Easy Rawlins, starting with *Devil in a Blue Dress* (1990); these novels emphasize racial inequity in Rawlins's inability to move as freely as his white counterparts. Speculative fiction and mystery writers also highlight environmental issues. Rudolfo Anaya's *Jemez Spring* (2005), one of his Sonny Baca mysteries, is about issues related to water use in the arid Southwest. Also promoting environmental awareness are the novels of Frank Herbert, David Brin, and Ursula K. Le Guin, who write speculative fiction.

As writers search for fresh ways to tell stories, they have blended genres. Stephanie Meyer's Twilight series, which includes *Twilight* (2005), *New Moon* (2006), *Eclipse* (2007), and *Breaking Dawn* (2008), combines Gothic vampire elements and romance. Detective fiction has proven malleable enough to combine with other genres as well. Romantic suspense, for example, has long been a popular subgenre of romance. Science-fiction versions of detective fiction have proven popular, too. Android bounty hunter Rick Deckard in Philip K. Dick's *Do Androids Dream of Electric Sheep?* (1968) was among the first science-fiction detectives, providing a model for private investigators such as Albert Morris in David Brin's *Kiln People* (2002). Michael Chabon's detective novel *The Yiddish Policemen's Union* (2007) uses an element of speculative fiction in his creation of Alaska, instead of Israel, as the site of Jewish settlement after World War II. Frank Miller's *Batman: The Dark Knight Returns* (published in four issues of DC Comics from February to June 1986) combines detection, crime fighting, and Gothic elements with the graphic novel.

Students interested in genre fiction or in one particular form should first gain an understanding of the plot, character, and thematic conventions associated with the genre. The RESOURCES section provides resources for several genres. To locate works not included in this essay, students may wish to consult various professional organizations devoted to promoting genre fiction. All of these sites include discussion or links to sources about the conventional features of their genres. The Western Writers of America, founded in 1953, is the oldest of these types of organizations; its website is <www.westernwriters.org>, and it lists winners of its annual Spur, Lariat, and Branding Iron Awards. The website for the Science Fiction & Fantasy Writers of America, founded in 1965, can be found at <www.sfwa.org>. This site includes a list of works awarded the organization's Nebula Awards and a special section, "For Educators," with lesson plans for specific works. Mystery Writers of America can be found at <www.mysterywriters.org>; the site has a section with advice for book clubs that suggests books and discussion questions and lists winners of the Edgar Allan Poe Awards. The Romance Writers of America (RWA), established in 1981, offers descriptions of the genre and its subgenres, statistics about its industry and readers, and links to author websites at <www.rwanational.org>; it lists winners of the annual RITA (named for the RWA's first president, Rita Clay Estrada) and Golden Heart (for unpublished fiction) Awards. The Horror Writers Association at <www.horror.org> also lists writers and winners of the Bram Stoker Awards given annually for outstanding horror writing in various categories. These websites can also direct students to the numerous fanzines and "prozines" (professional or industry magazines) devoted to each genre; these sources offer reviews of work using criteria appropriate to each genre.

## TOPICS FOR DISCUSSION AND RESEARCH

1. In *Writing Fiction: A Guide to Narrative Craft* (2007) Janet Burroway expresses disdain for genre fiction: "dealing in the conventions and hackneyed phrases of romance, horror, fantasy, and so forth can operate as a form of personal denial, using writing as a means of avoiding rather than uncovering your real concerns." Students may wish to engage Burroway in an examination of one or more examples of genre fiction. In what ways is a work escapist or not? Do the conventions related to plot, character, and theme provide a way for readers to avoid serious issues? Does the entertainment value or formulaic aspect of genre fiction prevent it from addressing serious issues?

2. Students might want to try their hand at writing in one of the genres. After studying several short stories or a novel, create a short story following the conventions of the genre. Include a reflection in which you discuss the genre aspects of the plot. What is the most important part of the story you wrote—action, dialogue, character, or setting? Did you focus on one aspect more than another? To what effect? In your story, do you pay equal attention to character and plot, do you develop character at the expense of plot, or use their actions just to further the plot?

3. Students interested in mystery fiction can find many fascinating topics for exploration. Those drawn to hard-boiled fiction might read a work by Dashiell Hammett (perhaps *Red Harvest* [1929] or *The Maltese Falcon* [1930]) or Raymond Chandler (*The Big Sleep* [1939] or *Farewell, My Lovely* [1940]) and compare it to Walter Mosley's Easy Rawlins series, which begins with *Devil in a Blue Dress*, or Sara Paretsky's V. I. Warshawski series, the first of which is *Indemnity Only* (1982). These authors all use the hard-boiled mystery genre to explore the dynamics of corruption. Where does that corruption originate in each author's view? Is it a result of greed, of prejudice, of other factors? Or, one might compare Easy Rawlins with any of the other lead characters to examine how an African American protagonist changes the typical plot or other aspects

of the hard-boiled conventions. Along these same lines, one could offer a gender comparison, investigating the effect of having a female detective, as in Paretsky's novels. Similar questions related to other genres might be explored.

4. Students interested in the sociology of reading and the blurring of lines between high culture and popular culture might wish to investigate the history and dynamics of "Oprah's Book Club," sponsored by popular and influential television talk-show host Oprah Winfrey. Begun in 1996, it became powerful enough to catapult Winfrey's selections immediately onto best-seller lists. Although sometimes accused of promoting texts focusing on situations of domestic abuse, the list has ranged from works by Nobel Prize winners such as William Faulkner, Gabriel García Márquez, and Toni Morrison to popular romance writers such as Maeve Binchy and Anita Shreve. At least two major controversies have sprung up over Winfrey's selections: in 2001 she chose Jonathan Franzen's *The Corrections* (2001), but he publicly disavowed the choice, saying that while some of her choices were good books, he did not like the idea of being in the same company as many of the other "schmaltzy" choices she had made and that he had been hoping to attract a male audience. Students might research and examine this controversy for what it tells us about assumptions regarding "good" literature versus "reading for the masses" and about how male and female audiences are targeted. The article by Timothy Aubry, which focuses on Winfrey's discussion of Toni Morrison's *Paradise* (1998), would be useful for this undertaking. The second Winfrey controversy arose over James Frey's *A Million Little Pieces* (2003). A story of alcoholism, drug addiction, and a criminal career, it was published as a memoir. After Winfrey's show focused on it, allegations surfaced that much of it was fiction. Winfrey eventually confronted Frey and his publisher, Nan Talese, on another show. This controversy could be explored to examine contemporary attitudes toward fact and fiction, and where and how we draw that line. Several other topics might be developed from an exploration of Oprah's Book Club, including why it has been so popular, why she has made some of the choices she has, and, from a sociological perspective for advanced students, how and why people bond over the books that they read.

## RESOURCES

### Criticism

M. Keith Booker and Anne-Marie Thomas, *The Science Fiction Handbook* (Malden, Mass.: Wiley-Blackwell, 2009).
Provides a brief introduction to the genre, including discussions of various subcategories and representative authors and texts.

Mark Bould, Andrew M. Butler, Adam Roberts, and Sherryl Vint, eds., *The Routledge Companion to Science Fiction* (New York: Routledge, 2009).
Comprehensive resource that includes a chronological overview of the genre.

Ken Gelder, *Popular Fiction: The Logics and Practices of a Literary Field* (New York: Routledge, 2004).

Focusing on romance, crime fiction and science fiction, identifies the literary features of popular fiction while arguing that it is a distinctive field of literature; for advanced readers.

Jeet Heer and Kent Worcester, eds., *A Comics Studies Reader* (Jackson: University Press of Mississippi, 2009).
Twenty-eight critical essays using a variety of approaches to examine the history of comic forms, including cartoons, comic strips, comic books, Japanese manga, and graphic novels, with excellent discussions of thematic interests, narrative craft, and visual techniques. Some essays are more appropriate for advanced students.

Jerold E. Hogle, ed., *The Cambridge Companion to Gothic Fiction* (New York: Cambridge University Press, 2002).
Useful resource providing historical overview of the Gothic genre, complete with chronology and guide to further reading, from the late eighteenth to the twenty-first century; offers various interpretive approaches. The introduction provides a concise overview with discussion of variations, while chapters 13 and 14 discuss contemporary fiction.

Edward James and Farah Mendlesohn, eds., *The Cambridge Companion to Science Fiction* (New York: Cambridge University Press, 2003).
Defines science fiction as a literary genre; traces its history; describes four critical approaches drawing from Marxism, Postmodernism, feminism, and queer theory; and examines various themes.

Kathleen Gregory Klein, ed., *Diversity and Detective Fiction* (Bowling Green, Ohio: Bowling Green University Popular Press, 1999).
Collection of essays and critical introduction that examine the way writers explore issues related to racial and ethnic diversity within the context of detective fiction.

Paul Lopes, *Demanding Respect: The Evolution of the American Comic Book* (Philadelphia: Temple University Press, 2009).
An essential overview of comic-book culture, covering the last seventy-five years of production and interest on the part of readers, fans, and scholars. Chapters 4, 5, and 6 are most relevant to the contemporary period.

Patrick McGee, *From* Shane *to* Kill Bill: *Rethinking the Western* (Malden, Mass.: Blackwell, 2007).
Analysis of representative films from the 1930s to the present that focuses on the history of the American Western film and provides a discussion of the genre that is applicable to literature as well as of social and historical contexts affecting the genre.

Steven McVeigh, *The American Western* (Edinburgh, Scotland: Edinburgh University Press, 2007).
Examines the importance of the Western in American literature and film in the twentieth century, pinpointing recurrent uses, subversions, and revisions of myths and symbols. The last three chapters are particularly useful for the contemporary period.

Tania Modleski, *Loving with a Vengeance: Mass Produced Fantasies for Women,*
     revised edition (New York: Routledge, 2007).
An updated and expanded edition of the classic 1992 study of women readers and
their reading practices. Modleski examines Harlequin romances, Gothic novels,
and soap operas.

Martin Priestman, ed., *The Cambridge Companion to Crime Fiction* (New York:
     Cambridge University Press, 2003).
Focusing on British and American literature, describes fiction in which crime
plays a significant role such as the thriller, spy fiction, police procedural, and mystery. The book also includes chapters on black detectives and female detectives,
and film and television versions.

Matthew Pustz, *Comic Book Culture: Fanboys and True Believers* (Jackson: Univer-
     sity Press of Mississippi, 1999).
Study of comic-book readers and their practices, interviews, history of comic
books, and analysis of the works themselves.

Janice A. Radway, *Reading the Romance: Women, Patriarchy, and Popular Literature*
     (Chapel Hill: University of North Carolina Press, 1991).
Essential study of female reading practices that challenges stereotypical notions
of why women read romance novels.

Pamela Regis, *A Natural History of the Romance Novel* (Philadelphia: University of
     Pennsylvania Press, 2003).
An excellent study that argues for the legitimacy of the genre while defining its
formal features and tracing its variations and major themes.

Charles J. Rzepka, *Detective Fiction,* Cultural History of Literature (Malden,
     Mass.: Polity Press, 2005).
Useful for its basic overview of the genre and its features but offers relatively little
discussion of contemporary American fiction.

Corinne J. Saunders, *A Companion to Romance: From Classical to Contemporary*
     (Malden, Mass.: Blackwell, 2004).
Although focusing on British examples, offers discussions of genre variations,
identifying their main features and association with women writers and readers.

John Scaggs, *Crime Fiction: The New Critical Idiom* (New York: Routledge, 2005).
A thorough overview that delineates the various permutations including crime
narratives, mystery and detective fiction, hard-boiled, police procedural, crime
thriller, and historical crime fiction.

David Seed, ed., *A Companion to Science Fiction* (Malden, Mass.: Blackwell, 2005).
Excellent resource divided into sections on the development, issues, genres and
movements, and films of science fiction.

John Sutherland, *Bestsellers: A Very Short Introduction* (New York: Oxford Univer-
     sity Press, 2007).
An easy-to-read historical overview of popular fiction. The book does not treat
contemporary American literature specifically, although definitions in chapter 1
and the historical overview of American bestsellers in chapter 4 are helpful.

Jane Tompkins, *West of Everything: The Inner Life of Westerns* (New York: Oxford University Press, 1992).
Overview of the genre and discussion of representative texts (not contemporary). The identification of the elements of the genre in part 1 is especially useful.

Bradford W. Wright, *Comic Book Nation: The Transformation of Youth Culture in America* (Baltimore: Johns Hopkins University Press, 2001).
Comprehensive study of comic books and reader practices, and analysis of the ways comic books reflect national concerns such as war, drug use, and racism.

## PEOPLE OF INTEREST

**Rudolfo A. Anaya** (1937–   )
Best known for *Bless Me, Ultima* (1972). His other works include *Heart of Aztlan* (1976), *Tortuga* (1979), *The Silence of the Llano: Short Stories* (1992), *The Legend of La Llorona* (1984), *The Adventures of Juan Chicaspatas* (1985), *Lord of the Dawn: The Legend of Quetzalcóatl* (1987), *Alburquerque* (1992), and *Jalamanta: A Message from the Desert* (1996). His series of detective novels featuring detective Sonny Baca includes *Zia Summer* (1995), *Rio Grande Fall* (1996), *Shaman Winter* (1998), and *Jemez Springs* (2005). He has also written plays (*The Season of La Llorona* [1987] and *Matachines* [1992]), and travel essays, such as *A Chicano in China* (1986).

**Philip K. Dick** (1928–1982)
Science-fiction author of thirty-six novels and more than one hundred short stories, known for his explorations of morality and metaphysics. Many of his works have been adapted into films, including *Do Androids Dream of Electric Sheep?* (1968), which was adapted as *Blade Runner* (1982).

**Frank Miller** (1957–   )
Writer and film director best known for his graphic novels *Ronin* (1987), *Batman: The Dark Knight Returns* (2002), and *Sin City* (1992–2000).

**Walter Mosley** (1952–   )
Writer of crime fiction, science fiction, erotica, and literary fiction; best known for the Easy Rawlins series, which begins with *Devil in a Blue Dress* in 1990 and ends with *Blonde Faith* in 2007, consisting of nine novels, all with a color in the title, and two short-story collections. Three Fearless Jones novels are also crime fiction, while three Socrates Fortlow books are best described as a cross between crime fiction and novel. Notable among his other works are the novels *RL's Dream* (1995) and *The Man in My Basement* (2004), an homage to Ralph Ellison's *Invisible Man* (1952), and nonfiction on issues including writing and peace.

**Barbara Neely** (1941–   )
Novelist and short-story writer, author of Blanche White mysteries. The first, *Blanche on the Lam* (1992), won the Agatha, Macavity, and Anthony Awards, three of the four major awards recognizing a first mystery novel.

**Art Spiegelman** (1948–   )

Comic artist and editor best known for the comic-book memoir *Maus: A Survivor's Tale* (volume 1, *My Father Bleeds History* [1986]; volume 2, *And Here My Troubles Began* [1991]), which won a special Pulitzer Prize in 1992.

*—Linda Trinh Moser and Kathryn West*

# Literature and the Environment

Nature and the environment are traditional themes in American literature and have a long history on the North American continent. Native American oral narratives invoke plant and animal life, weather patterns, and particular places, often viewing these elements of the natural world as animated by life spirits similar to those of human beings. The writings of early European explorers and early settlers contain descriptions of the physical world and people. Nature and environmental literature, however, does not encompass all writing that features descriptions of the natural environment. Robert Finch and John Elder note that nature writing is defined by the "personal element—that is, the filtering of experience through an individual sensibility." By the nineteenth century, writers such as Henry David Thoreau combined observations of nature with their emotional, spiritual, and psychological responses to it. Contemporary nature and environmental literature continues to record the interrelationships that exist between the external and internal, the physical and metaphysical, providing a record of what one sees and of the self in the act of seeing.

The description "environmental" is a more inclusive term than "nature" when applied to literature. It underscores a relationship between human and nonhuman life, an idea supported by scientific discoveries about the interconnectedness of all living things. The term also encompasses writing about both rural and urban environments and encourages one not to treat "culture" and "nature" as mutually exclusive terms. As writers in the late 1960s and 1970s began incorporating more social criticism into works about nature, environmentalism became associated with radical politics. In the introduction to *Teaching Environmental Literature: Materials, Methods, Resources,* Frederick Waage argues, however, that describing literature as environmental does "not imply a particular ideological or political bias." Although this body of literature reveals a great diversity of attitudes and perceptions, it is true that the tone of post-1970 nature writing changes. Starting in the previous decade, conservationist and preservationist movements had helped to generate a growing awareness of environmental degradation. Poets could no longer "write poems of pure celebration," notes Denise Levertov in the foreword to *The Life around Us: Selected Poems on Ecological Themes* (1997); instead, she "is driven inevitably to lament, to anger, and to the expression of dread."

After 1970 writers could not ignore increases in nuclear testing, industry, agribusiness, and the growth of suburbs and parallel loss of wilderness spaces. Although impelled to expose the ways human activities threaten natural environments, they also express commitment to, appreciation, and often love of the natural world. But literary images of nature belie a multiplicity of perspectives that move beyond simplistic division between pro- and anti-environment. For example, the role of "protector" befits characters in Edward Abbey's *The Monkey Wrench Gang* (1975); the novel advocates what came to be known as "monkey-wrenching," or any activity, legal or, more often, not, that preserves wilderness from human development. Wendell Berry's work, however, promotes the role of "steward." In *The Art of the Commonplace: The Agrarian Essays of Wendell Berry* (2002), he defends sustainable agricultural practices, calling on us to become good stewards of the earth and its limited resources. The essays in Lewis Thomas's *The Lives of a Cell* (1974) suggest a "dependent" role when he writes "we are not the masters of nature that we thought ourselves; we are as dependent on the rest of life as are the leaves or midges or fish."

Several anthologies and studies serve as introductory guides to the world of nature or environmental writing while highlighting representative writers and works. *The Norton Book of Nature Writing* (1990), edited by Finch and Elder, contains key nature writers such as Annie Dillard, Barry Lopez, and Peter Matthiessen. Their introduction also identifies ways to delineate and categorize nature writing, a difficult task considering the vastness of this field. Finch and Elder trace a literary genealogy back to pastoral poetry and the natural history essay. In *This Incomparable Land: A Guide to American Nature Writing* (2001), Thomas Lyons categorizes works based on the "relative weight or interplay" of three characteristics he finds in environmental literature: "natural history information, personal responses to nature, and philosophical interpretation of nature." The focus of these two important works, however, is almost exclusively limited to nonfiction prose. For a rich selection of poems, students can consider *Poems for a Small Planet: Contemporary American Nature Poetry* (1993), which features established nature poets Maxine Kumin, Dana Gioia, Joy Harjo, and Gary Snyder. Despite their differences in tone and style, all respond to the destruction of nature.

Until the late 1990s studies of nature and environmental literature, like the anthologies previously described, focused on nonfiction prose with some attention to poetry. Making assumptions about the practical purposes and uses of writing, critics and editors tended to privilege works whose purposes were more didactic than entertaining, distinctions made by Finch and Elder, who exclude works that are imaginative rather than "real" because "the purposes of fiction differ sufficiently from those of nonfiction." Laurence Buell also discusses this distinction in *The Environmental Imagination: Thoreau, Nature Writing, and the Formation of American Culture* (1995). In *Farther Afield in the Study of Nature-Oriented Literature* (2000), however, Patrick D. Murphy challenges this oversight. Noting the "fiction" involved in the aesthetic restructuring of journals, chronicles, and natural histories such as Thoreau's *Walden* (1854), he offers a more inclusive taxonomy of nature-oriented literature that includes work previously neglected in the field of environmental literary criticism. Students interested in identifying fiction that treats environmental issues will find Murphy's study of contemporary science fiction and fantasy, ethnic American, and Postmodernist works useful.

Interest in nature and environmental writing has given rise to ecocriticism, a term coined in the 1970s to describe criticism sensitive to environmental themes. An interdisciplinary strategy, it considers history, ethics, philosophy, science, and psychology in addition to literary analysis to uncover explicit and implicit attitudes toward the environment. Ecocriticism promotes the value of writing concerned with nature (by identifying important texts), while also attempting to effect change by creating awareness of the interconnectedness between humanity and the natural world (as expressed in the works they study). *The Ecocriticism Reader: Landmarks in Literary Ecology* (1996), edited by Cheryll Glotfelty and

Harold Fromm, provides examples from the field and traces the development of this critical movement from the 1960s. Additional trends and debates in the field are addressed in *Beyond Nature Writings: Expanding the Boundaries of Ecocriticism* (2001) and *The ISLE Reader: Ecocriticism, 1993–2003* (2003).

## TOPICS FOR DISCUSSION AND RESEARCH

1. The 1970s ushered in the first wave of environmental legislation. Earth Day was established in 1970, as was the Clean Air Act. The Endangered Species Act was passed in 1973. This context can be a starting point for considering the relationship between nature writing and ecological awareness and environmental justice. *American Earth: Environmental Writing since Thoreau* (2008), edited by Bill McKibben, includes an array of primary works that describe and question humanity's impact on the environment. As students read these selections, they might consider the following questions: How do the writers define terms like environment and nature? What kinds of environment are each of the writers interested in (wild, domestic, urban, suburban, agricultural)? What are the writers' attitudes toward these environments? What are the writers' attitudes toward human activities within these environments? How do these attitudes support and/or challenge those held by the mainstream culture? What actions do they propose?

2. *Pastoral* is a term traditionally applied to poetry about shepherds and rural folk but now used more broadly to describe literary works that contrast rural life, usually idealized, with urban life. In addition to describing form and content, pastoral can also impart a pejorative attitude when applied to works whose ideal representations ignore the material reality of the environment. In *Pastoral* (1999) Terry Gifford defines the various definitions and uses of pastoral. Students might wish to apply Gifford's criteria to contemporary works about the environment, paying particular attention to how pastoral elements function with regard to theme, tone, and style.

3. Women writers have been wary of invoking nature in their work because of stereotypical representations of their gender as controlled by nature that often reinforced the notion that they lacked reason and should be confined to domestic spaces. Since 1970 more women "have begun to invoke nature for feminist purposes or have used nature as an agent of resistance," as noted by Barbara J. Cook in her introduction to *Women Writing Nature: A Feminist View* (2007). Students might be interested in using ideas from the essays collected by Cook to examine the ways nature writing by women challenges the dual exploitation of the environment and women, questions the stereotypical association of women with wilderness, proposes alternative relationships between humanity and the environment, and ultimately, "questions the traditional notion that the wilderness is 'no place for women.'" Suggested works for further study include Terry Tempest Williams's *Refuge: An Unnatural History of Family and Place* (1991), Barbara Kingsolver's *Animal Dreams* (1990), Mary Clearman Blew's *Balsamroot: A Memoir* (1994), Toni Morrison's *Jazz* (1992), Gloria Naylor's *Mama Day* (1988), and poetry by Mary Oliver.

4. In her introduction to *American Indian Literature, Environmental Justice and Ecocriticism: The Middle Place* (2001) Joni Adamson argues that American Indian literature offering "insider" perspectives expands and challenges those of "outsiders" or European Americans, writing: "The outsider and the insider may view the same piece of ground, but where one sees mountains or valleys, the other sees the 'invisible landscape' of local and lived significance. The outsider follows a map's pattern of contours, symbols, and colors over geographical surface, but the insider annotates the map, tracing the invisible landscape." This idea can be the starting point for considering connections between Native American identity and the land and parallels between environmental degradation and loss of indigenous culture in works such as Louis Owens's *Wolfsong* (1991), Leslie Marmon Silko's *Ceremony* (1977), Louise Erdrich's *Tracks* (1988*)*, and Joy Harjo's *She Had Some Horses* (1983) or *Secrets from the Center of the World* (1989). For suggestions about African American writers and environmental issues, see Sylvia Mayer's *Restoring the Connection to the Natural World: Essays on the African American Environmental Imagination* (2003).

5. In "The Non-Alibi of Alien Scapes: SF and Ecocriticism" in *Beyond Nature Writings: Expanding the Boundaries of Ecocriticism* (2001) Patrick D. Murphy discusses the ways science fiction promotes awareness of environmental issues. By presenting conflicts whose resolutions depend upon human and nonhuman relationships, these and other works of speculative fiction function as "ecological parables" highlighting our own environmental problems and choices. Focusing on a particular work, students can analyze its presentation of the environment, human responses to it, and consequences of those responses. Appropriate works include those by Ursula K. Le Guin, particularly *The Word of World Is Forest* (1972) and the Earthsea Trilogy; the six novels comprising David Brin's Uplift Universe series; the six novels in Frank Herbert's Dune saga; and Octavia Butler's *Parable of the Sower* (1993). Students could extend Murphy's argument to other kinds of genre and popular forms of fiction. Nevada Barr's series of mysteries featuring park ranger Anna Pigeon, for example, all take place in a different national park and feature a mystery highlighting an environmental issue.

## RESOURCES

**Primary Works**

Robert Finch and John Elder, eds., *The Norton Book of Nature Writing*, second edition (New York: Norton, 2002).

A well-annotated anthology, focusing on nonfiction prose, with broad selections from the best-known nature writers and useful introductions.

Bill McKibben, ed., *American Earth: Environmental Writing since Thoreau* (New York: Library of America, 2008).

Collection of works by key writers that focuses on environmental conservation and activism; includes a chronology of the environmental history movement.

Robert Pack and Jay Parini, eds., *Poems for a Small Planet: Contemporary American Nature Poetry* (Hanover, N.H.: University Press of New England, 1993).
Provides a wide variety of nature poems and an afterword, "Taking Dominion over the Wilderness."

## Criticism

Joni Adamson, ed., *American Indian Literature, Environmental Justice and Ecocriticism: The Middle Place* (Tucson: University of Arizona Press, 2001).
Investigation of American Indian literature from the perspective of environmental studies that challenges and expands Anglo-American notions of culture and place.

Karla Armbruster and Kathleen R. Wallace, eds., *Beyond Nature Writings: Expanding the Boundaries of Ecocriticism* (Charlottesville: University Press of Virginia, 2001).
Scholarly essays that challenge earlier criticism related to environmental concerns.

*ASLE Online Bibliography,* The Association for the Study of Literature & Environment (ASLE) <http://www.biblioserver.com/asle/index.php> [accessed 22 March 2010).
An extensive and useful resource that provides "citations and abstracts of scholarly and creative works in various media, as well as public documents, related to the study of relationships between language and literature, broadly conceived, and the environment."

Michael P. Branch and Scott Slovic, eds., *The ISLE Reader: Ecocriticism, 1993–2003* (Athens: University of Georgia Press, 2003).
Essays examining debates and trends in the field of ecocriticism.

Laird Christensen, Mark C. Long, and Frederick O. Waage, eds., *Teaching North American Environmental Literature* (New York: Modern Language Association, 2008).
Collection of scholarly essays that expands and revises the 1985 version, *Teaching Environmental Literature: Materials, Methods, Resources.* The book includes course descriptions and approaches.

Barbara J. Cook, ed., *Women Writing Nature: A Feminist View* (Lanham, Md.: Lexington Books, 2008).
Collection of critical essays on particular writers and works, collectively considering women's nature writing in the context of feminist and ecofeminist theory.

Terry Gifford, *Pastoral* (New York: Routledge,1999).
Summarizes the history of the genre from its origins to the contemporary period.

Cheryll Glotfelty and Harold Fromm, eds., *The Ecocriticism Reader: Landmarks in Literary Ecology* (Athens: University of Georgia Press, 1996).
Explains ecocriticism—its practices, concerns, key texts, and changes in it.

George Hart and Scott Slovic, eds. *Literature and the Environment, Exploring Social Issues through Literature* (Westport, Conn.: Greenwood Press, 2004).
Introduction to literature about the environment with chapters devoted to single authors and texts.

Kent P. Lundquist, "Nature and Landscape," in *Encyclopedia of American Literature,* edited by Steven R. Serafin (New York: Continuum, 1999), pp. 809–812.
Broad overview of writing about nature in America.

Thomas J. Lyon, ed., *This Incomparable Land: A Guide to American Nature Writing* (Minneapolis: Milkweed, 2001).
Expanded and updated from the 1988 edition, providing a critical overview of the field and approaches to reading but omitting primary sources.

Patrick D. Murphy, *Farther Afield in the Study of Nature-Oriented Literature* (Charlottesville: University Press of Virginia, 2000).
Challenges the focus on nonfiction writing in the field of ecocriticism while also offering readings of works—mostly fiction—previously ignored in the field.

## PEOPLE OF INTEREST

**Edward Abbey** (1927–1989)
Best known for work featuring environmental concerns, including nonfiction *Desert Solitaire* (1968) and the novel *The Monkey Wrench Gang* (1975).

**Nevada Barr** (1952–   )
Author of the "Anna Pigeon" series of mystery novels, each set in a different U.S. National Park. *Track of the Cat* (1993) won an Agatha Award for best first mystery novel.

**Wendell Berry** (1934–   )
Prolific essayist, poet, fiction writer, and farmer whose essay collections include *A Continuous Harmony: Essays Cultural and Agricultural* (1972) and *The Unsettling of America: Culture & Agriculture* (2004). His poetry collections include *Collected Poems 1957–1982* (1985), *A Timbered Choir: The Sabbath Poems, 1979–1997* (1998), and *Given* (2005).

**David Brin** (1950–   )
Scientist and award-winning author of the science-fiction series The Uplift Novels.

**Annie Dillard** (1945–   )
Pulitzer Prize–winning writer best known for her narrative nonfiction, including *Pilgrim at Tinker Creek* (1974), and her memoir *An American Childhood* (1987). Her works also include novels, poetry, and literary criticism.

**Dana Gioia** (1950–   )
Poet, New Formalist critic, and chairman of the National Endowment for the Arts from 2004 to 2009. His collection *The Gods of Winter* (1991) won the 1992 Poets' Prize.

**Joy Harjo** (1951–   )
Muscogee (Creek) poet and musician who plays saxophone with her band, Poetic Justice.

**Frank Herbert** (1920–1986)
Highly acclaimed science-fiction writer whose best-known work, *Dune* (1965), is the first of a series that includes *Dune Messiah* (1969), *Children of Dune* (1976), *God Emperor of Dune* (1981), *Heretics of Dune* (1984), and *Chapterhouse: Dune* (1985).

**Maxine Kumin** (1925–   )
Poet who won the Pulitzer Prize in 1973 for her collection *Up Country*.

**Ursula K. Le Guin** (1929–   )
Science-fiction writer who received the Hugo and Nebula Awards for *The Left Hand of Darkness* (1969) and for *The Dispossessed: An Ambiguous Utopia* (1974). In 1972 she won the National Book Award for *The Farthest Shore*, part of her Earthsea Trilogy.

**Denise Levertov** (1923–1997)
Politically active poet and essayist who was born in England and immigrated to the United States in 1948. Her poetry collections include *Relearning the Alphabet* (1970), *Footprints: Poems* (1972), and *A Door in the Hive* (1989).

**Barry Lopez** (1945–   )
Writer of nonfiction prose and novels best known for *Arctic Dreams: Imagination and Desire in a Northern Landscape* (1986), which won the National Book Award.

**Peter Matthiessen** (1927–   )
Naturalist and writer known for *The Snow Leopard* (1978), a National Book Award nonfiction winner; *In the Spirit of Crazy Horse* (1983); and *Shadow Country* (2008), a National Book Award fiction winner.

**Mary Oliver** (1935–   )
Acclaimed poet whose works include the Pulitzer Prize–winning *American Primitive* (1983) and the National Book Award–winning *New and Selected Poems* (1992). In 1998 she received the Lannan Literary Award for poetry.

**Louis Owens** (1948–2002)
Literary scholar and a writer known for novels that draw from his mixed Choctaw, Cherokee, and Irish background, including *Wolfsong* (1995), *Bone Game* (1996), and the American Book Award winner *Nightland* (1996). His criticism includes *Other Destinies: Understanding the Native American Novel* (1992) and *Mixedblood Messages: Literature, Film, Family, Place* (2001).

**Gary Snyder** (1930–   )
Poet and activist who draws inspiration from nature and non-Western philosophies; his works include *Turtle Island* (1974), which won the Pulitzer Prize, and *Mountains and Rivers without End* (1996), which was awarded the Bollingen Prize.

**Lewis Thomas** (1913–1993)

Biologist and physician who was president of Memorial Sloan-Kettering Cancer Center in New York City. His works include *The Lives of a Cell* (1974), *The Medusa and the Snail* (1979), and *Late Night Thoughts on Listening to Mahler's Ninth Symphony* (1983).

**Terry Tempest Williams** (1955–   )

Naturalist and environmental activist who writes nonfiction prose and poetry. Her best-known work is *Refuge: An Unnatural History of Family and Place* (1991).

*—Linda Trinh Moser*

# Multiculturalism and Globalization

Since 1970 American literature has been characterized by an extraordinary proliferation of imaginative writing, a good deal of it by African, Native, Asian, and Latino Americans who have found success in all literary genres—fiction, poetry, memoir and autobiography, and drama. Many of these works appear on best-seller lists and are featured as required reading for colleges and secondary schools. While this body of texts continues to grow, scholars have been looking backward to recover and recuperate lost or forgotten works, some of them non-English-language texts or those that were transmitted orally, including songs of enslaved African Americans or Asians imported for their labor, Hawaiian chants, the graffiti poems of Angel Island detainees, Native American orations, and travel accounts by Spanish explorers, some dating back to the sixteenth century. With such diversity, one could argue that American literature has always been multicultural, perhaps even "global"; expressions of literary multiculturalism and globalization, however, do not merely involve acknowledging the presence of writers with diverse backgrounds and histories. Understanding multicultural-ism merely as the existence of "minority" groups or as "a synonym of pluralism" (Palumbo-Liu) divests it of its connection to movements for social justice and change embodied by the Civil Rights movement of the 1960s. Acknowledging cultural diversity not only uncovers a rich literary history; it brings into focus the monocultural or racist thinking that had been and is responsible for the erasure of works, while also helping us to reconsider how we interpret "canonical" works that had never been neglected or lost—those by writers such as Mark Twain, T. S. Eliot, Ernest Hemingway, and William Faulkner. Thinking in multicultural or global terms helps not only to expand the American literary canon but also to transform the way it is interpreted. While writing and scholarship of the 1970s focused on defining overlooked and marginalized literary traditions, history, and identity, over time literary study has expanded to encompass transnationalism, compara-tive race and ethnic studies, and Postmodernist/poststructuralist ideas.

The increasing attention to and availability of multicultural literary texts in the 1970s were a reflection of the social movements of the previous decades. In this and the preceding decade, writers sought to define separate literary tradi-tions associated with their different racial and ethnic groups. (In this volume the essays "African American Literature" and "Native American Renaissance" trace two of these traditions.) Many Americans insisted that all blacks were alike, as were Asians, Latinos, and Indians—that they were non-American regardless of ancestry and nativity, bound together by cultural otherness and their inability or unwillingness to assimilate. To combat invisibility and resist stereotypes, many wrote autobiographies and coming-of-age novels, emphasizing their historical presence in the United States as well as ethnic or cultural pride. For instance, the title character of Nicholasa Mohr's *Nilda* (1973) feels the humiliation of being Puerto Rican and poor in New York City; yet, the use of Spanglish and portray-als of an extended family and community in the autobiographical novel express a vibrant cultural synthesis. In Tomás Rivera's Spanish-language novel *. . .y no se lo tragó la tierra* (1971; translated as *. . . and the Earth Did Not Devour Him*, 1987),

Rudolfo A. Anaya's *Bless Me, Ultima* (1972), and Rolando Hinojosa-Smith's *Estampas del valle y otras obras* (1973; translated as *Sketches of the Valley and Other Works;* rewritten in English as *The Valley,* 1983) the writers draw a connection between Chicanos and the landscape of the Southwestern United States, a part of Mexico until the mid nineteenth century. Likewise, in *Homebase* (1979) Shawn Wong traces the contributions of four generations of a Chinese immigrant family to American history as agricultural workers and builders of the cross-continental railroad.

The struggle to define an alternative identity and positive presence in American letters led to a type of cultural nationalism that promoted strict and usually narrow visions of identity. For some, insisting on a unitary identity, however, seemed the only effective—albeit limited—means of opposing and defending oneself against marginalization. Wong, Jeffery Paul Chan, Frank Chin, and Lawson Fusao Inada, the editors of *Aiiieeeee! An Anthology of Asian American Writers* (1974) and its expanded 1991 version, *The Big Aiiieeeee!,* posited the notion of an "Asian universal knowledge" embedded in "Cantonese operas and Kabuki" and other "artistic enterprises" of Asian immigrants. In the anthology and their respective works, these writers focused on American-born, non-Christian, male writers; in addition, they identified writers only of Chinese and Japanese descent, the most established Asian American groups. Likewise, works by Chicanos (a category of Hispanic American writing) tended to define identity narrowly. Luis Valdez, in plays such as *Los Vendidos* (1976) and in his work with the grassroots theater company *El Teatro Campesino,* for example, distinguished Chicano identity as "exclusively working-class, Spanish-speaking or bilingual, rurally oriented, and with a strong heritage of pre-Columbian culture" (Kanellos). Representations of other Latinos or Asian ethnic groups were obviously excluded by these definitions, as were female and gay experiences. Even in their later expanded anthology, Chan and his colleagues singled out their contemporaries Maxine Hong Kingston and Amy Tan for what they considered to be "fake" versions of Chinese culture and history and described David Henry Hwang's *M. Butterfly* (1986; published, 1988) as "the fulfillment of white male homosexual fantasy," charges that ignore the writers' concerns with combating stereotypes based on gender and sexuality in addition to race. Chicanas such as Gloria Anzaldúa and Cherríe Moraga, too, felt the sting of cultural nationalism when they spoke out against sexism and "were identified as man haters, frustrated women, and 'agringadas,' Anglo-cized."

Just as it is impossible to speak of American literature as a singular entity, it is impossible to describe the literary traditions of various racial or ethnic groups as homogenous. Writers emerging after the early attempts to establish cultural literary traditions began to recognize the limitations of narrowly defined Latino, black, Native American, or Asian American identity. While cultural nationalisms formed a critical response to the racism and ethnocentrism of the dominant culture, they failed to recognize that ethnic and racial identity has always been linked to class, gender, sexual orientation, national origin, and age. The diversity within racial and ethnic categories became increasingly more obvious as writers added their voices. Arte Público Press, founded in 1979, for example, brought attention to both Cuban American and Puerto Rican, or "Nuyorican," literature in addition to Chicano/a writers. Works by Puerto Rican American writers represent the second largest contributions to Hispanic American literature and include writers Judith Ortiz Cofer, Sandra María Esteves, Victor Hernández Cruz, Tato Laviera, Esmeralda Santiago, Piri Thomas, and Ed Vega. The next largest belongs to Cuban Americans, who include Gustavo Pérez Firmat, Cristina García, and Oscar Hijuelos, the first Hispanic American to be awarded the Pulitzer Prize, for *The Mambo Kings Play Songs of Love* (1989). Asian Americans are equally diverse; among them are writers whose ancestors come from China, Japan, Korea, the Philippines, India, Vietnam, Cambodia, Laos, Thailand, and Burma. Hwang and Gish Jen are Chinese Americans; Theresa Hak Kyung Cha and Chang-rae Lee are Korean American writers; Jessica Hagedorn is Filipino American; Japanese Americans include Kimiko Hahn, Garrett Kaoru Hongo, Jeanne Wakatsuki Houston, and Janice Mirikitani; Americans with roots in India include Meena Alexander, Bharati Mukherjee, and Jhumpa Lahiri. Writers with Asian heritage who grew up in Hawaii, described as "local," are Nora Okja Keller, Chris McKinney, Cathy Song, and Lois-Ann Yamanaka. Gay Latino and Asian Americans added their voices to further underscore diversity. Just as women writers delineated a "double marginalization" as women and racial/ethnic others, works by Arturo Islas, Rane Arroyo, Kitty Tsui, and Andrew Lam describe being outsiders in terms of race and sexuality, which also led to their ostracization by both their root and the mainstream cultures.

Since the 1990s works by ethnic Americans have brought increasing attention to international factors that affect the cultural makeup of the United States. Political instability in the Dominican Republic is represented in the works of Julia Alvarez and Junot Díaz, as is the exile experience of Vietnamese immigrants in works by Lan Cao and Andrew X. Pham. Other changes also affect the cultural landscape of America. Steven George Salaita notes that since the terrorist attacks of 11 September 2001, Arab Americans "are being analyzed widely and systematically as a discrete ethnic community." Literary works by Arab Americans resist orientalist stereotypes while also revealing the diversity of their authors. In terms of religion, for example, Arab America is not monolithic. As Salaita notes, they "are Muslim (Shia and Sunni and Alawi and Isma'ili), Christian . . . , Jewish . . . , Druze, Bahai . . . immigrants and fifth-generation Americans . . . religious and secular, White and Black, Latin American and Canadian." And, he adds, "Sometimes [they] are non-Arabs such as Circassians, Armenians, Berbers, Kurds, and Iranians." Arab American poetry has a long tradition in American letters and includes works by Naomi Shihab Nye and Agha Shahid Ali. Arab American fiction writers include Kathryn K. Abdul-Baki, Diana Abu-Jaber, Rabih Alameddine, Laila Halaby, and Laila Lalami.

While the lines between foreign nationals, immigrants, and those born in America (first-generation vs. second-generation, Asian vs. Asian American, or

Chicano vs. Mexican, for example) were important to writers in the 1960s and 1970s, those lines are increasingly being blurred as writers adopt transnational perspectives, exploring pan-Pacific, transatlantic, and other cross-cultural connections and identities. Writers in all genres continue to address issues of identity, assimilation, and cultural heritage, but they do so with increased attention to craft and experimentation with form. Although more-recent writers are less inclined to focus on the social inequities that earlier generations wrote about, they are not blind to them. Their inclination, however, is to focus on the creative possibilities of hybridity in culture as well as form. The dynamic process of identity formation is reflected in the fragmentation of Cha's *Dictee* (1982), which combines prose and poetry interspersed with photographs, diagrams, and documents. Linguistic play, a mixture of Spanish, English, and Spanglish, in the poetry of Alberto Ríos and the fiction of Díaz and Ana Castillo transforms literary English to suggest the multiple textures of different cultural perspectives. Kiana Davenport includes legends and rituals as markers of a Hawaiian identity rooted in place rather than in the images on tourist postcards. Within the narrative of *Dogeaters* (1990), Hagedorn interweaves poetry, excerpts from letters and other works, news items, and a gossip column to get at different perspectives of postcolonial Filipinos. These works and others continually remind readers of the changing nature of America's cultural negotiations and the continuities between the United States and other nations.

The emphasis on considering race and ethnicity as a central subject of interest has also led to a reexamination of the social, political, and economic conditions which historically shaped (and continue to shape) identity in literary works by Americans with Jewish, Italian, and Irish backgrounds. More recently, "whiteness" has become a focus for studying racial formation. Toni Morrison's *Playing in the Dark* (1992), for example, suggests how the social and political category of "white" has been constructed and protected in relation to those defined as racial "others."

The richness of works by writers of different cultural backgrounds makes it impossible to speak of American literature as a monolithic or unified entity. Any interpretation needs to situate ethnic American literature within the historical and cultural contexts of its cultural tradition while also working through parallels and connections to other ethnic American discourses. The emphasis must always be on plurality. Although this makes the categorization and analysis of American literature a more complicated task, it is ultimately more rewarding than accepting the illusion of homogeneity.

## TOPICS FOR DISCUSSION AND RESEARCH

1. In Maxine Hong Kingston's *The Woman Warrior* (1976) the narrator protests stereotypical and racist labels, "'chink' words and 'gook' words" because, as she says, "they do not fit my skin." Other ethnic American writers have sought to dismantle shallow stereotypes through their works by presenting complex characters in particular social and historical situations. Students interested in exploring how writers resist racist images might begin with an investigation of

stereotypes about particular ethnic groups. Good starting points are offered in *The Greenwood Encyclopedia of Multiethnic American Literature* (2005) entries "African American Stereotypes," "Arab American Stereotypes," "Chinese American Stereotypes," "Italian American Stereotypes," "Jewish American Stereotypes," "Mexican American Stereotypes," and "Native American Stereotypes." Using a novel, short stories, a play, or poem(s) mentioned in this essay or in listed critical works and anthologies, students might consider the following questions: Are these stereotypes reflected or addressed in the work? Does the writer challenge the stereotype? If so, in what ways? How does the writer represent his/her cultural or ethnic identity? One might also compare how stereotypes are challenged or co-opted in works by two different writers from similar traditions or across different cultural traditions.

2. Coming-of-age novels trace the development of the protagonist from childhood or adolescence into adulthood and usually involve disillusionment as he or she moves from innocence to experience, ignorance to knowledge, or idealism to realism. The identities of ethnic American adolescents are shaped by the culture(s) of their families as well as by dominant society. The volatility of adolescence combined with cultural negotiations that ethnic Americans undertake make the genre particularly powerful and appealing to American writers of diverse cultural backgrounds. Analyzing coming-of-age novels draws out the unique challenges that race and ethnicity impose on the development of nonwhite protagonists. What happens when characters realize that their skin color, religion, food, and habits are different from those of their friends? How does this awareness affect their sense of self and/or their attitudes toward their family members and root culture? How is the process of growing up complicated by the realization of "minority" status in a predominantly white society? Is the awareness of cultural difference empowering or disabling to the individual? Why or why not?

3. Students might also consider comparing a coming-of-age novel from the 1970s to one written more recently, paying close attention to attitudes about race and ethnicity. Do you see a change in attitude on the part of the protagonists? What social or historical reasons might there be for differences/similarities? Another way to approach this topic is to consider the way ethnic American writers use the coming-of-age novel to counteract historical and social marginalization. In other words, how does the act of self-definition challenge those who would define them stereotypically? Some suggested works and comparisons: Kingston's *The Woman Warrior* (1976) or Wong's *Homebase* (1979) with Chin's *Donald Duk* (1991) or Gish Jen's *Mona in the Promised Land* (1996); Tan's *The Joy Luck Club* (1989) with Keller's *Comfort Woman* (1997); Mukherjee's *Jasmine* (1989) with Lahiri's *The Namesake* (2003); Houston's *Farewell to Manzanar* (1973) with Julie Otsuka's *When the Emperor Was Divine* (2002); Rivera's *. . . y no se lo trágo la tierra* (1971), Anaya's *Bless Me, Ultima* (1972), or Mohr's *Nilda* (1973) with Alvarez's *How the García Girls Lost Their Accents* (1991), Helena María Viramontes's *Under the Feet of Jesus* (1995), or Díaz's *The Brief Wondrous Life of Oscar Wao* (2007).

4. Like coming-of-age novels, memoir and autobiography by ethnic American writers trace the development of identity, tracing similar movements from innocence to experience, ignorance to knowledge, or idealism to realism, with an emphasis on ethnicity and race. In *The Hunger of Memory* (1982), for example, Richard Rodriguez describes his education as a transformation into "a public man" which entails loneliness, and "a movement away from the company of family," from the Spanish language of his parents and Mexican traditions, and from "private" or ethnic identity. In this work, Rodriguez describes his intellectual development within an "either/or" context; he either becomes an "assimilated man" or remains forever alien and unsuccessful. Other writers have conceived different models of cultural contact, finding alternatives to binaries that make, for example, "nonwhite" and "white" or "minority" and "majority" mutually exclusive terms. Meena Alexander in *Fault Lines: A Memoir* (1993), Jimmy Santiago Baca's *A Place to Stand: The Making of a Poet* (2001), and Diana Abu-Jabar in *The Language of Baklava* (2005) all exhibit more hybrid and heterogeneous understandings of ethnic American identity, as does Richard Rodriguez in his second book, *Days of Obligation* (1992). Focusing on a memoir or autobiography, students could consider creative ways writers express multicultural identity. How do they demonstrate the ways "majority" and "minority," foreign and native cultures, come together to challenge, alter, and revitalize one another? For help in identifying primary works, students might consult Joe Rodriguez's "United States Hispanic Autobiography and Biography: Legend for the Future," in Francisco Lomelí's *Handbook of Hispanic Cultures in the United States: Literature and Art* (1993), and Guiyou Huang's *Asian American Autobiographers* (2001).

5. The British Indian writer Salman Rushdie has described magical realism as the "commingling of the improbable and the mundane." An important aspect in contemporary fiction, magical realism is a term applied to realistic narratives that include "magical" and supernatural happenings as accepted and integrated aspects of everyday life. In her introduction to *Ordinary Enchantments: Magical Realism and the Remystification of Narrative* (2004) Wendy Faris offers this definition: "Very briefly defined, magical realism combines realism and the fantastic so that the marvelous seems to grow organically within the ordinary, blurring the distinction between them. Furthermore, that combination of realistic and fantastical narrative, together with the inclusion of different cultural traditions, means that magical realism reflects, in both its narrative mode and its cultural environment, the hybrid nature of much postcolonial society. Thus the mode is multicultural." Students interested in this topic might begin by examining the elements of magical realism of a particular work. How do these elements challenge or revise Western European notions of reality? How do magical realist techniques help writers to bridge cultural differences and gaps? How do writers "integrate them into contemporary U.S. culture in order to enrich or remedy it?" (Lois Parkinson Zamora, "Magical Romance/Magical Realism: Ghosts in U.S. and Latin American Fiction," in Zamora and Wendy B. Faris, eds.,

p. 542). Works to consider include (but are not limited to) Sherman Alexie's *Reservation Blues* (1995), Rudolfo Anaya's *Bless Me, Ultima* (1972), Ana Castillo's *So Far from God* (1993), Kiana Davenport's *Shark Dialogues* (1994), E. L. Doctorow's *Loon Lake* (1980), Cristina García's *Dreaming in Cuban* (1992), Chitra Divakaruni's *Mistress of Spices* (1997), Toni Morrison's *Song of Solomon* (1977), Gloria Naylor's *Mama Day* (1988), and Charles Johnson's *Middle Passage* (1990).

6. In his introduction to *MultiAmerica* (1996) Ishmael Reed challenges readers to imagine "a new, inclusive definition of the common [American] culture" that takes into consideration cultural, racial, and ethnic differences. He writes: "I think that a new definition of a common culture is possible, and that because of their multicultural status, Latinos, African Americans, and Asian Americans with knowledge of their own ethnic histories and cultures as well as those of European cultures are able to contribute to the formation of a new, inclusive definition." Students might consider engaging Reed's proposition by analyzing works by ethnic Americans. How does the particular work contribute to "a new, inclusive definition" of American literature? How does the work insist upon a broader definition of American identity that includes racial and ethnic difference? Another way to approach this topic would be to focus on the forms and narrative techniques that ethnic American writers use. A common feature is the use of multiple forms and genres in a single work. As Maria Lauret notes in the introductory essay to *Beginning Ethnic American Literature* (2001), "frequently autobiography functions as theory, prose is shot through with poetry and song, narrative is also (counter-) historiography. Linguistic mixtures occur too, most obviously in the bilingual texts of Chicano/a writers, but also when African American writers make use of the black vernacular as a 'native tongue,' or when Asian Americans and Native Americans intersperse their English with words and phrases from their first language." How do writers use these techniques and mixtures to challenge and revitalize monocultural definitions of American literature and identity? How does form express cultural hybridity? In analyzing a work, consider whether a writer is calling for the inclusion of ethnic American writers as part of mainstream America or is challenging the very defination of America.

# RESOURCES

## Primary Works

Asian Women United of California, ed., *Making Waves: An Anthology of Writings by and about Asian American Women* (Boston: Beacon, 1989).

Collection of fiction, poetry, and essays by fifty-three women, representing the diversity of Asian American writers whose cultural roots are in China, India, Japan, Korea, the Philippines, Vietnam, and other Asian countries. Also included are a useful timeline of events important to Asian American history and essays tracing historical and social contexts.

Wesley Brown and Amy Ling, eds., *Imagining America: Stories from the Promised Land: A Multicultural Anthology of American Fiction* (New York: Persea Books, 2002).
Revised and updated version of the 1991 edition that provides a basic introduction to multicultural American literature, in the form of short stories from writers of various ethnic backgrounds linked by the immigrant experience.

Jules Chametzky, John Felstiner, Hilene Fanzbaum, and Kathryn Hellerstein, eds., *Jewish American Literature: A Norton Anthology* (New York: Norton, 2001).
Includes the section "Wandering and Return: Literature since 1973," the introduction to which provides an overview of the development of more-recent writing and discussion of thematic concerns.

Maria Mazziotti Gillan and Jennifer Gillan, eds., *Unsettling America: An Anthology of Contemporary Multicultural Poetry* (New York: Penguin, 1994).
Divided into the sections "Uprooting," "Performing," "Naming," "Negotiating," and "Re-envisioning." This collection features up-and-coming and established poets such as Lucille Clifton, Rita Dove, Louise Erdrich, Lawrence Ferlinghetti, and Gary Soto.

Pauline Kaldas and Khaled Mattawa, eds., *Dinarzad's Children: An Anthology of Contemporary Arab American Fiction* (Fayetteville: University of Arkansas Press, 2004).
Short fiction by nineteen American authors of Egyptian, Lebanese, Libyan, Palestinian, and Syrian descent. Themes addressed include immigration, alienation, and assimilation.

Nicholás Kanellos, ed., *En otra voz: Antología de literatura hispana de los Estados Unidos* (Houston: Arte Público Press, 2002).
Spanish-language anthology tracing the history of Hispanic writing in the United States from the colonial times to the present. The book is divided chronologically into three sections, each addressing a different aspect of the U.S. Hispanic experience, from those born in the country, those who have immigrated, and those living in exile.

Kanellos, ed., *Herencia: The Anthology of Hispanic Literature of the United States* (New York: Oxford University Press, 2002).
Comprehensive anthology of writing from colonial times to the present that underscores the diversity of Hispanic literature in the United States through its representation of Chicano, Nuyorican, Cuban American, and Latino writings. The book is organized chronologically, and each section is also divided by content to underscore cultural, historical, and political issues influencing writers.

Elaine H. Kim, Lilia V. Villanueva, and Asian Women United of California, *Making More Waves: New Writing by Asian American Women* (Boston: Beacon, 1997).
Comprehensive anthology of fiction, poetry, and essays by writers of Asian descent that updates and expands *Making Waves*.

Michael P. Kramer and Hana Wirth-Nesher, eds., *The Cambridge Companion to Jewish American Literature* (New York: Cambridge University Press, 2003).
Highlights contributions that expand definitions of American literary and popular culture. The book includes a chronology and guide to further reading.

## Criticism

Mary Jo Bona and Irma Maini, eds., *Multiethnic Literature and Canon Debates* (Albany: State University of New York Press, 2006).
Useful collection of essays charting the growth of ethnic American writers and the academic fields that study them. Beginning with an essay on the history of the Society for the Study of Multi-Ethnic Literatures of the United States (MELUS) and its journal, this volume provides individual chapters on Chicano/a, Italian American, African American, Native American, and Asian American literatures.

Louis Freitas Caton, *Reading American Novels and Multicultural Aesthetics: Romancing the Postmodern Novel* (New York: Palgrave Macmillan, 2008).
Uses theory derived from European Romanticism to analyze contemporary works, which Caton argues allows for a focus on aesthetic form as well as themes related to politics and history.

King-kok Cheung and Stan Yogi, eds., *Asian American Literature: An Annotated Bibliography* (New York: Modern Language Association, 1993).
Useful list of primary sources divided by ethnicity and geographical region, secondary sources, and literature about Asians and Asian Americans written by non-Asians.

Teresa Córdova, "Roots and Resistance: The Emergent Writings of Twenty Years of Chicana Feminist Struggle," in *Handbook of Hispanic Cultures in the United States: Sociology,* edited by Félix Padilla (Houston: Arte Público Press, 1994), pp. 175–202.
Overview of the efforts of feminists within the Chicana movement that provides excellent historical context for discussing literary works.

Christopher Douglas, *A Genealogy of Literary Multiculturalism* (Ithaca, N.Y.: Cornell University Press, 2009).
Interprets African American, Native American, Chicano, and Asian American literary texts in the context of theories derived from sociology and anthropology.

Wendy B. Faris, *Ordinary Enchantments: Magical Realism and the Remystification of Narrative* (Nashville: Vanderbilt University Press, 2004).
Comprehensive examination of magical realism as a trend in contemporary fiction from around the world, identifying its major characteristics and narrative traits.

Andrew Furman, *Contemporary Jewish American Writers and the Multicultural Dilemma: Return of the Exiled* (Syracuse, N.Y.: Syracuse University Press, 2000).

Exploration of contemporary Jewish American literature within the context of current debates about multicultural literature; provides a historical overview of Jewish American fiction.

Helena Grice, Candida Hepworth, Maria Lauret, and Martin Padget, *Beginning Ethnic American Literature* (Manchester, England & New York: Manchester University Press, 2001).

Examines the work of African Americans, Asian Americans, Chicanos/as, and Native Americans within cultural, historical, and literary contexts; divided into four sections, each focused on a literary tradition offering a brief overview, a discussion of critical issues, and essays on individual novels.

Guiyou Huang, *Columbia Guide to Asian-American Literature since 1945* (New York: Columbia University Press, 2006).

Traces the literature of Asian America from the end of World War II to the beginning of the twenty-first century within historical contexts. In addition to fiction, poetry, and drama, the work discusses major anthologies and memoir/autobiography.

Huang, ed., *Asian American Autobiographers: A Bio-Bibliographical Critical Sourcebook* (Westport, Conn.: Greenwood Press, 2001).

Alphabetically arranged entries that provide biographical, critical, and bibliographical information on Asian American memoirists and autobiographers.

Huang, ed., *Asian-American Poets: A Bio-Bibliographical Critical Sourcebook* (Westport, Conn.: Greenwood Press, 2002).

Entries on forty-eight Asian American poets, each entry consisting of a short biography, discussion of major themes, a summary of critical reception, and critical sources.

Huang, ed., *The Greenwood Encyclopedia of Asian American Literature*, 3 volumes (Westport, Conn.: Greenwood Press, 2008).

Comprehensive resource featuring entries on Asian American writers, individual works, topics, events, and terms.

Nicholás Kanellos, *Hispanic Literature of the United States: A Comprehensive Reference* (Westport, Conn.: Greenwood Press, 2003).

Essential resource on the history of U.S. Hispanic literature with useful discussion of major trends, movements, and themes. The "Who's Who of Hispanic Authors of the United States" will help students quickly identify important literary figures.

Jeff Karem, *The Romance of Authenticity* (Charlottesville: University of Virginia Press, 2004).

Discusses the problems of using authenticity when assessing the value of ethnic American literature for both writers and literary critics. Examples are given from works by African American, Latino, and Native American literatures.

A. Robert Lee, *Multicultural American Literature: Comparative Black, Native, Latino/a and Asian American Fictions* (Jackson: University Press of Mississippi, 2003).

Comparative analyses of recent ethnic writing that has enlarged the spectrum of American literature.

Shirley Geok-lin Lim, John Blair Gamber, Stephen Hong Sohn, and Gina Valentino, eds., *Transnational Asian American Literature: Sites and Transits* (Philadelphia: Temple University Press, 2006).
Collection of thirteen essays on the transnational and diasporic aspects of Asian American literature. Writers discussed include Ha Jin, Maxine Hong Kingston, Jhumpa Lahiri, Chang-rae Lee, and Karen Tei Yamashita.

Francisco Lomelí, ed., *Handbook of Hispanic Cultures in the United States: Literature and Art* (Houston: Arte Público Press, 1993).
Collection of fifteen essays examining Hispanic literature (from the sixteenth century to the present) with a variety of approaches.

Emmanuel S. Nelson, ed., *The Greenwood Encyclopedia of Multiethnic American Literature: A–Z* (Westport, Conn.: Greenwood Press, 2005).
Accessible resource providing information on hundreds of ethnic American authors, works, topics, and traditions.

David Palumbo-Liu, ed., *The Ethnic Canon: Histories, Institutions, and Interventions* (Minneapolis: University of Minnesota Press, 1995).
Essays that delineate the historical, theoretical, and practical considerations of canon formation for ethnic American literatures. Overall, they suggest strategies of incorporating texts without losing a sense of their historical specificity and differences.

Ishmael Reed, ed., *MultiAmerica: Essays on Cultural Wars and Cultural Peace* (New York: Viking, 1997).
Anthology of essays, including personal reflections, by writers who argue against monoculturalism in American society and art. The introduction by Reed sets forth an argument for multiculturalism.

Steven George Salaita, *Arab American Literary Fictions, Cultures, and Politics* (New York: Palgrave Macmillan, 2007).
Focuses on the development of contemporary Arab American literature with the purpose of defining it in more-complex ways than has been done in previous studies. Salaita uses interpretive methods drawn from Native American literary studies to propose new interpretive approaches.

Jelena Šesnić, *From Shadow to Presence: Representations of Ethnicity in Contemporary American Literature* (Amsterdam & New York: Rodopi, 2007).
Describes four comparative approaches to multicultural literature: cultural nationalism, ethnic feminism, borderlands and contact zones, and the diasporic model.

Bonnie TuSmith, *All My Relatives: Community in Contemporary Ethnic American Literatures* (Ann Arbor: University of Michigan Press, 1994).
Proposes alternatives to the practice of reading works by ethnic Americans through Euro-American contexts.

Lois Parkinson Zamora and Wendy B. Faris, eds., *Magical Realism: Theory, History, Community* (Durham, N.C.: Duke University Press, 1995).
Anthology of essays offering a variety of approaches. Taken together, they trace the origins of magical realism from Germany to contemporary literature, demonstrating the international scope of magical realism in works from Europe, Latin America, North America, Africa, the Caribbean, Asia, and Australia.

## PEOPLE OF INTEREST

**Kathryn K. Abdul-Baki** (?–   )
Daughter of a Palestinian father and American mother who was born in Washington, D.C., and raised in Iran, Kuwait, Beirut, and Jerusalem. She is a journalist and fiction writer whose works include the short-story collection *Fields of Fig and Olive: Ameera and Other Stories of the Middle East* (1991) and the novels *Tower of Dreams* (1995), *Ghost Songs* (2000), and *Sands of Zulaika* (2007).

**Diana Abu-Jaber** (1960–   )
Born in Syracuse, New York, to a Jordanian father and Irish American mother. Her works include two novels, *Arabian Jazz* (1993) and *Crescent* (2003); *The Language of Baklava* (2005) is a memoir.

**Rabih Alameddine** (1959–   )
Lebanese American fiction writer who was born in Jordan. He is the author of *KOOLAIDS: The Art of War* (1998), *The Perv: Stories* (1999), *I, The Divine: A Novel in First Chapters* (2001), and *The Hakawati* (2008).

**Meena Alexander** (1951–   )
Poet and fiction writer born in India as Mary Elizabeth Alexander and raised there and in Sudan. She has written *The Bird's Bright Ring* (1976), *Without Place* (1978), *Stone Roots* (1980), *Fault Lines: A Memoir* (1993), *Manhattan Music* (1997), and *Raw Silk* (2004).

**Agha Shahid Ali** (1949–2001)
Poet whose works include *Bone-Sculpture* (1972), *A Walk through the Yellow Pages* (1987), *The Beloved Witness: Selected Poems* (1992), *Rooms Are Never Finished* (2002), and *Call Me Ishmael Tonight: A Book of Ghazals* (2003).

**Julia Alvarez** (1950–   )
Writer who was born in New York but spent her first ten years in the Dominican Republic, which her family fled after her father's involvement in a political rebellion. Her novels include *How the García Girls Lost Their Accents* (1991), *In the Time of the Butterflies* (1994), *¡Yo!* (1997), *In the Name of Salomé* (2000), and *Saving the World* (2006). Her poetry collections are *The Housekeeping Book* (1984) and *The Woman I Kept to Myself* (2004). Autobiographical essays make up *Something to Declare* (1998). She has also written for young-adult audiences in *Return to Sender* (2009).

**Rudolfo A. Anaya** (1937–   )
Chicano writer best known for *Bless Me, Ultima* (1972). His other works include *Heart of Aztlan* (1976), *Tortuga* (1979), *The Silence of the Llano: Short Stories*

(1982), *The Legend of La Llorona* (1984), *The Adventures of Juan Chicaspatas* (1985), *Lord of the Dawn: The Legend of Quetzalcóatl* (1987), *Alburquerque* (1992), and *Jalamanta: A Message from the Desert* (1996). His series of detective novels featuring detective Sonny Baca includes *Zia Summer* (1995), *Rio Grande Fall* (1996), *Shaman Winter* (1998), and *Jemez Spring* (2005). He has also written the plays *The Season of La Llorona* (1987) and *Matachines* (1992) and a collection of travel essays, *A Chicano in China* (1986).

**Rane Arroyo** (1954– )
Poet and playwright born in Chicago to Puerto Rican parents. He is the author of the poetry collections *Columbus's Orphan* (1993), *The Singing Shark* (1996), *Pale Ramón* (1998), and *Home Movies of Narcissus* (2002).

**Jimmy Santiago Baca** (1952– )
Born in Santa Fe, New Mexico, to Indio-Chicano parents. After being sentenced to five years in prison, he learned to read and write. He is a prolific writer whose works include *Martín; and, Meditations on the South Valley* (1987), which was awarded the Before Columbus American Book Award for poetry, and *Winter Poems along the Rio Grande* (2004). He is also the author of a screenplay, *Bound by Honor* (1993), and a memoir, *A Place to Stand: The Making of a Poet* (2001).

**Ana Castillo** (1953– )
Chicana poet, essayist, and fiction writer. Her novels include *The Mixquiahuala Letters* (1986), *Sapogonia* (1990), *So Far from God* (1993), *Peel My Love like an Onion* (1999), and *The Guardians* (2007). *Loverboys* (1996) is a collection of short stories. She also published *My Father Was a Toltec and Selected Poems, 1973–1988* (1995).

**Lorna Dee Cervantes** (1954– )
Chicana–Native American poet who is the author of *Emplumada* (1981), which won the American Book Award, and *Cables of Genocide: Poems on Love and Hunger* (1991). She is also the founder of *Mango*, the name of both her poetry magazine and press.

**Theresa Hak Kyung Cha** (1951–1982)
Korea-born and California-raised writer known for the experimental novel *Dictée* (1982).

**Jeffery Paul Chan** (1942– )
Chinese American writer who coedited *Aiiieeeee!* (1974) and *The Big Aiiieeeee!* (1991) and cofounded the Asian American Studies Department at San Francisco State University. He is the author of the novel *Eat Everything before You Die: A Chinaman in the Counterculture* (2004).

**Denise Chávez** (1948– )
Chicana author who began her career as a writer of one-act plays but found recognition for *The Last of the Menu Girls* (1986), a collection of interrelated stories published as a novel. Her other works include *Face of an Angel* (1994) and *Loving Pedro Infante* (2001).

**Frank Chin** (1940–   )
Chinese American playwright and fiction writer. He coedited *Aiiieeeee!* (1974) and *The Big Aiiieeeee!* (1991) and is the author of *The Chickencoop Chinaman and The Year of the Dragon: Two Plays* (1981), *The Chinaman Pacific & Frisco R.R. Co.* (1988), *Donald Duk* (1991), *Gunga Din Highway* (1994), and *Bulletproof Buddhists and Other Essays* (1998).

**Judith Ortiz Cofer** (1952–   )
Writer of poetry, fiction, and nonfiction who was born in Puerto Rico and raised there, as well as in New Jersey and Georgia. Her poems have been collected in *Latin Women Pray* (1980), *Reaching for the Mainland* (1987), *Terms of Survival* (1989), *The Latin Deli: Prose & Poetry* (1993), and *The Year of Our Revolution: New and Selected Stories and Poems* (1998). She is also the author of the young-adult book *An Island Like You: Stories of the Barrio* (1995).

**Victor Hernández Cruz** (1949–   )
Poet who was born in Puerto Rico and moved with his family to the United States in 1954. He is the cofounder of New York's East Harlem Gut Theatre. His works include *Snaps* (1969), *Mainland* (1973), *Tropicalization* (1976), *By Lingual Wholes* (1982), *Rhythm, Content and Flavor* (1988), *Red Beans* (1991), *Panoramas* (1997), *Maraca* (2001), and *The Mountain in the Sea* (2006).

**Kiana Davenport** (?–   )
Born Diana Davenport in Hawaii. Of part-Hawaiian descent, she is the author of the novels *Shark Dialogues* (1994), *Song of the Exile* (1999), and *House of Many Gods* (2006).

**Junot Díaz** (1968–   )
Born in the Dominican Republic and immigrated to New Jersey in 1974. His works include *Drown* (1996) and *The Brief Wondrous Life of Oscar Wao* (2007).

**Sandra María Esteves** (1948–   )
A founder of the Nuyorican poetry movement who has published six collections of poetry: *Yerba Buena* (1980), *Tropical Rain: A Bilingual Downpour* (1984), *Bluestown Mockingbird Mambo* (1990), *Undelivered Love Poems* (1997), *Contrapunto in the Open Field* (1998), and *Finding Your Way* (1999).

**Gustavo Pérez Firmat** (1949–   )
Poet, novelist, and literary critic who was born in Havana and grew up in Miami. His poetry collections include *Carolina Cuban* (1987), *Equivocaciones* (1989), *Bilingual Blues* (1995), and *Scar Tissue* (2005). *Anything But Love* (2000) is a novel, and *Next Year in Cuba* (1995; revised, 2000) is a memoir.

**Cristina García** (1958–   )
Cuban American author of the novels *Dreaming in Cuban* (1992), *The Agüero Sisters* (1997), *Monkey Hunting* (2003), *A Handbook to Luck* (2007), and *The Lady Matador's Hotel* (2010). *The Lesser Tragedy of Death* (2010) is a collection of poems.

**Jessica Hagedorn** (1949–    )
Filipino American writer whose works include the poetry collection *Pet Food &*
*Tropical Apparitions* (1981) and the novels *Dogeaters* (1990), a National Book
Award recipient; *The Gangsters of Love* (1996); and *Dream Jungle* (2003). She is
the editor of *Charlie Chan Is Dead: An Anthology of Contemporary Asian American*
*Fiction* (1993).

**Kimiko Hahn** (1955–    )
Born in New York to a Japanese American mother who had been raised in Hawaii
and a German American father. Her poetry collections include *We Stand Our*
*Ground* (1988), with Gale Jackson and Susan Sherman; *Air Pocket* (1989); *Earshot*
(1992); *The Unbearable Heart* (1995); *Volatile* (1998); *Mosquito and Ant* (1999);
and *The Artist's Daughter* (2002).

**Laila Halaby** (?–    )
Born in Lebanon to a Jordanian father and American mother and grew up mostly
in Arizona. Her novels are *West of the Jordan* (2003) and *Once in a Promised Land:*
*A Novel* (2007).

**Oscar Hijuelos** (1951–    )
Cuban American fiction writer whose *Mambo Kings Play Songs of Love* (1989)
earned him the distinction of being the first Hispanic American to be awarded
the Pulitzer Prize in fiction. His other works are *Our House in the Last World*
(1983), *The Fourteen Sisters of Emilio Montez O'Brien* (1993), *Mr. Ives's Christmas*
(1995), *Empress of the Splendid Season* (1999), and *A Simple Habana Melody* (2002).
*Dark Dude* (2008) is for young-adult readers.

**Garrett Kaoru Hongo** (1951–    )
Japanese American poet born in Hawaii and raised in California. His works
include *The Buddha Bandits down Highway 99* (1978), with Lawson Fusao Inada
and Alan Chong Lau; *Yellow Light* (1982); and *The River of Heaven* (1988). *Vol-*
*cano* (1995) is a memoir.

**Jeanne Wakatsuki Houston** (1934–    )
Japanese American writer who was imprisoned with her family in a Japanese
Relocation Camp during World War II, an experience she writes about in the
autobiographical *Farewell to Manzanar* (1973), coauthored with her husband, James
Houston. Her other works are *Beyond Manzanar and Other Views of Asian-American*
*Womanhood* (1985) and the novel *The Legend of the Fire Horse Woman* (2003).

**David Henry Hwang** (1957–    )
Chinese American playwright best known for *M. Butterfly* (1988), for which he
was the first Asian American to be awarded the Tony Award for best play.

**Lawson Fusao Inada** (1938–    )
Japanese American poet who coedited *Aiiieeeee!* (1974) and *The Big Aiiieeeee!*
(1991). He is also author of the poetry collections *Before the War: Poems as They*
*Happened* (1971); *The Buddha Bandits down Highway 99* (1978), with Garrett

Kaoru Hongo and Alan Chong Lau; *Legends from Camp* (1992); and *Drawing the Line* (1997).

**Gish Jen** (1956– )
Chinese American fiction writer whose works include the novel *Typical American* (1991); its sequel, *Mona in the Promised Land* (1996); and a collection of short stories, *Who's Irish?* (1999).

**Charles Johnson** (1948– )
African American writer who began his career as a journalist and cartoonist and then turned to fiction. His novels include *Faith and the Good Thing* (1974), *Oxherding* (1982), *Middle Passage* (1990), and *Dreamer* (1998). *The Sorcerer's Apprentice: Tales of Conjurations* (1986) is a collection of stories, and *Being and Race: Black Writing since 1970* (1988) is a critical study.

**Nora Okja Keller** (1965– )
Novelist born in Korea to a Korean mother and German father. *Comfort Woman* (1997) and *Fox Girl* (2002) are the first two works in a planned trilogy. She is also the coeditor of *Intersecting Circles: The Voices of Hapa Women in Poetry and Prose* (1999).

**Laila Lalami** (1968– )
Fiction writer born in Morocco. Her works are *Hope and Other Dangerous Pursuits* (2005) and *Secret Son* (2009).

**Tato Laviera** (1951– )
Playwright and poet who was born in Puerto Rico but has lived in New York City since 1960. His poetry is collected in *La Carreta Made a U-Turn* (1979), *Enclave* (1981), *AmeRícan* (1985), and *Mainstream Ethics* (1988). *Olú Clemente* (1979) is a play.

**Chang-rae Lee** (1965– )
Writer who was born in Seoul, South Korea, and came to the United States with his family in 1968. His novels are *Native Speaker* (1995), *A Gesture Life* (1999), and *Aloft* (2004).

**Chris McKinney** (?– )
Hawaii-born novelist of mixed Korean, Japanese, and Scottish descent. His works include *The Tattoo* (1999), *The Queen of Tears* (2001), *Bolohead Row* (2005), and *Mililani Mauka* (2009).

**Janice Mirikitani** (1942– )
Japanese American poet. Her collections are *Awake in the River* (1978), *Shedding Silence* (1987), *We the Dangerous* (1995), and *Love Works* (2001).

**Nicholasa Mohr** (1938– )
Graphic artist and writer born in New York to Puerto Rican parents. Her works include *Nilda* (1973), *El Bronx Remembered* (1975), *In Nueva York* (1977), *Felita* (1979), *Rituals of Survival: A Women's Portfolio* (1985), *Going Home* (1986), *All*

*for the Better: A Story of El Barrio* (1993), and *A Matter of Pride and Other Stories* (1997).

**Pat Mora** (1942–   )
Chicana poet, essayist, and children's book author whose works include *Chants* (1984), *Borders* (1986), *Communion* (1991), *Nepantla: Essays from the Land in the Middle* (1993), *Agua Santa/Holy Water* (1995), *House of Houses* (1997), and *Aunt Carmen's Book of Practical Saints* (1997).

**Cherríe Moraga** (1952–   )
Chicana playwright, poet, and essayist whose writings include *The Last Generation: Poetry and Prose* (1993) and *Heroes and Saints and Other Plays* (1994).

**Bharati Mukherjee** (1940–   )
Fiction writer born into a Bengali Brahmin family in Calcutta. Her novels include *The Tiger's Daughter* (1972), *Wife* (1975), *Jasmine* (1989), *The Holder of the World* (1993), *Leave It to Me* (1997), *Desirable Daughters* (2002), and *The Tree Bride* (2004). Her other works include the nonfiction *Days and Nights in Calcutta* (1977; revised, 1986), coauthored with her husband, Clark Blaise, and *The Sorrow and the Terror: The Haunting Legacy of the Air India Tragedy* (1987). Her short stories are collected in *Darkness* (1985) and *The Middleman* (1988).

**Naomi Shihab Nye** (1952–   )
Daughter of a Palestinian father and Anglo American mother. Her poetry collections include *Hugging the Jukebox* (1982), *Red Suitcase* (1994), *Fuel* (1998), *19 Varieties of Gazelle: Poems of the Middle East* (2002), and *You and Yours* (2005).

**Julie Otsuka** (1962–   )
Japanese American author of *When the Emperor Was Divine* (2002).

**Ishmael Reed** (1938–   )
Poet, fiction writer, essayist, and playwright best known for coining the term *Neohoodooism* to describe an African American aesthetic philosophy. His poems are collected in *New and Collected Poems* (1988). His novels include *The Freelance Pallbearers* (1967), *Yellow Back Radio Broke-Down* (1969), *Flight to Canada* (1976), and *Japanese by Spring* (1993). His nonfiction works are *Shrovetide in Old New Orleans: Essays* (1978), *God Made Alaska for the Indians: Selected Essays* (1982), *Writing Is Fighting: Thirty-Seven Years of Boxing on Paper* (1988), and *Airing Dirty Laundry* (1993). He is also the editor of *The Before Columbus Foundation Fiction Anthology* (1992), *The Before Columbus Foundation Poetry* (1997), and *Multi-American: Essays on Cultural Wars and Cultural Peace* (1997).

**Alberto Ríos** (1952–   )
Chicano poet whose works include *Elk Heads on the Wall* (1979), *Sleeping on Fists* (1981), *Whispering to Fool the Wind* (1982), *Five Indiscretions* (1985), *The Lime Orchard Woman* (1988), *The Warrington Poems* (1989), *Teodoro Luna's Two Kisses* (1990), *The Smallest Muscle in the Human Body* (2002), *The Theater of Night* (2005), and *The Dangerous Shirt* (2009).

**Tomás Rivera** (1935–1984)
Writer, teacher, and administrator born in Texas to Mexican farm laborers. He wrote the novel . . .*y no se lo tragó la tierra* (1971; translated as . . . *and the Earth Did Not Devour Him*, 1987), *The Harvest: Short Stories* (1989), and *The Searchers: Collected Poetry* (1990).

**Richard Rodriguez** (1944–   )
Chicano author of *Hunger of Memory: The Education of Richard Rodriguez* (1982), *Days of Obligation: An Argument with My Mexican Father* (1992), and *Brown: The Last Discovery of America* (2002).

**Esmeralda Santiago** (1948–   )
Puerto Rico–born author of the memoirs *When I Was Puerto Rican* (1993), *Almost a Woman* (1998), and *The Turkish Lover* (2004) and the novel *América's Dream* (1996).

**Cathy Song** (1955–   )
Chinese-Korean American poet who was raised in Hawaii. Her first poetry collection, *Picture Bride* (1983), was selected for the Yale Younger Poet Series. Her other works are *Frameless Windows, Squares of Light* (1988), *School Figures* (1994), *The Land of Bliss* (2001), and *Cloud Moving Hands* (2007).

**Gary Soto** (1952–   )
Poet who also writes fiction, plays, and children's books. His works include *The Elements of San Joaquin* (1977), *The Tale of Sunlight* (1978), and *New and Selected Poems* (1995). His memoir, *Living up the Street* (1985), received the Before Columbus Foundation's American Book Award.

**Amy Tan** (1952–   )
Chinese American writer whose works include the novels *The Joy Luck Club* (1989), *The Kitchen God's Wife* (1991), *The Hundred Secret Senses* (1995), and *The Bonesetter's Daughter* (2001). She has also written the children's books *The Moon Lady* (1992) and *Sagwa: The Chinese Siamese Cat* (1994) and a collection of essays, *The Opposite of Fate: A Book of Musings* (2003).

**Piri Thomas** (1928–   )
Born Juan Pedro Tomás to Puerto Rican and Cuban parents in New York City's Spanish Harlem. He is best known for his influence in the Nuyorican literary movement and for the autobiography *Down These Mean Streets* (1967). His other works are the sequel *Seven Long Times* (1974) and *Stories from El Barrio* (1978). He is the subject of Jonathan Robinson's film *Every Child Is Born a Poet: The Life and Work of Piri Thomas* (2002).

**Luis Valdez** (1940–   )
Mexican American playwright whose works have been collected as *Luis Valdez—Early Works: Actos, Bernabé and Pensamiento Serpentino* (1990), *Zoot Suit and Other Plays* (1992), and *Mummified Deer and Other Plays* (2005).

**Ed Vega** (1936–2008)
Novelist and short-story writer born Edgardo Vega Yunqué in Puerto Rico. His works include *Comeback* (1985), *Mendoza's Dreams* (1987), and *Casualty Report* (1991).

**Helena María Viramontes** (1954– )
Mexican American fiction writer whose works include *The Moths and Other Stories* (1985), *Paris Rats in E.L.A.* (1993), and *Under the Feet of Jesus* (1995).

**Shawn Wong** (1949– )
Chinese American writer who was one of the coeditors of *Aiiieeeee!* (1974) and *The Big Aiiieeeee!* (1991) and is the author of the novels *Homebase* (1979) and *American Knees* (1995).

**Lois-Ann Yamanaka** (1960– )
Hawaii-born Japanese American fiction writer whose works include *Saturday Night at the Pahala Theatre* (1993), *Wild Meat and the Bully Burgers* (1996), *Blu's Hanging* (1997), *Name Me Nobody* (1999), *Father of Four Passages* (2001), and *Behold the Many* (2006). She wrote the screenplay for the film *The Silent Years* (2004).

**Karen Tei Yamashita** (1951– )
Japanese American writer whose nine-year residence in Brazil was the inspiration for the novels *Through the Arc of the Rain Forest* (1990) and *Brazil-Maru* (1992). Her other novels include *Tropic of Orange* (1997) and *I Hotel* (2010). *Circle K Cycles* (2001) blends memoir, short stories, and photographs.

—*Linda Trinh Moser*

# The Native American Renaissance

An issue of much debate and contention is how to refer to people whose heritage goes back to pre-Columbian times on the North and South American continents. The term *Indian* is based on Christopher Columbus's mistaken belief that he had reached the West Indies, and many people object to it on those grounds; it also has a history of being used derogatorily. *Native American* came into use a few decades ago as a remedy, but it raises objections as yet another example of an enforced label—*American* is derived from the name of the Italian navigator Amerigo Vespucci—and as an example of "political correctness." The most widely accepted and respectful practice is to refer to people by their tribe of origin—Cherokee, Ojibwa, Sioux, Pueblo, and so forth. If that information is unknown, or if one is referring to members of more than one tribe, a reasonable choice is to alternate between *American Indian* and *Native American*. (In Canada, the preferred collective term is *First Nations*.)

The emergence of a body of Native American literature and art significant enough to be designated a "renaissance" was signaled by three distinct occurrences. The first was the escalation of activism by the American Indian Movement (AIM) in the 1960s and 1970s. Drawing inspiration from the African American Civil Rights movement, and in protest of the loss of 3.3 million acres of land between 1948 and 1957 owing to reservation-termination policies, American Indians began organizing and staging demonstrations, land takeovers, and occupations of federal buildings. The most famous of these events were the 1969 takeover of Alcatraz Island in San Francisco Bay, the former site of the infamous prison, which lasted for nineteen months, and the 1973 standoff at Wounded Knee, South Dakota, on the Oglala Sioux Pine Ridge Indian Reservation, when for ten weeks national television news showed AIM protesters surrounded by heavily armed soldiers. The awareness raised by these protests was bolstered by the publication of two nonfiction works: Vine Deloria Jr.'s *Custer Died for Your Sins: An Indian Manifesto* (1969), which dissected stereotypes of American Indians and called for acknowledgment of the negative ramifications of American "Manifest Destiny" on indigenous populations, and Dee Brown's *Bury My Heart at Wounded Knee* (1970), a history of the American West from an Indian perspective. For many Americans who thought of native culture and people as part of America's past, these events brought a new awareness of the existence and living conditions of American Indians—rates of unemployment, infant mortality, alcoholism, homelessness, and poverty all much higher than national averages, resulting in an average lifespan of forty years. For many peoples of native heritage, they brought a renewed urge toward self-expression.

The other two signals of a Native American Renaissance were more specifically literary in character. In 1969 N. Scott Momaday, a Kiowa, received the Pulitzer Prize in fiction for his novel *House Made of Dawn* (1968)—the first major national honor for a literary work by a Native American. The third signal came fifteen years later: in 1983 Kenneth Lincoln published *Native American Renaissance*, which recognized in the previous two decades "a written renewal of oral traditions translated into Western literary forms . . . transitional continuities emerging from the old." In addition to the writings of Momaday, Lincoln discussed those of James Welch (Blackfoot/Gros Ventre), Simon J. Ortiz (Acoma Pueblo), Wendy Rose (Hopi/Miwok), and Leslie Marmon Silko (Laguna Pueblo). Although not treated in *Native American Renaissance*, the Paiute poet Adrian Louis and the Pueblo scholar and poet Paula Gunn Allen may also be considered early voices in the Native American Renaissance. Lincoln also noted several anthologies of Native American literature that had been published in the 1970s and early 1980s and the contemporaneous establishment of journals focused on Native American studies, including *SAIL: Studies in American Indian Literature* (1977), the *American Indian Quarterly* (1977), and the *Wíazo Ša Review* (1985).

Lincoln added a preface to the 1985 paperback edition of his text in which he discussed the Ojibwa (also known as Anishinaabe or Chippewa) Louise Erdrich's *Love Medicine*, which had been published the previous year; his excitement about the novel is palpable. As the first best seller by an American Indian, it ushered in a second generation of writers to follow those Lincoln had recognized. In addition to Erdrich, this generation includes Joy Harjo (Creek), Michael Dorris (Modoc), Linda Hogan (Chickasaw), Greg Sarris (Coastal Miwok/Pomo), Luci Tapahonso (Navajo), Sherman Alexie (Spokane/Coeur d'Alene), Susan Power (Sioux), and David Treuer (Ojibwa).

Momaday commands virtually unanimous respect among American Indian writers as the founder of the Native American Renaissance. *House Made of Dawn* combines the spiritual beliefs of the Kiowa with the conditions faced by a young Kiowa veteran after World War II. Its depiction of the characters' relationships to the land and their tribal heritage, as well its blending of oral and written traditions, inspired methods and themes in many later works. Momaday followed *House Made of Dawn* with *The Way to Rainy Mountain* (1969) and *The Names: A Memoir* (1976), volumes that weave together memoir, illustrations, photographs, and poetry in an innovative, highly structured form. *The Names* directly influenced Silko's *Storyteller* (1981), a combination of family photographs, family history, tribal stories, fiction, and poetry. Readers will also find Momaday's collection *The Man Made of Words: Essays, Stories, Passages* (1997) a rich selection of ruminations on language and voice, land ethics, hatred of American Indians, place and the sacred, and storytelling and storytellers.

Like the fiction of Momaday and Silko, Welch's novels *Winter in the Blood* (1974) and *The Death of Jim Loney* (1979) explore traditional spiritual beliefs and rituals within a harsh landscape of contemporary Blackfoot problems of poverty and lack of regard by the majority community. Welch's fiction highlights a feature that is also prominent in the work of many later American Indian writers: a strong, if dark, sense of humor. Many consider his greatest work to be *Fools Crow* (1986), a historical novel set in the 1870s, when the Blackfeet were facing extinction because of smallpox and attacks by U.S. troops. Like the fiction writers, the prominent poets of the early years of the Native American Renaissance, Rose (who was an AIM activist in the 1970s) and Ortiz combine an interest in traditional native spirituality with attentiveness to social issues and problems facing contemporary Native Americans. Ortiz, in particular, demonstrates a deep awareness of geography and its interrelationship with history. Both poets have a habit of adding epigraphs, which often contain disturbing historical information, to sections of their poems.

On 21 April 1997 *The New York Times* published an article by Dinitia Smith, "The Indian in Literature Is Catching Up," in which Sarris is quoted as delineating a major difference in the generations of Native American writers: "Momaday and Silko were very spiritual. But Erdrich was dealing with the drinking and funkiness we all know from everyday life. Before then, Indian writers didn't want to think of Indians as fooling around, cheating on each other, the way everyone else does." While they are heavily influenced by Momaday, Silko, Welch, Ortiz, and Rose, the later writers are less likely to set their works on reservations (Erdrich is a notable exception) and are more likely to include pop-culture references and to pepper their work with humor of all sorts—satire, farce, dark comedy, and belly laughs—a practice that reaches back many centuries in traditional American Indian storytelling.

Native American writers also experiment with techniques often associated with Postmodernism. While employing many native tropes and themes, especially the use of tricksters, the work of the Ojibwa poet and novelist Gerald Vizenor is also markedly Postmodernist—playful and ironic as it dismantles the concept of, and stereotypes surrounding, the idea of *Indian*. Vizenor's earliest novel, *Darkness in Saint Louis Bearheart* (revised as *Bearheart: The Heirship Chronicles*, 1990)—one of the few science-fiction novels by a native writer—appeared in 1978, but he only began to receive significant attention for his fiction in the 1990s. He has also published several works of literary criticism, typically from a mixed Postmodernist and Native American perspective.

Other writers have combined activism for Native American rights with other movements for social justice. Hogan, for example, in novels such as *Mean Spirit* (1990), a finalist for the Pulitzer Prize, and *Solar Storms* (1995); in volumes of poetry such as *Seeing through the Sun* (1985), an American Book Award winner; in the essays in *Dwellings: A Spiritual History of the Living World* (1995); and in her memoir, *The Woman Who Watches over the World* (2001), writes from a feminist perspective on women's roles, environmental issues, and poverty.

Among the younger writers, Sarris has spent time as a street-gang member, a model, an actor (his best-known role was on the television series *CHiPs*), an academic who earned tenure at UCLA in one year, and a tribal chief. His scholarly books, such as *Keeping Slug Woman Alive: A Holistic Approach to American Indian Texts* (1993), combine personal narrative with academic critique. In *Mabel McKay: Weaving the Dream* (1994) he tells the story of a Pomo healer and basket maker who had several works on display in the Smithsonian Institution but also peeled apples six days a week at a cannery during harvest season. Sarris followed *Mabel McKay* with two novels, *Grand Avenue: A Novel in Stories* (1994), which was adapted as a highly rated HBO miniseries in 1996, and *Watermelon Nights* (1998). Also of this generation is Power; her *The Grass Dancer* (1995), which received the PEN/Hemingway Award for best first fiction, is more traditional in many respects than the novels of her contemporaries, with a strong emphasis on Sioux spirituality.

Several of the fiction writers—Erdrich, Hogan, Alexie, Silko, and Welch—have also published poetry. Alexie frequently cites the Paiute poet Louis as an important influence: Alexie's poetry, like Louis's, is known for its sharp satire. Tapahonso, acclaimed as a storyteller and performance poet, grounds much of her poetry in Navajo history and systems of belief. Perhaps the most acclaimed poet is Harjo, who cites Ortiz and Silko as major influences. Harjo combines the realistic and social—poverty, time spent in bars, substandard housing, and relationships strained by lack of material necessities—with mythic conceptions of the moon, femininity and masculinity, and the power of land. She also plays saxophone and flute and performs her poetry with the band Poetic Justice, which has released several CDs.

One of the thorniest controversies in Native American literature centers on issues of authenticity: who is entitled to speak for whom. In "An Old-Time Indian Attack Conducted in Two Parts: Part One—Imitation 'Indian' Poems/ Part Two—Gary Snyder's *Turtle Island*" (1979), Silko accused Snyder and other white poets of appropriating native material without truly understanding it. Silko also published a highly critical review of Erdrich's *The Beet Queen* (1986), arguing that Erdrich's writing was skillful and poetic but that the novel focused too little on the racism Native Americans face. In a *Los Angeles Times* book review (23 January 2000) Alexie castigated Ian Frazier's best-selling *On the Rez* (2000): Frazier had spent months researching the history of the Pine Ridge Reservation and conditions there, but Alexie claimed that the writer had no right to tell these stories because he had not lived on or near a reservation and had no Indian heritage. These sentiments were echoed by many others. In some of her prose writings Rose discusses *whiteshamanism;* the term, which was coined by the Quapaw/Cherokee/Chickasaw writer Geary Hobson, refers to non-Indians adopting a literary "shaman" identity and claiming a fundamental knowledge they do not possess and to which they have no right. Rose sees the taking on of the voice of someone from a different culture as inherently exploitative and unjust. In her collection *Bone Dance* (1994) she explains that *whiteshamanism* represents a lack of ability to speak from one's own position and thus is unworthy as an artistic stance. Alexie takes up a similar theme in his novel *Indian Killer* (1996).

Stereotypes and the most effective response to them pose another point of contention and challenge. The two extreme stereotypes—the stoic noble savage always "in tune" with nature and the lazy, dissolute primitive—stretch back to first contact experiences, with traces of their beginnings to be found in Columbus's journals. Contemporary writers often confront these stereotypes but sometimes find themselves misunderstood or criticized for doing so. For instance, Erdrich and Alexie have been criticized for the number of alcoholic native characters in their works; Alexie responds that he writes about what he witnessed growing up on the Spokane reservation. He also tries to dispel the notion that American Indians have an automatic spiritual connection to nature and the land. While traditional Native American concepts of land, nature, and ownership are different from those of European Americans, to view this difference as an inherent spiritual one overidealizes natives and refuses to see them as fully-faceted human beings. The literature that has come out of the Native American Renaissance works to dispel stereotypes while acknowledging real problems, and to deepen understandings between and among cultures of the United States while offering inventive formal creations and, often, vivid storytelling.

## TOPICS FOR DISCUSSION AND RESEARCH

1. Many contemporary American Indian writers confront the traditional version of American history in their stories, especially the concept of Manifest Destiny—the belief held by white eighteenth- and nineteenth-century Americans that the United States and people of Anglo-European heritage were destined and ordained by God to expand across the North American continent. Often unexpressed in mainstream histories is the resultant decline in Native American populations, land, and cultures. Historical references in native literary works may include incidents such as the biological warfare carried out through the "gift" of smallpox-infected blankets, wars carried out against native tribes, government policies (for instance, the General Allotment, or Dawes, Act) that steadily eroded the native land base, and the plethora of treaties never honored by the U.S. government. Such references can be found especially in the work of Sherman Alexie, James Welch, Adrian C. Louis, and Simon J. Ortiz and in Leslie Marmon Silko's *Almanac of the Dead* (1991) and *Gardens in the Dunes* (1999). More specific instances include Silko's *Ceremony* and N. Scott Momaday's *House Made of Dawn*, which focus on the circumstances of American Indian soldiers who fought for the United States in World War II but on their return were met with the same prejudice they had always experienced. Linda Hogan's *Mean Spirit* uncovers the history of ruthless oil speculators who married Osage women and discarded them after gaining control of their mineral rights. Alexie discusses Colonel George Wright's 1858 massacre of Spokanes and more than eight hundred of their horses in "A Drug Called Tradition" and "The Trial of Thomas Builds-the-Fire," both included in *The Lone Ranger and Tonto Fistfight in Heaven* (1993), as well as in many of his poems. Students can read any of these authors for their historical references and ask such questions as: how do the writers revise standard versions of American history by presenting it from a native perspective? What previously "hidden" history do they help bring to light? How effective are their strategies? Silko's and Momaday's depictions of fictional veterans might be compared to the true stories of the Iwo Jima veteran Ira Hays or the World War II Navajo code talkers. Peter Nabokov's *Native American Testimony: A Chronicle of Indian-White Relations from Prophecy to the Present, 1492–2000* (1999) would be an invaluable resource for any of these undertakings: it provides primary resources, as well as useful overviews of Native American history. Students interested in pre-Columbian Native American history should consult Charles C. Mann's *1491: New Revelations of the Americas before Columbus* (2005), while those who want to investigate contemporary history will find Joane Nagel's *American Indian Ethnic Renewal: Red Power and the Resurgence of Identity and Culture* (1996) useful. The first three essays in Joy Porter and Kenneth M. Roemer's *The Cambridge Companion to Native American Literature* (2005) also offer historical context.

2. A classic theme in American literature is the intersection of individual identity with the needs and identity of the community. In many examples this intersection becomes a conflict, with a protagonist asserting his or her individual identity and desires by pushing against those of the community. Students will find that this theme often takes a different shape in writing by American Indians, such as almost any of Momaday's works, Silko's *Ceremony* (1977), Louise Erdrich's *Tracks* (1988) or *The Plague of Doves* (2008), Greg Sarris's *Grand Avenue* (1994), Jay Hogan's *Solar Storms* (1995), or Joy Harjo's poems "The Deer Dancer" and "The Woman Hanging from the Thirteenth Floor Window." Students might consider any of those texts with these questions in mind: to what extent is the community privileged over the individual? When, where, and why is the individual as individual asserted and valued? How are individual and community needs balanced? A similar theme, focusing on individual needs in conflict with family rather than community pressures, could be explored in Michael Dorris's *A Yellow Raft in Blue Water* (1987) or Erdrich's *Tales of Burning Love* (1996) or *Love Medicine.* For secondary sources, both of the books by Kenneth Lincoln, as well as those by Louis Owens, James Ruppert, and Jace Weaver, would provide helpful analysis to support this topic. Part 4 of *The Columbia Guide to American Indian Literatures of the United States since 1945* (2006) looks at self and community in Native American autobiographies.

3. In "'The Grace That Remains': American Indian Women's Literature" (*Book Forum: An International Transdisciplinary Quarterly,* 5, no. 3 [1981]: 376–382) Paula Gunn Allen notes that "A sense of familiarity with what is strange, a willingness to face, to articulate what is beyond belief, to make it seem frightening and natural at the same time lies in much of the writing of American Indian women." The same could also be said of much writing by American Indian men: dreams, myths, and magic play an important role in many Native American texts. Students might choose one or two works in which these features are prominent and consider the extent to which they may or may not be considered magical realism: the mingling of the marvelous and inexplicable with the mundane. Magical realism immerses readers in the experience of what it is like to live in the world with magic as part of one's reality, and a part that is not necessarily frightening or disruptive. Strong candidates for such analysis include any of Erdrich's novels; *The Grass Dancer* (1994), by Susan Power (Sioux); Silko's *Ceremony* or short stories or poems in her collection *Storyteller,* including "Lullaby" and "Yellow Woman"; Sarris's nonfictional *Mabel McKay: Weaving the Dream;* Welch's *Fools Crow;* and Momaday's *The Way to Rainy Mountain.* Stuart Cochran discusses supernatural and spiritual elements in poetry by Simon J. Ortiz (for instance, "From Sand Creek") and in Silko's *Ceremony.* Those wishing to focus on poetry could investigate Harjo's "The Deer Dancer" or *The Woman Who Fell from the Sky,* or works by Luci Tapahonso or Linda Hogan. In these texts, does the presence of magic or the inexplicable grow out of cultural beliefs? Does it arise, as does much Latin American magical realism, from the clash of preindustrial with industrialized cultures? Beyond the issue of the literary mode of magical realism, students may wish to explore the role of dreams, magic, and

the supernatural in these texts. In addition to Cochran, useful secondary sources include Ruppert's *Mediation in Contemporary Native American Fiction* (1995), which discusses the roles of tangible and intangible realms in American Indian writing, and Allen's *The Sacred Hoop: Recovering the Feminine in American Indian Traditions* (1986).

4. The concept of hybridity is important in Native American literature on several levels. The exigencies of history have made insistence on full-blood status next to impossible; yet, people of mixed blood nevertheless find themselves stigmatized, often by both white and native cultures. Many of the major novels of the Native American Renaissance have explored what it means for one's personal and communal identity to be of mixed blood; characters who deal with this issue include Tayo in Silko's *Ceremony*, the title character of Welch's *The Death of Jim Loney*, John Smith in Alexie's *Indian Killer*, and Pauline in Erdrich's *Tracks*. Another form of hybridity involves growing up on a reservation in the midst of the United States. These issues are explored in Dorris's *A Yellow Raft in Blue Water* and Alexie's *The Absolutely True Diary of a Part-Time Indian*. Students might examine any of these works and ask: What conflicts arise because of mixed heritage or mixed cultures? What does mixed status or hybridity mean for the character's personal identity, and what does it mean for communal identity? In what ways is it depicted as a strength, and in what ways as a weakness? In the examples involving living in two overlapping cultures, what role does U.S. popular culture play in the formation of identity? How are characters expected to demonstrate allegiance to the different cultures in which they partake, and what conflicts arise from these expectations? Lincoln's *Native American Renaissance* and the works by Nagel, Ruppert, and James H. Cox can provide useful insights for exploring aspects of hybridity and mixed-blood status.

5. Students could compare a traditional story with a contemporary one through any of several elements that have historically been important to Native American storytelling: the relationship to oral traditions, the use of tricksters, and the role of humor. Allen's *Spider Woman's Granddaughters: Traditional Tales and Contemporary Writing by Native American Women* (1989) offers juxtapositions of traditional with contemporary stories; John L. Purdy and Ruppert's *Nothing but the Truth: An Anthology of Native American Literature* (2001) might also be consulted. Silko's frequently anthologized "Yellow Woman" could be compared to the Pueblo legends about Yellow Woman. Lincoln's *Indi'n Humor: Bicultural Play in Native America* (1993) would be useful for topics exploring tricksters or humor. The interviews in Laura Coltelli's *Winged Words: American Indian Writers Speak* (1990) address oral traditions and humor. Susan Berry Brill de Ramírez also deals with the oral tradition.

6. Students interested in literary history might wish to compare the Native American Renaissance to other American literary "renaissances," such as the American Renaissance of the 1850s, in which Nathaniel Hawthorne, Herman Melville, Henry David Thoreau, and Walt Whitman came to prominence; the Harlem Renaissance of the 1920s, highlighted by such figures as Langston Hughes and Zora Neale Hurston; or the Southern Renaissance of the mid

twentieth century, which included William Faulkner, Flannery O'Connor, Robert Penn Warren, and Eudora Welty. Specific topics that might be pursued include a comparison of the social forces that generated the movements or the extent to which each group saw itself as a literary movement in its own time. Lincoln's *Native American Renaissance* would be most useful for this undertaking.

# RESOURCES

**Primary Works**

Paula Gunn Allen, ed., *Spider Woman's Granddaughters: Traditional Tales and Contemporary Writing by Native American Women* (Boston: Beacon, 1989).
Juxtaposes traditional tales with contemporary stories by such writers as Leslie Marmon Silko, Louise Erdrich, and Linda Hogan and includes a useful introduction.

Laura Coltelli, ed., *Winged Words: American Indian Writers Speak* (Lincoln: University of Nebraska Press, 1990).
Interviews conducted in 1985 with eleven native writers—Paula Gunn Allen, Michael Dorris, Louise Erdrich, Joy Harjo, Linda Hogan, N. Scott Momaday, Simon J. Ortiz, Wendy Rose, Leslie Marmon Silko, Gerald Vizenor, and James Welch—some of whom had not yet come to prominence. Each discusses the oral tradition and its impact on written literature, the role of humor, and his or her own creative process.

Mimi D'Aponte, ed., *Seventh Generation: An Anthology of Native American Plays* (New York: Theatre Communications Group, 1999).
Seven plays from the contemporary era by Kiowa, Choctaw, Kuna/Rappahanock, Ojibwa, Assiniboine/Nakota, Hawaiian, and Cherokee authors, including Hanay Geiogamah's *Body Indian* (1972), notable as one of the first to depict contemporary native lives in a drama, and Diane Glancy's *The Woman Who Was a Red Deer Dressed for the Deer Dance* (1995).

John L. Purdy and James Ruppert, eds., *Nothing but the Truth: An Anthology of Native American Literature* (Upper Saddle River, N.J.: Prentice-Hall, 2001).
Comprises twelve nonfiction essays and works of literary criticism, followed by generous selections of fiction and poetry, mostly by contemporary writers, and a play by Gerald Vizenor. It is probably the best selection currently available.

**Criticism**

Paula Gunn Allen, *The Sacred Hoop: Recovering the Feminine in American Indian Traditions* (Boston: Beacon, 1986).
Examines the female rituals, traditions, and figures of strength across various Native American traditions and their incarnations in contemporary literatures.

Susan Berry Brill de Ramírez, *Contemporary American Indian Literatures and the Oral Tradition* (Tucson: University of Arizona Press, 1999).

Argues for becoming "listener-readers," active participants in written stories in order to comprehend the oral dimensions of works by Sherman Alexie, N. Scott Momaday, Leslie Marmon Silko, Luci Tapahonso, Anna Lee Walters (Pawnee/ Otoe-Missouria), Della Frank (Navajo), Lee Maracle (Salish/Cree), and Louis Owens (Choctaw/Cherokee and Irish American).

Susan Pérez Castillo, "Postmodernism, Native American Literature, and the Real: The Silko-Erdrich Controversy," *Massachusetts Review*, 32 (1991): 285–294 (also available in the anthology edited by Purdy and Ruppert, pp. 15–22).
A careful analysis of Leslie Marmon Silko's criticisms of Louise Erdrich's *The Beet Queen*. The article is also useful for its discussion of the relationship of Postmodernism and Native American writing.

Eric Cheyfitz, ed., *The Columbia Guide to American Indian Literatures of the United States since 1945* (New York: Columbia University Press, 2006).
Considers Native American literatures in a postcolonial context, focusing on issues of identity, sovereignty, and land. Part 1, a long essay by Cheyfitz, deals with American Indian literatures in the context of federal Indian law; part 2 consists of essays by other scholars on fiction, poetry, drama, nonfiction, and autobiography.

Stuart Cochran, "The Ethnic Implications of Stories, Spirits, and the Land in Native American Pueblo and Aztlán Writing," *MELUS*, 20 (Summer 1995): 69–91.
Discusses the relationship to land and the conception of a spirit world in the writing of Native American authors Leslie Marmon Silko, Simon J. Ortiz, and Jimmy Santíago Baca (Apache and Chicano) and the Chicano writer Rudolfo Anaya.

James H. Cox, *Muting White Noise: Native American and European American Novel Traditions*, American Indian Literature and Critical Studies Series, volume 51 (Norman: University of Oklahoma Press, 2006).
Excellent close readings of works by Gerald Vizenor, Thomas King, and Sherman Alexie, demonstrating how they resist and revise the colonialist ideas that native peoples were conquered and then disappeared from history. Attempting to avoid imposing European American methodologies and philosophies, Cox works through the lens established by native critics to offer "red readings" of American classics such as Herman Melville's *Moby-Dick* (1851).

Kathleen M. Donovan, *Feminist Readings of Native American Literature* (Tucson: University of Arizona Press, 1998).
Looks at Native American literature and feminist literary theory as areas with many common concerns, including the question "who in a society can speak, and under what circumstances?" Among the authors whose works are discussed are N. Scott Momaday, Joy Harjo, and Paula Gunn Allen.

Kenneth Lincoln, *Indi'n Humor: Bicultural Play in Native America* (New York: Oxford University Press, 1993).

Covers five hundred years of Indian humor to challenge the stereotypes of American Indians as "wooden" and "stoic." Lincoln particularly focuses on the last quarter of the twentieth century and Louise Erdrich, James Welch, N. Scott Momaday, Paula Gunn Allen, and Linda Hogan.

Lincoln, *Native American Renaissance* (Berkeley: University of California Press, 1983).

Landmark study that laid the groundwork for understanding the major issues, themes, and forms that have characterized the Native American Renaissance. Lincoln focuses especially on Black Elk (Oglala Sioux), N. Scott Momaday, Simon J. Ortiz, James Welch, Wendy Rose, and Leslie Marmon Silko.

Charles C. Mann, *1491: New Revelations of the Americas before Columbus* (New York: Random House, 2005).

In-depth reportage of the past thirty years of scholarship, which has shown that the 1491 population was much higher than ever before realized (between 100 and 200 million), and which dispels many of the myths about Native Americans—for instance, that they had no cities and no significant impact on the landscape.

Peter Nabokov, ed., *Native American Testimony: A Chronicle of Indian-White Relations from Prophecy to the Present, 1492–2000,* revised edition (New York: Penguin, 1999).

Invaluable collection of passages from stories, legends, letters, memoirs, personal accounts, manifestos, and histories by American Indians from first contact to the end of the twentieth century.

Joane Nagel, *American Indian Ethnic Renewal: Red Power and the Resurgence of Identity and Culture* (New York: Oxford University Press, 1996).

Although not about literature, a good resource for information on American Indian history in the contemporary period. Nagel also offers accessible theories for understanding ethnicity and culture.

Louis Owens, *Other Destinies: Understanding the American Indian Novel,* American Indian Literature and Critical Studies Series, volume 3 (Norman: University of Oklahoma Press, 1992).

Readings of works spanning 1854 to the 1990s, focusing on themes of self-discovery and cultural recovery. Contemporary authors discussed are N. Scott Momaday, James Welch, Leslie Marmon Silko, Louise Erdrich, Michael Dorris, and Gerald Vizenor.

Joy Porter and Kenneth M. Roemer, eds., *The Cambridge Companion to Native American Literature* (New York: Cambridge University Press, 2005).

Excellent collection, including an informative introduction and a time line by Roemer; three essays on historical and cultural contexts, including one on translation and one on women writers and gender issues; essays on nonfiction, life writing, poetry, pre-1968 fiction, post-1968 fiction, and theater; and essays on N. Scott Momaday, Simon J. Ortiz, James Welch, Leslie Marmon Silko, Gerald Vizenor, Louise Erdrich, Joy Harjo, and Sherman Alexie.

James Ruppert, *Mediation in Contemporary Native American Fiction*, American Indian Literature and Critical Studies Series, volume 15 (Norman: University of Oklahoma Press, 1995).
Readings of works by N. Scott Momaday, James Welch, Leslie Marmon Silko, Gerald Vizenor, D'Arcy McNickle (Cree/French and Scots-Irish), and Louise Erdrich that demonstrate how these writers draw on techniques and philosophies from both European American and Native American traditions and aim for mediation, a kind of healing, and cross-cultural understanding that maintains respect for difference.

Leslie Marmon Silko, "Here's an Odd Artifact for the Fairy-Tale Shelf," *SAIL: Studies in American Indian Literatures*, first series, 10 (Fall 1986): 178–184.
Highly critical review of Louise Erdrich's second novel, *The Beet Queen*, accusing Erdrich of ignoring native historical and social issues in favor of a focus on individual psychology.

Dinitia Smith, "The Indian in Literature is Catching Up," *New York Times*, 21 April 1997, pp. B1, B4.
Discusses a generational shift in Native American literature to an urban-oriented group of writers.

David Treuer, *Native American Fiction: A User's Manual* (St. Paul, Minn.: Graywolf Press, 2006).
Breaks with established criticism to consider Native American literary works as literature rather than as expressions of culture and sociology or interrogating them for authenticity. Among the writers discussed are Louise Erdrich, Leslie Marmon Silko, James Welch, and Sherman Alexie.

Jace Weaver, *That the People Might Live: Native American Literatures and Native American Community* (New York: Oxford University Press, 1997).
A survey of works from 1768 to the 1990s, considering contemporary writers such as Leslie Marmon Silko, Vine Deloria Jr., and Gerald Vizenor, and arguing for a commitment to community and its survival as central to Native American writing. Weaver, a scholar of religion, also offers context for native religious traditions and considers their conflicts and compatibilities with Christianity.

## PEOPLE OF INTEREST

**Paula Gunn Allen** (1939–2008)
Laguna/Sioux and Lebanese scholar and poet; the author of *The Sacred Hoop: Recovering the Feminine in American Indian Traditions* (1986), *The Woman Who Owned the Shadows* (1983), *Coyote's Daylight Trip* (1978), *Grandmothers of the Light: A Medicine Woman's Sourcebook* (1991), and *Life Is a Fatal Disease: Collected Poems, 1962–1995* (1996).

**Michael Dorris** (1945–1997)
Scholar, fiction and popular nonfiction writer, and poet of Modoc, German, and Irish descent who became director of the Native American studies program at

Dartmouth College in 1972. He married author Louise Erdrich in 1981; they separated in 1995. His National Book Critics Circle Award–winning *The Broken Cord: A Family's Ongoing Struggle with Fetal Alcohol Syndrome* (1989) details the couple's experiences with the first of the three children Dorris had adopted before their marriage. His other works include the novel *A Yellow Raft in Blue Water* (1987), with an African American/American Indian protagonist; its sequel, *Cloud Chamber* (1997); short-story collections; and works for children.

**Joy Harjo** (1951–  )
Muscogee Creek poet, playwright, and musician. Her books include *The Last Song* (1975); *In Mad Love and War* (1990), winner of the American Book Award; *The Woman Who Fell from the Sky* (1994); *The Spiral of Memory: Interviews* (1996); *A Map to the Next World: Poems and Tales* (2000); and *How We Became Human: New and Selected Poems, 1975–2001* (2002).

**Linda Hogan** (1947–  )
Chickasaw poet, playwright, novelist, and environmentalist. She is the author of the novels *Mean Spirit* (1990), a finalist for the Pulitzer Prize; *Solar Storms* (1995); *Dwellings: A Spiritual History of the Living World* (1995); *The Woman Who Watches over the World* (2001), a memoir; and several volumes of poetry and essays.

**Adrian C. Louis** (1947–  )
Lovelock Paiute author of *Skins* (1995), *Wild Indians and Other Creatures* (1996), *Logorrhea* (2006), and editor of *Shedding Skins: Four Sioux Poets* (2008). He is a cofounder of the Native American Journalists Association.

**N. Scott Momaday** (1934–  )
Born Novarro Scotte Mommedaty. Of Kiowa and Cherokee decent, he won the Pulitzer Prize for *House Made of Dawn* (1968) in 1969 and received the National Medal of Arts in 2007. His other works include *The Way to Rainy Mountain* (1969), *The Names: A Memoir* (1976), *The Ancient Child* (1989), *The Man Made of Words: Essays, Stories, Passages* (1997), *In the Presence of the Sun* (1992), and *In the Bear's House* (1999).

**Simon J. Ortiz** (1941–  )
Full-blooded member of the Acoma Pueblo tribe and one of the most respected poets of his generation. Ortiz is the author of *Going for the Rain* (1976), *A Good Journey* (1977), *Fight Back: For the Sake of the People, for the Sake of the Land* (1980), *From Sand Creek* (1981), *Fightin': New and Collected Short Stories* (1983), *The People Shall Continue* (1988), and *Out There Somewhere* (2002).

**Susan Power** (1961–  )
Standing Rock Sioux poet and novelist best known for her novel *The Grass Dancer* (1995), which received the PEN/Hemingway Award for best first fiction. Her *Roofwalker* (2002) is a collection of short stories.

**Wendy Rose** (1948–  )
Poet, artist, activist, and anthropologist of Hopi, Miwok, and European descent, born Bronwen Elizabeth Edwards. Her poetry collections include *Hopi Road-*

*runner Dancing* (1973); *Long Division: A Tribal History* (1976); *Academic Squaw: Reports to the World from the Ivory Tower* (1977); *Lost Copper* (1980), nominated for the Pulitzer Prize; *What Happened When the Hopi Hit New York* (1982); *Bone Dance: New and Selected Poems, 1965–1992* (1994); and *Itch Like Crazy* (2002).

### Greg Sarris (1952–   )
Writer of Miwok/Pomo/Filipino and German-Jewish/Irish descent, best known for *Keeping Slug Woman Alive: A Holistic Approach to American Indian Texts* (1993); *Mabel McKay: Weaving the Dream* (1994); *Grand Avenue: A Novel in Stories* (1994), adapted as an HBO miniseries; and the novel *Watermelon Nights* (1998).

### Luci Tapahonso (1953–   )
Navajo poet and short-story writer whose collections include *Seasonal Woman* (1982), *A Breeze Swept Through* (1987), *Sáani Dahataal: The Women Are Singing* (1993), *Blue Horses Rush In* (1997), and *A Radiant Curve* (2008). In 1995 she was named "Storyteller of the Year" by the Wordcraft Circle of Native Writers.

### David Treuer (1970–   )
Novelist and critic of Ojibwa and Jewish descent. He is the author of the novels *Little* (1995), *The Hiawatha* (1999), and *The Translation of Dr. Apellas* (2006), as well as *Native American Fiction: A User's Manual* (2006).

### Gerald Vizenor (1934–   )
Minnesota Chippewa poet, novelist, literary critic, and native theorist known for his Postmodernist sensibilities. His books include *Darkness in Saint Louis Bearheart* (1978; revised as *Bearheart: The Heirship Chronicles,* 1990); *The Heirs of Columbus* (1991); *Griever: An American Monkey King in China* (1987), winner of the American Book Award; and *Manifest Manners: Postindian Warriors of Survivance* (1999). He also edited *Narrative Chance: Postmodern Discourse on Native American Indian Literatures* (1993).

### James Welch (1940–2003)
Blackfoot who won the American Book Award for his novel *Fools Crow* (1986). He is also the author of the poetry collection *Riding the Earthboy 40* (1970); the novels *Winter in the Blood* (1974), *The Death of Jim Loney* (1979), and *The Indian Lawyer* (1990); and the nonfiction work *Killing Custer: The Battle of Little Bighorn and the Fate of the Plains Indians* (1994).

*—Kathryn West*

# Poetry—Debates and Developments

American poetry published since 1970 features a broad range of voices as a result of demographic and social changes in American culture that allow for fuller equality of, and hence fuller representation of, previously disenfranchised groups, including women, members of ethnic minorities, gay people, and recent immigrants. Prior to the early 1970s the formal study of literature was restricted almost entirely to the study of white poets, and poets studied were far more likely to be men than women. Poetry published since 1970 exhibits many voices that resist traditional categories and classifications. Despite this resistance and a flourishing of poetic forms and thematic issues, it is possible to identify certain literary groupings, such as the postconfessional poets, and the language poets, and to identify distinctive approaches, such as slam poetry, and feminist poetry. The emergence of ethnic writers introducing new idioms and new social concerns to American poetry must also be considered.

For most of the twentieth century and into the twenty-first, American poetry has been divided between that written in traditional verse forms (including rhyme and meter) and that written in free verse. Free verse rejects traditional rhyme and meter, and with, at times, varying line lengths and uneven (or missing) stanza patterns, may not read or sound at all like conventional poetry, although it still includes properties of rhythm and musical sound. This distinction is important between poets who describe their work as experimental, concerned with breaking standards for logic and syntax, for example, and poets who see themselves as innovative within the conventions of preexisting traditions. Cole Swenson and David St. John, in *American Hybrid: A Norton Anthology of New Poetry* (2009), describe experimental poetry as including such features "as non-linearity, juxtaposition, rupture, fragmentation, immanence, multiple perspective, open form, and resistance to closure," all of which can be confusing when approached by a reader schooled in more-traditional forms. By contrast, Swenson and St. John describe more-traditional poetry as that which demonstrates "coherence, linearity, formal clarity, narrative, firm closure, symbolic resonance, and stable voice."

These two tendencies appear in the work of two schools, the Language poets and the New Formalists or neoformalists. On the forefront of experimental poetry are poets associated with the school of Language (or, L=A=N=G=U=A=G=E, the name of the magazine published from 1978 to 1982) poetry. Language poets, although a diverse group, tend to downplay the importance of the individual speaking voice in poetry, believing instead that language speaks us as much as we speak language, and that language is fraught with contradictory meanings. Two poets associated with this school are Michael Palmer and Susan Howe. In contrast, the 1980s brought renewed interest to formalism in American poetry. *Strong Measures* (1986), edited by Philip Dacey and David Jauss, featured structured works by contemporary American poets; not since the 1960s had a major anthology been devoted to poetry featuring traditional forms. It was followed by *Ecstatic Occasions, Expedient Forms: 65 Leading Contemporary Poets Select and Comment on Their Poems*

(1987), edited by David Lehman, featuring work by X. J. Kennedy, Dana Gioia, and Marilyn Hacker, poets most often associated with neoformalism.

Another division in contemporary poetry, suggested by poet and translator Paul Auster, is between poets influenced by the British Romantic tradition beginning with William Wordsworth and those influenced by more-experimental French traditions beginning with Stéphane Mallarmé and Charles Baudelaire. Among American Modernist poets, Robert Frost was most clearly in the British tradition with his emphasis on describing the natural world, on plain speech in poetry, and on accessibility to a more general audience. T. S. Eliot, on the other hand, was clearly influenced by French traditions, an influence that can be seen in the fragmentation of his poetry, his emphasis on urban themes, and his tendency to have poems written in many voices. Drawing on a description by the French poet Yves Bonnefoy of "English as a 'mirror' and French as a 'sphere,'" the one Aristotelian in its acceptance of the given, the other Platonic in its readiness to hypothesize 'a different reality, a different realm,'" Auster posits a distinction related not merely to style but to sensibility. Swenson and St. John later use the words "immanent" and "transcendent" to describe the difference between these two groups, the first referring to poets who attempt to reflect the world, the second whose works seek to shape and transform it.

An additional debate that follows, in part, from the distinctions noted above concerns the issue of "accessibility" in poetry. Critics (and poets) who champion "accessibility" in poetry prefer poems that do not place excessive demands on the reader to look up unfamiliar words or to gloss unfamiliar allusions, references to previous literature or history. The call for accessibility stems, in part, from a continuing reaction against the unusual difficulties presented in modern poetry. But the call for accessibility is also deployed, legitimately, against poems that seem to have significance only to the author who wrote the poem, without an apparent concern for a larger audience.

Admirers of Billy Collins have praised his work for qualities associated with accessibility. His poems feature the quotidian, ordinary, even trivial, as is evident in just a sampling of titles from his oeuvre: "A Portrait of the Reader with a Bowl of Cereal," "Splitting Wood," and "I Chop Some Parsley While Listening to Art Blakey's Version of 'Three Blind Mice.'" Beyond Collins's aim for accessibility in his own poetry, he has used his influence as U.S. poet laureate from 2001 to 2003, among other positions he has held, to make poetry less a mystery and more an everyday pleasure for the public. In 2003 he published the anthology *Poetry 180: A Turning Back to Poetry;* its 180 poems provide one for each day of the high-school year. Its success was followed in 2005 with *180 More: Extraordinary Poems for Every Day.* The poems can be freely accessed online, one per day, at <http://www.loc.gov/poetry/180/165.html>. Another poet laureate, Robert Pinsky, started the *Favorite Poem Project* (<http://www.favoritepoem.org/>), in which Americans of all ages read and discuss their favorite poems.

The work of Jorie Graham, on the other hand, focus on an individualistic perspective instead of accessibility. In the title poem of *The Dream of the Unified Field: Selected Poems, 1974–1994* (1995), the use of a varied line and the free association of disparate images—often idiosyncratic—make meaning more difficult to grasp. That, however, may be precisely the point; the poem illustrates the mind—the "unified field"—through which all individuals receive and sort through reality in order to make meaning.

In their *American Hybrid* Swenson and St. John challenge the categorization of poets into mutually exclusive camps. They note the emergence of what amounts to a new school in American poetry—poets who combine techniques of the traditional and the experimental, poets who "access a wealth of tools, each one of which can change dramatically depending on how it is combined with others and the particular role it plays in the composition." According to Swenson and St. John, "Hybrid poems often honor the avant-garde mandate to renew the forms and expand the boundaries of poetry—thereby increasing the expressive potential of language itself—while also remaining committed to the emotional spectra of lived experience." Poets such as Ortiz, Pinsky, Gwendolyn Brooks, Louise Glück, and Cathy Song have demonstrated the ability to absorb a variety of influences, moving between formalism and experimentalism, in and out of free verse and traditional forms. Furthermore, the forms are no longer solely Anglo-European in origin. Lorna Dee Cervantes, Sandra Cisneros, Alberto Ríos, and Gary Soto incorporate Spanish language while also echoing its rhythms. Native American oratory and storytelling can be heard in the work of Ortiz, Louise Erdrich, Joy Harjo, and Wendy Rose. Audre Lorde draws from African oral traditions of chant and call, while Nikki Giovanni, Michael S. Harper, Yusef Komunyakaa, Ishmael Reed, and Natasha Trethewey infuse their poems with the rhythms of jazz and blues. In *The Veiled Suite: The Collected Poems* (2009), the Kashmiri American poet Agha Shahid Ali demonstrates a wide variety of poetic forms, including most notably the *ghazal,* an ancient Persian form consisting of couplets with a strict rhyme scheme and requiring that the poet include his own name, as well as references to love and to wine.

Finally, debates about the nature of poetic quality, or aesthetics, predominate in discussions of contemporary poetry. The editors of the *Norton Anthology of Contemporary Poetry* note, "Aesthetic criteria are notoriously impossible to pin down," before offering an inclusive and useful list of characteristics: "creative daring, figurative reach, verbal dexterity, formal skill, historical responsiveness, social significance, psychological complexity, emotional richness, and the inventive engagement with, and revision of, literary and extraliterary genres and discourses." This description is broad enough to include both traditional and experimental poetry and takes into account many features of the poetry that engage (or even emotionally move) individual readers. American poetry in the contemporary period embraces a diverse group of poets who offer multiple and varying attributes and contributions. Taken together, their work suggests the imaginative power of poetry in the contemporary period and its potential to entertain, enlighten, move, and transform audiences.

## TOPICS FOR DISCUSSION AND RESEARCH

1. Poetry since 1970 has been labeled "postconfessional." In general, American poetry published after 1945 or the end of World War II tends to be more personal than poetry published roughly between 1900 and 1945. Although poetry after 1970 tends to move away from the shocking self-revelation and articulation of individual psychological despair of the generation of poets labeled "confessional" (Sylvia Plath, Anne Sexton, John Berryman, and Robert Lowell), contemporary poets continue to place a premium on individual experience and expression while tempering the excesses and despair found in the work of the previous generation. In his introduction to *The Post-Confessionals: Conversations with American Poets of the Eighties,* Stan Sanvel Ruben delineates differences between confessional and post-confessional poets: "While it is often highly personal experience that first prompts these poets to poetry [. . .] the general thrust is nearly always away from the personal and toward something sensed to be larger." As with the work of the previous generation of poets, their work is a "mix of personal and public." *The Post-Confessionals* provides a useful working definition for students interested in examining the ways the self and subjectivity are depicted. Students might focus on poets interviewed in the collection or on others such as Rita Dove, Li-Young Lee, Sharon Olds, Natasha Trethewey, and/or Franz Wright, exploring the ways these poets use personal history in their poetry, and how their approaches vary. How do their works merge "personal and public"? How does a particular poem move beyond the self to address larger issues related to history and society?

2. American poetry is sometimes characterized by regional differences, exemplified in the work of poets as different as Ted Kooser, who writes about the landscape of rural Nebraska, and Mary Oliver, who writes about the spiritual and natural landscapes of Cape Cod and more specifically of the area around Provincetown, Massachusetts. Kooser, who served as poet laureate in 2004 and won the Pulitzer Prize in 2005 for *Delights and Shadows* (2004), writes in a deliberately plain style, believing that his words should be accessible to common readers and should never require the use of a dictionary or reference works. Oliver, one of the best-selling writers among contemporary poets, won the Pulitzer for *American Primitive* (1983), which might be described as a book of spiritual geography. Students interested in geography and poetry might ask the question of how regional differences influence the work of Oliver and Kooser, and alternately, how these poets delineate regional differences in their work.

3. Since 1970 there have been various efforts to move poetry from academic institutions and to make poetry more accessible and available to the general public. Poetry-writing groups and workshops encourage people to try their hand at writing poetry. The proliferation of audio and visual recordings

of poets reading their work (on video, CD, DVD, and via the Internet) make poems more available while also focusing on orality and performative qualities. Open readings, poetry slams, recitations, and performances, in venues as diverse as school auditoriums, libraries, clubs, bookstores, parks, and coffee shops, have encouraged larger groups to participate. In addition, poetry now appears on the sides of city buses and buildings, over speakers in elevators, and on signs in public parks. Starting with a particular attempt to connect poetry to the everyday world, students might evaluate its effectiveness at generating public participation with poetry while also analyzing how these efforts have influenced the form and theme of poetry. For background information about such movements and their effect on poetic form, students can consult Dana Gioia's *Disappearing Ink* (2004). Another way to approach this topic would be to take part in or organize a poetry reading, slam, recitation, or performance. A report on such activities would include a discussion of the history of poetry performance and readings and the criteria used to evaluate work or set up a performance/reading. Resources associated with promoting poetry to the public include the Academy of American Poets website at <http://poets.org>; NEA and Poetry Foundation's Poetry Out Loud website at <http://poetryoutloud.org>; the Poetry Foundation's webste at <http://www.poetryfoundation.org>. Students interested particularly in poetry slams might consult Glazner and Poetry Slam, Inc.'s website <http://www.poetryslam.com>.

4. As the United States has become more diverse, so too has its poetry. First are poets who draw on their international backgrounds. Among these poets are Aga Shahid Ali, Naomi Shihab Nye, and Meena Alexander. Poems by these writers frequently treat themes related to exile, migration, and multicultural or global identity; students might consider examining how these poets address such themes. Students might also consider how poets call attention to international events, in particular how events in the Middle East, India, and the region of Kashmir are played out in the work of Nye, Alexander, and Ali, respectively. Other global influences emerge through the efforts of poets to incorporate non-European or non-Western elements and through translation. The poetry of Robert Bly incorporates Latin surrealism while Gary Snyder infuses Zen Buddhism. Both Robert Pinsky and Jane Hirshfield have translated works from other languages, Pinsky adapting the terza rima of *The Inferno of Dante* (1994) for American audiences and Hirshfield, with Mariko Aratani, translating *The Ink Dark Moon: Poems by Ono no Komachi and Izumi Shikibu, Women of the Ancient Court of Japan* (1990). Students could examine these works and poets for traces of "global influences."

5. Adrienne Rich has noted, "Poetry has the capacity to remind us of something we are forbidden to see. A forgotten future: a still uncreated site whose moral architecture is founded not on ownership and dispossession, the subjection of women, outcast and tribe, but on the continuous redefining of freedom." Other contemporary American poets are interested in the transformative ability of poetry, its potential to shape human perception

and enact change on personal, social, and political levels. Poets, of course, take different approaches to connections between poetry and change in the world. The Black Power poetry of Amiri Baraka and Nikki Giovanni and feminist poetry of Adrienne Rich and Marge Piercy (and Giovanni) have helped to expand notions about identity to encompass race, gender, and sexuality, adding to conversations in politics. Pinsky demonstrates a broad engagement with the political, especially with questions of civic virtue. Other poets have taken on specific causes. Mark Doty writes to raise awareness about the AIDS epidemic and gay civil rights, and Ali, about Kashmir. Other poets have protested war (see Study Guide on Vietnam War and antiwar literature) and the degradation of the environment (see John Felstiner and Topic essay on environmental literature). The anthology *An Eye for An Eye Makes the Whole World Blind: Poets on 9/11* (New York: Regent Press, 2002) offers poems from one hundred different poets working to better understand the human condition through the lens of such a great tragedy. Students interested in the relationship between poetry and change might consider how poetry can indeed raise awareness about social and political issues. How may it help us grapple with such events as 9/11? How can poetry help readers think differently about complex questions?

## RESOURCES

### Primary Works

Billy Collins, ed., *Poetry 180: A Turning Back to Poetry* (New York: Random House, 2003).
An anthology of contemporary poetry designed to offer a poem a day for the 180 days in the high-school year.

Philip Dacey and David Jauss, eds., *Strong Measures: Contemporary American Poetry in Traditional Forms* (New York: Harper & Row, 1986).
An excellent collection of poetry in a wide variety of forms that includes works by major poets. The book would be extremely helpful to students exploring differing forms; clear explanations of forms are included.

Gary Mex Glazner, ed., *Poetry Slam: The Competitive Art of Performance Poetry* (San Francisco: Manic D Press, 2000).
Anthology of pieces by national poetry slam champions. The book also includes essays with practical information about organizing a poetry slam and preparation tips.

Earl G. Ingersoll, Judith Kitch, and Stan Sanyel Ruben, eds., *The Post-Confessionals: Conversations with American Poets of the Eighties* (Cranbury, N.J.: Associated University Presses, 1989).
Interviews with nineteen poets, all of them past participants in the Writers Forum program at the State University of New York College at Brookport, in which they

discuss their craft. Ruben's introduction provides a useful overview of pre-1970 American poetry and its legacy.

Bill Moyers, *The Language of Life: A Festival of Poets* (New York: Doubleday, 1995).
A companion volume to the PBS series of the same name that includes transcriptions of Moyers's "conversations" with thirty-four poets who share insights into their work and lives. Students might wish to locate the video or audio recordings of interviews with poets they are interested in studying.

Moyers, ed., *Fooling with Words: A Celebration of Poets and Their Craft* (New York: Perennial, 2000).
Based on interviews Moyers conducted at the Dodge Poetry Festival in 1998 with eleven poets, provides insights into the poets' craft and samples of their work. Students might wish to locate the recordings of interviews with poets they are interested in studying.

Jahan Ramazani, Richard Ellmann, and Robert O'Clair, eds., *The Norton Anthology of Modern and Contemporary Poetry,* volume 2: *Contemporary Poetry* (New York: Norton, 2003).
Offers a broad and definitive survey of contemporary poetry, both traditional and experimental.

Cole Swenson and David St. John, eds., *American Hybrid: A Norton Anthology of New Poetry* (New York: Norton, 2009).
Introduces a wide range of contemporary experimental and hybrid poets.

## Criticism

Christopher Beech, *Poetic Culture: Contemporary American Poetry between Community and Institution* (Evanston, Ill.: Northwestern University Press, 1999).
Places debates about contemporary poetry in their sociocultural contexts.

John Felstiner, *Can Poetry Save the Earth? A Field Guide to Nature Poems* (New Haven, Conn.: Yale University Press, 2009).
Contextualizes poetry, including the contemporary, with environmental concerns.

Dana Gioia, *Disappearing Ink: Poetry at the End of Print Culture* (St. Paul, Minn.: Graywolf Press, 2004).
Collection of essays that examine the form and thematic concerns of poetry beyond print culture.

David Lehman, ed., *Ecstatic Occasions, Expedient Forms: 85 Leading Contemporary Poets Select and Comment on Their Poems,* second edition (Ann Arbor: University of Michigan Press, 1996).
Updated edition that features eighty-five contributors. The introduction provides an overview of forms represented ("villanelles, pantoums, prose poems,

sonnets . . ."); comments by poets demonstrate a range of attitudes toward the relationship between form and content.

Adrienne Rich, *Poetry and Commitment*, afterword by Mark Doty (New York: Norton, 2007).
Presents a provocative discussion of the poet's political responsibility.

## PEOPLE OF INTEREST

**Meena Alexander** (1951– )
Poet and fiction writer born in India as Mary Elizabeth Alexander and raised there and in Sudan. Her first books of poems were printed in Arabic translation when she was still a teenager. She has written *The Bird's Bright Ring* (1976), *Without Place* (1977), *Stone Roots* (1980), *Fault Lines: A Memoir* (1993), *Manhattan Music* (1997), and *Raw Silk* (2004).

**Aga Shahid Ali** (1949–2001)
Poet whose works include *Bone-Sculpture* (1972), *A Walk through the Yellow Pages* (1987), *The Beloved Witness: Selected Poems* (1992), *Rooms Are Never Finished* (2002), and *Call Me Ishmael Tonight: A Book of Ghazals* (2003).

**Paul Auster** (1947– )
Writer of fiction, poetry, translations, and screenplays. Among his works are *The New York Trilogy* (1987), *Disappearances: Selected Poems* (1988), *The Music of Chance* (1990), *Smoke* (1995), and *Collected Poems* (2007).

**John Berryman** (1914–1972)
Poet associated with the confessional school. His collection *77 Dream Songs* (1964) received the Pulitzer Prize in 1965. His other works include *The Dispossessed* (1948), *His Thoughts Made Pockets and The Plane Buckt* (1958), *Berryman's Sonnets* (1967), *Homage to Mistress Bradstreet and Other Poems* (1968), *Delusions, Etc.* (1972), *Henry's Fate and Other Poems* (1977), and *Collected Poems 1937–1971* (1989).

**Lorna Dee Cervantes** (1954– )
Chicana poet who received the American Book Award for *Emplumada* (1981), a collection of bilingual free verse. She is also the author of *From the Cables of Genocide: Poems on Love and Hunger* (1991) and *DRIVE: The First Quartet* (2006).

**Billy Collins** (1941– )
Poet who has served two terms as poet laureate of the United States and was described by *The New York Times* in 1999 as "the most popular poet in America." His poetry has been collected in *Pokerface* (1977), *Video Poems* (1980), *The Apple That Astonished Paris* (1988), *Questions about Angels* (1991), *The Art of Drowning* (1995), *Picnic, Lightning* (1998), *Sailing Alone around the Room: New and Selected Poems* (2001), *Nine Horses* (2002), *The Trouble with Poetry* (2005), *She Was Just*

*Seventeen* (2006), and *Ballistics* (2008). See the topic devoted to him in Part III of this volume.

**T. S. Eliot** (1888–1965)
American-born poet, critic, and dramatist who won the Nobel Prize in literature and the Order of Merit in 1948. His works include *The Love Song of J. Alfred Prufrock* (1915), *The Waste Land* (1922), *The Hollow Men* (1925), *Ash Wednesday* (1930), *Four Quartets* (1943), *Murder in the Cathedral* (1935), and *The Cocktail Party* (1949).

**Dana Gioia** (1950–   )
Poet associated with New Formalism. He served as the chairman of the National Endowment for the Arts from 2003 to 2009 and is the author of *Daily Horoscope* (1982), *The God of Winter* (1991), and *Interrogations at Noon* (2001), which won an American Book Award in 2002.

**Jorie Graham** (1951–   )
Poet, the author of *Hybrids of Plants and of Ghosts* (1980), *Erosion* (1983), *The End of Beauty* (1987), *Region of Unlikeness* (1991), *Materialism* (1993), *The Errancy* (1997), *Swarm* (2000), *Never* (2002), and *Sea Change* (2008). Her collection *The Dream of the Unified Field: Selected Poems, 1974–1994* (1995) received the Pulitzer Prize in 1996.

**Marilyn Hacker** (1942–   )
Poet, was awarded the National Book Award in 1975 for her first collection of poetry, *Presentation Piece* (1974). Her other works include *Separations* (1976), *Taking Notice* (1980), *Assumptions* (1985), *Love, Death and the Changing of the Seasons* (1986), *Going Back to the River* (1990), *The Hang-Glider's Daughter: New and Selected Poems* (1991), *Selected Poems* (1994), *Winter Numbers: Poems* (1995), *Squares and Courtyards* (2000), *Desesperanto: Poems 1999–2002* (2003), and *Essays on Departure: New and Selected Poems* (2006).

**Joy Harjo** (1951–   )
Member of the Muscogee Creek tribe who is a poet, playwright, and musician (her band is Poetic Justice). Her books include *The Last Song* (1975), *In Mad Love and War* (1990), *The Woman Who Fell from the Sky* (1994), *The Spiral of Memory: Interviews* (1996), *A Map to the Next World: Poems and Tales* (2000), *The Good Luck Cat* (2000), and *How We Became Human: New and Selected Poems 1975–2001* (2002).

**Jane Hirshfield** (1953–   )
Poet and author of *Alaya* (1982), *Of Gravity and Angels* (1988), *The October Palace* (1994), *The Lives of the Heart* (1997), *Nine Gates: Entering the Mind of Poetry* (1997), *Given Sugar, Given Salt* (2001), *After* (2006), and *Hiddenness, Uncertainty, Surprise: Three Generative Energies of Poetry* (2008).

**Susan Howe** (1937–   )
Poet associated with the L=A=N=G=U=A=G=E school of poetry and with Postmodernism. Her works include *Singularities* (1990), *The Nonconformist's Memorial*

(1993), *Frame Structures: Early Poems 1974–1979* (1996), *Pierce-Arrow* (1999), *The Europe of Trusts* (2002), *Kidnapped* (2002), and *The Midnight* (2003).

**X. J. Kennedy** (1929– )
Poet whose work has been collected in *Nude Descending a Staircase* (1961), *Celebrations after the Death of John Brennan* (1974), *Dark Horses: New Poems* (1992), and *The Lords of Misrule: Poems 1992-2002* (2002).

**Galway Kinnell** (1927– )
Poet, was awarded the Pulitzer Prize and National Book Award for *Selected Poems* (1982) in 1983; his other works include *What a Kingdom It Was* (1960), *Body Rags* (1968), *The Book of Nightmares* (1971), *Mortal Acts, Mortal Words* (1980), *The Past* (1985), *When One Has Lived a Long Time Alone* (1990), *Imperfect Thirst* (1996), *A New Selected Poems* (2000), *Strong Is Your Hold* (2006).

**Ted Kooser** (1939– )
Former poet laureate. His collection, *Delights and Shadows* (2004), won the Pulitzer Prize in 2005. Other works include *Sure Signs* (1980), *One World at a Time* (1985), *Weather Central* (1994), and *Winter Morning Walks: One Hundred Postcards to Jim Harrison* (2000).

**Audre Lorde** (1934–1992)
Poet and essayist. Her works of poetry include *The First Cities* (1968), *Cables to Rage* (1970), *From a Land Where Other People Live* (1972), *New York Head Shop and Museum* (1974), *The Black Unicorn* (1978), *The Cancer Journals* (1980), *Chosen Poems, Old and New* (1982), *Our Dead Behind Us* (1986), and *A Burst of Light* (1988), which won a National Book Award.

**Robert Lowell** (1917–1977)
Considered a founder of the confessional-poetry movement. His *Lord Weary's Castle* (1946) received the Pulitzer Prize in 1947. His other works include *Land of Unlikeness* (1944), *Poems, 1938–1949* (1950), *The Mills of the Kavanaughs* (1951), *Life Studies* (1959), *Imitations* (1961), *For the Union Dead* (1964), *Selected Poems* (1965), *Near the Ocean* (1967), *The Voyage and Other Versions of Poems by Baudelaire* (1968), *Notebooks, 1967–1968* (1969), *History* (1973), *The Dolphin* (1973), *For Lizzy and Harriet* (1973), *Selected Poems* (1976), and *Day by Day* (1977).

**Naomi Shihab Nye** (1952– )
Daughter of a Palestinian father and Anglo American mother, whose works include *Hugging the Jukebox* (1982), *Red Suitcase* (1994), *Fuel* (1998), *19 Varieties of Gazelle: Poems of the Middle East* (2002), and *You and Yours* (2005).

**Sharon Olds** (1942– )
Poet whose works include *Satan Says* (1980), *The One Girl at the Boys' Party* (1983), *The Dead and the Living* (1984), *The Gold Cell* (1987), *The Father* (1993), *The Wellspring* (1996), *Blood, Tin, Straw* (1999), *The Unswept Room* (2002), *Strike Sparks: Selected Poems* (2004) and *One Secret Thing* (2008).

**Mary Oliver** (1935–  )
Received the Pulitzer Prize in 1984 for *American Primitive* (1983). A prolific poet, since 2000 she has written and published *The Leaf and the Cloud* (2000), *What Do We Know* (2002), *Owls and Other Fantasies: Poems and Essays* (2003), *Why I Wake Early: New Poems* (2004), *Blue Iris: Poems and Essays* (2004), *Long Life: Essays and Other Writings* (2004), *New and Selected Poems, Volume Two* (2005), *Thirst: Poems* (2006), *Our World* (2007), *Red Bird* (2008), and *Evidence* (2009).

**Simon J. Ortiz** (1941–  )
Poet and member of the Acoma Pueblo tribe. He is the author of *Going for the Rain* (1976), *A Good Journey* (1977), *Fight Back: For the Sake of the People, for the Sake of the Land* (1980), *From Sand Creek* (1981), *Fightin': New and Collected Short Stories* (1983), *The People Shall Continue* (1988), and *Out There Somewhere* (2002).

**Michael Palmer** (1943–  )
Poet often associated with the L=A=N=G=U=A=G=E school of poetry. Some of his more significant works are *Blake's Newton* (1972), *The Circular Gates* (1974), *Without Music* (1977), *Notes for Echo Lake* (1981), *First Figure* (1984), *Sun* (1988), *At Passages* (1996), *The Lion Bridge: Selected Poems 1972–1995* (1998), *The Promises of Glass* (2000), *Codes Appearing: Poems 1979–1988* (2001), and *Company of Moths* (2005).

**Sylvia Plath** (1932–1963)
Poet and novelist often described as a confessional poet. *The Collected Poems* (1981) won the Pulitzer Prize in 1982, making Plath the first poet to receive the award posthumously. She is the author of *The Colossus* (1960), *Ariel* (1965), *Crossing the Water* (1971), and *Winter Trees* (1972) and a novel, *The Bell Jar* (1963).

**Alberto Ríos** (1952–  )
Poet whose works include *Elk Heads on the Wall* (1979), *Sleeping on Fists* (1981), *Whispering to Fool the Wind* (1982), *Five Indiscretions* (1985), *The Warrington Poems* (1989), *The Lime Orchard Woman* (1988), *Teodoro Luna's Two Kisses* (1990), *The Smallest Muscle in the Human Body* (2002), *The Theater of Night* (2006), and *The Dangerous Shirt* (2009).

**Anne Sexton** (1928–1974)
Often classified as a confessional poet, was awarded the Pulitzer Prize in 1967 for *Live or Die* (1966). Her other works include *To Bedlam and Part Way Back* (1960), *All My Pretty Ones* (1962), *Selected Poems* (1964), *Love Poems* (1969), *Transformations* (1971), *The Book of Folly* (1973), *The Death Notebooks* (1974), *The Awful Rowing toward God* (1975), *45 Mercy Street* (1976), *Words for Dr. Y.: Uncollected Poems* (1978), and *The Complete Poems* (1981).

**Cathy Song** (1955–  )
Poet whose first poetry collection, *Picture Bride* (1983), was selected for the Yale Series of Younger Poets. Her other works are *Frameless Windows, Squares of Light* (1988), *School Figures* (1994), *The Land of Bliss* (2001), and *Cloud Moving Hands* (2007).

**Natasha Trethewey** (1966–    )
Poet who was awarded the Pulitzer Prize in 2007 for *Native Guard* (2006). Her books include *Domestic Work* (2000) and *Bellocq's Ophelia* (2002).

**Franz Wright** (1953–    )
Poet who received the Pulitzer Prize in 2004 for *Walking in Martha's Vineyard* (2003). His other works include *Tapping the White Cane of Solitude* (1976), *The Earth without You* (1980), *8 Poems* (1982), *The One Whose Eyes Open When You Close Your Eyes* (1982), *Going North in Winter* (1986), *Entry in an Unknown Hand* (1991), *The Night World and the Word Night* (1993), *Ill Lit: Selected & New Poems* (1998), *God's Silence* (2006), *Earlier Poems* (2007), and *Wheeling Motel* (2009).

*—Jane Hoogestraat*

# Postmodernism

Students who wish to explore Postmodernism will first want to familiarize themselves with the larger cultural meanings of the term and then explore its manifestations in exemplary authors and works. While few scholars and critics are likely to dispute the significance of Postmodernism in contemporary American literature and culture, it remains a vexed term about which there is much debate. Some critics argue for a temporal definition: Postmodernism is the art and literature that come after Modernism, both extending and reacting to the principles that infused that movement. But if a temporally based definition is accepted, all art and literature produced after about 1950 would be "Postmodernist," and the term would lose its conceptual power.

More useful definitions of Postmodernism are those that describe it in terms of a set of philosophical assumptions and approaches to art and culture. One of the most influential of these definitions is that by Jean-François Lyotard in *La Condition postmoderne: Rapport sur le savoir* (1979; translated as *The Postmodern Condition: A Report on Knowledge*, 1984). Lyotard says that the basic premise of Postmodernism is a lack of belief in the overarching, all-encompassing explanations that he calls "metanarratives"; this stance maintains that there can be no absolute truth. Other critics conceptualize Postmodernism in political and economic terms. In his influential *Postmodernism; or, The Cultural Logic of Late Capitalism* (1991) Fredric Jameson argues that Postmodernism describes the kind of cultural artifacts that are created in "late capitalism," a period characterized by multinational corporations and mass consumption. Consumer culture and the "Information Age," according to Jameson, have created a superabundance of disconnected images and styles, resulting in a sense of fragmentation and depthlessness. All experience is commodified; art reflects that commodification, blurring and even erasing the distinction between "high" art and popular culture.

A third major interpretation of Postmodernism comes from Jean Baudrillard and looks back to the linguistic insights of Ferdinand de Saussure. Overturning the common-sense notion of language, wherein a word refers directly and inherently to a thing that exists in the world, Saussure argued that a word (or signifier) refers instead to a concept of the thing. This notion allows for great ambiguity in the use of apparently stable language: words do not mean anything in isolation but only in relation to other words; language is, finally, the only reality. Baudrillard extends this notion by arguing that the world is a simulacrum: an image of an image. Ideas and concepts refer not to the physical world but to other forms of representation. One finds oneself looking at copies or images for which no ultimate reality exists; Baudrillard calls these images "hyperreal." The popular *Matrix* movie trilogy (1999–2003) was heavily influenced by, and makes allusions to, Baudrillard's notion of the simulacrum. The Internet has accelerated this sense of the world. The idea of the simulacrum is useful for understanding the roles that intertextuality, parody, pastiche, and allusion play in Postmodernist fiction. The principal points of reference in a text are to other texts; there is little—perhaps no—reference to an independent reality. This phenomenon, along with the blurring of lines between high and popular culture, leads to the mixing of genres:

the thriller, the detective story, the myth saga, the science-fiction and speculative novel, fantasy, romance, the realistic psychological novel, and even pornography may intertwine in a given work.

Literary and artistic movements typically react to what came before them. Therefore, even though a purely temporal definition may not be satisfactory, it can be helpful to an understanding of Postmodernism to delineate its similarities to, and differences from, Modernism. Like Modernist fiction by authors such as William Faulkner, Katherine Anne Porter, Ernest Hemingway, James Joyce, and Virginia Woolf, many Postmodernist texts feature scrambled chronologies, stream of consciousness, neologisms and other wordplay, and multiple perspectives. Yet, there is a fundamental difference in philosophical outlook and, thus, a difference in the uses to which these techniques are put. The Modernists believed in the power of art to save, to heal, and to make things whole; Postmodernists do not share this faith. Modernists also believed in the possibility of a grand narrative; Postmodernists do not. Furthermore, while both Modernist and Postmodernist writers use fragments of the art and literature of the past in their own works, Modernists do so respectfully; Postmodernists tend to use such fragments ironically.

Students will find that criticism of American Postmodernist literature from the 1960s through the early 1990s tends to discuss only a small group of white male writers: John Barth, Donald Barthelme, Robert Coover, Don DeLillo, William Gass, Thomas Pynchon, and Kurt Vonnegut. These authors wrote self-reflexive works that downplay characterization and story in favor of irony, metafiction, game playing, and fragmentation. Barth, whose fictions are unrelentingly metafictional and self-referential, published two essays in the *Atlantic Monthly* that are influential in discussions of Postmodernism. "The Literature of Exhaustion" (1967) appeared to declare that the novel form was "used up." In "The Literature of Replenishment" (1980) Barth claimed that his earlier point had been misconstrued: he merely meant that literary conventions grow stale and need to be "retired, subverted, transcended, transformed, or even deployed against themselves to generate new and lively work." Coover's novel *The Universal Baseball Association, Inc., J. Henry Waugh, Prop.* (1971) delights in play while asking large questions about theology and the creative act. His *The Public Burning* (1977) satirizes Richard Nixon and the Julius and Ethel Rosenberg spy case, exemplifying the Postmodernist deflating of authority. Vonnegut's works provide many examples of Postmodernist forays into genre fiction, particularly science fiction. Pynchon's *V.* (1963), *The Crying of Lot 49* (1966), and *Gravity's Rainbow* (1973) demonstrate early Postmodernist expressions of paranoia and interest in ferreting out underlying systems and structures that ultimately prove to be elusive if not imaginary. The critic Patrick O'Donnell believes that paranoia is the "symptomatic condition of postmodernity" rather than a personal psychological state. Most early Postmodernist works employ parody, although in these works it does not necessarily carry the sense of ridicule traditionally associated with it; the student should consult the books by Jameson and Linda Hutcheon for extended discussions of parody in Postmodernism. With the publication in 1989 of Molly Hite's *The Other Side of the Story: Structures and Strategies of Contemporary Feminist*

*Narrative* more attention began to be paid to Postmodernist writing by women and people of color.

One can also divide literary Postmodernism into stages by decade, beginning in the 1960s with the Black Humor and absurdist experiments of Barth, Barthelme, Coover, Gass, Pynchon, and Vonnegut. The critic Ihab Hassan was a key figure in the delineation of the characteristics of this early stage. These trends continued in the 1970s, but in the 1980s more emphasis was placed on simulacra in the work of DeLillo and E. L. Doctorow. Also in the 1980s Hutcheon and Brian McHale published important studies of Postmodernist fiction. Hutcheon introduced the phrase "historiographic metafiction" to describe self-reflexive works that include historical personages and events; examples include Doctorow's *The Book of Daniel* (1971) and *Ragtime* (1975) and Coover's *The Public Burning*. In the 1990s and early 2000s the sophisticated self-awareness, wryness, and irony of early Postmodernism continued, but telling an engaging story with fully realized characters came to be just as important; instances include works by Paul Auster, Tim O'Brien, and David Foster Wallace.

For a recently proposed alternative view students may consult Rachel Adams's "The Ends of America, the Ends of Postmodernism" (2007). Adams argues that Postmodernism ended in the late 1980s, giving way to a new paradigm, "American literary globalism," in which ethnic writers and a rejuvenated emphasis on emotional storytelling become prominent; while the Postmodernist reacts to a sense of hidden connections behind the surface of life with paranoia, as in Pynchon's *The Crying of Lot 49* or DeLillo's *Underworld* (1997), American literary globalism upholds the interconnectedness of life all across the planet.

The Postmodernist skepticism regarding grand narratives and ideas of progress, rationality, and scientific objectivity grows in part out of the fact that those ideas historically failed to take cultural differences into account. Accordingly, Postmodernism opens the door to more perspectives. Until well into the 1990s, however, most criticism treated Postmodernism and multiculturalism as parallel but separate manifestations of contemporary American literature. More-recent criticism has begun to recognize that ethnic writers of the contemporary period are responsible for some extremely thought-provoking writing that is also strongly Postmodernist. Ana Castillo combines the "high" form of the family saga with pop-culture *telenovelas* (soap operas) in her novel *So Far from God* (1993), while her fellow Chicana writer Sandra Cisneros uses pastiche in "Little Miracles, Kept Promises" and techniques such as genre-blending, parody, and a strong sense of irony in many of the other stories in her collection *Woman Hollering Creek* (1991). Maxine Hong Kingston blurs the line between memoir and novel in *The Woman Warrior* (1975) and offers Postmodernist play throughout *Tripmaster Monkey: His Fake Book* (1989). Michael Chabon explores Jewish identity while interpolating adventure stories, detective fiction, and comic-book narratives in *The Amazing Adventures of Kavalier and Clay* (2000) and combines detective fiction and an alternate-universe plot in *The Yiddish Policemen's Union* (2007). Native American authors Gerald Vizenor, Louise Erdrich, and Leslie Marmon Silko employ Postmodernist techniques and sensibilities along with a historically grounded sense of the philosophies and traditions of their respective tribes. Among African

American writers, Ishmael Reed has engaged in Postmodernist game playing, metafiction, and parody from the beginning of his career in the 1960s, and Toni Morrison, Colson Whitehead, and Trey Ellis are often mentioned in discussions of Postmodernism. The Jewish writer Philip Roth created an alter ego, Nathan Zuckerman, who appears as the narrator and a character in several of his novels, highlighting the metafictional and self-reflexive nature of those works. Although it would be exaggerating to claim that everything in contemporary American literature is Postmodernist, one can trace a Postmodern sensibility—particularly the strong presence of irony and sense of self-consciousness—in many of the major writers discussed in this volume.

## TOPICS FOR DISCUSSION AND RESEARCH

1. Students might find it profitable to become familiar with some literary techniques that frequently appear in Postmodernist writing and then explore works by authors who are known for being particularly adept at those strategies. Probably the most commonly mentioned techniques are metafiction and self-reflexivity: they refer to fiction that calls attention to its own artificiality. While not invented by Postmodernists—self-reflexivity reaches back to the earliest history of the novel in Henry Fielding's *The History of Tom Jones, a Foundling* (1749) and Laurence Sterne's *The Life and Opinions of Tristram Shandy, Gentleman* (1760–1767)—it has become quite prevalent in their writing. Barth's short story "Lost in the Funhouse" (1968) is a typical coming-of-age/initiation story but is constantly interrupted by the author with comments about his process of writing the story. In Kurt Vonnegut's *Slaughterhouse-Five* (1969) a character named Kurt Vonnegut speaks to the reader in the first chapter and sporadically through the rest of the novel. O'Brien appears as a character and muses on the process of writing in many of his works. Patricia Waugh's *Metafiction: The Theory and Practice of Self-Conscious Fiction* (1984) and Hutcheon's *The Poetics of Postmodernism* (1988) offer helpful discussions of metafiction. Students might also explore parody, pastiche, irony, and intertexuality as they appear in Postmodernist writing.

2. Students might read one of the works about which a full essay appears in Part III of this volume, look at some of the criticism in its "Resources" list, and consider why the work is or is not considered Postmodernist. What techniques does it display? If the work is designated "Postmodernist" by the critics, does that designation seem to be a matter of style, content, or both? How does it deepen your understanding of the work to think of it as Postmodernist? If the work is generally considered "multicultural," does it also fit into the Postmodernist camp?

3. For authors who are engaged in an explicitly Postmodernist project, students might find it instructive to compare one of their early works to one of their more-recent texts: for instance, Pynchon's *V.* or *The Crying of Lot 49* to *Mason & Dixon* (1997) or *Inherent Vice* (2009), or DeLillo's *White Noise* (1985) to *Cosmopolis* (2003) or *Falling Man* (2007). How has the representation of the

material world and its impact on human consciousness changed over time in these authors' works?

4. Genre blending is a common strategy in Postmodernist fiction. In addition, many "serious" writers have chosen to write within the confines of what is commonly considered genre fiction. For instance, Chabon has published a detective novel, *The Final Solution* (2004), and an alternate-universe novel, *The Yiddish Policemen's Union*. Vonnegut commonly employed science-fiction conventions and tropes in his novels. Reed parodies the Western in his *Yellow Back Radio Broke-Down* (1969) and other genres in many of his other works. Students might choose any of these texts and consider whether it stretches the boundaries of the given genre, and, if so, how it does so. Such genre blurring usually also blurs the distinction between "high" art and popular culture. What does the author gain or lose by admitting popular-culture references and conventions into his or her fiction? Theo D'haen and Hans Bertens offer several essays on genre blurring in their anthology *Narrative Turns and Minor Genres in Postmodernism* (1995). A useful discussion, especially of science-fiction tropes, can be found in McHale's *Postmodernist Fiction* (1987).

5. Students might also wish to consider the shifting boundary between fact and fiction in Postmodernist writing. The selections in Paula Geyh, Fred G. Leebron, and Andrew Levy's *Postmodern American Fiction* (1998) offer many useful examples of this. Authors to explore for this topic include Vonnegut, Norman Mailer, Kingston, O'Brien, and Theresa Hak Kyung Cha.

## RESOURCES

### Primary Works

R. V. Cassill and Joyce Carol Oates, eds., *The Norton Anthology of Contemporary Fiction*, second edition (New York: Norton, 1998).

A collection of more than forty short stories by Postmodernist, multicultural, realist, and other writers. Useful biographical sketches appear at the end of the book.

Paula Geyh, Fred G. Leebron, and Andrew Levy, eds., *Postmodern American Fiction: A Norton Anthology* (New York: Norton, 1998).

Wide-ranging selections of fiction from the contemporary period, divided into the sections "Breaking the Frame," "Fact Meets Fiction," "Popular Culture and High Culture Collide," "Revisiting History," "Revising Tradition," and "Technoculture." Ten critical readings by key theorists of Postmodernism are also included.

Oates and Christopher R. Beha, eds., *The Ecco Anthology of Contemporary American Short Fiction* (New York: HarperPerennial, 2008).

Forty-eight short stories, most published in the twenty-first century, with a brief but valuable preface by Oates in which she argues that the short stories of the 1980s through the early 2000s are less self-consciously experimental than those of the 1960s and 1970s. She identifies the simulation of memoir and "vernacular urgency" as literary strategies that entice readers.

**Criticism**

Rachel Adams, "The Ends of America, the Ends of Postmodernism," *Twentieth-Century Literature*, 53 (Fall 2007): 248–272.
Argues that Postmodernism gave way as a primary literary mode in the late 1980s to "American literary globalism," a new paradigm with differing assumptions.

John Barth, "The Literature of Exhaustion," *Atlantic Monthly*, 220 (August 1967): 29–34; and "The Literature of Replenishment: Postmodernist Fiction," *Atlantic Monthly*, 245 (January 1980): 65–71; both reprinted in his *The Friday Book: Essays and Other Nonfiction* (New York: Putnam, 1984), pp. 62–76, 193–206.
Two articles that discuss trends in fiction in contemporary literature, the first focusing on the need for new approaches and the second on who and what is Postmodernist.

Steven Best and Douglas Kellner, *Postmodern Theory: Critical Interrogations* (New York: Guilford Press, 1991).
Provides accessible readings of Michel Foucault, Gilles Deleuze and Félix Guattari, Jean Baudrillard, Jean-François Lyotard, Frederic Jameson, Theodor W. Adorno, Jürgen Habermas, and others for the advanced student who wishes to understand the theories surrounding Postmodernism.

Steven Connor, *Postmodernist Culture: An Introduction to Theories of the Contemporary* (Cambridge, Mass.: Blackwell, 1989).
Accessible, respected overview of Postmodernist debates in philosophy, political theory, architecture, art, photography, literature, drama, film, television, popular culture, and cultural politics.

Connor, ed., *The Cambridge Companion to Postmodernism* (New York: Cambridge University Press, 2004).
Offers an introduction by Connor, a chronology, and ten essays on Postmodernism in philosophy, film, literature, art, performance, space, science and technology, religion, ethics, and law.

Marianne DeKoven, *Utopia Limited: The Sixties and the Emergence of the Postmodern* (Durham, N.C.: Duke University Press, 2004).
Argues that the 1960s embodied simultaneously the full, final expression of the Modern and the beginning of the Postmodern and that Postmodernism grew out of the politics of the 1960s rather than as a reaction to Modernism. DeKoven offers readings of many classic 1960s texts by authors such as William S. Burroughs, Norman Mailer, E. L. Doctorow, and Hunter S. Thompson, as well as Bob Dylan's music, the *Port Huron Statement* (1962), and Toni Morrison's post-1960s *Beloved* (1987).

Theo D'haen and Hans Bertens, eds., *Narrative Turns and Minor Genres in Postmodernism*, Postmodern Studies, 11 (Amsterdam & Atlanta: Rodopi, 1995).

Collects essays on the structuring of Postmodernism in works by Jerome Klinkowitz, Donald Barthelme, and Raymond Carver; the relationship between history and fiction in Postmodernism; the Postmodernist American sports novel; Postmodernism and detective fiction in the work of Paul Auster; and Postmodernism and science fiction in works by Philip K. Dick and Ursula K. Le Guin.

Thomas Docherty, ed., *Postmodernism: A Reader* (New York: Columbia University Press, 1993).
Useful collection with helpful introductions to the selections, which represent the major articulations of Postmodernism across many of the arts.

Madhu Dubey, *Signs and Cities: Black Literary Postmodernism* (Chicago: University of Chicago Press, 2003).
Discusses works by Octavia Butler, Samuel Delaney, Trey Ellis, Charles Johnson, Toni Morrison, Gloria Naylor, Ishmael Reed, Sapphire, and John Edgar Wideman in the context of Postmodernism and urbanity.

Emily Griesinger and Mark Eaton, eds., *The Gift of Story: Narrating Hope in a Postmodern World* (Waco, Tex.: Baylor University Press, 2006).
Collection edited from a Christian perspective that goes against the grain of most Postmodernist resistance to the idea of a grand narrative underpinning reality. The book includes essays on films and novels, including works by Don DeLillo, Amy Tan, and John Okada.

Donna Haraway, *Simians, Cyborgs, and Women: The Reinvention of Nature* (New York: Routledge, 1991).
A landmark work on feminism and Postmodernism.

Ihab Hassan, *The Dismemberment of Orpheus: Toward a Postmodern Literature* (New York: Oxford University Press, 1971).
One of the earliest analyses of Postmodernism in American literature, including an often-cited table of comparisons to Modernist writing and identifications of key writers.

Molly Hite, *The Other Side of the Story: Structures and Strategies of Contemporary Feminist Narrative* (Ithaca, N.Y.: Cornell University Press, 1989).
Important discussion of the intersections between Postmodernism and feminism. Until the publication of this work, studies of Postmodernism had been almost exclusively male and masculinist.

W. Lawrence Hogue, *Race, Modernity, Postmodernity: A Look at the History and the Literatures of People of Color since the 1960s* (Albany: State University of New York Press, 1996).
Looks at multiculturalism and Postmodernity as intertwined, rather than separate, impulses and offers readings of works by Toni Morrison, N. Scott Momaday, Richard Rodriguez, Andrea Lee, Maxine Hong Kingston, David Bradley, and Richard Perry within that context.

Linda Hutcheon, *A Poetics of Postmodernism* (New York: Routledge, 1988).
One of the most important and influential studies of Postmodernist literature, introducing the concepts of "historiographic metafiction" and "minoritarian" racial, ethnic, sexual, and gendered voices.

Hutcheon, *The Politics of Postmodernism* (New York: Routledge, 1989).
Continues the work of Hutcheon's previous volume but focuses on the political implications of Postmodernist strategies, particularly in feminist and other minoritarian works. The introduction provides a particularly useful description of the debates about defining and understanding Postmodernism.

Frederic Jameson, *Postmodernism; or, The Cultural Logic of Late Capitalism* (Durham, N.C.: Duke University Press, 1991).
One of the key documents in Postmodernist theory. Jameson discusses Postmodernism as the manifestation of the values and assumptions of a late-capitalist economy, an economy dominated by consumerism in which everything is commodified.

Brian McHale, *Postmodernist Fiction* (New York: Routledge, 1987).
Influential study that looks at Postmodernist fiction by American, British, and European writers, including William S. Burroughs, Don DeLillo, E. L. Doctorow, Thomas Pynchon, Kurt Vonnegut, John Barth, Robert Coover, and Ishmael Reed, among the Americans. McHale argues that Postmodernist writing concerns itself with questions of being (ontology), as opposed to Modernism, which focuses on questions of the nature and limits of knowledge (epistemology).

Patrick O'Donnell, *Latent Destinies: Cultural Paranoia and Contemporary U.S. Narrative* (Durham, N.C.: Duke University Press, 2000).
Examines the prevalence of paranoia and conspiracy theories in contemporary American writing, film, and television, focusing on the roles of nationalism, gender, and criminality in such novels as Thomas Pynchon's *The Crying of Lot 49* (1966), Norman Mailer's *The Executioner's Song* (1979), and Don DeLillo's *Libra* (1988) and *Underworld* and films such as *In the Realm of the Senses* (1976), *The Killer Inside Me* (1976), *JFK* (1991), *Reservoir Dogs* (1992), *Groundhog Day* (1993), and *The Truman Show* (1998).

Susan Strehle, *Fiction in the Quantum Universe* (Chapel Hill: University of North Carolina Press, 1992).
Argues that a strain of contemporary American literature has developed out of concepts from quantum physics in which reality is seen as discontinuous, dynamic, relative, statistical, indeterminate, subjectively observed, and uncertainly known. Naming this fiction "actualism," Strehle uses this framework to read major novels by Thomas Pynchon, Robert Coover, William Gaddis, John Barth, Margaret Atwood, and Donald Barthelme.

Patricia Waugh, *Metafiction: The Theory and Practice of Self-Conscious Fiction* (New York: Methuen, 1984).
Seminal study of metafiction and self-reflexivity as Postmodernist techniques.

# PEOPLE OF INTEREST

**Paul Auster** (1947– )
Fiction writer and poet who often employs a sense of the absurd and the crime-fiction genre to comment on the search for identity. His works include *City of Glass* (1985), *Ghosts* (1986), and *The Locked Room* (1986), published as *The New York Trilogy* in 1987; *Moon Palace* (1989); *The Music of Chance* (1990); *The Book of Illusions* (2002); *Oracle Night* (2004); and *The Brooklyn Follies* (2005).

**John Barth** (1930– )
Novelist, short-story writer, and essayist whose works include *The Floating Opera* (1957); *The End of the Road* (1958); *The Sot-Weed Factor* (1960); *Giles Goat-Boy* (1966); *Lost in the Funhouse: Fiction for Print, Tape, Live Voice* (1968); *Chimera* (1972), winner of the National Book Award; *LETTERS* (1979); *Sabbatical* (1982); and *The Tidewater Tales* (1987).

**Donald Barthelme** (1931–1989)
Author of short stories and novels, editor, and journalist. His stories have been published in *The New Yorker* and collected in *City Life* (1970), *Sadness* (1972), *Amateurs* (1976), *Great Days* (1979), *Overnight to Many Distant Cities* (1983), and *Sixty Stories* (1981). His novels include *The Dead Father* (1975) and *Paradise* (1986).

**Ana Castillo** (1953– )
Chicana poet, essayist, and fiction writer. Her works include the novels *The Mixquiahuala Letters* (1986), *Sapogonia* (1990), *So Far from God* (1993), *Peel My Love Like an Onion* (1999), and *The Guardians* (2007); the short-story collection *Loverboys* (1996); and *My Father Was a Toltec and Selected Poems, 1973–1988* (1995).

**Theresa Hak Kyung Cha** (1951–1982)
Korean American author known for the experimental novel *Dictee* (1982).

**Robert Coover** (1932– )
Writer and cofounder of the Electronic Literature Organization, established in 1999 to promote and facilitate the writing, publishing, and reading of electronic literature. His most acclaimed works include *The Origin of the Brunists* (1966), *The Universal Baseball Association, Inc., J. Henry Waugh, Prop.* (1968), *Pricksongs and Descants* (1969), *The Public Burning* (1977), *Gerald's Party* (1986), and *A Night at the Movies; or, You Must Remember This* (1987).

**Don DeLillo** (1936– )
Prolific and wide-ranging novelist who reworks various narrative genres. His books include *White Noise* (1985), *Underground* (1997), *Cosmopolis* (2003), and *Falling Man* (2007).

**Trey Ellis** (1962– )
Novelist, essayist, memoirist, and blogger whose *Right Here, Right Now* received an American Book Award in 1999. *Bedtime Stories: Adventures in the Land of Single-Fatherhood* (2008) is a memoir of his life as a single father of two.

**William Gass** (1924–   )
Novelist, short-story writer, and essayist known especially for his linguistic and narrative experimentation and metafictional tendencies (he coined the term *metafiction*). His most acclaimed works are the novels *Omensetter's Luck* (1966) and *The Tunnel* (1995) and the essay collections *Habitations of the Word* (1985), *Finding a Form* (1997), and *Tests of Time* (2003). Among his many awards are the American Book Award for *The Tunnel*, the PEN/Nabokov Lifetime Achievement Award, and the Lannon Lifetime Achievement Award; he has received the National Book Critics Circle Award for Criticism three times.

**Fredric Jameson** (1934–   )
Marxist theorist, best known for *Sartre: The Origins of Style* (1961), *Marxism and Form: Twentieth-Century Dialectical Theories of Literature* (1971), *The Political Unconscious: Narrative as a Socially Symbolic Act* (1981), *Postmodernism; or, The Cultural Logic of Late Capitalism* (1991), and *Valences of the Dialectic* (2009).

**Thomas Pynchon** (1937–   )
Much-admired but reclusive novelist and short-story writer best known for *V.* (1963); *The Crying of Lot 49* (1966); *Gravity's Rainbow* (1973), winner of the 1974 National Book Award; *Slow Learner* (1984), a collection of short stories with an autobiographical essay; *Mason & Dixon* (1997); and *Inherent Vice* (2009).

**Ishmael Reed** (1938–   )
Prolific African American fiction writer, poet, anthologist, and recipient of a MacArthur Fellow grant noted for his satire and unrelenting critique of contemporary intellectual life. His best-known novels are *Yellow Back Radio Broke-Down* (1969), *Mumbo Jumbo* (1972), and *The Last Days of Louisiana Red* (1974). His poetry is collected in *New and Collected Poems* (1988).

**Kurt Vonnegut** (1922–2007)
Novelist and essayist known particularly for his satire and blending of science-fiction elements into his fiction. His novels include *Player Piano* (1952), *Mother Night* (1961), *God Bless You, Mr. Rosewater* (1965), *Slaughterhouse-Five; or, the Children's Crusade* (1969), *Breakfast of Champions* (1973), and *Hocus Pocus* (1990). His essays and occasional writing are collected in *A Man without a Country* (2005) and *Armageddon in Retrospect* (2008).

**David Foster Wallace** (1962–2008)
Novelist, short-story writer, and essayist whose works include the novels *The Broom of the System* (1987) and *Infinite Jest* (1996), the short-story collection *Brief Interviews with Hideous Men* (1999), and the essay collection *A Supposedly Fun Thing I'll Never Do Again* (1997). He received a MacArthur Foundation Fellowship Award in 1997.

**Colson Whitehead** (1969–   )
African American novelist and MacArthur Fellow known for his Postmodernist sensibility in *The Intuitionist* (1999), *John Henry Days* (2001), and *Apex Hides the Hurt* (2006).

—*Kathryn West*

# Vietnam War (and Antiwar) Literature

Literature of the Vietnam War crosses genres, appearing in poetry, fiction, drama, memoir, and other nonfiction literary forms. The complex and varied literary images in these works match the public's complicated and conflicting views of the war with representations echoing the changes in American popular and political culture. No monolithic version of the Vietnam War exists in literature. Depicted instead are a wide variety of experiences and equally diverse perspectives offered by both combatants and noncombatants. Despite their differences, literary works about the conflict in Vietnam try to make sense of, and come to terms with, the war as it progressed and changed over time. Through writing, authors, often veterans themselves, hope to convey the experiences of those involved while also understanding the cultural and political reasons behind the war and the reactions to it at home.

As the number of American troops began to increase in Vietnam in the mid 1960s, writers began using their work to protest the war, denouncing it on moral, political, and social grounds. Norman Mailer's novel *Why Are We in Vietnam?* (1967) answers the title's question in its depiction of a character's unfair hunting tactics and obsessive desire to kill a grizzly bear; the war for him reflects the nation's arrogance and immorality. Robert Bly, who helped found American Writers against the Vietnam War in 1966, used poetry to decry what he considered America's unjust participation in the war. *The Teeth-Mother Naked at Last* (1970), one of Bly's best-known collections, captures the chaos and violence of combat while questioning the authority that condones it. Bly was joined by other poets who actively protested the war in their writing and participated in antiwar groups on and off college campuses; these poets include Muriel Rukeyser, Adrienne Rich, W. S. Merwin, and Denise Levertov.

Those who served in Vietnam also began publishing before the last troops came home on 29 March 1973. Like those of novelists and poets who did not serve, the works of veterans provide an alternative to official accounts and explanations. Deriving from the writers' service "in country," they tend to refrain from making explicit political statements about the war. Michael Casey's collection *Obscenities* (1972), winner of the Yale Series of Younger Poets award, displays frightening images from the war zone inspired by his experience as a military police officer in Quang Ngai province but without moral judgments or comments. Similarly, David Rabe, who also served in Vietnam, did not write his plays to make a political statement about the situation there but rather to highlight the struggle of individuals faced with powers beyond their control and to question the incongruity of idealism and war in general. His Vietnam War trilogy includes *Sticks and Bones* (first produced as *Bones,* 1969; revised, 1971), *The Basic Training of Pavlo Hummel* (produced, 1971; published, 1973), and *Streamers* (produced, 1976; published, 1977).

Works written by veterans continued to appear after the war ended with the fall of Saigon on 30 April 1975. Using a variety of genres and experimenting with style, voice, and narrative structure, writers continued to seek the truth about America's role in Vietnam. Several writers used memoir to convey personal experiences and the effects of the war on individuals to the American public, who, they felt, did not understand what veterans had gone through. Tim O'Brien's *If I Die in the Combat Zone* (1973) explores the conflict the author faced between his moral objections to war and reluctance to ignore his draft notice. In *Born on the Fourth of July* (1976) Ron Kovic explains his progression from innocent and idealistic teen soldier, to wounded and wheelchair-bound veteran, to social activist. Philip Caputo's autobiographical *A Rumor of War* (1977) provides an account of his 1965–1966 tour of duty as a marine lieutenant. Characterizing the work as "a story about war, about the things men do in war and the things war does to them," Caputo describes events leading to his court-martial (charges were eventually dropped) and confronts the notion that moral decay is a by-product of war. In the fast-paced *Dispatches* (1977) journalist Michael Herr moves beyond reportage to convey the terror, violence, and senselessness of war, memories he brought to the screenplays for *Apocalypse Now* (1979) and *Full Metal Jacket* (1987), on which he collaborated.

Much of the fiction and poetry published after the war also deals directly with combat and its effects. In *The 13th Valley* (1982) John M. Del Vecchio uses meticulous battle details, maps, and historical reports to re-create war operations in a realistic fashion. Just as significant are the emotional responses of his characters, which he contrasts with historical reports about battles. Indeed, veteran-writers became equally, if not more, interested in conveying subjective, rather than objective, experience. In *Paco's Story* (1986), for example, Larry Heinemann uses flashback and the narrative voices of members of the title character's dead platoon to convey Paco's guilt and the haunting memory of war for survivors.

Heinemann's novel begins with the assertion that "War stories are out," setting the stage for the novel's overt critique of idealistic stories about war and those who believe in these simplistic versions. Also focusing on subjective experience and storytelling are O'Brien's *Going after Cacciato* (1978), considered by many the definitive Vietnam War novel, and *The Things They Carried* (1990). The interplay between fact and imagination is evident in O'Brien's work as he explores the ways historical events are transformed by memory, imagination, and retelling. His work highlights the relevance of storytelling as a way not merely to recount events but to "save" those who tell and listen. Through stories, survivors cope with traumatic events such as war.

Other writers sought to depict the war through poetry while also trying to make sense of, and recover from, their experiences. In the war poems in *Caliban in Blue* (1976) and *After the Noise of Saigon* (1988) Walter McDonald spares readers sentimental and moral interpretations of war; the later book, especially, includes darker and more-disturbing imagery than his previous works as he seeks recovery from wartime violence. Bruce Weigl's poems, collected in *A Romance* (1979), *The Monkey Wars* (1985), and *Song of Napalm* (1988), provide the conflicting images and emotions faced by soldiers from their military induction to their return home from the war. His poems also expose, and attempt to exorcise, wartime experiences, as do those by poet W. D. Ehrhart, whose collections include *A Generation of Peace* (1975). While conveying the brutality of war, Kevin Bowen's collection *Playing Basketball with the Viet Cong* (1994) is deeply sympathetic toward those affected by war, soldier and civilian alike. Like Bowen, John Balaban offers a more complex look at the Vietnamese. His experience as a conscientious objector, working as a teacher and humanitarian in Vietnam, provides him a perspective unavailable to soldier veterans. The poems collected in *After Our War* (1974) stand out for their sympathetic portrayals that contrast the beauty of Vietnam village life with the war's disruption of it.

Other writers explore the often unseen or untold aspects of war, presenting perspectives influenced by race, ethnicity, and/or gender. The poetry of Yusef Komunyakaa shows the complexity of emotions felt by African American servicemen. An established poet by the time he published his first war poems, collected in *Dien Cai Dau* (1988—the title is taken from a Vietnamese expression roughly meaning "crazy")—Komunyakaa explores experiences with racism and relationships with Vietnamese civilians that lead to complex responses ranging from identification and ambivalence to abhorrence. Other voices that often go unheard include those of female veterans such as Lynda Van Devanter, whose memoir *Home before Morning* (1983) recounts her one-year service as a nurse in Vietnam. Also important are the perspectives of those who did not serve but were deeply affected by war. In the novel *In Country* (1985) Bobbie Ann Mason reflects on the legacy of the war for younger generations. Taking place during the summer of 1984, *In Country* features teenager Samantha Hughes's attempt to deal with her father's death in Vietnam—which happened when she was in the second grade. Sam's attempts to understand the war through popular culture and interaction with her veteran uncle, Emmett, dramatize the importance of the Vietnam War on the national and personal history of all Americans. Maxine Hong Kingston also dramatizes this importance in *The Fifth Book of Peace* (2003), which combines memoir and fiction in its exploration of loss and healing.

Recent writings about America's involvement in Vietnam pay more attention to Vietnamese and Vietnamese immigrant perspectives. Each of the stories that make up the Pulitzer Prize–winning collection *A Good Scent from a Strange Mountain* (1992) by veteran Robert Olen Butler features a Vietnamese immigrant living in Louisiana. Vietnamese immigrant writers have not remained silent about the war either. Expressing a wide range of personal reasons and perspectives, Vietnamese immigrant writers recount life in war-torn Vietnam, immigration to the United States, and postwar returns to Vietnam in memoir, fiction, and poetry. These writers include Lan Cao, Le Ly Hayslip, Andrew Lam, Christian Langworthy, lê thi diêm thúy, Aimee Phan, Andrew X. Pham, and Dao Strom. For Vietnamese who left their homeland or whose parents left, Lam notes, the conflict "is long over, yet hasn't, in many ways, ended. It continues to divide as well as claim us." The imaginative literature about the Vietnam War seeks to heal this divide by allowing those who experienced the war to tell their stories, thus creating connections between them and all affected, directly and indirectly, by war.

Students interested in the literature of the Vietnam War should first develop a solid understanding of the political, social, and military aspects of the conflict. Frances Fitzgerald's award-winning sociological study of the war, *Fire in the Lake* (1972), had a significant impact on writers reacting to American involvement in Vietnam; it should be read along with Stanley Kranow's more traditional history. A survey of periodicals of the period, beginning with popular newsmagazines such as *Time* and *Newsweek* and extending, perhaps, to publications that span the political spectrum, such as the right-wing *National Review* and the left-wing *Ramparts*, will provide a reliable sense of the emotionalism of the period. Stewart O'Nan's *The Vietnam Reader* is an excellent anthology of fiction and nonfiction about the war, prepared specifically for students.

## TOPICS FOR RESEARCH AND DISCUSSION

1. In *Visions of War, Dreams of Peace: Writings of Women in the Vietnam War* (1991) Lynda Van Devanter recalls the response she got when trying to publish an account of her one-year service as a wartime nurse: "What could a woman have to say about the Vietnam War?" Like their male counterparts, women who served "in country" risked their lives and health and suffered post-traumatic stress disorder. They also endured sexual harassment, lack of veteran services, and the insult of having their wartime contributions doubted, ignored, or forgotten because of their gender. Students exploring gender issues will be interested in Van Devanter's memoir *Home before Morning* (1983) and *A Piece of My Heart* (1986), edited by Keith Walker, which includes the narratives of twenty-six women who served in Vietnam. Le Ly Hayslip's memoir, *When Heaven and Earth Changed Places* (1989), coauthored with Jay Wurts, provides a Vietnamese woman's perspective on war and its aftermath. To identify women writers, students can consult Deborah Butler's *American Women Writers on Vietnam: Unheard Voices: A Selected Annotated Bibliography* (1990). Also useful for its discussion of strategies used in female literary representations of the war is Carol Acton's "Dangerous Daughters: American Nurses and Gender Identity in World War One and Vietnam." Students may alternately wish to consider images of women in literature about the Vietnam War and/or the construction of "masculinity" and its connection to definitions of heroism. See Kali Tal, and Gina Weaver's "The Vietnam War Film, Victimized Veterans, and the Disappearing Woman" (in Mark A. Heberle, pp. 42–52).

2. Representations of the war by nonwhite writers offer complex attitudes that challenge stereotypical accounts about the war and race. Students interested in investigating African American perspectives might consider the poems of Yusef Komunyakaa, especially those collected in *Dien Cai Dau* (1988), and the narratives in Wallace Terry's *BLOODS: An Oral History of the Vietnam War* (1984). The narratives of Chicano vets in Charley Trujillo's *Soldados: Chicanos in Viet Nam* (1990) offer a variety of responses to the war. For help identifying narrative strategies in African American and Chicano Vietnam War literature, students can consult, respectively, Shirley A. J. Hanshaw's "Refusal to Be Can(n)on Fodder: African American Representation of the Vietnamese War and Canon Formation" and Catherine Calloway's "In Their Own Voices: The Chicano Experience in Vietnam War Literature" (in Heberle, pp. 123–141, 142–158).

3. After the Vietnam War ended, it became a popular topic at the box office. For inspiration, filmmakers looked to books. Stanley Kubrick's *Full Metal Jacket* (1987) is based on Gustav Hasford's *The Short-Timers* (1979); Oliver Stone's *Born on the Fourth of July* (1989) adapts Ron Kovic's 1976 memoir of the same

name; Ted Kotcheff's *First Blood* (1982), starring Sylvester Stallone, is based on David Morrell's *First Blood* (1982); and Norman Jewison's *In Country* (1989) is adapted from the 1985 novel by Bobbie Ann Mason. Students might consider comparing a film to its original source, paying particular attention to changes in plot and how they affect overall representations of, and perspectives on, war. Students might also consider whether Hollywood versions are more or less effective than their literary counterparts in conveying the experience of war. A thematic approach to film and literature would also be worthwhile. The induction of soldiers in films such as *Platoon* (1986), *Apocalypse Now* (1979), and *Hamburger Hill* (1987) could be examined alongside Philip Caputo's *A Rumor of War* (1977). Images of the returning soldier in Hal Ashby's film *Coming Home* (1978) could be compared to those from its source, George Davis's 1975 novel of the same name, or works such as *Paco's Story* (1986), by Larry Heinemann. Good starting points for identifying additional works and critical approaches are offered in Mark Taylor and Catherine Calloway.

4. In "Novels about the 'Other Side'" (in Marc Jason Gilbert, pp. 115–120) Gilbert W. Berkley notes that most works about the Vietnam conflict feature "Vietnamese characters [who] are either absent, peripheral, or drawn from Western stereotypes." This observation can serve as the starting point for examining the representations of the Vietnam conflict in works by Vietnamese American writers. By echoing the work of Tim O'Brien, Andrew Lam's essay "The Stories They Carried," included in *Reflections on the Vietnamese Diaspora* (2005), suggests that the experiences of "boat people" are no less important than those of former American soldiers. They, too, have survived war. Other Vietnamese immigrant works that depict the war and its aftermath from a bicultural perspective include Andrew Pham's memoir *Catfish and Mandala* (1999), Lan Cao's autobiographical novel *Monkey Bridge* (1997); Dao Strom's *Grass Roof, Tin Roof* (2003); lê thi diêm thúy's *The Gangster We Are All Looking For* (2003); and Aimee Phan's short-story collection *We Should Never Meet* (2004). Students might also compare these depictions to those in *A Good Scent from a Strange Mountain* (1992) by Anglo-American veteran Robert Olen Butler. In addition, students might consider how the perspectives of those who left Vietnam contribute to a larger understanding of the war and its aftermath.

5. Maxine Hong Kingston's *The Fifth Book of Peace* (2003) juxtaposes a section about the fictional war protester and draft dodger Wittman Ah Sing and his experiences living in Hawaii with a section describing Kingston's own writing workshops, in which participants include Vietnam veterans from both sides of the conflict and those who, like herself, protested the war. Similar workshops, such as those hosted by the William Joiner Center Writers' Workshop at the University of Massachusetts, Boston, have allowed veterans to practice the process of writing in order to promote healing and peace. Examining prose and poetry written by veterans, students might consider how writing about and retelling war experiences promote healing and peace. Works by amateur writers are included in the anthologies edited by Kevin Bowen and Bruce Weigl and by Kingston. For a discussion about the connection between writing and healing from war, students can also consult Tal.

## RESOURCES

**Primary Works**

Kevin Bowen and Bruce Weigl, eds., *Writing between the Lines: An Anthology on War and Its Social Consequences* (Amherst: University of Massachusetts Press, 1997).
Includes works by veterans from both sides of the battle lines.

Maxine Hong Kingston, ed., *Veterans of War, Veterans of Peace* (Kihei, Hawaii: Koa Books, 2006).
Autobiographical accounts and fictional writing collected from Kingston's healing workshops; written by veterans and victims of other trauma (substance abuse and gang and domestic violence).

Stewart O'Nan, ed., *The Vietnam Reader: The Definitive Collection of American Fiction and Nonfiction on the War* (New York: Anchor, 1998).
An essential collection with works written mostly by veterans. The introductions to each section provide a useful chronology of war literature that charts changes in thematic and stylistic interests.

**Criticism**

Carol Acton, "Dangerous Daughters: American Nurses and Gender Identity in World War One and Vietnam," *War, Literature, and the Arts: An International Journal of the Humanities*, 13, 1–2 (2001): 87–113.
Discusses the way female writers challenge the marginalization of women in literary accounts of war.

Ronald Baughman, ed., *Dictionary of Literary Biography Documentary Series*, volume 9: *American Writers of the Vietnam War: W. D. Ehrhart, Larry Heinemann, Tim O'Brien, Walter McDonald, John M. Del Vecchio* (Detroit: Bruccoli Clark Layman/Gale, 1991), pp. 275–340.
Provides unique perspectives on the work and lives of five veteran-writers through previously unpublished material documenting their military service, including letters, drafts for published works, and service records.

Deborah Butler, *American Women Writers on Vietnam: Unheard Voices: A Selected Annotated Bibliography* (New York: Routledge, 1989).
An exhaustive list of entries with informative annotations identifying works featuring the perspective of women.

Catherine Calloway, "Vietnam War Literature and Film: A Bibliography of Secondary Sources," *Bulletin of Bibliography*, 43 (September 1986): 149–158.
A useful and exhaustive resource for locating reviews and critical essays about film and literature.

Marc Jason Gilbert, ed., *The Vietnam War: Teaching Approaches and Resources* (Westport, Conn.: Greenwood Press, 1991).

Part of the Contributions in Military Studies series, this unique collection of essays examines the Vietnam conflict from multiple disciplines, including history, literary analysis, and military studies.

Mark A. Heberle, ed., *Thirty Years After: New Essays on Vietnam War, Literature and Film* (Newcastle upon Tyne, England: Cambridge Scholars Publishing, 2009).
Excellent collection of essays, including pieces on the Vietnamese diaspora and on African American and Chicano representations in Vietnam War literature.

Stanley Karnow, *Vietnam: A History,* revised edition (New York: Penguin, 1997). A well-written and comprehensive overview of the war that will help students familiarize themselves with history of America's involvement in Vietnam.

Kali Tal, "The Mind at War: Images of Women in Vietnam Novels by Combat Veterans," *Contemporary Literature,* 31 (Spring 1990): 76–96; also available at <http://www.kalital.com/Text/Articles/womenvn.html> [accessed 19 March 2010].
Essay that examines the connection between healing and images of women in novels written by veterans.

Mark Taylor, *The Vietnam War in History, Literature, and Film* (Tuscaloosa: University of Alabama Press, 2003).
An excellent overview of trends in depicting the Vietnam conflict in various media.

## PEOPLE OF INTEREST

**John Balaban** (1943– )
Has written poetry, fiction, and nonfiction and has translated Vietnamese poetry. He served as a civilian in Vietnam and later for the Quaker and Mennonite Committee of Responsibility to Save War-Burned and War-Injured Children. His works include *After Our War* (1974), *Blue Mountain* (1982), *The Hawk's Tale* (1988), *Words for My Daughter* (1991), and a memoir, *Remembering Heaven's Face: A Moral Witness in Vietnam* (1991).

**Robert Bly** (1926– )
Poet known for his activism who founded American Writers against the Vietnam War. His collection *The Light around the Body* (1967) won the National Book Award in 1968. Other works include *Old Man Rubbing His Eyes* (1974), *Gratitude to Old Teachers* (1993), *Holes the Crickets Have Eaten in Blankets: A Sequence of Poems* (1997), and *Eating the Honey of Words* (1999).

**Kevin Bowen** (1947– )
Poet and translator whose works include a poetry collection, *Playing Basketball with the Viet Cong* (1994), and *Writing between the Lines: An Anthology on War and Its Social Consequences* (1997), which he coedited. He served in Vietnam in 1968–1969.

**Robert Olen Butler** (1945–   )
Fiction writer who became fluent in Vietnamese while working in counter-intelligence during the Vietnam War. *A Good Scent from a Strange Mountain*, a collection of short stories, won the Pulitzer Prize in 1993. Other works include *Tabloid Dreams* (1997), *The Deep Green Sea* (1999), *Had a Good Time: Stories from American Postcards* (2004), and *Severance* (2006).

**Lan Cao** (1975–   )
Attorney who was born in Saigon and writes fiction and nonfiction. She is the author of *Monkey Bridge* (1997) and coauthor of *Everything You Need to Know about Asian Americans* (1996).

**Michael Casey** (1947–   )
Poet who served as a military policeman in Vietnam from 1968 to 1970. He has written *Obscenities* (1972), *On Scales* (1972), *My Youngest That Tall* (1972), and *My Brother-in-Law and Me* (1974).

**John M. Del Vecchio** (1947–   )
Journalist and fiction writer served who as a combat correspondent in Vietnam in 1969 and earned a Bronze Star. He is the author of *The 13th Valley* (1982) and *For the Sake of All Living Things* (1990).

**W. D. Ehrhart** (1948–   )
Known mostly as a "Vietnam War poet." He enlisted in the United States Marine Corps in 1966 and served in Vietnam for thirteen months. His poetry collections include *A Generation of Peace* (1975), *The Samisdat Poems* (1980), *To Those Who Have Gone Home Tired* (1984), and *Just for Laughs* (1990). His work also appears in *Winning Hearts and Minds: War Poems by Vietnam Veterans* (1972), edited by Larry Rottmann, Jan Barry, and Basil T. Paquet, and he has written *Vietnam-Perkasie: A Combat Marine Memoir* (1983).

**Le Ly Hayslip** (1949–   )
Born Phùng Thi Lê Lý in South Vietnam and immigrated to the United States after marrying an American serviceman. She has written two memoirs, *When Heaven and Earth Changed Places* (1989), with Jay Wurts, and *Child of War, Woman of Peace* (1993), with her son James Hayslip, that were adapted by the director Oliver Stone for the film *Heaven and Earth* (1993).

**Larry Heinemann** (1944–   )
Writer who served in Vietnam in 1967–1968. He has written two novels about the war, *Close Quarters* (1977) and *Paco's Story* (1986), and a memoir, *Black Virgin Mountain: A Return to Vietnam* (2005). *Paco's Story* won the National Book Award in 1987.

**Michael Herr** (1940–   )
Journalist and screenplay writer who was a correspondent for *Esquire* magazine during the Vietnam War. *Dispatches* (1977) is his memoir about that experience. He has also written *The Big Room* (1986) and *Walter Winchell* (1990). He cowrote the screenplays for *Apocalypse Now* (1979) and *Full Metal Jacket* (1987).

**Yusef Komunyakaa** (1947–   )
Born James Willie Brown Jr., a poet who received the Pulitzer Prize in 1994 for *Neon Vernacular: New & Selected Poems, 1977–1989* (1993). He served in Vietnam with the United States Army (1965–1967) and was awarded a Bronze Star. His works include *Copacetic* (1983), *I Apologize for the Eyes in My Head* (1986), *Dien Cai Dau* (1988), *Talking Dirty to the Gods* (2001), and *Pleasure Dome: New & Collected Poems, 1975–1999* (2001).

**Ron Kovic** (1946–   )
Writer and activist who served in Vietnam from 1965 to 1968 and was awarded a Bronze Star with the "V" device for valor and a Purple Heart. His memoir, *Born on the Fourth of July* (1976), was adapted into the 1989 film of the same title. For this work, Kovic and Oliver Stone received a Golden Globe Award for best screenplay and were nominated for an Academy Award for best adapted screenplay.

**Andrew Lam** (1964–   )
Writer and editor with Pacific News Service and regular commentator on National Public Radio's *All Things Considered*. His essays have appeared in *The Nation*, *The New York Times*, *Mother Jones*, *The San Francisco Chronicle*, and the *Baltimore Sun*. Some of them are collected in *Reflections on the Vietnamese Diaspora* (2005). He was born in Saigon and left in the 1975 exodus.

**Christian Langworthy** (1967–   )
Poet and writer of prose, born Nguyên Văn Phương in Vietnam and adopted in 1975 by American parents after being brought to the United States in Operation Babylift. He is the author of the chapbook *The Geography of War* (1995).

**lê thi diêm thúy** (1972–   )
Performance artist, poet, and author of *The Gangster We Are All Looking For* (2003). She was born in Phan Thiet, South Vietnam, and raised in Southern California after leaving Vietnam in 1978.

**Denise Levertov** (1923–1997)
Poet who became a naturalized American citizen. She helped found the Writers and Artists against the War in Vietnam movement. Poems from her career have been collected in *Poems 1972–1982* (2001) and *Selected Poems* (2002*)*.

**Norman Mailer** (1923–2007)
Writer whose *The Armies of the Night* (1968), about his participation in an anti–Vietnam War march on the Pentagon in 1967, won the Pulitzer Prize and National Book Award in 1969.

**Bobbie Ann Mason** (1940–   )
Fiction writer and literary scholar whose works include *Shiloh and Other Stories* (1982), *In Country* (1986), *Spence + Lila* (1989), *Love Life: Stories* (1989), and *Feather Crowns* (1993).

**Walter McDonald** (1934–   )
Writer who served in Vietnam in 1969–1970. He has published one collection of stories, *A Band of Brothers* (1989), and twenty-two collections of poems, including

*Caliban in Blue* (1976), The *Flying Dutchman* (1987), *Rafting the Brazos* (1988), *After the Noise of Saigon* (1988), *Night Landings* (1989), *Where Skies Are Not Cloudy* (1993), *Counting Survivors* (1995), *Blessings the Body Gave* (1998), *Climbing the Divide* (2003), *A Thousand Miles of Stars* (2004), and *Faith Is a Radical Master* (2005).

**W. S. Merwin** (1927–   )
Poet and translator who won Pulitzer Prizes for *The Carrier of Ladders* (1970) and *The Shadow of Sirius* (2008).

**Andrew X. Pham** (1967–   )
Writer who was born in Vietnam and immigrated to the United States with his family after the war. His memoir, *Catfish and Mandala*, was the winner of the 1999 Kiriyama Pacific Rim Book Prize. He has also written a biography of his father, *The Eaves of Heaven: A Life in Three Wars* (2008), and a translation of *Last Night I Dreamed of Peace: The Diary of Thuy Dang Tram* (2007).

**Aimee Phan** (1977–   )
Fiction writer whose parents immigrated to California from Vietnam before she was born. Her collection of interrelated stories, *We Should Never Meet* (2004), was named a Notable Book by the Kiriyama Prize in fiction and a finalist for the 2005 Asian American Literary Awards.

**David Rabe** (1940–   )
Playwright best known for *The Basic Training of Pavlo Hummel* (1969), *Sticks and Bones* (1972; revised, 1979), *The Orphan* (1975), and *Streamers* (1975). He received a Tony Award for best play for *Sticks and Bones* in 1972. His works are influenced by his experiences in Vietnam, where he served for two years.

**Muriel Rukeyser** (1913–1980)
Poet who was politically and socially active throughout her life. Her works include *The Gates* (1976) and *The Collected Poems* (1978).

**Dao Strom** (1973–   )
Fiction writer and folksinger who was born in Saigon, which she left in 1975. Her books include a novel, *Grass Roof, Tin Roof* (2003), and a collection of stories, *The Gentle Order of Girls and Boys* (2006); her first album is *Send Me Home* (2004).

**Wallace Terry** (1938–2003)
Journalist who wrote and worked for *The Washington Post* and *Time*. He was also one of the founders of *USA Today*. He wrote the Pulitzer Prize–nominated *BLOODS: An Oral History of the Vietnam War* (1984).

**Lynda Van Devanter** (1947–2002)
Writer and activist. In 1980 she established the Women's Project with the Vietnam Veterans of America. Her experience as an army nurse during the Vietnam War is the source for her memoir, *Home before Morning* (1983).

**Bruce Weigl** (1949–   )

Poet who served in the United States Army in Vietnam from 1967 to 1970 and received a Bronze Star. His works include *A Sack Full of Old Quarrels* (1976), *Executioner* (1986), *A Romance* (1979), *The Monkey Wars* (1985), and *Song of Napalm* (1988).

—*Linda Trinh Moser*

# Part III
# Study Guides
# on Works and Writers

# Sherman Alexie, *The Lone Ranger and Tonto Fistfight in Heaven*
(New York: Atlantic Monthly Press, 1993)

Sherman Joseph Alexie Jr., an enrolled Spokane from his mother, a social worker, and Coeur d'Alene on his father's side, was born hydrocephalic (commonly known as "water on the brain") in October 1966. When he underwent brain surgery at six months of age, doctors expected him to suffer severe brain damage in the unlikely event that he survived. He not only survived but reports having read John Steinbeck's *The Grapes of Wrath* (1939) at age five, a novel he still claims as one of his favorites. As a child he suffered seizures and abuse at the hands of bullies due to his medical problems and his propensity for pastimes, particularly reading, that were not popular on his reservation. These are all experiences he gives to Arnold Spirit, the protagonist of his National Book Award–winning young adult novel, *The Absolutely True Diary of a Part-Time Indian* (2007).

Alexie credits his father, who worked at various times as a truck driver and logger and died in 2003 as a result of alcoholism and diabetes, with instilling in him a love of reading. His relationship with his father was both significant and frustrating to him, as suggested by the closing words of his introduction to the tenth-anniversary edition of *The Lone Ranger and Tonto Fistfight in Heaven:* "the sons in this book really love and hate their fathers." A son struggling with feelings of abandonment by his father is the central concern in the film *Smoke Signals* (1998), for which Alexie wrote the screeplay, adapting the story "This Is What It Means to Say Phoenix, Arizona," from *The Lone Ranger and Tonto Fistfight in Heaven*. Alexie became an alcoholic at age eighteen but quit drinking five years later. He attended Gonzaga University, then transferred to Washington State University in Pullman. After fainting in human anatomy classes, he gave up his aspirations to become a doctor and instead became interested in writing poetry through a class with Alex Kuo, whose gift to him of an anthology titled *Songs From This Earth on Turtle's Back,* edited by Joseph Bruchac (1983), opened Alexie's eyes to the realization that his experiences could be a subject for literature.

In 1996 *Granta* magazine named Alexie one of the "Best Young American Novelists." By that time he had published more than three hundred poems, six volumes of poetry, two novels, one short-story collection, and numerous stories, essays, and reviews. When asked how he was so prolific, he noted that the average life expectancy of an American Indian man is forty-nine years, and given how much he felt he had to say and how little time he might have, he needed to get it out there quickly. This comment illustrates prominent characteristics in much of Alexie's writing: his desire to educate the American public about Native American history and about living conditions on reservations; his wry, acerbic sense of humor; and his combination of these elements to critique and sometimes to satirize contemporary culture, especially as it relates to U.S. attitudes about American Indians.

A younger member of the Native American Literary Renaissance, Alexie frequently and with passion points to the Indian authors (he prefers the term "Indian" to "Native American") who influenced him, including Leslie Marmon

Silko, Joy Harjo, Simon Ortiz, and Adrian Louis. He also speaks enthusiastically about Emily Dickinson, Walt Whitman, and F. Scott Fitzgerald, and claims Stephen King, John Steinbeck, and *The Brady Bunch* as significant influences. He sharply criticizes non–Native American contemporary authors who feature Indians in their work, arguing that is one more form of the colonization and co-optation historically experienced by American Indians. (For more on this controversy, see the Study Guide on the Native American Renaissance in Part II of this volume.)

*The Lone Ranger and Tonto Fistfight in Heaven*, which received the PEN/ Hemingway Award for Best First Book of Fiction, consists of twenty-two stories, most set on the Spokane Indian reservation. Victor Joseph, Thomas Builds-the-Fire, and "Junior" Polatkin appear at various ages in many (although not all) of the stories. (In a joke repeated across many of his works, Alexie claims that if you call out the name "Junior" on a reservation, seventeen men and three women will turn around in response). The volume loosely approximates a short-story cycle or sequence, but it does not quite have the sense of connection and coherence characteristic of most works typically given that label. Certain themes do appear across many stories, however, including the difficulty of negotiating the present and a future out of a tribal past filled with loss, the effect of poverty on loving relationships, and the relationship between alcoholism and despair. His prose has been acclaimed for its humor, convincing dialogue, and metaphorically powerful images. His critics have accused him of stereotyping for his depiction of so much drunkenness and despair among contemporary Indians; he replies that he writes what he has witnessed.

In addition to more than a dozen volumes of poetry, Alexie has published the novels *Reservation Blues* (1995), *Indian Killer* (1996), and *Flight* (2007). He is also the author of three other short-story collections: *The Toughest Indian in the World* (2000); *Ten Little Indians* (2003), including "What You Pawn I Will Redeem," which won an O. Henry Prize; and *War Dances* (2009). Students interested in learning more about Alexie's life and his views will find many interviews available online, including those at his own website, <www.fallsapart.com>. Under "Academic Center" there are links to many scholarly articles.

## TOPICS FOR DISCUSSION AND RESEARCH

1. Alexie has commented on the important role father/son relationships play in many stories in *The Lone Ranger and Tonto Fistfight in Heaven*. Students might examine such aspects as conflict, role-modeling, abandonment, holding onto or trying to forget the past, and other factors that have an impact on those relationships, perhaps most especially poverty and violence. Another angle is to consider how Alexie uses the dynamics of father/son relationships to comment on other aspects of contemporary native culture. For instance, in the story "Because My Father Always Said He Was the Only Indian Who Saw Jimi Hendrix Play 'The Star-Spangled Banner' at Woodstock," the narrator remarks, "On a reservation, Indian men who abandon their children are treated worse than white fathers who do the same thing. It's

because white men have been doing that forever and Indian men have just learned how. That's how assimilation can work." In addition, students might wish to view the film *Smoke Signals* and compare its treatment of father/son relationships.

2. Alexie weaves into his stories references to many social and historical events, such as Woodstock, the Battle of the Little Big Horn, Colonel George Wright's slaughter of eight hundred native horses in 1858, and the Ghost Dance of 1890. Students might find it fruitful to research the historical events referenced in the stories and then consider what light they cast on the characters and their lives. Much of the history of American Indians in contact with Europeans has been, despite some moments of pride, a history of loss—the loss of land and the loss of culture through assimilation. What do Alexie's characterizations suggest about what it feels like today to be Indian and look back on that history of loss? A related subject for analysis is the role of popular culture for contemporary reservation life; the article by James Cox will be useful.

3. Students might assess the extent to which Alexie draws on traditional native storytelling themes and methods, and how he may revise them for his own purposes. For instance, how does Alexie employ the traditional trickster figure? Karl Kroeber's *Native American Storytelling: A Reader of Myths and Legends* (Malden, Mass.: Blackwell, 2004), the PBS website <www.pbs.org/circleofstories>, and the articles by Joseph L. Coulombe and Jerome DeNuccio, cited below, are useful resources for study of the trickster figure. Study of the complex depiction of the contemporary reservation storyteller, Thomas Builds-the-Fire, could provide a more focused topic, as could the role of tricksters in *The Lone Ranger and Tonto Fistfight in Heaven*.

4. Alexie often dramatizes situations in which people who care deeply about one another also experience deep conflict. In "Every Little Hurricane," Victor describes his two uncles fighting: "Strangers would never want to hurt each other that badly." Trace the various causes Alexie identifies for these situations. How do they relate to the American Indian past, poverty, and reservation life? Why are love and violence so intertwined in these stories? Poverty and alcohol are often triggers for such conflicts, and Alexie has been accused of perpetuating the stereotypical image of the drunken Indian. See the article by Stephen F. Evans and determine how you would weigh that charge.

5. Alexie's humor is a a notable characteristic of his writing, but readers and critics sometimes disagree about its effect. Does his acerbic sense of humor merely puncture pretensions and point out inequities? Or does it go further and use satire to offer a corrective? The articles by Coulombe, DeNuccio, and Ron McFarland and the chapter by Louis Owens, all cited below, should be helpful to students examining this question.

6. "Witnesses, Secret or Not" is the final story in the original edition of *The Lone Ranger and Tonto Fistfight in Heaven*. (In the tenth-anniversary edition two additional stories that were considered for, but not included in, the original have been added.) In this story, a young boy describes how his father is questioned by the Spokane police on an annual basis about a murder that happened

several years before, questioned not so much as a suspect but as someone who might have information. At the end of the story, after Junior and his father return home to the reservation from one such ordeal, the family is gathered around the dinner table when the father begins to cry. The story ends with, "and we all watched him. All of us." Just as this man's family bears witness to his pain, the idea of bearing witness runs through many of the stories in *The Lone Ranger and Tonto*, starting with the very first, "Every Little Hurricane," in which young Victor witnesses the emotional turmoil of his reservation community during a large party. What other examples of witnessing, of watching difficult events and emotions, occur in the collection? What is significant about the act of witnessing or bearing witness to pain? What is the relationship between witnessing and history, and how is it similar to or different from the relationship between witnessing and contemporary events? In what ways might the collection itself be described as an act of bearing witness? The article by DeNuccio and the interview with Dave Welch, among others, should be helpful.

## RESOURCES

### Primary Works

Erik Himmelsbach, "The Reluctant Spokesman," *Los Angeles Times*, 17 December 1996 <http://www.fallsapart.com/art-lat.html> [accessed 16 November 2009].
Discusses Alexie's fraught relationship with his home reservation, his novel *Indian Killer*, and the problems associated with being seen as "speaking for" a particular ethnic group.

Jim Lehrer, "A Dialogue on Race with President Clinton," with Alexie, Richard Rodriguez, Roger Rosenblatt, Clarence Page, Cynthia Tucker, Roberto Suro, Kay James, and Elaine Chao, *Online NewsHour*, 9 July 1998 <http://www.pbs.org/newshour/bb/race_relations/OneAmerica/oneamerica.html> [accessed 16 November 2009].
Panel discussion of issues of race in the contemporary United States.

John Purdy, "Crossroads: A Conversation with Sherman Alexie," *Studies in American Indian Literature*, 9 (Winter 1997): 1–18.
Discusses Alexie's work on the film *Smoke Signals;* his belief that new, Indian-centered approaches to Indian literatures need to be developed; and his discomfort with writing novels instead of poetry.

Tavis Smiley, "Sherman Alexie," *Tavis Smiley Show*, 27 April 2007 <http://www.pbs.org/kcet/tavissmiley/archive/200704/20070427_alexie.html> [accessed 16 November 2009].
Includes discussions of Alexie's 2007 novel, *Flight;* his family; his feelings about the United States; and issues of alcoholism in his own family and in Native American communities.

Dave Welch, "Revising Sherman Alexie," interview held on 15 May 2007 in Portland, Oregon, *Powell's Books*, <http://www.powells.com/interviews/shermanalexie.html> [accessed 16 November 2009].

Discusses Alexie's considering himself a "colonized mind" as a writer, using the types of metaphors and situations that typify writing from colonial and postcolonial situations (such as an orphaned protagonist); his unconventional public readings and stand-up comic performance style; and his desire to rewrite and republish his novel *Flight* every few years.

## Criticism

Kathleen L. Carroll, "Ceremonial Tradition as Form and Theme in Sherman Alexie's *The Lone Ranger and Tonto Fistfight in Heaven:* A Performance-Based Approach to Native American Literature," *Journal of the Midwest Modern Language Association,* 38 (Spring 2005): 74–84.

Advocates using a performance-based approach to Alexie's work in the classroom, focusing on the art of Native American storytelling, to overcome student discomfort with his use of stereotypes and his sometimes confrontational tone.

Joseph L. Coulombe, "The Approximate Size of His Favorite Humor: Sherman Alexie's Comic Connections and Disconnections in *The Lone Ranger and Tonto Fistfight in Heaven,*" *American Indian Quarterly,* 26 (Winter 2002): 94–115.

Thoroughly examines Alexie's complex deployment of humor, arguing that it operates much like Trickster, embodying "shifting meanings and serv[ing] conflicting ends," and that it is ultimately most valuable for creating dialogue about social and moral issues significant to Indian communities.

James Cox, "Muting White Noise: The Subversion of Popular Culture Narratives of Conquest in Sherman Alexie's Fiction," *SAIL,* 9 (Winter 1997): 52–70.

Discusses how Alexie's fiction illustrates that contemporary Indians are damaged by the stereotypical depictions of them in popular culture—particularly movie and television—and how he critiques and refutes these characterizations.

Jerome DeNuccio, "Slow Dancing with Skeletons: Sherman Alexie's *The Lone Ranger and Tonto Fistfight in Heaven,*" *Critique,* 44 (Fall 2002): 86–96.

Close reading of many stories in the collection, highlighting themes of subjectivity and reconciling a painful past (tribal and personal) with present existence and hope for the future, arguing that stories "teach survival."

Andrew Dix, "Escape Stories: Narratives and Native Americans in Sherman Alexie's *The Lone Ranger and Tonto Fistfight in Heaven,*" *Yearbook of English Studies,* 31 (2001): 155–167.

Compares Alexie's writing to that of Leslie Marmon Silko, contrasting their differing depictions of storytelling and seeing Alexie as much more skeptical about the political and social power of storytelling.

Stephen F. Evans, "'Open Containers': Sherman Alexie's Drunken Indians," *American Indian Quarterly*, 25 (Winter 2001): 46–72.
Thorough consideration of the depiction of alcohol use and drunkenness across most of Alexie's work; also debates the question of whether or not Alexie offers any kind of corrective or sense of hope along with his critique.

Jennifer Gillan, "Reservation Home Movies: Sherman Alexie's Poetry," *American Literature*, 68 (March 1996): 91–110.
Offers carefully considered examination of major themes in Alexie's work, especially the struggle to find an identity within the competing claims of tribal pasts and contemporary U.S. culture. This article is specially recommended for those interested in exploring Alexie's poetry.

Patrice Hollrah, "Sherman Alexie's Challenge to the Academy's Teaching of Native American Literature, Non-Native Writers, and Critics," *Studies in American Indian Literature*, 13 (Summer–Fall 2001): 23–36.
Through analyses of various characters, discusses Alexie's often harsh criticism of white writers and scholars attempting to discuss American Indian texts and issues, while critiquing Alexie's refusal to offer solutions or suggestions for those wishing to engage with native texts authentically and without arrogance. Hollrah also highlights Alexie's sympathetic depictions of strong women and gender complementarity in native cultures.

Ron McFarland, "Sherman Alexie's Polemical Stories," *Studies in American Indian Literature*, series 2, 9 (Winter 1997): 27–38.
Noting the discomfort Alexie often invokes in readers and listeners, argues that Alexie couches anger in satiric humor, eschews dense texture and description for an accumulation of character traits and actions, and demonstrates a flair for aphorism and metaphor to create his distinctive style.

Jacqueline L. McGrath, "'The Same Damn Stories': Exploring a Variation on Tradition in Sherman Alexie's *The Lone Ranger and Tonto Fistfight in Heaven*," *Southern Folklore*, 57 (January 2001): 94–105.
Excellent article challenging definitions of folklore to argue that Alexie's writing is an actual embodiment of folklore. (Folklorists argue that any written text cannot be folklore, but only a folklore text.) McGrath also provides a useful perspective on Alexie's negative view of non-Native American writers using native characters, as well as analysis of some innovative features of Alexie's prose.

Louis Owens, *Mixedblood Messages: Literature, Film, Family, Place* (Norman: University of Oklahoma Press, 1998).
Particularly important for the final chapter, in which Owens recognizes Alexie's talent but doubts his ability to offer work that is positive and useful, especially when compared to such figures as N. Scott Momaday and Leslie Marmon Silko.

*—Kathryn West*

# Maya Angelou, *I Know Why the Caged Bird Sings*
## (New York: Random House, 1970)

In a 1977 interview with Jeffrey M. Elliot, Maya Angelou revealed that "I decided many years ago to invent myself. I had obviously been invented by someone else—by a whole society—and I didn't like their invention. I just didn't. So I continued to invent myself every day."

Born Marguerite Annie Johnson on 4 April 1928 in St. Louis, Missouri, and raised primarily in Stamps, Arkansas, by her grandmother, Angelou continued to define and invent herself anew in response to the abuse and hardship she faced growing up black and female in the South during the Jim Crow era. Adding to the injury of racism were feelings of displacement, "the rust on the razor that threatens the throat," related to a broken home, separation from her parents, and insecurity about her looks. Angelou was raped as a child and became an unwed mother in her teens. Despite these experiences, she channeled her talents to find success as a dancer and singer performing Off Broadway and touring Europe and as an Emmy-nominated actress, teacher, and acclaimed memoirist and poet. In her life and writing, she provides an enduring testament to human resiliency and the ability not only to survive but also to rise above and overcome difficult circumstances.

Angelou recounts her childhood in *I Know Why the Caged Bird Sings* (1970), the first volume of her autobiography and her most popular work. Her divorced parents, Vivian Baxter and Bailey Johnson, shuttled her and older brother Bailey back and forth between St. Louis and Stamps, where they were cared for by their paternal grandmother, Annie "Momma" Henderson, who owned the only African American general store in town. Arkansas became Angelou's permanent home when she was three. During a visit with her mother in Chicago when she was seven, Angelou was raped by her mother's boyfriend. After she named her rapist and endured his trial, her attacker was found murdered—presumably by her uncles. Feeling responsible for the death, Angelou did not speak for five years, her silence a manifestation of guilt, insecurity, and feelings of worthlessness. Against these early difficulties, however, Angelou sets in her memoir the positive and life-affirming qualities embodied by her grandmother and by African American cultural traditions. Returned to her grandmother after her rape, Angelou eventually regained her speech and spirit, also discovering what would become a life-long passion for writing and reading. This renewal, however, was threatened by a move with her mother and brother to San Francisco where she struggled again to find acceptance. The work also describes her job as the first African American streetcar conductor and a growing passion for drama and dance. It ends with the birth of her son, Guy, a week after she graduated from Mission High School at age sixteen.

Angelou continues the story of her life in subsequent books. *Gather Together in My Name* (1974) picks up shortly after *I Know Why the Caged Bird Sings* leaves off, depicting the bleakest period recounted in her autobiographical works. In contrast to the sense of optimism that pervades the end of *I Know Why the Caged Bird Sings* are descriptions of her guilt over having a child outside of marriage and of a series of relationships with men she describes in retrospect as "dangerous." She also describes low-end jobs as a cook, a dancer, and for one week, as a prostitute. Angelou's third volume, *Singin' and Swingin' and Gettin' Merry Like Christmas* (1976), reflects her climb out of the spiraling descent of unhealthy relationships and choices depicted in the previous volume. Attempting to claim middle-class respectability for her son, she married former sailor Tosh Angelos in 1952. Although the marriage ended in divorce, she kept a variant of his surname as her own, combining it with Maya, her brother's childhood nickname for her. Angelou balances optimism and a sense of worry as she addresses the split between work and family life experienced by many women. While touring with the cast of *Porgy and Bess* in Europe, she regained a positive sense of self; however, guilt over leaving Guy to go on tour led again to depression.

The *Heart of a Woman* (1981), Angelou's follow-up, chronicles her involvement in the Civil Rights movement and growth as a writer. After moving to Brooklyn, she joined the Harlem Writer's Guild, where fellow member James Baldwin encouraged her to write what would become *I Know Why the Caged Bird Sings*. After meeting Martin Luther King Jr., she became the northern coordinator of the Southern Christian Leadership Conference, a position she left to travel with South African activist Vusumzi Make. With him and her son, Angelou moved to Egypt, where she became editor of the English-language *Arab Observer*. When her relationship with Make ended, she decided to stay in Africa, feeling it offered her a sense of home she had never felt in the United States. *All God's Children Need Travelin' Shoes* (1986) chronicles her life in Ghana, where she encountered other African American expatriates and served as an administrator at the University of Ghana; the book also recounts her distress as nineteen-year-old Guy seeks independence from his mother. *A Song Flung up to Heaven* (2002) describes the personal grief she experienced following the assassinations of Martin Luther King Jr. and Malcolm X (she had worked with both of them) and the solace she finds in writing.

Angelou lives up to her website's description of her as a "Global Renaissance Woman," in the success she has found in other areas of the arts. Her poetry has been collected in *Just Give Me a Cool Drink of Water 'fore I Diiie* (1971), *Oh Pray My Wings Are Gonna Fit Me Well* (1975), *Still I Rise* (1978), *Shaker, Why Don't You Sing?* (1983), and *I Shall Not Be Moved* (1990). *Wouldn't Take Nothing for My Journey Now* (1993) and *Letter to My Daughter* (2008) are other works of prose, and *My Painted House, My Friendly Chicken, and Me* (1994) is a children's book. She has also written for television, most notably, *Black, Blues, Black* (1968), a series for PBS; a teleplay of *I Know Why the Caged Bird Sings* (1979); and *Sister, Sister* (1982). She wrote the screenplays for *Georgia, Georgia* (1972) and *Down on the Delta* (1997), which she directed. As an actress she has appeared in *Roots* (1977), for which she earned an Emmy nomination, and *Poetic Justice* (1993). In 1993 Angelou read her poem "On the Pulse of Morning" at the inauguration of President Bill Clinton; it was commissioned for the occasion. Angelou has been awarded the Presidential Medal for the Arts (2000), the Lincoln Medal (2008), and more than thirty honorary degrees for her achievements. Dr. Angelou, as she likes to be called, is the Reynolds Professor of American Studies at Wake Forest University in North Carolina.

Useful for students who want a quick overview is "Maya Angelou: Global Renaissance Woman," her official website at <http://mayaangelou.com> [accessed 16 December 2009]. It provides a comprehensive description of her career, photographs from different stages of her life, a list of books and films, and links to videos of recent interviews and readings.

## TOPICS FOR DISCUSSION AND RESEARCH

1. In the opening passage of *I Know Why the Caged Bird Sings* the narrator fantasizes about emerging "out of my black ugly dream, and my real hair, which was long and blond, would take the place of the kinky mass that Momma wouldn't let me straighten[.] My light blue eyes were going to hypnotize them. . . ." Later in the autobiography, she reveals being jealous of her brother and mother who both have fairer complexions. Her conception of physical beauty is the exact opposite of everything she is. Given the choice, she would exchange dark hair, skin, and eyes for blue eyes and blondeness. How do these prevalent beauty standards affect the narrator's self-perception and sense of self? Similar notions about beauty affect characters in Toni Morrison's *The Bluest Eye* (1970) and Rita Dove's *Through the Ivory Gate* (1992). Students might compare the experiences of characters in one or both works to Angelou's, analyzing the effects of white beauty standards on black identity. Sidonie Smith and the book-length study by Mary Jane Lupton offer helpful starting points on this topic.

2. The theme of motherhood appears throughout *I Know Why the Caged Bird Sings* in Angelou's representations of her own mother Vivian Baxter, her paternal grandmother Annie "Momma" Henderson, mother-figure Mrs. Bertha Flowers, and her own role as mother to Guy. Smith describes Angelou's attitude toward motherhood in positive terms: "With the birth of her child Maya is herself born into a mature engagement with the forces of life." Yet, the work also reveals ambivalence on her part, perhaps directly related to feelings of abandonment. Students would find it beneficial to look further into the depiction of motherhood. One way to start would be to consider her relationships with the various mother figures she has throughout the work. How do her own experiences being "mothered" translate to her feelings and actions toward her pregnancy and to her son? What must be done to avoid making the same mistakes her mother did with her children? How might the interactions with her grandmother and Mrs. Flowers provide alternative models of mothering for the unwed mother? Lupton (both works), Dolly A. McPherson, and Carol E. Neubauer all provide insight on this topic. Lupton's essay also traces this theme in Angelou's later works.

3. The title of Angelou's first book is taken from an 1899 poem, "Sympathy," by Paul Laurence Dunbar, which uses the line at the beginning and ending of each stanza. "Sympathy" can be found at <http://www.csustan.edu/english/reuben/pal/chap6/dunbar.html> [accessed 16 December 2009]. The poem depicts a bird who persists in beating and thus injuring its wings against the cage even though it may never be free. Why is this a fitting metaphor for the experiences depicted in Angelou's autobiography? Which of the narrator's actions are akin to

the beating of wings in the poem? Who or what encourages her to keep striving, and what inner resources does she draw upon in her persistence to be free?

4. Angelou has said, "I write for the Black voice and any ear which can hear it" (quoted in Evans). Yet, in much of *I Know Why the Caged Bird Sings* the narrator confronts her own silence. After she names her rapist and he is murdered, she takes a vow of silence, because she believes her words have killed him; she says, "Just my breath, carrying my words out, might poison people and they'd curl up and die like the black fat slugs that only pretended." She overcomes the silence with the help of Mrs. Flowers, "the aristocrat of Black Stamps," with whom she reads literary classics. What is it about Mrs. Flowers and her lessons that help the narrator speak again? Later, upon learning she is pregnant, the narrator, unable to tell anyone, again goes silent and must relearn to speak. What induces silence in this work and why must it constantly be overcome? Helpful to students interested in this topic are essays in both works by Lupton, as well as those by Johnson, McPherson, Smith, and essays by Selwyn R. Cudjoe and Sondra O'Neale in Mari Evans's book.

5. The end of *I Know Why the Caged Bird Sings* suggests that the narrator will succeed. Having overcome various obstacles, readers sense that she will be able to "fly" free. The other volumes of Angelou's autobiographical series prove her eventual success but not without revealing further difficulties. The other works trace her struggles against the same kinds of dangers she faced in the first book. Threatening her identity, independence, and positive sense of self are racism, shame, and dependent relationships with men—all present in *I Know Why the Caged Bird Sings*. Students may wish to compare the first installment of Angelou's autobiography to another in the series. How are the trials in each of the works similar? What does this suggest about the ease (or lack thereof) of overcoming trauma and hardship? What role do family and community play in this process? What is the role of the individual? The essays by Cudjoe, Lupton, and Smith would serve as particularly helpful guides. Students interested in focusing on racism could consult Johnson, and those interested in reading *Heart of a Woman* will find useful the essay by Neubauer.

## RESOURCES

### Primary Work
*Conversations with Maya Angelou,* edited by Jeffrey M. Elliot (Jackson: University Press of Mississippi, 1989).
Collection of significant interviews with Angelou about her work and life.

### Biography
Marcia Ann Gillespie and others, *Maya Angelou: A Glorious Celebration* (New York: Doubleday, 2008).
Focuses largely on Angelou's private life through pictures and comments from those closest to her.

## Criticism

Joanne M. Braxton, *Maya Angelou's* I Know Why the Caged Bird Sings: *A Casebook* (New York: Oxford University Press, 1999).
Useful essays focused on thematic issues in the autobiography. The book includes two interviews that shed light on Angelou's career.

Mari Evans, ed., *Black Women Writers (1950–1980): A Critical Evaluation* (Garden City, N.Y.: Anchor, 1984).
Collection of essays and biographical and bibliographic information on African American writers. The section on Angelou includes the writer's self-evaluation of her works as well as two essays by literary critics: Selwyn R. Cudjoe's "Maya Angelou and the Autobiographical Statement," which discusses her writing within the context of the tradition of slave narratives; and Sondra O'Neale's "Reconstruction of the Composite Self: New Images of Black Women in Maya Angelou's Continuing Autobiography," which discusses how Angelou challenges and breaks free from stereotypes of black women.

George E. Kent, "Maya Angelou's *I Know Why the Caged Bird Sings* and Black Autobiographical Tradition," *Kansas Quarterly*, 7 (1975): 72–78.
Traces Angelou's use of the gospel and blues traditions in the development of her life story.

Mary Jane Lupton, *Maya Angelou: A Critical Companion* (Westport, Conn.: Greenwood Press, 1998).
Essential guide to all of Angelou's autobiographical works except *A Song Flung up to Heaven*.

Lupton, "Singing the Black Mother: Maya Angelou and Autobiographical Continuity," *Black American Literature Forum*, 24, 2 (1990): 257–276.
Shows how the theme of motherhood is developed in Angelou's works, particularly *I Know Why the Caged Bird Sings*, and discusses earlier scholarship on Angelou.

Dolly A. McPherson, *Order out of Chaos: The Autobiographical Works of Maya Angelou* (New York: Peter Lang, 1990).
Evaluation of narrative technique and style that connects five of Angelou's autobiographical works (through *All God's Children Need Traveling Shoes*).

Carol E. Neubauer, "Displacement and Autobiographical Style in Maya Angelou's *The Heart of a Woman*," *Black American Literature Forum*, 17 (Autumn 1983): 123–129.
Notes parallels between the childhoods of the narrator and her son, Guy, and argues that the narrator's feelings of instability and displacement are transferred to her son.

Sidonie Smith, "The Song of the Caged Bird: Maya Angelou's Quest after Self-Acceptance," *Southern Humanities Review*, 7 (Fall 1973): 365–375.
Early critical essay that highlights and identifies important thematic concerns.

*—Jaimie Young*

⚭

# T. Coraghessan Boyle, *The Tortilla Curtain*
## (New York: Viking, 1995)

A prolific writer of both short and long fiction—usually with a comic or satiric edge—Thomas John Boyle was born on 2 December 1948, in Peekskill, New York; he changed his middle name to the ethnically Irish "Coraghessan" when he was seventeen and publishes as both T. Coraghessan Boyle and T. C. Boyle. By his own account, his working-class Catholic family provided little access to intellectual or cultural capital, and he was an indifferent student through his college years at the State University of New York at Potsdam. Boyle had intended to study music as an undergraduate but discovered both a greater talent and interest in literature and history. Upon completing his bachelor's degree in 1968, Boyle taught high-school English, began writing, and published his first short story, "The OD & Hepatitis RR or Bust," in *The North American Review* (Fall 1972). Boyle leveraged this story into admission to the renowned Iowa Writers' Workshop, where he received his M.F.A. in 1974; he then completed his Ph.D. in English at University of Iowa in 1977. Despite a declared emphasis in nineteenth-century British literature, his dissertation was a creative project that developed into his first book publication, the short-story collection, *Descent of Man* (1979).

Since 1978 Boyle has taught in the English department at the University of Southern California, where he helped found that institution's undergraduate creative writing major. Married since 1974 and the father of three children, Boyle and his family live near Santa Barbara, California, in a Frank Lloyd Wright–designed home that they have restored. Boyle tours widely to promote and read his fiction, continues to teach regularly at USC, gives interviews generously, and maintains an active website with links to reviews, summaries, and study questions about his work. He is a working writer who follows a daily regimen—a four-hour stint at the computer every morning—that is more than simply discipline. In "This Monkey, My Back," (1999) Boyle asserts that, for him, writing "is a habit, an addiction, as powerful and overmastering an urge as putting a bottle to your lips or a spike in your arm. Call it the impulse to make something out of nothing, call it an obsessive-compulsive disorder, call it logorrhea" (http://www.tcboyle. com/page2.html?4).

Whether understood as writing junkie or disciplined craftsman, Boyle has had a highly productive career. As of summer 2009 he had published eight volumes of collected short fiction, twelve novels, and frequent short stories in *The New Yorker, Harper's, The Atlantic Monthly, Granta,* and other prestigious literary venues. Ironically, such a large oeuvre can bring scorn from the literary establishment, but Boyle's productivity has been well rewarded. He is the recipient of, among many honors, two National Endowment for the Arts Fellowships and a Guggenheim Fellowship; numerous O. Henry Awards for his short fiction; a PEN/Faulkner Award for best novel of the year (1988 for *World's End*); and, for *The Tortilla Curtain,* the French *Prix Medicis Etranger* for best foreign novel. A self-styled "wild man of American fiction," Boyle often incorporates historical characters into his work—for example, explorer Mungo Park in *Water Music* (1981); physician and pioneering nutritionist John Harvey Kellogg in *The Road to Wellville* (1993); Stanley, the troubled son of inventor and industrialist Cyrus McCormick, in *Riven Rock* (1998); sex researcher Dr. Alfred C. Kinsey in *The Inner Circle* (2004); and architect Frank Lloyd Wright in *The Women* (2008)—but the author's creative interests also take him in more-contemporary directions. *Drop City* (2003) explores the 1970s drug scene, *A Friend of the Earth* (2000) looks at environmental and ecological crises from both the 1980s and 1990s and an imagined 2025, and *Talk Talk* (2006) considers the psychological as well as financial impact of identity theft. While these topics may seem wildly dissimilar, Boyle claimed in a 2003 interview with Robert Birnbaum that all his "books are allied in one way or another."

Like Boyle's other novels set in contemporary times, *The Tortilla Curtain* is a satire that, while it focuses specifically on illegal immigration, critiques modern American society in other ways as well. Two worlds—those of the privileged white citizens of Los Angeles and of illegal Mexican immigrants—literally collide in the first pages of the novel when Delaney Mossbacher hits Candido Rincon with his car. Delaney and his real-estate agent wife, Kyra, live in an exclusive upper-middle-class suburb, Arroyo Blanco Estates; Candido and his pregnant wife, America, survive in hand-to-mouth fashion by camping in Topanga Canyon and seeking day-labor as they try to raise enough money to secure a modest apartment, their symbol of the American dream of financial safety. The two couples' lives intersect in both accidental and intentional ways; the novel culminates as fire and flood devastate their (unequally) shared environment.

## TOPICS FOR DISCUSSION AND RESEARCH

1. Boyle appears to maintain ironic neutrality while exploring the nature of cultural and social misunderstanding, economic struggle and middle-class materialism, and personal and environmental catastrophe. Critics often consider his ironic detachment a successful approach to such provocative content. *Chicago Tribune* critic Jeff Kunerth affirms that the novel "takes an unflattering look at the politically charged issue of immigration from two divergent perspectives and comes up with a compelling story of myopic misunderstanding and mutual tragedy." Tobias Jones of the *London Literary Review* agrees: "Boyle has written a political novel that is both funny and serious; he hits his targets with venomous prose and parody, whilst his humor always pulls him up short of sentimentalism. He sketches the whole panorama of animalistic activity and, above all, he shows what happens to liberal humanism when the 'human' is forgotten." Other critics are less enamored. Scott Spencer contends that because the Mossbachers are so socially unconscious and narcissistic, the novel's commentary "rings hollow." Indeed, "where the socially engaged novel once offered critique, Mr. Boyle provides contempt. . . . Contempt is a dangerous emotion, luring us into believing that we understand more than we do. Contempt causes

us to jeer rather than speak, to poke at rather than touch." For a more detailed look at critical response, consult both Boyle's website (where multiple reviews are easily available) and Spencer's 1995 *New York Times* assessment. Defend or attack one or more of these responses using examples from the novel to support your opinion.

2. Scholars also examine the success of the novel as a work of art and explore the implications of Boyle's satiric take on modern social issues. Does the structure of multiple narrators work, or does the authorial voice intrude and thereby disrupt the subjectivity? Are the Mossbachers relatively flat (and therefore unsympathetic) as characters, while our compassion is drawn to Candido and America because we know their complicated personal histories, their tragedies? How does the image of the coyote as both predator and survivor expose and illuminate naturalist-writer Delaney's understanding—and that of the reader—of the migration of the human species? Is the end of the novel left open to the possibilities of a shared future, an ironic gesture, or an unsatisfying cop-out? For an insightful close reading of the novel as well as a measured critique of its strengths and shortcomings, see Peter Freese's "T. Coraghessan Boyle's *The Tortilla Curtain:* A Case Study in the Genesis of Xenophobia" (2000).

3. The timeliness and political nature of the novel continue to engage scholarly interest. The novel takes place in an explosive era, when the Los Angeles riots of 1992, the Malibu/Topanga fire of 1993, and the passage in 1994 of the anti-immigrant California Proposition 187 were immediately relevant. However, not only current political and social events ground the narrative; Boyle's deep literary knowledge enables him to connect this highly contemporary story thematically to earlier landmark fictions. One is French Enlightenment philosopher Voltaire's 1759 satire *Candide: or, The Optimist;* Voltaire's eponymous hero is, like Boyle's, "a hapless picaro traveling in search of the best of all possible worlds" (Elisabeth Schäfer-Wünsche, p. 404). Two American Depression-era classics also offer context. John Steinbeck's 1939 opus *The Grapes of Wrath* provides the epigraph as well as themes of migration and exploitation and the formal structure that alternates the narrative voice from chapter to chapter. The protagonist of William Faulkner's 1932 *Light in August,* the racially mixed Joe Christmas, becomes *The Tortilla Curtain's* Jose Navidad, a parallel though now secondary character who reflects the disturbing impact of racism. For a reading of the novel that not only explores its literary connections but also gives a Marxist interpretation of class conflict and eco-racism by comparing the novel to the contemporary work of social commentator Mike Davis, see Gregory Myerson's "*Tortilla Curtain* and *The Ecology of Fear*" (2004). Elisabeth Schäfer-Wünsche also reads the novel as in dialogue with Davis's work. How does a reading of the novel change when put in the context of such literary references, or when comparing *The Tortilla Curtain* to the work of Davis?

4. Boyle's examination of contemporary American society invites interdisciplinary academic inquiry. Students might find particularly fruitful an engagement with one such methodology, whiteness studies, which asserts that the concept of race is a social construct conferring privilege on those identified as white

while simultaneously keeping nonwhites in subordinated positions. This approach argues that Kyra and Delaney Mossbacher enjoy forms of unearned privilege of which they are largely unaware but intensely protective. Despite their self-perception as people of enlightened, liberal leanings, the Mossbachers increasingly identify loss of privilege (material goods, safety, access to nature) with the presence of nonwhites. The Arroyo Blanco homeowners build a gate and then walls to keep out the undifferentiated undesirables (both coyotes and the poor), though ironically it is these privileged few who abuse the Mexican laborers (America is paid for fewer hours than she works, Candido is cheated out of a day's pay, white teens destroy the couple's camp) and impede the Rincons' ability to achieve financial stability. For a more complete discussion, consult "On Whiteness in T. Coraghessan Boyle's *The Tortilla Curtain*," by Heather J. Hicks. Do the Mossbachers enjoy privileges because they are white, or is their race incidental to their material success?

5. Scholars engaged in studies of immigration into the United States from Mexico and other Latin American countries have found *The Tortilla Curtain* to be an illuminating literary text against which to read historical, political, and social concerns. In such readings, the walled and gated community of Arroyo Blanco Estates becomes a microcosmic representation of the dominant culture of the United States. For example, like the United States as a whole, the residents of Arroyo Blanco—note how all homes in the development must be painted in one of three shades of white—not only financially exploit desperately needy immigrants like Candido but also hypocritically fear and blame the poor for imagined crimes. See Kathy Knapp's article, cited below, for more information on both the phenomenon of the gated community and American immigration policy over the decades of the twentieth century as both relate to *The Tortilla Curtain*. Are your ideas about immigration altered by this novel?

# RESOURCES

## Primary Works

*T. C. Boyle* <www.tcboyle.com/> [accessed 13 November 2009].
Boyle's official website; it includes interviews, reviews, summaries, and more.

"T. C. Boyle: Author of *Drop City* Talks with Robert Birnbaum," *identitytheory. com* (19 March 2003) <http://www.identitytheory.com/interviews/birnbaum94.html> [accessed 13 November 2009].
A lengthy interview covering several of Boyle's works.

"This Monkey, My Back" <http://www.tcboyle.com/page2.html?4> [accessed 13 November 2009].
Boyle discusses his mentors and his method.

## Criticism

Peter Freese, "T. Coraghessan Boyle's *The Tortilla Curtain:* A Case Study in the Genesis of Xenophobia," in *English Literatures in International Contexts,*

edited by Heinz Antor and Klaus Stierstorfer (Heidelberg: Winter, 2000), pp. 221–243.
Traces Delaney Mossbacher's fear-driven descent into racial intolerance.

Heather J. Hicks, "On Whiteness in T. Coraghessan Boyle's *The Tortilla Curtain,*" *Critique,* 45 (Fall 2003): 43–64.
Argues that Boyle attempts "to delineate the contemporary meanings of whiteness through a set of metaphoric relations and satirical figures."

Kathy Knapp, "'Ain't No Friend of Mine': Immigration Policy, The Gated Community, and the Problem with the Disposable Worker in T. C. Boyle's *Tortilla Curtain,*" *Atenea,* 28 (December 2008): 121–134.
Explores the hypocrisy of American immigration policy and the desire of the dominant culture to "render . . . workers [like America and Candido] invisible."

Gregory Meyerson, "*Tortilla Curtain* and *The Ecology of Fear,*" *Contracorriente: A Journal on Social History and Literature in Latin America,* 2 (Fall 2004): 67–91.
Looks at Boyle's literary referents, as well as the intersections of his novel and Southern California urban theorist Mike Davis's *City of Quartz* (1990) and *Ecology of Fear* (1998).

Elisabeth Schäfer-Wünsche, "Borders and Catastrophes: T. C. Boyle's Californian Ecology," in *Space in America: Theory, History, Culture,* edited by Klaus Benesch and Kerstin Schmidt (Amsterdam & New York: Rodopi, 2005), pp. 401–417.
Interprets Boyle's "fictionalization of Californian spaces" as both ironic nature writing and a "dialogic reading" of texts by urban theorist Mike Davis, who writes about the effect of built environments on natural settings.

Scott Spencer, "The Pilgrim of Topanga Creek," *New York Times,* 3 September 1995 <http://www.nytimes.com/books/98/02/08/home/boyle-tortilla.html?_r=1&scp=1&sq=Tortilla%20Curtain&st=cse> [accessed 13 November 2009].
Review that questions the success of the novel.

*—Patricia L. Kalayjian*

꒰◯◯◯꒱

# Octavia Butler, *Kindred*
(Garden City, N.Y.: Doubleday, 1979)

Octavia Estelle Butler, a decidedly unsentimental writer dubbed the "Black Oracle" of science fiction/fantasy, was born in Pasadena, California, on 22 June 1947 but had roots in Louisiana. Her father, a shoe-shine man, died when she was young, so Butler was raised by her mother, a domestic worker. Nicknamed "Junie" as a child (short for Junior, perhaps, as her mother was also Octavia),

Butler read voraciously, despite being diagnosed with dyslexia. Extremely shy and introspective, she began writing short stories at age ten, using her writing to stave off loneliness. Butler graduated from Pasadena City College with an associate of arts degree in 1968; she later attended California State University, Los Angeles, and took creative-writing classes at UCLA. During the early years of her career, Butler lived alone in Los Angeles, cared for her mother, and wrote and worked at various jobs, including dishwasher and telemarketer. Later, while she regularly gave lectures on various college campuses, contributed to National Public Radio programs, and granted numerous interviews, she claimed to be "comfortably asocial, a hermit in the middle of Los Angeles."

A self-proclaimed "slow writer" with "limited literary talent," Butler has said that she had to "learn my craft." In 1976 she published her first novel, *Patternmaster*, part of a five-book series about telepaths connected to each other in a rigid hierarchical structure; this foreshadowed Butler's interest in hierarchies dictated by race and class. In 1999, a few years after her mother's death, Butler moved to Seattle, where she continued to publish her work. Little else is known about Butler's personal life. Butler credits the portrayal of limited and often deficient black characters in science fiction for her early inspiration: she remarked in a 2000 *New York Times* interview that there were only "occasional characters or characters who were so feeble-witted that they couldn't manage anything. I wrote myself in, since I'm me and I'm here and I'm writing."

A prodigious feminist writer, Butler is one of the first African American women to secure membership in this male-dominated science-fiction club, as well as the first to address race and gender and its impact on future generations in a substantial way. Using science fiction as a medium for social commentary, Butler authored fourteen books—of which *Fledgling* (2005) was her final—and published several short stories in anthologies and magazines, for which she won the most esteemed awards in the science-fiction world. "Speech Sounds" won a Hugo Award for best short story of 1984, and "Bloodchild" won the 1984 Nebula Award and the 1985 Hugo for best novella. She also became the first science-fiction writer to receive the prestigious MacArthur Foundation Fellowship or "Genius Award" in 1995 following publication of *Parable of the Sower* (1993), a novel about the perils of not paying attention to the world around us—inevitable social, environmental, and economic decay. Butler's books have been translated into ten languages and offer powerful multicultural revisions of history, with complex articulations of human nature and provocative visions of the future.

As she does in many of her other works, Butler interrogates the relationship among race, politics, and sexuality in *Kindred* (1979) not only by uncovering some historical truths about American slavery but also by reflecting the binaries presented by race (and gender) in the 1960s and 1970s. She is among several black writers, including Tananarive Due, Nalo Hopkinson, Phyllis Alesia Perry, Toni Morrison, Gloria Naylor, Jewelle Gomez, Steven Barnes, Charles Johnson, Toni Cade Bambara, and Maryse Condé, to use themes and experiences from the African diaspora in fantasy or "speculative" fiction. *Kindred* was the first of Butler's novels to garner critical acclaim, leading to its republication in the Beacon Black

Women Writers Series in 1988 and the publication of a twenty-fifth anniversary edition in 2004.

*Kindred* was initially rejected by several publishers who were unable to envision a science-fiction novel set in the antebellum South as opposed to one set on a planet in the future. Engaging multiple audiences, including science-fiction aficionados as well as those in the disciplines of women's studies and African American studies, *Kindred's* popularity is attributable in part to its accessibility and its hybrid nature. Butler often bristled at "boring" questions about how to define this novel. She consistently responded by saying that she was a "writer," suggesting that the important question is whether she tells a good story.

*Kindred* employs time travel to send narrator Edana "Dana" Franklin from 1976 to the nineteenth century to experience plantation life in Maryland. There, Dana must make the difficult choice of saving the life of the slave owner Rufus Weylin, who will one day father the children of her ancestor Alice Greenwood. The resulting birth of Rufus and Alice's daughter Hagar ensures Dana's existence in the present. Critics see *Kindred* as somewhat of a departure from Butler's typical futuristic narratives from *Patternmaster* (1975) to *Clay's Ark* (1984); in fact, it is her only novel, besides *Wild Seed* (1980), that is set in the past.

Butler began working on *Kindred* while in college. It was a black classmate's critical attitude and disdain for his parents' "humility" and acquiescence that motivated her to tell this story. *Kindred* draws on this disconcerting attitude—one that reveals the palpable disillusionment and the failure to assess the historical context that disconnects the younger generation from its predecessors—to explore the meaning of *lived* history. Butler notes, too, that *Kindred* helped her "to resolve [her own] feelings" toward the indignities her mother willingly suffered in her position as a domestic worker: in a 2004 interview with Daniel Burton-Rose she said, "What I wanted to teach in writing *Kindred* was that people who did the work my mother did were not frightened or timid or cowards; they were heroes." Timothy Spaulding argues that Butler "use[s] the fantastic as a vehicle for conflating the past and the present" in order to emphasize the lasting effect of slavery on twentieth-century African American identity. Even as the past is central to Dana's mission, Butler insists that her work "is not about the past; it's about the present and the future" (Burton-Rose Interview).

Butler died on 24 February 2006 in Seattle. Her work is inherently interdisciplinary, her themes are universal, and it speaks to many of the existing underlying implications of race.

*Kindred* has attracted a significant amount of critical attention. In addition to the articles listed in RESOURCES, some two dozen studies are cited in the MLA bibliography. Students interested in general approaches to her work might consult Christopher N. Okonkwo's *A Spirit of Dialogue: Incarnations of Ogbanje, the Born-to-Die, in African American Literature* (University of Tennessee Press, 2008) for a study of the uses of myth in African American literature and Ashraf H. A. Rushdy's *Remembering Generations: Race and Family in Contemporary African American Fiction* (University of North Carolina Press, 2001), which discusses *Kindred* with regard to slave-family relationships.

## TOPICS FOR DISCUSSION AND RESEARCH

1. *Kindred* is the first novel to have a contemporary character confront the reality of history and experience slavery. The novel opens: "The trouble began long before June 9, 1976, when I became aware of it, but June 9 is the day I remember. It was my twenty-sixth birthday. It was the day I met Rufus—the day he called me to him for the first time." Apparently, Dana's "trouble" began "long before" her violent physical encounter with the past. Butler's narrative structure challenges her protagonist (and readers) to examine actively the relationship between slavery and contemporary America. How do you understand this relationship? How well are you able to negotiate the ambiguities presented by the conflation of time? Why does Dana travel through time? Why is her first interaction with the past rendered so ambiguously? What is the "trouble" to which she refers? Why does the past intrude so violently on Dana's present?

2. There is critical consensus that *Kindred* is a feminist re-envisioning of nineteenth-century black women's slave narratives, such as Mary Prince's *The History of Mary Prince, a West Indian Slave* (1831), Harriet Jacobs's *Incidents in the Life of a Slave Girl* (1861), and Lucy Delaney's *From the Darkness Cometh the Light* (1891). Students will find it profitable to research slave narratives and then consider how Butler rewrites the traditional narrative through the "enslaved" Alice and the "emancipated" Dana. In what ways do these characters challenge those designations? How do they invite us to think through present social concerns? What do you see as this narrative's relevancy? Is this narrative technique the best vehicle to illustrate the connection between the past and the present? For background reading on the structure of slave narratives, consult Robert Levine's "The Slave Narrative and the Revolutionary Tradition of American Autobiography," in *The Cambridge Companion to the African American Slave Narrative,* edited by Audrey A. Fisch (Cambridge, England: Cambridge University Press, 2007). See also Frances Smith Foster's introductions to *Witnessing Slavery: The Development of Ante-Bellum Slave Narratives* (Madison: University of Wisconsin Press, 1994) and *Written by Herself: Literary Production by African American Women, 1746–1892* (Bloomington: Indiana University Press, 1993).

3. Critic Guy Mark Foster argues that some scholars focus their critical readings of *Kindred* almost entirely on slavery to the exclusion of "the narrative of consensual interracial desire," that is, Dana and Kevin's marriage. Yet, in Dana's character, Butler has constructed a contemporary black woman who reflects the complexity of her past and present. Her marriage to a white male adds another layer to this complexity. What is Butler's purpose? What do you make of Dana's silence on issues of race and politics? What does this narrative suggest about the possibilities for Dana and Kevin's relationship and, by extension, black/white relationships?

4. Influenced by the politics of its time—the 1960s black arts and power movements (resistance to integrationist principles represented by mainstream culture) and the emergence of "colorblind" principles of the 1970s, but well before critical whiteness studies (whiteness as a racial construct that functions as invisible power) in the 1990s—*Kindred* is even more important today in the

wake of changing conceptions of multiculturalism. How have civic discourses about race changed over time? How has the 2008 election of the first black president of the United States complicated your reading of the novel?

5. Butler's protagonist loses her left arm on her last trip home. Philosopher Paul Ricoeur suggests that "the past survives by leaving its trace." If Dana's dismemberment functions as a trace of memory, what does this dismemberment signify? How might the loss of an arm encourage her to re-member herself and the past, and to take control of her own agency? How might this loss afford Dana a new and unique perspective on her history? How will her loss contribute to Dana's "re-memory," making her past part of her present?

## RESOURCES

### Primary Works

Daniel Burton-Rose, "Reinventing Our Heroes," *LiP Magazine* (Summer 2004) <http://www.lipmagazine.org/articles/octaviabutlerinterview_2004.pdf> [accessed 16 November 2009].
An interview covering hierarchy, relevancy of slave narratives, and various aspects of several of Butler's novels.

Randall Kenan, "An Interview with Octavia E. Butler," *Callaloo*, 14, 2 (1991): 495–514.
Interview covering biographical and creative elements in Butler's works.

Charles H. Rowell, "An Interview with Octavia E. Butler," *Callaloo*, 20, 1 (1997): 47–66.
A lengthy interview covering biographical and creative elements related to Butler's works.

### Criticism

Dorothy Allison, "The Future of Female: Octavia Butler's Mother Lode," in *Reading Black, Reading Feminist: A Critical Anthology*, edited by Henry Louis Gates Jr. (New York: Meridian, 1990), pp. 471–478.
Explores Butler's construction of "femaleness."

Robert Crossley, Introduction to Butler's *Kindred* (Boston: Beacon, 1988).
A critical introduction later used as an afterword in the twenty-fifth anniversary edition. Crossley provides an overview of the novel and its issues and places it in a critical context.

Anne Donadey, "African American and Francophone Postcolonial Memory: Octavia Butler's *Kindred* and Assia Djebar's *La femme sans sépulture*," *Research in African Literatures*, 39 (Fall 2008): 65–81.
Examines important elements in the work of both authors—the need to represent the unspeakable and to resist historical amnesia.

Frances Smith Foster, "Octavia Butler's Black Female Future Fiction," *Extrapolation: A Journal of Science and Fantasy*, 23 (Summer 1982): 37–49.
Analyzes Butler's work with a specific focus on race and gender.

Guy Mark Foster, "'Do I Look Like Someone You Can Come Home to from Where You May Be Going?': Re-mapping Interracial anxiety in Octavia Butler's *Kindred*," *African American Review*, 41 (Spring 2007): 143–165.
Analyzes the subversive nature of Butler's depiction of a bi-temporal interracial relationship.

Sandra Govan, "Homage to Tradition: Octavia Butler Renovates the Historical Novel," *MELUS*, 13, 1–2 (1986): 79–96.
Examines the similarities between the nineteenth-century female emancipatory narrative and Butler's narrative.

Angelyn Mitchell, "Not Enough of the Past: Feminist Revisions of Slavery in Octavia E. Butler's *Kindred*," *MELUS*, 26 (Fall 2001): 51–75.
Examines Butler's revision of dominant themes such as sexuality, motherhood, individualism, and community in the nineteenth-century female emancipatory narrative.

Sarah Eden Schiff, "Recovering (from) the Double: Fiction As Historical Revision in Octavia E. Butler's *Kindred*," *Arizona Quarterly*, 65 (Spring 2009): 107–138.
Examines the ways that Butler attempts to destabilize the master narrative of American history and rewrite it as a curative narrative of memory and history.

A. Timothy Spaulding, *Re-forming the Past: History, The Fantastic, and the Postmodern Slave Narrative* (Columbus: Ohio State University Press, 2005).
Offers a Postmodernist approach to reading and understanding the slave narrative by examining contemporary revisions of those narratives that use elements of the fantastic to conflate the past and the present.

Marc Steinberg, "Inverting History in Octavia Butler's Postmodern Slave Narrative," *African American Review*, 38 (Fall 2004): 467–477.
Analyzes Butler's work in the context of Postmodernist writing.

Kelley Wagers, "Seeing 'from the Far Side of the Hill': Narrative, History, and Understanding in *Kindred* and *The Chaneysville Incident*," *MELUS*, 34 (Spring 2009): 23–45.
Argues that two contemporary African American historical novels, by Butler and David Bradley, use the intersections between imaginative narrative and historical knowledge to teach their protagonists a lesson about the enduring presence of American slavery.

—*Annette Harris Powell*

## Raymond Carver, *Where I'm Calling From*

(New York: Atlantic Monthly Press, 1988)

"Get in, get out. Don't linger. Go on!" is how Raymond Carver (1938–1988) has described the "unmistakable signature" of his writing. Acknowledged as a writer who helped rescue the short story as an art form from its extensive lull, Carver is considered the most influential American short-story writer since Ernest Hemingway. Carver's style is marked by precision of language and realistic, often stark, description. He drew inspiration for his fiction from life; his characters' bouts with alcoholism, financial struggles, and destructive relationships parallel his own. Although Carver began to concentrate on poetry late in his career—publishing six collections of poetry during his lifetime, including *Where Water Comes Together with Other Water* (1985) and *Ultramarine* (1986)—he was best known for his short fiction, published in six collections during his lifetime. One of these, *Cathedral* (1984), was nominated for both a National Book Award and a Pulitzer Prize. His other honors include a National Endowment for the Arts Discovery Award (1970), a Guggenheim Fellowship (1978), a Wallace E. Stegner Fellowship (1972), and a National Endowment for the Arts Fellowship for fiction (1980). He taught at numerous institutions, including the Iowa Writers Workshop; the Berkeley, Santa Cruz, and Santa Barbara campuses of the University of California; and Syracuse University and was a Distinguished Writer-in-Residence at the University of Texas, El Paso. In May 1988 Carver was inducted into the American Academy and Institute of Arts and Letters.

Raymond Clevie Carver was born on 25 May 1938 in Clatskanie, Oregon, on the Columbia River, where his father, Clevie Raymond "C. R." Carver, worked in a sawmill, and his mother, Ella Casey Carver, worked as a waitress and sales clerk. His parents struggled economically, and Carver's early life was marked by his father's alcoholism and domestic violence. In 1942 Carver's family moved to Yakima, Washington, where he grew up hunting, fishing, and reading Mickey Spillane novels and magazines such as *Sports Afield* and *Outdoor Life*. Soon after graduating from Davis High School in 1956, Carver followed his father to California to work in a sawmill. In June 1957 Carver married his sixteen-year-old high-school sweetheart, Maryann Burk, and moved them both to California. Their first child, Christine La Rae, was born in December 1957 at the same hospital where Carver's father was being treated for alcoholism. A son, Vance Lindsay, was born the next year. With a wife and family to support, he worked a series of "crap jobs"— custodian, deliveryman, dictionary salesman, and library assistant. Scenes from his family life permeate Carver's fiction. "Distance," for example, reflects the divide growing between the couple because of parental responsibilities; "Chef's House" mirrors their attempts at reconciliation; and "The Bath," later rewritten and retitled "A Small, Good Thing," elaborates an accident in which his daughter was hit by a car.

In 1958 Carver began taking classes at Chico State College in California, where he enrolled in a creative-writing course taught by John Gardner, who remained a major influence; Carver later admitted he "had felt Gardner looking over his shoulder when he wrote, approving or disapproving of certain words, phrases, and strategies" (McInerney). Carver transferred to Humboldt State College, where he earned a bachelor's degree in English in 1963; while there, he published his first story, "The Pastoral," in the *Western Humanities Review* in the spring of 1962. In the same year, his first poem, "The Brass Ring," was published in *Targets*. With the help of a modest scholarship ($500), he attended the Iowa Writers' Workshop, where later, in 1973, he returned as a visiting lecturer and taught with John Cheever. Later, Carver admitted that mostly the two writers drank heavily.

Carver's drinking, which began long before his return to Iowa, accompanied other problems. In 1967 he was working as a textbook editor when his father died after several hospitalizations. In debt, he was forced to declare bankruptcy. (He filed again in 1974.) In the same year, some brightness in the form of recognition and validation of his work appeared; his story "Will You Please Be Quiet, Please?" was included in *The Best American Short Stories 1967*. Many of Carver's characters who struggle with alcoholism were self-inspired. Carver experienced the same tremors that Tiny, in "Where I'm Calling From," has when he tries to stop drinking, and "Gazebo" reflects the same kind of poor decisions made by Carver while drinking.

Carver's first collection, *Will You Please Be Quiet, Please?* (1977), was nominated for a National Book Award, solidifying his reputation as an exemplary writer. Soon after its publication, he quit drinking with the help of Alcoholics Anonymous, separated from his wife, and began a relationship with the poet Tess Gallagher, whom he married in 1988. Carver's next collection, *What We Talk about When We Talk about Love*, was published in 1981. Edited by Gordon Lish (a highly regarded writing coach with whom Carver had become acquainted earlier when trying to publish a short story in *Esquire*), the collection drew critical attention for what was deemed Carver's "minimalist" approach to writing, a description Carver later protested and tried to correct. By this time Carver was a professor of English at Syracuse University. When the American Academy and Institute of Arts and Letters awarded him its first Mildred and Harold Strauss Livings Fellowship in 1983, Carver left teaching to become a full-time writer.

In 1982 John Gardner selected "Cathedral" for *The Best American Short Stories* series. Carver cites the writing of this story as a pivotal moment in his career. He soon switched editors after a falling-out with Lish and published *Cathedral* (1984), a collection of stories with a more expansive style than found in his previous writing. In 1986 Carver served as guest editor of *The Best American Short Stories*. The following year, he was diagnosed with lung cancer. Carver died on 2 August 1988. Later that year, Gallagher published his posthumous collection of selected works, *Where I'm Calling From* (1988), regarded by many critics as his capstone work. With these stories, Carver made a deliberate effort to move away from the "minimalist" narrative and diction of the stories published while working with Lish. Like Carver's earlier stories, they realistically depict loneliness, pain, and despair without authorial commentary, but the suffering of his characters is lessened by a movement toward healing and sometimes redemption as characters look for and find connection to others.

Raymond Carver has attracted as much critical attention as any modern short-story writer. The MLA bibliography lists some 280 critical articles about his work. Students beginning study of Carver's stories must first seek reliable guidance. Ewing Campbell and Kirk Nesset, cited below are good starting points, and Arthur M. Saltzman's *Understanding Raymond Carver* is perhaps the best. Carver's relationship with his heavy-handed editor Gordon Lish is an interesting study. The Library of America edition of Carver's works (2009) includes "Beginners," the unedited version of "What We Talk about When We Talk about Love" that Carver submitted to Lish, which indicates the significant role Lish played in shaping Carver's writing style.

## TOPICS FOR DISCUSSION AND RESEARCH

1. Like his earlier work, most of the stories in *Where I'm Calling From* feature working-class characters. Carver affectionately referred to his working-class characters as "my people," those who, despite their lack of social mobility and economic restrictions, lived their lives the best way they could manage, as in "Chef's House," "Feathers," and "Elephant." Students interested in Carver's people would benefit from Ben Harker's analysis of images of "socio-economic disempowerment and diminished class consciousness" in Carver's work. Also useful is Paul Lauter's "Under Construction: Working-Class Writing," in *New Working Class Studies,* edited by John Russo and Sherry Lee Linkon (Ithaca, N. Y.: Cornell University Press, 2005), pp. 63–77. Although Lauter does not specifically address Carver, he identifies features of working-class writing that provide an excellent framework for discussing Carver's fiction. Lauter reminds students to consider how class is related not only to thematic issues but also narrative form.

2. Surely inspired by his life experience, alcoholism remains a major theme throughout Carver's fiction, many of his characters suffering from various degrees of alcoholism as they struggle to overcome the "dis-ease" in their lives. In "Why Don't You Dance?" a middle-aged man relinquishes the possessions from his failed marriage, presumably ending because of his drinking. The two couples in "What We Talk about When We Talk about Love" use gin as a social lubricant that enables them to speak candidly about their definitions of love. "Chef's House" represents an alcoholic's denial of his addiction. A man is inspired to reconcile his marriage which failed due to excessive drinking after listening to the story of a fellow patient at a treatment center in "Where I'm Calling From." Students interested in investigating the realism of Carver's depiction of alcoholism can use as a model John Magee's interpretation of "Chef's House"; those interested in tracing the effects of Carver's own struggles with alcoholism and recovery will find useful the biographical-based analysis in Chad Wriglesworth's "Raymond Carver and Alcoholics Anonymous: A Narrative Under the 'Surface of Things,'" in Sandra Lee Kleppe and Robert Miltner's collection (pages 132–153). Students may also wish, as some literary critics have, to trace the symbolic and narrative functions of alcohol and drinking in Carver's fiction. As Kirk Nesset observes, drinking often fills in when characters "cannot speak their pain."

3. Raymond Carver's work has been adapted for the screen in *Short Cuts* (1993), directed by Robert Altman, and *Jindabyne* (2006), directed by Ray Lawrence. Both films change Carver's Pacific Northwest setting to, respectively, Los Angeles and the town of Jindabyne in New South Wales, Australia. *Jindabyne* is based on "So Much Water So Close to Home"; *Short Cuts* uses that story, as well, combining it with eight others, five of which are also in *Where I'm Calling From*. Students may wish to view one or both films with the aim of comparing them to the original stories, paying particular attention to changes in plot and character (Altman changes and collapses characters, even inventing new ones) and how these changes affect overall theme. Students might also consider whether the screen versions are more or less effective than their literary counterparts in conveying certain themes such as love, family, death, marriage, and voyeurism, and whether or not the film versions are able to capture Carver's distinctive narrative style.

4. Arthur M. Saltzman describes Carver as a "diligent refiner of sentences," a quality that critics connect to "minimalism." Carver, however, loathed the minimalist "tag" and felt it "suggests the idea of a narrow vision of life, low ambitions, and limited cultural horizons" (interview with Del Pozzo in Stull). A controversy regarding Carver's minimalist style jeopardized the acclaim that positioned Carver as the "father of minimalism." Motoko Rich's *New York Times* article, "The Real Carver: Expansive or Minimal," describes how Carver's style was altered by the severe editing of Lish, Carver's editor at Alfred A. Knopf, who published *What We Talk about When We Talk about Love*. Students can view Lish's alterations by examining "Beginners," the original version of "What We Talk about When We Talk about Love" submitted to Lish; it is available in *Raymond Carver: Collected Stories* (2009). Students may also wish to examine versions of the Lish-edited stories in *Where I'm Calling From*. For this collection he revised "So Much Water So Close to Home," and the story "The Bath" is restored, added to, and renamed "A Small, Good Thing." After comparing versions of the stories, students may wish to weigh in on the discussion of minimalism in Carver's fiction. For more on minimalism and Raymond Carver, consult Arthur Bethea's volume (especially the conclusion, which distinguishes between technical and ideological versions of minimalism), Nesset, Saltzman, and Trussler.

5. Many of Carver's characters are hindered by silences and inarticulateness. In "'What's to Say': Silence in Raymond Carver's 'Feathers,'" Laura Champion outlines studies of Carver's uses of silence, while also advancing her own. She notes: "Often it is not direct discourse, words spoken between characters, but characters' inability to communicate that becomes important in developing characters' attitudes, motives, weaknesses, or hopelessness." In stories such as "Gazebo" and "Why Don't You Dance?" characters arrive on the cusp of verbal expression only to fail with open-ended silence, highlighting their own inadequacies and those of language. Silence in stories such as "Feathers" and "A Small, Good Thing" contribute to the development of characters and advance meaning in the same manner as negative space in a photograph. Students may wish to extend Champion's examination to other stories that feature silence: "Careful," "Where I'm Calling From," "A Serious Talk," and "Cathedral."

## RESOURCES

### Primary Works

Marshall Bruce Gentry and William L. Stull, eds., *Conversations with Raymond Carver* (Jackson: University Press of Mississippi, 1990).
The most comprehensive collection of interviews with Carver.

*Raymond Carver: Collected Stories,* edited by William L. Stull and Maureen Carroll (New York: Library of America, 2009).
A comprehensive collection of Carver's stories, including sketches and works discovered after his death. Original and published versions of stories allow readers to see the extent of Gordon Lish's editing of Carver's work.

Stull, "Prose as Architecture: Two Interviews with Raymond Carver," *Clockwatch Review,* 10, 1–2 (1995) <http://titan.iwu.edu/~jplath/carver.html> [accessed 18 November 2009].
Two interviews translated into English, one conducted in Paris in 1987 by French journalist Claude Grimal, titled "Stories Don't Come out of Thin Air," and the second conducted by Silvia Del Pozzo for *Panorama,* a Milanese weekly, in 1986, titled "I'm Sort of Their Father." Both appeared upon the publication of a foreign-language translation of Carver's work.

### Biography

Sam Halpert, *Raymond Carver: An Oral Biography* (Iowa City: University of Iowa Press, 1995).
A collection of vignettes about Carver by his family, friends, and colleagues, arranged in chronological order. These stories shed light on Carver's life and reveal connections between the stories and biographical details.

Carol Sklenicka, *Raymond Carver: A Writer's Life* (New York: Scribner, 2009).
The most detailed look at Carver's life available, with generous attention to the writing.

### Criticism

Arthur Bethea, *Technique and Sensibility in the Fiction and Poetry of Raymond Carver* (New York: Routledge, 2001).
Critical approaches to Carver's fiction and poetry. Bethea considers stylistic concerns such as Carver's use of unreliable narrators, symbolism, and omission, as well as themes such as alcoholism, family, death, and marriage.

Ewing Campbell, *Raymond Carver: A Study of the Short Fiction* (New York: Twayne, 1992).
A critical study of short fiction tracing stages in Carver's development as a writer from what Campbell refers to as his "apprenticeship" through his "mastery and continued growth." Also included are Carver's essay "On Writing," an interview conducted by Larry McCaffery, and several critical essays.

Laurie Champion, "'What's to Say': Silence in Raymond Carver's 'Feathers,'" *Studies in Short Fiction,* 34 (Spring 1997): 193–201.
Focuses on the various meanings of silences in Carver's "Feathers" and provides a more positive reading of them than in previous scholarship; offers insights that could be applied to other stories by Carver featuring silence.

Ben Harker, "'To be there, inside and not be there': Raymond Carver and Class," *Textual Practice,* 21, 4 (2007): 715–736.
Critical examination of class in Carver's work through a biographical context.

Sandra Lee Kleppe and Robert Miltner, eds., *New Paths to Raymond Carver: Critical Essays on His Life, Fiction, and Poetry* (Columbia: University of South Carolina Press, 2008).
Collection of critical essays addressing Carver's poems and fiction from an international group of scholars. They cover a range of thematic and aesthetic issues shedding light on his thematic concerns (death, voyeurism, television, alcohol) and technique (diction, humor, musical quality).

John Magee, "Carver's 'Chef's House,'" *Explicator,* 56, 2 (1997): 111–112.
Interpretation of Carver's "Chef's House" as "an accurate step-by-step portrayal of an alcoholic's denial"; a similar approach could be taken to other stories about alcoholic characters.

Jay McInerney, "A Still, Small Voice," *New York Times Book Review,* 6 August 1989, p. 1.
Recapitulation of Carver's life and influence by a former student.

Adam Meyer, *Raymond Carver* (New York: Twayne, 1995).
A literary biography of Carver, including critical summaries of selected stories from each volume of his published work and a chapter devoted to his poetry.

Kirk Nesset, *The Stories of Raymond Carver: A Critical Study* (Athens: Ohio University Press, 1995).
Critical examination of Carver's work with attention to the themes of love, the minimalist aesthetic, insularity and self-enlargement, and communication and control.

Motoko Rich, "The Real Carver: Expansive or Minimal?" *New York Times,* 17 October 2007, p. 1.
Identifies Gordon Lish, Carver's former editor, as the creator of Carver's minimalist writing style and explains Tess Gallagher's attempts to republish the stories collected in *What We Talk about When We Talk about Love* in their original expansive form.

Randolph Paul Runyon, *Reading Raymond Carver* (Syracuse, N.Y.: Syracuse University Press, 1992).
Critical readings of stories from *Will You Please Be Quiet, Please?, What We Talk about When We Talk about Love, Cathedral,* and Carver's later stories.

Arthur M. Saltzman, *Understanding Raymond Carver* (Columbia: University of South Carolina Press, 1988).

A frequently cited comprehensive study of Carver's work, including an excellent biographical section. Saltzman critically analyzes Carver's stories and some of his poetry.

Michael Trussler, "The Narrowed Voice: Minimalism and Raymond Carver," *Studies in Short Fiction*, 31 (Winter 1994): 23–37.

Uses the "maximalism versus minimalism" debate to analyze Carver's fiction, in particular, "Why Don't You Dance?"

—*Steve Rucker*

c⬿⬾ↄ

# Michael Chabon, *The Amazing Adventures of Kavalier and Clay*
(New York: Picador, 2000)

When Michael Chabon's first novel, *The Mysteries of Pittsburgh* (1988), was in progress as his master's thesis at the University of California at Irvine, his adviser, Donald Heiney (who writes under the pen name MacDonald Harris), sent the unfinished manuscript to his own literary agent, who negotiated an advance of $155,000, an extraordinary amount for a first novel. A best seller, it is a first-person coming-of-age story set in the summer after the protagonist's graduation from the University of Pittsburgh, Chabon's own undergraduate alma mater. The main character has a sexual relationship with a man, leading *Newsweek* to publish an article hailing Chabon as one of the best new gay novelists. Chabon corrected this, but now says he is grateful for the mistake, because it brought him a loyal gay readership.

Chabon was born on 24 May 1963 to a pediatrician father and lawyer mother, both Jewish. He grew up in Columbia, Maryland, in a planned community and then, after his parents divorced when he was eleven, split his time between Maryland and Pittsburgh, Pennsylvania. He describes himself as a comic-book geek until the age of sixteen, when music became his passion. He says of his two summers before graduating from the University of Pittsburgh that they "rattled my nerves and rocked my soul and shook my sense of self—but in a good way. I had drunk a lot, and smoked a lot, and listened to a ton of great music, and talked way too much about all of those activities and about talking about those activities. I had slept with one man whom I loved, and learned to love another man so much that it would never have occurred to me to want to sleep with him. . . . those summers . . . had shocked the innocent, pale, freckled Fitzgerald who lived in the great blank Minnesota of my heart" ("My Back Pages," in *Maps and Legends*, 2008). He married poet Lollie Groth in 1987, the year he graduated from Irvine; they divorced in 1991. In 1993 he married

Ayelet Waldman, with whom he now has four children. They make their home in Berkeley, California. Several of these biographical details are developed into major themes in Chabon's writing: divorce, abandonment, father/son relationships, Jewish identity, and gay relationships.

After struggling with a long second novel, Chabon abandoned it and wrote *Wonder Boys* (1995), in part about a novelist struggling with a manuscript that has ballooned to thousands of pages. It received strong reviews and was made into a movie starring Michael Douglas, Tobey Maguire, Katie Holmes, and Robert Downey Jr. (2000). He has also published two short-story collections, *A Model World and Other Stories* (1991) and *Werewolves in Their Youth* (1999). *The Amazing Adventures of Kavalier and Clay* (2000) established him as a major voice in contemporary fiction, winning the Pulitzer Prize for 2001. Since then, his published fiction includes a children's novel, *Summerland* (2002); a novella based on an aged (although unnamed) Sherlock Holmes, *The Final Solution* (2004); a murder mystery positing an alternate history Jewish community in Alaska, *The Yiddish Policemen's Union* (2007); and an adventure novella, first serialized in the *New York Times Sunday Magazine*, *Gentlemen of the Road* (2007).

*The Amazing Adventures of Kavalier and Clay* marks two important turns in Chabon's writing. Beginning with it, his novels have moved from having some Jewish elements to engaging themes often identified as Jewish. In addition, *Kavalier and Clay* marks the beginning of his full-fledged engagement with genre fiction as both subject and style. Feeling that it is under-regarded, his ambition is to use some of its conventions and topics with strong, careful prose in "real" novels. This interest has seen fruition through the genre connections of the novels since *Kavalier and Clay* and through his editorship of *McSweeney's Mammoth Treasury of Thrilling Tales* (2003), *McSweeney's Enchanted Chamber of Astonishing Stories* (2004), and a limited series of comic books based on the superheroes created by his *Kavalier and Clay* main characters.

Chabon and his wife, a novelist and former lawyer, each entered the discourse surrounding gender roles and parenting in a major way in 2009. In May of that year Waldman published *Bad Mother: A Chronicle of Maternal Crimes, Minor Calamities, and Occasional Moments of Grace*. A frequent blogger, Waldman had initiated a controversy in 2005 when she wrote in an essay that she loves her husband more than her children and believes the relationship between husband and wife should be primary and the relationship with children secondary. *Bad Mother* revisits that controversy and expands on her beliefs that our culture constantly places guilt on women, regardless of what they do as mothers. Chabon followed in November with *Manhood for Amateurs: The Pleasures and Regrets of a Husband, Father, and Son*. Its interlinked essays form an autobiography focused on the roles enumerated in its title.

## TOPICS FOR DISCUSSION AND RESEARCH

1. The theme in *The Amazing Adventures of Kavalier and Clay* that most prominently announces itself from the beginning is, as the epigraph from Nathaniel

Hawthorne puts it, "Wonderful escape!" Escape takes many, many forms here: as Houdini-style magic tricks; as Jews fleeing from the Nazis; as escapist entertainment offered by comic books; as emotional and/or literal abdication, running away from commitment; as attempting to escape your sexual identity, or attempting to escape society's disapproval of that sexual identity; or even, as stated at the beginning of the novel, "It was never just a question of escape. It was also a question of transformation." Bernard Kornblum, Josef Kavalier's magic teacher, tells him, "Never worry about what you are escaping *from*. Reserve your anxieties for what you are escaping *to*." Yet, of course, Joe cannot forget the family he left behind when he escaped from Czechoslovakia, nor can Sammy forget the father who "escaped" life with him and his mother. Toward the end of the novel, reflecting on comic books, Joe thinks, "Having lost his mother, father, brother, and grandfather, the friends and foes of his youth, his beloved teacher Bernard Kornblum, his city, his history—his home—the usual charge leveled against comic books, that they offered *merely an easy escape from reality*, seemed to Joe actually to be a powerful argument on their behalf. . . . The escape from reality was, he felt—especially right after the war—a worthy challenge." Students could find fruitful trajectories for topics by following any one of these tropes of escape in the novel. For an extra-textual topic, advanced students might explore comic-book history and assess Joe Kavalier's argument that this kind of escapist entertainment is valuable. The articles by Hillary Chute and Lee Behlman should be useful, along with the history by Gerard Jones. At the end of *Kavalier and Clay* Chabon offers a list of histories and biographies he consulted while writing the book; students will find there sources on Houdini, the Holocaust, comic-book history, and gay life in mid-twentieth-century New York City.

2. One of Sammy's comic-book-artist friends refers to their creations as "wishful figments" (a malapropism for "wish fulfillment"), pointing out that Sammy, who is lame from polio, gave his creation, the lame Tom Mayflower, a magic key that made him strong and whole, able to walk without a limp. Sammy "wondered what other wishes he might have subsumed unknowingly into the character." Another example of a wishful figment is Joe's first cover, depicting the Escapist delivering a powerful punch to the jaw of Adolf Hitler. In what ways does Chabon play with the notion of wish fulfillments in this novel? How does it serve as an investigation of the relationship between desire and imagination? How are Kavalier and Clay's many character creations alter egos for them, and in what ways does each young man's creations speak to his fears, desires, and perceived shortcomings? Another approach would be to focus on Luna Moth, Joe's imagining of Rosa Saks. In what way is the Luna Moth character a "wishful figment," and in what ways does Luna Moth accurately represent the character of Rosa? Advanced students might tackle this question in relation to the psychological impact of escapist art.

3. Chabon has demonstrated a steadily increasing interest in the mixing of genres, as well as in genre fiction itself. (Genre fiction refers to romance, science fiction, fantasy, horror, westerns, and mystery.) For instance, *The Final Solution* narrates a mystery being investigated by a figure clearly meant to be

an aged Sherlock Holmes. *The Yiddish Policemen's Union* interpolates science fiction and alternate universe fantasy, as well as a murder mystery. How does Chabon "mix" genres within *The Amazing Adventures of Kavalier and Clay*? For instance, in the chapters that relate the story portion of the first Escapist and first Luna Moth comics, as readers begin these chapters nothing introduces the fact that we are "overhearing" what Sammy and Joe create as they walk through the streets of New York City. Are those chapters that tell just the comic book stories different from the writing in the rest of the novel? In what ways does Chabon use comic-book styles or methods in other places within the novel? Are there cliffhangers? Does the pacing follow that of superhero stories? What genre does the fifth section, "Radioman," embody? The article by Chute would be useful here, as would Scott McLoud's *Understanding Comics* (1994) and Will Eisner's *Comics and Sequential Art: Principles and Practices from the Legendary Cartoonist* (1985).

4. History plays an important role in this novel, and points of interest that arrive out of its strong presence can lead to a great many topics of research. Although Samuel Klayman and Josef Kavalier are the products of Chabon's imagination, the artists and writers of the early comic-book age were often young men, and several of the most notable—for example, the creators of Superman, Joe Schuster and Jerry Siegel—were also Jewish. (Similar to Sammy and Joe, Schuster and Siegel sold the rights to the character of Superman for $130 and profited little from the millions generated by the character they had drawn for decades.) They, along with many other historical people involved in the comic-book industry, are mentioned or make brief appearances. Chabon weaves many non-comic-book-industry-related historical figures into his novel, as well, including the Surrealist painter Salvador Dali, First Lady Eleanor Roosevelt, Alfred E. Smith (politician and president of the corporation that owned the Empire State Building), German boxer Max Schmeling, director and actor Orson Welles, comic-book opponent Dr. Frederick Wertham, Senator Estes Kefauver, and, of course, escape artist Harry Houdini. History also appears in the persecution of Jews in Joe Kavalier's homeland of Czechoslovakia, Pearl Harbor, the Surrealist movement, the "fairy raids" on gay groups—and places—the Empire State Building, the 1939–1940 World's Fair, and Louis Tannen's Magic Shop. Chabon also plays with history by inserting footnotes into the novel—some provide fictitious history about his characters and the comic books they create (for instance, sales figures), while others provide factual information about real history. How does the weaving together of history and fiction affect how we understand the history? How does the presence of historical figures affect our view of the fictional characters? Does it make them more realistic? More sympathetic? Students might choose a specific historical figure or place or event and assess how its story enriches a particular theme in the novel. In another vein, much of the history that these character bump up against—the persecution of Jews during World War II, the persecution of gays—is traumatic. What does the novel offer in terms of examples of how people cope with traumatic history? The sources mentioned by Chabon in

his "Author's Note" at the end provide examples of the histories he consulted. The article by Chute would also be helpful.

5. Once Sammy and Joe are established and their assignment expands to two more comic lines, they "went for a series of long strolls, in and out of the streets of Manhattan and Empire City, talking and dreaming and walking in circles in the prescribed manner of golem makers." At the beginning of the novel, we hear of Joe's escape from Czechoslovakia in the coffin of the famous Golem of Prague. In Jewish lore, golems were created of clay and animated by various means, usually through walking and ritual language, and were often employed to battle intruders and protect communities. How is the idea of the golem important in this novel? What other examples of golem-like figures or images are there? Is it significant that Sammy's real last name is "Klayman"? What is suggested at the end by Joe's creation of a massive "comic book novel" featuring "The Golem"? The article by D. G. Myers and the Lisa Simeone interview would be helpful to an exploration of the theme of golems, as would Chabon's essays "The Recipe for Life" and "Golems I Have Known, or, Why My Elder Son's Middle Name is Napoleon: A Trickster's Memoir," both found in *Maps and Legends*.

6. Consider the role of money in the novel. Sheldon Anapol and Jack Ashkenazy take advantage of the creative abilities of Kavalier and Clay, giving them only a very small share of the millions Empire Comics earns from these young men's work. In what ways is class exploitation a topic in this novel? Is the exploitation they experience due to class or to some other factor? The article by Daniel Punday will be useful. What other roles does economics play in the story? What is Sammy's reason for wanting to be successful? Joe's? What role does Joe's status as an immigrant play in his attitude toward economics? George Deasey tells Sammy and Joe that the only way to avoid disappointment and disillusionment is to work only for the money; yet, he is one of the most disillusioned figures in the novel. What things are ultimately most valuable in the economy of this novel?

## RESOURCES

### Primary Works

Mark Binelli, "The Amazing Story of the Comic-Book Nerd Who Won the Pulitzer Prize for Fiction: A Conversation with Michael Chabon," *Rolling Stone*, 27 September 2001, pp. 58–62, 78.
Wide-ranging interview that includes discussion of Chabon's childhood, early publications, interest in comics and music, and the writing of *The Amazing Adventures of Kavalier and Clay*.

Lisa Simeone, "Michael Chabon Talks about the Legend of the Golem and about His Book, *The Amazing Adventures of Kavalier and Clay*," *NPR Weekend All Things Considered*, 2001 May 6 <www.npr.org/templates/story/story.php?storyId=1122517> [accessed 23 November 2009].

Discusses golems and the analogy he has come to see between them and novels, as well as how contemporary audiences tend to view all writing as autobiographical.

### Criticism

Lee Behlman, "The Escapist: Fantasy, Folklore, and the Pleasures of the Comic Book in Recent Jewish American Holocaust Fiction," *Shofar,* 22 (Spring 2004): 56–72.

Investigates how *The Amazing Adventures of Kavalier and Clay* both dramatizes the use of fantasy and escapism in art as a response to the Holocaust and presents a running debate on the value and relevance of such popular culture escapism. Behlman also discusses Nathan Englander's *For the Release of Unbearable Urges* (1999) and Jonathan Safran Foer's *Everything Is Illuminated* (2002).

Hillary Chute, "*Ragtime, Kavalier and Clay,* and the Framing of Comics," *Modern Fiction Studies,* 54 (Summer 2008): 268–301.

Argues that graphic narratives and contemporary fiction share a valuing of the popular, an obsession with history, and even some stylistic and narrative practices, and that E. L. Doctorow's novel *Ragtime* and Chabon's *The Amazing Adventures of Kavalier and Clay* participate in this through dramatizations of how the popular—that is, comic books in *Kavalier and Clay*—articulates traumatic histories. The article is stronger on theory than on close reading.

Gerard Jones, *Men of Tomorrow: Geeks, Gangsters, and the Birth of the Comic Book* (New York: Basic Books, 2004).

History of the early comic-book industry focusing particularly on the many Jewish figures involved as writers, artists, and financiers, with emphasis on the story of Joe Schuster and Jerry Siegel, the creators of Superman who sold the rights to the character for $130 and spent decades writing the stories but not profiting from the millions the character generated.

D. G. Myers, "Michael Chabon's Imaginary Jews," *Sewanee Review,* 116 (Fall 2008): 572–588.

Largely biographical article that is quite critical of Chabon's use of Jewish elements and themes in his works, despite seeing him as "immensely talented"; argues that there is a "fundamental incoherence" at the heart of *Kavalier and Clay*'s message about Jews and the golem.

Daniel Punday, "*Kavalier & Clay,* the Comic-Book Novel, and Authorship in a Corporate World," *Critique,* 49 (Spring 2008): 291–302.

Looks at a number of contemporary novels that feature the comic-book industry or comic-book characters and argues that *Kavalier and Clay* offers a new way of imagining the individual against the economic landscape, one that harkens back to something more possible before the twentieth century than during it.

Marc Singer, "Embodiment of the Real: The Counterlinguistic Turn in the Comic-Book Novel," *Critique,* 49 (Spring 2008): 273–289.

For advanced students, a complex discussion of how Chabon, Jonathan Lethem, and Rick Moody go beyond metaphor and metonymy to engage in a kind of hypostasis, using comics to "challenge some of the most basic tenets of the linguistic turn of twentieth-century critical theory."

*—Kathryn West*

# Sandra Cisneros, *The House on Mango Street*
(Houston, Tex.: Arte Público, 1983)

In an essay titled "Only Daughter," Chicana author Sandra Cisneros describes looking back at a self-description she had written for an anthology early in her career; it reads, "I am the only daughter in a family of six sons. *That* explains everything." She says that for the reader's sake, she should have written, "I am the only daughter in a *Mexican* family of six sons" or "I am the only daughter of a working-class family of nine." In the first printings of *The House on Mango Street* Cisneros's author biography states, "The daughter of a Mexican father and a Mexican-American mother, and sister to six brothers, she is nobody's mother and nobody's wife." The emphases and variations in these self-descriptions highlight Cisneros's major concerns as a writer: societal, cultural, and familial expectations of women, the role of class and poverty on identity and self-perception, and perhaps most poignantly, the intersections between gender and culture for a Chicana. As the first and perhaps still most influential writer to articulate this story, she stands at the forefront of such contemporary Latina writers as Helena María Viramontes, Ana Castillo, Denise Chávez, Lorna Dee Cervantes (all Chicana), Julia Alvarez (Dominican American), Judith Ortiz Cofer, Esmeralda Santiago (Puerto Rican), and Cristina García (Cuban).

Cisneros was born in Chicago on 20 December 1954. She spent her childhood traveling back and forth between impoverished Chicago neighborhoods and the large and comfortable home of her paternal grandparents in Mexico. Despite economic difficulties, her parents managed Catholic-school tuition for their children, even, as she points out in the essay mentioned above, for her as "*only* a daughter." Cisneros attended Loyola University in Chicago, where she majored in English, receiving a B.A. in 1976. With encouragement from an English teacher, she applied to and was accepted to the University of Iowa Writers' Workshop, where she earned an M.F.A. in 1978. She did, not, however, find the Iowa program a comfortable experience. She says, "*The House on Mango Street* started when I was in graduate school, when I realized I didn't have a house. I was in this class, we were talking about memory and the imagination. . . . I remember sitting in the classroom, my face getting hot and I realized, 'My god, I'm different! I'm different from everybody in this classroom.' . . . It wasn't as if I didn't know who I was. I knew I was a Mexican woman. But, I didn't think that had anything to do with why I felt so much imbalance in my life, whereas it had everything to do with it. My race, my gender, and my class! And it didn't make sense until that moment, sitting in that seminar. That's when I decided I would write about something my classmates couldn't write about" (Pilar R. Rodríguez Aranda interview).

After finishing her graduate degree, Cisneros worked as a college recruiter, a teacher to high-school dropouts, a poet-in-the-schools, and an arts administrator, as well as filling visiting-writer positions at a number of universities. Her earliest publications were poetry, but it was the 1984 appearance of *The House on Mango Street* that brought her to national prominence. She followed it with a volume of poetry, *My Wicked, Wicked Ways,* in 1987, and an acclaimed collection of short stories, *Woman Hollering Creek and Other Stories,* in 1991. While *Mango Street* channels beautifully the voice of a young girl, the short stories in *Woman Hollering Creek* are told by narrators ranging from young girls to more mature women negotiating cultural stereotypes, abusive marriages, love, and family. Although Spanglish, the representation of the mixture of English and Spanish vocabulary in the speech of many people who live on both sides of the border, appears in a few instances in *Mango Street,* Cisneros uses it more frequently and deliberately in *Woman Hollering Creek,* where it serves to highlight themes of border crossings and hybridity. In 1994 Cisneros published a book for children, *Hairs/Pelitos,* and another collection of poetry, *Loose Woman.* As the titles of her volumes of poetry suggest, her poetic voice expresses passion, sexuality, and rebellion. In 1995 Cisneros received a MacArthur Foundation "genius" award.

In her 2002 novel *Caramelo, or Puro Cuento* Cisneros redefines the meaning of "border culture," depicting the life and family of Lala Reyes, a descendant of a family of renowned *rebozo,* or shawl, makers. Lala's family makes an annual trip from their home in Chicago to visit family "on the other side," in Mexico City, which for many Midwestern Mexican Americans becomes a kind of "suburb" of the Midwest, despite its distance. Much longer than Cisneros's other works (more than four hundred pages), it nevertheless shares the use of many short chapters and vignettes, songs, Spanglish, poetic prose, rich sensory details, and focus on the intimate and often fraught negotiations of family life that characterize much of her other work. It is dedicated to her father, an upholsterer like Lala's father, who was diagnosed with terminal cancer during the writing of the novel.

In addition to her writing, Sandra Cisneros influences the world of art and literature through other avenues. She is the founder and president of the Macondo Foundation (begun in 1998 around her kitchen table and incorporated in 2006, it is named for the village in Gabriel García Márquez's *Cien años de soledad* [1967; translated as *One Hundred Years of Solitude,* 1970]), which "works with dedicated and compassionate writers who view their work and talents as part of a larger task of community-building and non-violent social change [and attempts] to serve our under-served communities through our writing" (its website is <www.sandracisneros.com/macondo.php>). In 2000 she also founded the Alfredo Cisneros Del Moral Foundation in honor of her father; it provides awards to writers with connections to Texas who are judged to take the same pride in craftsmanship that her father did in his craft as an upholsterer. Cisneros has made her home in San Antonio, Texas, for many years.

When Cisneros was eleven, her family bought a small house, their first permanent home, in Humboldt Park, a Puerto Rican neighborhood on the north side of Chicago. Later, while working at the Latino Youth Alternative High School in Chicago, Cisneros discovered students whose lives made hers feel "comfortable and privileged," for she never had to worry about being beaten by a father or boyfriend, or avoiding gangs in the hall of her school, or being asked to drop out of school to help support her family. Feeling emotionally overwhelmed at times and, she says, not knowing what else to do with her students' stories but needing to do something, she combined them with her own childhood experiences in Humboldt Park into *The House on Mango Street*. While Esperanza, the narrator, lives in a supportive family that cares very much about education, in the neighborhood around her she sees poverty, neglected children, domestic abuse, and young girls using their sexuality to try to break out of the prisons created by their environments. Consisting of a series of vignettes, most one to three pages long, it has been translated around the world and is widely taught in middle schools, high schools, and universities.

Highly recommended for any of the following topics on *The House on Mango Street* is Cisneros's introduction to the twenty-fifth-anniversary edition of the novel. She maintains a useful website at <http://www.sandracisneros.com>. The chapter by Alvina E. Quintana would also be useful for any of these topics.

## TOPICS FOR DISCUSSION AND RESEARCH

1. *The House on Mango Street* is both a bildungsroman, a coming-of-age story, and a *künstlerroman*, a more specific type of coming-of-age story, in which the protagonist grows into an awareness of him- or herself as an artist or writer. Students interested in coming-of-age stories or comparative analysis might wish to research definitions of these types of stories and consider how Cisneros revises or expands the tradition. Another avenue of research would be to compare the coming-of-age elements in *The House on Mango Street* to those in other examples, such as Mark Twain's *The Adventures of Huckleberry Finn* (1884), Ernest Hemingway's Nick Adams stories, J. D. Salinger's *The Catcher in the Rye* (1951), or Harper Lee's *To Kill a Mockingbird* (1960). For an example of another bildungsroman from a Latino writer, students could read and compare Rudolfo Anaya's *Bless Me, Ultima* (1972). For the latter, consult Dianne Klein's "Coming of Age in Novels by Rudolfo Anaya and Sandra Cisneros," *English Journal*, 81 (September 1992): 21–26.

2. In a 1990 interview Cisneros says of *The House on Mango Street*, "I wrote it as a reaction against those people who want to make our barrios look like Sesame Street, or some place really warm and beautiful. Poor neighborhoods lose their charm after dark, they really do. It's nice to go visit a poor neighborhood, but if you've got to live there every day, and deal with garbage that doesn't get picked up, and kids getting shot in your backyard, and people running through your gangway at night, and rats, and poor housing. . . . It loses its charm real quick!" (Rodríguez Aranda interview). While Esperanza's family is loving and supportive, her surroundings do not offer her a secure environment. From being

shamed by the nun who says, "You live *there?*" to the rape in "Red Clowns," Esperanza is threatened emotionally and physically. Students would find it fruitful to examine what factors, and what intersection of factors, create these threats to her sense of identity. In other words, what role do race, class, and gender play in Esperanza's life, and where and how do those things intersect? What does Esperanza learn from her examination of the neighborhood and neighbors around her? The articles by Felicia J. Cruz, Jacqueline Doyle, Robin Ganz, and Leslie Petty would be helpful to this set of topics.

3. Told through a series of forty-four vignettes, *The House on Mango Street* has been described as a novel, a novella, and a short-story cycle. Many readers and critics have commented on the poetic qualities of the prose and the use of "voice" over character. What is Cisneros doing with traditional notions of genre and divisions between poetry and prose? What is the impact of her choices on the story she tells? What aspects of the story do her structural and formal choices highlight? The articles by Cruz, Julián Olivares, Margot Kelley, and Deborah Madsen should be of assistance. Students interested in comparative analysis might compare Cisneros's genre experimentations with those by Tim O'Brien in *The Things They Carried* (1989) or Louise Erdrich in *Love Medicine* (1993).

4. By the end of *The House on Mango Street* Esperanza has determined that her future is to be a writer, and to write about these lives she has known on Mango Street. Her final words take the reader back to the beginning of the novel. Students would find it fruitful to trace Esperanza's evolving relationship to storytelling and writing through the text. Which characters encourage her to write? What do those figures have in common? What other experiences not directly about writing help shape her identity as a writer? Doyle and Madsen would be useful for this undertaking.

5. In "The Family of Little Feet" and "Hips" a young Esperanza and her friends explore questions of gender and sexuality, trying on high-heeled shoes and discovering they have "legs, all our own, good to look at, and long," wondering about the function of women's hips. What other episodes lead to Esperanza's growing awareness of sexuality, as well as of gender? Where do gender and sexuality meet, and where do they diverge? How does her Chicano community define gender roles and expectations, and how are those expectations enforced? How do the models of female experience around Esperanza lead to her conclusion in "Beautiful & Cruel" that "I have decided not to grow up tame like the others who lay their necks on the threshold waiting for the ball and chain"? Students could consult the articles by Doyle, Petty, Eva Paulino Bueno, and Ellen McCracken for a variety of views on this question.

6. Houses play a significant role in Esperanza's consciousness. Students would find it fruitful to consider the many manifestations of houses in *Mango Street*, from the literal to the figurative. When and where do houses offer safety? When and where and why do they not, but rather function as prisons? How are relationships to houses shaped by gender in this text? More than once Esperanza is told she will have a "home in the heart"—what does this mean? Students interested in this exploration should consult McCracken, Olivares, and Alvina E. Quintana.

# RESOURCES

## Primary Works

"Only Daughter," in *Latina: Women's Voices from the Borderlands,* edited by Lillian Castillo-Speed (New York: Simon & Schuster, 1995), pp. 156–160.

Discusses her feelings about being described as the only daughter and only a daughter, and her father's eventual pride in her success as an author.

Pilar E. Rodríguez Aranda, "On the Solitary Fate of Being Mexican, Female, Wicked, and Thirty-Three: An Interview with Writer Sandra Cisneros," *Americas Review,* 18 (Spring 1990): 64–80.

Extensive interview discussing *The House on Mango Street* and Mexican American culture.

"Sandra Cisneros," in *Interviews with Writers of the Post-Colonial World,* edited by Feroza Jussawalla and Reed Way Dasenbrock (Jackson: University Press of Mississippi, 1993).

A collection of interviews in which Cisneros discusses her life and provides insight into her work.

## Criticism

Eva Paulino Bueno, "The Importance of Being Sandra (Cisneros)," in *A Companion To US Latino Literatures,* edited by Carlota Caulfield and Darién J. Davis (Rochester, N.Y.: Boydell & Brewer, 2007), pp. 37–50.

Analysis of Cisneros's work that places her in the context of the feminist movements.

Felicia J. Cruz, "On the 'Simplicity' of Sandra Cisneros's *House on Mango Street,*" *Modern Fiction Studies,* 47, 4 (2001): 910–946.

Examines responses to the novel in order to explain its "widespread appeal." In doing so, the essay resists simplistic readings that focus on depictions of "reality," and encourages readers to look at the novel's "ideological and narrative intricacies." The review of the reception of *The House on Mango Street* is also useful.

Jacqueline Doyle, "More Room of Her Own: Sandra Cisneros's *The House on Mango Street,*" *MELUS,* 19 (Winter 1994): 5–35.

A critical essay that situates *The House on Mango Street* within the context of a women's literary tradition and compares it to the work of Virginia Woolf.

Robin Ganz, "Sandra Cisneros: Border Crossings and Beyond," *MELUS,* 19 (Spring 1994): 19–29.

A critical overview of Cisneros's development as a writer who introduces and makes accessible culturally specific details within mainstream themes.

Margot Kelley, "A Minor Revolution: Chicano/a Composite Novels and the Limits of Genre," in *Ethnicity and the American Short Story,* edited by Julia Brown (New York: Garland, 1997), pp. 62–84.

Examines the form of *The House on Mango Street* and places it in the context of other Chicano writing that experiments with the composite novel, or short-story cycle.

Deborah Madsen, "Sandra Cisneros," in *Understanding Contemporary Chicana Literature* (Columbia: University of South Carolina Press, 2000), pp. 105–134.
A useful overview of major themes and motifs in both prose and poetry by Cisneros.

Ellen McCracken, "'Sandra Cisneros' *The House on Mango Street:* Community-Oriented Introspection and the Demystification of Patriarchal Violence," in *Breaking Boundaries: Latina Writing and Critical Reading,* edited by Asunción Delgado, Eliana Ortega, Nina M. Scott, Nancy Saporta Sternbach, and Elaine N. Miller (Amherst: University of Massachusetts Press, 1989), pp. 62–71.
Still valuable for its analyses of the motif of the house and of feminist and women's issues, although its framing argument, suggesting reasons why *The House on Mango Street* did not receive much critical attention, is moot now that the novel has been well received and is widely taught.

Caryn Mirriam-Goldberg, *Sandra Cisneros: Latina Writer and Activist* (Berkeley Heights, N.J.: Enslow, 1998).
Written for an adolescent audience, an overview of Cisneros's life and works that focuses on her development as a writer and the relationship between biography and thematic issues in her work.

Julián Olivares, "Sandra Cisneros' *The House on Mango Street,* and the Poetics of Space," *The Americas Review,* 15 (Fall–Winter 1987): 160–170.
Examines the idea of house as both literal and metaphorical space in the novel; includes some discussion of form and genre.

Leslie Petty, "The 'Dual'-ing Images of la Malinche and la Virgen de Guadalupe in Cisneros's *The House on Mango Street,*" *MELUS,* 25 (Summer 2000): 119–32.
Useful tracing of the way female figures offer models of "La Malinche" (the traitorous or promiscuous woman) and of the Virgin of Guadalupe (the good or pure woman) for Esperanza and how she negotiates a role for herself that partakes of both and neither.

Alvina E. Quintana, *Home Girls: Chicana Literary Voices* (Philadelphia: Temple University Press, 1996).
Includes the chapter on Cisneros, "*The House on Mango Street:* An Appropriation of Word, Space, and Sign," which offers a clear analysis of the major themes of the text.

—*Kathryn West*

# Billy Collins (1941–   )

The only child of William Collins, an electrician and later an insurance broker, and Katherine Collins, a nurse, Billy Collins was born in New York City on 22 March 1941. Although he was named after his father, he never goes by William—a habit that mirrors the informality of his poems and the familiarity of his subject matter. His poems feature such commonplace activities as eating cereal for breakfast, listening to music (most often jazz), and walking in the park. They usually start with an observation about the world and are written in the first-person singular, in unrhymed everyday language, and in a rhythm that matches normal speech patterns. Even when his descriptions verge on the metaphysical, they do so in a way that brings the subject down to earth: in Collins's vision, angels deliver mail and Buddha shovels snow. In "The Flight of the Reader" he muses on the appeal of his poems: they do not "pester you / with the invisible gnats of meaning"; instead, they settle on concrete images and the matter-of-factness of everyday life—much like the poetry of William Carlos Williams, who, Collins likes to point out, was a pediatrician at the New York City hospital where he was born.

Collins attended Catholic schools through college, receiving a B.A. from the College of the Holy Cross in Massachusetts. He earned his M.A. and Ph.D. from the University of California at Riverside, where he wrote a dissertation on the Romantic poets. In 1971 he began teaching at Lehman College of the City University of New York, where he is today distinguished professor of English. Collins began publishing poetry in small magazines in the 1970s and cofounded the *Mid-Atlantic Review* with Michael Shannon in 1975; he remained relatively unknown, however, until the poet Edward Hirsch chose his *Questions about Angels* (1991) as the winner of the National Poetry Series competition. After Garrison Keillor read selections from Collins's *Picnic, Lightning* (1997) on National Public Radio and invited him to appear on Keillor's show, *A Prairie Home Companion,* sales of his books and requests for readings increased. Bruce Weber calls Collins "the most popular poet in America"; his enormous appeal is credited to his entertaining public readings and the ease of understanding his work. This appeal has garnered Collins not only popularity but also financial rewards: in what Weber describes as "an expression of confidence virtually unheard of in commercial publishing for a serious poet," Random House paid him six-figure sums for *Sailing Alone around the Room: New and Selected Poems* (2001), *Nine Horses: Poems* (2002), and *The Trouble with Poetry and Other Poems* (2005).

Plain language and straightforwardness make Collins's poetry highly accessible—a word often used to describe his work. "I try very assiduously to court the reader and engage him," Collins has said. "I am interested more in a public following than a critical one." The accessibility can also be ascribed to his propensity for humor. In "Care and Feeding" the speaker says that he "will turn 420 in dog years" and imagines taking himself out for "a long walk." In "Introduction to Poetry" Collins pokes fun at his students' attempts at literary interpretation, which he likens to "torture": "beating [a poem] with a hose / to find out what it really means." But Collins told Elizabeth Farnsworth that "humor . . . is really a gate of departure. It's a way of enticing a reader into a poem so that less funny things can take place later. It really is not an end in itself, but a means to an end." Underlying his humor is something darker. In the frequently anthologized "I Chop Some Parsley While Listening to Art Blakey's Version of 'Three Blind Mice'" the lighthearted image of the speaker musing on the blindness of nurseryrhyme creatures leads into a meditation on loss and empathy. Other poems are more consistently serious in tone. In "Forgetfulness" Collins imagines the loss of memory that comes with aging, and he ponders mortality in "Boy Shooting at a Statue." "The Names," a moving poem that he read to a special joint session of Congress in September 2002, lists the victims of the 11 September 2001 terrorist attacks.

Collins has also done much to encourage Americans to make poetry a part of their everyday lives. As U.S. poet laureate for two terms, from 2001 to 2003, Collins was influential in shaping American reading tastes through Poetry 180, a program designed to encourage high-school students to read poetry aloud rather than analyzing it. He was named a "Literary Lion" by the New York Public Library in 1992, received the Poetry Foundation's first Mark Twain Award for his use of humor in 2004, and served as New York State poet laureate in 2004–2005. Collins does have some detractors: Jeredith Merrin, for example, concedes that he is "not without some rhetorical skills, charm, and wit" but ultimately finds his work "disappointingly monotonous and slight." Despite such criticism, Collins's appeal remains strong, and through his writing and his efforts to promote the work of others he has helped to broaden the appeal of poetry and make it relevant to the lives of more people.

Students interested in learning more about Collins and in sampling his work will find "Billy Collins: Online Resources" at the Library of Congress website (<http://www.loc.gov/rr/program/bib/collins/>) useful. Maintained by Peter Armenti, it provides extensive links to biographies, press releases, criticism, interviews, poems, and audio and video recordings. Also offering biographical information and samples of Collins's work are the websites of the Academy of American Poets (<http://poets.org/poet.php/prmPID/278>) and the Poetry Foundation <http://www.poetryfoundation.org/archive/poet.html?id=80600>. A book-length study of Collins's work has not yet been published, but reviews of particular collections can be found in publications such as *The New York Times.* Longer essays, dealing with several books, include those by Merrin and Ernest Hilbert, both of whom take a negative view of Collins's oeuvre. The chapter on Collins in Michael D. Sharpe's *Popular Contemporary Writers* (2006), which is geared toward young-adult readers, takes a more objective view. Interviews, the Poetry 180 website, and the introductions to anthologies Collins has edited provide insights into his life, experience as a teacher, influences, and writing process.

## TOPICS FOR DISCUSSION AND RESEARCH

1. Collins is an entertaining and talented reader of his own work. Students can listen to recordings of him delivering his own poems on *The Best Cigarette* (1997), which can be downloaded at <http://www.bestcigarette.us/>, and in the audiobook *Billy Collins Live: A Performance at the Peter Norton Symphony Space* (2005), with an introduction by Bill Murray. A list of other audio and

video recordings and links to them can be found at the Library of Congress website. Students might consider the difference between reading a Collins poem in a book and hearing him read it aloud. Is it more understandable, accessible, and/or enjoyable when he performs it? Do you find that Collins's reading makes his humor more obvious? Dwight Garner does: Garner has dubbed Collins a "stand-up poet" and described his readings as comedy routines. Does hearing a poem read aloud rather than seeing it laid out on a page make it seem less like a poem? Ernest Hilbert writes: "There is very little to indicate that what he recites is, in fact, poetry, aside from the occasional announcement of itself as a poem." In his reading of his own poems, what qualities does Collins emphasize, and what does this emphasis suggest about Collins's views on poetry?

2. Several of Collins's poems respond to the work of well-known earlier poets. "Monday Morning" comments on Wallace Stevens's "Sunday Morning"; "Lines Composed over Three Thousand Miles from Tintern Abbey" calls to mind William Wordsworth; "Musée des Beaux Arts Revisited" takes its point of departure from W. H. Auden's "Musée des Beaux Arts"; Petrarch is mentioned in "Sonnet"; "Dancing toward Bethlehem" undercuts the seriousness of W. B. Yeats's "The Second Coming"; and "Taking off Emily Dickinson's Clothes" imagines and echoes the nineteenth-century poet. Hilbert describes these poems as "pastiches, or parodies"; students might examine the originals to see what Collins is parodying. Alternatively, students might consider how Collins's playful tone accompanies a critique of the way readers—including students, teachers, and poets—approach, interpret, and/or define poetry. How might Collins's poems challenge the way we approach so-called canonical works? How might we read the works of earlier poets differently if we take a hint from Collins? In what ways would this approach be positive? Negative? Collins comments on his parodies in his interview with Joel Whitney.

3. Various artists have produced short videos animating Collins's poems "Budapest," "Forgetfulness," "Hunger," "No Time," "Now and Then," "Some Days," "The Best Cigarette," "The Country," "The Dead," "Today," and "Walking across the Atlantic"; these videos are accompanied by Collins reading the works and can be viewed at "Billy Collins: Action Poetry" (<http://www.bcactionpoet.org/>). Students might analyze the clips to determine which aspects of the poems are lost and which are highlighted in these interpretations. Why do Collins's poems lend themselves so easily to visual interpretation? How do they support the views on poetry he has expressed in interviews and in his introductions to *Poetry 180: A Turning Back to Poetry* (2003) and *The Best American Poetry, 2006* (2006)? Alternatively, students may wish to try to create visual adaptations of one or more of Collins's poems themselves.

4. As poet laureate Collins encouraged high-school students to read poetry through Poetry 180, a project named for the number of days in a typical school year but also for the number of degrees in a complete about-face turn, the effect he envisioned reading the poems would have on students' attitudes toward poetry. The project called for students to hear or read a poem each

school day. The anthologies *Poetry 180: A Turning Back to Poetry* and its follow-up, *180 More: Extraordinary Poems for Every Day* (2005), both edited by Collins, feature poems that, as he says in the introduction to the first volume, "any listener could basically 'get' on first hearing—poems whose injection of pleasure is immediate." The poems can be accessed online at the Library of Congress website. Students may wish to compare some of Collins's selections in regard to form and subject matter. Alternatively, students might consider choosing from among Collins's choices to create their own anthologies on a smaller scale: *Poetry 30* with a month's worth of poems, or *Poetry 7* for a week. Like Collins, students should include critical introductions that explain the criteria for selection.

5. In "Art over Easy" Jeredith Merrin gives three reasons for not liking Collins's work: sameness, self-centeredness, and his "esthetic of easiness." Students might discuss whether or not they agree with Merrin's assessments. Questions to consider include: Are Collins's poems (those discussed in the article and others) alike in terms of form and content? If so, does this similarity add to or detract from their overall effect? Does the predominant use of the first-person singular prevent readers from identifying with the sentiments in Collins's poems—that is, are they *too* personal? Are his poems "easy"? Is a poem's difficulty related to its quality?

## RESOURCES

### Primary Works

*The Apple That Astonished Paris* (Fayetteville: University of Arkansas Press, 1988).
Collins's first book of poems.

Grace Cavalieri, "An Interview with Billy Collins" (December 2001) <http:// www.gracecavalieri.com/poetLaureates/billyCollins.html> [accessed 26 February 2010].
Transcript of an interview that originally aired on the National Public Radio series *The Poet and the Poem at the Library of Congress*. Collins discusses the role of the poet laureate, his use of humor in poetry, and teaching.

Elizabeth Farnsworth, "Elizabeth Farnsworth Talks to the New Poet Laureate, Billy Collins," *Online NewsHour* (10 December 2001) <http://www.pbs. org/newshour/bb/entertainment/july-dec01/collins_12-10.html> [accessed 26 February 2010].
Transcript of an interview in which Collins discusses his "accessibility," humor, and quick writing process ("in one sitting only").

George Plimpton, "The Art of Poetry No. 83: Billy Collins," *Paris Review*, 159 (Fall 2001): 182–216 <http://www.theparisreview.org/viewinterview.php/ prmMID/482> [accessed 26 February 2010].
Discusses the process of writing a poem. For Collins "it's a very sporadic activity."

"Poetry, Pleasure, and the Hedonist Reader," in *The Eye of the Poet: Six Views of the Art and Craft of Poetry*, edited by David Citino (New York: Oxford University Press, 2001), pp. 1–33.

Essay in which Collins considers "what exactly—or even vaguely—happens to us" psychologically and physically "when we *do* read a poem."

Robert Potts, "A Conversation with Billy Collins," *Coachella Review* (Fall 2009) <http://thecoachellareview.com/poetry/interview_billycollins_fall09.html> [accessed 26 February 2010].

Short interview in which Collins discusses influences on his poetry and why he believes people are turning more to poetry.

*Sailing Alone around the Room: New and Selected Poems* (New York: Random House, 2001).

Includes poems from previous collections, providing an excellent sampling of Collins's work.

"Seventy-Five Needles in the Haystack of Poetry," in *The Best American Poetry, 2006*, edited by Collins (New York: Scribner Poetry, 2006), pp. xv–xxiii.

Introduction in which Collins describes his criteria of selection, giving an insight into what he values in poetry and what he does not.

*She Was Just Seventeen* (Lincoln, Ill.: Modern Haiku Press, 2006).
A chapbook of haiku.

*Taking off Emily Dickinson's Clothes* (London: Picador, 2000).
The first collection of Collins's work published outside the United States. It includes poems from his first four books.

Joel Whitney, "A Brisk Walk: Billy Collins in Conversation," *Guernica: A Magazine of Art and Politics* (2006) <http://www.poets.org/viewmedia.php?prm-MID/19796> [accessed 26 February 2010].

Excellent resource in which Collins discusses his childhood, first attempts at poetry, influences, and views on difficult poetry.

## Criticism

David Baker, "Smarts," in *Heresy and the Ideal: On Contemporary Poetry* (Fayetteville: University of Arkansas Press, 2000), pp. 119–136.

Chapter dealing with Collins, Susan Howe, Andrew Hudgins, Mark Doty, and Lynda Hall. An analysis of the meanings of Collins's poetry and of the strategies he employs to convey them comprises the last four pages of the chapter.

Dwight Garner, "Stand-Up Poet," *New York Times*, 29 September 2001 <http://www.nytimes.com/2001/09/23/books/stand-up-poet.html?pagewanted=all> [accessed 26 February 2010].

A mostly positive review of *Sailing Alone around the Room*, with discussions of several individual poems.

Ernest Hilbert, "Wages of Fame: The Case of Billy Collins," *Contemporary Poetry Review* (2006) <http://www.cprw.com/Hilbert/collins2.htm> [accessed 26 February 2010].
Describes a shift in American poetry in the 1980s from being an "academic affair" to a more popular one. Hilbert provides an overview and evaluation of Collins's poetry, finding it positive with regard to its accessibility and humor but negative in its unvaried form and theme.

Adam Kirsch, "The Taste of Silence," *Poetry*, 191 (January 2008): 340–347 <http://www.poetryfoundation.org/journal/article.html?id=180561> [accessed 26 February 2010].
For advanced students. Kirsch traces the influence on poetry of the thought of the philosopher Martin Heidegger, ending with a discussion of Collins's work and his ability to make the "ordinary" image "extraordinary."

Katherine Marsh, "The Selling of Billy Collins," *New York Times*, 18 November 2001 <http://www.nytimes.com/2001/11/18/nyregion/citypeople-the-selling-of-billy-collins.html> [accessed 26 February 2010].
Charts Collins's "fairy-tale transformation from local literary loner" to popular poet whose public readings are "the literary equivalent of Beatlemania," identifying and discussing qualities that contribute to the success of Collins's poetry.

Janet Maslin, "Tripping To and Fro, Happily Skewering Poetry," *New York Times*, 2 October 2008 <http://www.nytimes.com/2008/10/02/books/02masl.html> [accessed 26 February 2010].
Review of *Ballistics* (2008) that identifies features of Collins's poetry not just in this collection but also throughout his work: realism, the use of everyday images, humor, and playfulness.

Jeredith Merrin, "Art over Easy," *Southern Review*, 38 (Winter 2002): 202–214.
Review of *Sailing Alone around the Room: New and Selected Poems* that discusses the controversy surrounding the inclusion of works from Collins's three previous books, which were published by a different firm. Although Merrin acknowledges qualities that make Collins's poetry popular, she criticizes it as "elevator music."

Michael D. Sharpe, "Billy Collins," in his *Popular Contemporary Writers* (Tarrytown, N.Y.: Marshall Cavendish, 2006), pp. 453–466.
Most extensive critical overview of the poet's life and works, with reading guides to *The Art of Drowning, Questions about Angels, Nine Horses*, and *Picnic, Lightning*.

Marion K. Stocking, "Books in Brief: Another Kind of Best," *Beloit Poetry Journal*, 57 (Winter 2006–2007): 42–48.
Review of Collins's anthology *The Best American Poetry, 2006*, in which his criteria for choosing the poems are identified and evaluated. Although the essay does not discuss Collins's own poetry, it serves as a guide to the poetic forms and themes that most interest Collins.

Bruce Weber, "On Literary Bridge, Poet Hits a Roadblock," *New York Times,* 19 December 1999 <http://www.nytimes.com/1999/12/19/us/on-literary-bridge-poet-hits-a-roadblock.html?pagewanted=1> [accessed 26 February 2010].
Recounts the controversy surrounding the publication of *Sailing Alone around the Room,* offers a sample of Collins's work and an overview of his career, and describes him as "the most popular poet in America."

—*Linda Trinh Moser*

# Don DeLillo, *White Noise*
(New York: Viking, 1985)

Don DeLillo is often one of the first names mentioned when discussions turn to literary Postmodernism. Critics debate many different definitions of Postmodernism, yet what they all share is a concern with how language and other forms of representation shape us and separate us from reality. Although it is far too simplistic to say that DeLillo belongs to any one camp of Postmodern thought—and he, while neither accepting nor rejecting the label, says he is "a novelist, period. An American novelist" (DePietro)—his novels certainly seem to be more in the vein of critics such as Fredric Jameson who see Postmodernism as a recent stage of capitalist transformation, one in which all experience is commodified, made commercial. DeLillo's project, in terms of the entire range of his novels, is to rethink the history of the post–World War II era. Thus, several of his books focus either on specific historical moments—*Libra* (1988) with its reimagining of President Kennedy's assassination or *Falling Man* (2007) and its treatment of the 9/11 terrorist attacks—or on the feel of a moment in the recent past, as in *Mao II* (1991), *Underworld* (1997), and *White Noise* (1985).

Don DeLillo was born in New York City on 20 November 1936. The son of Italian immigrants, DeLillo grew up in the Bronx and for a brief time in Pennsylvania. His was the typical childhood for working-class boys of the time, complete with makeshift sports in the streets, card games and pool, punctuated by Catholic Mass on a regular basis. DeLillo has said that he was not a voracious reader as a child, but a high school summer job as a park attendant gave him the time he needed, and he eagerly read Faulkner, Joyce, Melville, and found his interest in the function and feel of language stimulated. After graduating from Fordham University with a degree in communication arts, DeLillo went to work as a copywriter in an advertising agency, a job he pursued for five years before deciding that he wanted to try something else. His first short story was published in 1960; eleven years later his first novel, *Americana,* was published.

In 1975 DeLillo married Barbara Bennett; they live outside of New York City. Between 1972 and 1982 he published seven more novels, mostly well reviewed but none reaching the level of acclaim and interest achieved by *White Noise* in 1985. It received the National Book Award and was a finalist for the National Book Critics Circle Award. His follow-up in 1988, *Libra,* was a National Book Award finalist, appeared on *The New York Times* Best Books of the Year list, and received the Aer Lingus International Fiction Prize in 1989. It also received much media attention due, largely, to its subject matter—Lee Harvey Oswald and a myriad of plots and conspiracies leading up to the assassination of John F. Kennedy. Its treatment of our cultural relationship to history and the strong strains of paranoia in contemporary American culture resonated with audiences and critics alike. DeLillo followed *Libra* with *Mao II* in 1991; it won the PEN/Faulkner Award in 1992. Many consider *Underworld* (1997) to be DeLillo's magnum opus, although at more than eight hundred pages, it is less commonly taught on high-school and college campuses than is *White Noise. Underworld* was a finalist for the National Book Award and the Pulitzer Prize and received the American Book Award, the Jerusalem Prize, and the William Dean Howells Medal. Under the title "Pafko at the Wall" the first section originally appeared as a novella in *Harper's* magazine in October 1992. A brilliant evocation of the intermingling personalities, famous and ordinary, historical and fictional, at the 1951 Giants-Dodgers pennant game, culminating in a ninth-inning homerun "heard round the world," the first section of *Underworld* also documents the moment when news comes that the Soviets have detonated a nuclear bomb. These elements are intertwined throughout the novel *Underworld:* the Cold War, baseball and the young man who caught the game-winning ball, bombs, historical figures such as Lenny Bruce and J. Edgar Hoover, and ordinary people, all literally and figuratively trying to deal with the "waste" produced by their world.

DeLillo has followed *Underworld* with four short novels: *The Body Artist* (2001), *Cosmopolis* (2003), *Falling Man,* and *Point Omega* (2010). He is also the author of four plays. One of his novels, *Amazons* (1980), was written under the pseudonym Cleo Birdwell and presents itself as the memoir of the first woman to play in the National Hockey League.

As his influences DeLillo names New York City, the paintings in the Museum of Modern Art, jazz, and the movies of Federico Fellini, Jean-Luc Godard, and Howard Hawks. In addition, the assassination of John F. Kennedy and the existence of the Zapruder film have been a long-term fascination and explain in part his interest in the idea of the simulacrum, the image of an image. In a 1988 interview with William Goldstein he says that the Zapruder film (the home movie taken of the Kennedy assassination by private citizen Abraham Zapruder) was "one of the things that informed my subsequent, or all my work. . . . The notion of a medium between an event and an audience, film and television in particular. The irony is that we have film of the assassination and yet it is still remote" (*Publishers Weekly,* 19 August 1988).

At the center of *White Noise* is Jack Gladney, professor of Hitler Studies at the fictional College-on-the-Hill, and his family and extended families that have developed through marriages, divorces, and remarriages. As they go about their daily lives, Jack's family operates in the midst of a constant barrage of "white noise"—the sound of their clothes dryer, toasters, television, radios, brand names. It is a world in which all experience, even sex, seems to be mediated; only the fear of death offers heightened awareness.

Early in *White Noise* DeLillo introduces the idea of the simulacrum when Jack and his colleague Murray Siskind visit a barn billed as "The Most Photographed Barn in America." As they stand near the "slightly elevated spot set aside for viewing and photographing," Murray says to Jack, "No one sees the barn." Instead, they "are taking pictures of taking pictures." We live in an age of the mechanical reproduction of art and images; thus, we find the image further removed from its referent. The referent (the barn in this case) has completely disappeared beneath the images of it and the images of those images. DeLillo highlights the role of commodification in this disappearance of reality: Near the viewing site for the barn, "A man in a booth sold postcards and slides—pictures of the barn taken from the elevated spot." Reality is buried under layers of signification and the endless commodification of all experience.

On 23 October 1995 Don DeLillo sent a reply to a reading group's questions about *White Noise,* giving his permission for it to be posted online. Addressed to Jon Jackson, it explains his preference for language over plot: "For me, well-behaved books with neat plots and worked-out endings seem somewhat quaint in the face of the largely incoherent reality of modern life; and then again fiction, at least as I write it and think of it, is a kind of religious meditation in which language is the final enlightenment, and it is language, in its beauty, its ambiguity and its shifting textures, that drives my work" ("Don DeLillo on Writing").

## TOPICS FOR DISCUSSION AND RESEARCH

1. Students interested in structure and genre might enjoy investigating these topics in DeLillo's *White Noise.* He mingles several genres in this novel: the beginning a combination of academic novel and domestic comedy; the "Airborne Toxic Event" reads somewhat like a disaster novel; and in the final sections there are overtones of a thriller with absurdist sensibilities. All these genres are delivered metafictionally and ironically. Students could investigate where DeLillo uses conventions of any one of these genres and to what purpose, and could also trace where he diverges from them and what he reveals about them by doing so. A related topic would look at the idea of "plot" as Jack Gladney repeatedly, obsessively plans his attack on Willie Mink, and what DeLillo questions about the very idea of plot in a Postmodern world. DeLillo's *Paris Review* interview, the articles by Cornel Bonca and Tom LeClair, and Leonard Orr's guide will be useful resources.

2. In his treatment of contemporary themes and issues in his novels DeLillo routinely employs defamiliarization, painting a picture of contemporary life that looks like the real world but is slightly exaggerated or altered so that the absurdities are more readily apparent. Nowhere is that process of making the reader stop and recognize anew something seen every day more apparent than in *White Noise.* DeLillo commented after returning from three years in Greece that he was surprised by "something on television which I hadn't noticed before. This was the daily toxic spill—there was the news, the weather and the toxic spill. This was a phenomenon no one mentioned. It was simply a television reality. It's only the people who were themselves involved in these terrible events who seemed to be

affected by them." *White Noise* results from that observation. Students would find it fruitful to track instances of defamiliarization and examine how they remind a numbed audience about the reality that they inhabit. What do you take for granted that *White Noise* makes you notice anew? What do those reminders suggest about the preoccupations of late twentieth-century American lives? John N. Duvall's "The (Super)Marketplace of Images" (1994) and the essay by Michael Valdez Moses in Frank Lentricchia, ed., *New Essays on* White Noise (1991) will be useful for developing this topic, as will several pieces in *Approaches to Teaching DeLillo's* White Noise (2006), edited by Tim Engles and Duvall.

3. The culture DeLillo paints in *White Noise* is filled with simulacra, a culture where an actual emergency evacuation serves an evacuation planning team (SIMU-VAC) as a practice for their next simulated evacuation, a world where a band plays live Muzac, where passengers who survive an airliner's near crash are more moved by the retelling of the event than they were by the actual experience, a world where if a disaster does not get coverage on TV, it is not real. It is also a novel populated by countless lists of the stuff that identifies our existence: "open cartons, crumpled tinfoil, shiny bags of potato chips, bowls of pasty substances covered with plastic wrap, flip-top rings and twist ties, individually wrapped slices of orange cheese." Moreover, in the same way that our lives are interrupted by commercials, DeLillo randomly inserts in his narrative lists of brand-name products: "The Airport Marriott, the Downtown Travelodge, the Sheraton Inn and Conference Center." Students might consider how the "simulacra" and the proliferation of commodities shape the personalities of the characters in the novel. What is the impact on emotional lives? Why does Jack Gladney go shopping, and why does he throw away piles and piles of things in one scene? What is the role of the supermarket in this novel? The essays by Lentricchia and Thomas J. Ferraro in *New Essays on* White Noise, several essays in Duvall's *The Cambridge Companion to Don DeLillo* (2008), the article by Haldar Eid, and the chapter on *White Noise* in Douglas Keesey's book are worth consulting. For a different approach, students might investigate how DeLillo's use of brand names and references to popular culture differs from such usages in other contemporary fictions—perhaps, for instance, in minimalist works such as those by Raymond Carver and Bobbie Ann Mason.

4. In "The Question Concerning Technology" the philosopher Martin Heidegger asserts that "Everywhere we remain unfree and chained to technology, whether we passionately affirm or deny it. But we are delivered over to it in the worst possible way when we regard it as something neutral; for this conception of it, to which today we particularly like to do homage, makes us utterly blind to the essence of technology." The mysterious drug Dylar, taken by Jack's wife Babette and eventually an object of desire and obsession on the part of Jack, is described as a high-tech "drug delivery system" designed to rid its takers of their fear of death. What does DeLillo have to say about the human relationship to technology in the latter half of the twentieth century? In the letter to Jon Jackson, DeLillo says, "the book is driven by a connection I sensed between advanced technology and contemporary fear. By the former, I don't mean bombs and missiles alone but more or less

everything—microwaves, electrical insulation etc." Students interested in this topic might start with analysis of the drug Dylar, its side effects and its effect on the relationship between Babette and Jack. How does DeLillo support Heidegger's position in *White Noise*? Useful criticism includes the article by Moses in *New Essays on* White Noise; several pieces in *The Cambridge Companion to Don DeLillo*, and Lentricchia's *Introducing Don DeLillo* (1991) discuss the treatment of technology in DeLillo's work.

5. Alternatively, students might start with the role of Dylar to consider the novel's exploration of the fear of death. After returning to America after some time living abroad, DeLillo noted something distinctive in contemporary American culture: "a sense of death had begun to permeate not only television but the media in general. Death seems to be all around us—in the newspapers, in magazines, on television, on the radio. . . . I can't imagine a culture more steeped in the idea of death." How does Jack's fear of death relate to his choice of Hitler as the focus of his academic work? Consider the scene on pages 168–169 of the Vintage paperback, when Jack hears of the death of a colleague. Does DeLillo convincingly demonstrate that technology has increased our fear of death, rather than softening it, in *White Noise*? Students might examine such scenes as that when the family sees Babette leading an exercise class on a silent television, or Steffie's tears over the fight between a sitcom husband and wife. What does media saturation mean for real emotion? Jack's town experiences brilliantly beautiful sunsets after the airborne toxic event—is there anything not mediated by the media or by technology in the world of this novel? The article by Karen Weekes will be useful for this topic.

6. Jack Gladney is at the center of a family made up of several branches due to his four marriages to five different wives (and Babette, his current wife, has also been married multiple times). Students will find it fruitful to explore what DeLillo has to say about the nature of family in the latter half of the twentieth century. The family scenes, especially early in the novel, are often comic. The family is also depicted as the site of the proliferation of much misinformation. In the interview with William Goldstein in *Conversations with Don DeLillo* (2005), edited by Thomas DePietro, DeLillo says, "I don't know exactly how to summarize my work but I would say it's about danger, modern danger." What endangers family in *White Noise*? In this context students might also consider such questions as Jack's sense of masculinity. See various essays in Engles and Duvall, the essay on masculinity in *The Cambridge Companion to Don DeLillo*, and Tom LeClair.

## RESOURCES

### Primary Works

Adam Begley, "Don DeLillo: The Art of Fiction," *Paris Review*, 35 (Fall 1993): 274–306.

Discusses his early influences, working habits, methods of composition, dialogue, characterization, and audience, as well as the idea of "plots," the impact of the

Kennedy assassination, the Warren Report, paranoia, and most of his novels published to 1993.

Thomas DePietro, ed., *Conversations with Don DeLillo* (Jackson: University Press of Mississippi, 2005).
Invaluable collection of interviews ranging from 1982 to 2001 that belie DeLillo's reputation as interview-shy. He does tend to avoid personal questions, but is generous in his discussions of his work, his work habits, his views on contemporary culture, and passions such as baseball, movies, and jazz.

"Don DeLillo on Writing," *Don DeLillo's America—A Don DeLillo Site* <http://perival.com/delillo/ddwriting.html> [accessed 23 November 2009].
A collection of brief statements by the author from various sources.

## Criticism

Cornel Bonca, "Don DeLillo's *White Noise:* The Natural Language of the Species," *College Literature*, 23 (June 1996): 25–44.
Helpful essay arguing that DeLillo demonstrates the redemptive powers of language in *White Noise*.

John N. Duvall, "The (Super)Marketplace of Images: Television As Unmediated Mediation in DeLillo's *White Noise*," *Arizona Quarterly*, 50 (Autumn 1994): 127–153.
Analysis of the role of television and the idea of the simulacrum, with some helpful explanation of Murray Siskind.

Duvall, ed., *The Cambridge Companion to Don DeLillo* (New York: Cambridge University Press, 2008).
Includes one essay devoted to *White Noise*. Several others include discussions of *White Noise* within considerations of DeLillo and Modernism, Postmodernism, media culture, apocalyptic satire, masculinity, and the power of language.

Haidar Eid, "Beyond Baudrillard's Simulacral Postmodern World: *White Noise*," *Undercurrents*, 7 (Spring 1999).
Discusses DeLillo's adaptation and transformation of Jean Baudrillard's idea of the simulacrum, the image of the image.

Tim Engles and John N. Duvall, eds., *Approaches to Teaching DeLillo's* White Noise (New York: Modern Language Association, 2006).
Includes the section "Materials," which suggests helpful readings and resources for students and teachers. "Approaches" offers eighteen essays on technological, cultural, and theoretical contexts, as well as comparisons to other works by DeLillo and suggestions for classroom strategies.

Douglas Keesey, *Don DeLillo* (New York: Twayne, 1993).
Biographical overview and a chapter on each of the novels published through 1992. The readings tend to focus on issues of media culture and language.

Tom LeClair, "Closing the Loop: *White Noise*," in his *In the Loop: Don DeLillo and the Systems Novel* (Urbana & Chicago: University of Illinois Press, 1987), 207–236.

Interesting analysis of the novel's structures and response to contemporary structures and systems, arguing for its emotional resonance.

Frank Lentricchia, *Introducing Don DeLillo* (Durham, N.C.: Duke University Press, 1991).

Includes twelve articles, one of which is the famous *Rolling Stone* essay coauthored with Anthony DeCurtis. The critical essays tend to focus on themes and philosophies rather than on one individual novel, so *White Noise* is discussed in several.

Lentricchia, ed., *New Essays on* White Noise (New York: Cambridge University Press, 1991).

In addition to an overview of the novel's critical reception by Lentricchia, includes four essays covering such topics as family, perceptions of Adolf Hitler in the twentieth century, technology, and postmodern America.

Jeffrey MacIntyre, "Don DeLillo," *Salon.com* (23 October 2001) <http://www.salon.com/people/bc/2001/10/23/delillo/index1.html> [accessed 23 November 2009].

Overview of DeLillo's career with an emphasis on his importance as a cultural critic and his prescience in identifying the developing preoccupations of his age.

Leonard Orr, White Noise: *A Reader's Guide* (New York: Continuum, 2003).
Brief but helpful analysis and close reading of the novel.

Karen Weekes, "Consuming and Dying: Meaning and the Marketplace in DeLillo's *White Noise*," *LIT: Literature, Interpretation, Theory*, 18 (October 2007): 285–302.

Discusses the role of consumerism in the novel, drawing on the use of the term "white noise" in the discipline of economics.

*—John Orr and Kathryn West*

◦⟨✖⟩◦

# Joan Didion, *We Tell Ourselves Stories in Order to Live: Collected Nonfiction*
## (New York: Knopf, 2006)

"I am so physically small," Joan Didion writes, "so temperamentally unobtrusive, and so neurotically inarticulate that people tend to forget that my presence runs counter to their best interests." So Didion explains her "only advantage as a reporter" with a directness of voice that has become her trademark. She has won acclaim for her Hollywood screenplays and novels, which include *Run River* (1963), *Play It as It Lays* (1970), *A Book of Common Prayer* (1977), *Democracy*

(1984), and *The Last Thing He Wanted* (1996). Yet, her literary reputation rests most solidly on her nonfiction, which extends from her first collection of essays, *Slouching towards Bethlehem* (1968), to her memoir *The Year of Magical Thinking* (2005). The success of her memoir led to renewed interest in Didion's essays, thus prompting the republication of seven of Didion's earlier nonfiction collections as *We Tell Ourselves Stories in Order to Live* (2006), a title taken from the first sentence of *The White Album* (1979). Filled with compelling social commentary, political critique, and reflections on her native California, these works register, above all, a writer's personal search for identity and self-understanding. Didion's particular genius has been to craft a style that captures and reflects the spare, hard truths she has uncovered from a lifetime of unobtrusive observation of herself, her home state, and her country.

Didion was born in Sacramento, California, in 1934. Her family traces its ancestry in the West to Nancy Hardin Cornwall, who traveled to Oregon by wagon train in 1846. This lineage helped give Didion entrée into exclusive social circles, including (at fourteen years old) the Mañana Club, a sorority whose initiation took place at the California governor's mansion during the tenure of Earl Warren (later chief justice of the United States). The rustic California of Didion's childhood—the years immediately before and after World War II—serve as a potent foil in her writing for the great social changes that occurred in that state in the latter half of the twentieth century.

In 1956 Didion graduated from the University of California at Berkeley with a degree in English and won *Vogue* magazine's Prix de Paris contest; the prize included a job at the magazine. Her eight-year stay in New York had an enormous influence on her writing and personal life. Writing for *Vogue* taught her "less was more, smooth was better, and absolute precision essential to the monthly grand illusion" (Winchell). She also met John Gregory Dunne, a writer for *Time* magazine. They married in 1964 and moved to Southern California. The two collaborated throughout their respective careers on magazine columns in *The Saturday Evening Post* (1967–1969), *Esquire* (1976–1977), and *New West* (1979–1980). They also cowrote several Hollywood films, including *Play It as It Lays* (1972), based on her 1970 novel; *Panic in Needle Park* (1971); *A Star Is Born* (1976); and *True Confessions* (1981), based on Dunne's 1977 novel. Dunne's death in 2003 inspired Didion's *The Year of Magical Thinking,* which won the 2005 National Book Award for nonfiction and was a finalist for the 2006 Pulitzer Prize. In 2005 she also received the Gold Medal for Belles Lettres from the American Academy of Arts and Letters. In 2007 she received the National Book Foundation's Medal for Distinguished Contribution to American Letters, a lifetime-achievement award.

In her essays Didion reports on a wide breadth of subject matter from early West Coast settlers, John Wayne, the Doors, and political figures such as Ronald Reagan, the Clintons, and El Salvadorian dictators, to shopping centers, Hawaii, Cuban exiles, and other journalists. Despite this diversity of topics, her nonfiction exhibits several stylistic hallmarks. The essays tend to be highly readable and fast-moving, a blend of journalistic facts and critical opinion. Her style shows the influence of the New Journalism that became prominent in the late

1960s, a literary movement that applied the techniques of fiction writers (scene, dialogue, first-person perspective) to nonfiction. The result boosted journalism to a recognized art form and freed writers such as Didion to report on people and cultural events through a subjective gaze. When Didion stated that her presence as a reporter always ran counter to her subjects' "best interests," she added: "That is one last thing to remember: *writers are always selling somebody out.*" The severity with which Didion constantly scrutinizes her own motives, however, gives the reader confidence in her vision when she applies it in laser-like fashion to others. Filtered through her vision are several motifs that emerge and reappear throughout her work: social commentary, California, and politics.

"On the Mall" in *The White Album* is a typical example of how Didion's social commentary flows from her personal narrative. The essay recounts her naive dream of managing shopping malls as a way of funding her other dream: fiction writing. Trying to be sensible, she enrolled in a correspondence course on "shopping-center theory" while working at *Vogue*. Didion deftly blends her personal dream with the more mythic ones of California developers who believe that

> The solution was in sight. The frontier had been reinvented, and its shape was the subdivision, that new free land on which all settlers could recast their lives *tabula rasa*.

The mall in Didion's mind takes on larger significance as part of a new wave of westward migration and development, part also of the naive dreams (like her own) of financial success in the promised land of California. Although this particular dream of hers will go unfulfilled, her personal narrative transcends a simple critique of real-estate development. She reclaims for malls across the country the therapeutic role of sedating anxiety: "In each of them, one moves for a while in an aqueous suspension not only of light but of judgment, not only of judgment but of 'personality.'" Didion herself finds the temporary escape offered by malls particularly useful; she was diagnosed in 1968 as "a personality in process of deterioration with abundant signs of failing defenses," a literal fact as well as a metaphor for the social unrest of the 1960s.

Didion's writing about California runs throughout her corpus. She devotes a major section in *Slouching towards Bethlehem, The White Album,* and *After Henry* (1992), to her home state. Didion's memoir *Where I Was From* (2003) remains her most comprehensive study of California. She returns to the more personal prose of her earlier essays, describing the work as "an exploration into my own confusions about the place and the way in which I grew up, confusions as much about America as about California, misapprehensions and misunderstandings so much a part of who I became that I can still to this day confront them only obliquely."

As always, Didion begins her examination into the public record through questions about her personal life. In *Where I Was From* she digs up her matrilineal roots, tracing pioneer women who did not have "much time for second thoughts, without much inclination toward equivocation." These hardscrabble traits of her forbearers are alive and well in Didion's prose. As Didion charts her family tree through California history, she evokes the vitality of events (the wagon trains, the railroads, the gold rush) and people (Josiah Royce, Jack London, the Bohemian Club) that have given the thirty-first state its glorious and tragic history. She then takes a hard look at how California has changed in the post–World War II era, reporting on the rise and fall of Lakewood, a Los Angeles suburb, a growing prison system, and the economic downturn in the 1990s. She closes her memoir with a return to her family roots, in particular the death of her mother, who embodies in many ways "the confusions and contradictions in California life." Didion leaves us then not with a resolution to her initial confusions about her home state but with a much deeper understanding of the reasons for those confusions.

Although Didion mentions politics in her early writing—Communism in "Comrade Laski, C.P.U.S.A. (M.-L.)" in *Slouching towards Bethlehem* and the Black Panthers in the title essay of *The White Album*—her engagement with politics did not become pronounced until the 1980s, with the publication of *Salvador* (1983) and *Miami* (1987). Both were based on essays commissioned by the *New York Review of Books*. In *Salvador* Didion uncovers the "dreamwork" or ideological fictions that promote the involvement of the United States in the violence and human-rights abuses perpetrated in El Salvador. In *Miami* she implicitly criticizes successive U.S. administrations who have "repeatedly used and repeatedly betrayed" exiles from Cuba.

Didion returns to politics in *Political Fictions* (2001). The eight essays included range historically from Ronald Reagan's presidency (1980–1988) to the 2000 campaigns of Al Gore and George W. Bush. The format departs from her earlier essay collections: the essays are longer and less personal. Didion turns what she calls "a somewhat doubtful eye" on the Right ("Newt Gingrich, Superstar"), on the Left ("Clinton Agonistes"), and on such journalists as Bob Woodward ("Political Pornography") and Michael Isikoff ("Vichy Washington"). Her observations of such figures aim higher than exposing individual foibles. Her goal, instead, is focused on "the ways in which the political process did not reflect but increasingly proceeded from a series of fables about American experience." Her real scorn is directed at those who spin fables for the sake of staying in business, "the nation's permanent professional political class"—the politicians, the political machines, the press—all of whom she feels are out of touch with the American people.

"*Style is character,*" Didion wrote about Georgia O'Keeffe's art in *The White Album*. Didion's own style, sharp as a scalpel, reveals as much about the author's ongoing attempt to clarify the murky waters of her identity as about society, California, or politics. Her writing continues to be a valuable resource because her deep sense of personal fragmentation has captured an essential element of our cultural history.

In addition to the criticism cited in RESOURCES, students interested in general comparative studies are advised to consult Lynne Hanley's *Writing War: Fiction, Gender, and Memory* (Amherst: University of Massachusetts Press, 1991), which focuses on Didion, Virginia Woolf, and Doris Lessing among women writing about armed conflict, and Barbara Lounsberry's *The Art of Fact: Contemporary*

*Artists of Nonfiction* (Westport, Conn.: Greenwood Press, 1990), which compares Didion's nonfiction with that of Tom Wolfe, Norman Mailer, Gay Talese, and John McPhee.

## TOPICS FOR DISCUSSION AND RESEARCH

1. Didion has discussed mythic notions about the West in her writing about California featured in large sections of *Slouching towards Bethlehem, The White Album,* and *After Henry;* the state and Western ideals are also the subject of *Where I Was From.* Elyse Blankley invites readers to question Didion's use of the metaphor of California as the "final frontier" and the traditional Western belief in "unfettered individualism." Should readers accept these ideals or "deconstruct" them as myths? Although Blankley focuses on Didion's novels, students could pose similar questions about Didion's essays about California. Is Didion calling for a return to these ideals or dismantling them? Students should also be mindful of any changes in Didion's presentation of the West. How do Didion's representations of the West in *Slouching towards Bethlehem* or *The White Album* compare to those in *Where I Was From?*

2. Students might consider comparing Didion's depictions of California to those of other writers whose perceptions about the state are grounded in different histories and experiences. A starting point could be Richard Rodriguez's memoir *Days of Obligation* (1984), in which he compares his experience to Didion's. Rodriguez observes that her version "was about ghostly ladies who perched on the veranda of the Senator Hotel and about their husbands, who owned the land and were selling the land. Joan Didion's Sacramento was nothing to do with me; families like mine meant the end of them." In addition to Rodriguez's memoir, students might consider Maxine Hong Kingston's *The Woman Warrior* (1976) and *China Men* (1980).

3. Didion has been criticized for the lack of objectivity in her nonfiction. In his analysis of Didion's nonfiction prose, however, Mark Z. Muggli defends her subjective stance, writing: "In 'Alicia and the Underground Press,' Didion writes that the Underground Press is not read for its facts. Neither should Didion be read for hers. Literal facts are usually her starting point, but figurality gives her journalism much of its interest." Students can apply this observation in an examination of literal and figurative (metaphoric or symbolic) meanings in one of Didion's collection or several of her essays. Which details are literal and can be verified by other sources as objective facts? When Didion elaborates or embellishes facts with metaphor, what meaning is added to her writing? How does metaphor allow her to develop themes and perspectives unavailable in purely factual, literal, or objective reportage?

4. Krista Comer notes that Didion's view of gender "presents critics with more of a problem, for Didion is no feminist. She disdains the category 'woman writer.' In more than one essay she ridicules the women's movement. All of these factors make Didion a problematic candidate for feminist endorsement." And yet, Comer observes, in her California fiction, Didion does

not merely depict cultural changes but also the effect of those changes on women, an interest that could be described as feminist. Other critics who address feminist concerns in Didion's fiction are Patricia Merivale and Janis P. Stout (in Sharon Felton, ed., pp. 99–105, 210–227). Students might wish to apply observations about Didion's fictional depictions of gender to her essays. The middle section of *The White Album*, "The Woman's Movement," is Didion's most direct criticism of 1970s feminism. Compare the essays in this section to her self-presentation and the fusing of public and personal in her other writing, a trait associated with feminism. Other areas to explore Didion's interest in evaluating gender issues include her depictions of pioneer and other women in *Where I Was From* and her attention to connections between patriarchy and war in *Salvador*. See Lynne Hanley's essay in Felton, ed., pp. 171–187.

5. Bruce Bawer takes Didion to task in his review of *We Tell Ourselves Stories in Order to Live*, concluding: "Many of the works collected in it purport to relate some very grim facts about the lives of real people; yet, the omnibus's title shifts the focus from those people and their predicaments to the 'storyteller'—to Didion—who thereby becomes not only author but protagonist." Compare Bawer's negative observations to those who defend Didion's use of the personal (examples of positive reviews are included in Felton), analyzing what criteria are used to measure the worth of Didion's writing. Students should pay attention to those aspects of her writing that are invoked by those who view her in a positive light and which ones by those who do not. Do reviewers cite similar or different criteria when judging her work? Students may wish to discuss the relative merits for each position or alternately, to defend a particular position.

## RESOURCES

### Primary Works

"Dave Eggers Talks with Joan Didion," in *The Believer Book of Writers Talking to Writers*, edited by Vendela Vida (San Francisco: Believer, 2005), pp. 59–77.
Transcript of a fall 2003 interview, one in a series of interviews with writers in San Francisco presented by City Arts & Lectures. Didion discusses her then most recent book, *Where I Was From*.

Michiko Kakutani, "Joan Didion: Staking out California," *New York Times Magazine*, 10 June 1979, pp. 34–50; reprinted in Ellen G. Friedman, ed., pp. 29–40.
Review of *The White Album* that also describes and quotes from an interview with Didion.

Natasha Wimmer, "Joan Didion: Telling It Like It Is (or Should Be)," *Publishers Weekly*, 15 October 2001, pp. 41–42.
An essay that interweaves quotations from an interview with Didion with descriptions of *Political Fictions*.

## Criticism

Bruce Bawer, "Didion's Dreamwork," *Hudson Review,* 60 (Spring 2007): 85–103.
A negative review of *We Tell Ourselves Stories in Order to Live* that analyzes Didion's self-presentation in her nonfiction.

Elyse Blankley, "Clear-Cutting the Western Myth: Beyond Joan Didion," in *San Francisco in Fiction: Essays in a Regional Literature,* edited by David M. Fine and Paul Skenazy (Las Cruces: University of New Mexico Press, 1995), pp. 177–197.
Compares Didion's writing to works by other women and nonwhite writers and reveals the relationship of Didion's writing to myths about the West.

Krista Comer, "Joan Didion," in *Updating the Literary West,* sponsored by the Western Literature Association (Fort Worth: Texas Christian University Press, 1997), pp. 346–351.
Focuses on images of California and feminism in Didion's work.

Sharon Felton, ed., *The Critical Response to Joan Didion* (Westport, Conn.: Greenwood Press, 1994).
A particularly useful collection of reviews and essays on Didion's work from her first novel, *Run River* (1963), to *After Henry* (1992). It includes an extensive bibliography of secondary sources.

Ellen G. Friedman, ed., *Joan Didion: Essays and Conversations* (Princeton: Ontario Review Press, 1984).
Focusing primarily on Didion's fiction (only three of the fourteen essays included examine her nonfiction), an anthology of interviews and critical essays that offers insights into the writer's craft, sensibility, and thematic concerns.

Merritt Moseley, "Joan Didion's Symbolic Landscapes," *South Carolina Review,* 21 (Spring 1989): 55–64; reprinted in Felton, ed., pp. 133–143.
Examines the symbolic resonance of "surroundings. . . . The setting, the weather, the wind, the animal life" in Didion's writing, particularly *Slouching towards Bethlehem* and *The White Album.*

Mark Z. Muggli, "The Poetics of Joan Didion's Journalism," *American Literature,* 59 (October 1987): 402–421; reprinted in Felton, pp. 143–158.
Provides an in-depth analysis of Didion's nonfiction and categorizes her uses of metaphor while arguing for the need to consider "the sophisticated poetics of factual literature."

Robert Ward, "Remembering Memoir: California(s) in Joan Didion's *Where I Was From,*" *Lifewriting Annual: Biographical and Autobiographical Studies,* 2 (2008): 113–125.
Describes Didion's role as memoirist as putting together the "I"—her own personal crises and the way she has used writing to grapple with them—and the "Not I," her gathering of master narratives in the history of California and the more fragmentary history represented by women's diaries and journals, letters, quilts, and other objects of material history to create a collage-like structure.

Mark Royden Winchell, *Joan Didion*, revised edition (Boston: Twayne, 1989). A study of Didion's life and work with valuable notes and references. The concluding chapter, "Threescore Miles and Ten," describes a shift in the critical reception of Didion's work in the 1980s.

—*Patrick Moser*

# E. L. Doctorow, *Ragtime*
## (New York: Random House, 1975)

While a student at the Bronx High School of Science, E. L. Doctorow was assigned to write an essay about a "colorful person." His description of the German-Jewish refugee Karl, a Carnegie Hall stage doorman beloved by all of the performers, so impressed his English teacher that she wanted to publish the essay in the school newspaper. Pressed for more information and a photograph, Doctorow admitted that he had made Karl up; the teacher changed his grade to an "F." Despite this early failure, Doctorow's penchant for elaboration and invention led to his success as a writer who blurs the lines between fact and fiction. Doctorow told Christopher D. Morris, "History written by historians is clearly insufficient"—a conviction borne out in his historical novels, including *Ragtime* (1975), which was awarded the National Book Critics Circle Award in fiction. Often described as Postmodernist, these works fuse fiction, history, and Doctorow's own biography to confront questions of epistemology. Overall, Doctorow's works suggest that history is only as truthful or accurate as the perspective from which it is presented.

Named for Edgar Allan Poe, Edgar Lawrence Doctorow was born in the Bronx on 6 January 1931; his parents were second-generation Americans whose own parents were Russian Jews. He majored in philosophy at Kenyon College in Ohio, where he studied English under the poet John Crowe Ransom. After graduating with honors in 1952, he did graduate work at Columbia University but did not take a degree. Drafted into the army, he served in Germany from 1953 to 1955; in 1954 he married a fellow former Columbia student, Helen Selzer. After his military service, he returned to New York and took a job as a reader for Columbia Pictures, looking for books that could be adapted as movies. This work was unsatisfying but provided lessons about narrative structure and technique that later informed his writing. In 1959 Doctorow became a senior editor for the New American Library. His first novel, *Welcome to Hard Times* (1960), parodies the plots of many of the Westerns with which he had become familiar—and been frustrated by—in his Columbia Pictures job. In 1964 he moved to Dial Press as editor in chief. He left publishing in 1969 to concentrate on his own writing. His novel *The Book of Daniel* (1971) was based on the case of Julius and Ethel Rosenberg, who were arrested in 1950 on espionage charges and executed in 1953. Historical figures mingle with fictional ones, and fact is mixed with fantasy, calling into question the "reality" Doctorow and his narrator create, which, in turn, challenges the "official" version of the Rosenbergs' guilt.

*Ragtime* (1975), Doctorow's best-known work, questions nostalgic or limited perceptions of earlier times. The novel is set in New York City during the heyday of ragtime music, roughly from 1902 to the beginning of World War I. It depicts a vast array of historical figures, including Presidents William Howard Taft and Theodore Roosevelt, the African American educator Booker T. Washington, Archduke Franz Ferdinand of Austria, the industrialist Henry Ford, the illusionist and escape artist Harry Houdini, the psychologists Sigmund Freud and Carl Gustav Jung, the oil tycoon John D. Rockefeller, the financier J. P. Morgan, the inventor Thomas A. Edison, the anarchist Emma Goldman, the radical labor leader "Big Bill" Haywood, the African American ragtime composer Scott Joplin, the chorus girl and artist's model Evelyn Nesbit, and the explorer Robert E. Peary, who cross paths with the members of three fictional families. Published during a time of social upheaval when Americans questioned traditional gender roles, racial identity, and the reliability of the government, the novel depicts a period that seems to be disciplined and peaceful, a time when "Patriotism was a reliable sentiment":

> Trains and steamers and trolleys moved them from one place to another. That was the style, that was the way people lived. Women were stouter then. They visited the fleet carrying white parasols. Everyone wore white in summer. Tennis racquets were hefty and the racquet faces elliptical. There was a lot of sexual fainting. There were no Negroes. There were no immigrants.

This perception of uniformity and efficiency is embodied by the archetypal upper-middle-class WASP family introduced to readers as Father, Mother, Little Boy, and Mother's Younger Brother. Appropriately, their money comes from the manufacture of fireworks, flags, and bunting—the trappings of patriotism. This vision, however, is interrupted when Father, setting off with Peary on an expedition to the North Pole, sees an incoming ship carrying immigrants: "Thousands of male heads in derbies. Thousands of female heads covered with shawls. It was a rag ship with a million dark eyes staring at him. Father, a normally resolute person, suddenly foundered in his soul. A weird despair seized him."

The narrative structure of *Ragtime* further challenges Father's vision of an order that puts him at the top of the social hierarchy. Doctorow introduces two families who are marginalized by society and by mainstream historical accounts: the poor immigrant Jews Tateh, Mameh, and Daughter; and the African Americans Coalhouse Walker Jr., Sarah Walker, and their baby. The lives of the three families become entangled when Mother's Younger Brother joins in a search for Tateh and the little girl and Mother takes in the Walkers' baby. This intersection dismantles Father's assumed superiority based on race, class, and gender. Similarly, the novel's narrative voice, with its shifting perspectives and unclear identities, demonstrates the limitations of historical perspective. The narrator knows Little Boy's thoughts but does not claim any specific relationship to Father, Mother, or Mother's Younger Brother. In later sections the narration shifts from third-person to first-person plural, using "we" to refer to the WASP family. Most interesting is the way the narrator filters the past through a 1970s perspective that shapes Coalhouse with a Black Panther sensibility and Younger Brother as a Weatherman-like conspirator. These techniques highlight racism, sexism, and class bias, while also contributing to the novel's questioning of the nature of narrative and its place in shaping historical reality.

*Ragtime* takes its epigraph from Joplin: "Do not play this piece fast. It is never right to play Ragtime fast." Yet, the novel is filled with descriptions of fast-paced progress and technological developments: assembly-line production and the invention of faster modes of travel from trains to automobiles to airplanes. Ragtime music itself "never stood still a moment," and Peary can play *The Minute Waltz* in forty-eight seconds. The advances in technology are matched by the social transformations of characters such as the destitute Tateh, who becomes movie mogul Baron Ashenazy; Mother, who develops an identity independent from Father; and Houdini, who escapes from the chains and social attitudes that would imprison him. The novel negatively portrays stagnation in its unfavorable depiction of those unwilling to accept change, while celebrating social transformation and diversity through the use of music as a metaphor. The complexity and richness of *Ragtime* invite multiple interpretive approaches, all of which add to the reader's understanding of American history and attitudes.

Doctorow's other novels include *Big as Life* (1966); *Loon Lake* (1980); *World's Fair* (1985), winner of the National Book Award; *Billy Bathgate* (1989), winner of the PEN/Faulkner Award, the National Book Critics Circle Award, and the William Dean Howells Medal of the American Academy of Arts and Letters; *The Waterworks* (1994); *City of God* (2000); *The March* (2005), winner of the PEN/Faulkner and National Book Critics Circle Awards; and *Homer & Langley* (2009). He has also published the short-story collections *Lives of the Poets: Six Stories and a Novella* (1984) and *Sweet Land Stories* (2004) and a play, *Drinks before Dinner* (1979). His essays are collected in *Reporting the Universe* (2003) and *Creationists: Selected Essays 1993–2006* (2006). *Three Screenplays* (2003) comprises adaptations of *The Book of Daniel, Ragtime,* and *Loon Lake.* Doctorow holds the Lewis and Loretta Glucksman Chair in English and American Letters at New York University.

Students interested in learning more about Doctorow might begin with the overviews of his life, work, and critical reception by Douglas Fowler, Carol C. Harter and James R. Thompson, Paul Levine, and John G. Parks. Doctorow has explained his work and discussed his writing process and literary influences in interviews. Morris collects interviews from throughout Doctorow's career up to 1997 in *Conversations with E. L. Doctorow* (1999); the interviews conducted by Allen Weinstein also offer valuable insights. Students interested in the critical reception of Doctorow's works can consult newspaper, magazine, and journal reviews of his books; John Williams provides a detailed overview of the reception. Essays on particular themes or critical approaches to Doctorow's works have been collected by Richard Trenner; many of them deal with *Ragtime.* Berndt Ostendorf traces the importance of music in the novel, as does William Matheson, who also sees "rags" as a metaphor for poverty. Marshall Bruce Gentry highlights gender representations. Kathleen M. Puhr and David Segal focus on the Postmodernist techniques Doctorow uses in the novel. Students interested in comparing the novel to the 1981 film adaptation will find the articles by Anthony B. Dawson, Leonard and Barbara Quart, and Joanna E. Rapf useful. Hillary Chute discusses the foregrounding of visual images in *Ragtime* and compares the work to graphic novels. Doctorow's papers are in the Special Collections Department of New York University's Fales Library; a description of the holdings can be found at the website <http://dlib.nyu.edu/findingaids/html/fales/doctorow_restricted.html>, which also features a useful biography.

## TOPICS FOR DISCUSSION AND RESEARCH

1. Critics tend to view the title, *Ragtime,* either as a metaphor for a historical period or as the musical style on which the structure of the novel is based. That structure, which Parks describes as "repetition colliding with change, convention with innovation," reproduces ragtime's syncopated rhythms. Focusing on "non-musical usages," Matheson sees the title as a reference to the "rags" worn by the poor—an interpretation supported by the emphasis in the novel on social injustice. Ostendorf, however, asserts the importance of the literal meaning: tracing the history of ragtime music, he draws out the novel's affirmation of African American cultural contributions. Students might examine the various meanings of *ragtime* in the novel, considering their relationships to one another and the ways they emphasize or de-emphasize certain themes. Does the novel support multiple complementary meanings of *ragtime,* or do the various meanings negate each other?

2. Toward the end of *Ragtime* the narrator announces that "the time of the era of Ragtime had run out, with the heavy breath of the machine, as if history were no more than a tune on a player piano." The description suggests the Postmodernist idea of history as art—as a construction of the past rather than an objective view of it. Puhr identifies another sign of a Postmodernist sensibility in the "blurring of the . . . line between historical narrative and fictional narrative. Doctorow accomplishes this in part by inventing details using historical figures and also by deliberately imposing a 1970s consciousness on the events of the first two decades of the twentieth century." While some critics, including Puhr, view these techniques positively, others, such as Richard Todd and Barbara Foley, find them irresponsible. Inventions and anachronisms in the novel include Little Boy's request that Houdini warn the archduke about his impending assassination, which will lead to World War I; Coalhouse Walker's racial pride and acts of violence that are reminiscent of 1960s-era Black Panthers; Freud and Jung riding through the Tunnel of Love at Coney Island; the meeting of Nesbit and Goldman; Ford and Morgan discussing reincarnation; and Peary's need for a player piano on his Arctic voyage. Examine several of the inventions or anachronisms in *Ragtime* and evaluate their effect. How do they help to convey a "subjective" rather than "objective" view of history? Do they detract from or support the overall message of the novel? With which critics do you agree, and why? Helpful in this study would be Doctorow's discussions of his opposition to

"objective" versions of histories in his interviews with Weinstein and, in Morris's *Conversations with E. L. Doctorow*, with Levine, Mel Gussow, and Jared Lubarsky. The chapter "Postmodernism" in Part II of the present volume offers more information about the styles and techniques of this movement.

3.  Students may wish to investigate the historical personages and events Doctorow blends into his novel, such as the murder of architect Stanford White by Nesbit's millionaire husband, Harry Kendall Thaw, in the Madison Square Roof Garden; Houdini's escape artistry; and the early days of American cinema and photography. Compare historical accounts of the era to Doctorow's manipulation of them. What is his purpose, besides entertainment? What characteristics and qualities are emphasized in his invented stories about the real-life figures? How do Doctorow's made-up aspects show readers not what happened but how it felt to live at the beginning of the twentieth century? Students might also consider the relationship between Doctorow's inventions and his interest in highlighting social inequality based on gender, race, and class.

4.  In crafting *Ragtime* Doctorow drew not only from historical figures and events but also from other literary works, including the German writer Heinrich von Kleist's 1811 novel *Michael Kohlhass*—a title obviously echoed in the first name of Doctorow's character Coalhouse Walker—and John Dos Passos's *U.S.A.* trilogy: *The 42nd Parallel* (1930), *1919* (1932), and *The Big Money* (1936). Critics such as Foley consider the use of these sources "derivative" and "close to the point of imitation"; others view them as a hallmark of Postmodernist "pastiche," a technique that suggests the lack of an independent or objective reality. How does *Ragtime* compare to the works by Kleist and Dos Passos? Is Doctorow merely borrowing characters and plots, or does his use of them help to highlight certain themes in *Ragtime*? Good starting points for this discussion can be found in Foley's essay; she also cites other critics who have pointed out connections between Doctorow's novel and those of Kleist and Dos Passos. In Morris's *Conversations with E. L. Doctorow* Doctorow discusses his use of Kleist's work in the interview with Herwig Friedl and Dieter Schulz and mentions Kleist and Dos Passos in the interview with Lubarsky.

5.  The film *Ragtime* (1981) was directed by Milos Forman, who rejected a screenplay by Doctorow that had originally been commissioned by the director Robert Altman; instead, he used a script by Michael Weller. Doctorow, who did not like the movie, revised his screenplay and published it in *Three Screenplays* (2003); in the introduction to the volume he describes the differences between his screenplay and the one used for the film. Students might compare the novel, the film, and Doctorow's revised screenplay. How do changes in the plot and the emphasizing or de-emphasizing of characters, events, or themes in the three treatments affect the message of the work? Also helpful are essays by Leonard and Barbara Quart, who criticize the film, and Joanna E. Rapf, who is much more favorable to it. Students interested in theater may want to investigate the critical reception of the musical adaptation of *Ragtime,* with book by Terence McNally, music by Stephen Flaherty, and lyrics by Lynn Ahrens, that premiered in Toronto in 1996 and was revived on Broadway in 2009.

# RESOURCES

## Primary Works

Boris Kachka, "E. L. Doctorow on *Ragtime*," *New York*, 41 (14 April 2008): 69.
Interview in which Doctorow discusses his sources of inspiration for *Ragtime:* his childhood home in the New York suburb of New Rochelle and novels by John Dos Passos and Saul Bellow. He also responds to criticisms of the novel.

Christopher D. Morris, ed., *Conversations with E. L. Doctorow* (Jackson: University Press of Mississippi, 1999).
Highly useful resource with interviews from 1975 to 1997, a chronology, and an introduction that provides an overview of Doctorow's biography and the critical reception of his work.

Allen Weinstein, "American Conversations with the Archivist of the United States: E. L. Doctorow" (25 September 2008) <http://www.archives.gov/about/archivist/conversations/>.
Video and transcript of a lengthy and informative interview conducted by former archivist Weinstein at the National Archives in Washington, D.C. Doctorow discusses the intersections between mythology and history, his college education, and how he began to use history in his fiction.

## Criticism

Laura Barrett, "Compositions of Reality: Photography, History, and *Ragtime*," *Modern Fiction Studies*, 46 (Winter 2000): 801–824.
Examines photography as a trope in the novel.

Hillary Chute, "*Ragtime, Kavalier & Clay*, and the Framing of Comics," *Modern Fiction Studies*, 54 (Summer 2008): 268–301.
Compares Doctorow's and Michael Chabon's novels, emphasizing the two writers' attention to twentieth-century visual media.

Anthony B. Dawson, "*Ragtime* and the Movies: The Aura of the Duplicable," *Mosaic*, 16 (Winter–Spring 1983): 205–214.
Focuses on the depiction of social and economic relationships in the film and the novel.

Barbara Foley, "From *U.S.A.* to *Ragtime:* Notes on the Forms of Historical Consciousness in Modern Fiction," *American Literature*, 50 (1978): 85–105; reprinted in Trenner, pp. 158–179.
Compares *Ragtime* unfavorably to John Dos Passos's trilogy.

Douglas Fowler, *Understanding E. L. Doctorow* (Columbia: University of South Carolina Press, 1992).
Discusses Doctorow's intentions, inventions, and politics in his works. Chapter 4 is an extended analysis of *Ragtime*.

Marshall Bruce Gentry, "Elusive Villainy: *The Waterworks* as Doctorow's Poesque Preface," *South Atlantic Review*, 67 (Winter 2002): 63–90.

Discusses the "paradoxical" treatment of gender in *The Waterworks*, in which women are "praiseworthy but silenced," and uses that novel as a way to view gender in Doctorow's other works. In regard to *Ragtime* the characters Mother, Emma Goldman, and Evelyn Nesbit are discussed.

Carol C. Harter and James R. Thompson, *E. L. Doctorow* (Boston: Twayne, 1990). Useful synthesis of scholarly opinion on Doctorow's works, with an annotated bibliography and a chapter devoted to biography.

Paul Levine, *E. L. Doctorow* (London: Methuen, 1985). Ninety-six-page critical discussion of the author's works, with biographical information.

William Matheson, "Doctorow's *Ragtime,*" *Explicator*, 42 (1984): 21–22. Extends the meaning of the title of the novel to include not only a style of music but also a period in history marked by "rags"—that is, poverty and social inequities.

Christopher D. Morris, *Models of Misrepresentation: On the Fiction of E. L. Doctorow* (Jackson: University Press of Mississippi, 1991). For advanced students. Morris uses a poststructuralist approach to interpret Doctorow's fiction and nonfiction, with references to Jacques Derrida, J. Hillis Miller, and Paul de Man.

Berndt Ostendorf, "The Musical World of Doctorow's *Ragtime,*" *American Quarterly*, 43 (December 1991): 579–601. Highly detailed discussion of the importance of African American musical traditions in understanding the discussion of race in the novel.

John G. Parks, *E. L. Doctorow*, Literature and Life: American Writers (New York: Continuum, 1991). Excellent introduction to Doctorow's novels that presents them in a positive light. The first chapter provides a biographical overview.

Kathleen M. Puhr, "Postmodernism for High-School Students," *English Journal*, 81 (January 1992): 64–66. Highlights the Postmodernist techniques used in *Ragtime* and compares it to other well-known Postmodernist works. The essay is directed toward teachers rather than students.

Leonard Quart and Barbara Quart, "*Ragtime* without a Melody," *Literature/Film Quarterly*, 10 (1982): 71–74. Analysis of the film version of *Ragtime* that finds fault with its lack of overall vision and purpose.

Joanna E. Rapf, "Volatile Forms: The Transgressive Energy of *Ragtime* as Novel and Film," *Literature/Film Quarterly*, 26 (1998): 16–22. Analyzes the ways in which the film employs cinematic equivalents for the narrative fragmentation of the novel.

David Segal, "The Time Travels of E. L. Doctorow," *Washington Post,* 1 October
    2005 <http://www.washingtonpost.com/wp-dyn/content/article/2005/09/30/
    AR2005093001847.html> [accessed 2 March 2010].
Focuses on *The March* but provides an excellent overview of Doctorow's oeuvre
and his "impish disregard for the wall between fact and fiction."

Ben Siegel, ed., *Critical Essays on E. L. Doctorow* (New York: G. K. Hall, 2000).
Collection of essays and reviews with an introduction that summarizes them.

Richard Todd, "The-Most-Overrated-Book-of-the-Year-Award and Other Lit-
    erary Prizes," *Atlantic Monthly,* 237 (January 1976): 95–96.
Argues against the critical acclaim garnered by *Ragtime.*

Richard Trenner, ed., *E. L. Doctorow: Essays and Conversations* (Princeton: Ontario
    Review Press, 1983).
Critical essays on various themes in Doctorow's works, including the American
dream, history, literary influences, and music.

John Williams, *Fiction as False Document: The Reception of E. L. Doctorow in the
    Post-Modern Age* (Columbia, S.C.: Camden House, 1996).
Surveys critical responses to Doctorow's works from his first novel, *Welcome to
Hard Times,* to the mid 1990s.

*—Linda Trinh Moser*

# Rita Dove, *Selected Poems*
(New York: Pantheon, 1993)

In the preface to her *Selected Poems* Rita Dove tells readers, "In books, I could
travel anywhere, be anybody, understand worlds long past and imaginary colonies
of the future." Books were central to Dove's intellectual formation while growing
up. She transfers her own reading experiences into poetry in which she imagines
different perspectives, bringing to life many subjects and people who have been
overlooked, forgotten, or erased from history and daily life. Never shying away
from difficult, painful, or unusual topics, she uses a disinterested manner and
controlled cadences to articulate the connections between the events of public
history and personal experiences. Born on 28 August 1952, in Akron, Ohio, she
is the second child of Ray A. Dove (who worked as an elevator operator before
becoming the first African American chemist in the tire industry) and Elvira
Hord Dove. As a high school senior, she was a presidential scholar, an honor
given to the top one hundred high-school students that year. In 1973 she graduated summa cum laude with a B.A. from Miami University in Oxford, Ohio.
After graduation she studied at the University of Tübingen in West Germany as
a Fulbright-Hays fellow, and then was admitted to the Iowa Writers' Workshop,
where she earned the M.F.A. in 1977.

In 1979 Dove married German-born writer Fred Viebahn, whom she met at the University of Iowa; they have one daughter. Dove has traveled extensively in Europe, and to Israel and Africa, and has taught at the University of Iowa, Tuskegee, and Arizona State University. She is currently Commonwealth Professor of English at the University of Virginia. Dove is the second African American to be awarded the Pulitzer Prize in poetry—for her third collection, *Thomas and Beulah* (1986)—and the first to serve as poet laureate of the United States (from 1993 to 1995). She was also poet laureate of the Commonwealth of Virginia from 2004 to 2006. In addition to these honors, Dove has been awarded a Guggenheim Fellowship, a Walt Whitman award, the Lavan Younger Poets award, the National Humanities Medal, and the Fulbright Lifetime Achievement Medal.

Dove conceived her first collection, *The Yellow House on the Corner* (1980), "as a very domestic title, but one on the edge of domesticity. I mean, the house is on the corner. There's a sense of something beyond that—outside of that boundary there is something else" (interview with Helen Vendler). The description describes a hallmark of Dove's poetic strategy in this and other collections: the ability to move beyond the personal and immediate to other ways of understanding and seeing the world. Even semiautobiographical poems transcend individual experience. The frequently anthologized "Adolescence—I" and "Adolescence—II" delineate feelings of expectation common to all girls coming of age, thus "refus[ing] any overt racial/cultural frames" (Malin Pereira). In the historical poems that make up section three, Dove moves beyond being a "consumer" or "tourist" of history by extending her imagination to understand and empathize with those from other places and times. "Belinda's Petition," "The House Slave," "The Transport of Slaves from Maryland to Mississippi," and "Kentucky, 1833" deal with the trauma and history of American slavery. In "David Walker (1785–1830)" Dove juxtaposes quotations from abolitionist ideals expressed in Walker's pamphlet *Appeal in Four Articles* (1829) with harsh details from his life, the protest and disbelief he encounters when he insists that "*Men of colour. . . are also of sense.*"

In her second full-length collection, *Museum* (1983), Dove also moves from the personal to include "perspectives that cross history, cultures, genders, socioeconomic positions, races and ethnicities," as Pereira notes. Functioning like a museum, her poems allow a specific subject to come under scrutiny. Using fable, legend, ekphrastic poetry (in which she responds to an artistic image), and objective musing, the collection explores the early classical Greeks, Saints Catherine and Alexandria, Shakespeare, and the Cold War. In poems like "Why I Turned Vegetarian" and "To Bed," she presents autobiographical moments, while other poems register the consciousness of historical personages. In "Parsley," perhaps Dove's most famous poem, she presents Rafael Trujillo, the dictator of the Dominican Republic from 1930 to 1961, who ordered the massacre of some thirty thousand Haitians for reasons seemingly both racist and ethnocentric: the Francophone Haitians—unlike Trujillo's mother, who "could roll an R like a queen"—were unable to pronounce *perejil*, the Spanish word for parsley. The poem, which ends the collection, warns against Trujillo's dangerously narrow vision, his inability to appreciate difference.

For her third book, *Thomas and Beulah* (1986), Dove depicts in forty-four poems the lives of her maternal grandparents. The linked poems narrate events from 1919 when Thomas leaves Tennessee, his marriage to Beulah, and their lives in Akron, Ohio, until his death in 1963 and Beulah's in 1969. The work is divided into two sections, with the first, "Mandolin," consisting of twenty-three poems about Thomas; the second, "Canary in Bloom," has twenty-one poems featuring Beulah's life. The poems are told by an omniscient narrator in third-person but include quoted monologue and dialogue to showcase multiple perspectives. Details, such as changing her grandmother's name, Georgianna, to Beulah, suggest an attempt to move beyond historical specificity. Indeed, part of Dove's purpose in depicting her grandparents' lives is to limn the realities of the Great Migration of African Americans from the rural South to the North in search of opportunities. The chronology included at the end further emphasizes the intersections between personal lives and public history. Here Dove lists the moments described in the poems against historical events such as World War II and the assassination of John F. Kennedy.

With her next two collections of original works, *Grace Notes* (1989) and *Mother Love* (1995), Dove reworks scenes from her personal life. With the first, Dove tried "to counter the heavy weight of *Thomas and Beulah*, which has such a big scope" (Vendler). Many of the poems here focus on domestic scenes and familiar spaces: homes, kitchens, porches, yards; they feature private scenes that become revelatory of women's lives. In "After Reading *Mickey in the Night Kitchen* for the Third Time Before Bed," a simple moment between mother and daughter delivers an innocent comparison of bodies and a reminder of female vulnerability: "this . . . is what a stranger cannot touch / without her yelling." *Mother Love* (1995) expands upon the mother-daughter relationship through an exploration and revision of the myth of Persephone and Demeter. In her foreword, "An Intact World," Dove explains the reason for her subject matter: "[T]here comes a point when a mother can no longer protect her child, when the daughter must go her own way into womanhood." For Dove, the mother-daughter separation represents both loss and possibility, which she investigates in spare, controlled rhythms. Most of the poems are sonnets in various forms.

In subsequent collections, *On the Bus with Rosa Parks* (1999), *American Smooth* (2004), and *Sonata Mulattica* (2008), Dove continues to use her craft to discover connections between the personal and private with subjects that are also public and political. Although Dove is most known for her poetry, she has also written prose works: *Fifth Sunday* (1992), a short-story collection; *Through the Ivory Gate* (1992), a novel; and *The Darker Face of the Earth: A Verse Play in Fourteen Scenes* (1994). These works address many of the themes Dove treats in her poetry—music, growing up female and black, cultural limitations—yet have not received the same critical attention or acclaim as Dove's poetry.

## TOPICS FOR DISCUSSION AND RESEARCH

1. Although coming to consciousness and serious writing during the Black Arts movement, Dove resists having her work categorized as part of this important

movement. In an interview with Malin Pereira (in Earl G. Ingersoll, ed., pp. 148–173), she states: "I have nothing against anyone in the Black Arts movement.... Not even artistically. I see how it was absolutely necessary, and I think a lot of it is really wonderful work, too." She uses the expression "Don't fence me in" to explain her feelings, meaning, of course, that she would write what she chose and not be proscribed artistically by an agenda not her own. *The Yellow House on the Corner* features poems that address the Black Arts movement, including "Upon Meeting Don L. Lee, In a Dream" and "Nigger Song: An Odyssey." Students interested in this topic might consider examining the stance Dove takes in these poems and others toward the Black Arts movement, considering which aspects of the movement she rejects and/or embraces. She talks more about her stance with Pereira in Ingersoll (pp. 148–173). For more on the history of the movement and writers associated with it, students can consult *The Black Arts Movement: Literary Nationalism in the 1960s and 1970s,* edited by James Edward Smethurst (Chapel Hill: University of North Carolina Press, 2005); *New Thoughts on the Black Arts Movement,* edited by Lisa Gail Collins and Margo Natalie Crawford (New Brunswick, N.J.: Rutgers University Press, 2006); and part 1 of Larry Neal's useful essay "The Black Arts Movement" (1968); reprinted in "The Black Aesthetic: Background" in *The Black Aesthetic Movement,* edited by Steven Serafin, *Dictionary of Literary Biography Documentary Series,* volume 8 (Detroit: Gale Research, 1991).

2. Dove has significant musical training and has provided the texts for major musical works by composers Tania León (1996 and 2006) and Bruce Adolphe (1997). Her song cycle *Seven for Luck,* with music by John Williams, premiered with the Boston Symphony Orchestra and at Tanglewood on 25 July 1998; some of the songs and a conversation between writer and composer were featured in the popular PBS television series *Boston Pops.* Dove also collaborated with John Williams on Steven Spielberg's *The Unfinished Journey* and read her text live at the premiere of this documentary during "America's Millennium" at the Lincoln Memorial in Washington on New Year's Eve 1999. In 2001 the Museum for Contemporary Art in Chicago premiered *Thomas and Beulah,* set to music by Amnon Wolman. Students with interests in music themselves might analyze some of Dove's poetry for its musical qualities. What forms/ patterns does she draw on in structuring her collections and in the individual poems themselves? How does musical metaphor help Dove to explore and develop themes in her work? Alternatively, students might investigate Dove's use of dance imagery and forms in her poems (particularly in *American Smooth*); Dove includes video of her dancing on her faculty homepage at the University of Virginia. The interview with Robb St. Lawrence will be helpful to an investigation of the intersections between dance or music and Dove's poetry.

3. Dove's work often features historical figures. Some examples are the abolitionist and dealer in used clothes featured in "David Walker (1785–1830)" (in *The Yellow House on the Corner*); African American mathematician, astronomer, and farmer Benjamin Banneker in "Banneker" (in *Museum*); blues singer Billie Holliday in "Canary" (in *Grace Notes*); and civil-rights activist Rosa Parks in

the series of poems titled "On the Bus with Rosa Parks" (in the collection of the same title). Students might investigate one or several of these figures in order to compare Dove's poetic representations with biographical details, paying particular attention to her use of historical accuracies and departures from them. Why does Dove choose certain details and not others from the historical record? What themes do her chosen details allow her to elaborate? Pat Righelato's essay "Rita Dove and the Art of History" (in "Rita Dove: *American Poet,*" pp. 760–775) offers insight into Dove's use and elaboration of history.

4. In a 2006 interview with Robb St. Lawrence, Dove discussed the thought she puts into her arrangement of poems within a collection, her structuring of the male/female voices on two sides of the page in "Rhumba" (found in *American Smooth*), the importance of epigraphs to her, her use of "almost dramatic monologues"—in other words, many issues having to do with the structural, formal side of her poetry. Students might find it interesting to explore one of these questions of structure and form in any of her collections. For instance, possible approaches could focus on the "almost dramatic monologues" of *Thomas and Beulah,* where the voice is third-person but with very strong first person elements; her adaptation of the sonnet cycle in *Mother Love* to suit her purposes; or the importance of the epigraphs from Tuvok the Vulcan of the *Star Trek* television series to how the reader moves through the poems in *American Smooth*. She also discusses with St. Lawrence the ways in which the rhythms of speech can be incorporated into poetry, and how Langston Hughes achieved that. One could analyze her own interpolation of speech rhythm into her poetry, or compare how she does this with how it appears in poetry by Hughes.

5. About Dove's first three collections Elizabeth Alexander observes, "The right to speak, in Dove's poems, is preceded by her articulation of her right to think beyond the immediate world she lives in and the limited expectations of a dominant culture." Alexander focuses her study on the confines of domesticity and gender norms. For example, she notes that "Canary in Bloom," the second part of *Thomas and Beulah,* "explores that tension between confined domestic space and outside vistas." John Shoptaw also investigates how the historical separation of genders contributes to this collection. Students might apply the insights of Alexander and Shoptaw to Dove's other works that feature female experience in order to analyze how they register restrictions related to gender while at the same time suggesting alternatives. Students might ask similar questions about images of confinement and restrictions related to race in Dove's work.

## RESOURCES

### Primary Works

Earl G. Ingersoll, ed., *Conversations with Rita Dove* (Jackson: University Press of Mississippi, 2003).

A selection of interviews spanning the years 1905 to 2002 in which Dove discusses her work, inspirations and interests, including music, crossword puzzles, and dancing.

Robb St. Lawrence, "'Taking the Cards You're Dealt and Building a House': An Interview with Rita Dove," *Bellingham Review*, 29 (Fall 2006): 77–84; also available at <http://people.virginia.edu/~rfd4b/Bellingham%20Review.pdf> [accessed 24 November 2009].

Fascinating discussion of Dove's interests in form and arrangement, and reflecting the interplay of cultures in poetry, including her representations of guns, war, and dancing.

Helen Vendler, "An Interview with Rita Dove," in *Reading Black, Reading Feminist*, edited by Henry Louis Gates Jr. (London: Penguin, 1990), pp. 481–491.

Discusses craft and aesthetics for her work up to the late 1980s.

## Criticism

Elizabeth Alexander, "*The Yellow House on the Corner* and Beyond: Rita Dove on the Edge of Domesticity," in *Power and Possibility: Essays, Reviews, and Interviews* (Ann Arbor: University of Michigan Press, 2007).

Excellent overview of Dove's first three collections that analyzes how Dove's "girlhood persona" challenges the confines of domesticity.

*Rita Dove* <http://people.virginia.edu/~rfd4b> [accessed 24 November 2009].

Dove's faculty homepage at the University of Virginia. It provides a comprehensive look at her career, complete with links to selected criticism, audios of the poet's readings, and videos of her ballroom dancing.

"Rita Dove: *American Poet*," special issue of *Callaloo*, 31 (Summer 2008).

Includes several poems and prose pieces by Dove, a two-part interview by Charles Henry Rowell, critical essays, a selected bibliography, and current and childhood photographs of Dove with her family and friends.

Lotta Lofgren, "Partial Horror: Fragmentation and Healing in Rita Dove's *Mother Love*," *Callaloo*, 19 (Winter 1996): 135–142.

Explores *Mother Love* through an examination of relationships between mothers and daughters and between women.

Robert McDowell, "The Assembling Vision of Rita Dove," in *Conversant Essays: Contemporary Poets on Poetry*, edited by James McCorkle (Detroit: Wayne State University Press, 1990), pp. 294–302.

Discusses intersections between the personal and public in three of Dove's collections—*The Yellow House, Museum*, and *Thomas and Beulah*—with attention to the relationship between her poems and myths.

Malin Pereira, *Rita Dove's Cosmopolitanism* (Urbana: University of Illinois Press, 2003).

Argues that Dove transcends "racial specificity" in an attempt to touch upon universal themes; includes chapters devoted to each of Dove's major collections through *Mother Love* and an interview conducted by Pereira. This work is especially useful for its summaries of the critical appraisal of each of Dove's works.

Pat Righelato, *Understanding Rita Dove* (Columbia: University of South Carolina Press, 2006).
A thorough and useful examination of Dove's poetry from the first book to *American Smooth*.

John Shoptaw, "Segregated Lives: Rita Dove's *Thomas and Beulah*," in *Reading Black, Reading Feminist*, edited by Henry Louis Gates Jr. (New York: Penguin, 1990), pp. 374–381.
Attributes the difficulties of integrating the volume's two sections of poems ("Mandolin" and "Canary in Bloom") to issues related to the historical separation of genders.

Therese Steffen, *Crossing Color: Transcultural Space and Place in Rita Dove's Poetry, Fiction, and Drama* (New York: Oxford University Press, 2001).
The first full-length critical reaction to Dove's work. Steffen explores Dove's writing up to the new century with an emphasis on its internationality and U.S.-European reach.

*—Billy Clem, Linda Trinh Moser, and Kathryn West*

# Louise Erdrich, *Love Medicine*
(New York: Holt, Rinehart & Winston, 1984;
revised, New York: Holt, 1993).

In a series of interrelated novels and short stories Louise Erdrich has detailed the lives and histories of families on and around an Ojibwe reservation in North Dakota over the course of the twentieth century. She dramatizes her characters' loves, losses, foibles, feats, and tragedies with a mixture of humor that ranges from the subtle to the outrageous, with a clear-eyed sympathy that refuses sentimentality, with an interwoven mixture of the marvelous and the mundane, and with a deep awareness of history. Even in her works that are not part of the reservation series, characters familiar from the reservation make an appearance. Erdrich's reservation series began with *Love Medicine*, winner of the National Book Critics Circle Award (as well as a host of other awards) and the first novel by a Native American to become a best seller.

Karen Louise Erdrich was born on 7 June 1954 to an Ojibwe and French mother and a German American father. She grew up primarily in Wahpeton, North Dakota, near the Turtle Mountain Reservation, where she is an enrolled member of the Pembina band. Both of her parents taught at the Bureau of Indian Affairs school on the reservation. Her maternal grandfather, Patrick Gourneau, was tribal chair of the Turtle Mountain Reservation and one of several sources of fine storytelling during her childhood. Her family encouraged her at a young age to tell stories, with her father offering her a nickel per story and her mother helping her to make book covers.

Erdrich entered Dartmouth College in 1972, the first year it admitted women. She graduated in 1976 and went on to earn a master's degree in creative writing from Johns Hopkins University in 1979. In 1981 she married Michael Dorris, director of the Native American Studies Program at Dartmouth (the first such program in the United States). He had adopted three Native American children, Abel, Madeline, and Jeffrey Sava; in 1989 Dorris published the National Book Award–winning *The Broken Cord,* detailing Abel's struggles growing up with fetal alcohol syndrome. Together Erdrich and Dorris had three daughters, Persia, Pallas, and Aza.

Erdrich and Dorris's marriage created a fruitful literary partnership. Early on, they wrote romance stories under the pen name "Milou North," and Dorris set himself up as Erdrich's agent. They talked through story and character ideas with each other and published one novel, *The Crown of Columbus* (1991), under both their names. They separated in 1995, and in 1997 Dorris committed suicide. Erdrich said that she knew from the second year of their marriage that Dorris suffered from depression severe enough to result in suicide. She gave birth to a fourth daughter in 2001. In addition to her writing career, she has established an independent bookstore, Birchbark Books, in Minneapolis, where she resides.

Erdrich's reservation novels—*Love Medicine; The Beet Queen* (1986); *Tracks* (1988); *The Bingo Palace* (1994); *The Last Report on the Miracles at Little No Horse* (2001), nominated for the National Book Award; and *Four Souls* (2004)—dramatize the lives, loves, and feuds of the Pillager, Kashpaw, Nanapush, Lamartine, Morissey, and Lazarre families, all Ojibwe or mixed Ojibwe and French. *Tales of Burning Love* (1997) is not set on a reservation; but several key characters come from the world of the reservation novels, and one scene retells the story of June Kashpaw's death, the opening scene of *Love Medicine,* from a different perspective. Her other novels are *The Antelope Wife* (1998); *The Master Butchers Singing Club* (2003), which dramatizes the lives of German immigrants living near the reservation; *The Painted Drum* (2005); and *The Plague of Doves* (2008). Erdrich's short stories are collected in *The Red Convertible: Selected and New Stories* (2009). She has written five children's books set in early Native American cultures and has published three volumes of poetry. She also wrote a memoir of pregnancy, *The Blue Jay's Dance: A Birthyear* (1995). Of interest to students wishing to learn more about Ojibwe culture is her *Books and Islands in Ojibwe Country* (2003).

Several of the chapters in *Love Medicine* were first published as short stories, leading some scholars to suggest that the work should be considered a short-story cycle. Erdrich revised the stories as she wove them into a larger narrative; in 1993 she added four new chapters and expanded a fifth to delineate the relationships among characters in greater detail and to strengthen ties to the reservation novels published after it. In 2009 she published another revision, deleting two of the chapters added in the 1993 edition. Students might wish to compare the versions of *Love Medicine* to determine the impact of the revisions on the cohesiveness and the focus of the story. Alternatively, students could compare one of the original short stories to its revision as a chapter in the novel. The copyright page provides information as to where to find the stories.

While *Love Medicine* provides a compelling reading experience on its own, students will have an even richer one by reading other reservation novels. Although published first chronologically, *Love Medicine* dramatizes events that take place after much reservation land has been whittled away owing to the Allotment Acts and unscrupulous timber companies and while the Ojibwe are seeking ways to sustain their traditoin but also survive within the U.S. economy. *Tracks* and *Four Souls* depict events prior to those in *Love Medicine* and provide context for understanding the feuds among the reservation families. *The Beet Queen* overlaps with the early years depicted in *Love Medicine,* while *The Bingo Palace* follows it in time. *The Last Report on the Miracles at Little No Horse* covers the entire twentieth century and is told primarily through the perspective of the reservation priest.

*Love Medicine* follows three generations and fifty years (1934 to 1984) in the lives of several Ojibwe families, with the primary emphasis on the Kashpaws and the Lamartines. The eighteen chapters are mostly narrated in the first person by various characters. The four "elements"—fire, earth, water, and air—serve as potent sources of imagery in the reservation novels, with water taking the dominant and transformative role in *Love Medicine.* Along with its multiplicity of narrators, which allows the reader to learn of family and individual histories from varied and sometimes conflicting sources, the novel blends humor and tragedy in a complex swirl of events.

*Love Medicine* has generated a large amount of scholarship; the works cited below are meant to provide an entry into that body of criticism, which can be carried further by exploring articles and essays cited in their bibliographies. Note that Erdrich's Native characters are alternately referred to as Ojibwe, Chippewa, and Anishinaabeg, and each of those terms is found with alternate spellings. *Ojibwe* once referred to the more northern people, roughly those living in Minnesota and Canada, and *Chippewa* to those in North Dakota, but the two terms have become increasingly interchangeable. *Anishinaabeg* is the name the people traditionally used for themselves, probably meaning "spontaneous people," and it refers to their language. In RESOURCES, spellings of tribal names are not regularized; in the essay above the spellings are Erdrich's.

## TOPICS FOR DISCUSSION AND RESEARCH

1. A fruitful topic for exploration is the concept of home in *Love Medicine.* At the end of the first section of the novel, one finds the sentence "The snow fell deeper that Easter than it had in forty years, but June walked over it like water and came home." Near the end of the novel June's son, Lipsha, has discovered that his biological parents were June and Gerry Nanapush, and he brings home the car June's other son had bought with her insurance money. Rivals Lulu Lamartine and Marie Kashpaw both make homes for many children over the years; several scenes focus on their housekeeping. Lulu's extremely orderly home, which seems to contrast with her love life, burns down. What does home mean to various characters? In what respects

is it a physical place, and how does Erdrich use the concept metaphorically? The essays by James Ruppert, Mark Shackleton, and the third section of essays in Hertha D. Sweet Wong's book provide various perspectives on this topic, as does Lorena L. Stookey's discussion in her second chapter. For a different approach, students might consider how the larger story—the larger history—of losing the tribal land connects to the concept of home. Erdrich's own essay, "Where I Ought to Be: A Writer's Sense of Place," originally published in *The New York Times Book Review* in 1985 and reprinted in Wong, will be helpful.

2. Students might consider the title, *Love Medicine*, in its many and varied implications. What does the term suggest when broken into its two parts, and what does it suggest as a phrase, both in Native and non-Native contexts? Why does the chapter "Love Medicine" share its title with the book? In what ways might this novel be considered an example of love medicine? Is it something that heals? Students will find widely divergent views as to whether the end of the novel and the idea of "love medicine" offers redemption or resonates with the failure to save June and the land or to overcome religious and cultural oppression, alcoholism, and poverty. Advocate for one or the other point of view. Articles by Karen Jane McKinney, Lissa Schneider, John S. Slack, and the chapter by Ruppert offer entries into the debate.

3. Several critics have commented on the powerful women in this novel. What kind of power do these female characters wield? How does this affect their relationships with men? With other women? What does the older generation of women pass on to the younger? Students could consult Susan Castillo, Karen Castellucci Cox, Michelle Pacht, Kristan Sarvé-Gorham, Karah Stokes, and the essay by Annette Van Dyke, "Of Vision Quests and Spirit Guardians: Female Power in the Novels of Louise Erdrich," found in Allan Chavkin's *Chippewa Landscape*. Alternately, students might wish to explore the kinds of power wielded by the men of *Love Medicine*, and their relationship to power.

4. *Love Medicine* offers humor, sometimes even in the face of the most tragic circumstances. What kinds of humor can be found in the novel? Erdrich has described it as "survival humor"—what does she mean by that description? In what ways might it make a political or social statement? How are tricksters related to humor? Claudia Gutwirth and Slack, among others, discuss the role of tricksters in Erdrich's fiction.

5. Students interested in matters of form will find many promising avenues for analysis in *Love Medicine*. For instance, what is the impact of having so many different narrators? What techniques does Erdrich use to make each voice distinctive—are they in fact distinctive? What does the presence of several different voices as opposed to a single narrator accomplish? What implications does this have for thematic and social issues in the novel? Lydia A. Schultz and Schneider will be helpful in approaching these questions. Or one could explore the lyricism that characterizes Erdrich's prose or analyze her use of metaphor and other poetic techniques. You might consider how the novel blends the

short-story cycle and novel genres; the articles by Cox, Slack, and Suzanne Ferguson will be especially useful for this study.

6. Erdrich's grandfather, Patrick Gourneau, served as tribal chair of the Turtle Mountain Band and mingled Catholicism with tribal religious customs—smoking the pipe, using traditional medicine. This blending she saw enacted in her family and community is an important element in her fiction. Thus students might find it fruitful to ponder not only instances of cultural conflict but also the significance of cultural blendings in her imagined worlds. Patricia Riley's article on mixed bloods will be useful here; also helpful is Dennis Walsh, "Catholicism in Louise Erdrich's *Love Medicine* and *Tracks*," *American Indian Culture and Research Journal*, 25, no. 2 (2001): 107–127, as well as the articles by Shackleton, Ruppert, and McKinney. How are these blendings enacted on a personal level (for instance, the alliance between Lulu and Marie) and how on a tribal or communal level? What values ultimately make blendings and alliances possible, and what new values do such cultural blendings make possible? The articles by Schneider and Schultz, although centered on other topics, should also be consulted for their readings of community.

## RESOURCES

### Primary Work

Allan Chavkin and Nancy Feyl Chavkin, eds., *Conversations with Louise Erdrich and Michael Dorris* (Jackson: University Press of Mississippi, 1994).
Collection of interviews with Erdrich and Dorris, separately and together, conducted between 1985 and 1994. The book includes a useful introduction and chronology.

### Criticism

Peter G. Beidler and Gay Barton, eds., *A Reader's Guide to the Novels of Louise Erdrich* (Columbia: University of Missouri Press, 1999).
Detailed genealogies, time lines, geographies, and a dictionary of characters for each of Erdrich's first six novels; useful given the many characters and the complexities of their relationships.

Susan Castillo, "Women Aging into Power: Fictional Representations of Power and Authority in Louise Erdrich's Female Characters," *SAIL: Studies in American Indian Literatures*, 8 (Winter 1996): 13–20.
Notes that, unlike in many traditional American texts where female protagonists die at a young age, in Erdrich's works female characters are presented at various stages of life.

Allan Chavkin, ed., *The Chippewa Landscape of Louise Erdrich* (Tuscaloosa: University of Alabama Press, 1999).
Focuses on games of chance in Erdrich's novels; the role of the carnivalesque; hunting; and female power; offers an essay comparing the two versions of *Love Medicine*, although fails to take into account the role of retelling in native oral traditions.

Karen Castellucci Cox, "Magic and Memory in the Contemporary Short Story Cycle: Gloria Naylor and Louise Erdrich," *College English*, 60 (February 1998): 150–172.
Discusses Erdrich's use of the short-story cycle for *Love Medicine* and notes the way matters of form heighten the sense of community over individuality. Also contains useful insights into the roles of women.

Suzanne Ferguson, *Studies in Short Fiction*, 33 (Fall 1996): 541–555.
Compares the original short-story versions to their revisions as chapters in the novel for how they "mean" in each context.

Claudia Gutwirth, "'Stop Making Sense': Trickster Variations in the Fiction of Louise Erdrich," in *Trickster Lives: Culture and Myth in American Fiction*, edited by Jeanne Campbell Reesman (Athens: University of Georgia Press, 2001), pp. 148–167.
Focuses on Lipsha and the humor of the trickster-like verbal play.

P. Jane Hafen, *Reading Louise Erdrich's* Love Medicine, Boise State University Western Writers Series, 158 (Boise, Idaho: Boise State University, 2003).
Works through the novel section by section, offering readings and explanations; particularly strong in making connections to Ojibwe backgrounds.

Karen Jane McKinney, "False Miracles and Failed Vision in Louise Erdrich's *Love Medicine*," *Critique*, 40 (Winter 1999): 152–161.
Argues against a communal vision and highlights the destructiveness of Catholicism for the Chippewa.

Louis Owens, "Erdrich and Dorris's Mixedbloods and Multiple Narratives," in his *Other Destinies: Understanding the American Indian Novel* (Norman: University of Oklahoma Press, 1992), pp. 192–224.
Traces the theme of search for self and authenticity in Erdrich's first three novels.

Michelle Pacht, "Creating Community: Motherhood and the Search for Identity in Louise Erdrich's *Love Medicine*," *Narratives of Community: Women's Short Story Sequences*, edited by Roxanne Harde (Newcastle upon Tyne, England: Cambridge Scholars Press, 2007), pp. 152–172.
Discusses the central role of June, Marie, and Lulu in the novel, also arguing that Erdrich's chosen form leads to a narrative of community.

Patricia Riley, "There Is No Limit to this Dust: The Refusal of Sacrifice in Louise Erdrich's *Love Medicine*," *SAIL: Studies in American Indian Literatures*, 12 (Summer 2000): 13–23.
Argues that historically most texts featuring mixed bloods have insisted on sacrificing them but that Erdrich takes a markedly different path, insisting on a "synergistic mythic resistance." Riley provides a useful reading of the interaction between Marie Lazarre and Sister Leopolda in "Sister Marie."

James Ruppert, "Celebrating Culture: *Love Medicine*," in his *Mediation in Contemporary Native American Fiction* (Norman: University of Oklahoma Press, 1995), pp. 131–150.

Sees *Love Medicine* as "overcoming Otherness" through its bicultural blendings, offering different but mutually beneficial readings for Native and non-Native readers.

Karla Sanders, "A Healthy Balance: Religion, Identity, and Community in Louise Erdrich's *Love Medicine," MELUS,* 23, 2 (1998): 129–155.
Traces cultural blendings and forms of power.

Kristan Sarvé-Gorham, *Bucknell Review,* 39, 1 (1995): 167–190.
Argues that *Tracks*, set earlier in time than *Love Medicine*, establishes two lines of power in the characters of Fleur and Pauline and that those lines and their much different motivations and goals can be traced into their descendants in *Love Medicine*.

Lissa Schneider, "*Love Medicine:* A Metaphor for Forgiveness," *SAIL: Studies in American Indian Literatures,* 4 (Spring 1992): 1–13.
Focuses on storytelling as act and as form in the novel, arguing that stories help lead to forgiveness and thus the novel becomes a kind of healing or "love medicine" itself.

Lydia A. Schultz, "Fragments and Ojibwe Stories: Narrative Strategies in Louise Erdrich's *Love Medicine," College Literature,* 18 (October 1991): 80–95.
Discusses multi-perspectivity in *Love Medicine,* considering its lineage from Modernism but ultimately deciding that rather than signaling the fragmentation typical there, it constructs a sense of community.

Mark Shackleton, "'June Walked over It Like Water and Came Home': Cross-Cultural Symbolism in Louise Erdrich's *Love Medicine* and *Tracks,"* in *Transatlantic Voices: Interpretations of Native North American Literatures,* edited by Elvira Pulitano (Lincoln: University of Nebraska Press, 2007), pp. 188–205.
Argues that readers must pay attention to bicultural codes—for instance, to Native spiritual beliefs and Catholicism—to appreciate the complexity of Erdrich's work; includes analysis of the water imagery in *Love Medicine*.

John S. Slack, "The Comic Savior: The Dominance of the Trickster in Louise Erdrich's *Love Medicine," North Dakota Quarterly,* 61, 3 (1993): 118–129.
Argues for seeing the trickster in various manifestations as occupying a crucial role in *Love Medicine* and for an ultimately comic and thus redemptive tone; also takes up the question of whether to see the work as a short-story cycle or as a novel.

Karah Stokes, "What about the Sweetheart?: The 'Different Shape' of Anishinabe Two Sisters Stories in Louise Erdrich's *Love Medicine* and *Tales of Burning Love," MELUS,* 24 (Summer 1999): 89–105.
Compares characters and relationships in *Love Medicine* to figures in traditional Anishinaabe myths, focusing particularly on female characters.

Lorena L. Stookey, *Louise Erdrich: A Critical Companion* (Westport, Conn.: Greenwood Press, 1999).

Geared toward students and general readers. The book offers a biographical chapter, a chapter tracing themes of community and storytelling through Erdrich's works, and a chapter on each of the novels published through 1998. The chapter on *Love Medicine* focuses on issues of genre, plot, character, and reader response.

Hertha D. Sweet Wong, ed., *Love Medicine: A Casebook* (New York: Oxford University Press, 2000).

Essential collection, gathering the most important essays published on the novel through 2000. The book is divided into four sections: "Contexts: History, Culture, and Storytelling"; "Mixed Identities and Multiple Narratives"; "Individual and Cultural Survival: Humor and Homecoming"; and "Reading Self/Reading Other." It includes three essays by Erdrich, especially her crucial "Where I Ought to Be: A Writer's Sense of Place." Students will find the essays helpful in addressing all the topics suggested above.

— *Kathryn West*

# Ernest J. Gaines, *A Gathering of Old Men*
(New York: Knopf, 1983)

In his short stories and novels, Ernest J. Gaines draws from his experiences growing up on the River Lake Plantation near Oscar in Louisiana's Pointe Coupée Parish, where his family and ancestors had lived and labored for at least four generations as slaves and, later, as sharecroppers. Gaines, born on 15 January 1933, was the eldest of twelve siblings, eight of whom were raised by his disabled aunt, Augusteen Jefferson, or "Aunt 'Teen," who would become, he has said, "the greatest influence on me, as an artist, as well as a man" (Academy of Achievement interview). By the time he was eight, Gaines was cutting sugarcane in the fields. Because his parish did not have a high school for African Americans, when he was fifteen, he joined his mother and stepfather in Vallejo, California, where he continued his education. To stay off the streets and out of trouble, Gaines spent time in the public library, where reading also became a way to fend off feelings of homesickness for Louisiana. After high school, Gaines spent two years at a community college in Vallejo, followed by two years in the army. The GI Bill allowed him to attend San Francisco State College, where he began writing short stories for *Transfer*, the campus literary magazine. After graduating with a B.A. in 1957, Gaines was awarded a Wallace Stegner Fellowship to attend Stanford University.

Gaines remembers, "There were no books [at the library] by or about blacks, but I read the books that were there. There were lots of books there, but none by and about blacks" (Academy of Achievement interview). Instead, he read the works of Russian writers Leo Tolstoy, Anton Chekhov, and Ivan Turgenev, whose work reminded him of the social divisions in the South. He also acknowledges the influence of American writers Ernest Hemingway, Eudora Welty, and William Faulkner. Like Faulkner's Yoknapatawpha County, Gaines's rural St. Raphael Parish and its central town of Bayonne connects all his works and characters. Most important to his development as a writer, however, is the storytelling or "porch talk" he heard while growing up in "the quarters." His characters' speech patterns, physical appearances, and mannerisms are modeled on the people he has known. "I'm very very proud of my Louisiana background," he has said, "the people I come from—my uncle and the people we drink with, the people I talk with, and the people I grew up around, and their friends" (Lowe). This pride shows in Gaines's literary representations of African American speech patterns, a hallmark of his style and work.

Gaines's work typically features ordinary people plagued by circumstances beyond their control. Despite racism, lack of formal education, poverty, and ill health, they achieve dignity and provide inspiration—like his Aunt 'Teen, who "did not walk a day in her life, but who taught me the importance of standing." This tribute to his aunt serves as the dedication to *The Autobiography of Miss Jane Pittman* (1971), Gaines's third novel, in which the 108-year-old title character recounts events from her birth in slavery to the era just before desegregation. Framing her story is that of the white historian to whom she tells her story. Many readers believed the novel to be true, a testament to its realism. Gaines's ability to reproduce the tenor and variation of African American speech patterns contributes to the realism of all his stories and novels, most of which are told in the first person; only his first novel, *Catherine Carmier* (1964), and fourth, *In My Father's House* (1978), are narrated in third person.

In his writing Gaines combines the "theme of commitment, of responsibility" with the related motif of "someone teaching someone younger something about life" (Academy of Achievement interview). Teaching occurs by example as in the short story "The Sky Is Gray" in *Bloodline* (1968) when a boy watches his mother interact with others during a trip to town. It also happens indirectly through storytelling through which important lessons are transmitted. To underscore the importance of teaching, Gaines makes many of his characters teachers who, ironically, often need to learn as much as, if not more than, their students. *A Lesson before Dying* (1993), for example, features schoolteacher Grant Wiggins, whose "lessons" for a young convict sentenced to death for a murder he did not commit are as much for him as they are for the innocent prisoner. Against the themes of teaching and responsibility, Gaines's fiction provides an implicit criticism of racial hierarchies. His first two novels, *Catherine Carmier* and *Of Love and Dust* (1967), feature biracial couples whose romantic relationships are thwarted by racism. Gaines also elaborates the complex system of social codes dividing Louisiana's African American, Cajun, and Creole communities, revealing not only conflict but surprising alliances as well. In A *Gathering of Old Men* (1983), for example, Gaines reveals the interdependency of Louisiana's unique and varied cultural communities.

In 1993 Gaines received the John D. and Catherine T. MacArthur Foundation Fellowship or "genius award." That year *A Lesson before Dying* won the

National Book Critics Circle Award for fiction. Gaines has also been awarded the National Humanities Medal of the United States, and is a Chevalier de l'Ordre des Arts et des Lettres, one of France's highest honors. In 2007 the Baton Rouge Foundation established the Ernest J. Gaines Award for Literary Excellence in his honor to recognize new fiction by African American authors. Gaines is emeritus writer-in-residence at University of Louisiana at Lafayette, where he began teaching creative writing in 1983.

In his fifth novel, *A Gathering of Old Men,* Gaines reworks the popular genre of the detective story while depicting the actions of a rural community after an African American man kills Beau Boutan, a Cajun farmer. Hindering the investigation by Sheriff Mapes is the expected retribution by Boutan's father, a vigilante whose past acts of violence against the black community are well known. In addition, eighteen elderly black men and one white woman declare responsibility for the death, thus preventing the immediate arrest of the obvious suspect, Mathu. The novel is the culmination of Gaines's most popular themes and narrative techniques. It uses a range of first-person narrators, fifteen in all, who each take turns "speaking," to highlight the relationships across generations and ethnic communities. Eight of the African American narrators are among the "old men" of the title. Also included are an African American boy and two women, one white, the other black. The other narrators are white men, two of whom are sympathetic to the African American community and two who are not. In that context, an interesting study in addition to those cited below is Suzanne W. Jones's *Race Mixing: Southern Fiction since the Sixties* (Baltimore: Johns Hopkins University Press, 2004), which considers interracial relationships as treated in Gaines's novels, including *A Gathering of Old Men,* along with works by both black and white writers, such as Josephine Humphreys, Ellen Douglas, Randall Kenan, and Chris Wiltz.

## TOPICS FOR DISCUSSION AND RESEARCH

1. Gaines's departures from the genre of detective fiction underscore themes related to race, community, and responsibility on the part of both individuals and society. Students interested in genre-related issues might consider how Gaines's depiction of setting, structure, and characterization compare to these elements in typical detective fiction. For definitions and elements of detective novels, students can consult Charles J. Rzepka, *Detective Fiction* (Cambridge, England: Polity Press, 2005), especially the first chapter, "What Is Detective Fiction?," and George N. Dove, *The Reader and the Detective Story* (Bowling Green, Ohio: Bowling Green State University Popular Press, 1997).

2. *A Gathering of Old Men* addresses a theme prevalent in most of Gaines's work: black masculine identity or manhood. Keith Clark has noted that "Gaines does not merely digest and regurgitate shopworn definitions of masculinity," those that emphasize physical strength, intimidation, and power. Instead, he redefines African American manhood to emphasize responsibility to the self, family, and community. "A man got to do what he think is right," Mathu says, "That's what part him from a boy." Using discussions of mas-

culinity in Gaines's fiction included in the volumes by Keith Clark, Karen Carmean, or David C. Estes, students might develop an analysis of definitions of African American manhood in *A Gathering of Old Men*. Questions to consider include: How do racial stereotypes undercut African American masculinity? Which of Mathu's characteristics lead others to describe him as a "man"? As the elderly men transform, which of Mathu's characteristics do they emulate? How does the humorous treatment of stereotypical masculine traits (or lack of them as in Lou Dimes's inability to influence or control Candy) help undermine stereotypical images of manhood? Students might also consider the universal nature of this theme, how the search for manhood serves as a metaphor for what Gaines has described as "the importance of standing."

3. The events of *A Gathering of Old Men* take place in 1973, highlighting challenges that continue to divide communities despite the Civil Rights Movement. Not just older but younger generations of white supremacists, represented respectively by Fix Boutan and Luke Will, echo outdated notions of race. Vigilantism in the rural South is still expected and acceptable by some during this time. Gaines, however, complicates descriptions of racism as merely something whites do to blacks, noting racial and ethnic divisions within both the African and Anglo American communities. He also notes the way class and gender affect relationships between and within ethnic and racial communities. Gaines addresses issues related to race in Michael Sartisky's "Writing about Race in Difficult Times: An Interview with Ernest J. Gaines" (in John Lowe, pp. 253–275). This could be a starting point for an examination of connections between attitudes about race and divisions within and between communities.

4. As the elderly men tell their stories and "work out their gall," to use Sheriff Mapes's description, they describe threats to their rural values and way of life while revealing their commitment to the land. Even Bea, descendant of the white landowning class, says: "The land has not been the same since they brought those tractors here." In "Of Machines and Men: Pastoralism in Gaines's Fiction" (in Estes, pp. 12–29) Frank W. Shelton discusses Gaines's use of pastoral elements. Students could use this essay as a point of departure for exploring how characters define themselves, their community, and the past through a relationship to the land. Alternatively, students might consider how Gaines challenges the dual exploitation of rural environments and African Americans and explores the role shared land use might play in bridging differences between different cultural groups.

5. In "A Breed Between: Racial Mediation in the Fiction of Ernest Gaines" Maria Hebert-Leiter traces the historical relationships of Louisiana's unique racial and ethnic groups, which include African Americans, Cajuns, and Creoles. Students might wish to use this historical context to examine the connections and mutual dependence between black and white communities in *A Gathering of Old Men*. A consideration of cross-racial relationships within and across generations could reveal historical variations in attitudes about race or ways to challenge racism. These relationships include those that cross genera-

tions, such as the one shared by Mathu and Candy; between older characters like Mathu and Sheriff Mapes or Miss Merle; or younger characters like Gil "Salt" Boutan and Cal "Pepper" Harrison—teammates on Louisiana State University's winning football team.

## RESOURCES

### Primary Works

"Ernest Gaines Interview," *Academy of Achievement* <http://www.achievement. org/autodoc/page/gai0int-1> [accessed 24 November 2009].
Discussion of Gaines's life and work.

Marcia Gaudet and Carl Wooton, eds., *Porch Talk with Ernest Gaines: Conversations on The Writer's Craft* (Baton Rouge: Louisiana State University Press, 1990).
Interviews organized thematically. The book includes photographs of the author and of the plantation on which he grew up.

John Lowe, ed., *Conversations with Ernest Gaines* (Jackson: University Press of Mississippi, 1995).
Useful resource that provides an overview of Gaines's work and critical reception in an introduction and a biographical chronology. The interviews span the period from 1969 to 1994.

### Criticism

Valerie Melissa Babb, *Ernest Gaines* (Boston: Twayne, 1991).
Places Gaines within the *griot* tradition. Chapters are devoted to his novels from *Catherine Carmier* to *A Gathering of Old Men* and his collection of short stories.

Jerry H. Bryant, "Ernest J. Gaines: Change, Growth, and History," *Southern Review*, 10 (October 1984): 851–864.
Analyzes Gaines's novels, with particular attention to the major themes and elements that make him a classic Southern American writer.

Karen Carmean, *Ernest J. Gaines: A Critical Companion* (Westport, Conn.: Greenwood Press, 1998).
A thorough study of Gaines's fiction through *A Lesson before Dying* (1994). The book includes a useful bibliography of interviews, reviews, and criticism.

Keith Clark, *Black Manhood in James Baldwin, Ernest J. Gaines, and August Wilson* (Carbondale: Southern Illinois University Press, 2002).
Provides an extended analysis in chapter 3 of depictions of black men and masculinity in Gaines's fiction including *A Gathering of Old Men.*

Mary Ellen Doyle, *Voices from the Quarters: The Fiction of Ernest J. Gaines* (Baton Rouge: Louisiana State University Press, 2002).
Traces "Gaines's evolution as an artist" from short-story writer to novelist, including biographical details related to his craft.

David C. Estes, ed., *Critical Reflections on the Fiction of Ernest J. Gaines* (Athens: University of Georgia Press, 1994).
Essays by fourteen scholars providing thoughtful analyses of Gaines's work.

Marcia Gaudet, "Gaines' Fifteen Narrators: Narrative Style and Storytelling Technique in *A Gathering of Old Men*," *Louisiana Folklore Miscellany*, 6, 3 (1990): 15–22.
Close examination of Gaines's use of oral tradition.

Maria Hebert-Leiter, "A Breed Between: Racial Mediation in the Fiction of Ernest Gaines," *MELUS*, 31 (Summer 2006): 95–117.
Provides historical information about the ethnic communities in Louisiana and their interdependence.

Charles J. Heglar and Annye L. Refoe, "Aging and the African-American Community: The Case of Ernest J. Gaines," in *Aging and Identity*, edited by Sara Munson Deats and Lagretta Tallent Lenker (Westport, Conn.: Praeger, 1999), pp. 139–148.
Examines how Gaines challenges stereotypes of the elderly.

—*Linda Trinh Moser*

# Louise Glück (1943–    )

Louise Elisabeth Glück (pronounced *glick)* does not shy away from autobiographical elements in her work. Her poems are often centered on scenes from childhood and her relationships with parents and other family members, lovers, her son, and the natural world. Her method, however, is not to reproduce life events exactly as they happened but to reshape them through art. In *Proofs and Theories: Essays on Poetry* (1994) she observes, "The source of art is experience, the end product truth, and the artist, surveying the actual, constantly intervenes and manages, lies and deletes, all in the service of truth." Her attempts to uncover the truth include its darker aspects, and she writes most frequently about loss, pain, rejection, disappointment, and betrayal. She avoids, however, the myopic and self-indulgent tendencies of the confessional mode by deflecting the autobiographical self in her use of archetypes from Greek myth, the Bible, and fairy tales. Speaking through various personae, Glück finds liberation from a singular perspective or subjectivity. As critic Helen Vendler notes, she "trie[s] in her poetry to give experience the permanent form of myth" without attempting to make the autobiographical or personal mythic.

Despite the autobiographical nature of her poetry, Glück has remained quiet about the particulars of her life in interviews and essays. Born in New York City on 22 April 1943, she was raised on Long Island. Her mother attended Wellesley and her father, Daniel Glück, was a businessman who invented the X-Acto knife;

his Jewish father emigrated from Hungary and settled in New York. She is one of three sisters, the middle between the youngest, Tereze, and the eldest, who died before she was born and who is the subject of many of Glück's poems. As a teenager, Glück suffered from anorexia, an oft-discussed theme in her work. In her senior year of high school, she began psychoanalysis which lasted for seven years, a process that she says taught her to think and to pay close attention to speech. She attended Sarah Lawrence College in 1962, transferring to Columbia University where she studied with poet Stanley Kunitz (whose work she has written about in *Proofs and Theories,* 1994). Her talents were recognized early on, and in 1967 she was awarded the Columbia University Academy of American Poets Prize; publication of her first poetry collection, *Firstborn* (1968), came soon after. Since then, Glück has been recognized with fellowships from the Guggenheim Foundation, the Rockefeller Foundation, and the National Endowment for the Arts. Her awards include the National Book Critics Circle Award for *The Triumph of Achilles* (1985), the Library of Congress's Rebekah Johnson Bobbitt National Prize for Poetry for *Ararat* (1990), the Pulitzer Prize for *The Wild Iris* (1992), the PEN/Martha Albrand Award for Nonfiction for *Proofs and Theories* (1994), the Lannan Literary Award for Poetry (1999), and the Bollingen Prize (2001). A former U.S. poet laureate (2003–2004), Glück serves as judge for the Yale Series of Younger Poets (a position she has held since 2003) and teaches creative writing at Boston and Yale Universities. She has been married and divorced twice and has one son, Noah, who was born in 1973.

Glück's attempts to transform private experiences into broader social concerns can be traced throughout her work. In her second collection, *The House on Marshland* (1975), the confessional mode of *Firstborn* continues; but she transforms personal into public narratives by adopting the perspectives of various literary figures. In terms of tone, these poems are less grim. Diseased landscapes, relationships, and self of *Firstborn* are replaced with Eden-like imagery and poems about birthing. Not all is rosy, however; poems featuring autumn suggest an ever-present awareness of death. Glück continues this theme in *The Descending Figure* (1980), the title of which refers to images of falling and destruction, from dying biblical cities such as Jerusalem to those of the sister who died at birth. Glück followed it with *The Triumph of Achilles,* which marks her first extended use of literary personae to treat traditional lyrical themes related to loss and betrayal in love; she perfected this technique in the collections published during the 1990s.

The mythic mode seems to provide the kind of detachment encouraged by the psychoanalytic process she underwent as a young adult. Although Glück adopts a more personal tone in *Ararat,* invoking the deaths of her sister and father, she explores feelings of grief and loss with an awareness of her lack of objectivity. In the "Untrustworthy Speaker," for instance, she warns, "Don't listen to me; My heart's been broken. / I don't see anything objectively . . . / When I speak passionately, / that's when I'm least to be trusted." Glück returns to an extended use of other voices and perspectives in *The Wild Iris* and *Meadowlands* (1996). The poems of the first collection describe a garden from early spring to the first frost of autumn with flowers representing different aspects of human feeling but also providing a medium for a divine speaker. *Meadowlands* juxtaposes *The Odyssey* against the banal particulars of a failing marriage in an American suburb, allowing Glück to embrace multiple viewpoints and avoid sensational or mundane domestic details.

Glück continues to investigate domestic life in *Vita Nova* (1999) in which she writes about the process of recovery from the trauma of divorce, a house fire, and relocation. Here, she pays more attention to the simple joys found in everyday life, a theme she continues to expand upon in the poems collected in *The Seven Ages* (2001). In contrast, *Averno* (2006) is "a retraction of the hard-won truce it seemed she had made with nature, mortality, the body, and the pleasures of the quotidian" in her previous two volumes. Returning to what Daniel Morris calls a "uniformly bleak, even apocalyptic" language, the poems depict nature as malevolent rather than healing, a movement suggested by the title, a reference to a lake in Italy that in myth is the gateway to Hades. In *The Village Life* (2009) Glück again registers a connection between the natural cycles of days and seasons with the patterns of human relationships. When the speaker of "Pastoral" says, "No one really understands / the savagery of this place, / the way it kills people for no reason, / just to keep in practice," she could be talking about herself as much as the landscape. But, as in her most successful poems, the potentially narcissistic impulse of personal details gives way to embrace a greater social vision.

An excellent resource for students wishing a general overview of the author's life and work is "Louise Glück: Online Resources" at the Library of Congress website. Maintained by Peter Armenti, it provides an extensive list of links to biographies, interviews, press releases, audio, and video recordings and is available at <http://www.loc.gov/rr/program/bib/gluck/> [accessed 20 November 2009].

## TOPICS FOR DISCUSSION AND RESEARCH

1. Glück adopts different perspectives through the use of personae as diverse as Moses, Joan of Arc and Gretel (in *The House on Marshland*), Persephone and Demeter (in *Ararat*), and Odysseus and Penelope (in *Meadowlands*). This allows her to move outside her own subjectivity in order to come to terms with death, pain, divorce, and the mutability of life. Students interested in this topic might look up original myths, biblical stories and fairy tales, paying particular attention to her revisions and elaboration while also considering how they inform Glück's examination of personal experience. How does Glück's use of these sources create the distance necessary to understand and put into perspective life's losses and difficulties? Think about how they invite the reader's participation by asking us, in the words of Helen Vendler reviewing the book in *New Republic,* to "fill out the story, substitute ourselves for the fictive personages, invent a scenario from which the speaker can utter her lines, decode the import, 'solve' the allegory." Morris's study focusing on Glück's use of "masks" will be especially useful to students interested in this topic as would essays in Joanne Feit Diehl's collection, in particular Bonnie Costello's "*Meadowlands:* Trustworthy Speakers" (pp. 48–62) and Diehl's own "'From One World to Another': Voice in *Vita Nova*" (pp. 151–164).

2. Tony Hoagland discusses Glück's "prosecutorial logic," her use of "an inter-twining deductive sequence of propositions and conclusions." Although Hoagland's analysis refers to the title poem of *The Triumph of Achilles* and "Love Poem" from *The House on Marshland*, it describes a "syllogistic sequence" found in much of her work. Students interested in examining the structural logic of one or more of Glück's poems might begin by paraphrasing it/them in the same way that Hoagland does before analyzing how she modifies sentence structure and uses line breaks and diction to enhance meaning. Also useful for this topic are Stephen Burt's "'The Dark Garage with the Garbage': Louise Glück's Structures" (in Diehl, pp. 74–89) and Helen Vendler's essay.

3. Much of Glück's poetry ponders natural images. From the central floral images in "Mock Orange" in *The Triumph of Achilles* and the talking flowers in *The Wild Iris*, to the conjuring up of an apple tree, bonsai, grass, and the earth in "Nostos" (from *Meadowlands*), Glück employs nature in some of her most successful and beautiful work. Beyond engaging the pastoral tradition or representing nature, Glück utilizes natural elements as metaphors for human existence. Students may be interested in examining how the natural world functions in one or several of her poems. What larger observations about life does Glück draw from natural images? Students might consult the works by Mary Kate Azcuy and Daniel Morris for starting points. Azcuy demonstrates a feminist impulse in Glück's association between nature and the mythic. Morris's "*The House on Marshland:* Second Nature Writing and the Entrance into the Symbolic" (pp. 151–177) and "Should I Say It with Flowers? *Ararat* and the Work of Mourning through Nature Poetry" (pp. 178–190), chapters 6 and 7 of his book, identify thematic concerns associated with the use of natural images in Glück's work.

4. "Legend" in *The Triumph of Achilles* concerns Glück's Jewish grandfather who emigrated from Hungary, and *Ararat* features the burial of her father in a Jewish cemetery. She also conjures Holocaust images in "Gretel in Darkness" and "The Fortress" (in *First Four*). Little scholarship, however, exists that examines the relationship between Glück's work and Judaism. Morris notes that she does not write about Judaism as either religious practice or ethnicity, describing her as "an assimilated Jew who seems as comfortable writing about Achilles, or a red trillium growing between rocks in a suburban garden in Vermont, as she does about Moses or David or Solomon." Students may find it worthwhile to consider the significance of Jewish identity, or lack thereof, in Glück's poetry. Morris provides insights into this topic in "Visions and Revisions: Commentary and the Questions of Being a Contemporary Jewish Poet" (pp. 60–97). This essay provides the first extensive treatment of Jewish themes, exploring Glück's ambivalence toward religious discourse and her reflection of the ancient rabbinic Midrash tradition of reading Scripture in order to discover new meanings and relevance.

5. While Glück has de-emphasized Judaism as a religious practice, her work does ponder matters of a spiritual nature. *The Wild Iris*, for example, as been described as a "contemporary prayer sequence" (Morris) in which Glück ponders the metaphysical. Students may choose to research and discuss the metaphysical nature

of Glück's work, focusing particularly on *The Wild Iris*, whose poems meditate upon death and the mutability of life. Students should pay particular attention to the ways the flowers in the poems suggest or voice a divine force beyond human comprehension. How do these voices critique the gardener-poet and humanity in general? How does Glück employ poetic form and narrative reflection as a way to overcome fears about death? For helpful starting points, students can consult Morris, chapter 8, "Errand in the Spiritual Wilderness: *The Wild Iris* as Contemporary Prayer Sequence" (pp. 191–230), and William V. Davis. Alan Williamson's discussion of the poem "Celestial Music" in his essay "Splendor and Mistrust" (in Diehl, pp. 63–73) also provides useful insights.

## RESOURCES

### Primary Works

Grace Cavalieri, "In the Magnificent Region of Courage: An Interview with Louise Glück," *Beltway Poetry Quarterly*, 10 (Fall 2009) <washingtonart. com/beltway/gluckinterview.html> [accessed 20 November 2009].
Transcript of a 2006 interview that originally aired on the NPR series *The Poet and the Poem from the Library of Congress*. Glück discusses *The Wild Iris*, the interdisciplinary aspects of her poetry, and her "two methods of writing."

Dana Levin, "For a Dollar: Louis Glück in Conversation," *The Academy of American Poets* <http://www.poets.org/viewmedia.php/prmMID/20961> [accessed 20 November 2009].
Originally appearing in *American Poet*, 36 (2009), includes discussion of Glück's influences and the collection *A Village Life*, about which she says: "That's what the book feels like to me: the whole of a life, but not progressive, not narrative: simultaneous."

*Proofs & Theories: Essays on Poetry* (Hopewell, N.J.: Ecco Press, 1994).
Focuses on Glück's thematic, academic, popular, and lyric concerns. The collection includes sections on influences she finds crucial to both contemporary poetry at large and her own.

### Criticism

Mary Kate Azcuy, "Louise Glück, Feminism and Nature in Firstborn's 'The Egg,'" in *Women Writing Nature: A Feminist View*, edited by Barbara J. Cook (Lanham, Md.: Lexington Books, 2008), pp. 57–66.
Close reading of the three-part poem that reveals how the poet moves away from traditional spirituality (which is patriarchal) through an understanding of the relationship between the mythic and the environment which redefines the feminine.

William V. Davis, "'Talked to by Silence': Apocalyptic Yearnings in Louise Glück's *The Wild Iris*," *Christianity and Literature*, 52 (2002).
Examines what is described as the "three powerful and visionary apocalyptic sequences" in *The Wild Iris*, to underscore the poet's "craving" for the immutable.

Joanne Feit Diehl, ed., *On Louise Glück: Change What You See* (Ann Arbor: University of Michigan Press, 2005).
Essential collection featuring essays by leading critics, poets, and scholars. The volume also includes Diehl's interview with the poet.

Elizabeth Dodd, "Louise Glück: The Ardent Understatement of Post Confessional Classicism," in her *The Veiled Mirror and the Woman Poet: H.D., Louise Bogan, Elizabeth Bishop, and Louise Glück* (Columbia: University of Missouri Press, 1992), pp. 149–197.
Situating Glück's position within women's and contemporary poetry, examines the poet's reliance on silence and omission, which allows her to use the mythic and archetypal without losing personal voice.

Tony Hoagland, "Three Tenors: Glück, Hass, Pinsky, and the Development of Talent," *American Poetry Review*, 32 (July–August 2003): 37–42.
An excellent and concise overview of Glück's work from *Firstborn* through *Meadowlands*, provided by the last third of the essay.

Lynn Keller, "'Free / of Blossom and Subterfuge': Louise Glück and the Language of Renunciation," in *Word, Self, Poem: Essays on Contemporary Poetry from the "Jubilation of Poets,"* edited by Leonard M. Trawick (Kent, Ohio: Kent State University Press, 1990), pp. 120–129.
Uses examples from Glück's first four volumes of poetry to examine themes conveyed by her negative images of womanhood—as both biologically and socially determined experience.

Daniel Morris, *The Poetry of Louise Glück: A Thematic Introduction* (Columbia: University of Missouri Press, 2006).
Essential book-length study of Glück's poetry examines her use of "masks," or personae, drawn from the Bible, fairy tales, and history. Each chapter focuses on an overall thematic issue and how it is treated in Glück's individual collections.

Lisa Sewell, "'In the End, The One Who Has Nothing Wins': Louise Glück and the Poetics of Anorexia," *Literature Interpretation Theory*, 17 (2006): 49–76.
Draws from psychoanalytic and literary theory to interpret images of anorexia in the poet's work within the context of poststructuralist accounts of subjectivity. Glück's work shows how "it is not gender per se that makes women vulnerable to eating disorders, but the way social norms and expectations construct femininity."

Helen Vendler, "Louise Glück, Stephen Dunn, Brad Leithauser, Rita Dove," in *The Music of What Happens: Poems, Poets, Critics* (Cambridge, Mass.: Harvard University Press, 1988), pp. 437–454.
Essay that places Glück in the context of her contemporaries and treats her unique contributions to poetic form and technique.

—*D. Gilson and Linda Trinh Moser*

## Barbara Kingsolver, *The Bean Trees*

(New York: Harper & Row, 1988)

Barbara Kingsolver was born in Maryland, 8 April 1955, and raised in rural Carlisle, Kentucky. She began her studies at DePauw University as a music major but switched to biology before graduating magna cum laude, in 1977. After living in France for a time, she returned to the United States and studied at the University of Arizona, where she earned a master's degree in ecology and evolutionary biology in 1981, after which she did additional graduate work in her field.

Kingsolver has established herself as a writer with an engaging, homey voice that attracts many readers, as well as a writer passionately invested in social-justice issues. In 1999 she used the advance for one of her books to establish the Bellwether Prize to advocate literary fiction that addresses issues of social justice. Awarded in even-numbered years, the prize consists of a cash award of $25,000 to the author and publication by a major publisher. In 2000 Kingsolver received the National Humanities Medal for being "a leading voice for human rights, social responsibility and the environment in contemporary American fiction." Kingsolver's 2008 nonfiction book, *Animal, Vegetable, Miracle: A Year of Food Life*, written with her husband, Steven L. Hopp, and daughter, Camille Kingsolver, argues for the necessity of sustainable agricultural practices, recounting a year in which the family vowed to eat only food they grew themselves or could obtain locally. In her two volumes of essays, *High Tide in Tucson* (1995) and *Small Wonder* (2002), she writes of domestic joys and travails alongside national and international political issues, such as 9/11 and nuclear disarmament, often alternating between the two within one essay to make the same kind of statement that characterizes her fiction: the local and the global are inextricably intertwined, and our seemingly individual acts have implications well beyond our personal lives. Her writing has been published in sixty-five countries and translated into twenty-three languages.

Kingsolver clearly inherited some of her strong sense of social justice from her father, who took the family to the Congo for several months and later to St. Lucia in the Caribbean in order to donate his services as a medical doctor. These experiences gave her an expanded vision of the world and the varied circumstances in which people may live. She began writing a novel while suffering from insomnia during her first pregnancy; negotiations for publication of the work were going on while she was in labor, and she signed her contract with Harper & Row the day she came home from the hospital. Linda Wagner-Martin sees Kingsolver's trajectory from that point as grappling with being a mother and a novelist simultaneously; certainly, mother/daughter themes permeate much of her writing.

The year after *The Bean Trees* appeared, Kingsolver published *Holding the Line: Women in the Great Arizona Mine Strike of 1983* (1989), a journalistic work she had been preparing for several years, as well as a collection of short stories, *Homeland and Other Stories* (1989). Her second novel, *Animal Dreams* (1990), again visited issues of corruption and human-rights abuses in Central America, focusing more closely than did *The Bean Trees* on people involved in the Sanctuary movement. *Pigs in Heaven* (1993) returns readers to the story of Taylor Greer and Turtle; it was written in response to the criticism that in allowing her *Bean Trees* protagonist to adopt a Cherokee child she flouted the importance of the Indian Child Welfare Act of 1978, which gives tribes precedence over state and federal entities in the placement of native children. She has said she recognized her mistake in neglecting the moral and legal implications of Turtle having been taken away from the Cherokee, and, as Wagner-Martin notes, she wrote *Pigs in Heaven* to encourage readers to hear "sympathetically the claims of the Indian community."

Some readers thought that Kingsolver had taken a departure with *The Poisonwood Bible* (1998), producing a longer novel with political turmoil in another country as its backdrop. The story of four sisters who, along with their mother, are brought by their evangelical Baptist father, Nathan Price, to the Belgian Congo in 1959, it received the National Book Prize of South Africa and was shortlisted for the Pulitzer Prize and the PEN/Faulkner Award. Kingsolver has also published a book of poetry, *Another America* (1992, enlarged in 1998), which features each poem in English on one side of the page and Spanish on the other. Her novel *Prodigal Summer* appeared in 2000 and *The Lacuna*, also a novel, in 2009.

Kingsolver names as her major influences Doris Lessing, Bobbie Ann Mason, Flannery O'Connor, and Maxine Hong Kingston. In an interview with David King Dunaway she stated, "In high school, I learned that there are three great themes in literature: man against man; man against nature; and man against himself. So it was all 'man' and it was all 'against'; and yet so much of my life has no 'against' in it. It's mostly 'with.' I'm usually figuring out how I can get something done with the help of somebody else, and that is not one of the great themes of literature" she was taught. In her writing, she replaces "against" with a sense of connectedness.

*The Bean Trees* opens with Marietta Greer—she will change her name to Taylor during her trip, adopting the name of the town where she runs out of gas—striking out from her home in rural Kentucky for new territory, in traditional American fashion. What is not traditional about her journey, however, is that unlike James Fenimore Cooper's Natty Bumppo, Mark Twain's Huck Finn, Ernest Hemingway's Nick Adams, and countless other American protagonists who have fled confining homes for new land, Taylor is female; rather than shedding commitments she gains an enormous one on the road when an abused Cherokee child is given to her; and once she arrives in Tucson, Arizona, she finds herself slowly but surely enveloped in community. Taylor learns to be a mother to Turtle and becomes educated about the plight of Latin American political exiles such as Esteban and Esperanza, who lost their child in Guatemala and are now seeking sanctuary with Mattie, the tire-store owner who employs Taylor.

In an essay in *Small Wonder* Kingsolver describes having her mother read the typescript for *The Bean Trees* when she came to see her new grandchild. Addressing her mother, she explains, it is "the longest letter to you I've ever written. Finally, after a thousand tries, I've explained everything I believe in, exactly the way I always wanted to: human rights, Central American refugees, the Problem

That Has No Name, abuse of the powerless, racism, poetry, freedom, childhood, motherhood, Sisterhood is Powerful. All that."

In addition to the works cited below that focus on *The Bean Trees*, students would be well served by consulting general studies of Kingsolver's works. Mary Jean DeMarr's *Barbara Kingsolver: A Critical Companion* (Westport, Conn.: Greenwood Press, 1999) is a reliable introduction to the author's works, as is Mary Ellen Snodgrass's *Barbara Kingsolver: A Literary Companion* (Jefferson, N.C.: McFarland, 2004), which places Kingsolver's fiction in a social context.

## TOPICS FOR DISCUSSION AND RESEARCH

1. *The Bean Trees* presents several examples of women in the process of mothering and learning to mother, most of them in nontraditional situations. Taylor becomes a mother accidentally, having an abused Cherokee child thrust into her car and into her arms when she stops for a meal in Oklahoma—ironically, in the process of fleeing what she sees as the only future for young women in her rural Kentucky hometown: pregnancy. Although she bonds with the child she dubs Turtle and begins to bring her out of her shell, Taylor herself withdraws when Turtle is threatened by a possible molester in the park and must renegotiate what being a mother means to her. Lou Ann has a baby boy, separates from her husband, is visited by her own cantankerous mother and grandmother, and worries incessantly over dangers to her child. Slowly, through taking a job—something many conservative views see as inappropriate for a woman with a small child—Lou Ann develops a stronger sense of self-esteem. Mattie, an older woman who provides sanctuary for Guatemalan political refugees, might be considered in this line of thought for the ways in which she offers nurturing, protection, and education to not only the refugees staying with her but also to Taylor, who goes to work in Mattie's Jesus-is-Lord Used Tires business. Thus, students would find it fruitful to explore ideas of motherhood and mothering in *The Bean Trees*. What does Kingsolver depict as positive and as negative about these various nontraditional versions of motherhood? By extension, what does Kingsolver have to say about gender and community in this novel?

2. In leaving her small hometown and heading west, Taylor Greer seems to be falling into a long tradition of American individualism. Yet, unlike most literary travelers west, Taylor acquires a child along the way and continues amassing friends once she settles in Tucson. In what ways does Kingsolver rewrite the traditional American saga of heading west? This might be considered in terms of different oppositions: How do opportunities, desires, and approaches change according to whether the protagonist is male or female, rich or poor, white or a person of color? How are the tensions between individual desires and community needs played out? Students might find Kingsolver's interview with David Gergen a useful springboard for examining such issues in *The Bean Trees;* the articles by Catherine Himmelwright, Magali Cornier Michael, and Loretta Martin Murrey should also prove helpful.

3. Linda Wagner-Martin notes a tendency in Kingsolver's interviews and essays for the writer to consider herself an outsider, a misfit. Most of the major characters in *The Bean Tree* can be seen as outsiders or misfits in some way. While being an outsider or a social "misfit" can be painful in ways both emotional and physical, what perspectives do Kingsolver's characters gain from their social perspectives and status? What are they able to see and do that someone who feels quite comfortable socially and economically might not? In addition to Wagner-Martin's work, the article by Bob J. Frye would be helpful in exploring this question, particularly in terms of class distinctions.

4. Driving home from a picnic at which Taylor, Turtle, Lou Ann, Mattie, Estevan, and Esperanza have begun to bond, the group sees a mother quail herding her dozens of babies across a road to safety. When a doctor who has examined Turtle explains to Taylor the extent of the abuse the child had suffered in the past (several broken bones, physical and emotional deprivation), she looks out a window and sees a bird who has built her nest in spiny cactus and thinks, "You just couldn't imagine how she'd made a home there." Many other instances occur in the novel in which the emotions, perceptions, and insights of the characters are analogized in a scene in nature. In other words, the natural world often helps characters, especially Taylor, understand what they are hearing. Examining this narrative strategy should prove fruitful. How effective is it, and what are its implied messages?

5. Kingsolver has been criticized for making her characters mouthpieces for certain political views (see Maureen Ryan); she has been praised, on the other hand, for illustrating how interwoven are personal decisions and major social and political issues. Students might research political oppression in Guatemala, the Sanctuary movement in the United States, or controversies surrounding the adoption of native children out of their tribe in order to assess how Kingsolver makes these real issues in her characters' lives. See Wagner-Martin, Gergen, and Michael.

6. In a 1988 *New York Times Book Review* essay Jack Butler started a theme that continues in Kingsolver criticism: the idea that she has brought together the tradition of the Southern novel with that of Southwestern and Western writing. Where and how do these two disparate traditions exist in *The Bean Trees*? How successfully are they melded, and what new insights are available because they are brought together? Himmelwright and Frye would be helpful here.

## RESOURCES

### Primary Work

David Gergen, "Interview with Barbara Kingsolver," 24 November 1995 <www. pbs.org/newshour/gergen/kingsolver.html> [accessed 24 November 2009]. Discusses Kingsolver's decision to live in Spain for a while during the Persian Gulf War. She describes the United States as struggling to balance its cultural idealization of the individual with the need for strong communities.

## Biography

David King Dunaway and Sara L. Spurgeon, eds., "Barbara Kingsolver," in their *Writing the Southwest* (New York: Plume, 1995), pp. 93–107.
Based on interviews done by Dunaway for a radio documentary. The piece provides an overview of Kingsolver's work and career with samples of her and Dunaway's discussion of her childhood, influences, political awareness, and sense of the possibilities of community.

## Criticism

Mary Jean DeMarr, "Mothers and Children in Barbara Kingsolver's *The Bean Trees*," in *Women in Literature: Reading through the Lens of Gender*, edited by Jerilyn Fisher and Ellen S. Silber (Westport, Conn.: Greenwood Press, 2003), pp. 26–28.
Brief article arguing that *The Bean Trees* appeals to female readers because it depicts several models of mothering.

Bob J. Frye, "Nuggets of Truth in the Southwest: Artful Humor and Realistic Craft in Barbara Kingsolver's *The Bean Trees*," *Southwestern American Literature*, 26 (March 2001): 73–83.
Argues for more critical attention to be paid to Kingsolver's work and furthers that project by focusing on her narrative art. Frye claims that Kingslover combines an effective use of humor with several "artful" means for encouraging reader identification—attention to the realities of low social class, satire, cultural criticism, valuing exemplary role models—thus creating an "aesthetics of the ordinary."

Catherine Himmelwright, "Gardens of Auto Parts: Kingsolver's Merger of American Western Myth and Native American Myth in *The Bean Trees*," *Southern Literary Journal*, 39 (Spring 2007): 119–139.
Sees Kingsolver starting with the archetypal American story of a protagonist heading west for adventure but then reversing all the major points of that story, with Taylor accumulating friends and community as she makes her way. Himmelwright profitably focuses on the diametric opposites running through the novel—for example, junkyards and gardens in the same space, a Southern sensibility in a Western setting—and her references to historical women's experiences of going west add context.

Magali Cornier Michael, *New Visions of Community in Contemporary American Fiction: Tan, Kingsolver, Castillo, Morrison* (Iowa City: University of Iowa Press, 2006).
Reads *The Bean Trees* and *Pigs in Heaven* as depicting healthy, vibrant communities of extended families not necessarily created due to blood ties or kinship and argues that Kingsolver successfully promotes multiculturalism without erasing difference.

Loretta Martin Murrey, "The Loner and the Matriarchal Community in Barbara Kingsolver's *The Bean Trees* and *Pigs in Heaven*," *Southern Studies*, 5 (March 1994): 155–164.

Considers *The Bean Trees* through the lens of the tradition of loners in American literature, typically male and moving away from community.

Maureen Ryan, "Barbara Kingsolver's Lowfat Fiction," *Journal of American Culture*, 18 (Winter 1995): 77–82.
Accuses Kingsolver of offering endings that are too "easy" in both *The Bean Trees* and *Pigs in Heaven*, of offering "political correctness" rather than deep political analysis.

Linda Wagner-Martin, *Barbara Kingsolver* (Philadelphia: Chelsea House, 2004).
A critical overview of Kingsolver's writing with biography woven throughout. The chapter on *The Bean Trees* emphasizes the role of women's communities and the parallels between individual personal circumstances and national issues in such acts as providing sanctuary to political refugees.

*—Kathryn West*

⌒◯◯◯⌒

# Maxine Hong Kingston, *The Woman Warrior: Memoirs of a Girlhood among Ghosts*
(New York: Knopf, 1976)

Maxine Hong Kingston's best-known work, *The Woman Warrior*, opens with an injunction to silence: "You must not tell anyone." The narrator, however, proceeds to reveal her family's history and secrets but in a way that combines historical reality and fantasy inspired by imagination and stories told to her about China. Kingston cites her parents' status as illegal immigrants as the reason for her obfuscation of fact. "I was thinking," she admits, "that if immigration authorities read my books they could not find evidence to deport my parents" (Alegre). Kingston's parents both emigrated from China but at different times. Her father, Thom Hong, arrived in New York City in 1924; her mother, Ying Lan Hong, arrived about fifteen years later. Maxine Ting Ting Hong was born on 27 October 1940 in Stockton, California, the eldest of her parents' six American-born children; two had died in China. The Hongs supported their family with a laundry business, but Kingston's father also sometimes ran a gambling operation, while her mother, who had practiced medicine in China, found seasonal work as a field hand.

Kingston's love of literature and storytelling was inspired by her father's educational background—he had trained to be a poet and scholar—and her mother's storytelling. She learned about Chinese culture and her family's history through her mother's "talkstory"; what she heard became inspiration for the written works she eventually published. Kingston's first writing success came early. When still a teenager, she won a $5 prize for the essay "I Am an American," published in *The American Girl*, a magazine for the Girl Scout organization. Although her interest in writing persisted, a facility with math led her to major first in engineering at the University of California; she switched later to English. After graduating in 1962, she married Earll Kingston, an actor; their only child, Joseph Lawrence Chung Mei, was born in 1964. Kingston began her teaching career in 1966 at Sunset High School in California. In 1967 she and her family relocated to Hawaii where she taught English and writing at several schools, including Mid-Pacific Institute and the University of Hawaii. While in Hawaii, she published her first book, *The Woman Warrior*, inspired by the experiences of women in her family. This was followed by a companion work, *China Men* (1980), which recounts the lives of her male relatives who left behind their homeland. These first two works weave together elements of fiction, myth, biography, and history; however, despite their fictive elements both works were initially received as nonfiction. Both books continue the theme of her first publication, "I Am an American," in their depiction of Chinese immigrant experience.

Kingston's third book and first novel, *Tripmaster Monkey: His Fake Book* (1989), also weaves together Chinese immigrant and mainstream American experience. The name of her fifth-generation Chinese American protagonist, Wittman Ah Sing, pays obvious tribute to Walt Whitman. The double narrative threads reflect Kingston's interests in cultural fusion. Interspersed with descriptions of Wittman's struggles as a playwright after graduating from Berkeley during the radical heyday of the 1960s is the story of the Monkey King, a legendary figure who brought Buddhist scriptures to China from India. In his attempt to merge East and West and to create a Chinese American language in his work, Wittman is like the Monkey King who brought "foreign" rhythms westward from India. Kingston planned to continue Wittman's story in her next book, but the manuscript was destroyed by the 1991 fires that ravaged the Oakland-Berkeley hills in California and destroyed her home. But she does finally "make [him] grow up" in *The Fifth Book of Peace* (2003), which features "his life as a husband and as a responsible father" (Alegre). Like her previous works, it combines biographical and imaginative aspects while describing the reconstruction of her lost novel-in-progress alongside the process of recovery from the loss of her home and possessions.

*The Fifth Book of Peace* describes Kingston's participation in writing workshops for war veterans. Having focused on thematic issues related to speaking out in her writing, Kingston turned to helping others find voice in order to translate their experiences into poems, novels, and essays. Since 1993 Kingston has worked with more than five hundred veterans of every American war since World War II (though Vietnam veterans represent the largest number). Some of the works by workshop participants have been collected and edited by Kingston in *Veterans Of War, Veterans Of Peace* (2006). As Bill Moyers has noted, "For many of them it has been a life-changing, even life-saving experience." Her project moves beyond individual needs and reflects her enduring activism as, along with veterans, she seeks to create "a literature of peace." Her activism moves beyond the written page and workshop setting. In March 2003 she was arrested while participating in a Washington, D.C., protest against the war in Iraq; her cellmate was fellow writer Alice Walker.

Kingston has published two volumes of essays. The earliest, *Hawai'i One Summer* (1987; republished in 1998), includes essays she wrote in 1978 for *The New York Times* and offers insights into her life in Hawaii and her teaching. Those collected in *To Be the Poet* (2002) are based on her William E. Massey Lectures in 2000 at Harvard University and explore her growing experimentation with writing in verse and attempts to live a poet's life. Kingston has been recognized for her work. *The Woman Warrior* was awarded the National Book Critics Circle Award for Nonfiction in 1976, *China Men* was the 1981 National Book Award Winner for General Nonfiction, and *Veterans of War, Veterans of Peace* (2006) was awarded the Northern California Book Award Special Award in Publishing. She is the recipient of an American Academy of Arts and Letters Award in Literature. In 1997 then-president Bill Clinton presented her with a National Humanities Medal from the National Endowment for the Humanities. In 2002 Kingston retired from the University of California, having taught there since 1990.

The Woman Warrior, Kingston's most popular work, was described in 1987 by poet laureate Robert Hass as "the book by a living author most widely taught in American universities and colleges." In part, its popularity on campuses comes from its relevance to many different disciplines: literature, history, Asian American studies, women's studies, and anthropology. Yet, this popularity also signals the pleasure many readers have found in her engaging prose, her evocation of the challenges posed by growing up amidst two very different cultures, and her insistence that myth and story may have as much reality in our lives as do facts and events. The book is divided into five interconnected stories, each featuring a different female figure. In the first, "No Name Woman," the narrator describes the suicide of her paternal aunt after she gave birth to an illegitimate child. The second, "White Tigers," features an allegorical fantasy in which the narrator imagines herself as a version of the legendary Chinese woman warrior, Fa Mu Lan. "Shaman," the third section, depicts the experiences of Brave Orchid, the narrator's mother, in China where she was a doctor and in the United States. The fourth section, "At the Western Palace," features her maternal aunt Moon Orchid's mental breakdown after she immigrates to the United States from China in order to find her estranged husband. "A Song for a Barbarian Reed Pipe," the last, features the narrator's childhood experiences before closing with an image of cultural fusion: a re-telling of the story of early-third-century Chinese poet Ts'ai Yen, who, like the narrator, learns to sing in a foreign tongue.

## TOPICS FOR DISCUSSION AND RESEARCH

1. Despite being highly acclaimed, *The Woman Warrior* has received criticism centering on a debate over Kingston's representation of Chinese and Chinese American culture. Perhaps her most vocal critic has been playwright and novelist Frank Chin, who accuses Kingston of inventing a "fake" Chinese American culture to appeal to white readers. Benjamin R. Tong in an 11 May 1977 article in the *San Francisco Journal* ("Critic of Admirer Sees Dumb Racist") describes Kingston as a "sell-out" who lacks any "organic connection" to Chinese American history. Those on the other side of the debate include Deborah L. Madsen, who challenges notions of cultural "authenticity" by examining different traditions in Chinese immigrant writing. Madsen argues that Kingston subverts "racial authenticity" in representations that combine both Chinese and American elements. King-kok Cheung defends Kingston against what she

perceives to be exclusionary definitions of Chinese American identity based on masculine or "heroic" traits. Students might consider examining *The Woman Warrior* with this controversy over "authenticity" in mind, paying particular attention to aspects in the work most often criticized. Important to consider are the narrator's exploration of Chinese and American culture and her stance toward them, in particular, the questioning, undercutting, and revision of all her stories (as in the story of the "no name" aunt and of tongue cutting). Students might also discuss the ways *The Woman Warrior* can be and has been "misread," considering the consequences of these misreadings, and offering a remedy. Kingston addresses these in "Cultural Misreading by American Reviewers" as does Li. Other helpful works are Grice and Wong; the former provides a summary of the criticism against Kingston in a chapter devoted to *The Woman Warrior*, and the latter includes essays both criticizing and praising the work. Students could also consult Jeehyun Lim, who challenges Kingston's critics for "misread[ing] her play with ideas of foreignness and nativeness," and Kingston's own comments about her critics (made during an interview with Marilyn Chin, included in Skenazy and Martin).

2. The narrator juxtaposes the Fa Mu Lan story against a comment about her own life. "My American life," she says, "has been such a disappointment." Students might want to examine how the narrator's revision of Fa Mu Lan allows her to explore and reconcile the paradoxical version of female identity represented by what she has observed in Chinese and American cultures, her mother's "talk-story," and the myths she has been told. How does her revision of the story help her to shape a positive identity that is female and Chinese American? Another way to approach Kingston's version of Fa Mu Lan would be to compare it to the original (Frank Chin provides a translation, "The Ballad of Mulan," in his essay, pp. 5–6) and other revisions, such as the Disney animated film *Mulan* (1998) and Jeanne Lee's illustrated children's book *The Song of Mu Lan* (1995). Students can show what elements Kingston has added to the story and how her revision compares with others. In addition, students might consider how changes, additions, and/or deletions highlight certain themes. How do the changes help the narrator define herself and her Chinese American identity? For critical discussions about Kingston's representation of Fa Mu Lan, see Dong and Lan.

3. Critics have praised Kingston for her attention to the subjectivity of Chinese women who have long been oppressed by Chinese male tradition. This approach, however, may ignore other thematic concerns in *The Woman Warrior*. Maureen Sabine argues that Kingston's first work should be read alongside *China Men*, citing Kingston's own description of how she conceived of and wrote the two works together. Kingston decided to separate the male and female narratives when she felt that the "men's stories seemed to interfere. They were weakening the feminist point of view. So I took all the men's stories out, and then I had *The Woman Warrior*." Sabine's study (especially the introduction and first chapter) would serve as a starting point for students interested in comparing *The Woman Warrior* and *China Men*. Students should pay close attention to the connections between male and female immigrant experiences, for example, the ways both are subject to immigration laws, stereotypical thinking, and silenc-

ing by dominant American culture. Another approach would be to show how thematic issues in one work "speak to" or reveal similar issues in the other. For example, how are characters in *China Men* subject to the same silencing as the "no name" aunt and other characters from *The Woman Warrior*? How do they eventually find voice? Also worth considering is the way male characters are emasculated or feminized by mainstream American culture. Is this process similar to the narrator's in *The Woman Warrior* as she looks for ways to subvert what is Chinese and/or American feminine? How do the brief vignettes in *China Men* like "The Ghostmate" and "The Wild Man of the Green Swamp" highlight concerns similar to those in *The Woman Warrior*, such as Brave Orchid's battle with a sitting ghost and the captivity story of Ts'ai Yen?

4. In her interview with Miel Alegre and Dave Weich, Kingston says: "I feel that I have had to translate a whole Eastern culture and bring it to the West, then bring the two cultures together seamlessly. That is how one makes the Asian American culture." This "fusion" of Chinese and Western images and metaphors is a hallmark of Kingston's style. Choosing one story from *The Woman Warrior*, students can explore the ways she transplants and transforms Chinese "talkstories" to make them relevant to an American setting. Alternatively, students might consider how stories about China help her overcome racial oppression. Useful approaches to this topic are suggested in the essays by Cheung, Petit, and Winsbro.

5. The critical debate surrounding *The Woman Warrior* touches upon the book's generic status. Subtitled a "memoir," it was initially published as nonfiction. More-recent editions label it as fiction, acknowledging its blending of biography and history with fantasy and myth. How do these labels impact the way you read and understand the story? How do they create certain expectations about the shape and content of the book? Students might alternatively wish to examine another unstable boundary in *The Woman Warrior*: the one between Chinese and American culture. Early in the work the narrator asks: "Chinese-Americans, when you try to understand what things in you are Chinese, how do you separate what is peculiar to childhood, to poverty, insanities, one family, your mother who marked your growing with stories, from what is Chinese? What is Chinese tradition and what is the movies?" Students might also consider the connection between Kingston's blurring of genres and the narrator's confusion about what is Chinese (and American). How does one reflect the other? Helpful discussions of shifting perspectives and genres can be found in chapters about *The Woman Warrior* in Grice, Huntley, and Simmons.

## RESOURCES

### Primary Works

Miel Alegre and Dave Weich, "Powell's Book Interview: Maxine Hong Kingston After the Fire" <http://www.powells.com/authors/kingston.htm> [accessed 24 November 2009].
A 2003 interview in which Kingston discusses writing, touching on reasons for the narrative style in *The Woman Warrior*.

Shirley Geok-lin Lim, "Reading Back, Looking Forward: A Retrospective Interview with Maxine Hong Kingston," *MELUS,* 33 (Spring 2008): 157–170.
A 2006 interview highlights Kingston's development as a writer.

Bill Moyers, "Bill Moyers Interview," *Bill Moyers Journal* (25 March 2007) <http://www.pbs.org/moyers/journal/05252007/transcript1.html> [accessed 24 November 2009].
An interview in which Kingston and participants of her writing workshops for veterans discuss how writing facilitates healing and helps them "come home" from war.

Paul Skenazy and Tera Martin, eds., *Conversations with Maxine Hong Kingston* (Jackson: University Press of Mississippi, 1998).
Collection of sixteen interviews with Kingston, from 1977 to 1996, dealing with *The Woman Warrior, China Men,* and *Tripmaster Monkey.* The chronology and introduction provide a concise summary of all the interviews.

## Criticism

King-Kok Cheung, "Provocative Silence: *The Woman Warrior* and *China Men,*" in *Articulate Silences: Hisaye Yamamoto, Maxine Hong Kingston, Joy Kogawa* (Ithaca, N.Y.: Cornell University Press, 1993), pp. 74–125.
An essential discussion of Kingston's varied uses of silences.

Frank Chin, "Come All Ye Asian American Writers of the Real and the Fake," in *The Big Aiiieeeee! An Anthology of Chinese American and Japanese American Literature,* edited by Jeffrey Paul Chan, Frank Chin, Lawson Fusao Inada, and Shawn Wong (New York: Meridian, 1991), pp. 1–92.
Essay in which Chin defines "real" Asian Americans in opposition to those who are "fake." According to Chin, the latter are assimilated and mirror "white racist" stereotypes.

Lan Dong, "Writing Chinese America Into Words and Images: Storytelling and Retelling of the Song of Mu Lan," *The Lion and the Unicorn,* 30 (April 2006): 218–233.
Useful essay that compares three re-creations of the Chinese story: Jeanne Lee's *The Song of Mu Lan* (1995), Kingston's *The Woman Warrior,* and the Disney animated film *Mulan* (1998).

Helena Grice, *Maxine Hong Kingston* (Manchester, England & New York: Manchester University Press, 2006).
An overview of Kingston's life with attention to her development as a writer and activist; includes a summary of the debate concerning the genre of *The Woman Warrior* and chapters about each of Kingston's works through *The Fifth Book of Peace.*

E. D. Huntley, *Maxine Hong Kingston: A Critical Companion* (Westport, Conn.: Greenwood Press, 2001).
Critical overview of thematic and stylistic issues in Kingston's first three works: *The Woman Warrior, China Men,* and *Tripmaster Monkey;* includes an overview

of Asian American literary history and a bibliography of works by and about Kingston.

Feng Lan, "The Female Individual and the Empire: A Historicist Approach to Mulan and Kingston's *Woman Warrior*," *Comparative Literature*, 55 (Summer 2003): 229–245.
Presents the evolution of the Chinese legend in an attempt to rehistoricize Kingston's version.

David Leiwei Li, "Can Maxine Hong Kingston Speak? The Contingency of *The Woman Warrior*," chapter 2 of *Imagining the Nation: Asian American Literature and Cultural Consent* (Stanford, Cal.: Stanford University Press, 1998), pp. 44–62.
Discusses the "disastrous" results when the oppression of Asian and Asian American women is viewed only as a product of their root culture.

Jeeyun Lim, "Cutting the Tongue: Language and the Body in Kingston's *The Woman Warrior*," *MELUS*, 31 (22 September 2006): 49–65.
Focusing on images of tongue cutting, addresses critics who see the novel as a misrepresentation of the Chinese American community as abusive and barbaric.

Shirley Geok-lin Lim, ed., *Approaches to Teaching Kingston's "The Woman Warrior"* (New York: Modern Language Association, 1991).
Although geared toward teachers, includes seventeen essays in part 2, "Approaches," that are also useful for general readers because they provide the historical, cultural, and literary contexts in which to study and interpret the novel.

Debra Madsen, "Chinese American Writers of the Real and the Fake: Authenticity and the Twin Traditions of Life Writing," *Canadian Review of American Studies*, 36, 3 (2006): 257–271.
A thorough overview of the dispute between Kingston and Frank Chin. Madsen also discusses their stances within the context of two distinct traditions of Chinese writing and within the historical context of Chinese immigrant communities.

Angela Petit, "Words So Strong: Maxine Hong Kingston's 'No Name Woman' Introduces Students to the Power of Words," *Journal of Adolescent and Adult Literacy*, 46 (March 2003): 482–493.
Describes the "rich reading experiences" and insights of the author's high-school students inspired by the novel and discusses the "classic themes of adolescence" in the work.

Maureen Sabine, *Maxine Hong Kingston's Broken Book Life: An Intertextual Study of* The Woman Warrior *and* China Man (Honolulu: University of Hawai'i Press, 2004).
Argues that feminist readings of *The Woman Warrior* obscures discussion of other political and thematic issues that become obvious when the interplay between *The Woman Warrior* and *China Men* is considered.

Diane Simmons, *Maxine Hong Kingston* (New York: Twayne, 1999).
Informative study of Kingston's work through *Tripmaster Monkey*, providing historical and biographical contexts.

Bonnie C. Winsbro, "Writing with Ghosts: Power through Individuation in Maxine Hong Kingston's *The Woman Warrior*," in *Supernatural Forces: Belief, Difference, and Power in Contemporary Works by Ethnic Women* (Amherst: University of Massachusetts Press, 1993), pp. 154–180.
Examines the use of the supernatural in the novel and the way it challenges Western and Judeo-Christian notions of reality.

Sau-ling Cynthia Wong, ed., *Maxine Hong Kingston's* The Woman Warrior: *A Casebook* (New York: Oxford University Press, 1999).
Overview of multiple ways of interpreting the novel, critical debates, and a discussion of its reception. Also included is a 1977 interview with Kingston in which she discusses the novel.

—*Linda Trinh Moser*

# Tony Kushner, *Angels in America: A Gay Fantasia on National Themes*

*Part One: Millennium Approaches* (London: National Theatre/Nick Hearn, 1992); *Part Two: Perestroika* (London: National Theatre/Nick Hearn, 1994)

Pulitzer Prize–winning dramatist, screenwriter, opera and musical librettist, director, and essayist Tony Kushner was born in New York City on 16 July 1956. His family soon moved to Lake Charles, Louisiana, where he spent his childhood. His parents were classically trained musicians. Kushner credits his career in theater to his mother, whom he saw perform in local productions. He was set apart from other children by his Jewish background, his artistic and political interests, and his homosexuality, of which he was aware from age six and certain by eleven.

He hid his sexual orientation from family and friends throughout his undergraduate career, begun in 1974 at Columbia University. While a student, he sought treatment for his homosexuality through psychotherapy before accepting who he was and informing those close to him. In 1981 he called his mother from a pay phone in New York to tell her he was gay, an event he re-created in *Angels in America, Part One: Millennium Approaches*. While at Columbia, he read widely—Bertolt Brecht's plays, the works of Walter Benjamin and Karl Marx, medieval literature, and classical Greek drama. He received his bachelor of arts degree in English literature in 1978. Six years later, he earned a master of fine arts degree in directing at New York University's Tisch School of the Arts.

Kushner has written plays since the early 1980s. In the dramatic tradition of Brecht, Henrik Ibsen, and George Bernard Shaw, he uses his stage to stimulate thought and social discussion in audiences on such complex, controversial topics as religion, prejudice, power, history, hypocrisy, morality, homosexuality, AIDS, and, especially, politics; for him, "all theatre is political" (quoted in

Fisher, 2001). Despair over the reelection of President Ronald Reagan in 1984 inspired his first significant play. He set *A Bright Room Called Day* (1985) in 1930s Berlin during the rise to power of Adolf Hitler but used "Interruptions" between certain scenes to criticize the Reagan administration's conservative policies. In 1987 Kushner was commissioned to write a play for San Francisco's Eureka Theatre about the impact of AIDS on that city's gay community; the disease had been first recognized in 1981. After workshops and productions in California, London, and New York, *Angels in America* was produced on Broadway in 1993. *Part One: Millennium Approaches* opened in May and received the Antoinette Perry (Tony) Award for best play and the Pulitzer Prize in drama. *Part Two: Perestroika* opened on Broadway six months later and won the 1994 Tony for best play. *Angels in America* established Kushner as a preeminent American playwright.

Kushner called his play a fantasia, describing, as in music, a work in which the composer's imagination, or fantasy, moves unrestricted by a specific form. In that spirit, Kushner, using a nonlinear structure, shifts easily, often quickly, between and among intersecting plots, styles (realism, surrealism, farce), tones (serious, comic), and staging techniques (single locales, simultaneous settings with overlapping dialogue, visible scene changes, spectacular theatrical effects). The "National Themes" of the subtitle comprise the political and religious conservatism of the 1980s during the presidency of Ronald Reagan as well as the gay culture and the AIDS epidemic in that decade. Critic John Lahr observed in his review in *The New Yorker* (31 May 1993) that Kushner "honors the gay community by telling a story that sets its concerns in the larger historical context of American political life."

*Angels in America* has been called an epic play for both its thematic breadth and its structural scope. Its two parts have a combined running time of seven hours. The action spans more than four years (October 1985–January/February 1990), in such disparate settings as a funeral home, bedrooms, offices, hospital wards, New York, Salt Lake City, a hallucinatory Antarctica, Moscow, heaven, and, briefly, hell or purgatory. The twenty to twenty-five characters in each play are interpreted by eight actors taking several roles. The play's four main stories focus on the gay couple Louis Ironson and Prior Walter, the married couple Joe and Harper Pitt, the devious New York lawyer Roy Cohn, and God and his angels. Each plot illustrates the complete work's principal theme of change.

Part 2 of *Angels in America—Perestroika*—takes its title from the Russian word for "restructuring," used to describe Soviet leader Mikhail Gorbachev's economic and political reforms in the mid 1980s. In the opening scene, set in the Kremlin in January 1986, Aleksii Antedilluvianovich Prelapsarianov, "the World's Oldest Living Bolshevik," acknowledges "we all desire that Change will come," but, until he reads the new political "Theory" that will "reorder the world," he exclaims, "we MUST NOT move ahead!"

In the celestial realm God, "Bewitched by Humanity" and its "Potential for Change," has deserted his angels and disappeared. Prior Walter, whom the Angel of America greets as "Prophet," is charged with telling humanity to cease moving so that God will return to his rightful home. Prior refuses, informing the angelic Continental Principalities, "We can't just stop. We're not rocks—progress, migration, motion is . . . modernity. It's *animate*, it's what living things do. We desire."

The epilogue to *Perestroika* (and to *Angels in America* as a whole), set four years later in early 1990, marks significant changes. International evidence includes the fall of the Berlin Wall, perestroika, and the end of the Cold War. On the personal level, Prior has lived with AIDS for five years (likely benefiting from Roy Cohn's unused AZT pills—purloined and presented to Prior by a friend). To society at large he proclaims that he and others with the disease "are not going away" and "won't die secret deaths anymore. The World only spins forward. We will be citizens. . . . The Great Work Begins." Many of Kushner's plays, *Angels in America* among them, deal unflinchingly with suffering, loss, and death, but hope, as a complementary theme to change, regularly lightens those works. Prior asserts, "We live past hope."

In 1994 Kushner wrote *Slavs! Thinking about the Longstanding Problems of Virtue and Happiness*, which he called a "coda" to *Angels in America*. The ninety-minute play, crafted largely from material not used in *Perestroika* and covering the period 1985 to 1992, explores the collapse of the Soviet Union and its aftermath. Since then Kushner has written such works as *Homebody/Kabul* (1999; revised, 2004), a four-hour political drama on Afghanistan; the book and lyrics for *Caroline, or Change* (2002), a semi-autobiographical musical; and the play *The Intelligent Homosexual's Guide to Capitalism and Socialism with a Key to the Scriptures* (2009).

## TOPICS FOR DISCUSSION AND RESEARCH

1. Kushner has frequently acknowledged the significance of Bertolt Brecht's plays and dramatic theories in his development as a playwright. To measure the extent of Brecht's influence on *Angels in America* and its coda, *Slavs!*, students could first read one or more of his major plays, such as *Mother Courage and Her Children* (translated, 1966), *The Good Person of Setzuan* (translated, 1993), and *The Caucasian Chalk Circle* (translated, 1948), as well as his theories on epic theater, political theater, and the "alienation effect." Then students could compare and contrast the chosen Brechtian play(s) and theories with relevant examples from Kushner's plays. Helpful sources include *Brecht on Theatre*, edited and translated by John Willett (New York: Hill & Wang, 1964); and two essays in the volume edited by Deborah R. Geis and Steven F. Kruger—Janelle Reinelt, "Notes on *Angels in America* as American Epic Theatre," pp. 234–244, and Art Borreca, "'Dramaturging' the Dialectic: Brecht, Benjamin, and Declan Donnellan's Production of *Angels in America*," pp. 245–260.

2. In light of political references in *Angels in America*, students might research history of the spread and treatment of AIDS in the United States since the discovery of the disease in the early 1980s. A useful starting place is Randy Shilts's *And the Band Played On* (1987).

3. Critic James Fisher claims that "Belief in progress, in compassion, in the transformative power of love, in true community is the religion Kushner offers for the new millennium." Students might analyze *Angels in America* from the perspective of each belief in Fisher's quotation to gauge its accuracy. Students could also determine how these beliefs constitute a religion of sorts. A precise definition of "religion" is a necessary element of the analysis.

4. Consider discussing the ways in which *Angels in America* is not only a gay/AIDS play but also a drama about discrimination on the basis of gender, race, and religion, as well as sexual orientation. Part of this discussion might profitably focus on the moral message concerning bigotry and tolerance. See the four essays grouped under the heading "'I I I I': Identities in *Angels*," in Geis and Kruger, pp. 103–169.

5. A major character in both parts of *Angels in America* is the conservative lawyer Roy Cohn. (He also appears in Kushner's short play *G. David Schine in Hell* [1996].) As Kushner notes in the similarly worded disclaimers in *Millennium Approaches* and *Perestroika*, he based Cohn on a real person of that name and attributed to the stage version acts committed by him. The playwright states, however, that the Cohn of *Angels* is "a work of fiction; his words are my invention, and liberties have been taken." Research the life of the real Cohn, including his homosexuality and his role in the espionage trial of Ethel and Julius Rosenberg (also in *Angels in America*). How much artistic license does Kushner exercise in drawing his Cohn? To what extent, and how, does he succeed in making Cohn a believable, three-dimensional, dynamic—even appealing—character? To what degree is he flat and static? How accurate is it to label him the villain of *Angels in America*? Sources to consult include Nicholas von Hoffman, *Citizen Cohn* (New York: Doubleday, 1978); Michael Cadden, "Strange Angel: The Pinklisting of Roy Cohn," in Geis and Kruger, *Approaching the Millennium*, pp. 78–89; Atsushi Fujita, "Queer Politics to Fabulous Politics: Pinklisting and Forgiving Roy Cohn," in James Fisher, ed., *Tony Kushner: New Essays on the Art and Politics of the Plays* (2006), pp. 112–136.

## RESOURCES

### Primary Work
Robert Vorlicky, ed., *Tony Kushner in Conversation* (Ann Arbor: University of Michigan Press, 1998).
Twenty-two interviews that present Kushner's interests, opinions on social and political issues, and other topics.

### Criticism
Harold Bloom, ed., *Tony Kushner* (Philadelphia: Chelsea House, 2005).
Collects eleven essays about *Angels in America* and other plays as historical, epic, gay, Jewish, and medieval drama.

John M. Clum, *Still Acting Gay: Male Homosexuality in Modern Drama* (New York: St. Martin's Press, 2000).
Includes a lengthy positive analysis of *Angels in America*.

James Fisher, *The Theatre of Tony Kushner: Living Past Hope* (New York: Routledge, 2001).
Major study of Kushner's works through 2000, with production histories and an extensive bibliography.

Fisher, ed., *Tony Kushner: New Essays on the Art and Politics of the Plays* (Jefferson, N.C.: McFarland, 2006).
Twelve essays discussing Kushner's work and its connections to plays by Tennessee Williams, William Inge, and Adrienne Kennedy.

Deborah R. Geis and Steven F. Kruger, eds., *Approaching the Millennium: Essays on* Angels in America (Ann Arbor: University of Michigan Press, 1997).
Eighteen essays on such subjects as racial and religious identities, AIDS and politics, and *Angels in America* in performance.

Randy Shilts, *And the Band Played On: Politics, People, and the AIDS Epidemic* (New York: St. Martin's Press, 1987).
Detailed history and examination of the origins and spread of AIDS.

—*John Spalding Gatton*

⌐✺⌐

# Jhumpa Lahiri, *Interpreter of Maladies*
(Boston: Houghton Mifflin, 1999)

It is rare for a debut book, especially a short-story collection, to achieve international best-seller status and to win such major literary awards as the Pulitzer Prize and the PEN/Hemingway Award. Jhumpa Lahiri's *Interpreter of Maladies* achieved these distinctions. Consisting of nine stories, the collection features characters, mostly South Asian, whose lives are marked by cultural hybridity, migration, and increasing globalization. While some are newly arrived in America from India, others are second generation, some have returned, and still others have never left. Despite their geographical or cultural locations, all have ties to the subcontinent. These pieces have been honored for Lahiri's precise, evocative prose, her skilled use of sensuous details—especially foods, fabrics, sounds—and her depictions of the emotional complexities of love, family relationships, and immigration.

Of Bengali descent, Lahiri was born in London in 1967 but immigrated to the United States when she was three and was raised primarily in Kingston, Rhode Island. She describes frequent family trips to Calcutta, India, while she was growing up but also says she identifies strongly with her Bengali heritage because she grew up in her parents' household: "I feel Indian not because of the time I spent in India or because of my genetic composition but rather because of my parents' steadfast presence in my life" ("My Two Lives"). She attended Barnard College, majoring in English, then earned three master's degrees and a Ph.D. in Renaissance studies from Boston University. She lives in New York City with her husband, journalist Alberto Vourvoulias-Bush, with whom she has two children.

Lahiri's first novel, *The Namesake* (2003), follows forty years in the life of Gogol Ganguli as he negotiates life as the child of immigrant parents. It was made into a movie of the same title, released in 2007, directed by Mira Nair. In 2008 Lahiri published a second collection of short stories, *Unaccustomed Earth*, which—unprecedented for a short-story collection—debuted at number one on *The New York Times* best-seller list.

Awareness of aspects of South Asian history heightens appreciation for nuances in Lahiri's writing. Contemporary India, Pakistan, and Bangladesh came under the control of the British East India Company, and then the British crown, in the eighteenth century. As with any such situation of colonization, the presence of the British led to clashes, blendings, and irrevocable changes to both British and South Asian cultures. In 1947, after years of struggles led by such figures as Mahandas Gandhi, the area was declared independent of Great Britain. At the same time partition occurred, dividing the land into two countries: India, where the primary religion is Hindu; and Pakistan, which is primarily Muslim. Pakistan was geographically divided, however, into west and east, with the much larger area of India between its two parts. In 1971 Pakistan experienced a civil war that led to East Pakistan (which had originally been called East Bengal) becoming the separate country of Bangladesh. In Lahiri's story "When Mr. Pirzada Came to Dine" Mr. Pirzada is a Pakistani Muslim while Lilia's family is Indian and, most likely, Hindu. Lilia's parents search phone directories looking for names familiar to their part of the world and issue dinner invitations to those they find, regardless of religion despite the fact that for many, in their respective home countries, "the idea of eating in the other's company was still unthinkable." Together they watch news reports of Pakistan at civil war on Lilia's family's television and later witness their two countries going to war against one another.

While many contemporary American prose writers are acclaimed for the lyricism and complexity of their prose styles—some on the far side of the Post-modernist spectrum even being noted for convoluted writing—Lahiri's prose is both plain and yet simultaneously rich and evocative. She explained to interviewer Isaac Chotiner, "I like it to be plain. It appeals to me more. There's form and there's function and I have never been a fan of just form." Many critics have noted that the significances of her stories often arise more from key images than from plot. Small but powerful gestures speak volumes: in "Sexy" the cocktail dress that Miranda buys because she thinks it is the sort of clothing a mistress should have will not stay on its hanger, suggesting something is wrong with adultery. When the title character of "When Mr. Pirzada Came to Dine," who is visiting the United States on an academic fellowship while his family remains at home in

Pakistan, hears that India is threatening to go to war with Pakistan, his shock is evoked when his hand slips and he cuts a huge gash across the jack-o'-lantern he has offered to carve. In "A Temporary Matter" Shoba comes in from work, kicks off her tennis shoes, and leaves them and her bag in a heap on the floor, signaling she no longer cares about this space she shares with her husband. Lahiri reveals the complicated nature of cultural identity through the use of irony. For instance, ironies abound in the title story, as the Indian American couple with three children visit the land of their parents but epitomize "ugly Americans"; they show no sensitivity to the landscape or the history of the country they are touring, to the people they meet, nor even among themselves. And in "Sexy" Miranda, who is American, hears her Indian friend Laxmi describe the pain her cousin feels because the cousin's husband is having an affair; yet, she does not seem to recognize that she could be causing the same pain to her married boyfriend's family. In another irony, while she acts selfishly and blindly in having the affair, she finds her horizons expanded by her explorations of her lover's Indian culture.

In some ways the title (of the collection and of its third story) acts as a kind of metaphor for what Lahiri as novelist is performing: she interprets the "maladies" of her characters, translating for readers multiple perspectives to highlight the complexity of cultural communication and hybridity. First- and second-generation Indian Americans interact with one another and their relatives in India, an Anglo American woman has an affair with a Bengali man, and two stories about Indian women are set in India. Lahiri also presents perspectives from both genders; her protagonists are sometimes male and sometimes female; sometimes happy in an arranged marriage and sometimes not; sometimes happy in a marriage of choice and sometimes not. Noelle Brada-Williams argues that these multiple perspectives are set in a narrative dialogue of care and neglect, with examples of each playing off the other within and between stories. For instance, the neglect of the marriage in the first story, "A Temporary Matter," is contrasted with the unnamed narrator's courtesy and care first for the elderly Mrs. Croft, and then for his new wife. Her perception spans generations, as well; children play key roles in three stories, while the final story includes a woman who is 103.

## TOPICS FOR DISCUSSION AND RESEARCH

1. A fruitful topic would be the cross-cultural connections and disconnections that Lahiri tracks through her stories. Around what types of things do people of different backgrounds, different religions, connect? In "When Mr. Pirzada Came to Dine" Mr. Pirzada is from a different country and different religion from the family he visits; how does Lilia's list of the many things she sees that he has in common with her parents explain the connection that is made? What other elements indicate that Lilia may be too young to understand explain it? What kind of connection is made between Mrs. Croft and the unnamed narrator of "The Third and Final Continent" despite the vast differences in their ages and the cultures they have experienced, and why? In

the title story Mr. Kapasi and Mrs. Das each imagine very different connections with the other person. What leads to the complete disruption of any connection between them—is it individual personalities, or cultural influences, or some mix of the two? Other stories that offer profitable avenues for such a consideration include "Mrs. Sen's" and "Sexy." What do these and other examples suggest about cross-cultural connections? The articles by Jennifer Bess, Noelle Brada-Williams, and Simon Lewis will be helpful to those interested in this topic.

2. Similarly, one might consider the following statements by Lahiri in her essay "My Two Lives," cited below: "While I am American by virtue of the fact that I was raised in this country, I am Indian thanks to the efforts of two individuals [her parents]. . . . Their passing will mark not only the loss of the people who created me but the loss of a singular way of life, a singular struggle. The immigrant's journey, no matter how ultimately rewarding, is founded on departure and deprivation, but it secures for the subsequent generation a sense of arrival and advantage." What aspects of the immigrant's journey does Lahiri reveal in these stories? What struggles are particular to the immigrant, and what to their children? Does she suggest or imply strategies for negotiating these struggles? "Mrs. Sen's," the husband in "This Blessed House," and "The Third and Final Continent" are particularly relevant, while the articles by Judith Caesar, Madhuparna Mitra, and Laura Anh Williams, as well as the various interviews, should be helpful to these topics.

3. Caesar, in "Beyond Cultural Identity in 'When Mr. Pirzada Came to Dine,'" cited below, asserts that "the plot of the story is slim because the meaning of the story resides in its images and emblems, not in its story line." This could be argued for many—perhaps all—of the stories in *Interpreter of Maladies*. Images and emblems that could provide fruitful exploration for the way they build a theme or reveal a character include the dress that will not stay on the hanger in "Sexy," Shukumar's recipe book in "A Temporary Matter," Lilia's ritual with the candy Mr. Pirzada gives her, Mrs. Sen's chopping, the religious artifacts in "This Blessed House," and Mrs. Croft's "splendid," among others. Consult the articles by Williams and Jennifer Bess.

4. Food plays a major role in many of the stories in *Interpreter of Maladies*. The first story, "A Temporary Matter," has a young husband using the recipes his wife cooked with such care before their child was stillborn, relying on her notations in her cookbook. He refers to "back when she used to cook," signaling they are now moving in different directions. "When Mr. Pirzada Came to Dine" has the Pakistani Muslim visitor presenting candy to the young narrator every night, an act she imbues with great ritual significance. Mrs. Sen, in the story of that name, spends a great deal of time chopping vegetables and other ingredients, focused on finding the freshest fish as she tries to figure out her identity in her new land. Her complicated food preparation also reminds her of—perhaps helps her feel connected to—the community of women she once prepared food with back in India. These and other instances of food or food preparation as metaphor (Mrs. Croft's pans of soup in the final story) could prove productive for research and analysis. One might also consider how food

becomes tied to ritual. The article by Williams would be most useful; Mitra's should be consulted for "Mrs. Sen's."

5. Students might trace instances of defamiliarization in Lahiri's writing. Defamiliarization is the process by which an author elicits new recognition of something familiar and typically taken for granted. For instance, Mr. Pirzada's impatience with Americans constantly thanking him suggests how meaningless expressions may become when overused. One of the most powerful examples of defamiliarization comes in "Sexy," when Rohin, whose father has abandoned his family for a woman he met on a plane, tells Miranda that "sexy" means "loving someone you don't know." What does Lahiri accomplish through the strategy of defamiliarization? How might this relate to her preference for a "plain" style, as noted above?

6. Most Americans find the idea of an "arranged marriage" offensive, believing marriage should be based on companionate love rather than economics, family ties, or parents' views of a good match. Yet, the practice continues in some other parts of the world with some success, while the United States experiences a 50 percent divorce rate. In these stories some marriages are arranged, others come about through individuals meeting on their own, and a few are somewhere between these two possibilities, with parents making introductions but nothing more formal. What outcomes does Lahiri depict for these marriages? What evidence is there that she considers arranged marriages a viable option or an intrusive mistake? Beyond this cultural difference issue, students will find good material in these stories for analyzing what Lahiri dramatizes as necessary for healthy relationships.

## RESOURCES

**Primary Works**

Isaac Chotiner, "Jhumpa Lahiri," *Atlantic*, 18 March 2008 <http://www.theatlantic.com/doc/200802u/jhumpa-lahiri> [accessed 24 November 2009].
Interview in which Lahiri discusses her interest in the position of immigrants and their children, her own reading interests, and her views on criticism and reviewers.

Liane Hansen, "Jhumpa Lahiri's 'Interpreter of Maladies,'" *NPR: Weekend All Things Considered*, 22 August 1999 <www.npr.org/templates/story/story.php?storyId=1057437> [accessed 24 November 2009].
Interview in which Lahiri discusses her family and particularly "Mrs. Sen's" and "The Third and Final Continent."

Steve Inskeep, "Jhumpa Lahiri's Struggle to Feel American," *NPR: Morning Edition*, 25 November 2008 <http://www.npr.org/templates/transcript/transcript.php?storyId=97418330> [accessed 24 November 2009].
Interview in which Lahiri discusses her parents' inability to feel "American" despite raising a family in the United States and coming to think of it as their home; the ways she felt "different" growing up, both internally and externally; and her own "halfway feeling" about identifying as American.

## Criticism

Jennifer Bess, "Lahiri's *Interpreter of Maladies,*" *Explicator,* 62 (Winter 2004): 125–128.
Discusses "Mrs. Sen's," "This Blessed House," and "The Third and Final Continent," illustrating how characters' relationships to small details—a cutting knife, a Jesus trivet, the word "splendid"—signify cultural identity, individual identity, and human connection or its lack.

Noelle Brada-Williams, "Reading Jhumpa Lahiri's *Interpreter of Maladies* as a Short Story Cycle," *MELUS,* 29 (Fall/Winter 2004): 451–464.
Through strong close readings, points to dialogues between the stories in the collection to argue that they form a short-story cycle not through the more common unity of setting or recurring characters but through pattern and motif, "including the recurring themes of the barriers to and opportunities for human communication; community . . . and the dichotomy of care and neglect."

Judith Caesar, "American Spaces in the Fiction of Jhumpa Lahiri," *ESC,* 31 (March 2005): 50–68.
Discusses "The Third and Final Continent" and "Nobody's Business," a short story published in *The New Yorker* (12 March 2001), in terms of the ways they rewrite the traditional American motif of the confining enclosure of houses.

Caesar, "Beyond Cultural Identity in Jhumpa Lahiri's 'When Mr. Pirzada Came to Dine,'" *North Dakota Quarterly,* 70 (Winter 2003): 82–91.
Argues that Lahiri's fiction does not fit into the categories of postcolonial, Asian American, or American literature because it goes beyond those forms in offering recognitions of growth and suggesting that the past can, in fact, be learned from and then moved beyond or that, like Mr. Pirzada, one can go home again.

Brewster L. Fitz, "Bibi's Babel: Treating Jhumpa Lahiri's 'The Treatment of Bibi Haldar' as the Malady of Interpreters," *South Asian Review,* 26, 2 (2005): 116–131.
Examines the use of a first-person-plural female narrator, arguing it is a kind of "ghost interpreter-translator of maladies" that cures Bibi Haldar.

Joel Kuortti, "Problematic Hybrid Identity in the Diasporic Writings of Jhumpa Lahiri," in *Reconstructing Hybridity: Postcolonial Studies in Transition*, edited by Jopi Nyman (Amsterdam, Netherlands: Rodopi, 2000), pp. 205–219.
Focusing primarily on "This Blessed House" but with references to others, Kuortti examines the engagement with translation and spaces of hybridity in Lahiri's writing.

Simon Lewis, "Lahiri's *Interpreter of Maladies,*" *Explicator,* 59 (Summer 2001): 219–221.
Discusses how the characters, plot, and setting of a tourist excursion in India of "Interpreter of Maladies" rewrite E. M. Forster's *A Passage to India* (1924) to place the cause of human disconnection and misunderstanding in sources other than geography and race.

Madhuparna Mitra, "Lahiri's Mrs. Sen's," *Explicator,* 64 (Spring 2006): 185–189.
Brief but helpful close reading of the details in "Mrs. Sen's" that speak to the
character's struggles with her new life as a Bengali American.

Laura Anh Williams, "Foodways and Subjectivities in Jhumpa Lahiri's *Interpreter
of Maladies,*" *MELUS,* 32 (Winter 2007): 69–79.
Traces the importance of food and food preparation in "A Temporary Matter,"
"Mrs. Sen's," and "This Blessed House," illustrating the ways in which choices
about food and food preparation represent assertions of identity and subjectivity.

Bonnie Zare, "Evolving Masculinities in Recent Stories by South Asian Ameri-
    can Women," *Journal of Commonwealth Literature,* 42 (September 2007):
    99–111.
Argues that Lahiri and Meera Nair differ from other contemporary South Asian
American women writers in depicting male protagonists and in showing those
characters working through "internalized colonialist, consumerist and patriarchal
norms"; discusses "Interpreter of Maladies" and "This Blessed House."

—*Kathryn West*

# Li-Young Lee, *Rose*

(Brockport, N.Y.: BOA Editions, 1986)

In his foreword to Li-Young Lee's first book of poetry, *Rose,* the renowned poet
Gerald Stern writes, "What characterizes Lee's poetry is a certain humility, a
kind of cunning, a love of plain speech, a search for wisdom and understanding." This humility and desire for understanding may result from Lee's turbulent
childhood. Lee was born to Chinese parents in Jakarta, Indonesia, in 1957. His
mother was from a wealthy landowning family whose property was seized during
the communist takeover. His father had been personal physician to Mao Tse-tung
and later was imprisoned and tortured under Sukarno in Indonesia. In 1959 the
family fled Indonesia; from 1959 to 1964 they moved from place to place, living
in Hong Kong, Macau, and Japan until finally settling in the United States. From
this peripatetic and unstable childhood Lee emerged with a contemplative view
of human life and poetry. In an interview published shortly after the release of
*Rose* (1986) he said, "I have to say that I'm concerned just as much with ideas and
with making sense of my world as I am with language. [Writing poetry] isn't mere
*play* for me" (Ingersoll). This earnestness pervades Lee's work, making his poems
as much philosophical meditations as literature.

Lee studied poetry with Stern at the University of Pittsburgh from 1978 to
1979 and later attended the University of Arizona and the State University of
New York at Brockport. During this period Stern noticed in him a propensity
toward "the deep seriousness" one observes in spiritual poets such as John Keats
and Rainer Maria Rilke. Rather than writing in a particular tradition, Lee was

creating a poetic of somber spiritual devotion—a devotion on full display in his first book, *Rose*.

Lee's first book is a small but attentively crafted collection of which he once said, "Now that I look at it and it's so thin I wish I would have put more in. But I just couldn't. I am such a slow writer. I think for somebody who writes this way the danger is writing anecdotes" (Ingersoll). Many critics have discussed the subject matter of Lee's work, but too few have acknowledged Lee's meticulous technique. The poems in *Rose* were not written in haste, nor mindlessly selected for their inclusion in the collection. It stands a book constructed with care and constructed of poems composed and revised with patience.

Lee's impact on contemporary American literature is significant—particularly his perspective as an Asian man who immigrated to the United States as a child. Xiaojing Zhou claims, "Lee's poems and poetics are largely shaped by his experience as a refugee and immigrant and by his readings in English, being educated from grade school through college in the United States." Lee's poetry represents a multicultural perspective on the American experience and is compelling because it blurs cultural stereotypes. Taken together, the poems in *Rose* reflect on both Asian and American ideals as well as on feelings of cultural aimlessness. Lee alludes to this aimlessness in his memoir, *The Winged Seed: A Remembrance* (1995), when recounting a story about his arrival in the United States as a child. He writes, "And by the time we got to America, my feet were tired. My father put down our suitcase, untied my shoes, and rubbed my feet, one at a time and with deep turns of the wrist I heard the water in him through my soles. Since then I have listened for him in my steps." Lee describes a life of constant travel that ends with rest in the United States—rest symbolized by both settlement in America and peace within his family.

Three major themes transcend *Rose*: the conflicts of simultaneously occupying multiple cultural communities, the importance of family, and the grief of loss. Throughout the text Lee intertwines these three themes so that they all become synonymous with one another. Often flowers, plants, and other natural objects represent these themes. These characteristics are on display best in Lee's most anthologized poem, "Persimmons," which is exemplary of *Rose* as an entire collection. In the poem the persimmons become symbols for his aging parents, Chinese heritage, and difficulty finding acceptance in the United States.

The importance of natural images—particularly flowers—as representations of Lee's major themes continues in "The Weight of Sweetness" and "From Blossoms," in which peaches and peach blossoms signify hope for a speaker haunted by death. In "Falling: The Code," "My Indigo," "Irises," "Eating Alone," "Visions and Interpretations," and the poem sequence "Always a Rose," fruit and flowers represent life's mutability. Like Modernist poets Walt Whitman, H.D., and Marianne Moore, as well as like the highly influential poet Elizabeth Bishop, Lee finds meaning in the natural world. For him, a persimmon or a rose is not a mere clipping of vegetation but a mirror in which he sees himself and those he loves. In "Always a Rose" Lee writes, "if I adore you, Rose, / with adoration become nonsense become / praise, could I stop our dying?" Of course, the speaker is asking a rhetorical question, but what we see in such a question is Lee's hope to preserve beauty for the reader, praise that beauty, pray for it, and then accept that he must let it go.

The greatest strength of the poems collected in *Rose* is their ability to function on two levels: one level concerning the specific experience of the speaker and another concerning the speaker's similarities with greater mankind. This complexity and Lee's careful attention to craft did not go unnoticed by critics, and the collection won him New York University's Delmore Schwartz Memorial Poetry Award in 1987. His other collections have also garnered him significant critical acclaim; his second collection, *The City in Which I Love You* (1990), was the Lamont Poetry Selection of The Academy of American Poets. His other works are *Book of My Nights* (2001), winner of the 2002 William Carlos Williams Award, and *Behind My Eyes* (2008). His memoir, *The Winged Seed: A Remembrance*, also shows the influence of his craft; it has been described as a book-length lyric prose poem. In the works published since *Rose*, Lee continues to deal with his primary subjects of family, his Chinese-American heritage, and loss. To these subjects he also adds his own evolution into fatherhood.

## TOPICS FOR DISCUSSION AND RESEARCH

1. Li-Young Lee is often discussed in light of his Chinese-American background as well as his attempt to reconcile his multicultural identity with his role as a child, parent, and poet. This is seen in the poem "Persimmons," in which the speaker of the poem is punished because of his confusion with language: "In sixth grade Mrs. Walker / slapped the back of my head / and made me stand in the corner / for not knowing the difference / between *persimmon* and *precision*." The struggle to reconcile the compound cultural identities on display in this poem permeates Lee's book. His speaker finds himself calling a country home that does not accommodate his cultural diversity, and so his poems show the frequent ramifications of that conflict. The poem continues with the speaker's memory of teaching his wife how to speak Chinese, an intimate expression of his love for her, but this intimacy is not without sadness. In trying to teach his wife, he realizes how much of his first language he has forgotten, and his grief over this loss inspires him to appreciate where and what he is right now—in love with his wife. Fortunately, the poem's representation of diversity does not lack joy. The speaker also realizes that his heritage and experience can be assets for him. When the poem returns to the classroom with the speaker as a child, Mrs. Walker brings in a persimmon for the class to taste, but the speaker refuses to eat, "knowing / it wasn't ripe or sweet . . ." but watched the other faces. What first caused the speaker ridicule earlier in the poem now protects him. A cultural shortsightedness still exists within the classroom, but the speaker does not face the same cruel ridicule displayed earlier. Here the speaker acts as a keen observer of those around him, admiring how their faces react violently to the taste of the unripe fruit. Again, this keen observance carries through the book. Though the speaker's awareness of his own heritage alienates him, he still finds moments to celebrate his identity. Students might compare the speaker's multiple feelings toward his cultural background

in "Persimmons" with other poems in *Rose,* explaining their connection to themes related to language and expression, generational perspectives, loss, and empowerment.

2. In *Rose* flowers serve as symbols for relationships and for emotional, spiritual, physical, and cultural conditions. Students might want to explore the different flowers used throughout the collection and explicate the role that these plants play in the individual poems. They could also explore what purpose the use of flowers serves for the collection as a whole. In this vein, students might also be interested in exploring how the use of flowers or nature as significant symbols connects Lee to the poetic heritage of Romanticism and the image-driven Modernist poets. Research regarding poets including the Romantics William Wordsworth and John Keats might be helpful as well as research into the work of Modernist poets such as H.D. and Moore.

3. *Rose* could be viewed as a historical artifact of immigration or an act of political activism calling for the embrace of immigrants and multicultural persons in the United States. Students might be interested in contemplating the implications of writing from the perspective of an immigrant and expressing the social or emotional conflicts that arise from immigration. Starting points for this topic include essays by Slowik and Zhou, and Lee's interviews with Chang and with Moyers (the latter included in Ingersoll, pp. 20–43). Students might also be interested in tracing the different ways Lee depicts immigrant identity throughout his career. Notable poems from other collections to be compared to those in *Rose* include "For a New Citizen of the United States" and the title poem from *The City in Which I Love You* and "Self-Help for Fellow Refugees" and "Immigrant Blues" from *Behind My Eyes.* The film *The Power of the Word: Voices of Memory Featuring Li-Young Lee* may also provide fruitful insights.

4. Stern observes the importance of Lee's father in the poems, writing: "I think, in fact, that understanding, even accepting, the father is the critical event, the critical 'myth' in Lee's poetry." Lee's poems function on both private and public levels. David Baker insists that "Lee's finest achievement as a poet, in fact, is his persistent blending of cultural politics and personal desire, a doubled subject that seems to me essential to American poetry." Students might explore the continuity between personal moments and larger cultural, social, psychological, and historical contexts. How do poems that are encapsulated within a specific personal history speak to the experiences of others? Suggested poems include "Dreaming of Hair," "Persimmons," "The Gift," "I Ask My Mother To Sing," and "Rain Diary."

5. Some might consider Lee a religious or Christian poet, especially as he was raised in a Christian home and his father was a minister. He also discusses issues related to spiritual belief and practice throughout his body of work. Students interested in this topic might review Lee's interview with Reamy Jansen or Ingersoll's introduction (both in Ingersoll, pp. 74–85 and 9–15, respectively). Alternatively, students might also be interested in comparing the different portrayals of Christianity and religion in general across Lee's first three books, *Rose,*

*The City in Which I Love You,* and, most notably, *Book of My Nights.* Again, what may be most interesting here is the evolution from book to book.

## RESOURCES

### Primary Works
Tina Chang, "The Totality of Causes: Li-Young Lee and Tina Chang in Conversation" (2007) <http://www.poets.org/viewmedia.php/prmMID/19802> [accessed 24 November 2009].
Interview in which Lee discusses poetry as a political act or a companion act to political activism. Lee and Chang also discuss *Book of My Nights,* the physical decline of Lee's parents, religion, and Lee's views of poetry as meditation.

Earl G. Ingersoll, *Breaking the Alabaster Jar: Conversations with Li-Young Lee* (Rochester, N.Y.: BOA, 2006).
A collection of interviews spanning the period from the beginning of Lee's career through the publication of his poetry collection *Book of My Nights.* The interviews explore the poet's Chinese heritage, immigration to the United States, writing practices, literary influences, education, and views on religion. This book also includes a notable interview with Bill Moyers from *The Language of Life: A Festival of Poets.*

James Kyung-Jin Lee, "Li-Young Lee," in *Words Matter: Conversations with Asian American Writers* (Honolulu: University of Hawai'i Press, 2000), pp. 270–280.
Interview in which Lee discusses his craft and challenges faced while writing.

Bill Moyers, *The Power of the Word: Ancestral and Voices of Memory* (Alexandria, Va.: PBS Video, 1989).
Video series featuring Lee speaking about and reading his poetry. He also discusses his struggle with his Chinese cultural heritage. (Other poets featured are Garrett Kaoru Hongo, Mary Tall-Mountain, and Joy Harjo.)

### Criticism
David Baker, "Culture, Inclusion, Craft," *Poetry,* 158 (June 1991): 158–175.
A review of *The City in Which I Love You* that claims Lee's poetry combines both personal and cultural or political ambitions. Baker also reflects on the achievements and limitations of the poet's lyric and meditative voice.

King-Kok Cheung, "Art, Spirituality, and the Ethic of Care: Alternative Masculinities in Chinese American Literature," in *Masculinity Studies and Feminist Theory: New Directions,* edited by Judith Kegan Gardiner (New York: Columbia University Press, 2002), pp. 261–289.
Article discussing Lee's representation of "alternative masculinities" in his depiction of Ba, his father, in *The Winged Seed.* Cheung discusses Lee specifically on pages 271–276; her ideas might be applied to a reading of the poems in *Rose.*

Gerald Stern, Foreword to *Rose,* by Li-Young Lee (Rochester, N.Y.: BOA, 1986), pp. 8–10.
Discusses Stern's relationship with Lee and what he claims are Lee's literary influences. Stern also touches on the major themes of family, race, and spirituality observed in Lee's collection.

Xiaojing Zhou, "Inheritance and Invention in Li-Young Lee's Poetry," *MELUS,* 21 (Spring 1996): 113–132.
Examines how the speakers in *Rose* and *The City in Which I Love You* are shaped by their experiences as immigrants in the United States and by their development as poets.

*—Isaiah Vianese*

## David Mamet, *Glengarry Glen Ross*
(Performed 1984; New York: Grove, 1983)

For playwright David Mamet the connection between language and action is crucial. He has said, "Actually, my main emphasis is on the rhythm of language—the way action and rhythm are identical. Our rhythms describe—no, our rhythms *prescribe* our actions. I became fascinated—I still am—by the way, the way the language we use, its rhythm, actually determines the way we behave, more than the other way around" (Leslie Kane, ed., *Mamet in Conversation*). Mamet is most known for his attention to the sounds and sense of everyday speech rhythms. He excels at the use of simple, sparse, direct, and often clipped dialogue. A critic of his early plays advised audiences to "remember that name," correctly predicting the vital role Mamet would come to play in American theater. He is one of the most important playwrights to emerge in the 1970s; his reputation rests on a large body of work in which he portrays the moral, spiritual, and emotional corruption of contemporary society.

David Alan Mamet was born in Chicago on 30 November 1947. He attributes his fascination with language to his upbringing in a predominately Jewish Southside neighborhood, where his grandmother spoke to shopkeepers "in what could have been Yiddish, Polish, or Russian." His father, Bernard Morris Mamet, was a labor attorney who also instilled in him the importance of language by encouraging him to learn complex rhymes from a recording produced by the International Society for Semantics; his father later insisted that one of these rhymes inspired *Duck Variations* (produced, 1972; published, 1978). His mother, Lenore June Silver Mamet, was a teacher. Although his parents were the children of Ashkenazi Jews from Poland, Judaism did not play the major part in their home that it does in Mamet's adult life. Mamet has described his childhood as difficult. His parents, undemonstrative and critical of him and his younger sister, Lynn (who also became a playwright), divorced in 1959. Soon after, his mother remarried and relocated the family to Olympia Fields, a suburb of Chicago. He did not get along with his stepfather, who was psychologically and physically abusive, especially to Mamet's sister. When Mamet was fourteen, he returned to Chicago to live with his father, stepmother, and two stepbrothers, Tony (whom Mamet has cast in several productions) and Bobby (a jazz musician).

The teenaged Mamet discovered acting when his uncle Henry, a radio and television producer for the Chicago Board of Rabbis, gave him and his sister, Lynn, bit parts on television and radio playing Jewish children. Through this uncle Mamet also became involved in community theater. During high school (he attended the progressive Francis W. Parker School) he worked at Chicago's Hull House Theatre and the Second City, now renowned for comedy improvisation. In his spare time he honed his writing skills by writing dialogue on a typewriter in his father's office. He earned a B.A. in 1969 at Goddard College in Vermont, where he wrote his first play, "Camel," to fulfill an English requirement. During a hiatus from school he studied acting with Sanford Meisner at the Neighborhood Playhouse School of Theater in New York City. In 1970 Mamet was hired as a one-year replacement at Marlboro College in Vermont partly on the basis of a play he claimed to have completed (but had not). That one-act play, *Lakeboat* (revised and produced, 1979; published, 1981), was staged later that year with his students. The next academic year found him back at Goddard, where he staged *Duck Variations* with students, one of them actor William H. Macy, who would make his career with roles written by Mamet. Between these two academic posts Mamet returned to Chicago, where he worked in an office selling real estate over the phone to elderly couples. This experience became the foundation for *Glengarry Glen Ross* (published, 1983; produced, 1984).

In 1972 Mamet returned to Chicago, where several of his plays were produced in small, experimental theaters. *Sexual Perversity in Chicago* (performed 1974; published 1978) won the Joseph Jefferson Award (given each year to the best new play in Chicago). This play, along with *Duck Variations*, was produced on Off Off Broadway in 1975 and 1976. Another Mamet play, *American Buffalo* (produced, 1975; published, 1976), which premiered in Chicago and won Mamet his second Jefferson award, followed a similar trajectory to New York. In 1976 he was also awarded Obies for *Sexual Perversity in Chicago* and *American Buffalo*. The latter, which features three men plotting to steal a rare and valuable buffalo-head nickel, became his first work to appear on Broadway and established Mamet's place on the American stage.

Not all of Mamet's plays have been equally successful or well reviewed. Throughout his work, however, he creates characters whose failure to express themselves parallels their inability to connect with others. They use obscenities (for which Mamet is notorious) and tell stories that ultimately have no meaning to disguise the fact that they have little to say. Their speech is filled with aphorisms and clichés that disguise and justify immoral actions. In many of the plays Mamet also explores the way social rules related to gender inhibit and prevent communication between men, family members, and men and women. Another theme running through Mamet's oeuvre is the emptiness of the American dream. *American Buffalo* and *Glengarry Glen Ross* are both negative examinations of American business and greed and explore men's capacity for immorality.

*Speed-the-Plow* (produced, 1987; published, 1988) picks up on these themes in its unflattering portrayal of the film industry where profit motivates more than artistry and ideals. Mamet's plays frequently make his audiences uncomfortable. His depiction of a student who accuses her professor of sexual harassment in *Oleanna* (1992; film adaptation, 1994) incited fierce debate. While some audience members perceived the student as manipulative, wielding accusations of sexual misconduct as a way to gain power, others were angered by what they saw as an unfair attack on women who try to defend themselves.

Mamet's best-known play is *Glengarry Glen Ross*, for which he was awarded the Pulitzer Prize and two Tony Awards, for Best Play and Best Director. The play, which takes its title from a conflation of two of the real-estate developments being peddled, Glengarry Highlands and Glen Ross Farms, features four real-estate agents (Levene, Roma, Moss, and Aaronow) and their supervisor (Williamson). All go to great lengths (legal and illegal) to sell undesirable real estate at inflated prices. Motivating them is the prospect of either winning a Cadillac (the prize for the top seller) or being fired (the penalty for the two who produce the least number of sales). As the play progresses it charts the degradation of the salesmen as they resort to lies, bribery, theft, and trickery. Meanwhile, their supervisor manipulates them without pity. Williamson baits Levene with false promises of "good leads," abusing his position of power. Even acts of benevolence are calculated and heartbreakingly false; Roma shows kindness to Levene only in hopes of earning a greater profit.

In addition to his other works cited below, Leslie Kane's *Weasels and Wisemen: Ethics and Ethnicity in the Work of David Mamet* (New York: St. Martin's Press, 1999) is a good general study of Jewish ethnicity and moral principles in Mamet's plays and is recommended for students seeking a general perspective. *Glengarry Glen Ross* has attracted a broad range of criticism; students are encouraged to consult the MLA bibliography for additional sources after consulting those cited below.

## TOPICS FOR DISCUSSION AND RESEARCH

1. Robert Lublin argues that the stage and film versions of *Glengarry Glen Ross* are distinct enough to warrant their treatment as separate works. (James Foley directed the 1992 film adaptation.) In "'By Indirections Find Directions Out': Uninflected Cuts, Narrative Structure, and Thematic Statement in the Film Version of *Glengarry Glen Ross*" in Kane, *David Mamet's* Glengarry Glen Ross (1996), Christopher C. Hudgins also examines differences between the two versions. Students interested in comparing the film and print versions of the play will find both essays useful as starting points for examining the way narrative structure in film creates a different thematic focus. Students should pay attention to editing techniques, visual symbols, the use of music, and the actors' particular handling of the written material. Students might also wish to engage Hudgins's argument regarding the film's ability to evoke more complex motives behind the men's irresponsible and immoral behavior, arguing whether or not they agree with his assessment of the film characters' redeeming qualities.

2. Almost all discussions of Mamet's plays note his adept use of language. Anne Dean observes, "the sharklike salesmen in *Glengarry Glen Ross* are constantly propelled forward by their language; to them, to talk is to survive. As the words spill out, so their behavior endeavors to match them." Indeed, to sell the worthless property, they themselves must sell out. Language in this play is no longer a means of reliable communication and has been corrupted by the salesmen; however, it not only reveals their corruption but serves further to corrupt them. Using Dean's discussion of *Glengarry Glen Ross* (pp. 189–221) as a starting point, students could analyze a particular speech or scene to determine various uses of language and its role in furthering the corruption of the characters. What does a character reveal about himself and his values (or lack thereof) in his speech? How do characters use language to persuade themselves and others? What does their language conceal? Students should pay close attention to the salesmen's use of jargon, fast-paced and overlapping dialogue, rhetorical questions, inspirational sayings, incomplete sentences, silences, and obscenities. Many scenes in *Glengarry Glen Ross* lend themselves well to this type of analysis, including Moss's manipulation of Aaronow in act 1, scene 2; Roma's monologue-like speech to Lingk in act 1, scene 3; Levene's speech about the great sale in act 2. Students might also consult David Worster's "How to Do Things with Salesmen: David Mamet's Speech-Act Play" in Kane (pp. 19–45).

3. In *Glengarry Glen Ross* the salesmen become so divorced from their own needs that they are able to justify their existence by their sales records. After the play's appearance at London's National Theatre in 1983, a reviewer described the men as "microcosms of a system so distorted that it martials considerable human resources and intelligence in pursuit of the grand con. So this is a morality play" (quoted in Sauer, p. 145). Morality plays traditionally refer to medieval allegorical dramas in which sermons are dramatized and characters represent not individual personalities but abstract personifications (Everyman, Truth, King, Mercy, Greed). Later morality plays included scenes of broad comedy satirizing or burlesquing political or social situations of everyday life. Using the characteristics of traditional and later morality plays, students could examine the play to see how well the play fits this characterization. In particular, students should consider what abstract qualities are personified by the characters and to what end and the ways the play makes fun of or satirizes contemporary political or social situations or ideas.

4. *Glengarry Glen Ross* features an all-male cast; women have only a presence offstage. This fact, coupled with the macho way characters speak and act, has been cited as evidence of Mamet's gender bias. Hudgins and Leslie Kane provide an overview of the complexity of the "critical and popular debate about Mamet's work [which] often centers on whether or not he is a misogynist, or, more broadly, on whether we should read his often misogynist, unlovable, and unloving characters as reflecting his own misogyny or should recognize some Mametian irony in his depiction of these figures of his fertile imagination." Hersh Zeifman argues the latter, viewing the play as an exploration and undercutting of "American masculinity myths." These critical works would be useful for the student wishing to examine the construction of gender in Mamet's play. Closely

examining male behavior, speech, and interactions with one another, students could extrapolate how Mamet defines American manhood and related myths while also taking a position on whether the play supports or undermines his definition.

5. In *Glengarry Glen Ross* Mamet examines the potentially destructive aspects of the American dream by linking its promise of freedom, social equality, and prosperity to the world of capitalism. In an interview Mamet explains "We are finally reaching a pointwhere there is nothing left to exploit. . . . The dream has nowhere to go so it has to start turning in on itself" (Savran, p. 133). Most critical works about Mamet address his preoccupation with the American dream. Students interested in pursuing this topic will do well to consider the way the play evokes both "ideal" and "real" manifestations of the American dream. Students might also consider the differences between what Glengarry Highlands actually is and what it represents and its relation to the American dream. Alternatively, students might consider comparing Mamet's vision of the degradation of the American dream to an earlier work such as Arthur Miller's *Death of a Salesman* or to one by a Mamet contemporary, Sam Shepard's *True West* (1981) or August Wilson's *The Piano Lesson* (1990, both of which offer competing versions of the American dream.

## RESOURCES

### Primary Works

Leslie Kane, ed., *David Mamet in Conversation* (Ann Arbor: University of Michigan Press, 2001).
Essential and comprehensive collection of interviews with Mamet, who is notorious for his avoidance of them.

David Savran, "David Mamet," in *In Their Own Words: Contemporary American Playwrights* (New York: Theatre Communications Group, 1988), pp. 132–144.
An 11 February 1987 interview in which Mamet discusses his influences, work, and ideas that he is interested in; it is preceded by an overview of his life and work.

### Biography

Ira Nadel, *David Mamet: A Life in the Theatre* (New York: Palgrave, 2008).
A comprehensive biography exploring Mamet's ideas about acting, directing, and writing as well as key discussions about thematic issues and productions of his work.

### Criticism

Christopher Bigsby, ed., *The Cambridge Companion to David Mamet* (New York: Cambridge University Press, 2004).
Essential collection of essays providing an excellent introduction to the plays as well as discussions of Mamet as actor, director, and fiction writer. Benedict

Nightingale's *"Glengarry Glen Ross"* (pp. 89–102) is a useful discussion of the play and its critical reception.

*The David Mamet Society* <http://mamet.eserver.org/> [accessed 16 November 2009].
Website featuring the society's newsletter, which publishes performance and publication reviews and updates related to Mamet studies. Also included are links to other sites related to David Mamet including the blog he posted for the *Huffington Post*.

Anne Dean, *David Mamet: Language as Dramatic Action* (Rutherford, N.J.: Fairleigh Dickinson University Press, 1990).
An analysis of Mamet's use of dialogue in his now classic plays *Sexual Perversity in Chicago, American Buffalo, A Life in the Theatre, Edmond,* and *Glengarry Glen Ross.*

Katharine Hibbert, "Unreal Estate," *Times Literary Supplement,* 2 November 2007, p. 18.
Review of the 2007 revival of *Glengarry Glen Ross* that provides a glimpse of a stage production.

Christopher Hudgins and Leslie Kane, eds., *Gender and Genre: Essays on David Mamet* (New York: Palgrave, 2001).
Collection of essays that do not feature *Glengarry Glen Ross* but offer various approaches to and critical positions on the topic of gender in Mamet's plays.

Kane, ed., *David Mamet: A Casebook* (New York: Garland, 1992).
A collection of important essays treating major themes and questions raised by Mamet's plays. The book includes interviews with critic Gregory Mosher (pp. 231–247) and actor Joe Mantegna (pp. 249–269).

Kane, ed., *David Mamet's* Glengarry Glen Ross: *Text and Performance* (New York: Garland, 1996).
Offers critical studies, bibliographies, and interviews from a wide variety of perspectives. Particularly useful is Janice A. Sauer, "Bibliography of *Glengarry Glen Ross* (1983–1995)," pp. 263–273.

Robert Lublin, "Differing Dramatic Dynamics in the Stage and Screen Versions of *Glengarry Glen Ross," American Drama,* 10 (Winter 2001): 38–55.
An analysis of the differences between the stage and film versions of *Glengarry Glen Ross,* arguing that they are separate works with related but different thematic concerns.

David K. Sauer and Janice A. Sauer, eds., *David Mamet: A Research and Production Sourcebook* (Westport, Conn.: Greenwood Press, 2003).
Comprehensive work that includes production history, overview of all reviews (including excerpts from them), and criticism of each of Mamet's plays. *Glengarry Glen Ross* is discussed primarily on pp. 143–180.

Hersh Zeifman, "Phallus in Wonderland: Machismo and Business in David Mamet's *American Buffalo* and *Glengarry Glen Ross,"* in *Modern Dramatists: A*

*Casebook of Major British, Irish, and American Playwrights,* edited by Kimball King (New York: Routledge, 2001), pp. 167–176.
Examines Mamet's exploration of "American masculinity myths" as a vehicle for indicting exploitative business practices.

*—Linda Trinh Moser and Chelsea Russell*

⸎

# Cormac McCarthy, *All the Pretty Horses*
## (New York: Knopf, 1992)

In Cormac McCarthy's *All the Pretty Horses* the death of a small doe leads protagonist John Grady to ponder the relationship between pain and beauty: "He thought that in the beauty of the world were hid a secret. He thought the world's heart beat at some terrible cost and that the world's pain and its beauty moved in a relationship of diverging equity and that in this headlong deficit the blood of multitudes might ultimately be exacted for the vision of a single flower." In all his work, McCarthy reenacts the "blood of multitudes" in his depiction of the West as an indifferent landscape that offers much less beauty and meaning than his searching characters wish and need to find. Using language both sparse and lyrical, he creates a dispassionate world where human experience is marked by violence and death, and where redemption and transcendence play little if any part. Although he is criticized for extreme images of violence, especially in the earlier works, both literary critics and popular readers have come to embrace his revision of the traditional Western.

Most of McCarthy's works take place in Tennessee, Texas, or Mexico. Those written from 1959 to 1979, what critic Dianne C. Luce calls his "Tennessee period," draw from his experiences in the state he moved to as a child. Born Charles Joseph McCarthy Jr. on 20 July 1933 in Providence, Rhode Island, the third child of Charles Joseph (his namesake) and Gladys McGrail McCarthy, he was called Cormac after an Irish king and because it means "son of Charles." When he was four the family moved to Knox County, just outside of Knoxville, Tennessee, where two more children were born into the family. Like the other children he grew up around, McCarthy participated in outdoor activities—hunting, fishing, riding horses—despite being somewhat of an outsider, considered different because of his family's economic status. Charles Sr. was Yale-educated, an attorney whose jobs with the U.S. Justice Department and the Tennessee Valley Authority provided comfortably for the family in an area where most people lived in two- or three-room shacks.

After graduating from a Roman Catholic high school in Knoxville, McCarthy attended the University of Tennessee for a year (1951–1952) as a liberal arts major. He then spent another year working a series of odd jobs before joining the U.S. Air Force in 1953. McCarthy spent two of his four years of service in Alaska, where he worked as a radio-show host and devoted himself to an intensive reading program. After his military service McCarthy returned to the University of Tennessee with renewed focus, enrolling in a course on fiction writing. His talent and unique perspective were recognized by the English department, and two of his short stories—"Wake for Susan" and "A Drowning Incident"—were published in *The Phoenix,* a campus literary magazine. He also began to work on his future novels. Despite his academic success, McCarthy left the university without a degree to pursue a writing career.

Five years passed before McCarthy's first novel, *The Orchard Keeper* (1965), was published. During this time he married and divorced Lee Holleman, a poet, with whom he had a son, Cullen; she later depicted their marriage in the collection *Desire's Door* (1991). He married his second wife, Anne DeLisle, in 1966; they divorced ten years later. Because of his reclusive nature and a desire to devote himself entirely to his craft (he is notorious for not allowing anything to interfere with writing), McCarthy refrained from holding a steady job and subsisted on a series of grants and awards, including the William Faulkner Foundation Award in 1965 (given to the best first novel by an American writer), a Rockefeller Foundation grant in 1966, a Guggenheim Fellowship in 1969, and the prestigious MacArthur Foundation "genius award" in 1981. These awards enabled McCarthy to make ends meet as he toiled away on critically successful yet commercially unprofitable novels such as *Outer Dark* (1968), *Child of God* (1973), *Suttree* (1979), and *Blood Meridian, Or, The Evening Redness in the West* (1985).

*Blood Meridian* is McCarthy's fifth novel and the first to take place outside of Tennessee. Having relocated to El Paso, Texas, he found new inspiration and a fresh setting for his writing. The story follows an unnamed "kid" from age fourteen to forty-three who roams the Southwest both alone and in the company of a ruthless gang of "scalp hunters" intent on exterminating Indians and Mexicans. Although the novel takes place in the Old West of the 1840s and 1850s, it runs counter to traditional Westerns. The protagonist is passive, swept up in violence that he neither willingly nor unwillingly participates in, and when given the chance to kill a villain, he cannot. Critics were enthusiastic about the novel. In 2005 *Time* magazine chose it as one of the one hundred best novels published since 1923, and in a 2006 survey conducted by *The New York Times Book Review* it was ranked the third "best work of American fiction published in the last twenty-five years."

The publication of *All the Pretty Horses* (1992), the first of his Border Trilogy, ushered in a much more lucrative phase of McCarthy's writing career and made him well known to the general reading public. Less dark and violent than his earlier works, the novel has the elements of a coming-of-age tale, romance, and action-filled Western. The combination proved to be more accessible to general reading audiences and became his most successful novel to date, selling 190,000 copies in hardcover within the first six months of publication. The book was on the *New York Times* best-seller list for twenty-one weeks and won both the National Book Award and the National Book Critics Circle Award. Although themes of violence, brutality, and the struggle against evil are present in *All the Pretty Horses,* it also features, for the first time, a protagonist with the makings of a hero. The self-reliant John Grady Cole embodies old-fashioned values; his capacity for violence is balanced by decency, kindness, and sense of responsibility for others.

*The Crossing* (1994) and *Cities of the Plain* (1998) are the other two volumes of the trilogy. *The Crossing,* which sold out its initial printing of two hundred thousand copies within a month of its publication, mirrors the coming-of-age theme set against the background of a changing West present in *All the Pretty Horses.* It tells the story of sixteen-year-old Billy Parham's three journeys to Mexico and his parallel search for freedom and justice, ideals that are, not surprisingly in a McCarthy novel, constantly undermined. *Cities of the Plain* (1998) unites the main characters from the trilogy's first two volumes, John Grady, now nineteen, and Billy, who is nine years older. The novel's title, a reference to Sodom and Gomorrah, reflects the theme of a West gone bad. As in McCarthy's other works, people, animals, and place meet a dark and gloomy end. In an epilogue that takes place fifty years later, however, he suggests the possibility of understanding and a brief moment of hope. Although *Cities of the Plains* was not as well received by critics as the first two volumes, it was nonetheless a commercial success. In the year *Cities of the Plain* was published, McCarthy married his third wife, Jennifer Winkley, with whom he has a son, John Francis McCarthy. They moved in 2001 to Santa Fe, New Mexico, where he wrote *No Country for Old Men* (2005). The novel retains a Western theme, but locates the drama into a modern desert setting where a drug deal has gone wrong. The book was adapted into a motion picture of the same name and won four Academy Awards. His next novel, *The Road* (2006), a postapocalyptic narrative featuring a father seeking safety for himself and young son, was adapted for film in 2009; it also won the Pulitzer Prize in fiction.

McCarthy has also tried his hand at writing plays. *The Stonemason* (1994) is a five-act play about a family of African American masons. *The Sunset Limited: A Novel in Dramatic Form* (2006) takes place in New York. He also wrote the screenplay for *The Gardener's Son,* broadcast on PBS in 1997.

Most helpful to students interested in researching Cormac McCarthy are general guides to his life and work by Edwin T. Arnold and Dianne C. Luce, Stephen Frye, Robert L. Jarrett, and James D. Lilley and Luce's entry on McCarthy in the *Dictionary of Literary Biography* (1994).

## TOPICS FOR DISCUSSION AND RESEARCH

1. John Grady's descent into Mexico has been compared to other coming-of-age tales, such as *The Adventures of Huckleberry Finn* (1884), by Mark Twain. Students familiar with Twain's novel may wish to explore its similarities to *All the Pretty Horses,* and more important, its differences. Do John Grady and Huck develop in similar ways? What qualities do the protagonists develop during the course of the novels? What role do violence, hardship, and lack of a strong father figure play in their development? Does John Grady's journey mirror Huck's? In what ways? What are their views about the West? What part does the physical environment and landscape play in their development as they come of age? Students might consult Vereen Bell, who examines a similarity

in the protagonists' desire to be free from the complications of modernity. For a discussion of coming-of-age themes, students might also see John Blair.

2. The title of McCarthy's sixth novel signals the importance of horses in that work. Indeed, their presence in *All the Pretty Horses* reflects both thematic and historical significance. Students could investigate the importance of horses to the history of the southwestern United States and/or their place within Native American culture (as suggested by the passage about "painted ponies and the riders of that lost nation," p. 5). How is this history of horses relevant to the overall concerns of the novel and what does it say about the contemporary West? Students should also consider various representations of horses as wild and domesticated, and as warriors and ranch animals. Also worth examining are the attitudes of characters about horses and their relationships to them, for example, Luís's belief that the souls of horses and men mirror each other and also the connection and interdependence of John Grady and horses. A useful discussion of the topic can be found in "Horses as Warriors in *All the Pretty Horses*" (see Sanborn, pp. 115–130). Stephen Tatum also discusses horses (see pp. 46–47) as does Georg Guillemin (in Arnold and Luce's *A Cormac McCarthy Companion: The Border Trilogy*, pp. 92–130), who focuses on the representation of horses in the context of pastoralism and its part in McCarthy's environmental critique. In *West of Everything: The Inner Life of Westerns* (New York: Oxford University Press, 1993, pp. 89–110) Jane Tompkins has a chapter titled "Horses" that would provide thought-provoking context for working with this topic.

3. In discussions of McCarthy's early novels *(The Orchard Keeper, Outer Dark,* and *Child of God)*, he is often compared to William Faulkner, Carson McCullers, and Flannery O'Connor, all of whom have been described as American Southern Gothic writers. Like its generic predecessor, Southern Gothic is characterized by horror, violence, and supernatural elements, which are used not only to create suspense in the narrative but also to explore social, historical, and cultural issues and psychological underpinnings of characters. Southern Gothic is also noted for its use of "grotesques," defined as characters, settings, and situations distinguished by extreme and disturbing qualities, which capture and often challenge underlying social problems. Although *All the Pretty Horses* is not described as a Southern Gothic novel, students might explore its connection to the genre, in particular, its use of features such as horror, supernatural elements, and the grotesque. Is there a connection between these elements and a social problem or issue? For example, what issues are highlighted by the images of bloody cruelty, terrible violence, and horrible depravity? Does the novel ultimately have a pessimistic or an optimistic view of humanity? What does the novel say about the nature of human beings? Are people naturally good or evil? Another way to approach this topic would be to compare the novel to one by a Southern writer. For example, how does Faulkner's story "Spotted Horses" compare to *All the Pretty Horses*? How has McCarthy been influenced by Faulkner?

4. In a 2008 interview on *The Oprah Winfrey Show* McCarthy explained his preference for simple, declarative sentence structure. He said that he uses capital letters, periods, and an occasional comma. He stays away from semicolons and does not use quotation marks for dialogue, referring to excess punctuation as "clutter." What effect does the sparse style of McCarthy's prose have on the narrative quality of *All the Pretty Horses* and how does it convey character traits and/or highlight thematic issues? Students interested in comparative topics might consider a comparison of prose style to that of Faulkner. McCarthy also chooses not to translate Spanish-language conversations into English. What effect does this stylistic choice have on the overall effect of the novel?

5. *All the Pretty Horses* is considered a Western, a typically American genre that usually features a solitary protagonist (traditionally male) adept at handling horses and guns who faces violence or hardship (often successfully overcoming it) against the landscape and history of the western United States. Using this description and previous experience with literary and film versions of the Western, students could analyze the ways the novel transcends traditional Westerns. Helpful for this topic is the essay by Tatum. Students might also view the film adaptation of *All the Pretty Horses* (2000), directed by Billy Bob Thornton and starring Matt Damon and Penélope Cruz, comparing their respective treatments of the Western genre.

6. In a discussion of the representation of Mexicans in *All the Pretty Horses* J. Douglas Canfield concedes that they may "still be too romantic, too primitive," but that ultimately, they are "indeed positive . . . but his reflexivity seems to me to reveal that [McCarthy] is aware of the problem of the exotic, that he has critiqued it" ("Crossing from the Wasteland into the Exotic in McCarthy's Border Trilogy," in Arnold and Luce, 2001). Daniel Cooper Alarcón, however, does not agree. In "All the Pretty Mexicos: Cormac McCarthy's Mexican Representations" (in Lilley) he takes McCarthy to task for his exotic or stereotypical portrayals. Students may wish to weigh in on the matter themselves, considering the positions of both scholars. Alternatively, students may wish to examine a similar discussion regarding the representation of women. A helpful essay is Nell Sullivan's "Boys Will Be Boys and Girls Will Be Gone: The Circuit of Male Desire in Cormac McCarthy's Border Trilogy" (in Arnold and Luce, 2001). What is the place of female characters in the novel? Are they realistic, fully fleshed-out characters in themselves or simply plot devices or accessories to the narrative?

## RESOURCES

### Primary Works

"Exclusive Interview with Cormac McCarthy," *Oprah Winfrey Show* (6 January 2008) <http://www.oprah.com/media/20080601_obc_267033502COR-MACWEBEA_O_VIDEO_1> [accessed 17 November 2009].

McCarthy's first television interview, which touches on the author's writing theories and his lifelong search for literary perfection.

Garry Wallace, "Meeting McCarthy," *Southern Quarterly,* 30 (Summer 1992): 134–139.
Featuring a series of conversations with the author and friends, the topics of this essay include McCarthy's reading and faith.

Richard B. Woodward, "Cormac McCarthy's Venomous Fiction," *New York Times Magazine,* 9 April 1992, pp. 28–31.
An often-cited essay in which McCarthy's life and work is explored with an emphasis on his violent themes.

## Criticism

Edwin T. Arnold and Dianne C. Luce, eds., *A Cormac McCarthy Companion: The Border Trilogy* (Jackson: University Press of Mississippi, 2001).
Essential collection of essays by nine scholars that explores issues related to gender, the environment, style, history, the cowboy tradition, and spirituality.

Arnold and Luce, eds., *Perspectives on Cormac McCarthy,* revised edition (Jackson: University Press of Mississippi, 1999).
Essential book-length study containing in-depth criticism, thematic explanations, and biographical information.

Vereen Bell, "Between the Wish and the Thing the World Lies Waiting," *Southern Review,* 28 (October 1992): 920–927.
An examination of characters in *All the Pretty Horses* and their desire to live in an uncomplicated world free from the struggles and demands of modern culture. Bell makes the typical comparison between the novel and Mark Twain's *Adventures of Huckleberry Finn.*

John Blair, "Mexico and the Borderlands in Cormac McCarthy's *All the Pretty Horses,*" *Critique,* 42 (2001): 301–307.
A discussion of the protagonist's journey into Mexico as a journey from boyhood into manhood; analyzes the border as a symbol of passage from a world that has been destroyed to one defined by "Otherness."

Vince Brewton, "The Changing Landscape of Violence in Cormac McCarthy's Early Novels and the Border Trilogy," *Southern Literary Journal,* 37 (Fall 2004): 121–143.
Insightful essay that presents the Border Trilogy as point of transition from McCarthy's previous works, noting the elements of hero and romance that are absent in his early works.

John Cant, *Cormac McCarthy and the Myth of American Exceptionalism* (New York: Routledge, 2007).
Essential overview of McCarthy's life and work, including novels, short fiction he published as a student, a play, and a television film script, with particular emphasis on the way his work challenges America's vision of its position as exceptional.

Kevin L. Cole, "McCarthy's *THE BORDER TRILOGY*," *Explicator,* 59, 3 (2001): 161–163.
Short essay focusing on images of absent, dead, or disempowered fathers, with comparison to similar images in other novels by other American writers.

*Cormac McCarthy Society* website <http://www.cormacmccarthy.com> [accessed 18 March 2010].
Provides information about McCarthy's life and work; links to relevant resources including the online *Cormac McCarthy Journal;* a bibliography of primary and secondary sources; updates about McCarthy conferences, and emerging scholarship.

Denis Donoghue, "Dream Work," *New York Review of Books,* 40 (24 June 1993): 5–6, 8–10.
Review of *All the Pretty Horses* that discusses the novel in relation to previous works.

Jay Ellis, *No Place for Home: Spatial Constraint and Character Flight in the Novels of Cormac McCarthy,* second edition (New York: Routledge, 2009).
Challenges interpretations of McCarthy's characters that view them as simplistic while focusing on images of space and domesticity and their relation to gender and family in nine of the novels.

Stephen Frye, *Understanding Cormac McCarthy* (Columbia: University of South Carolina Press, 2009).
Essential and comprehensive interpretation of each of McCarthy's novels to date, tracing his development as a writer, thematic and aesthetic interests, influences, and place within American Western literary traditions.

Georg Guillemin, *The Pastoral Vision of Cormac McCarthy* (College Station: Texas A&M University Press, 2004).
In-depth analysis of McCarthy's eight novels within the context of the pastoral tradition, paying particular attention to his descriptions of landscape and human relationships to it.

David Holloway, *The Late Modernism of Cormac McCarthy* (Westport, Conn.: Greenwood Press, 2002).
Extensive study that uses a literary Marxist approach to interrogate the formal aspects of the novels, including language and storytelling structure.

Robert L. Jarrett, *Cormac McCarthy* (New York: Twayne, 1997).
Overview of McCarthy's life and work, which Jarrett divides into two "phases," regional and postmodern; discusses *All the Pretty Horses* in the context of the latter in chapter 5, "The Border Trilogy: Individualism, History, and Cultural Crossing" (pp. 94–120).

Susan Lee, "The Search for Utopia: Blood Imagery in McCarthy's *All the Pretty Horses,*" *Explicator,* 66 (Summer 2008): 189–192.
Short essay arguing that McCarthy's use of blood is a symbol of life and of John Grady Cole's need to survive and "desire for utopia."

James D. Lilley, ed., *Cormac McCarthy: New Directions* (Albuquerque: University of New Mexico Press, 2002).
Collection of fourteen essays (of which five concern the Border Trilogy) that demonstrate a variety of critical approaches and tackle such issues as gender and race.

Dianne C. Luce, "Cormac McCarthy," in *Dictionary of Literary Biography*, volume 143: *American Novelists Since World War II, Third Series* (Detroit: Bruccoli Clark Layman/Gale, 1994): 118–136.
Provides biographical information and a summary of McCarthy's life as well as brief overviews of each of McCarthy's books published prior to 1994.

Luce, *Reading the World: Cormac McCarthy's Tennessee Period* (Columbia: University of South Carolina Press, 2009).
Discussion of works written from 1959 to 1979 (his "Tennessee period"), placing them within historical, geographical, and philosophical contexts; for the advanced student.

Wallis R. Sanborn III, *Animals in the Fiction of Cormac McCarthy* (Jefferson, N.C.: McFarland, 2006).
Examination of representations of animals in McCarthy's novels, plays, and short stories. Sanborn argues that animals reinforce a vision of a world organized by biological determinism, observing that animal survival in the works depends on distance from humans.

John Sepich and Edwin T. Arnold, *Notes on Blood Meridian*, Southwestern Writers Series, second edition (Austin: University of Texas Press, 2008).
Revised and expanded from the 1993 edition. This study explores key issues and themes and traces the historical context of the novel's events.

Ched Spellman, "Dreams As a Structural Framework in McCarthy's *All the Pretty Horses*," *Explicator*, 66 (Spring 2008): 166–170.
Short essay that analyzes the use of dreams as a way to bind together the major plot elements of the story.

Walter Sullivan, "The Last Cowboy Song: Cormac McCarthy's Border Trilogy," *Sewanee Review*, 108 (Spring 2000): 292–297.
Review of the Border Trilogy, providing a useful summary of the novels and assessment of McCarthy's literary skills.

Stephen Tatum, "Cormac McCarthy," in *Updating the Literary West*, sponsored by Western Literature Association (Fort Worth: Texas Christian University Press, 1997), pp. 475–488.
Explores the ways McCarthy's novels set in the Southwestern borderlands revise the traditional Western novel.

*—Magi I. Smith and Linda Trinh Moser*

# Toni Morrison, *Beloved*

(New York: Knopf, 1987)

In 2006 *The New York Times* asked around two hundred writers, critics, editors, "and other literary sages" to name "the single best work of American fiction published in the last 25 years." Toni Morrison's *Beloved* received the most votes by a significant margin. In an essay accompanying the results, critic A. O. Scott notes that the outcome was not a surprise, given the extent to which *Beloved* has "inserted itself into the American canon more completely than any of its potential rivals" (*New York Times,* 21 May 2006). It is widely taught on college campuses, received the Pulitzer Prize in fiction in 1988, and was cited in the announcement of its author as a Nobel Laureate in literature in 1993.

Morrison was born Chloe Anthony Wofford in Lorain, Ohio, on 18 February 1931 to working-class parents. In interviews over the years, Morrison has discussed her father's dislike and distrust of white people (he witnessed two lynchings as a young man in the South) and the major role storytelling, especially black folklore, played in her family's home life. After graduating from Howard University with a major in English and a minor in classics in 1953, she received her master's degree in English from Cornell University in 1955, where she wrote her thesis on the theme of death in works by William Faulkner and Virginia Woolf. She married Harold Morrison, a Jamaican architect, in 1958; they divorced in 1964. They have two sons, Harold Ford (born in 1961) and Slade Kevin (born in 1964). After teaching at Texas Southern University and then Howard, Morrison began a career as a textbook, then trade-book, editor for Random House. In that position she promoted the careers of many African American writers, including Toni Cade Bambara, Claude Brown, Angela Davis, and Gayl Jones. She also oversaw production of *The Black Book* (1974), edited by Middleton A. Harris, Ernest Smith, Morris Levitt, and Roger Furman, a landmark compilation of photographs, advertisements, newspaper articles, letters, handbills, posters, pictures of quilts, and other representations of the African American experience. It reprints the original accounts of Margaret Garner, the slave woman who killed her child to keep her from being taken back into slavery (the historical incident that inspired *Beloved*) and a photograph of a young girl in a coffin that inspired *Jazz* (1992); shot by a jealous lover at party, the girl refused to name him so that he would have time to escape. In 1987 Morrison was named the Robert F. Goheen Professor in the Council of Humanities at Princeton University, thus becoming the first black woman writer to hold a named chair at an Ivy League university. She retired from that position in 2006.

Morrison's first novel, *The Bluest Eye* (1970), generated immediate praise for its lyrical prose (words frequently encountered in Morrison reviews and criticism). That novel is the powerful story of a young, poor black girl who believes that having blue eyes would solve the deep problems in her family life and reverse the lack of regard shown by her community. Its 1970 publication coincided with a time when many Postmodern writers and critics were claiming that all the old stories and forms were used up and the only literary endeavor remaining was to experiment with language and structure. (See, for instance, John Barth, "The Literature of Exhaustion," *Atlantic Monthly* [August 1967]; reprinted in his *The Friday Book: Essays and Other Nonfiction* [Baltimore: Johns Hopkins University Press, 1997], pp. 62–76.) Yet, *The Bluest Eye* gave voice to an emotionally powerful experience not previously heard in American literature and ushered in an era when many previously silenced lives would be given voice. In an early interview, Morrison explains how she sees the focus of her work:

> I never asked Tolstoy to write for me, a little colored girl in Lorain, Ohio. I never asked Joyce not to mention Catholicism or the world of Dublin. Never. And I don't know why I should be asked to explain your life to you. . . . It is this business of being universal, a word hopelessly stripped of meaning for me. Faulkner wrote what I suppose could be called regional literature and had it published all over the world. It is good—and universal—because it is specifically about a particular world. That's what I wish to do. If I tried to write a universal novel, it would be water. Behind this question is the suggestion that to write for black people is somehow to diminish the writing (Thomas LeClair, "The Language Must Not Sweat: Conversation with Toni Morrison," *New Republic,* 184 [21 March 1981]: 25–29).

In 1973 Morrison published *Sula,* the story of an unconventional woman and her relationship with her more-conventional friend. That novel received fairly divided reviews, although still with much praise for Morrison's prose. *Song of Solomon* in 1977 firmly established her as a major voice in American letters. With a male protagonist and a plot based on traditional quest motifs but all set within distinctly African American culture and folklore, it introduced her to a wide readership and garnered significant critical praise, including the National Book Critics Circle Award.

Morrison is not a writer who hurries her work. *Tar Baby* appeared in 1981; *Beloved* in 1987; *Jazz* in 1992; *Playing in the Dark: Whiteness and the Literary Imagination; Paradise* in 1998; *Love* in 2003; and *A Mercy* in 2008. She has also written an opera libretto, *Margaret Garner* (2005); six children's books with her son Slade; and a frequently anthologized short story, "Recitatif" (1983), and has edited two collections of essays on issues of race and gender. She has produced a substantial body of essays and speeches, some of which are collected in her *What Moves at the Margin: Selected Nonfiction* (2008). Students wishing to more deeply understand her project, African American culture and history, white American presuppositions, and storytelling and narration, among other relevant contemporary topics, are urged to explore these writings.

The central story of *Beloved* is about Sethe, her life as a young woman on the Sweet Home plantation, her escape from slavery after the "benevolent" master dies and the farm falls into the hands of the sadistic Schoolteacher, and her twenty-eight days spent living free followed by the arrival of Schoolteacher. While free, Sethe murders her child. Her life after that event, including the departure of her sons, is interwoven with the present story of the arrival of

Paul D, a friend from her Sweet Home days, and the appearance of Beloved, possibly the embodied ghost of her murdered child. Practically every item in the novel has symbolic import, including the house number, 124—the 3, like her third child, is missing—making it a complex and challenging read both structurally and emotionally. Two-thirds of the way through the novel stream-of-consciousness chapters are presented, alternately representing the voices of Sethe, Denver (Sethe's remaining daughter), Beloved, and the consciousness of slaves being brought to America in wretched conditions on slave ships during the Middle Passage.

*Beloved* gives voice to the traumatic experience of blacks during slavery, long ignored in this country, at least at the level at which Morrison addresses it. She articulated a horrific history through a combination of graphic depictions of physical realities suffered by slaves, probing psychological explorations of the enslaved and their enslavers, the use of the supernatural as an evocation of the power of the past in present lives, and her distinctive, lyrical, poetic, complex prose. Her belief in the power of language is perhaps best expressed in her Nobel Prize acceptance speech: "We die. That may be the meaning of life. But we do language. That may be the measure of our lives."

Toni Morrison has attracted perhaps more criticism than any other living author. The MLA bibliography lists more than 1,800 critical works, including some 90 books, about her and her novels. *Beloved* alone is treated in more than 500 critical sources. The challenge for students is to find the most useful criticism for their needs. The collections edited by William L. Andrews and Nellie Y. McKay, Barbara H. Solomon, and Henry Louis Gates Jr. and K. A. Appiah are good starting places that offer reliable essays and secondary bibliographies that suggest further sources of interest.

## TOPICS FOR DISCUSSION AND RESEARCH

1. Students may ask, whose story is this? What happens to your understanding of the novel when you shift answers to that question? What are the novel's central concerns if Sethe is put at the center? Beloved? Denver? Paul D?

2. Students might find it interesting to research the Middle Passage, the experience of Africans brought to America on slave ships, and then consider how those experiences are depicted in *Beloved*. Why might Morrison have chosen to deal with these episodes in American history in dense, stream-of-consciousness prose? What are the connections between Sethe, Beloved, and Denver and these unnamed victims? (Note that she dedicates the novel to "Sixty Million and more.") Charles Johnson's novel *Middle Passage* (New York: Atheneum, 1990), a National Book Award winner, and *Black Imagination and the Middle Passage*, edited by Maria Diedrich, Henry Louis Gates Jr., and Carl Pedersen (New York: Oxford University Press, 1999), are excellent sources for the historical material required to address this topic.

3. More than once in the novel Sethe talks about her "rememory." Much critical attention has centered on this concept in *Beloved*. Students may find it interesting to explore the meanings of the term. In what ways is rememory

valuable, and in what ways is it destructive? For instance, when Paul D tells Sethe of seeing Halle at a churn, smearing butter on his face because he had witnessed Schoolteacher's nephews taking Sethe's breast milk, she thinks of her brain, "No misery, no regret, no hateful picture too rotten to accept? . . . her brain was not interested in the future. Loaded with the past and hungry for more, it left her no room to imagine, let alone plan for, the next day." Yet, painful as memories may be, they are also, arguably, necessary to any person's sense of self, and the very presence of the girl Beloved suggests that the past cannot be suppressed. An examination of the complexities of memory and of the role of the past in the present would be aided by the articles by Deborah Horvitz, "Nameless Ghosts: Possession and Dispossession in *Beloved*," and Jan Furman, "Sethe's Re-Memories: The Covert Return of What Is Best Forgotten," both in Barbara H. Solomon's *Critical Essays on Toni Morrison's* Beloved (1998); Caroline Rody and Ashraf H. A. Rushdy also address this topic.

4. Toni Morrison has said that before writing *Beloved* she intentionally did not research Margaret Garner's life, that her imagination was fired by reading two interviews with the historical person, and that she does not base her writing on real-life people, preferring the pleasure of invention. Of Garner she says, "Her real life was much more awful than it's rendered in the novel, but if I had known [then] all there was to know about her I never would have written it" (*Paris Review* interview). Nevertheless, investigating the historical person may enrich one's experience of the novel. Steven Weisenburger's *Modern Medea: A Family Story of Slavery and Child-Murder from the Old South* (2008) is an account of the historical Garner and her family. Students might also wish to compare how *Beloved* is inspired by the Garner story to how Morrison treats the same material in the libretto for the opera *Margaret Garner*.

5. Morrison has given several important lectures—her Nobel Prize address, "The Dancing Mind," and "The Future of Time" as the 1996 Jefferson lecturer—and has written literary criticism, most notably *Playing in the Dark*. How do the ideas in these texts illuminate the ideas and methods of *Beloved*?

# RESOURCES

## Primary Works

Carolyn Denard, ed., *Toni Morrison: Conversations* (Jackson: University Press of Mississippi, 2008).
Collects interviews from the 1970s to the present. For the years that overlap with the Danille Taylor-Guthrie volume, different interviews are provided.

Sheldon Hackney, "'I Come from People Who Sang All the Time': A Conversation with Toni Morrison," *Humanities*, 17 (March–April 1996): 4–9, 48–50.
Interview on the occasion of Morrison being named the 1996 Jefferson Lecturer. The discussion ranges over her family's love of music and storytelling, the role of the

past in the present, and Black English. The volume also includes a transcript of her Nobel Prize address and essays on her hometown and on her use of language.

Elisa Schappell, with additional material from Claudia Brodsky Lacour, "A Writers-at-Work/*Paris Review* Interview with Toni Morrison," *Paris Review*, 128 (Fall 1993).

Fascinating and wide-ranging interview in which Morrison talks about writing as a craft, her teaching, her views on many major literary figures, and all of her novels through *Jazz*.

Danille Taylor-Guthrie, ed., *Conversations with Toni Morrison* (Jackson: University Press of Mississippi, 1994).

Essential collection of interviews with the author covering 1974 to 1992, just before she received the Nobel Prize in literature.

*What Moves at the Margin: Selected Nonfiction*, edited by Carolyn Denard (Jackson: University Press of Mississippi, 2008).

Twenty-nine of Morrison's highly influential essays, reviews, and speeches from the beginning of her career as an author in 1971 to reflections on 9/11 in 2002, including the Nobel Prize address and "The Dancing Mind." The volume is divided into "Family and History," "Writers and Writing," and "Politics and Society."

## Criticism

William L. Andrews and Nellie Y. McKay, eds., *Toni Morrison's* Beloved: *A Casebook* (New York: Oxford University Press, 1999).

Essential collection of some of the best essays on *Beloved* published before 1999. Includes a conversation on the novel among three preeminent African American scholars: Barbara Christian, Deborah McDowell, and Nellie Y. McKay.

Henry Louis Gates Jr. and K. A. Appiah, *Toni Morrison: Critical Perspectives Past and Present* (New York: Amistad, 1993).

Offers contemporary reviews and critical articles on all the novels through *Jazz* as well as four interviews with Morrison. Essays focusing on *Beloved* in particular discuss images of slavery, history and narrative, and the novel's intertextuality with slave narratives.

Middleton A. Harris, Morris Levitt, Ernest Smith, and Roger Furman, eds., *The Black Book* (New York: Random House, 1974).

A compilation of artifacts from African American history—photographs, newspaper accounts, bills of sale, advertisements with stereotypical caricatures, quilts—providing a strong sense of the lived material history of African Americans through slavery and years of segregation and oppression.

Denise Heinze, *The Dilemma of "Double-Consciousness": Toni Morrison's Novels* (Athens: University of Georgia Press, 1993).

Accessible and insightful readings of the play of history, race, class, and gender across several Morrison works; consideration of *Beloved* includes its dramatization of family, community, and the supernatural.

*New York Times,* "What Is the Best Work of American Fiction of the Last 25 Years?" 21 May 2006 <www.nytimes.com/2006/05/21/books/fiction-25-years.html> [accessed 24 November 2009].
Lists the results of the *New York Times* survey on best of contemporary American fiction.

Philip Page, "Anything Dead Coming Back to Life Hurts: Circularity in *Beloved*," in his *Dangerous Freedom: Fusion and Fragmentation in Toni Morrison's Novels* (Jackson: University Press of Mississippi, 1995).
Discusses figurative and literal fragmentation in *Beloved,* demonstrating its role in character depictions and plot progression and at the level of prose.

Caroline Rody, "Toni Morrison's *Beloved:* History, 'Rememory,' and a 'Clamor for a Kiss,'" *American Literary History,* 7 (Spring 1995): 92–119.
Argues that *Beloved* is not a "historiographic metafiction" but rather an attempt to communicate authentic truth.

Ashraf H. A. Rushdy, "'Rememory': Primal Scenes and Constructions in Toni Morrison's Novels," *Contemporary Literature,* 31 (Fall 1990): 300–323.
Discusses how adult recollection constructs childhood memories as it relates to Morrison's fiction.

A. O. Scott, "In Search of the Best," *New York Times,* 21 May 2006 <www.nytimes.com/2006/05/21/books/review/scott-essay.html> [accessed 24 November 2009].
Essay describing and analyzing the outcome of the *New York Times* request to writers, editors, critics, and others to name the best book of the previous twenty-five years. Scott discusses reasons why *Beloved* received multiple votes along with works by Don DeLillo, Cormac McCarthy, Philip Roth, and John Updike.

Barbara H. Solomon, ed., *Critical Essays on Toni Morrison's* Beloved (New York: G. K. Hall, 1998).
Essential collection of criticism on *Beloved* plus all the major reviews of the novel. Seventeen essays cover such topics as the oral tradition, the supernatural and ghosts, narrative strategies in the novel, connections to slave narratives, symbolism, and memory. Also includes a brief piece in which Morrison herself discusses the significance of the opening paragraphs of *Beloved.*

Steven Weisenburger, *Modern Medea: A Family Story of Slavery and Child-Murder from the Old South* (New York: Hill & Wang, 1999).
History of the runaway slave Margaret Garner, her infanticide, and her trial.

*—Kathryn West*

# Joyce Carol Oates, *High Lonesome: New and Selected Short Stories*

(New York: Ecco, 2006)

Almost every discussion of Joyce Carol Oates makes note of her extraordinarily large literary output. In a career that began in 1963 with the collection of short stories *By the North Gate*, through 2009, Oates has published more than 128 books (novels, short-story collections, books of essays, other nonfiction, plays, and volumes of poetry). This oeuvre is almost unheard of among nongenre writers in contemporary times (although it would have been less unusual in the nineteenth century). In comparison, Philip Roth and John Updike, writers considered fairly prolific and of the same generation as Oates, published 30 and 60 books, respectively, during that same time span. Sheer numbers, however, are not the only notable fact about Oates's career. The breadth of her work is certainly worthy of note. While, as she says, she tends to write usually "about real people in a real society," she does so ranging in genres from straight realism to horror stories, mystery, and gothic. Finally, Oates is important not so much for how much she has written but for the depth with which she explores quintessentially American themes: violence, family life, and the American dream.

Oates was born on 16 June 1938 on a farm near Lockport, New York. Her childhood was not an easy one because of the family's poverty, and, as she has said, it was not "an environment that was particularly receptive to children being creative. . . . So I more or less just found my own way" ("Writing and Weaving an Emotional Thread"). As a child Oates wrote stories about her life on the farm and her cats and horses. At the age of fourteen, however, she began "a kind of apprentice life" by reading William Faulkner and Ernest Hemingway, an activity that helped develop her iconic authorial voice. Attending Syracuse University on a scholarship, she continued to fine-tune her craft. At nineteen she won a fiction-writing contest sponsored by the popular women's magazine *Mademoiselle*. Oates graduated valedictorian in 1960, after which she completed a master's degree in English from the University of Wisconsin-Madison in one year.

Oates published *With Shuddering Fall* (1964), her first novel, when she was twenty-six years old. She began the ambitious *Wonderland Quartet* with *A Garden of Earthly Delights* (1967), which received a National Book Award nomination, as did later novels in the series, *Expensive People* (1968), *them* (1969), and *Wonderland* (1971); *them* was awarded the National Book Award in 1970. Oates envisioned these works "as critiques of America—American culture, American values, American dreams—as well as narratives in which romantic ambitions are confronted by what must be called 'reality.'" ("Afterword" to 2006 edition of *Expensive People*). Three other novels have garnered Pulitzer Prize nominations: *Black Water* (1992), based loosely on the Chappaquiddick incident involving the late Senator Edward M. Kennedy; *What I Lived For* (1994), about a self-made millionaire; and *Blonde* (2000), the fictional retelling of Marilyn

Monroe's life and untimely death. The elusive American dream is central to each of these works.

Oates's most anthologized and most frequently discussed story, "Where Are You Going, Where Have You Been?," made its first appearance in the fall 1966 issue of *Epoch* magazine. The story, dedicated to Bob Dylan and written as a response to his song "It's All Over Now Baby Blue," joins five decades of Oates's best work in the collection *High Lonesome: New and Selected Short Stories* (2006). Oates has said she believes that this story is the one for which she will be most remembered. It documents the sexually charged power struggle between a girl and the strange man-devil who shows up at her door in a gold convertible to proposition her. Connie is depicted as a generic teenaged girl at odds with her mother, who constantly compares her to her sister, June. The only value Connie sees in herself is beauty, which she believes makes her mother favor her over the incorruptible June. Her father seems absent from family life even when he is physically present. Although evil seems to be the overriding theme of the story, like much of Oates's work, "Where Are You Going, Where Have You Been?" has family dynamics at its center: Connie is ultimately vulnerable to Arnold Friend because her identity is so generic, and he gives her the opportunity to become the girl "who saved her family" by going away with him.

The title story of Oates's massive collection is strikingly representative of her most pervasive theme: violence. "High Lonesome" documents the decline of a failed patriarch, his betrayal, his suicide, and a loved one's revenge against his betrayer. In it, Daryl, an unreliable narrator, describes how his cousin Drake, a police officer, is accidentally involved in a prostitution sting that busted Pop Olaffson, their pathetic and unassuming step-grandfather. Even though Daryl admits that Drake never intended to arrest Pop, he remains unmerciful to him in the story's cinematic, blood-spattered ending.

Another highlight of the collection is "Heat," which depicts the double homicide of twin sisters, barely in their adolescence. The killer is the gentle, kind, and mentally handicapped Roger Whipple, whose characterization belies the influence of the Gothic genre on Oates. Whipple, reminiscent of Frankenstein's creature, snaps after being overstimulated by the antagonizing Rhea and Rhoda Kunkel. Told from the perspective of an unnamed narrator, a childhood friend of the Kunkel twins, the story's sympathy clearly lies with Roger. The narrator recalls the numerous horrors the twins subjected her to, including the time they forced her to strip naked so they could feel power over her; she also describes the twins' cruelty to Roger in great detail.

Although she is known best as a writer, Oates prefers to think of herself as "a teacher. . . . That's a different kind of activity. Being a writer is something I would rather just do, instead of talking about being" ("Writing and Weaving an Emotional Thread"). In 1967, due to race relations and objections to the war in Vietnam, Oates left her job at the University of Detroit for a position at the Canadian University of Windsor. She moved back to the United States in 1978 to accept a teaching job at Princeton University, where she is now Roger S. Berlind Distinguished Professor of the Humanities.

Students interested in writing about the stories collected in *High Lonesome* might want to begin by learning about Oates's life and career. Greg Johnson's biography, *Invisible Writer*, provides the most extensive look, but many book-length studies of her work also provide introductions or chapters devoted to biographical matters, including those by Johnson and Elaine Showalter. These works also provide a variety of critical approaches to Oates's short fiction, considering gender, genre, and historical perspectives. The article by Brenda Daly focuses particularly on gender issues. Those interested in comparing Oates's short fiction to her novels could examine the studies by Gavin Cologne-Brookes and Joanne Creighton. Oates has written about her own process, craft, and thematic interests in *The Journal of Joyce Carol Oates: 1973–1982* and *The Faith of a Writer: Life, Craft, Art.* By consulting these and various interviews listed below, students can gain insight into the inspiration behind her short fiction.

## TOPICS FOR DISCUSSION AND RESEARCH

1. In "Why Is Your Writing So Violent?" in *The New York Times Book Review* Oates comments on the irony of being asked this question in Germany, "not many miles from where Adolf Hitler proclaimed the Second World War." She goes on, "The question was asked in Liége, in Hamburg, in London, in Detroit, in New York City. It would be asked in China if I went to China. It would be in Moscow. In Hiroshima." She considers this question "always insulting . . . always ignorant . . . always sexist." Students might choose to write about the effect violence has on Oates's work. Such students would be particularly interested in the short stories "Heat" and "High Lonesome" but could examine many other stories in the collection, including "The Fish Factory" and "The Cousins." How does violence function in her stories? Is it necessary? Is it paired with other common themes? Students may also choose to compare and contrast the stories' violent aggressors, such as Daryl and Roger. Another approach would be to compare the more-realistic physical violence of "Heat" and "High Lonesome" to the psychological violence present in "Where Are You Going, Where Have You Been?" An important consideration to all of these topics is whether or not the violence is occurring "onstage" or "offstage."

2. As an American writer who has been publicly skeptical about the politics of the United States, Oates's fictional commentaries on the American dream provide an interesting examination. Particularly relevant stories from *High Lonesome* include "Golden Gloves," "The Cousins," "*BD*11 1 87," and "The Hair." Advanced students interested in doing additional reading may want to consider the novel *We Were the Mulvaneys* (1996) or the book-length essay *On Boxing* (1994). Students writing on this topic would find it beneficial to listen to an audio in which Oates defines the American dream. The clip is available online through the Academy of Achievement website: <http://www.achievement.org/autodoc/page/oat0int-2> [accessed 19 February 2010].

3. In her review of *High Lonesome* Cathleen Schine challenges the description of Oates as a "social realist," describing her instead as a "fantasist. The stories in fact are often told by fantasists, from the point of view of unreliable narra-

tors, of uncomprehending children, of the unbalanced and the insane." Using two or three of the collection's stories described in the review, students might wish to consider Schine's assessment. In what ways is Oates a "fantasist," a writer of fantasy rather than social realism? Alternatively, students may wish to challenge Schine by showing how Oates's use of "fantasy" elements does not detract from the social realism of her stories.

4. Not all of the stories in *High Lonesome* were written for an adult audience. "Small Avalanches," for example, is the title story of a collection Oates wrote for young adults in 2002. Students might compare the depiction of adolescence in "Small Avalanches" to the depictions of adolescence elsewhere in the book. It may also be interesting to explore how the themes and content vary. Students may wish to read other books Oates has written for young-adult audiences, such as *Big Mouth and Ugly Girl* (2002) or *Freaky Green Eyes* (2005), for comparison.

5. Popular culture is a strong influence on Oates's work; students might find it interesting to explore to what effect it is being used. Students interested in this topic would want to read "Fat Man My Love," which Oates describes in a footnote as "purely fiction containing, in a transmogrified form, factual material from *The Dark Side of Genius: The Life of Alfred Hitchcock* by Donald Spoto and *The Encyclopedia of Alfred Hitchcock* by Gene D. Phillips and Thomas M. Leitch." "Where Are You Going, Where Have You Been?" takes inspiration from Don Moser's feature article "The Pied Piper of Tucson" in *Life* magazine (4 March 1966; reprinted in Showalter). Students could explore the original sources for the stories, paying particular attention to ways Oates departs from them. Students interested in additional reading may also consider *Blonde*, Oates's fictional retelling of Marilyn Monroe's life story, voiced posthumously by Monroe.

## RESOURCES

### Primary Works

Sarah Crown, "The Grandmother of Invention," *Guardian* (London), 10 September 2007 <http://www.guardian.co.uk/books/2007/sep/10/fiction.sarahcrown> [accessed 19 February 2010].
Oates on writing from personal experience in the novel *The Gravedigger's Daughter*.

*The Faith of a Writer: Life, Craft, Art* (New York: Ecco, 2003).
Includes twelve previously published essays and an interview, discussing "the process of writing more than the uneasy, uncertain position of being a writer."

*The Journal of Joyce Carol Oates: 1973–1982*, edited by Greg Johnson (New York: Ecco, 2007).
Sheds light on Oates's style and writing process.

Jessica McCort, "Interview with Joyce Carol Oates," *Arch Literary Journal* (2007) <http://archjournal.wustl.edu/node/32> [accessed 19 February 2010].
A good discussion of Oates's female adolescent narrators, feminism, and Sylvia Plath.

Lee Millazzo, ed., *Conversations with Joyce Carol Oates* (Jackson: University Press of Mississippi, 1989).
Compiles the major interviews given by Oates from 1973 to 1989. Oates discusses revision, major literary influences, and writing methods.

Robert Phillips, "Joyce Carol Oates: The Art of Fiction No. 72," *Paris Review* (Fall–Winter, 1978) <http://www.theparisreview.org/viewinterview.php/prmMID/3441> [accessed 19 February 2010].
Excerpts from an extended conversation on Oates's writing process and craft. The complete interview is available for download.

Deborah Solomon, "A Woman's Work," *New York Times Magazine,* 12 April 2009 <http://www.nytimes.com/2009/04/12/magazine/12wwln-q4-t.html> [accessed 19 February 2010].
Brief interview that includes Oates's thoughts on productivity, religious views, Southern Gothic, her autistic sister, her late husband, and the possibility of a memoir.

"Writing and Weaving the Emotional Thread" (20 May 1997), *Academy of Achievement* <http://www.achievement.org/autodoc/page/oat0int-1> [accessed 19 February 2010].
An extensive interview that focuses on Oates's early life, writing process, views on the American dream, and career highlights. The article also includes previously unpublished photographs and audio clips.

## Biography
Greg Johnson, *Invisible Writer: A Biography of Joyce Carol Oates* (New York: Dutton, 1998).
Well-reviewed biography covering Oates's personal life and career from birth to its time of publication, with her cooperation and that of her friends and family.

## Criticism
Gavin Cologne-Brookes, *Dark Eyes on America: The Novels of Joyce Carol Oates* (Baton Rouge: Louisiana State University Press, 2005).
Comprehensive examination of Oates's practical study of American social and personal problems within her novels.

A. R. Coulthard, "Joyce Carol Oates's 'Where Are You Going, Where Have You Been?' as Pure Realism," *Studies in Short Fiction,* 26, 4 (1989): 505–510.
Argues against the idea of supernatural evil in "Where Are You Going, Where Have You Been?"

Joanne V. Creighton, *Joyce Carol Oates: Novels of the Middle Years* (New York: Twayne, 1992).
Extensive examination of fifteen novels, including discussion of thematic interests and narrative style.

Brenda Daly, "Sexual Politics in Two Collections of Joyce Carol Oates's Short Fiction," *Studies in Short Fiction*, 32, 1 (1995): 83–93.
Discusses the sexual politics in "My Warsaza" and violence against women in Oates's work.

D. F. Hurley, "Impure Realism: Joyce Carol Oates's 'Where Are You Going, Where Have You Been?'" *Studies in Short Fiction*, 28, 3 (1991): 371–375.
Examines the element of magical realism in the story.

Greg Johnson, *Joyce Carol Oates: A Study of the Short Fiction* (New York: Twayne, 1994).
Thorough discussion of theme and style in Oates's short stories; includes biographical information.

Cathleen Schine, "People Who Hurt People," review of *High Lonesome: New & Selected Stories, 1966–2004*, New York Times Sunday Book Review, 30 April 2006, <http://www.nytimes.com/2006/04/30/books/review/30schine.html> [accessed 19 February 2010].
A review of the collection that describes the stories as a "coherent picture of her work" while focusing on the theme of "disappearance" and the fatalism in Oates's fiction.

Elaine Showalter, ed., *"Where Are You Going, Where Have You Been?"* Women Writers: Texts and Contexts (New Brunswick, N.J.: Rutgers University Press, 2002).
A useful "casebook" including a critical introduction by Showalter, a chronology of Oates's life, the *Life* article that inspired the story, essays examining important themes, and a bibliography.

*—Jake Helton and Linda Trinh Moser*

ᴄ◦⦙◦ᴐ

# Tim O'Brien, *The Things They Carried*
(Boston: Houghton Mifflin, 1990)

Tim O'Brien was born on 1 October 1946 and grew up in a small town in Minnesota where his father was an insurance salesman and his mother an elementary-school teacher. Both of his parents had served in World War II, his father in the navy and his mother in the WAVES. He attended Macalester College in St. Paul, where he majored in political science but also took courses in English and philosophy. He speaks of his alma mater with affection, describing it as a place where he learned to read eclectically and to broaden his sense of what he cared about, and thus what he wanted to read about. In the summer of 1968, with plans to enter the graduate program in political science at Harvard University, he received his draft notice. In fiction such as "On the Rainy River" in *The Things They Carried*, the memoir *If I Die in a Combat Zone, Box Me up and Ship Me Home* (1973), and essays such as "The Vietnam in Me" O'Brien describes himself as responding to the draft notice with disbelief and disgust—he had participated in some antiwar activities in college—and finally, with cowardice. Rather than standing up for what he believed, he went to Vietnam and spent a year as a foot soldier in a war he regarded as immoral. In "The Vietnam in Me" he says, "I have written some of this before, but I must write it again. I was a coward. I went to Vietnam." He served in the Forty-sixth Infantry, A Company, Third Platoon, of the Twenty-third ("Americal") Division. Although O'Brien's company did not know about the it until well into their tour of duty, in March 1968 another unit of the Americal Division massacred between three hundred and five hundred Vietnamese civilians, most of them women, children, and elderly people, in the village of My Lai.

O'Brien returned from Vietnam in 1970 and entered graduate school at Harvard. Leaving his dissertation unfinished, he took a job with *The Washington Post* as a national-affairs reporter, but stayed there only about a year. In 1973 he collected some of his published and unpublished writings to create the memoir *If I Die in a Combat Zone, Box Me up and Ship Me Home,* which was well reviewed. He followed it with the novel *Northern Lights* (1975), the story of two brothers trapped in a snowstorm; one had fought in Vietnam, the other had stayed home. His breakthrough was *Going after Cacciato* (1978), which won the National Book Award. Now considered a classic of war fiction, *Going after Cacciato* is the story of a soldier who decides to leave the Vietnam War and walk to Paris, of the men of his platoon who follow him to bring him back, and of Paul Berlin, standing sentry one night in Vietnam, whose fantasy about Cacciato and the platoon's adventure is intermingled with combat memories. Through these three intertwined strands O'Brien suggests that war is ultimately absurd, while also incalculably boring and peppered with moments of adrenaline and thrill. The novel *Nuclear Age* (1985) followed *Going after Cacciato.*

In 1990 O'Brien published *The Things They Carried,* which won the Prix du Meilleur Livre Étranger and was a finalist for both the Pulitzer Prize and the National Book Critics Circle Award. It solidified his position as one of the major, if not the most important, American literary voices to come out of the Vietnam War experience. It has since become much beloved on college campuses. A genre-blurring work, it is neither a collection of discrete short stories, nor is it a novel with a continuous plot. It most closely fits the category of the short-story cycle or composite novel. Many of the twenty-two named chapters can stand alone and have frequently been anthologized, in particular the title story; "On the Rainy River"; "How to Tell a True War Story"; "Sweetheart of the Song Tra Bong"; and "In the Field." But many of the stories interrelate, doubling back to comment on or even refute the action or assertions of earlier ones. For instance, "Notes," which follows "Speaking of Courage," purports to tell which events in the latter were true and which were not. Similarly, the experience of killing a Vietnamese soldier related in "The Man I Killed" is contradicted, confirmed, and revised later in the book. In a further move blurring the distinction between fact and fiction, the narrator is named "Tim O'Brien." These strategies have caused *The Things They Carried* to be honored as much for its Postmodernist sensibility as for what it has to say about the experience of a foot soldier in Vietnam.

An example of the Postmodernist impulse at work in *The Things They Carried* begins even before the stories proper: the dedication reads, "This book is lovingly dedicated to the men of Alpha Company, and in particular to Jimmy Cross, Norman Bowker, Rat Kiley, Mitchell Sanders, Henry Dobbins, and Kiowa." These names are also those of the main characters in most of the stories, leading readers to feel that they are meeting in the fiction the people with whom O'Brien served in Vietnam. The copyright page, however, carries the notice: "This is a work of fiction. Except for a few details regarding the author's own life, all the incidents, names, and characters are imaginary." *The Things They Carried* revels in Postmodernist play with its boundary-blurring strategies. Yet, the Postmodern also mirrors O'Brien's beliefs about the negative consequences of young men being sent to war. The facts about what it was like to be a young, scared boy at war in a foreign country provide only a shadow of the truth. But a fictional story comes much closer to conveying a sense of the emotional truth about war.

O'Brien followed *The Things They Carried* with *In the Lake of the Woods* (1994). Again Postmodernist in its approach, it is the story of John Woods, a politician who has kept hidden his involvement in the My Lai Massacre for years. It was named best novel of the year by *Time* magazine and received the James Fenimore Cooper Prize from the Society of American Historians. *Tomcat in Love* (1998) is the story of a promiscuous Vietnam veteran, and *July, July* (2002) relates the experiences of several characters from the Vietnam era at their thirtieth college class reunion.

Tim O'Brien holds the Roy F. and Joann Mitte Endowed Chair in Creative Writing at Texas State University—San Marcos. He maintains an active and helpful website at <www.illyria.com/tobhp.html> [accessed 6 December 2009] with many links to interviews, reviews, and critical sources. Students are encouraged to read fiction and nonfiction about the war by other writers to gain perspective on O'Brien's literary accomplishment. Ronald Baughman's *American Writers of the Vietnam War* (Detroit: Bruccoli Clark Layman/Gale, 1991), volume 8 in the *Dictionary of Literary Biography Documentary Series*, treats O'Brien along with four other war writers, including primary and secondary sources and a generous helping of illustrations. *Reporting Vietnam: American Journalism, 1959-1975* (New York: Library of America, 1998) is an invaluable source for placing O'Brien's fiction in context.

## TOPICS FOR DISCUSSION AND RESEARCH

1. Many critics and readers have remarked that *The Things They Carried* is at least as much about the process of writing as it is about serving in Vietnam. Thus students interested in Postmodernism might wish to explore the role of metafiction and self-reflexivity in *The Things They Carried*. What does the text have to say about the process of writing? Do the metafictional aspects of the text heighten the dramatizations of soldiers' lives in Vietnam, or do they draw energy and attention away? The articles by Catherine Calloway, Clara Juncker, Robin Silbergleid, and John H. Timmerman all offer useful perspectives on Postmodern techniques and metafiction in this book.

2. Timmerman posits that a key question addressed by *The Things They Carried* is, "Can one capture the reality of the event in such a way that the reader imaginatively participates in it?" O'Brien has said he believes the book has as much to do with epistemology as it does with war (Patrick Hicks interview). In various interviews and essays he has asserted that he can write a factual account of something that happened while he was a soldier in Vietnam, and readers will understand little, but that he can write a fictional account and come closer to the emotional truth of the experiences. Students would find it fruitful to read the essays by Calloway, Timmerman, and Benjamin Goluboff and then consider the status of fact, fiction, and truth as they are presented in *The Things They Carried*.

3. In "The Mystery of My Lai" in *Facing My Lai: Moving beyond the Massacre*, edited by David L. Anderson (Lawrence: University Press of Kansas, 1998), pp. 171–178, O'Brien says, "We live in this weird culture where we think everything can be helped and healed. . . . I think that we've healed the wounds too well, if anything. The country [America] has obliterated the horror that was Vietnam. To the Vietnamese people who lost whole families or lost legs and arms, we've healed it too damn well. We've obliterated it from the national consciousness, just as we obliterated what happened to the American Indians." In other essays and in interviews O'Brien has expressed his outrage over the lack of concern shown by most Americans over what happened to the Vietnamese people during the conflict, including his disgust at the American preoccupation with finding and identifying the remains of Americans who were missing in action while giving no thought to the thousands of Vietnamese killed but never identified nor acknowledged. Students could explore whether this awareness of the losses of the Vietnamese people is reflected in any of the stories in *The Things They Carried*. "The Man I Killed" is a good starting place. O'Brien's essay "The Vietnam in Me" will be helpful, as would the Debra Shostak and Daniel Bourne and the Patrick Hicks interviews.

4. The author of *The Things They Carried* is Tim O'Brien, who served as a foot soldier in Vietnam on a 1969–1970 tour of duty, has since become an internationally acclaimed writer, and now lives in Texas. The narrator of *The Things They Carried* is also named Tim O'Brien. This "Tim O'Brien" appears as a character in the collection at three different ages: as a nine-year-old boy in love with a young girl who dies of brain cancer, as a soldier in Vietnam, and as a forty-three-year-old writer looking back on his experiences in Vietnam and sometimes visiting with his former fellow platoon members, in particular Jimmy Cross and Norman Bowker. Students might find it interesting to explore the different Tim O'Briens associated with the book. How is each distinct from the others? What does this confusion of identities allow the actual writer to accomplish? The Calloway article, as well as those by Timmerman and Steve Kaplan, should be consulted.

5. Up to the Iraq War, a common first instinct was to think of war as a primarily masculine experience. Many scholars have offered fruitful gender analysis of *The Things They Carried* and other Vietnam War literature. The short story "Sweetheart of the Song Tra Bong" particularly invites gender analysis with its

comparison of the typical soldier with visiting girlfriend Mary Anne: "Seventeen years old. Just a child, blond and innocent, but then weren't they all?" Other stories also offer ground for analysis of constructions of masculinity and femininity—for instance, Martha in "The Things They Carried," the female letter recipient and the middle-aged women who attend the writer's readings in "How to Tell a True War Story," and the interactions among the various soldiers. Lorrie Smith argues that *The Things They Carried* "offers no challenge to a discourse of war in which apparently innocent American men are tragically wounded and women are objectified, excluded, and silenced." On the other hand, Susan Farrell contends that O'Brien critiques overly masculinist perspectives. The interview with Hicks, the article by Pamela Smiley, and the book by Alex Vernon offer helpful perspectives for exploring gender in *The Things They Carried*. Are women objectified? Is masculinity held up as a beacon, or is it critiqued?

6. O'Brien has identified Ernest Hemingway, William Faulkner, F. Scott Fitzgerald, and James Joyce as major influences and has expressed his admiration for, and some sense of influence from, Jorge Luis Borges, Gabriel García Márquez, Toni Morrison, and Anne Tyler. Students might compare O'Brien's writing with any of these figures to identify common techniques or themes. Or students could turn to other key American texts dealing with war, particularly those by Hemingway, Stephen Crane, or James Fenimore Cooper, and compare their depictions of soldiers and the experience of war with such depictions by O'Brien.

# RESOURCES

**Primary Works**

Patrick Hicks, "A Conversation with Tim O'Brien," *Indiana Review*, 27 (Winter 2005): 85–95.
Rich interview in which Hicks and O'Brien discuss the fiction, his sense of outrage over the way the Vietnamese were treated, his influences and reading preferences, the friend in Vietnam who served as the model for Curt Lemon, and his interest in magic.

Martin Naparsteck, "An Interview with Tim O'Brien," *Contemporary Literature*, 32 (Spring 1991): 1–11.
Discussion concentrates primarily on details in the books through *The Things They Carried*.

Debra Shostak and Daniel Bourne, "*Artful Dodge* Interviews Tim O'Brien," *Artful Dodge*, 22/23 (1991): 74–90; <www3.wooster.edu/ArtfulDodge/interviews/obrien.htm> [accessed 6 December 2009].
Extensive and fascinating interview with significant discussion of *The Things They Carried*.

"The Vietnam in Me," *New York Times Magazine*, 2 October 1994, pp. 48–57.
Powerful essay alternating descriptions of June 1994 struggles with depression and an account of a February 1994 trip to Vietnam with a girlfriend who had

since left him. They visited several areas where he had been as a soldier, including the site of the My Lai Massacre.

## Criticism

Catherine Calloway, "'How to Tell a True War Story': Metafiction in *The Things They Carried*," *Critique*, 36 (Summer 1995): 249–257.
Explores the versions of various stories O'Brien tells and retells through *The Things They Carried*, and discusses the purposes behind the metafictional strategies.

Jen Dunnaway, "'One More Redskin Bites the Dirt': Racial Melancholy in Vietnam War Representation," *Arizona Quarterly*, 64 (Spring 2008): 109–129.
One of very few works to take up the issue of race in O'Brien's work; also looks at Louise Erdrich's *Love Medicine;* much of the analysis is of the character Kiowa.

Susan Farrell, "Tim O'Brien and Gender: A Defense of *The Things They Carried*," *CEA Critic*, 66 (Fall 2003): 1–21.
Thoughtfully argues against the idea that the text is overly masculinist by separating the perspectives of the writer-narrator and what the reader discerns about him and the characters. Farrell suggests that O'Brien presents trauma as communicable through reading and storytelling, and that he implicitly critiques the characters' beliefs that they understand war and gender. The article provides close readings of many of the stories.

Benjamin Goluboff, "Tim O'Brien's Quan Ngai," *ANQ*, 17 (Spring 2004): 53–58.
Highlights the "realism" in O'Brien's texts by tracing the verifiable historical places and events mentioned.

Mark A. Heberle, *A Trauma Artist: Tim O'Brien and the Fiction of Vietnam* (Iowa City: University of Iowa Press, 2001).
Defining the contemporary period as an age of trauma, looks at O'Brien's work in this context.

Tobey C. Herzog, *Tim O'Brien* (New York: Twayne, 1997).
Like most volumes in the Twayne United States Authors series, includes a biographical chapter and a chapter on each major work; very accessible. Herzog went on to publish *Writing Vietnam, Writing Life: Caputo, Heinemann, O'Brien, Butler* (Iowa City: University of Iowa Press, 2008), which also offers useful perspectives on O'Brien and compares him to the other writers listed in its title.

Clara Juncker, "Not a Story to Pass On? Tim O'Brien's Vietnam," in *Transnational America: Contours of Modern U.S. Culture*, edited by Russell Duncan and Juncker (Copenhagen: Museum Tusculanum, 2004), pp. 111–124.
Discusses primarily Postmodernist elements in O'Brien's works, especially in comparison to Don DeLillo and Toni Morrison.

Steve Kaplan, "The Undying Uncertainty of the Narrator in Tim O'Brien's *The Things They Carried*," *Critique*, 35 (Fall 1993): 43–52.
Explores the obliteration of the line between fact and fiction in the text to show how O'Brien convinces readers they are hearing "truth" about what it was like for an American soldier to be in the Vietnam War.

Don Lee, "About Tim O'Brien: A Profile," *Ploughshares*, 21 (Winter 1995–1996); <www.pshares.org/issues/article.cfm?prmarticleid=3989> [accessed 6 December 2009].
Brief but informative profile of the author.

Farrell O'Gorham, "*The Things They Carried* As Composite Novel," *War, Literature, and the Arts*, 10 (Fall 1998): 289–309.
Argues that the fairly recent label "composite novel" best suits the form of *The Things They Carried* and that its goal is to explore, beyond the situational setting of a war, human experience and the human heart.

Robin Silbergleid, "Making Things Present: Tim O'Brien's Autobiographical Metafiction," *Contemporary Literature*, 50 (Spring 2009): 129–155.
Focuses on *The Things They Carried* as a Postmodernist text, discussing its play with notions of truth and the narrative ethics that arise from that play, and offers the term "autobiographical metafiction" as a descriptive label.

Pamela Smiley, "The Role of the Ideal (Female) Reader in Tim O'Brien's *The Things They Carried*," *Massachusetts Review*, 43 (Winter 2002–2003): 602–613.
Thought-provoking article that argues that O'Brien constructs his ideal reader within the text as female, and that he ultimately redefines masculinity.

Lorrie Smith, "'The Things Men Do': The Gendered Subtext in Tim O'Brien's *Esquire* Stories," *Critique*, 36 (Fall 1994): 16–40.
Provides close readings of some of the stories that make up *The Things They Carried* and argues that they ultimately take a masculinist perspective that leaves her "uncomfortable" as a female reader.

John H. Timmerman, "Tim O'Brien and the Art of the True War Story: 'Night March' and 'Speaking of Courage,'" *Twentieth Century Literature*, 46 (Spring 2000): 100–114.
Compares O'Brien's frequently anthologized "Night March," which was first published as "Where Have You Gone, Charming Billy?" and also appears as a chapter in *Going after Cacciato*, with "Speaking of Courage" in *The Things They Carried* to discuss the issue of telling a "true war story" and the "interplay between reality as data and the reality of the human spirit."

Alex Vernon, *Soldiers Once and Still: Ernest Hemingway, James Salter, and Tim O'Brien* (Iowa City: University of Iowa Press, 2004).
Discusses O'Brien's resistance to being a soldier and the role of storytelling, pilgrimage, and gender in his work, arguing in part that even the fiction not centered on war experiences is permeated by the views he gained as a soldier.

*—Kathryn West*

# Robert Pinsky (1940–    )

As a poet, literary critic, teacher, and translator, Robert Pinsky has sought to move poetry beyond the realm of academics and to make it accessible to all readers. Shortly after being appointed U.S. poet laureate (a position he held for three terms, 1997–2000), he founded the Favorite Poem Project, a large-scale effort to document and celebrate the strong presence of poetry in America. Over the course of a year, Pinsky solicited Americans to share their most cherished poems, resulting in over eighteen thousand responses. A highly public literary figure, Pinsky has appeared regularly as "America's Wordsmith" on PBS's *The NewsHour with Jim Lehrer* and contributed a "Poet's Choice" column for *The Washington Post*. He has participated in more-popular venues as well, appearing on the animated television show *The Simpsons* and on *The Colbert Report*. Through various activities, Pinsky seeks to make people's connections to poetry and its importance to their everyday lives obvious.

Pinsky was born on 20 October 1940 in Long Branch, New Jersey, "a decayed but still gaudy town" (Gibson Fay-LeBlanc interview) whose suburban images are featured in his work. He grew up in a "nominally Orthodox" Jewish family who "did keep kosher" but "didn't go to synagogue except on High Holidays, and sometimes not even then" (interview with Ben Downing and Daniel Kunitz). His father, Milford Simon Pinsky, was an optician. Although his mother, Sylvia (née Eisenberg), urged him to follow his father in his profession, Pinsky instead was drawn to the arts, finding pleasure in music, in "reading the dictionary and daydreaming about the sounds of words," and "imitating Yeats, Allen Ginsberg, Frost, Eliot" (interview with J. M. Spalding). While attending Rutgers University, Pinsky decided to concentrate on writing rather than on playing music. After performing badly at an audition, he decided, "I could not do the things I wanted to do on the horn or the keyboard so I faced what I might have been evading, my actual métier, the sounds and nature of words" (Fay-LeBlanc). In 1961 he married Ellen Jane Bailey, with whom he has three daughters, Nicole, Caroline Rose, and Elizabeth. After graduating from Rutgers with a B.A. in English, Pinsky went on to Stanford University as a Stegner fellow. There, he studied under Yvor Winters and earned an M.A. and a Ph.D. in creative writing. Pinsky now teaches creative writing at Boston University, where he is professor of English.

A self-described "compulsive explainer" (*An Explanation of America*, p. 6), Pinsky seeks to explore the world and its relationship to culture in both his poetry and literary criticism. Pinsky, however, does not ignore the difficulties of such an investigation. As interviewer Fay-LeBlanc notes, his "work is filled with efforts to get at the fragmentation, the forgetting, and the disconnection that accompanies our existence." In "Poem about People," in Pinsky's first collection, *Sadness and Happiness* (1975), he describes "the dark wind crossing / The wide spaces between us." Taken together, his work tries to close this distance by uncovering and explaining ideas and conditions that keep us apart. In *The Situation of Poetry: Contemporary*

*Poetry and Its Traditions* (1976) he challenges dominant trends in contemporary poetry (such as the use of free verse and a focus on the personal) by emphasizing the discursive possibilities of poetry. "The idea," he writes, "is to have all the virtues of prose, in addition to those qualities and degrees of precision which can be called poetic." In the long, three-part poem *An Explanation of America* (1979) Pinsky bridges the "apparently contradictory" aspects of the term "discursive" which can describe that "which is wandering and disorganized" and also "pointed, organized around a setting forth of material." The poem illustrates the former in its depiction of the diversity and disorder of America, its "Colonial Diners, Disney, films / Of concentration camps" and *"Deep Throat,"* the latter in his attempt to "tell [his daughter] something about our country, / Or my idea of it: explaining it."

The poem's vision of "our country like a common dream / To be between us," despite its contradictions, also reveals Pinsky's faith in poetry's potential to unite and ignite communities to action, a theme he returns to in later works. For example, in "The Unseen," a poem from *History of My Heart* (1984), Pinsky balances an autobiographical impulse and its attending attention to self with poems about political and social issues. In a description of a visit to a death camp in Kraków, the narrator observes, "the heaped-up meticulous / Mountains of shoes, toothbrushes, hair"; these become "the whole unswallowable / Menu of immensities." While Pinsky registers outrage and horror, he also refuses readers the comfort of self-righteousness, noting "a formal, dwindled feeling" of boredom and the capacity of all humans to resort to violence in an attempt to ward off that feeling.

Pinksy's work also shows a careful attention to form. To contain the vagaries of his explorations, Pinsky often employs strict form. In earlier work, he often chooses to stick to a regular pattern. *An Explanation of America,* for example, uses modified iambic pentameter, which lends stability to the disparate, chaotic, and potentially overwhelming images of American life. Pinsky, however, is not limited by a particular form, and his work incorporates a remarkable range of style. Unlike the long, discursive lines of *An Explanation of America,* the poems in *The Want Bone* (1990) are shorter and exhibit more language play than earlier poems. The title poem, for example, consists of quatrains that rhyme on the first and third lines (instead of on the conventional second and fourth), and "Visions of Daniel," employs short, terse lines to suggest the urgency of God's challenge to Daniel. Later collections *The Figured Wheel: New and Collected Poems, 1966–1996* (1996), *Jersey Rain* (2000), and *Gulf Music* (2007) continue Pinsky's exploration of form to convey such varying topics, from the joke telling in the elegy "Impossible to Tell" (1996) to rock 'n' roll music in "Louie, Louie" (2007).

Pinsky's interest in language and form is also evident in his best-selling translation of *The Inferno of Dante: A New Verse Translation* (1994), in which he re-creates the interlocked rhyme scheme of Dante's terza rima. It received the *Los Angeles Times* Book Award in poetry and the Howard Morton Landon Prize for translation. Pinsky is cotranslator of *The Separate Notebooks* (1983), poems by Nobel Prize winner Czesław Miłosz, and retells in prose biblical stories in *The Life of David* (2005). He is also author of the interactive game *Mindwheel* (1984), developed by Synapse Software and released by Broderbund. In addition to his imaginative works, Pinsky is the author of several works of literary criticism (in addition to *The Situation of Poetry*), including *Landor's Poetry* (1968), *Poetry and the World* (1988), and *The Sounds of Poetry: A Brief Guide* (1998). Pinsky's Tanner lectures at Princeton University were published as *Democracy, Culture, and the Voice of Poetry* (2002).

Students interested in sampling the variety of Pinsky's work will find useful "Robert Pinsky: Online Resources" (30 June 2009) at the Library of Congress website. Maintained by Peter Armenti, it provides an extensive list of links to biographies, interviews, and audio and video recordings of Pinsky and is available at <http://www.loc.gov/rr/program/bib/pinsky/> [accessed 16 December 2009].

## TOPICS FOR DISCUSSION AND RESEARCH

1. In *Poetry and the World* Pinsky discusses the connections between poetry and people, the "sociable presence" of poets that allows their work to reflect the world and to be a force in it. In "Poetry and Pleasure" from that collection he underscores the value of poetry that delights and entertains readers. In "Responsibilities of the Poet" he suggests the power of poetry to resist or transform cultural values. Students may use these essays as starting points for an examination of the ways Pinsky engages with the world or society in his poetry. How does he create a "sociable presence" in his poems? Students might also find useful the 1999 interview with Tom Sleigh in which he discusses the social and political role of the poet, the essay by J. Logenbrack, Pinsky's "Statement of Conscience," and his essays collected in *Democracy, Culture, and the Voice of Poetry*.

2. Another way to approach Pinsky's ideas regarding connections between poetry and the world is to consider his nonwriting efforts to promote poetry. Students might investigate these efforts, paying particular attention to ways poetry is presented and defined or redefined by them. Students could read contributions to the Favorite Poem Project: What are the values implicit in the descriptions of poems Americans choose? About his television appearances, students could consider: What notions about poetry and poets does Pinsky poke fun at in his appearances on *The Simpsons* and *The Colbert Report*? Information about the Favorite Poem Project is available at <http://favoritepoem.org> [accessed 16 November 2009]. Students can view Pinsky's appearance with actor Sean Penn in a "Meta-Free-Phor-All: Shall I Nail Thee to a Summer's Day?" (originally aired on 19 April 2007) on the *Colbert Nation* website <http://www.colbertnation.com/the-colbert-report-videos/85568/april-19-2007/meta-free-phor-all--shall-i-nail-thee-to-a-summer-s-day-> [accessed 16 November 2009]. His reading of "Impossible to Tell" appears in the "Little Girl in the Big Ten" *The Simpsons* (season 13, episode 20), which originally aired on 12 May 2002. Also useful is the interview with Keira Butler.

3. Pinsky pays great attention to the formal aspects of poetry. In a discussion of "The Want Bone" he writes: "Form in itself, like 'creativity' in itself, is cheap—

it is already there: the starting place. All day long forms keep droning that *x=x,* every fulfilled expectation makes a form. . . . It is the exception that exhilarates and inspires." Students may wish to analyze the formal aspects of his poetry. Pinsky often uses regular poetic form, whether in the traditional sense, as in a "Sonnet" from *The Want Bone,* or in a self-imposed sense, as in "Rhyme" from *Gulf Music,* in which he rhymes end words across stanzas instead of within them. While Pinsky does not shy away from strict forms, he is not always consistent. For instance, the strict form of "Sonnet," is preceded by "The Night Game," a narrative in free verse. What role do forms play in Pinsky's poetry? When using traditional forms, what rules does Pinsky break and to what effect? Does he include "the exception that exhilarates and inspires"? What is the relationship between form and content in Pinksy's work? Sources useful for this topic include Pinsky's *The Sounds of Poetry* and the essays by Logenbrack, Barry Goldensohn, and Tony Hoagland.

4. In interviews Pinsky addresses the Judaism of his childhood and its subsequent influence; he observes that "religion is a kind of surrounding reality, no more 'losable' in its own terms than the color of your eyes, or the force of gravity" (*Talking with Poets,* p. 25). Students might wish to consider to what degree Pinsky's work is influenced by Judaism. While his earliest works seem to avoid the subject, later collections note the poet's Jewish identity. In the title poem of *History of My Heart,* for example, Jewish identity is a theme running throughout as the narrator contemplates how it fits both inside and outside mainstream American culture. In "The Night Game" he pays homage to Jewish southpaw Sandy Koufax, who refused to pitch a World Series game because it fell on Yom Kippur. Unnamed in the poem, he is a hero not for Jews only but for all Americans. Pinsky also pays attention to historic and religious Judaism in his book of prose *The Life of David,* a creative chronicle of ancient King David. For starting points, students can consult the interview by Ben Downing and Daniel Kunitz and the essay by Charles S. Berger.

5. Though there is a serious tone to his work in terms of subject matter and form, humor is often at play in Pinsky's poetry, an approach that makes it more accessible and its darker themes more approachable. Consider the widely anthologized "ABC," which is a short meditation on death. The form, however, lightens the tone. Each word begins with the next letter in the alphabet (the first line begins: "Any body can die, evidently . . ."), thus providing a playful context in which to approach the topic. "Impossible to Tell," too, utilizes humor, in more-overt ways. An elegy, the poem interweaves two jokes in its remembrance of Elliot Gilbert, a friend who died prematurely. Pinsky juxtaposes incongruous subject matter and diction for humorous effect in "The Haunted Ruin" when he describes a computer using an ominous tone and language. Other poems to consider include "Poem of Disconnected Parts" and those in *Explanation of America.* How does humor help to convey darker themes? Students may find it helpful to consult secondary sources on literary uses of humor such as the entry on poetry in the *Encyclopedia of 20th-Century American Humor,* edited by Alleen Nilsen and Don L. F. Nilsen (Phoenix,

Ariz.: Oryx Press, 2000), pp. 224–228; also useful is the entry on the "Academic Study of Humor," pp. 1–6.

## RESOURCES

### Primary Works

Kiera Butler, "Spreading the Word," *Mother Jones* (16 October 2007) <http://www.motherjones.com/media/2007/10/spreading-word> [accessed 16 December 2009].
Pinsky discusses a range of topics from his mission to make poetry popular to his interests in "high" and popular culture (Emily Dickinson, hip-hop, *The Simpsons*).

Ben Downing and Daniel Kunitz, "The Art of Poetry No. 76," *Paris Review*, 144 (Fall 1997): 180–213.
Interview in which Pinsky discusses the role of Judaism in his childhood and didactic elements in his work.

Elizabeth Farnsworth, "America's Wordsmith," interview with Robert Pinsky, *The NewsHour with Jim Lehrer*, 2 April 1997, transcript and audio version available at <http://www.pbs.org/newshour/bb/entertainment/april97/poet_4-2.html> [accessed 16 December 2009].
Pinsky discusses his appointment as poet laureate and anticipates projects he will undertake in this role; he also recites "To Television."

Gibson Fay-LeBlanc, "Thrilling Difficulty: An Interview with Robert Pinsky," *Guernica* (November 2007) <http://www.guernicamag.com/interviews/430/thrilling_difficulty/> [accessed 16 December 2009].
Pinsky discusses his multiple influences, including the early influence of music, his ideas about accessibility or difficulty in poetry, and the role of political opinion in poetry.

"My Favorite Show; Robert Pinsky on 'The Simpsons,'" *New York Times*, 20 September 1998 <http://www.nytimes.com/1998/09/20/magazine/my-favorite-show-robert-pinsky-on-the-simpsons.html> [accessed 16 December 2009].
Discusses Pinsky's reasons for liking *The Simpsons.*

"Statement of Conscience," in *Poets against the War*, edited by Sam Hamill and others (New York: Thunder's Mouth Press, 2003), pp. 180–181; also available at <http://www.poetsagainstwar.com/chapbook.asp#Pinsky> [accessed 16 December 2009].
Written in February 2003, explains reasons for Pinsky's declining an invitation to the White House during the presidency of George W. Bush. They include protest against the war in Iraq and the Bush administration's tax proposals and policy on affirmative action.

"Robert Pinsky," in *Ecstatic Occasions, Expedient Forms: 85 Leading Contemporary Poets Select and Comment on Their Poems*, edited by David Lehman, second edition (1987; Ann Arbor: University of Michigan Press, 1996), pp. 175–177.
Discusses the relationship between form and content in "The Want Bone."

"Robert Pinsky," in *Talking with Poets,* edited by Harry Thomas (New York: Hansdel, 2002), pp. 12–40.
Interview conducted by several students enrolled in a course, "The Art of Poetry," taught by the editor, covering issues related to craft and theme. The interviewers demonstrate broad knowledge of Pinsky's oeuvre.

Tom Sleigh, "In the Intervals: Robert Pinsky and Tom Sleigh in Conversation," (1 October 1997) <http://www.poets.org/viewmedia.php/prmMID/15896> [accessed 16 December 2009].
Discusses the influence of jazz on Pinsky's poetry.

Sleigh, "Robert Pinsky," *Bomb,* 68 (Summer 1999) <http://www.bombsite.com/ issues/68/articles/2249> [accessed 16 December 2009].
Sketches out changes Pinsky sees in the field of poetry since writing *The Situation of Poetry* (1977) and discusses the social and political role of poetry.

Adam J. Sorkin, "An Interview with Robert Pinsky," *Contemporary Literature,* 25 (Spring 1984): 1–14.
An interview conducted relatively early in Pinsky's career that places his work within the context of contemporary American poetry and pinpoints themes that continue to appear in his later poems.

J. M. Spalding, "Interview with Robert Pinsky," *Cortland Review* (March 1998) <http://www.cortlandreview.com/pinsky.htm> [accessed 16 December 2009].
Traces Pinsky's reasons for becoming a poet, his involvement in the Favorite Poem Project, and his translation of Dante's *Inferno.*

## Criticism

Robert Archambeau, "Identity Politics and the Modern Self: Robert Pinsky's *An Explanation of America,*" *Mantis,* 4 (2004): 108–123.
Interprets Pinsky's poetry as ideologically appealing to a new "Bobo" (bourgeois/ bohemian) dominant class in American society.

Charles S. Berger, "Robert Pinsky," in *Contemporary Jewish-American Dramatists and Poets: A Bio-Critical Sourcebook,* edited by Joel Shatzky and Michael Taub (Westport, Conn.: Greenwood Press, 1999), pp. 443–447.
A short discussion of the role of Judaism in Pinsky's writing.

Robert Boyer, "Robert Pinsky [1997], [2000], [2001]," in *A Book of Common Praise* (Keene, N.Y.: Ausable, 2002), pp. 86–94.
Originally written as introductions to three public readings. This discussion of Pinsky's work is highly positive.

Barry Goldensohn, "Myriad Minded: The Poetry of Robert Pinsky," *American Poetry Review* (January/February 2009): 33–35.
Essential overview that traces a pattern of "theme and variation" throughout Pinsky's poetry collections. Goldensohn challenges the view of his early poems as merely straightforward and didactic.

Piotr Gwiazda, "'Beyond My Outrage or My Admiration': Postnational Critique in Robert Pinsky's *An Explanation of America*," *College Literature*, 35 (Spring 2008): 86–103.

In a counterintuitive move, uses Pinsky's expression of commitment to the idea of a unified American culture and nation to explain and explore postnational critique in the late twentieth century. For advanced students, it provides a close reading of the collection's poems.

Edward Hirsch, "A Fresh Hell," *New Yorker*, 70 (23 January 1995): 87–90.

Review of *The Inferno of Dante* that provides a positive assessment of the translation useful for students interested in Pinksy's poetic abilities.

Tony Hoagland, "Three Tenors: Glück, Hass, Pinsky, and the Development of Talent," *American Poetry Review*, 32 (July–August 2003): 37–42.

A concise discussion of Pinsky's mediation between subject and form, focusing on excerpts from *An Explanation of America*.

J. Logenbrack, "Robert Pinsky and the Language of Our Time," *Salmagundi*, 103 (Summer 1994): 157–177.

Discusses Pinsky's role within the context of contemporary American poetry, focusing particularly on his use of language to develop a social, political, and cultural dialogue in verse.

Marshall Toman, "Pinsky's *An Explanation of America*," *Explicator*, 42 (Spring 1984): 62–64.

Pinpoints quotations from and allusions to the work of other writers in Pinsky's long poem.

Jay Parini, "Explaining America: The Poetry of Robert Pinsky," *Chicago Review*, 33, 1 (1981): 16–26.

Praises Pinsky for his unique vision and originality and highlights important thematic concerns.

*—D. Gilson and Linda Trinh Moser*

꙰

# Annie Proulx, *Close Range: Wyoming Stories*
(New York: Scribners, 1999)

Annie Proulx's first novel, *Postcards* (1992), won the PEN/Faulkner Award; she was the first woman to receive it. Her second novel, *The Shipping News* (1993), received both the Pulitzer Prize and the National Book Award in fiction. In 1997 she received the John Dos Passos Prize, given to an author the prize committee deems the best underrecognized American writer in midcareer. Two stories from *Close Range: Wyoming Stories*, "Brokeback Mountain" and "The Mud Below," won the O'Henry Award; "Brokeback Mountain" also won the National Magazine

Award. And yet, Proulx did not begin her full-fledged literary career until she was in her fifties. She has continued to publish short stories and novels to great acclaim and has seen *The Shipping News* and "Brokeback Mountain" produced as major Hollywood films.

Edna Annie Proulx (pronounced "Proo") was born on 22 August 1935, in Norwich, Connecticut. Her mother, a painter and amateur naturalist, encouraged in her the habit of close observation and, she reports, introduced her at age three to metaphor, asking her to describe the picture she saw in her mind when she heard a piece of music. This practice created a lifelong passion for metaphor that she describes as fueling all her writing. Proulx earned her bachelor's degree at the University of Vermont and her master's at Sir George Williams University, now Concordia University, both in history. She began work toward a doctorate but did not complete it. She became immersed in the French *Annales* school approach to history, which, in her words, "pioneered minute examinations of the lives of ordinary people through account books, wills, marriage and death records, farming and crafts techniques, the development of technologies" (*Missouri Review* interview; for an analysis of this influence on her work, see Stéphanie Durrans's essay in Alex Hunt). Her creative writing takes this same approach, as she does extensive and minute research into the places and people about which she has written (rural Vermont, Newfoundland, Wyoming, Texas), living in those places, examining old records, and getting to know the residents. She has been married and divorced three times and has a daughter and three sons, the latter whom she raised mainly as a single parent. After living in Vermont for most of thirty years, she moved to Wyoming in 1994. She now divides her time between Wyoming and Newfoundland.

Proulx spent many years as a freelance journalist for magazines, covering topics as diverse as canoeing, gardening, mountain lions, mice, African beadwork, and weather. She also produced how-to books on carpentering, gardening, and food. During these years she published short stories at the rate of one or two a year, most typically in *Gray's Sporting Journal*, known for the literary quality of the outdoor fiction it publishes. Her first collection was *Heartsongs and Other Stories* (1988). She initially published as E. Annie Proulx and sometimes E. A. Proulx but now prefers Annie Proulx.

Since *Close Range*, Proulx has published two more collections of stories set in Wyoming: *Bad Dirt: Wyoming Stories 2* (2004) and *Fine Just the Way It Is: Wyoming Stories 3* (2008). In the latter collection her interest in, and influence from, the work and methods of Mark Twain appears prominently, especially in "I've Always Loved This Place" and "Swamp Mischief," both featuring the devil as a major character. In addition to those mentioned above, her other novels are *Accordion Crimes* (1996) and *That Old Ace in the Hole* (2002). She almost always writes in a third-person, limited perspective (in *Close Range*, the only exception to this is the first-person narrative, "A Lonely Coast").

The lead story in *Close Range: Wyoming Stories*, titled "The Half-Skinned Steer," was selected by Garrison Keillor for inclusion in *The Best American Short Stories 1998* (Proulx herself edited the 1997 edition of this series) and later by novelist John Updike for *The Best American Short Stories of the Century* (1999).

Along with "The Blood Bay," it is a takeoff on the traditional "tall tale" that was once central to Western American literature. While the eleven stories that compose the collection uniformly feature her sharp, evocative, metaphor-driven prose, they form a spectrum in terms of their relationship to realism and tone. At one end would be "Job History," an example of minimalism with its bare-bones recounting of a family's series of failed economic efforts and brief references to news stories they hear—Vietnam and Selma, Alabama, "religious cult members [who] have swallowed Kool-Aid and cyanide"—reflecting the degree to which these historical events remain on the periphery of their lives. In the traditionally realist camp are "A Lonely Coast," "The Mud Below," and "People in Hell Just Want a Drink of Water." At the other end are examples of magical realism, with the talking tractor in "The Bunchgrass Edge of the World" and the seductive spurs in "A Pair of Spurs." Yet, all the stories in the collection are in some way resonant with its epigraph, attributed to a retired Wyoming rancher: "Reality's never been of much use out here."

"Brokeback Mountain" has received the most attention of the stories in *Close Range,* in part because of the motion picture based on it; in part because its reputation as a "gay cowboy love story" sets it apart from most fiction of the West; but also simply for the quality of the story. Beginning in 1963, it is the story of two uneducated young men: Jack Twist aspires to become a rodeo star; Ennis Del Mar wants to be a rancher. They spend a summer isolated together on Brokeback Mountain, herding sheep, and fall in love. The story then records the next twenty years in their lives, as they take fishing and hunting vacations together a few times a year until Jack is killed, most likely in a hate crime based on homophobia. "Brokeback Mountain" exemplifies the hallmarks of Proulx's fiction: rural characters with little to no economic opportunities; detailed attention to the landscape, weather, and social history of the setting; and social commentary. It was first published in *The New Yorker* in October 1997, and has been frequently anthologized.

## TOPICS FOR DISCUSSION AND RESEARCH

1. In an interview with the *Missouri Review* in 1999, the same year *Close Range* appeared, Proulx said, "I like stories with three generations visible. Geography, geology, climate, weather, the deep past, immediate events, shape the characters and partly determine what happens to them, although the random event counts for much, as it does in life. . . . I watch for the historical skew between what people have hoped for and who they thought they were and what befell them." This comment suggests several fruitful topics. For instance, almost every story in *Close Range* does in fact have three generations "visible," even if only one is the focus of the story. How does Proulx use the surrounding generations to relate a sense of her characters and what happens to them? What does the reader learn about the lives of the older generations even when the focus is on the younger? "People in Hell Just Want a Drink of Water," "The Bunchgrass Edge of the World," and "Brokeback Mountain" would be particularly suited for this analysis. "Geography, geology, climate, weather" could

be examined in any of these stories for their impact on character both in the sense of personality and of what happens to characters. How does the detailed description of landscape and weather affect the reading experience? Are these elements ever sentimentalized? In what respects might this writing be seen as pastoral, and in what ways does her attention to the natural world work against traditional notions of the pastoral? The essay by Ginger Jones would be useful for the latter analysis, while examinations of landscape, weather, and geography would be illuminated by the essay by Alex J. Tuss and several of those in Alex Hunt's *The Geographical Imagination of Annie Proulx* (2009), especially O. Alan Weltzien's "Annie Proulx's Wyoming: Geographical Determinism, Landscape, and Caricature" and Elizabeth Abele's "Westward Proulx: The Resistant Landscapes of *Close Range: Wyoming Stories* and *That Old Ace in the Hole*."

2. Also in the *Missouri Review* interview Proulx responded to the critics who have questioned the amount of violence depicted in her writing: "America is a violent, gun-handling country. Americans feed on a steady diet of bloody movies, television programs, murder mysteries. Road rage, highway killings, beatings and murder of those who are different abound; school shootings—almost all of them in rural areas—make headline news over and over. . . . The point of writing in layers of bitter deaths and misadventures that befall characters is to illustrate American violence, which is real, deep and vast." Most of the stories in *Close Range* include scenes of violence and cruelty, some physical and some emotional. Students could interrogate these scenes of violence for their purpose and effect. Are they reasonable or gratuitous in the context? How does human violence correspond to the landscape, the weather, and/or the social climate? In "Brokeback Mountain" the sex between Ennis and Jack is described as violent more than once. How and why does violence become mixed up with love in this and other stories?

3. The Puritan work ethic and late-nineteenth-century celebrations of American drive, inventiveness, and will to progress have been inherited by contemporary generations to some degree, but with significant changes. What does hard work mean in the stories in *Close Range*? Is it typically rewarded? Why or why not? Are there examples of labor that characters find satisfying? "Job History" and "The Bunchgrass Edge of the World" would be particularly interesting to examine through this lens, although insightful examples of the human relationship to work might be found in almost all the stories. What does Proulx have to say about the human relationship to work? Karen L. Rood's *Understanding Annie Proulx* (2001) would be helpful to this undertaking.

4. Students interested in film studies might wish to compare the film version of *Brokeback Mountain* with the short story. Proulx has enthusiastically praised the film; she and others have noted that it is an unusually close adaptation of a story to film; however, the same story told in a different medium changes. Students might track the changes from the printed to the filmed version and assess how those differences serve to shift the emphasis on themes and issues. Which version more accurately depicts the hardscrabble life of ranch workers in the 1960s? Students could consult the interview with Matthew Testa, the

essays by Christopher Pullen (in Hunt's *The Geographical Imagination*), James Keller and Anne Goodwyn Jones, and the collection by Jim Stacy.

5. After their sexual relationship has begun, Jack and Ennis spend an evening talking by their campfire. Jack tells of being beaten and urinated on by his father when he was a small child and didn't make it to the bathroom in time. When Jack visits Ennis the first time and suggests they run a ranch together, Ennis tells of his father taking him to see a gay man who had been beaten to death by a tire iron. Both of these incidents suggest important rejections by father figures. Students would find it profitable to consider other interactions with fathers and father figures in "Brokeback Mountain" or compare them to issues with fathers in stories such as "The Mud Below," "People in Hell Just Want a Drink of Water," and "The Bunchgrass Edge of the World." What does Proulx suggest about the impact of a father's rejection on a young man? How does she depict it as shaping identity? For what aspects of identity is it important, and when is it perhaps not important? What if a father figure is vaguely supportive but ineffectual? Students could consult Keller and Anne Goodwyn Jones and, for any of these suggested topics, Rood.

## RESOURCES

### Primary Works

"An Interview with Annie Proulx," *Missouri Review*, 22, 2 (1999): 77–90. Discusses her approach to fiction in great depth.

Matthew Testa, "At Close Range with Annie Proulx," *Planet JH Weekly*, 7 December 2005 <www.planetjh.com/music_arts_culture/A_100138.aspx> [accessed 16 December 2009]. Focuses on "Brokeback Mountain" and Proulx's thoughts on the reception of the story and the resulting film. Proulx also discusses her interest in Wyoming.

### Criticism

Sara Friedman, "Names in Annie Proulx's *Accordion Crimes* and *Close Range: Wyoming Stories* and Their Hebrew Translation," *Bucknell Review*, 47, 1 (2004): 107–123. Interesting look at the unusual names of people and places found in these two works.

Alex Hunt, ed., *The Geographical Imagination of Annie Proulx: Rethinking Regionalism* (Lanham, Md.: Lexington Books, 2009). Useful and thoughtful collection. Most relevant to *Close Range* are the introduction and the essays by Margaret E. Johnson, "Proulx and the Postmodern Hyperreal"; O. Alan Weltzien, "Annie Proulx's Wyoming: Geographical Determinism, Landscape, and Caricature"; Elizabeth Abele's "Westward Proulx: The Resistant Landscapes of *Close Range: Wyoming Stories* and *That Old Ace in the Hole*"; and Christopher Pullen's "*Brokeback Mountain* As Progressive Narrative and Cinematic Vision: Landscape, Emotion, and the Denial of Domesticity."

Ginger Jones, "Proulx's Pastoral: Brokeback Mountain As Sacred Space," in *Reading* Brokeback Mountain: *Essays on the Film and the Story*, edited by Jim Stacy (Jefferson, N.C.: McFarland, 2007), pp. 19–28.
Thought-provoking reading of the story through the conventions of the pastoral as created by Theocritus, arguing in part that Jack takes on many of the experiences of one of Theocritus's greatest heroes, Herakles (Hercules).

James Keller and Anne Goodwyn Jones, "*Brokeback Mountain:* Masculinity and Manhood," *Studies in Popular Culture*, 30 (Spring 2008): 21–36.
Argues that Proulx highlights the masculinity of Jack and Ennis in order to make the sex scenes between two men more palatable to mainstream audiences. More attention is given to the film than to the story.

Karen L. Rood, *Understanding Annie Proulx* (Columbia: University of South Carolina Press, 2001).
Highly useful study of Proulx and her work through *Close Range*. After a chapter of biography, one chapter is devoted to each of Proulx's books. The chapter on *Close Range* includes commentaries on all of the stories.

Jane Rose and Joanne Urschel, "Understanding the Complexity of Love in *Brokeback Mountain:* An Analysis of the Film and Short Story," *Journal of Men's Studies*, 14 (Spring 2006): 247–251.
Brief but helpful in its focus on the causes of emotional repression in Jack and Ennis. The essay must be read with care, as the authors do not always make it clear when they are discussing the film and when the short story.

Julie Scanlon, "Why Do We Still Want to Believe: The Case of Annie Proulx," *JNT: Journal of Narrative Theory*, 38 (Winter 2008): 86–110.
Examines several of Proulx's works as fulfilling a contemporary desire for realism despite the prevalence of Postmodernism; for advanced students.

Jim Stacy, ed., *Reading Brokeback Mountain: Essays on the Story and the Film* (Jefferson, N.C.: McFarland, 2007).
Uneven collection with more emphasis on the film than the short story.

Alex J. Tuss, "Brokeback Mountain and the Geography of Desire," *Journal of Men's Studies*, 14 (Spring 2006): 243–246.
Traces the bifurcated landscape of the story—plains and mountains—to the divided lives Jack and Ennis lead. Tuss discusses both the story and the film.

—*Kathryn West*

# Adrienne Rich (1929–   )

In "Diving into the Wreck" Adrienne Rich describes the poet's search for "the thing itself and not the myth," a quest for truth hidden behind social myths that pervades her lifelong explorations of her identity as a woman, poet, mother, lesbian, and Jew. Adrienne Cecile Rich was born in Baltimore in 1929 to Helen

Jones Rich, a concert pianist who set aside her career to be a wife and mother, and Arnold Rice Rich, a professor of pathology at the Johns Hopkins University School of Medicine. Hers was a white, middle-class upbringing, privileged but marked by her father's denial of his Jewish identity, which led her to feel "split at the root, neither Gentile nor Jew." She "was sent to the Episcopal church," although neither of her parents belonged to it, and when she was applying for college, her Protestant mother advised her to "put down 'Episcopalian' rather than 'none'" on application forms ("Split at the Root: An Essay on Jewish Identity," included in the volume edited by Barbara Charlesworth Gelpi and Albert Gelpi). Encouraged by her parents to pursue intellectual and artistic interests, she began writing poems at an early age and read widely in her father's library, where she gravitated toward poetry. She attended Radcliffe College, where she continued to develop her craft while reading John Donne, Robert Frost, Wallace Stevens, W. B. Yeats, and W. H. Auden. In 1951 Auden chose Rich's first collection of poetry, *A Change of World*, for the esteemed Yale Series of Younger Poets. In 1953 Rich married Alfred Conrad, an economist at Harvard College, and, in what she has called a "radicalizing experience," gave birth to three sons in four years. Her second collection, *The Diamond Cutters and Other Poems*, was published in 1955, the year her first son was born; it was eight years before her next book, *Snapshots of a Daughter-in Law: Poems, 1954–1962*, appeared. Reflecting Rich's early education, her first two collections are formally conservative, elegant, and emotionally repressed. *Snapshots of a Daughter-in-Law* reveals Rich's experimentation with "a looser line" and "new subject matter" (Claire Keyes), paving the way for her later experimentation with style and more-explicit interest in female identity, qualities that would define her later work.

In 1966 Rich moved with her family to New York City, where she became an instructor in SEEK, a basic-writing program at City College for open-admissions students who were mostly blacks, Asians, and Latinos from low-income neighborhoods. Rich also became involved in the Civil Rights, antiwar, and women's-liberation movements, launching a lifelong commitment to social justice and activism. In 1970 her husband committed suicide; she writes indirectly of his death in "From a Survivor" (1973) and "Sources" (1986). The earlier poem appears in *Diving into the Wreck: Poems, 1971–1972* (1973), the best known of Rich's many collections and the one that established her place as a major American poet. In the title poem the androgynous speaker dives into the sea to explore the wreck of a ship; this image is a metaphor for the need for oppressed individuals, especially women, to reject the lies society tells about them. The speaker must undertake this dangerous journey to discover a more truthful account of her life, history, and the political machinations of the world.

"Diving into the Wreck" marks Rich's first explicit and extended rejection of patriarchal traditions in terms of theme and form while also modeling the act of "re-visioning," whereby women reclaim agency over their lives, bodies, and language by searching through the "wreck" of social myths, primarily those about gender (a process she had earlier described in the essay "When We Dead Awaken," 1972). *Diving into the Wreck* won the National Book Award in 1974; Rich initially refused the award as an individual but accepted it later along with two fellow nominees, both African American women, Audre Lorde and Alice Walker. Soon afterward, Rich "came out" as a lesbian; in 1976 she began a relationship with writer-activist Michelle Cliff and published *Twenty-One Love Poems*, a collection written explicitly for a lesbian audience. A prolific poet, Rich continued to use a subjective stance to uncover the relationship between individual and social identities, the personal and the political, in works such as *The Dream of a Common Language: Poems, 1974–1977* (1978), *Your Native Land, Your Life* (1986), *Time's Power: Poems, 1985–1988* (1989), *An Atlas of the Difficult World: Poems, 1988–1991* (1991), *Dark Fields of the Republic, 1991–1995* (1995), *Fox: Poems, 1998–2000* (2001), *The School among the Ruins: Poems, 2000–2004* (2004), and *Telephone Ringing in the Labyrinth: Poems, 2004–2006* (2007); the last is her seventeenth collection of original poems. In all, she exhibits care, sympathy, empathy, and formal innovation, grounded by a lesbian and Jewish-feminist vision.

In her prose, Rich has made significant contributions to late-twentieth- and early-twenty-first-century thinking about female experience, language, sexuality, power, and the connection between art and politics. In *Of Woman Born: Motherhood As Experience and Institution* (1976) she combines subjective and emotional experience (traditionally relegated to poetry and fiction) with academic research to expose the social myths and institutions that restrict and regulate female bodies and behavior. She continued the process of "re-visioning" female identity and women's place in society in *On Lies, Secrets, and Silence: Selected Prose, 1966–1978* (1979) and *Blood, Bread, and Poetry: Selected Prose, 1979–1985* (1986), turning her attention to women's education, a female literary tradition, and issues related to race and ethnicity.

Rich's essays, like her poetry, interrogate power structures and explore the relationships among oppression of all kinds, misrepresentations of women in literature, "the erasure of lesbian existence," her relationship to men (including her father, husband, and male poets), and Jewish identity. Her work has not been immune to criticism. Her stance on lesbian "separatism," her repudiation of male culture, and her conceptualization of separatism in racial terms have all been criticized, as has her formulation of "compulsory heterosexuality" as the main factor in female oppression. She has also been accused of emphasizing content rather than form, sacrificing poetic artistry for her political messages. Her response has been an ongoing and open attempt, as she wrote early in her career, "to carry my thoughts on feminism and racism beyond the confines of my own mind."

From the 1990s onward, Rich has increasingly turned her attention to connections between poetry and politics in her prose works. In *What Is Found There: Notebooks on Poetry and Politics* (1993), *Arts of the Possible: Essays and Conversations* (2001), and *A Human Eye: Essays on Art in Society, 1997–2008* (2009), Rich elaborates a rejection of the separation between artistic and practical expression, highlighting the role of creativity in the political process. She also upholds the need for resistance in art and life; in "Why I Refused the National Medal of the Arts," an open letter included in *Arts of the Possible*, she describes her act as a refusal to accept the politics of the U.S. government.

Rich has taught at many institutions, including Swarthmore College and Columbia, Brandeis, Bryn Mawr, Rutgers, Cornell, Stanford, and San Jose State

Universities, and she has received numerous awards and fellowships, among them Guggenheim Fellowships (1952–1953 and 1961–1962), a Bollingen Foundation Fellowship (1962), the Amy Lowell Traveling Fellowship (1962–1963), the Fund for Human Dignity Award (1981), a Ruth Lilly Poetry Prize (1986), a Brandeis Creative Arts Medal (1987), the Common Wealth Award in Literature (1991), the Lenore Marshall/*Nation* Award (1992), and a MacArthur Foundation "genius award." She has also received honorary doctorates from (among others) Smith College, the College of Wooster, Harvard University, Swarthmore College, and Brandeis University.

## TOPICS FOR DISCUSSION AND RESEARCH

1. A good deal of scholarship addresses the early and middle periods of Adrienne Rich's poetry, while not as much critical work exists at the moment for her work from the mid 1990s to the present. Rich's poetic oeuvre is one of great change, fluidity, and openness; readers of Rich's work can notice even in cursory glances dramatic shifts in thinking and form throughout her career. If the early work, poems such as "Aunt Jennifer's Tigers" from *A Change of World* (1951) and "The Roofwalker" from *Snapshots of a Daughter-in-Law* (1963), look conservative, they are so formally and only so politically when compared to the more-radical work of Rich's middle and later periods. Students interested in investigating changes in Rich's style and thematic focus over the course of her career will do well to consult Cheri Colby Langdell's book.

2. In "Trying to Save the Skein," a review of *Diving into the Wreck* included in the collection edited by Jane Roberta Cooper, Cheryl Walker called the title work "one of the most beautiful poems to come out of the feminist movement. . . . The poem is utterly personal but there is nothing in it which draws away into private life." Walker's observations serve as a starting point for understanding how Rich's work, this poem in particular, manifests the feminist dictum "the personal is political." Students might consider analyzing the ways Rich removes the division between what is happening to a person behind closed doors and what is happening to her in the outside world. How do this poem and others show that the personal and political are linked absolutely, shaping and reinforcing one another constantly?

3. Rich's prose is a source of interpretation of her poetry and is an excellent starting place for students interested in analyzing her work. Pinpointing an idea from her essays, students can begin to examine how the same or a similar idea is explored and elaborated in her poetry. For example, in "Split at the Root: An Essay on Jewish Identity" (1982) Rich explores her multiple, and often contradictory, personal and social identities. How do poems like "Sources," "Yom Kippur 1984," and "Eastern War Time" foreshadow or continue her observations? Another example would be to show how Rich extends in poetry the examination of the myth "the self-denying, self-annihilative role of the Good Mother" expressed in *Of Woman Born: Motherhood As Experience and Institution,* and its connection to "the 'death' of the woman or girl who once had hopes, expectations, fantasies for herself—especially when those hopes

and fantasies have never been acted-on." Poems to consider include "Living in Sin," "The Knight," "Snapshots of a Daughter-in-Law," and "The Burning of Paper Instead of Children."

4. In "When We Dead Awaken: Writing As Re-Vision" (1971) Rich lays the groundwork for a principle of feminist interpretation:

> Re-vision—the act of looking back, of seeing with fresh eyes, of entertaining an old text from a new critical direction—is for women more than a chapter in cultural history: it is an act of survival. Until we can understand the assumptions in which we are drenched we cannot know ourselves. And this drive to self-knowledge, for women, is more than a search for identity: it is part of our refusal of the self-destructiveness of male-dominated society.

Students may wish to look at how Rich practices "re-vision" in her own prose and poetry or consider how the concept of re-vision might be applied to other literature of this time. Where else do we see contemporary writers uncovering "assumptions" about female identity that prevent women from knowing themselves? Students could also analyze the importance of this process in challenging oppressive social roles with the goal of transcending them and developing new ones.

5. The radical nature of Rich's ideas about gender and sexuality is not always obvious to contemporary readers of her work. Students can get a sense for the historical importance of her contributions to feminism by comparing reviews of her work appearing before and after *Diving into the Wreck*. Before this collection, reviewers miss, for the most part, themes about women; after its publication, they react, both positively and negatively, to Rich's evolving feminism and her focus on gender issues. Students can begin to analyze attitudes about Rich's feminism and trace a historical shift in the reception and understanding of her ideas in these reviews. Cooper reprints a sampling in "Part Two: Reviews of Rich's Poetry, 1951–1981" (pp. 209–289) and provides a bibliography of other reviews (organized under the titles of the works being reviewed, pp. 352–364); some reviews also appear in the Gelpi volume. Susan Sheridan's outline of the critical reception of Rich's work would also be useful.

## RESOURCES

### Primary Works

Bill Moyers, "Adrienne Rich," in his *The Language of Life: A Festival of Poets* (New York: Doubleday, 1995), pp. 335–353.
Transcript of an interview in which Rich discusses her life, poetry, and creativity.

Matthew Rothschild, "Adrienne Rich: I Happen to Think Poetry Makes a Huge Difference," *Progressive*, 58 (January 1994): 30–35.
Interview in which Rich discusses the relationship between poetry and politics.

## Criticism

Jane Roberta Cooper, ed., *Reading Adrienne Rich: Reviews and Revisions, 1951–81* (Ann Arbor: University of Michigan Press, 1984).
An excellent collection of reviews and critical articles concerned with Rich's poetry and prose published through the late 1970s.

Barbara Charlesworth Gelpi and Albert Gelpi, eds., *Adrienne Rich's Poetry and Prose* (New York: Norton, 1993).
Critical anthology, useful for both research and teaching, offering a selection of Rich's poetry and prose as well as many reviews and critical articles.

Jane Hoogestraat, "'Unnameable by Choice': Multivalent Silences in Adrienne Rich's *Time's Power*," in *Violence, Silence, and Anger: Women's Writing As Transgression*, edited by Deidre Lashgari (Charlottesville: University Press of Virginia, 1995), pp. 25–37.
Excellent feminist analysis of Rich's uses of silences and the breaking of silences in *Time's Power* (1989). The critical approach is applicable to Rich's other works.

Claire Keyes, *The Aesthetics of Power: The Poetry of Adrienne Rich* (Athens: University of Georgia Press, 1986).
An incisive feminist examination of Rich's oeuvre through the mid 1980s.

Cheri Colby Langdell, *Adrienne Rich: The Moment of Change* (Westport, Conn.: Praeger, 2004).
The most comprehensive critical analysis on Rich's work to date. Langdell presents a feminist understanding of the poetic and political changes informing Rich's work published through the early twenty-first century.

Susan Sheridan, "Adrienne Rich and the Women's Liberation Movement: A Politics of Reception," *Women's Studies*, 35, 1 (2006): 17–45.
Examines reviews appearing between the publication of *Diving into the Wreck* in 1973 and *Dream of a Common Language* in 1978 in order to trace the impact of Rich's feminism on the critical reception of her work.

— *Billy Clem and Linda Trinh Moser*

# Philip Roth, *The Human Stain*

(New York: Houghton Mifflin, 2000)

Philip Roth, first known for *Goodbye, Columbus* (1959) and *Portnoy's Complaint* (1969), is one of the most celebrated authors of the twentieth and twenty-first centuries. He has won nearly every major award for American authors (including the Pulitzer Prize, the National Book Award twice, the National Book Critics Circle Award twice, the PEN/Faulkner Award three times, and the highest honor of the American Academy of Letters, the Gold Medal in Fiction), as well as numerous international awards. He is widely considered to be one of the most influential authors writing in America after World War II. *Portnoy's Complaint* is notorious for its sexual themes and humor, and when the novel made Roth a household name, the popular assumption was that in order to write such an indecent book, Roth would necessarily have had to participate in such indecent behavior. In response to that contention, Roth asserted the difference between fiction and reality: and to prove his point, he created Nathan Zuckerman, narrator of nine Roth novels. Zuckerman is often referred to as Roth's "alter-ego," because the two have striking biographical similarities that challenge readers to find differences between the two (and between fiction and reality). But, as in *The Human Stain*, Zuckerman's narration also illustrates how fictional stories are constructed. Many of Zuckerman's actions involve creating fictional stories, and watching him work can often show a reader the differences between fiction and reality and why it is important not to conflate the two. These issues play a major role in Roth's later fiction, and some of his most celebrated works come from the years after *Portnoy's Complaint*, years in which Roth's novels became more epic in both scale and theme.

Roth's 2000 novel, *The Human Stain*, is the final part of the "American Trilogy," a group of works that details the promises and failures of American life in the second half of the twentieth century. *The Human Stain* is set in the summer of 1998 amidst the sex scandals of the Clinton White House, when "a president's penis was on everyone's mind, and life, in all its shameless impurity, once again confounded America." Nathan Zuckerman narrates the story of his neighbor, Coleman Silk, and his affair with an illiterate janitor half his age, Faunia Farley. Faunia is an uneducated woman with two dead children and an abusive Vietnam veteran husband, Lester. Coleman, on the other hand, is the dean of faculty at Athena College and professor of classics, but his career ends abruptly. In the fifth week of the semester Coleman still has not seen two of the students enrolled in his class, prompting him to ask, "Do they exist or are they spooks?" The two absent students are African American, and Coleman's question about "spooks" is interpreted as a racial slur. Coleman subsequently leaves the college in disgrace and anger.

After the death of his wife and months of obsessive planning of a book on the "spooks" incident, Coleman begins to change his life. When picking up his mail at the post office one day, Coleman notices Faunia mopping the floors, and the two begin an affair. Thanks to Viagra, the seventy-one-year-old Coleman is able to maintain his affair with the thirty-four-year-old janitor, and the two seem happy enough together. But one of Coleman's former Athena colleagues, Delphine Roux, confronts him in an anonymous note: "Everyone knows you're sexually exploiting an abused, illiterate woman half your age." This confrontation is indicative of the disapproval that surrounds the Coleman-Faunia affair, for the two are gossiped about but never publicly confronted for their behavior. The affair lasts only four months, and it ends as abruptly as it began: the two die in a car wreck, and very few attend Coleman's funeral.

In the midst of this plot, Zuckerman also reveals Coleman Silk's biggest secret, one that Coleman has kept for the past fifty years. Coleman, who has presented himself as a middle-class Jewish man, was born an African American in East Orange, New Jersey. After returning from World War II, Coleman began pretending to be a white Jew living in New York City, a process that culminated in abandoning his birth family and marrying a Jewish woman named Iris Gittelman. Zuckerman discovers this secret at Coleman's grave, when Coleman's sister Ernestine introduces herself, and from the information she gives him, Zuckerman constructs a life story for Coleman Silk. Much of the novel narrates how Coleman made his decision to "pass" as a white man and the effects of that decision on his family. Instead of telling others the truth, that he is the son of a railroad dining car worker who read William Shakespeare and died at an early age, Coleman creates a very different elaborate backstory for himself: he pretends to be the son of a Jewish saloon owner who kept a blackjack and a dictionary behind the bar at all times. Ultimately, Zuckerman portrays Coleman's decision to pass as a move of supreme independence, not as one of embarrassment or selfishness: "The objective was for his fate to be determined not by the ignorant, hate-filled intentions of a hostile world but, to whatever degree humanly possible, by his own resolve. Why accept a life on any other terms?"

Students studying Philip Roth and *The Human Stain* should begin with the Roth Society website (<http://rothsociety.org>) and the Roth Society journal, *Philip Roth Studies,* published semiannually. The website bibliography is up-to-date and provides some full-text interviews and criticism. The journal periodically publishes theme issues, such as the Fall 2006 number, "Roth and Race."

## TOPICS FOR DISCUSSION AND RESEARCH

1. The most obvious instance of passing in the novel is Coleman pretending to be white instead of living as an African American, but many more subtle instances of passing are woven throughout the novel. Delphine Roux passes as smart, successful, and secure, but her stable exterior hides how truly insecure and lonely she is. The American public that passes judgment (on both Coleman and Bill Clinton) is superficially moral and pure, yet the discussions and judgments are certainly impure, in that the public still wants to gossip about and punish those who transgress. The novel itself can even be accused of passing as a true account: although the work has a narrator gathering pieces of biographical information about the downfall of Coleman Silk, it is important to remember that Nathan Zuckerman is a writer of fiction who is rendering scenes within the novel to suit his own needs and that Zuckerman himself is a fictional character. Students would find it fruitful to trace the implications of any of these instances of passing, to compare and contrast a few of them, or to compare the social with the psychological ramifications of any of the instances of passing. Patrice D. Rankine's essay may be thought-provoking with regard to this topic, and Jennifer Glaser's discussion of race theory will be stimulating.

2. The historical moment of the novel is one that focuses on the impurities of human sexuality: Bill Clinton's White House scandal is the topic on everyone's mind and in every public conversation. Underlying such conversations

and judgments is the assumption that there are impure, indecent actions that cannot be allowed within civilization. Coleman and Faunia's relationship, due to the age difference and educational differences, falls under this category. But the novel's actions and narration suggest that "impurity" is a state of being human, not a defect of it. As Faunia explains in the novel's title passage: "The human stain. . . . We leave a stain, we leave a trail, we leave our imprint. . . . It's why all the cleansing is a joke. A barbaric joke at that. The fantasy of purity is appalling." Students might consider how the book suggests that such impurities as "cruelty, abuse, error, excrement, semen," are simply part of the human condition. Can purification occur without ruining what makes us human in the first place? How does the novel argue various sides of this question? See D. A. Boxwell's article on cultural conflict in the novel to begin formulating an approach to this topic. Bonnie Lyons is useful in this context, as well.

3. Students might also consider the concept of tragedy in its various manifestations in *The Human Stain*. As a professor of classics, Coleman is intensely aware of Greek tragic conventions and even relates much of his life to the Greek tragedies that he has spent so much time studying. The epigraph from Sophocles invites readers to see this story as a tragedy, and students might look to Lyons's and Rankine's essays for more perspectives on this issue. We witness Coleman Silk's rise to power as dean of faculty, his fall at Athena College, and then a further fall into the depths of tragedy with his death. In addition to references to the classic Greek tragedies, the novel is also concerned with Shakespearean tragedies, specifically *Julius Caesar*. Coleman's father was intensely interested in Shakespeare (so much so that he gave all of his children Shakespearean middle names) and Coleman's story reads much like one of these tragedies: the tale is divided into five chapters (corresponding to the number of acts of a Shakespearean tragedy). Students might also consider how allusions to Shakespearean and classical tragedy affect their reading of Coleman Silk's life. Do these allusions make Coleman seem more tragic? Less tragic? How does Coleman's awareness of classical tragedy affect the way he reads his own life? Rankine discusses the relationship between Roth's novel and classical models, especially Sophocles' *Oedipus* cycle.

4. The novel can also be defined as metafictional, that is, a piece of fiction about fiction. The presence of Nathan Zuckerman establishes the fictional status of the story: readers recognize that Zuckerman is narrating the story and also that Zuckerman is a creation of Roth. Moreover, the reader is led through the actual gathering of information and writing of this novel by Nathan Zuckerman. In many ways, it is possible to see the novel as commentary on how stories are created and what makes them fictional in the first place, for the novel makes perfectly clear that the story is Zuckerman's imagination at work on events that he witnesses, hears about, or surmises. But Zuckerman's status as a fictional character also shows how Roth may use the same process in creating the novel we read. How do Zuckerman the narrator and Zuckerman the author differ, and why might Roth choose to highlight this separation?

5. Much is made in the book about a person's formal education: because Coleman is a professor and Faunia is illiterate, most people assume that he is

exploiting her. Delphine Roux is a hyper-educated French intellectual, but her life is entirely unfulfilling outside of her position in the college. Moreover, the book offers alternatives to formal education through the characters of Faunia and Lester Farley. Lester begins to understand himself through experience and emotional education, while Faunia's tragic life experiences help her to deliver some of the most powerful passages in the novel. Even Nathan Zuckerman, a highly educated novelist, relies on his experience and imagination for knowledge of Coleman. In what ways is formal education valued in the novel, and how do the characters' actions also speak to the importance of less-formal education, the education that comes from life experience? See James Wood's essay review for a thoughtful approach to this topic.

# RESOURCES

## Bibliography

Derek Parker Royal, "Philip Roth: A Bibliography and Research Guide" <http://rothsociety.org/resources.htm> [accessed 16 December 2009].

A full secondary bibliography of works about Roth's novels. It is up-to-date and currently lists more than forty articles about *The Human Stain*.

## Criticism

Geoffrey W. Bakewell, "Philip Roth's Oedipal Stain," *Classical and Modern Literature*, 24 (Fall 2004): 29–46.

Discusses the relationship between *The Human Stain* and Sophocles' *Oedipus* cycle.

D. A. Boxwell, "*Kulturkampf*, Now and Then," *War, Literature, and the Arts: An International Journal of the Humanities*, 12 (Spring–Summer 2000): 122–136.

Treats culture conflict in *The Human Strain*.

Jennifer Glaser, "The Jew in the Canon: Reading Race and Literary History in Philip Roth's *The Human Stain*," *PMLA*, 123 (October 2008): 1465–1478.

A discussion of critical-race theory with regard to Jewish writers, using *The Human Stain* as an example.

Bonnie Lyons, "Philip Roth's American Tragedies," in *Turning up the Flame: Philip Roth's Later Novels*, edited by Jay L. Halio and Ben Siegel (Newark: University of Delaware Press, 2005): 125–130.

Argues that Coleman Silk is a man whose tragic nature comes from trying to escape his cultural identity as an African American. Lyons argues also that this is a truly American tragedy because the setting for this novel displays the Puritanism surrounding Bill Clinton's impeachment in 1998.

Timothy L. Parrish, "Becoming Black: Zuckerman's Bifurcating Self in *The Human Stain*," in *Philip Roth: New Perspectives on an American Author*, edited by Derek Parker Royal (Westport, Conn.: Praeger, 2005), pp. 209–223.

Sees *The Human Stain* as "the logical outgrowth of Roth's lifelong aesthetic commitment to the fluidity of the American (or ethnic) self" (211). The fluidity of Coleman's sense of self is such that it allows him to show how inauthentic race designations can be in American society. Zuckerman is able to identify with Coleman when he believes the former dean is a Jew, but Zuckerman only writes the novel once he discovers that Coleman was born as an African American in East Orange, New Jersey.

Patrice D. Rankine, "Passing As Tragedy: Philip Roth's *The Human Stain,* the Oedipus Myth, and the Self-Made Man," *Critique,* 47 (Fall 2005): 101–112.
Links two of the more powerful themes of Roth's novel: racial passing and the influence of classical tragedy. Rankine sees Coleman's choice to pass as white as the novel's most tragic aspect, for this decision highlights the tragic situation of African Americans. Furthermore, she reads the novel as consistently reinforcing the human tragedy by alluding to Greek myths and tragedies.

Carlin Romano, "The Troves of Academe," *Nation,* 270 (12 June 2000): 53–56.
Discusses the qualities of academic life that attract Roth and novelist Francine Prose, suggesting that it is the gap between the ideal and the real vulgarities of life that entice them.

James Wood, "The Cost of Clarity," *New Republic,* 222 (17–24 April 2000): 70–78.
A review in which Wood takes Roth to task for his "grinding, unappeasable intelligence," which shows itself in his creation of characters who are curiously shallow.

—*David M. Borman*

⌐✦⌐

# Sam Shepard, *True West*
(Performed 1980; Garden City: Doubleday, 1981)

"You gotta be like a rock-and-roll Jesus with a cowboy mouth" insists a character in *The Cowboy Mouth* (1971), the frequently cited one-act play coauthored and acted by Sam Shepard and poet (and later, rock star) Patti Smith. People's desire for a rock messiah or other mythical hero to believe in is a running theme throughout Shepard's astonishingly large body of work, which includes more than forty one-act and full-length plays (thirty of them produced before he was thirty), poetry, short fiction, and autobiographical prose. As the image also reveals, his work bears the imprint of popular culture, populated by such iconic figures, often associated with the West, as the cowboy, gunslinger, outlaw, and rancher. In an exploration of the spiritual starvation and anomie of contemporary culture and its effects on identity, Shepard's characters are always transforming, changing clothes, and trying out different roles and parts. In this way, the plays also test the idealistic American notion that one can emerge from humble beginnings to become anything or anyone. In Shepard's dramatic world, however, transformation may promise wealth and fame but also, and more typically, dislocation and disassociation from the past and from others. Shepard's own life suggests an ongoing process of self-creation and invention. In addition to being a playwright, he is a musician (playing in the rock bands Moray Eels and Holy Modal Rounders in the late 1960s) and has toured with folk singer Bob Dylan and poet Allen Ginsberg, experiences he describes in *Rolling Thunder Logbook* (1977). Shepard is also an accomplished actor; his most famous role, perhaps, was playing test pilot Chuck Yeager in *The Right Stuff* (1983), a movie role that brought him an Oscar nomination and celebrity. He has also written screenplays for *Paris, Texas* (1984), directed by Wim Wenders, which was awarded the Palme d'Or at the Cannes Film Festival, and for *Far North* (1988), starring Jessica Lange, to whom Shepard has been married since 1986.

Born on 5 November 1943 on an army base in Fort Sheridan, Illinois, as Samuel Shepard Rogers VII, Shepard was nicknamed "Steve" to distinguish him from his father. As an adult he dropped both the nickname and Rogers to become Sam Shepard. His father was a pilot in the United States Army Air Corps in World War II, and his mother, Jane Elaine (Schook) Rogers, was a teacher. The family, which includes two younger sisters, Deedee and Sandy, was transferred from one army base to another in places as varied as Florida, Guam, South Dakota, and Utah, eventually moving to a farm in Duarte, California, a suburb of Pasadena, when his father retired in 1949.

After graduating from high school, Shepard spent a year at a junior college majoring in agricultural science. Despite limited acting experience, he quit school in 1962 to join the Bishop's Company Repertory Players, touring with them across the nation. In 1963, he left the troupe to stay in New York and, like many would-be actors, supported himself as a busboy. While working at The Village Gate (a job he got with the help of high-school friend, Charles "Charlie" Mingus Jr., son of the jazz musician), he met Ralph Cook, founder of Theatre Genesis, part of the Off-Off-Broadway circuit. Cook encouraged Shepard to write and produced his first plays, among them *Cowboys* (1964; revised as *Cowboys #2,* 1967), *Rock Garden* (1964), and *Chicago* (1965). In these early plays Shepard began using motifs that he continued to explore in later plays. The myth of the American West features largely, for example, as does sibling rivalry and dysfunctional father-son relationships. The competing brothers of *Cowboys #2* and the distant father in *Rock Garden* foreshadow elements of *True West.*

His early one-act plays established Shepard's reputation, and in 1966 he received Obie Awards for *Chicago, Icarus's Mother* (1965), and *Red Cross* (1966), making him the first playwright to win three in one year. This critical acclaim led to a commission for *Operation Sidewinder* (1970), produced at the Repertory Theatre of Lincoln Center in New York City. Shepard was unhappy with the result, and audiences were alienated by the play's complicated and surreal plot involving a covert military operation, sophisticated computers, Hopi ritual, and rock music. It was Shepard's first "flop" and received almost uniformly scathing reviews.

In the decades following Shepard's disappointing Broadway opening, he tried to avoid "the mainstream in the arts" (Kakutani), and his career choices suggest ambivalence toward fame and celebrity. To escape the theater scene in New York, in 1971 he moved to England with his wife, actress O-Lan Johnson (whom he had married in 1969 and divorced in 1986) and son, Jesse Mojo. Several of his plays were produced in London to positive reviews, and his work remains popular there. *Curse of the Starving Class* (1976), also awarded an Obie (his ninth), premiered in 1977 at London's Royal Court Theatre; its U.S. premiere in New York followed in 1978. After three years in England, Shepard and his family returned to North America, first to a farm in Nova Scotia and then to a twenty-acre horse ranch in northern California. As playwright-in-residence for the Magic Theatre in San Francisco, Shepard debuted several of his best-known and most successful plays; these include *Buried Child* (1978) which won him his tenth Obie and the Pulitzer Prize in 1979, *True West* (1980), and *Fool for Love* (1983). Shepard calls *Curse of the Starving Class, Buried Child,* and *True West* a "family trilogy." The first play dramatizes the disintegration of a preyed-upon farming family; the second uncovers a literal family skeleton that has been buried under barren farm soil; and the last features two brothers in violent competition with one another.

Critics often describe *Curse of the Starving Class* as point of transition between Shepard's earlier and later plays. Influenced by British director Peter Brook, whom he met while living in England, Shepard had begun in this play to focus on his characters, developing them more fully and placing them into more-realistic situations than in his previous plays. Throughout his career, however, Shepard has highlighted certain themes and experimented with strong visual or aural metaphor. In *Cowboys #2* one of the title characters describes the "all-American" breakfast, which appears again in *Curse of the Starving Class* and is juxtaposed against the family's empty refrigerator. In both works, it serves as a metaphor for spiritual starvation. The play also features two characters, Chet and Stu, whose competitive relationship is resurrected in brothers Lee and Austin of *True West,* as is the sound of a single cricket offstage. In *Curse of the Starving Class* Shepard begins with a realistic kitchen only to despoil it and leave any sense of normalcy behind as surreal elements take over in the form of garbage, food, and finally, the carcass of a lamb, which are strewn across the floor of the once-everyday setting. In the trilogy's next two plays, however, realistic elements dominate.

*True West,* the first play written after winning the Pulitzer Prize for *Buried Child,* marks Shepard's shift into the kind of realism he rejected as a young playwright. Consisting of two acts divided into nine scenes, the play replaces Shepard's usual large cast with just four characters—two major, brothers Austin and Lee, and two minor, Saul Kimmer and Mom. The dialogue features natural rhythms and the set design, "a kitchen and adjoining alcove of an older home in a Southern California suburb," is realistic. Shepard also underscores realism in his stage directions: "The set should be constructed realistically with no attempt to distort its dimensions, shapes, objects or colors. No objects should be introduced which might draw special attention to themselves other than the props demanded by the script." The play's realism and accessibility contribute to its enduring popularity with audiences and critics. So, too, does its story line. Austin is a screenwriter with a budding career and family, and Lee is a drifter and thief who lives alone in the desert. As Austin works on a screenplay in his mother's house (which he is house-sitting), Lee decides to return home, initially with the intention of stealing from his mother's neighbors. Intrigued by the prospect of emulating Austin's success, however, Lee pitches his own story to a Hollywood producer, Saul Kimmer, who then drops Austin's project for Lee's. What ensues is role reversal as Lee vainly attempts to transform his idea into a screenplay while Austin, despondent, goes on a drinking binge followed by a stealing spree. The brothers' rivalry soon becomes physically violent, and the play ends with the image of endless struggle between them.

Students should begin study of any of Shepard's works, including *True West,* by consulting the Sam Shepard website <http://www.departments.bucknell.edu/theatre_dance/Shepard/shepard.html>, which includes a good primary bibliography and a selected secondary bibliography that includes both reviews and critical works. This site, which is maintained with scholarly care, should not be confused with the site at <http://www.sam-shepard.com/>, which is for fans only.

## TOPICS FOR DISCUSSION AND RESEARCH

1. A stage production of *True West* was filmed and originally aired on public television's *American Playhouse* in 1984; it starred Gary Sinise as Austin and John Malkovich as Lee. It was also performed for television in 2002. View a copy of one of these performances and compare it to a reading copy of the play.

2. The battle that takes place between Austin and Lee echoes the struggles between Chet and Stu in *Cowboys #2* and those between Cavale and Slim in *The Cowboy Mouth.* The three plays also explore similar themes: the appeal and illusion of the Old West, commercialism versus artistry, the difference between "real life" and performance. The earlier plays, however, are stylistically very different from *True West.* In addition to being single-act plays, *Cowboys #2* and *The Cowboy Mouth* have less-developed characters and rely more on absurd and nonrealistic details. Students interested in tracing the development of Shepard's style could compare *True West* to one or both of these earlier plays, focusing on plot, setting, and character and paying close attention to Shepard's stage directions. For discussions that trace Shepard's evolving style, students can consult Bottoms, DeRose, Graham, Kimball, and Mottram.

3. In his biography of Sam Shepard, Don Shewey writes: "There's a lot about *True West* that is explicitly autobiographical. Like Austin, Shepard himself has put in time as a would-be screenwriter, but he's also been known to share in Lee's sticky fingers." In addition, the house where the events take place is "40 miles east of Los Angeles," directions that apply to Duarte, California, where Shepard spent his teenage years. Evocative of the biography of Shepard's father are the references to and stories about "the old man," including the one about

his dentures. Students interested in exploring Shepard's life might examine biographical details included in the play. Students should be sure to consider how Shepard uses biographical details to highlight and advance larger themes about American identity.

4. Bottoms notes a similarity between *True West* and the "dirty realism" of fiction by writers like Raymond Carver, Bobbie Ann Mason, and Tobias Wolff. The shared characteristics "include a tendency to describe trivial and mundane details with minute precision, and to focus on apparently inconsequential narratives, tales of minor, often rather grubby incidents in the lives of ordinary Americans." In addition, "a very sparse, unadorned approach to plot and dialogue" results in stories that "are conspicuously devoid of strong or heroic characters." Students interested in studying the plot and style of *True West* might trace these elements in the play, arguing for or against Bottoms's observations.

5. Critics have noted Shepard's seeming obsession with all things "West"— horses, cowboys, stories about traveling westward. Clearly at the heart of *True West* is a question about the nature of the "true west." As Wade writes, "The text provides a range of candidates, from the world of Kirk Douglas cowboy pictures, to the smog-soaked sprawl of Los Angeles, to the desolate aridity of the Mojave." Students might find it profitable to examine elements of these different versions of the West and the characters with which they are associated in the play. In addition, one might argue whether Shepard promotes a particular vision of the West. Another way to approach the Western theme is to examine its connection to notions about America as the land of "freedom, opportunity, and limitless open land" (Wade). How do Shepard's representations of the West call into question the American dream? How are different versions of the American dream and the West evoked by Austin's material success and Lee's physical mobility and freedom? Why is it important to recognize multiple versions of these ideals? Most critics address the appearance of these themes in *True West*; most helpful to students would be Marranca, Mottram, Wade, and Westgate.

6. In the beginning of *True West* Lee and Austin are presented as opposites so that when Austin tells his brother that Saul "thinks we're the same person," the observation seems ironic. As the play progresses, however, each brother adopts the characteristics of the other. Shepard has said that he "wanted to write a play about double nature . . . one that wouldn't be symbolic or metaphorical or any of that stuff. I just wanted to give a taste of what it feels like to be two-sided. It's a real thing, double nature" (quoted in Shewey). Students might use Shepard's comments as the starting point for an analysis of Lee and Austin that considers how they represent two sides of the same person. Indeed, as the play progresses, we see each brother transform into the other. As you review the play, pay particular attention to which characteristics are evoked by Austin and by Lee at the beginning and then at the middle and end of the play. How does their inability to synthesize seemingly opposite characteristics lead to problems between the brothers? How might a synthesis of qualities lead to a resolution between the brothers? Alternately, you might wish to explore

reasons for each of the brother's weak identity formation and consider the backstory about the father. How is each brother subconsciously either rebelling against or becoming the father figure? How does the father figure—despite being absent—continue to affect the brothers' individual identities and relationship to one another?

## RESOURCES

### Primary Works

Kenneth Chubb, "Metaphors, Mad Dogs and Old-Time Cowboys," *Theatre Quarterly*, 4 (August–October 1974): 3–16; included in Marranca, ed., pp. 187–209.

Interview in which Shepard describes his craft and award-winning plays.

Michiko Kakutani, "Myths, Dreams, Realities—Sam Shepard's America," *New York Times*, 29 January 1984, pp. B1, B26–B28.

Essay that incorporates parts of an interview with Shepard written just before the airing of *True West* on public television's *American Playhouse* and during its run Off-Broadway at the Cherry Lane Theatre. It provides a detailed and concise overview of his life, work, and critical reception.

### Biography

Don Shewey, *Sam Shepard* (1985; New York: Da Capo, 1997).

Revised and expanded version of a 1985 biography that explores Shepard's unique status within theater and popular culture. The discussion of *True West* points out the autobiographical elements of the play.

### Criticism

Stephen J. Bottoms, *The Theatre of Sam Shepard* (New York: Cambridge University Press, 1998).

A complete analysis of Shepard's plays from his early experimental one-acts through *Simpatico* (1994), describing his work as a series of crises reflecting Shepard's ambivalence toward writing and performance. Bottoms underscores important motifs and presents Shepard as innovative, influential, and culturally important. Chapter 6 provides thorough discussions of *True West* and *Fool for Love*.

David J. DeRose, *Sam Shepard* (New York: Twayne, 1992).

Analyzes Shepard's use of direction, stage imagery, and language, as well as providing biographical information. DeRose's focus on social fragmentation places the playwright strongly in the context of Postmodernism.

Laura J. Graham, *Sam Shepard: Theme, Image, and the Director* (New York: Peter Lang, 1995).

A valuable analysis of the playwright's work with close attention to influences and performance.

Kimball King, *Sam Shepard: A Casebook* (New York: Garland, 1988).
An essential collection of interesting and informative essays that expand on the many themes present in his work. The book also offers a chronology of Shepard's career and an interview with him.

Bonnie Marranca, ed., *American Dreams: The Imagination of Sam Shepard* (New York: Performing Arts Journal Publications, 1981).
An essential collection featuring essays and miscellaneous pieces by leading theater critics, directors, and actors on the plays and productions of Shepard, from the beginning of his career. An essay by the author about his own work is also included.

Jim McGhee, *True Lies: The Architecture of the Fantastic in the Plays of Sam Shepard* (New York: Peter Lang, 1993).
A study of Shepard for advanced students that interprets his work within the context of the fantastic.

Ron Mottram, *Inner Landscapes: The Theatre of Sam Shepard* (Columbia: University of Missouri Press, 1984).
One of the earliest book-length studies of Shepard's work. This thorough analysis focuses on the "family plays" and the playwright's use of less realistic aspects. The biographical information provided is useful.

Matthew Roudané, ed., *The Cambridge Companion to Sam Shepard* (New York: Cambridge University Press, 2002).
Essential collection of newly commissioned essays that cover Shepard's major plays (including *Curse of the Starving Class, Buried Child,* and *True West*) and aspects related to his poetry, fiction, music, acting, and film work. The chronology of Shepard's life, biographical chapters, and May 2000 interview with the editor are also useful.

Michael Taav, *A Body across the Map: The Father-Son Plays of Sam Shepard* (New York: Peter Lang, 2000).
A detailed look at the most prevalent conflict in Shepard's work, that between father and son. Taav traces Shepard's evolving view of the relationship in plays from *The Rock Garden* through *A Lie of the Mind,* finding a movement from pessimism to cooperation and acceptance.

Leslie A. Wade, *Sam Shepard and the American Theatre* (Westport, Conn.: Greenwood Press, 1997).
Presents Shepard as a new voice that helps to define American national characters while also examining the contradiction between his reputation as an outsider to the theater establishment and rise to prominence after being awarded the Pulitzer Prize for *Buried Child.*

J. Chris Westgate, "Negotiating the American West in Sam Shepard's Family Plays," *Modern Drama,* 48 (Winter 2005): 726–743.

An examination of the "competing, even contradictory, visions of the West" in Shepard's family trilogy that challenges readings that ignore negative Western images in the plays; appropriate for more-advanced students.

Leonard Wilcox, ed., *Rereading Shepard: Contemporary Critical Essays on the Plays of Sam Shepard* (New York: St. Martin's Press, 1993).
Includes a broad range of theoretical approaches, including feminist and structuralist.

*—Linda Trinh Moser and Chelsea Russell*

## Leslie Marmon Silko, *Ceremony*
### (New York: Viking, 1977)

Leslie Marmon Silko is recognized as one of the key voices in the Native American Renaissance and as a major contemporary American author both for her multicultural exploration of being, in her words, "mixed breed," as well as for her Postmodernist techniques. She is of Laguna Pueblo, Mexican, and white heritage. She was born in Albuquerque, New Mexico, on 5 March 1948 and grew up in a house on the edge of the Laguna Pueblo reservation. Her father, Lee Marmon, was a noted photographer. Her mother was Mary Virginia Leslie. Owing to her mixed heritage, Leslie Marmon was not allowed to participate in some of the sacred ceremonies of the Pueblo. Nevertheless, she recounts in *Storyteller* (1981) and in various essays and interviews how she grew up immersed in the Pueblo storytelling traditions from her grandmother, great-grandmother, and aunts. Silko combines characters and motifs from those traditional stories, legends, and myths with an awareness of contemporary social and political issues in her prose and her poetry. *Ceremony* is her most acclaimed novel, and is frequently taught on college campuses around the country.

Marmon attended the University of New Mexico, earning a B.A. in English with honors in 1969. She was married to Richard Chapman from 1966 to 1969; they had one son, Robert. She later began law school, planning to practice in the area of Native American law, but quit after three semesters, deciding she could achieve more through her writing. Her first published story, "The Man to Send Rain Clouds," became the title piece of one of the earliest anthologies of contemporary short fiction by Native writers; of the nineteen stories in the volume, Marmon wrote seven. In 1971 she married John Silko, and had a son, Cazimir, the next year. Also in 1972 the family moved to Ketchikan, Alaska. Finding herself homesick for family and the Pueblo culture and landscape, Silko turned to her writing, starting *Ceremony*. As she describes in her introduction to the thirtieth-anniversary edition, her vivid, color-rich depictions of the Southwestern landscape were a way to ward off the depression she felt in the rainy, often sunless Alaskan climate. Also during this era, Silko developed a close friendship with Chinese-American poet Mei-mei Berssenbrugge, to whom she dedicates several works.

John and Leslie Marmon Silko eventually divorced; in 1976 she returned to Laguna Pueblo. Through this period Silko was publishing poetry and short stories. Her first collection of poetry, *Laguna Woman,* was published in 1974. Frequently anthologized from this collection are the poems "Prayer to the Pacific" and "The Time We Climbed Snake Mountain." Students will find useful connections between themes in these poems and those found in *Ceremony.* In "Prayer to the Pacific" Silko invokes connections to Asian peoples—"Thirty thousand years ago / Indians came riding across the ocean." She would refer in *Ceremony* as well to the theory that American Indians are descendants of Asians who crossed either the Bering Strait or island-hopped across the Pacific thousands of years ago. In these and other Silko poems, the sense of history resides in land and water, and humans are only a part of that large sweep. "Slim Man Canyon" begins, "700 years ago / people were living here / water was running gently / and the sun was warm / on pumpkin flowers." Contemporary people ride through this landscape, "past cliffs with stories and songs / painted on rock / 700 years ago." Highlighting another theme prominent in much of Silko's writing, the links between earlier generations and the present are emphasized, all within a cyclical understanding of history. In these poems as in *Ceremony,* contemporary people often appear both as themselves and as avatars of figures in Pueblo myths and legends.

*Ceremony* earned Silko widespread praise, including from the "father" of the Native American Renaissance, N. Scott Momaday, and Western writer Larry McMurtry. After its publication, a letter of appreciation from Pulitzer Prize–winning poet James Wright sparked a correspondence which would continue until his death in 1980. In their letters, which have been collected as *The Delicacy of Strength and Lace: Letters between Leslie Marmon Silko and James Wright* (1986), edited by Anne Wright, they discuss a wide variety of personal concerns and talk deeply about their writing.

In 1981 Silko received a MacArthur Foundation Award, popularly known as the "genius" grant, enabling her to quit university teaching and devote most of her time to her writing career. Also in 1981 Silko's *Storyteller* appeared. It is unusual in format both in the material shape and size of the book (landscape instead of the typical portrait orientation), and in its combination of family photographs (taken by her father and by Silko herself), family history, poems, oral tradition, and short stories. Among others, it includes the often anthologized "Lullaby," "Yellow Woman," and "Storyteller." The table of contents appears at the end of the book, and Silko has said it should be read from the middle outward, in the pattern of circularity characteristic of Pueblo thought. As with the earlier poetry collection, students interested in *Ceremony* may find their understanding of it enhanced by exploring *Storyteller.*

Silko's next novel, *Almanac of the Dead,* did not appear until 1991. Long, complex, with many characters and a story line moving between ancient Mayan texts and contemporary drug trafficking, it met with mixed reviews. Given the complexity and length of *Almanac,* Silko describes *Garden in the Dunes* (1991) as "a treat" for readers who braved their way through *Almanac.* It tells the story of two sisters of the

Sand Lizard people who are separated, one ending up traveling Victorian Europe. Gardens and botanical interests connect characters from many different cultures.

Silko began her own company, Flood Plain Press, to publish works with nontraditional formats, combining text, photographs, and drawings. Through this enterprise she brought out a second edition of *Laguna Woman* in 1994 and published *Sacred Water* (1993), a combination of her photographs, drawings, and poetic-prose meditations on family history, personal history, and the human relationship to land and water.

*Ceremony* was launched to rave reviews, including one by Frank MacShane in *The New York Times Book Review* (12 June 1977), who praised her integration of the Western novel and traditional Laguna storytelling practices, calling her "the most accomplished Indian writer of her generation." Since that time, *Ceremony* has been studied from several angles: as Native American storytelling, as literature about war veterans, as literature focused on environmental concerns, and even as an example of nuclear war literature. Many critics have researched the roots in the Laguna culture of the symbolism, motifs, landscape, gender roles, animals, and characters of the novel. Thus, students exploring criticism of *Ceremony* will find many rich examples of close readings of the novel as well as studies that consider it in the traditions mentioned above.

## TOPICS FOR DISCUSSION AND RESEARCH

1. In "Language and Literature from a Pueblo Indian Perspective," found in *Yellow Woman and a Beauty of the Spirit* and reprinted in many anthologies of Native American writing, Silko describes the oral storytelling practices of the Pueblo people, invoking the image of a spider web. Rather than a linear pattern, the spider web is one in which a multitude of connections leads to complex interrelationships where what happens in one place reverberates in many others. How does this metaphor reflect on the structure of *Ceremony*? How does it help explicate the novel's structure? What does it suggest about the role and significance of storytelling in the novel? Other points of discussion in the essay may also offer helpful strategies for understanding and discussing the novel. In a related topic, students might also wish to consider in what ways Silko combines the traditional Western novel form with Pueblo myths and stories, and the effects created by combining, rather than using one or the other. Helpful articles cited below include those by Alanna Kathleen Brown and Jude Todd, and Edith Swan's "Laguna Symbolic Geography."

2. The cattle Uncle Josiah creates as a mix of breeds that will be able to withstand Southwestern droughts but still carry weight serve as an example of a trope running throughout *Ceremony*: the role of "mixed-breeds" in contemporary culture. Tayo has green eyes and is not a full-blood Laguna. Old Betonie is part Mexican. Many other examples of people and things that are of mixed heritage appear throughout the novel. Students would find it profitable to trace these examples and examine their significance in the story. What strengths and weaknesses come from being mixed? Why does Auntie feel ashamed of Tayo's

mixed status? What does Tayo's quest for the cattle ultimately reveal about having mixed heritage? Susan Blumenthal's article and Louis Owens's chapter would be helpful for this undertaking.

3. The female characters in *Ceremony* may be seen as incarnations of various female goddesses and other figures from Pueblo myths and legends. Students could research the stories of Yellow Woman, Thought Woman, Ts'eh, and others, and compare those legends to the roles of the women who appear in the novel. Silko's volume *Storyteller* would be helpful for this purpose, as would the article by Elizabeth Hoffman Nelson in Louise K. Barnett and James L. Thorson. Alternatively, students could investigate the masculine roles in the novel, including Uncle Josiah, Rocky, Emo, and Ts'eh's husband, the Hunter. Useful for the latter are Swan's "Laguna Prototypes of Manhood in *Ceremony*" and the article by Colleen Shapiro.

4. When Tayo meets Old Betonie in the novel, we are given a detailed description of what the medicine man keeps in his house, ranging from old telephone books, calendars, and newspapers to medicine pouches, sage, and mountain tobacco. Betonie explains the purpose of these things to Tayo and argues that ceremonies and rituals have changed many times over the years and must continue to do so. Why must they change? What is Betonie's reasoning? How does it reflect on other aspects of the rituals and ceremonies depicted in the novel? What does the novel suggest about people who do not want to see changes made in the traditional ways? The articles by Naomi R. Rand and by Daniel White in Barnett and Thorson could be consulted for this topic.

5. Students could research the development of the atomic bomb and its testing in the deserts of the Southwest, despite the proximity of Native American reservations. Also worthwhile to explore is the uranium mining that took place around the Pueblos. The Jackpile mine was located near the Laguna village of Paguate and was the largest instance of open pit uranium mining in the United States. What controversies have arisen out of that history? What have been the results of this mining? Did the Native communities profit? What problems were they left with when the mining was finished? How does Silko integrate this history into *Ceremony*, and how accurate is her depiction? Students will find information on the Jackpile mine through online searches, as well as in Connie Jacobs's "A Toxic Legacy: Stories of Jackpile Mine," in *American Indian Culture and Research Journal*, 28 (Winter 2001): 41–52. For an environmentalist perspective, students will want to consult the articles by Reyes Garcia and Lisa Orr.

6. Tayo's quest is to restore harmony and balance to his world so that the rain will come and life can continue. How are individual and community balanced in this novel? Is one more important than the other? Is Tayo's personal development more important than the health of his community, or does community take precedence? The story of Tayo's cousin Rocky might be considered as a contrast to Tayo's experiences. From another angle, one might consider why Silko places Native cosmology uppermost by claiming all the havoc was created by Native witchery. What does she gain, and what does she lose by this strategy? James Ruppert and Garcia would be helpful for these topics.

# RESOURCES

## Primary Works

Ellen L. Arnold, ed., *Conversations with Leslie Marmon Silko* (Jackson: University Press of Mississippi, 2000).

Sixteen interviews with Silko, plus a chronology of her life. Silko does not grant interviews often, but when she does so she talks in depth about her views of her writing and her desire to work for social justice in general and justice for American Indians in particular.

*Yellow Woman and a Beauty of the Spirit: Essays on Native American Life Today* (New York: Simon & Schuster, 1996).

Collects twenty-one essays on topics that range from Pueblo culture to the meaning and significance of land and water, from tribal politics to centuries of U.S. mistreatment of American Indians, from photography to murals to rocks and memoir. The book includes "Language and Literature from a Pueblo Indian Perspective."

## Criticism

Ellen L. Arnold, "An Ear for the Story, an Eye for the Pattern: Rereading *Ceremony*," *Modern Fiction Studies*, 45, 1 (1999): 69–92.

Recommends rereading *Ceremony* to appreciate the underlying patterns and historical perspectives of the novel. The article includes a focus on orality in the work.

Louise K. Barnett and James L. Thorson, eds., *Leslie Marmon Silko: A Collection of Critical Essays* (Albuquerque: University of New Mexico Press, 1999).

Focuses mainly on *Almanac of the Dead*. Elizabeth Hoffman Nelson and Malcolm A. Nelson's "Shifting Patterns, Changing Stories: Leslie Marmon Silko's Yellow Women," offers helpful reading of the integration of the yellow-woman myth in *Ceremony*, seeing affinities in both Tayo and T'seh. Although not directly about *Ceremony*, Daniel White's "Antidote to Desecration: Leslie Marmon Silko's Nonfiction" is helpful for understanding her version of indigenous philosophy and its differences from mainstream thought, while Robert Nelson's "A Laguna Woman" offers biographical insights.

Susan Blumenthal, "Spotted Cattle and Deer: Spirit Guides and Symbols of Endurance and Healing in *Ceremony*," *American Indian Quarterly*, 14 (Fall 1990): 367–377.

Argues for a spiritual connection between Tayo and the deer and highlights the importance of both the deer and the hybrid cattle in Tayo's recovery.

Alanna Kathleen Brown, "Pulling Silko's Threads through Time: An Exploration of Storytelling," *American Indian Quarterly*, 19 (Spring 1995): 171–179.

Discusses the process of coming to understand Native American beliefs about storytelling and demonstrates how useful Silko's poetry, the collection *Storyteller*, and her essays can be to a deeper understanding of *Ceremony*.

Allan Chavkin, ed., *Leslie Marmon Silko's* Ceremony: *A Casebook* (New York: Oxford University Press, 2002).
Fourteen essays and two interviews that cover a wide range of topics in criticism on *Ceremony*, including structure, landscape, animals, semiotics, and canonization.

Reyes Garcia, "Senses of Place in *Ceremony*," *MELUS*, 10, 4 (1983): 37–48.
Traces connection between Tayo's growing understanding of the land and the abuses it has suffered (stolen from natives and mined for uranium used for destructive purposes) and his sense of his own identity.

Lisa Orr, "Theorizing the Earth: Feminist Approaches to Nature and Leslie Marmon Silko's *Ceremony*,"*American Indian Culture and Research Journal*, 18, 2 (1994): 145–157.
Reads *Ceremony* in light of contemporary environmental and ecofeminist movements, and argues it neither vilifies nor glorifies technology, but advocates balance.

Louis Owens, "'The Very Essence of Our Lives': Leslie Silko's Webs of Identity," in his *Other Destinies: Understanding the American Indian Novel* (Norman: University of Oklahoma Press, 1992), pp. 167–191; reprinted in Chavkin, pp. 91–116.
Focuses on Tayo's position as a "mixed blood" and his growing awareness of the power he can access due to that position. Owens also provides readings of the many webs creating connections within *Ceremony*.

Naomi R. Rand, "Surviving What Haunts You: The Art of Invisibility in *Ceremony*, The Ghost Writer, *and* Beloved," *MELUS*, 20 (Fall 1995): 21–32.
Examines the role of ghosts in works by three major contemporary American authors from three different ethnic groups, arguing that the ghostly presences have to do with the importance of survivorship in their cultures.

James Ruppert, "No Boundaries, Only Transitions: *Ceremony*," in his *Mediation in Contemporary Native American Fiction* (Norman: University of Oklahoma Press, 1995), pp. 74–92; reprinted in Chavkin, pp. 175–191.
Very helpful piece that analyzes the blending of Native and non-Native stories, structures, and worldviews.

Colleen Shapiro, "Silko's *Ceremony*," *Explicator*, 61 (Winter 2003): 117–119.
Examination of the figure of the Hunter in *Ceremony*.

Edith Swan, "Feminine Perspective at Laguna Pueblo: Silko's *Ceremony*," *Tulsa Studies in Women's Literature*, 11, 2 (1992): 309–328.
Discusses both the historical and the mythological matrilineal structures of the Laguna in relation to the female characters in *Ceremony*, as well as the significance of family and clan stories, and the symbolism of the color yellow and the associations to Yellow Woman.

Swan, "Laguna Prototypes of Manhood in *Ceremony*," *MELUS*, 17, 1 (1991): 39–61.
Compares male figures in the novel to traditional masculine roles in Laguna culture; includes a focus on Tayo's relationship to the land and how that is gendered.

Swan, "Laguna Symbolic Geography and Silko's *Ceremony,*" *American Indian Quarterly,* 12, 3 (Summer 1988): 229–249.
Detailed examination of the traditional symbols of the Laguna and how those are interwoven into Silko's novel.

Jude Todd, "Knotted Bellies and Fragile Webs: Untangling and Re-spinning in Tayo's Healing Journey," *American Indian Quarterly,* 19 (Spring 1995): 155–170.
Focuses on the importance of Spider Woman and the belly, from where stories are spun and children are birthed, and notes that much of Tayo's sickness has to do with vomiting. In addition to the explanation of the importance of the belly, Todd offers useful explications of Night Swan and Ts'eh.

*—Kathryn West*

⌦✖⌫

# John Updike, *Rabbit Redux; Rabbit Is Rich; Rabbit at Rest*

(New York: Knopf, 1971; 1981; 1990)

When John Updike died in 2009, he was one of the most prominent American writers of his generation. While he was also respected as a poet and an essayist, he was most acclaimed for his novels and short stories. He was born on 18 March 1932 in Reading, Pennsylvania, and lived until age thirteen in the nearby small town of Shillington. This area serves as the setting for many of his works, including the Rabbit novels, where Shillington appears as Mt. Judge and Brewer stands in for Reading. Updike received a scholarship to attend Harvard University, where he majored in English. He originally wanted to be a cartoonist and spent a year at Oxford University's Ruskin School of Drawing and Fine Art. He then returned to the United States and became a staff writer for *The New Yorker,* which later published many of his short stories, poems, and essays. After two years, he decided to try to become a full-time author and moved to Ipswich, Massachusetts; he lived there for the rest of his life. Among the most notable of his more than sixty books are *Bech: A Book* (1970), *Bech Is Back* (1982), and *Bech at Bay: A Quasi-Novel* (1998), comic novels about a writer who is the opposite of Updike in every key respect (he is Jewish, a city dweller, reclusive, and not very prolific); *The Centaur* (1963), winner of the National Book Award; *Olinger Stories* (1964), dramatizing suburban and small-town lives; *Couples* (1968), an exploration of changing sexual mores and adultery; the memoir *Self-Consciousness* (1989); *Collected Poems, 1953–1993* (1993); the voluminous collection *The Early Stories: 1953–1975* (2003), winner of the PEN/Faulkner Award; and *Terrorist* (2006).

Updike described his popular novel *The Witches of Eastwick* (1984) as an attempt to please his "feminist detractors," but many readers considered it misogynistic. Updike's final novel was a sequel to that work; *The Widows of Eastwick*

(2008) was less well received than its predecessor. Updike's later novels are seen as more experimental than the earlier ones; for an example of this view, see John N. Duvall's "U(pdike) & P(ostmodernism)" in *The Cambridge Companion to John Updike* (2006).

Although preceded by a short-story collection, a poetry collection, and the novel *The Poorhouse Fair* (1959), *Rabbit, Run* (1960) was the work that established Updike as a major literary figure. He followed it over the years with three sequels: *Rabbit Redux* (1971); *Rabbit Is Rich* (1981), which received the American Book Award, the National Book Award, the National Book Critics Circle Award, and the Pulitzer Prize; and *Rabbit at Rest* (1990), which received the National Book Critics Circle Award and another Pulitzer Prize (Updike is one of only three writers to date to receive the Pulitzer for fiction twice; the others are William Faulkner and Booth Tarkington). In 1995 Everyman's Library published revised versions of the four novels in one volume, titled *Rabbit Angstrom*. The first edition of *Rabbit, Run* had been censored because of the concerns of the publisher and the advice of a lawyer, but the original explicit language was restored in the later editions. In 2001 Updike included the novella "Rabbit Remembered" in the collection *Licks of Love;* it revisits the family Harry "Rabbit" Angstrom left behind, including the illegitimate daughter he was never sure existed.

*Rabbit, Run* is set in 1959. Rabbit was a basketball star in high school; he is now twenty-six, working at a meaningless job, unhappily married to Janice Springer Angstrom, and the father of a two-year-old son, Nelson. He runs away from home and moves in with a prostitute, Ruth Leonard, for a couple of months. He begins playing golf with a minister enlisted by Janice's family to reunite the couple. Rabbit returns home when Janice gives birth to their daughter, Rebecca June, but runs away again one evening when she refuses to have sex with him. Janice, who has a recurring drinking problem, accidentally drowns the baby while bathing her; the novel ends with Rabbit running from the funeral. These events set the stage for themes and motifs that critics have noted throughout the rest of the tetralogy: infidelity, lost daughters, faith and grace, father-son relationships, sports culture, and the conflict between social responsibility and individual desires and fulfillment. The novels are written in the present tense, a technique that was new when the first one was published but is now quite common. Updike believed that the sense of immediacy produced by the present-tense narration matched Rabbit's impulsiveness. (*Rabbit, Run* is discussed in detail in *RGAL*, volume 6: *Postwar Literature, 1945–1970.*)

*Rabbit Redux* takes place in 1969; characters watch the *Apollo 11* moon landing on television and discuss its significance. Critics have noted that *Rabbit Redux* engages social history more pointedly than does its predecessor, with racial issues and debates about the Vietnam War playing a major role. Janice leaves Rabbit to live with a Greek man who works at her father's car dealership. Rabbit allows a runaway teenager, Jill, to move in with him and Nelson; later, an African American male friend of Jill's, Skeeter, also moves in. Racists burn the Angstroms' home; Jill dies in the fire, becoming the symbolic "lost daughter" of the novel—albeit one with whom Rabbit has had sex. In *Rabbit Is Rich*, which opens with the gasoline shortage of the late 1970s, the Angstroms have become wealthy. Father-son conflicts are heightened as Nelson becomes a cocaine addict and then experiences a religious conversion. Rabbit also spends a great deal of time trying to find out whether Ruth gave birth to a child by him. The novel ends with Rabbit's newborn granddaughter, Judy, being placed in his arms, replacing the real daughter lost in *Rabbit, Run* and the symbolic one lost in *Rabbit Redux*. Family issues, economics and class, and consumerism have been major topics in the criticism on the third novel. As *Rabbit at Rest* begins, the news reports the bombing of Pan Am flight 103 over Lockerbie, Scotland, on 21 December 1988, ushering in a new awareness of terrorism in American consciousness and casting a shadow of looming death over the novel. Continuing to experience conflicts with Nelson, whose irresponsibility and cocaine addiction are destroying the Toyota dealership Janice has handed over to him, Rabbit commits perhaps the ultimate betrayal of his family and his relationships to daughter figures by sleeping with his daughter-in-law. Kerry Ahearn's "Family and Adultery: Images and Ideas in Updike's Rabbit Novels" (1988) was published before the appearance of *Rabbit at Rest*, but students might adopt its analytic strategies to examine these family dynamics in the final novel.

In addition to a plethora of articles, students will find not only a great number of books of literary criticism of Updike's works in general but also at least nine book-length studies devoted to the Rabbit novels. The thirty-four essays and reviews in Jack De Bellis's *John Updike: The Critical Responses to the "Rabbit" Saga* (2005) offer a historical overview of the reception of the Rabbit novels and an invaluable guide to the major critical debates about them; it will help students to focus on a topic and to narrow down the resources to consult. The essays in Lawrence R. Broer's *Rabbit Tales: Poetry and Politics in John Updike's Rabbit Novels* (1998) will provide a similar entrée to the novels. Marshall Boswell's *John Updike's Rabbit Tetralogy: Mastered Irony in Motion* (2001) is a good starting place for its close readings of the novels and for its accessible explication of Updike's religious vision, which Boswell describes as "a complex matrix of ethical precepts, theological beliefs, and aesthetic principles that governs nearly all of his literary output." *The New York Times* maintains a website with links to essays by Updike, reviews of his works, transcripts of interviews, and audio clips at <http://www.nytimes.com/books/97/04/06/lifetimes/updike.html?_r=1>; free registration is required [accessed 4 March 2010].

## TOPICS FOR DISCUSSION AND RESEARCH

1. *Rabbit, Run* begins with Rabbit joining a pickup basketball game on his way home from work; the penultimate scene of *Rabbit at Rest* has Rabbit winning a game of twenty-one against a black youth he encounters while walking the streets of his Florida retirement town, but his victory results in a fatal heart attack. In all of the novels Rabbit remembers scenes from his glory days as a high-school basketball star. He learns to play golf in the first novel and plays the game in each of the others. Students could explore the role of sports in any or all of the novels, particularly as it relates to the idea of the American dream. Jack B. Moore's "Sports, Basketball, and Fortunate Failure in the Rabbit Tetralogy" in Broer's *Rabbit Tales* provides a helpful starting place for this topic.

2. Updike is generally thought of as a writer who has focused on white Protestant lives. Starting with *Rabbit Redux,* however, race plays an important role in Rabbit's consciousness. He has many debates with Skeeter, who articulates a Black Panther–type position. Rabbit and others make racist comments in all of the novels. Students could examine any or all of the novels to form an argument about what Updike wishes to say about race and racists. Jay Prosser's "Updike, Race, and the Postcolonial Project" in *The Cambridge Companion to John Updike* and the articles by Sally Robinson and Jan Clausen will provide helpful insights. Students might also follow Clausen's lead and compare Updike's portrayal of racial issues with that of another contemporary writer, such as John Edgar Wideman, Toni Morrison, or Philip Roth.

3. One of the most debated topics in Updike criticism is his engagement with Christian theology. Updike himself has pointed critics toward this topic by citing his interest in the writings of Søren Kierkegaard and Karl Barth. What role does faith, grace, or organized religion play in the Rabbit novels? Does Updike envision God as loving or punitive? How strong an influence do Updike's characters believe God has in their lives, and how do they conduct themselves in relation to this belief? Boswell's book, as well as his article "Updike, Religion, and the Novel of Moral Debate" in *The Cambridge Companion to John Updike* would be useful for this topic, as would Peter J. Bailey's *Rabbit (Un)Redeemed: The Drama of Belief in John Updike's Fiction* (2006); the articles by John Stephen Martin, John M. Neary, and Kyle A. Pasewark; and the interviews with Edney Silvestre and Jan Nunley in James Plath's *Conversations with John Updike* (1994).

4. History plays a role in the Rabbit novels both in the large national, political, and social sense and in the individual lives of the recurring characters. How do the characters understand the history happening around them—for instance, the Apollo moon landing in *Rabbit Redux,* the gasoline shortage in *Rabbit is Rich,* or the bombing of Pan Am flight 103 over Lockerbie, Scotland, in *Rabbit at Rest*? To what extent do the characters feel engaged with history or divorced from it, and why? Edward Vargo's "Updike, American History, and Historical Methodology" and Donald J. Greiner's "Updike, Rabbit, and the Myth of American Exceptionalism," both included in *The Cambridge Companion to John Updike,* should be consulted for this topic, as well as Vargo's "Corn Chips, Catheters, Toyotas: The Making of History in *Rabbit at Rest*" in Broer's *Rabbit Tales.* Dilvo I. Ristoff's *Updike's America: The Presence of Contemporary American History in John Updike's Rabbit Trilogy* (1988) considers the issue in the first three novels; Ristoff continues his analysis in *John Updike's* Rabbit at Rest: *Appropriating History* (1998).

5. Even after suffering a heart attack and being diagnosed with a serious heart problem, Rabbit continues to eat too much of the kinds of food his doctor has told him to avoid. What other examples of dangerous self-indulgence appear in *Rabbit at Rest*? Do the characters who overindulge share other personality traits, or is almost everyone overindulgent? This topic might be extended into a consideration of the 1980s, the period in which the novel is set. What is Updike suggesting about the Angstrom family's relationship to the larger cul-

ture in which it lives? The articles by Richard G. Androne and Stacey Olster should be consulted, along with Vargo's "Corn Chips, Catheters, Toyotas: The Making of History in *Rabbit at Rest*" in Broer's *Rabbit Tales.*

6. As is the case with any major writer, Updike has received his share of critique along with the acclaim. That critique has followed two primary lines: that his depictions of women are largely negative, not fully developed, and/or objectifying, and that he focuses too much on a white, Protestant, upper-middle-class perspective. Students might explore the terms in which either of these debates have been grounded and then argue for one side or the other, or perhaps for a third perspective. For the debate surrounding Updike's treatment of women, students could start with the articles by Jan Clausen and Sally Robinson and Michiko Kakutani's "Critic's Notebook: Updike's Long Struggle to Portray Women" (1988); Mary O'Connell's book-length analysis, *Updike and the Patriarchal Dilemma: Masculinity in the Rabbit Novels* (1996), should also be consulted. For the view that the self-absorption of characters such as Rabbit is also a fault of Updike himself, see the twin articles by the critic Sven Birkerts and the novelist David Foster Wallace. For a defense of Updike against these articles, see William H. Pritchard's "Updike's Way" (2000).

## RESOURCES

### Primary Works

Introduction, *Best American Short Stories of the Century,* edited by Updike and Katrina Kenison (New York: Hougton Mifflin, 1999).
Useful for understanding Updike's view of what was important and interesting in twentieth-century fiction.

Diane Osen, "Interview with John Updike," *National Book Foundation Archives* <http://www.nationalbook.org/authorsguide_jupdike.html> [accessed 4 March 2010].
Focuses on Updike's influences and the Rabbit novels, including themes of father-son conflict and genetic heritage.

James Plath, ed., *Conversations with John Updike* (Jackson: University Press of Mississippi, 1994).
Strong selection of thirty-two interviews conducted between 1959 and 1993. Although Updike described himself as disliking interviews, he is a generous interviewee, willing to talk about a wide range of subjects. The book includes a chronology of his life.

"Showing Ordinary Life As Being Worth Writing About," *Academy of American Achievement* (12 June 2004) <http://www.achievement.org/autodoc/page/upd0int-1> [accessed 4 March 2010].
Interview in which Updike discusses his childhood, early career, interest in realism, reading interests, advice to young writers, and conception of the American dream. He also talks about the Rabbit novels and explains his decision to end them.

## Criticism

Kerry Ahearn, "Family and Adultery: Images and Ideas in Updike's Rabbit Novels," *Twentieth Century Literature*, 34 (Spring 1988): 62–83.
Examines the impact of adultery on marriage and the community and Updike's choice to depict sex in an explicit fashion.

Richard G. Androne, "'Never the Right Food': Eating and Alienation in John Updike's Rabbit Angstrom Saga," in *You Are What You Eat: Literary Probes into the Palate*, edited by Annette M. Magid (Newcastle upon Tyne, England: Cambridge Scholars, 2008), pp. 330–345.
Examines food and eating as substitutes for satisfaction in the Rabbit novels.

Peter J. Bailey, *Rabbit (Un)Redeemed: The Drama of Belief in John Updike's Fiction* (Madison, N.J.: Fairleigh Dickinson University Press, 2006).
Examines conflicts between faith and doubt in Updike's works, with chapters on each of the Rabbit novels and the novella "Rabbit Is Remembered."

Sven Birkerts and David Foster Wallace, "Twilight of the Phallocrats," *New York Observer*, 12 October 1997.
Twin articles arguing that the self-absorption of characters such as Rabbit is also a fault of the author. Birkerts's contribution is not online, but Wallace's "John Updike, Champion Literary Phallocrat, Drops One; Is This Finally the End for Magnificent Narcissists?" can be found at <http://www.observer.com/node/39731> [accessed 4 March 2010].

Marshall Boswell, *John Updike's Rabbit Tetralogy: Mastered Irony in Motion* (Columbia: University of Missouri Press, 2001).
Treats the four novels as one cohesive work, emphasizing Updike's dialectical vision. Boswell gives strong, close readings of each novel, as well as demonstrating how they work together to form a unified whole.

Lawrence R. Broer, ed., *Rabbit Tales: Poetry and Politics in John Updike's Rabbit Novels* (Tuscaloosa: University of Alabama Press, 1998).
Twelve essays by leading Updike scholars, covering such topics as Rabbit as an Adamic hero and history, family psychology, sports, the work ethic, and the middle class in the Rabbit novels.

Jan Clausen, "Native Fathers," *Kenyon Review*, new series 14 (Spring 1992): 44–55.
Compares the Rabbit novels, particularly *Rabbit Redux* and *Rabbit at Rest*, with John Edgar Wideman's *Philadelphia Fire* (1990), offering a feminist critique and an assessment of the depth of their respective engagements with racial issues.

Jack De Bellis, *John Updike: The Critical Responses to the "Rabbit" Saga* (Westport, Conn.: Praeger, 2005).
Invaluable resource for tracing the history of the reception of the Rabbit novels. De Bellis shows that the acclaim grew with each installment and indicates resources to consult for each critical debate or issue.

Michiko Kakutani, "Critic's Notebook: Updike's Long Struggle to Portray Women," *New York Times*, 5 May 1988, C: 29 <http://www3.nytimes.com/books/97/04/06/lifetimes/updike-portraywomen.html> [accessed 4 March 2010].
Argues that Updike's effort to improve his portrayal of women has been a failure.

Brian Keener, *John Updike's Human Comedy: Comic Morality in* The Centaur *and the Rabbit Novels* (New York: Peter Lang, 2005).
Takes up the issue of comedy and its relationship to morality, arguing that Rabbit is a comic hero who slowly matures over the course of the novels.

John Stephen Martin, "Rabbit's Faith: Grace and the Transformation of the Heart," *Pacific Coast Philology*, 17 (November 1982): 103–111.
Reads the first two Rabbit novels through Blaise Pascal's Pensée 507, which provides the epigraph to *Rabbit, Run*, discussing Rabbit's sense of faith and examining demonstrations of grace in the novels.

John M. Neary, "'Ah: Runs': Updike, Rabbit, and Repetition," *Religion & Literature*, 21 (Spring 1989): 89–110.
Argues that Updike's use of repetition in the Rabbit novels—of adultery, the search for God, and materialism—is evidence of an ultimately affirmative vision on the part of the writer, rather than of the nihilism of which he is often accused.

Joyce Carol Oates, "So Young!" *New York Times*, 30 September 1990, VII: 1.
Insightful review of *Rabbit at Rest*, forecasting themes that have come to dominate criticism on the novel and the tetralogy as a whole.

Mary O'Connell, *Updike and the Patriarchal Dilemma: Masculinity in the Rabbit Novels* (Carbondale: Southern Illinois University Press, 1996).
Examines the role of gender in the Rabbit novels.

Stacey Olster, "Rabbit Rerun: Updike's Replay of Popular Culture in *Rabbit at Rest*," *Modern Fiction Studies*, 37 (Spring 1991): 45–60.
Discusses the significance of popular culture and historical references in the final novel, with mentions of the others.

Olster, ed., *The Cambridge Companion to John Updike* (Cambridge, England & New York: Cambridge University Press, 2006).
Comprises twelve essays, a chronology through 2004, and a bibliography. The work is useful for becoming familiar with the major topics in Updike criticism; it also provides in-depth analyses of religion and moral debates, race, history, American exceptionalism, and Postmodernism in Updike's works.

Kyle A. Pasewark, "The Troubles with Harry: Freedom, America, and God in John Updike's *Rabbit* Novels," *Religion and American Culture*, 6 (Winter 1996): 1–33.
Argues that Rabbit exemplifies the conflicts between redemption, religion, and the American dream in American culture, while Thelma, who appears as his lover

in *Rabbit Is Rich* and dies in *Rabbit at Rest,* transcends these conflicts to experience true grace.

William H. Pritchard, *Updike: America's Man of Letters* (Boston: University of Massachusetts Press, 2005).
Comprehensive and sympathetic overview of the author's life and the work, with a significant amount of discussion devoted to the Rabbit novels.

Pritchard, "Updike's Way," *New England Review,* 23 (Summer 2000): 55–63.
Defends Updike against the charges leveled by Birkerts and Wallace. A version of the article appears as the introduction to Pritchard's *Updike: America's Man of Letters.*

Dilvo I. Ristoff, *John Updike's* Rabbit at Rest: *Appropriating History* (New York: Peter Lang, 1998).
Continues the analysis of history in the Rabbit novels begun in *Updike's America.*

Ristoff, *Updike's America: The Presence of Contemporary American History in John Updike's Rabbit Trilogy* (New York: Peter Lang, 1988).
Considers history in the first three novels, arguing that they are the story of middle America as much as of the Angstrom family.

Sally Robinson, "'Unyoung, Unpoor, Unblack': John Updike and the Construction of Middle American Masculinity," *MFS: Modern Fiction Studies,* 44 (Summer 1998): 331–363.
Focuses on the dramatizations of masculinity in the Rabbit novels, with useful references to various theories of masculinity.

*—Kathryn West*

# Alice Walker, *The Color Purple*

(New York: Harcourt Brace Jovanovich, 1982)

Pulitzer Prize juror Peter Prescott heralded Alice Walker's *The Color Purple* as a work of "permanent importance." Indeed, it is said to have transformed the literary landscape in terms of its representation of "authentic folk voice" and was instrumental in establishing Walker as a canonical figure in American letters. *The Color Purple* has sold over five million copies, has been translated into more than two dozen languages, was awarded the 1983 American Book Award in fiction, and was awarded the Pulitzer Prize in fiction, making Alice Walker the first black woman to win this prestigious award.

Born in Winds Chapel, Eatonton, Georgia, to a sharecropping family in 1944, Alice Malsenior Walker attended Spelman College in Atlanta (founded in 1881 as a school for recently emancipated black women) until her junior year. Always unpretentious, Walker also possessed a rebellious spirit and resisted conformity to social norms. Unable to reconcile her political commitments with those of the institution, Walker withdrew from Spelman, a move she attributes to feeling "alienated by the naiveté and passiveness of the middle-class milieu." Despite this, she developed a lasting relationship with professors and historians Howard Zinn and Staughton Lynd. With the help of Lynd, Walker transferred to the elite (then) women's college Sarah Lawrence in 1964, from which she graduated in 1966.

In 1967 Walker married civil rights attorney Melvyn (Mel) Rosenman Leventhal, whom she met while working with the Student Nonviolent Coordinating Committee (SNCC) in Jackson, Mississippi. Leventhal also worked with the NAACP Legal Defense Fund. Their union produced a daughter, Rebecca Grant Leventhal (born 1969), and was tested by bigotry. Walker and Leventhal remained strong in the midst of the tensions surrounding interracial couples, and the general distrust of white people in the Civil Rights Movement. Together, they lived in Jackson for several years before moving to the Cambridge, Massachusetts, area; they divorced in 1977. Walker did not return to the South for some twenty years, when she was honored as a speaker at Spelman College.

A feminist author-activist, Walker claims Langston Hughes as her "literary father" and Zora Neale Hurston as a model for her work. It was Walker, in fact, who single-handedly resuscitated Hurston's memory and legacy as a major figure of the Harlem Renaissance. Walker's commitment to black life and experience in America is clear as both she and her work are rooted in Southern culture. It is through Walker's fiction that her passion about the suffering of black people is evident. Still, Walker is often critiqued by black scholars as having a primarily feminist perspective which, at times, puts her at odds with racial issues. She was among the first writers to integrate the predominantly white, feminist publication *Ms.* magazine, where she worked as a contributing editor. In addition to her editorial duties, Walker wrote several poems and essays for *Ms.* and *American Scholar*. Walker's other professional appointments included writer-in-residence at Jackson State College and lecturer at Wellesley College and the University of Massachusetts, Boston.

Walker's publications are an impressive body of essays, poems, and novels. Her first published work of fiction, "To Hell with Dying" (1967), chronicles the life of Mr. Sweet and the two children who keep him alive. This story, initially included in a collection edited by Langston Hughes, *The Best Short Stories by Negro Writers*, was published as a children's book in 1988. Walker's other works of children's literature include *Langston Hughes: American Poet* (1974), *Finding the Green Stone* (1991), and *Why War Is Never a Good Idea* (2007). Many of her essays address black nationalism and its connection to the Civil Rights Movement. Walker's essay "The Civil Rights Movement: What Good Was It?" won first prize for publication in the fall 1967 issue of *American Scholar. In Love & Trouble: Stories of Black Women* (1973), Walker's debut short-story collection, includes "Her Sweet Jerome" and "Everyday Use," her most widely anthologized and taught story. Both offer a veiled critique of the black nationalist movement as a platform for elevating "cultured" blacks over less-educated ones, and an explicit valorization of Southern folk through her characters. (See Barbara Christian's essay "The

Contrary Women of Alice Walker" for a discussion of how the women of these stories challenge existing images of "obedient and *unthinking* black women.") Walker's first novel, *The Third Life of Grange Copeland* (1970), chronicles the lives of a family of sharecroppers. *Revolutionary Petunias & Other Poems* (1973), Walker's second volume of poems, also reflects strong feminist and black Southern roots. Her novel *Meridian* (1976), set in the South against the backdrop of the Civil Rights Movement of the 1960s, speaks to the paradoxes of African American identity. In 1979 Walker edited *I Love Myself When I Am Laughing . . . and Then Again When I Am Looking Mean and Impressive: A Zora Neale Hurston Reader*, a collection of writings by and about Hurston.

In 1982 Walker published *The Color Purple,* an epistolary novel written in dialect, chronicling the life (and isolation) of its protagonist, Celie, an impoverished black girl in rural Georgia in the 1930s. Although initially overlooked, *The Color Purple* received winning reviews and widespread acclaim in mainstream America, despite considerable critical backlash against the novel (and Walker) in the black community. Many charged Walker with unwittingly presenting a negative portrait of the black family, especially black males, arguing that she provided no context for the abuse and cruelty exhibited by her characters. Yet, *The Color Purple* boldly depicted an authentic Southern folk voice and exposed its "formidable critique of patriarchy" (Salamishah Tillet, "The Color Precious," 12 November 2009 <http://www.theroot.com/views/color-precious>). Walker, often queried about her inspiration for the characters in this novel, has said that they are composites of people from her childhood, and embody several events purportedly experienced by her family members. Although *The Color Purple* is not autobiographical, in the sense that she knew almost no one exactly like its characters, it could be characterized as a "longing to be intimate with [her] ancestors," noting that she "always thought of it as a gift."

A movie version of *The Color Purple* was directed by Steven Spielberg in 1985. Almost twenty years after the film's release, *The Color Purple* was adapted for the stage as a musical, premiering in Atlanta's Alliance Theater in 2004 and winning the Tony Award. Like the stage version, the film, too, generated bitter debate about its "Disney-like portrayal of incest" (Tillet), and the more significant charge that its treatment of black male characters was racist. On an episode of *The Phil Donahue Show,* columnist and talk-show host Tony Brown famously declared it, "the most racist depiction of black men since *Birth of a Nation* and the most anti-black family film of the modern film era." See Walker's book *The Same River Twice—Honoring the Difficult* (1996), where she discusses the experience of adapting *The Color Purple* for film and responds to the charge that her novel is an unfair depiction of black men.

Other critics have argued that Spielberg's adaptation, while certainly popular, was nothing more than a sentimental rendering of an otherwise serious text about women's subjectivity and agency. For instance, Walker writes Shug Avery as a nomadic blueswoman who defies the prescribed gender roles of her day; however, at the end of the movie Shug, in her quest for salvation, walks down the aisle and genuflects to her literal and figurative male father. Shug receives the love and reacceptance she craves and the audience gets their heartwarming moment as father and daughter are reunited. This overly romanticized film ending is said to undermine the novel's primary premise.

The Color Purple was followed by In Search of Our Mothers' Gardens (1983); the title essay offers a passionate analysis of historical barriers to black women's creative expression. The Temple of My Familiar (1989) explores black women's spirituality, and Possessing the Secret of Joy (1992) tells the story of Tashi, who makes a brief appearance in The Color Purple. It details (and implicitly protests) the practice of female genital mutilation among some African peoples. Her more-recent works include The Way Forward Is with a Broken Heart (2000), Sent by Earth (2001), Absolute Trust in the Goodness of the Earth: New Poems (2003), A Poem Traveled down My Arm (2003), and Now Is the Time to Open Your Heart (2004).

In 2007 Alice Walker placed her archive, which includes journals, drafts of some of her early works of fiction, and correspondence between Walker and her editors, at Emory University. The author resides in Northern California and continues to support the work of emerging writers through her publishing company, Wild Trees Press, which she started in 1984.

A useful website to consult for information about Alice Walker and her work is Anniina's Alice Walker Page <http://www.luminarium.org/contemporary/alicew/> [accessed 19 March 2010], which includes a healthy selection of full-text interviews and critical articles, as well as excerpts from primary works. Alice Walker's Garden, <http://www.alicewalkersgarden.com/alice_walker_welcom.html> [accessed 19 March 2010], promoted as "The Official Alice Walker Website" and maintained by the Alice Walker Society, offers similar information, though in smaller helpings. Both websites offer a guide to secondary sources that should be supplemented by the MLA bibliography.

## TOPICS FOR DISCUSSION AND RESEARCH

1. The epigraph for The Color Purple comes from a Stevie Wonder song: "Show me how to do like you / Show me how to do it." Consider how the novel opens, with Celie's "stuttered utterances" as she negotiates language, comes to voice, and begins to tell her own story. To whom does she look for instruction? Who can show her how to do it? How is literacy disseminated in this community? How is this relevant to the themes of the novel? What kinds of role models are lacking in the novel, and why? Where does Celie eventually find role models, and what impact do they have on her life? By the end, does she become a role model herself? For other characters? For the audience of the novel? What does Walker have to say about role models?

2. At the heart of much of the criticism of The Color Purple is Walker's placement of her narrators' (Celie and Nettie) personal histories at the center of the narrative. Several critics argue that rather than emphasizing the "collective plight of black people" it abstracts issues of race and class. How does emphasizing personal history trump the advancement of black concerns? Does Celie's sexual oppression erase concerns regarding race and class, or does it offer a productive critique of race? What does it suggest about race relations within the black community? How does the use of the epistolary form contribute to

or displace concerns about race and class? Read bell hooks and Trudier Harris for ideas about how to develop this topic.

3. *The Color Purple* was published in the early 1980s, during the Reagan administration, a period in which many believed there was considerable abatement of the gains made by the Civil Rights Movement, such as cutting funding to federal programs supporting minorities (Aid to Families with Dependent Children and affirmative action), and gutting the Civil Rights Division of the Department of Justice. Students might consider researching how this context might have mediated public reception of the novel, and how that reception produced specific readings of it. Jaqueline Bobo discusses aspects of this topic and offers thought-provoking commentary.

4. Students interested in film studies might wish to view the film adaptation of Walker's novel and compare/contrast how both texts work to construct specific narratives. What are the differences between the two works? What are the differences in the way a film and a novel is experienced? What are the ways in which the public has responded to both? Students might also examine the stage adaptation of this work. How does the transfer of *The Color Purple* to this medium (musical) change, alter, reshape the politics of the text? Lauren Berlant's essay is a place to start considering this topic.

5. Students might find it interesting to contrast Celie's experiences in the rural South with those of her sister Nettie in Africa. What restrictions and (eventual) freedoms does each woman find in her respective environment? Students could read other of Walker's works, such as the short story "Everyday Use" or the novel *Possessing the Secret of Joy* to compare depictions of Africa and its possibilities for African Americans. Such an analysis might also research Walker's own experiences with the black nationalist movement and her feelings about it. Linda Selzer's essay might stimulate ideas regarding this topic.

## RESOURCES

### Biography
Evelyn C. White, *Alice Walker: A Life* (New York: Norton, 2004).
First full-length biography of the author's life and works.

### Criticism
Lauren Berlant, "Race, Gender, and Nation in *The Color Purple*," *Critical Inquiry*, 14 (Summer 1988): 831–859.
Examines the politics of history and national identity in the novel.

Jacqueline Bobo, "Sifting through the Controversy: Reading *The Color Purple*," *Callaloo*, 12 (Spring 1989): 332–342.
An overview of the discourse shaped by the debates over the film and the novel.

Barbara Christian, "The Contrary Women of Alice Walker," in *Black Feminist Criticism* (Elmsford, N.Y.: Pergamon, 1985).
Examines a shift in black writing through a review of Walker's female protagonists.

Trudier Harris, "On *The Color Purple*, Stereotypes, and Silence," *Black American Literature Forum*, 4 (1984): 155–161.
Argues that *The Color Purple* unknowingly contributes to a "cultural narrative of pathology," charting objections to the way it has been "canonized."

bell hooks, "Writing the Subject: Reading *The Color Purple*," in *Reading Black, Reading Feminist: A Critical Anthology*, edited by Henry Louis Gates Jr. (New York: Meridian, 1990), pp. 454–470.
Argues that by placing the emphasis on Celie's sexual oppression rather than "the collective plight" of black people, *The Color Purple* parodies the tradition of the slave narrative.

Candice M. Jenkins, "Queering Black Patriarchy: The Salvific Wish and Masculine Possibility in Alice Walker's *The Color Purple*," *Modern Fiction Studies*, 48, 4 (2002): 969–1000.
Analysis of *The Color Purple* as a text that engages in a "queering" of patriarchal power in the black community.

Peter Kerry Powers, "'Pa Is Not Our Pa': Sacred History and Political Imagination in *The Color Purple*," *South Atlantic Review*, 60 (May 1995): 69–92.
Examines Walker's revision of African American religious traditions.

Linda Selzer, "Race and Domesticity in *The Color Purple*," *African American Review*, 29 (Spring 1995): 67–82.
Examines the use of domestic, familial relations as a "textual trope" for reading race and class in a broader context.

—*Annette Harris Powell*

# August Wilson, *The Piano Lesson*
(New York: Dutton, 1990)

About himself August Wilson has said: "I always tell people I'm a struggling playwright. I'm struggling to get the next play down on paper." This sense of commitment and discipline allowed Wilson to become one of the most prolific playwrights in America. In his cycle of ten plays, each covering a different decade of the twentieth century, Wilson captures changes in twentieth-century African American life, depicting both its challenges and triumphs.

Named for his German American father, Wilson was born Frederick August Kittel on 27 April 1945, in Pittsburgh, Pennsylvania. The fourth of six children, Wilson spent his early years with his family in a two-room apartment behind a grocery store in a racially mixed neighborhood known as "the Hill." His father, a baker, was often absent from home so Wilson's mother, Daisy Wilson Kittel, supported the family with earnings from work as a cleaning woman. After his parents divorced, his mother married David Bedford, who moved the family to a white suburb where they faced overt racism that caused Wilson to move from school to school. Against his mother's wishes, he eventually dropped out of Gladstone High School in 1961 after being falsely accused of plagiarizing. In 1963 he joined the army and was discharged after only one year. Soon after, he moved back to the Hill, his childhood neighborhood.

With a used typewriter, purchased for $20 in 1965, Wilson embarked upon a writing career. Despite a lack of formal training, he began writing poetry, finding inspiration in the Black Power movement and jazz music. Around this time, Wilson also adopted the first name August and his mother's maiden name, signaling a growing identification and pride in his African American heritage. These influences appear in his first publication, the poem "For Malcolm X and Others" (1969). Wilson also found inspiration by working with and around other struggling writers. He helped form the Center Avenue Poets Theatre Workshop in 1965 and cofounded the Black Horizons Theatre Company in Pittsburgh.

A 1973 production of Athol Fugard's *Sizwe Bansi Is Dead* encouraged Wilson to try his hand at drama. His earliest works include *Recycle* (produced in 1973), *The Coldest Day of the Year* (eventually produced in 1989) and *The Homecoming* (eventually produced in 1989) whose subject matter foreshadows his first Broadway success, *Ma Rainey's Black Bottom* (produced, 1984). These early plays are marked by the influence of the mannerisms, experiences, and speech of the African American community in Pittsburgh's Hill neighborhood. But it was not until he moved to St. Paul, Minnesota, in 1977 to take a job writing children's plays for the Science Museum that Wilson "felt [he] could hear voices for the first time accurately." In St. Paul, Wilson wrote the musical satire, *Jitney!* (produced, 1978), *Black Bart and the Sacred Hills* (produced, 1981), and *Fullerton Street* (produced, 1980), submitting all three in different years to the Eugene O'Neill Theater Center's National Playwrights Conference. All were rejected. For *Jitney!*, however, Wilson was awarded a Jerome Fellowship to develop his work at the Playwrights' Center of Minneapolis, where staged readings of *Jitney!* and *Fullerton Street* were performed.

In 1982 the breakthrough leading to Wilson's repeated successes on Broadway came: Lloyd Richards, dean of the Yale School of Drama and artistic director of the Eugene O'Neill Theater Center's National Playwrights Conference accepted *Ma Rainey's Black Bottom* for the conference, where it was given a staged reading. Thus began a collaboration, with Wilson as writer and Richards as director, that led to a series of successful plays: *Ma Rainey's Black Bottom, Fences* (1985), *Joe Turner's Come and Gone* (1986), *The Piano Lesson* (1987), *Two Trains Running* (1990), and *Seven Guitars* (1995). All but the last took similar routes to Broadway—initial staging at the O'Neill Theater Center, followed by productions at regional theaters.

Wilson's use of blues and other structural elements of black American culture marks a shift in American dramatic tradition. In a 1987 interview he confessed: "I haven't read Ibsen, Shaw, Shakespeare—except *The Merchant of Venice* in ninth grade. The only Shakespeare I've ever seen was *Othello* last year at Yale Rep. I'm not familiar with *Death of a Salesman*. I haven't read Tennessee Williams. I very purposefully didn't read them." Unencumbered by tradition, Wilson created his own rules, relying instead on what he refers to as the "4 B's": the Blues, Amiri Baraka, Jorge Luis Borges, and painter Romare Bearden. Combined with personal experiences growing up in Pittsburgh, these influences are evident in the Pittsburgh, or "Decade Cycle," for which Wilson is best known. Within each play, Wilson is honest about poverty and racism while also celebrating the richness of African American life. Each of the cycle's ten plays is set in a different decade of the twentieth century; all but one take place in Pittsburgh. They are, in order of the decade covered: *Gem of the Ocean* (2003), *Joe Turner's Come and Gone, Ma Rainey's Black Bottom, The Piano Lesson, Seven Guitars, Fences, Two Trains Running, Jitney!, King Hedley II* (2000), and *Radio Golf* (2005).

Wilson was awarded Pulitzer Prizes for both *The Piano Lesson* and *Fences* and received many other awards and playwriting fellowships. The last of the "cycle" plays, *Radio Golf,* premiered at the Yale Repertory Theater the day after Wilson's sixtieth birthday. That year he was diagnosed with inoperable liver cancer. Wilson died on 2 October 2005, in Seattle, where he had lived since 1994. To honor his achievements, Broadway's Virginia Theater was renamed the August Wilson Theater.

Written in 1986, *The Piano Lesson* was Wilson's fourth play to be produced on Broadway. It is set in 1936 and focuses on the question of who has the right to a 137-year-old piano: Berniece Charles, a widow struggling to raise her daughter in Pittsburgh, or her brother, Boy Willie, a Southern sharecropper who would like to sell it to buy land made available by the recent drowning of Sutter, the descendant of the owner of the Charles family's ancestors. The piano has symbolic value and monetary worth, both of which are invoked as the play progresses. The history of the piano is intertwined with that of the Charles family. Papa Boy Willie, the siblings' great-grandfather and Boy Willie's namesake, carved portraits of his wife and son on the piano after their owner traded them for the piano. Years later, their father, Boy Charles, was murdered after reclaiming the piano; for him, Sutter's ownership of the piano symbolized and ensured his family's historical and current bondage. Berniece wants to keep the piano as a reminder of the past—in particular, her family's hardships; Boy Willie wants to exchange it for the promise of a future.

In *The Ground on Which I Stand,* an address delivered in 1996 to the Theatre Communications Group national conference at Princeton University and cited below, Wilson mapped out what can be an ambitious course of study. He said: "In one guise, the ground I stand on has been pioneered by the Greek dramatists—by Euripides, Aeschylus and Sophocles—by William Shakespeare, by Shaw and Ibsen, and by the American dramatists Eugene O'Neill, Arthur Miller and Tennessee Williams. In another guise, the ground that I stand on has been pioneered by my grandfather, by Nat Turner, by Denmark Vesey, by Martin Delaney, Marcus Garvey and the Honorable Elijah Muhammad." Students can fruitfully begin study of this play by identifying and describing the significance of those references and suggesting how they relate not only to *The Piano Lesson* but to Wilson's cycle of history plays as well. It is always important in studying a literary work to determine the ground the author stands on, and Wilson has provided an eloquent statement to guide students of his work.

## TOPICS FOR RESEARCH AND DISCUSSION

1. Pressed to take sides, Doaker, the siblings' uncle, remarks: "Ain't nobody said nothing about who's right and who's wrong." Students will do well to take Doaker's words to heart; indeed, each sibling's claim is valid. Instead of supporting one sibling over the other, Wilson dramatizes the emotional costs of the conflict on the family and by extension, the community. In a 1987 interview with David Savran (included in Jackson R. Bryer and Mary C. Hartig, pp. 19–37), Wilson pinpoints the "central question" of the play as: "How do you use your legacy?" Neither sibling alone offers a definitive answer. At first glance, Boy Willie's claims seem easily dismissed. Arrogant, brash, and disruptive, he has played a part in the death of Berniece's husband and seems willing to exploit others to get what he wants. His repeated insistence that he will cut the piano in half suggests a disregard for his family's struggles. And yet, Boy Willie clearly knows of and takes pride in his family's past, especially the heroics of his father and grandfather. For him, buying the land his grandfather farmed as a slave is a way to honor the past. Using Wilson's discussion of the play's central conflict and his assessment of Boy Willie and Berniece as starting points, students could develop an analysis of the merits of each of their positions.

2. In "Ma Rainey and the Boyz: Gender Ideology in August Wilson's Broadway Canon" (Marilyn Elkins, pp. 123–160), Kim Marra points out dichotomous images of black women, noting the ways Wilson supports the negative idea that "black matriarchy is . . . complicit with white supremacy in the economic and sexual emasculation of the black male." Focusing on images of women and women's roles in *The Piano Lesson*, students could develop an analysis arguing for or against Marra's assessment: Do Berniece and other female characters support and/or resist racism and mainstream culture? How do the actions of women affect the black male characters? Do they participate with mainstream culture to emasculate and disempower black men? Alternatively, students can examine male images in the play: How is masculinity performed in the play and does it undercut racist attitudes about black men? How do male characters speak about and treat the female characters? Is it respectful and/or demeaning? For additional criticism on female images, students can also consult Sandra G. Shannon's "The Ground on Which I Stand: August Wilson's Perspective on African American Women," Harry J. Elam's "August Wilson's Women," and Missy Dehn Kubitschek's "August Wilson's Gender Lesson" (Alan Nadel, pp. 150–199).

3. To counteract the "glancing manner" mainstream American culture casts upon blacks, Wilson interweaves Afrocentrist elements and perspectives into the play, what Mary L. Bogumil calls "the African roots, the atavistic connection, African Americans have to their ancestors." Symbolized by the supernatural, they stand out in this mostly realistic play. Berniece's adherence to mainstream values is underscored by her insistence that Boy Willie, and not an avenging spirit or ghost, killed Sutter. Doaker and the other men, however, insist on the latter. Despite her disavowal of the men's beliefs, Berniece understands the power of black cultural practices as suggested by her reluctance to marry Avery Brown, a former sharecropper turned preacher. Boy Willie criticizes Brown for his willingness to accept inferior social status for economic security, a "turkey at Thanksgiving" rather than

social and cultural equality. By having Brown's Christian-influenced attempts to exorcise Sutter's ghost fail, Wilson undercuts the value of Western belief systems in this context. In addition, the kiss Berniece shares with Lyman, who was also present at her husband's death, signals a movement toward African cultural roots. Focusing on Afrocentrist elements, students might explore the ways they help define African American identity and whether or not such definitions are effective in combating racism. Elam also discusses African cultural influence in Wilson's plays.

4. In the chapter "August Wilson As Teacher: The Piano Lesson" in her *The Dramatic Vision of August Wilson* (1994) Sandra G. Shannon discusses the original open-ended version of the play's final scene that director Lloyd Richards found unsatisfying; the curtain came down as Boy Willie wrestled Sutter's ghost. For Wilson, the ending "wasn't important. The important thing . . . was Boy Willie's willingness to engage the ghost in battle." Richards, however, argued that audiences needed to find out the fate of the piano, thus prompting Wilson's revision, which includes one of the siblings giving up the piano. Using Shannon's discussion of lessons in the play, students can consider whether or not the ending provides a resolution to the siblings' conflict. The end of the play shows Berniece and Boy Willie working together, but are their respective views about the piano (and what it stands for) reconciled? How does the ending revise our perspective on the play's central theme and conflict?

5. In a 1993 interview with Nathan L. Grant (Bryer and Hartig, pp. 172–187), Wilson pinpoints Berniece as the protagonist or object of the "lesson" indicated in the play's title, stating: "the play's about Berniece, it's not about Boy Willie. Berniece is the only character in the play who goes through any changes." Despite Berniece's desire to preserve the piano, she seems reluctant to embrace black culture and history. Afraid to touch or play the piano, she sees it and the legacy it symbolizes as a burden not be passed on to future generations. While the piano serves as homage to the sacrifice of past generations and survival, her refusal to play it suggests a repugnance of the piano's association with slavery and her family's oppression. Berniece furthermore expresses internalized racism when she associates blackness with backwardness, warning her daughter Maretha not to "show . . . your color." She later scolds her daughter for fidgeting while combing her hair: "If you were a boy I wouldn't be going through this." Using Wilson's comments to Grant as a point of departure, discuss what changes Berniece's character goes through and why. How do the actions and words of other characters promote a change in her? Alternately, students can argue against Wilson's assessment by showing how other characters change and why.

## RESOURCES

### Primary Works

Jackson R. Bryer and Mary C. Hartig, eds., *Conversations with August Wilson* (Jackson: University Press of Mississippi, 2006).
A collection of interviews spanning 1984, the year of Wilson's first major success, to September 2004, less than a year before he was diagnosed with inoperable liver cancer.

*The Ground on Which I Stand* (New York: Theatre Communications Group, 2001). An address given at the 1996 Theatre Communications Group national conference in which Wilson states his concerns about the lack of creative and financial support for African American artists in theater. The speech resulted in written and live debates between Wilson and Robert Brustein, drama critic for the *New Republic*.

## Criticism

Christopher Bigsby, ed., *The Cambridge Companion to August Wilson* (Cambridge, England: Cambridge University Press, 2007).
Along with chapters addressing Wilson's life and career and the wider context of his plays, provides individual chapters analyzing each of the plays in the Decade Cycle.

Mary L. Bogumil, *Understanding August Wilson* (Columbia: University of South Carolina, 1999).
Overview of six plays *(Ma Rainey's Black Bottom, Fences, Joe Turner's Come and Gone, The Piano Lesson, Two Trains Running,* and *Seven Guitars)* within the context of Wilson's concern with African American dramatic tradition, history, and identity.

Harry J. Elam Jr., *The Past As Present in the Drama of August Wilson* (Ann Arbor: University of Michigan Press, 2004).
Organized around ideas and themes featured in Wilson's plays, a book-length analysis of Wilson's ten-play cycle examining the ways his work intersects with other African American works published in the 1980s and 1990s.

Marilyn Elkins, ed., *August Wilson: A Casebook* (New York: Garland, 1994).
A collection of critical essays on diverse topics such as the role of gender, folk traditions, politics, religion, and influences in Wilson's plays.

Alan Nadel, ed., *May All Your Fences Have Gates: Essays on the Drama of August Wilson* (Iowa City: University of Iowa Press, 1993).
An early (the first) but still useful collection of essays that treat a variety of thematic issues in five of Wilson's plays written before 1993.

Kim Pereira, *August Wilson and the African-American Odyssey* (Carbondale: University of Illinois Press, 1995).
Analysis of four plays *(Ma Rainey's Black Bottom, Fences, Joe Turner's Come and Gone,* and *The Piano Lesson)* that draws out themes of separation, migration, and reunion.

Yvonne Shafer, *August Wilson: A Research and Production Sourcebook* (Westport, Conn.: Greenwood Press, 1998).
An important resource especially for those who are interested in the staging of Wilson's plays. Shafer provides biographical information and an overview of the critical reception of Wilson's plays.

Sandra G. Shannon, *The Dramatic Vision of August Wilson* (Washington, D.C.: Howard University Press, 1994).
An excellent overview of Wilson's work with attention to influences. The book also includes an interview.

Peter Wolfe, *August Wilson* (New York: Twayne, 1999).
Overview of Wilson's life and work, along with a concise synthesis of the critical assessment of his work. The annotated bibliography of secondary sources is particularly useful.

—*Linda Trinh Moser*

# Part IV
# Annotated
# Bibliography

John W. Aldridge, *Talents and Technicians: Literary Chic and the New Assembly-Line Fiction* (New York: Scribners, 1992).
Examination of contemporary literary fiction by writers who received critical attention and praise in the 1980s and early 1990s, such as Ann Beattie, T. C. Boyle, Raymond Carver, Bret Easton Ellis, Louise Erdrich, and Jay McInerney. Aldridge points out "flaws" in their work that he ascribes to cultural trends.

Houston A. Baker, ed., *Three American Literatures: Essays in Chicano, Native American, and Asian-American Literature for Teachers of American Literature* (New York: Modern Language Association of America, 1982).
Eight essays offering broad overviews of minority literary traditions and basic interpretations of important works.

Christopher W. E. Bigsby, *Contemporary American Playwrights* (New York: Cambridge University Press, 1999).
Accessible survey of the careers and discussions of the plays of John Guare, Tina Howe, Tony Kushner, Emily Mann, Richard Nelson, Marsha Norman, David Rabe, Paula Vogel, Wendy Wasserstein, and Lanford Wilson.

Charles Blackstone and Jill Talbot, eds., *The Art of Friction: Where [Non]Fictions Come Together* (Austin: University of Texas Press, 2008).
Innovative anthology that provides nineteen works—short stories, essays, and hybrids of the two—along with a commentary by each author on his or her own work. The anthology attempts to "survey the borderlands where fiction and nonfiction intersect, commingle, and challenge genre lines." Writers represented include Mary Clearman Blew, Junot Díaz, Jonathan Safran Foer, Wendy McClure, Cris Mazza, Ronald Sukenick, and Terry Tempest Williams.

Malcolm Bradbury, *The Modern American Novel,* revised edition (New York: Oxford University Press, 1992).
Presents the American novel in all its variety and diversity from the late nineteenth century to the late twentieth century. Chapter 9, "After the Post: American Fiction from the 1970s to the 1990s," is especially relevant to the concerns of this volume of the *Research Guide to American Literature.*

Julie Brown, ed., *Ethnicity and the American Short Story* (New York: Garland, 1997).
Fourteen essays, many with a focus on contemporary fiction, covering a wide range of authors of diverse cultural backgrounds—Chinese American, Native American, African American, Chicano/Chicana, Japanese American, Hawaiian, Indo-American, Arab American, and Jewish American—including Amy Tan, Louise Erdrich, Gloria Naylor, Alice Walker, Sandra Cisneros, Ramzi M. Salti, and N. Scott Momaday.

Héctor Calderón and José David Saldívar, eds., *Criticism in the Borderlands: Studies in Chicano Literature, Culture, and Ideology* (Durham, N.C.: Duke University Press, 1991).
Essays on Chicano literary criticism treating four pertinent issues: debates about the American literary canon and the situation of Chicano literary studies; repre-

sentations of Chicanos and Chicanas; genre, ideology, and history; and aesthetics. The volume includes an annotated bibliography of contemporary Chicano literary criticism.

R. V. Cassill and Joyce Carol Oates, eds., *The Norton Anthology of Contemporary Fiction,* second edition (New York: Norton, 1998).
Diverse collection of more than forty short stories by writers of various tendencies, including Postmodernist, multicultural, and Realist, with useful biographical sketches at the end.

Keith Clark, ed., *Contemporary Black Men's Fiction and Drama* (Urbana: University of Illinois Press, 2001).
Collection of essays on prose published since 1970 that examine the ways male African American writers challenge and expand the literary conventions of both black and mainstream American writing. The works of the recognized authors Ernest J. Gaines, Charles Johnson, Clarence Major, Ishmael Reed, and John Edgar Wideman and the lesser-known writers Melvin Dixon, Randall Kenan, and Brent Wade are discussed.

Jay Clayton, *The Pleasures of Babel: Contemporary American Literature and Theory* (New York: Oxford University Press, 1993).
Examines a wide array of novels from the 1970s, 1980s, and 1990s while also clearly explaining contemporaneous developments in criticism. Clayton argues that the novels constitute a "great period of writing" and that their power "lies in their participation in larger networks of discourse and in their ability to attract, to hold, and to shape particular communities of readers."

Samuel Chase Coale, *Paradigms of Paranoia: The Culture of Conspiracy in Contemporary American Fiction* (Tuscaloosa: University of Alabama Press, 2005).
Focuses on the roles played by anxiety, isolation, ambiguity, fragmentation, and information overload in works by Thomas Pynchon, Don DeLillo, Joan Didion, Tim O'Brien, Paul Auster, and Toni Morrison.

Nicholas Coles and Janet Zandy, eds., *American Working-Class Literature: An Anthology* (New York: Oxford University Press, 2006).
Excellent resource featuring fiction, poetry, drama, nonfiction, and songs. The seven sections and illustrated timeline highlight historical developments in American working-class life.

John Christopher Cunningham, *Race-ing Masculinity: Identity in Contemporary U.S. Writings* (New York: Routledge, 2002).
Examines race and gender in works by American male writers of color, uncovering the coexistence of antiracist themes with those of sexism and homophobia. Writers discussed include Frank Chin, Shawn Hsu Wong, Charles Johnson, Oscar Zeta Acosta, and Richard Rodriguez.

Philip Dacey and David Jauss, eds., *Strong Measures: Contemporary American Poetry in Traditional Forms,* foreword by Richard Wilbur (New York: Harper & Row, 1986).

Well-chosen collection of poetry in a wide variety of forms that includes works by major poets. The book is extremely helpful for its clear explanations of the various forms.

Christopher Douglas, *Reciting America: Culture and Cliché in Contemporary U.S. Fiction* (Urbana: University of Illinois Press, 2001).
Examines the ways contemporary literary works both repeat and challenge clichés about American identity and experience such as "one nation under God," "life, liberty, and the pursuit of happiness," and the "American dream."

Robert Durante, *The Dialectic of Self and Story: Reading and Storytelling in Contemporary American Fiction* (New York: Routledge, 2001).
Argues that the Realist impulse in American fiction from the 1980s and 1990s is accompanied by Postmodernist themes such as alienation, social disintegration, and authorial self-reflexivity.

Emory Elliott, Martha Banta, Houston A. Baker, and others, eds., *The Columbia Literary History of the United States* (New York: Columbia University Press, 1988).
Essays surveying themes, genres, and subject matter of American literature. Most relevant to the contemporary period is part 5, "1945 to the Present."

Elliott, Cathy N. Davidson, and others, eds., *The Columbia History of the American Novel* (New York: Columbia University Press, 1991).
Thirty-one essays examining the American novel from the sixteenth century. Relevant to the contemporary period are the essays in the section "The Late Twentieth Century."

Wendy B. Faris, *Ordinary Enchantments: Magical Realism and the Remystification of Narrative* (Nashville: Vanderbilt University Press, 2004).
Examination of magical realism in contemporary fiction from around the world, identifying its major characteristics and narrative traits.

Cecilia Konchar Farr, *Reading Oprah: How Oprah's Book Club Changed the Way America Reads* (Albany: State University of New York Press, 2005).
History and analysis of the cultural phenomenon of Oprah Winfrey's television book club, arguing that Winfrey has used it both to entertain and to enlighten her viewers.

Henry Louis Gates Jr., *The Signifying Monkey: A Theory of Afro-American Literary Criticism* (New York: Oxford University Press, 1988).
Traces the roots of African American literature to African folklore, traditions, and languages. Gates mainly examines works written before 1970, but his approach is relevant to works published more recently.

Paula Geyh, Fred G. Leebron, and Andrew Levy, eds., *Postmodern American Fiction: A Norton Anthology* (New York: Norton, 1997).
Devoted to post–World War II experimental fiction, including excerpts from novels, short stories, creative nonfiction, and access to hypertext fiction. The general introduction, section introductions, and author headnotes provide social, his-

torical, and biographical contexts for the readings, while the section "A Casebook of Postmodern Theory" suggests connections between fiction and literary theory.

James R. Giles, *The Spaces of Violence* (Tuscaloosa: University of Alabama Press, 2006).
Examines connections between violence and physical space in works by Russell Banks, Cormac McCarthy, Lewis Nordan, Dorothy Allison, Don DeLillo, Denis Johnson, Sherman Alexie, Robert Stone, Bret Easton Ellis, Jane Smiley, Toni Morrison, Edwidge Danticat, and Chuck Palahniuk.

Giles, *Violence in the Contemporary American Novel: An End to Innocence* (Columbia: University of South Carolina Press, 2000).
A study of eight contemporary American urban novels in which writers convey a sense of violence as an epidemic that threatens American society.

Daniel Grassian, *Hybrid Fictions: American Literature and Generation X* (Jefferson, N.C.: McFarland, 2003).
Argues for the emergence of a generation of American writers born from the late 1950s to the early 1970s—David Foster Wallace, Neal Stephenson, Douglas Coupland, Sherman Alexie, William T. Vollmann, and Dave Eggers—whose most distinctive characteristic is hybridity in psychological, philosophical, ethnic, and technological terms. Grassian also discusses the impact of the Internet and hypertext on the future of fiction.

Richard J. Gray, *A History of American Literature* (Malden, Mass.: Blackwell, 2004).
Accessible overview of American literature and its social and historical contexts, covering a broad range of genres and periods from Native American oral traditions to contemporary works. Chapter 5, "Negotiating the American Century: American Literature since 1945," examines recent developments such as Postmodernism and multiculturalism.

Gray, "Open Doors, Closed Minds: American Prose Writing at a Time of Crisis," *American Literary History*, 21 (Spring 2009): 128–148.
Identifies narrative techniques and structures—some effective, others not—that writers use to represent contemporary American identity in response to the increasing internationalization of American culture and to events such as 9/11 and the "war on terror." This essay is especially useful for students wishing to identify works responding to 9/11 and its aftermath.

Lee Gutkind, ed., *In Fact: The Best of* Creative Nonfiction (New York: Norton, 2005).
Collection of twenty-five essays originally published in the journal *Creative Nonfiction* (established in 1995). An introductory essay by the editor, "The Creative Nonfiction Police?" explores the controversies surrounding this emerging genre and the differences between fiction and nonfiction.

Josephine G. Hendin, ed., *A Concise Companion to Postwar American Literature and Culture* (Malden, Mass.: Blackwell, 2004).

Useful overviews of many topics in contemporary literature (although some essays, and the first halves of others, cover the pre-1970 period), including drama; Vietnam; Postmodernist fiction; and gay and lesbian, Jewish, African American, Italian American, Irish American, Native American, Hispanic, and Asian American writing. Essays on film and music offer helpful context.

Kathryn Hume, *American Dream, American Nightmare: Fiction since 1960* (Urbana: University of Illinois Press, 2000).
Discusses more than a hundred novels written between 1960 and 2000, the "Generation of the Lost Dream." By "breaking down the divisions among standard categories of race, religion, ethnicity, and gender," Hume identifies "shared core concerns, values, and techniques among seemingly disparate and unconnected writers." She looks at literary considerations of the immigrant experience, liberalism and lost innocence, scientific materialism, spiritual yearning, "tarnished morality," and the fear that American exceptionalism has been lost.

Nicolás Kanellos, ed., *Herencia: The Anthology of Hispanic Literature of the United States* (New York: Oxford University Press, 2002).
Comprehensive anthology spanning colonial times to the present that underscores the diversity of Hispanic literature in the United States through its representation of Chicano/a, Nuyorican, Cuban American, and Latino/a writings. Each section is organized chronologically and also divided by content to highlight the cultural, historical, and political issues that influenced the writers.

J. Gerald Kennedy, ed., *Modern American Short Story Sequences: Composite Fictions and Fictive Communities* (New York: Cambridge University Press, 1995).
Excellent collection of eleven essays, plus the introduction by Kennedy, that discuss the challenges of defining the short story and explore reasons for the increased production and popularity of the form in recent decades. The contributors discuss examples by earlier writers such as Henry James, Jean Toomer, Ernest Hemingway, Richard Wright, William Faulkner, Eudora Welty, J. D. Salinger, and John Cheever but also by more-contemporary writers, including John Updike, Louise Erdrich, and Raymond Carver.

Michael Kowalewski, "Contemporary Regionalism," in *A Companion to the Regional Literatures of America,* edited by Charles L. Crow (Malden, Mass.: Blackwell, 2003), pp. 7–24.
Discusses the mass appeal of literary works with a regional emphasis by writers such as Cormac McCarthy, Annie Proulx, Barbara Kingsolver, and Charles Frazier.

Wendy Lesser, "United States," in *The Oxford Guide to Contemporary Writing,* edited by John Sturrock (New York: Oxford University Press, 1996), pp. 406–431.
Idiosyncratic but stimulating overview of contemporary American literature that defines *contemporary* as 1965 to its publication in 1996 but reaches back to discuss earlier works. Lesser sees crime—ranging from personal ingratitude and ethnic disloyalty to murder—as a central preoccupation of fiction, language as the focus

in drama, and confession as central in poetry and autobiography. She includes discussion of less traditional forms, such as Art Spiegelman's graphic novel *Maus: A Survivor's Tale* (1981, 1986) and New Journalism such as that of Truman Capote, Norman Mailer, and Joan Didion.

Deborah L. Madsen, *Beyond the Borders: American Literature and Post-Colonial Theory* (London: Pluto Press, 2003).
Examines "how America's own imperial history has shaped the literatures that have emerged from within America," with a strong emphasis on issues of identity, multiculturalism, and immigration. Sixteen essays discuss works by Native Americans, Chicano/as, African Americans, Asian Americans, Chinese Americans, Filipino Americans, Hawaiians, Puerto Ricans, and Americans from the Caribbean and Southeast Asia; issues of immigration and assimilation; and comparisons to Canadian literatures.

Robert McRuer, *The Queer Renaissance: Contemporary American Literature and the Reinvention of Lesbian and Gay Identities* (New York: New York University Press, 1997).
Discusses novels, poetry, and plays by openly gay and lesbian writers in the last few decades of the twentieth century, with a focus on intersections between art and activism. The volume includes consideration of works by Audre Lorde, Edmund White, Randall Kenan, Gloria Anzaldúa, Tony Kushner, and Sarah Schulman, among others.

Kenneth Millard, *Contemporary American Fiction: An Introduction to American Fiction since 1970* (New York: Oxford University Press, 2000).
Survey of American fiction since 1970 offering interpretations of novels arranged around several themes including family, gender, the West, consumerism, and technology, among others.

Joyce Carol Oates and Christopher R. Beha, eds., *The Ecco Anthology of Contemporary American Short Fiction* (New York: Ecco/HarperPerennial, 2008).
Forty-eight short stories, most published in the twenty-first century, with a brief but valuable preface in which Oates argues that the contemporary short story is less self-consciously experimental than those of the 1960s and 1970s.

Stacey Michele Olster, *Reminiscence and Re-Creation in Contemporary American Fiction* (New York: Cambridge University Press, 1989).
Traces the influence of historical and political events on American Postmodernist writers, including Thomas Pynchon, John Barth, Robert Coover, and E. L. Doctorow.

Nancy J. Peterson, *Against Amnesia: Contemporary Women Writers and the Crises of Historical Memory* (Philadelphia: University of Pennsylvania Press, 2001).
Examines the ways women writers such as Louise Erdrich and Toni Morrison represent historical—often traumatic—events related to their racial and ethnic backgrounds to counteract what she perceives as the amnesia and nostalgia characterizing mainstream culture.

A. Poulin Jr. and Michael Waters, eds., *Contemporary American Poetry*, eighth edition (Belmont, Cal.: Wadsworth, 2005).
Influential anthology that presents seventy poets and more than five hundred poems published since 1960 and includes photographs, biographical sketches, bibliographies, and an overview essay.

Robert Rebein, *Hicks, Tribes, and Dirty Realists: American Fiction after Postmodernism* (Lexington: University Press of Kentucky, 2001).
Examines a range of Postmodernist techniques and perspectives in the use of realism in American works published since 1980.

Jeanne Campbell Reesman, ed., *Trickster Lives: Culture and Myth in American Fiction* (Athens: University of Georgia Press, 2001).
Excellent collection of essays examining the figure of the trickster in several American cultures, including Native American, Hawaiian, African American, and Latino/a, and in the work of such authors as Mark Twain, Jack London, Toni Morrison, and Louise Erdrich. The essays show that the trickster figure is not bound to any one culture but is a manifestation of a certain way of thinking, of turning things upside down in order to startle us into new knowledge and awareness, that crosses many cultures.

Kathleen Rooney, *Reading with Oprah: The Book Club That Changed America*, second edition (Fayetteville: University of Arkansas Press, 2008).
Thorough history of Oprah's Book Club, offering analysis of the choices and their presentation, and discussion of the book club's role and position in the contemporary blurring of lines between high and popular culture.

A. LaVonne Brown Ruoff and Jerry W. Ward Jr., eds., *Redefining American Literary History* (New York: Modern Language Association of America, 1990).
Emphasizing African American, American Indian, Asian American, and Latino/a literatures, argues for a definition of American literature that takes into account non-European cultures.

Annette J. Saddik, *Contemporary American Drama* (Edinburgh: Edinburgh University Press, 2007).
Focusing on representative plays and the theme of American identity, explores the development of American contemporary theater, placing plays within historical, political, and theoretical contexts. Playwrights discussed include Adrienne Kennedy, Sam Shepard, Tony Kushner, Anna Deavere Smith, Karen Finley, and Will Power.

José David Saldívar, *Border Matters: Remapping American Cultural Studies* (Berkeley: University of California Press, 1997).
Argues for a trans-Latin approach to the study of identity, political struggle, and history as represented in fiction, travel writing, ethnography, memoir, and film by Americans of Latino/a heritage.

Marc Shell, ed., *American Babel: Literatures of the United States from Abnaki to Zuni* (Cambridge, Mass.: Harvard University Press, 2002).

Twenty-five essays tracing Greek, Haitian, Irish Gaelic, Welsh, Spanish, Chinese, and other cultural influences on American literature. While they focus on works from earlier periods, the attention to the diverse and polyglot nature of American literature offers historical and multicultural contexts necessary for interpreting contemporary American literature. This work is for advanced students.

Jeanne Rosier Smith, *Writing Tricksters: Mythic Gambols in American Ethnic Literature* (Berkeley: University of California Press, 1997).
Taking the premise that tricksters provide the "the power to laugh at old worlds, and invent new ones," offers comparative readings of works by Toni Morrison, Louise Erdrich, and Maxine Hong Kingston.

Sandra Stanley, *Other Sisterhoods: Literary Theory and U.S. Women of Color* (Urbana: University of Illinois Press, 1998).
Fifteen essays that examine the literary and theoretical contributions of women writers of color, focusing on the impact of issues such as social construction and identity politics and on the intersections of race/ethnicity, class, gender, and sexuality.

Susan Strehle, *Fiction in the Quantum Universe* (Chapel Hill: University of North Carolina Press, 1992).
Argues that a strain of contemporary American literature has developed out of concepts from quantum physics, in which reality is discontinuous, dynamic, relative, statistical, subjectively seen, indeterminate, and uncertainly known. Naming this fiction "actualism," Strehle uses this framework to read major novels by Thomas Pynchon, Robert Coover, William Gaddis, John Barth, Margaret Atwood, and Donald Barthelme.

Cole Swenson and David St. John, eds., *American Hybrid: A Norton Anthology of New Poetry* (New York: Norton, 2009).
Introduces a wide range of contemporary experimental and hybrid poets.

Sean Kicummah Teuton, *Red Land, Red Power: Grounding Knowledge in the American Indian Novel* (Durham, N.C.: Duke University Press, 2008).
Arguing for a "tribal realist" approach to Native American literature that defines "knowledge" as a product of self-reflexive and communally mediated work engaged with the world.

Lex Williford, ed., *Touchstone Anthology of Contemporary Creative Nonfiction: Work from 1970 to the Present* (New York: Simon & Schuster, 2007).
Based on a survey identifying contemporary nonfiction most read and taught by "teaching writers," including examples of the personal essay, memoir, and journalism.

Williford and Michael Martone, eds., *The Scribner Anthology of Contemporary Short Fiction: 50 North American Stories since 1970*, second edition (New York: Touchstone/Simon & Schuster, 2007).
Notable for the aesthetic and cultural diversity of its selections.

Lois Parkinson Zamora and Wendy B. Faris, eds., *Magical Realism: Theory, History, Community* (Durham, N.C.: Duke University Press, 1995).
Anthology of essays offering a variety of approaches. Taken together, they trace the origins of magical realism from Germany to contemporary literature, demonstrating the international scope of magical realism in works from Europe, Latin America, North America, Africa, the Caribbean, Asia, and Australia.

# Part V
# Glossary

**Bildungsroman**   German word, meaning "novel of education," that has been taken into English. Traditionally the protagonist was a young man learning to make his way in the world, moving from innocence to experience, but in contemporary literature the protagonist is just as likely to be female. Sandra Cisneros's *The House on Mango Street* (1983) is both a bildungsroman and a *künstlerroman* (see below). John Barth's "Lost in the Funhouse" (1968) is a famous parody of the genre.

**Black humor**   Also known as **black comedy** or **dark comedy**. A style of writing prominent in the 1960s and 1970s, especially by writers such as John Barth, Thomas Pynchon, Philip Roth, and Kurt Vonnegut, it draws attention to the absurd, the morbid, and the grotesque. The black humorist attitude is that contemporary life presents so many absurd situations that the only possible response is laughter.

**Bricolage**   Like a collage, a work of art or literature put together through the juxtaposition of various pieces but with the added element that the pieces are found materials that happen to be available; the word is adapted from the French for "do-it-yourself."

**Carnivalesque**   A frequently encountered term in criticism of contemporary American literature. Coined by the literary theorist Mikhail Bakhtin, it refers to the presence of carnival-like activity: fun, play, and games; defiance of authority; humor; chaos; and **heteroglossia** (see below).

**Chicano/Chicana**   A man/woman of Mexican heritage in the United States; the term came into usage in the late 1960s. Prominent Chicano writers include Rudolfo Anaya, Gary Soto, and Dagoberto Gilb; among well-known Chicana authors are Sandra Cisneros, Ana Castillo, and Denise Chávez.

**Chick lit**   A fiction genre that became popular in the late 1990s and early 2000s. Typified by English writer Helen Fielding's novel *Bridget Jones's Diary* (1996), it features single women who struggle with careers and romantic relationships.

**Choreopoem**   A work that integrates dance, music, and poetry so that each element complements the others; it is more than simply poetry set to music with accompanying dance steps. Each performer of a choreopoem may improvise. The term first appeared in the subtitle of Ntozake Shange's *for colored girls who have considered suicide/when the rainbow is enuf: a choreopoem* (1975).

**Code-switching**   Occurs when speakers fluent in more than one language alternate among those languages in speech. The term also refers to the practice of moving between dialect and more-formal language, as between African American vernacular and standard English, in different social settings. Michael Chabon's *The Yiddish Policemen's Union* (2007) code-switches between English and Yiddish.

**Creative nonfiction**   A recently developed genre that employs the techniques of fiction to deal with factual subject matter. Among the forms it may take are memoir, journalism, and essay.

**Defamiliarization**    The process by which literature makes one see the familiar and everyday anew, thereby enhancing one's perceptions. The Russian Formalists coined the term, describing the effect as "making the stone stoney."

**Epistolary**    Adjective referring to a narrative told through letters. Many of the earliest British and American novels were epistolary works; Alice Walker's *The Color Purple* (1982) is a contemporary example.

**Gothic**    Dating back to the eighteenth century, refers to literature that involves the supernatural or the fear that the supernatural is present; the horror is often more psychological than physical. Traditional Gothic works feature haunted houses, ghosts, madness, and doubles. In contemporary examples, such as many works by Joyce Carol Oates, the sense of enclosure and the use of doubles is maintained.

**Graphic novel**    A long form of "sequential art," combining text and drawings to tell a story. Originally designating a narrative that was conceived as a whole from the start, it is now sometimes used to refer to compilations of comic-book narratives. The first important graphic novels were *Batman: The Dark Knight Returns* (1986), by Frank Miller; *Watchmen* (2005), by Alan Moore, Dave Gibbons, and John Higgins; and the two-volume *Maus: A Survivor's Tale* (1986, 1991), by Art Spiegelman, which was based on the author's father's struggles during the Holocaust and was awarded a special Pulitzer Prize in 1992.

**Heteroglossia**    The presence in a text of many voices and perspectives.

**Hip urban novels**    A popular genre of the 1980s featuring young city dwellers negotiating drug-laden and promiscuous lifestyles; Jay McInerney, Bret Easton Ellis, Tama Janowitz, and Donna Tartt are the major authors of these novels. The genre was **parodied** (see below) in 1989 by *Spy* magazine in the book *Spy Notes,* a take-off on *Cliffs Notes.* Cliffs Notes sued Doubleday, the publisher of *Spy Notes,* but lost the case.

**Hispanic**    Derived from the Latin word for "Spain"; refers to people who are from, or whose ancestors are from, Spanish-speaking countries. The term is used by the U.S. Census Bureau and is broader than *Latino,* which refers to people of Latin American origin. Thus, a person from Spain can be described as "Hispanic" but not as "Latino."

**Historical novel**    A novel set in a particular period in the past and frequently involving major events of that period. Historical novels often use actual figures as minor or peripheral characters or as characters who are on stage for a short period, while the main characters are fictional, as in Michael Chabon's *The Amazing Adventures of Kavalier and Clay* (2000). Alternately, they may dramatize events in the life of a historical person, as in T. C. Boyle's *The Road to Wellville* (1993), about Dr. John Harvey Kellogg, sanatorium director and coinventor of cornflakes, and *The Inner Circle* (2004), about the sex researcher Dr. Alfred Kinsey; and Thomas Pynchon's *Mason & Dixon* (1997), about the surveyors.

**Historiographic metafiction**    A term coined by Linda Hutcheon in *A Poetics of Postmodernism: History, Theory, Fiction* (1988) to describe works that are markedly **self-reflexive** (see below), calling attention to their own fictionality, but that also present—seemingly paradoxically—a strong backdrop of historical people and events.

**Hybridity**  A term popularized by postcolonial theory to refer to the merging of cultures that emerges from the contact between an indigenous culture and a colonizing group.

**Intertextuality**  Implicit and explicit relationships between texts that may take a variety of forms, including allusion, **parody** (see below), and **pastiche** (see below). Intertexts may be literary or cultural (for instance, allusions to films or advertising copy). Postmodernist thought sees all texts as referring to other texts, rather than to an external reality. Intertexts illuminate meanings by drawing on the connotations surrounding the text that is alluded to or parodied.

**Irony**  A difference between what is said and what is meant. It is a common stance in Postmodernism, and some scholars argue that it is a fundamental aspect of the Postmodern sensibility.

**Kmart realism**  Sometimes used interchangeably with **minimalism** (see below); a literary mode characterized by spare prose and frequent references to commercial surface details such as brand names, shopping malls, popular songs, movies, and television programs. It typically features working-class characters in bleak environments.

*Künstlerroman*  A specific type of **bildungsroman** (see above) in which the protagonist discovers that his or her destiny is to be an artist or writer.

**MacArthur "Genius" Awards**  The popular name for the MacArthur Fellowships, grants given annually by the John D. and Catherine T. MacArthur Foundation to Americans in any field who "show exceptional merit and promise for continued and enhanced creative work." They provide a generous stipend (currently $500,000), paid in quarterly installments over a period of five years. Recipients are nominated anonymously. Contemporary American writers who have received the award include Thomas Pynchon, Leslie Marmon Silko, Sandra Cisneros, Octavia Butler, Ernest J. Gaines, Edwidge Danticat, David Foster Wallace, and Cormac McCarthy.

**Magical realism**  The presence of the supernatural or inexplicable in an otherwise realistic everyday setting. Although often associated with authors of the Latin American Boom, such as the Colombian writer Gabriel García Márquez, versions appear in much contemporary American literature, including works by Toni Morrison, Gloria Naylor, Louise Erdrich, Tim O'Brien, and Alice Hoffman. The phrase is sometimes written as **magic realism.**

**Manifest Destiny**  The belief held by many white Americans in the nineteenth century that they were ordained by God to expand their sway across the North American continent. This view ignored the presence of American Indians or saw them as destined to die out to make way for Anglo-American civilization.

**Metafiction**  Fiction that takes as a central subject the creation of fiction, often referring to its own strategies in a **self-reflexive** (see below) manner. The strategy consistently reminds the reader that he or she is reading a work of fiction, denying him or her the ability to become "lost in the story" and highlighting questions about the relationship between fiction and reality. Metafiction stretches back through the history of the novel, including appearances in Miguel de Cervantes's *Don Quixote* (1605, 1615) and Laurence Sterne's *The Life and Opinions of Tristram Shandy, Gentleman* (1760–1767), but it has become a prominent aspect of much Postmodern writing. Contemporary examples include most of the work of John Barth and Kurt Vonnegut and Tim O'Brien's *The Things They Carried* (1990).

**Midrash**    An early form of Jewish commentary on or interpretation of a biblical text that explains or clarifies a moral principle or point of law; contemporary forms include new versions or retellings of stories from the Torah. Midrash plays an important role in the poetry of Louise Glück.

**Minimalism**    A style of writing featuring spare prose that focuses on surface details and in which the author refuses to signal to readers how they should feel about characters. The characters are typically of the working class, and the surface details include many popular-culture references. Raymond Carver, Ann Beattie, Bobbie Ann Mason, Grace Paley, and Frederick Barthelme are often classified as minimalists, although Carver disliked the term.

**New Journalism**    A form of nonfiction that arose in the 1960s and 1970s, combining literary techniques and, often, a subjective viewpoint with investigative reporting. Truman Capote, Tom Wolfe, Norman Mailer, Joan Didion, and Hunter S. Thompson are considered practitioners of New Journalism; Thompson called his style "Gonzo Journalism."

**Noble Savage**    A stereotype that sees Native Americans as inherently pure and good but also as simple and primitive. Both the positive and the negative poles of the stereotype fail to recognize American Indians as complex human beings.

**Nuyorican**    A term that blends *New York* and *Puerto Rican* to refer to the culture or people of the Puerto Rican diaspora who have settled in New York City. Esmeralda Santiago and Tato Laviera are Nuyorican writers.

**Parody**    As a noun: an imitation of a preexisting work that ridicules the conventions used in the original. As a verb: to create such a work.

**Pastiche**    A literary or artistic work that imitates the style of an earlier work without intent to ridicule (in contrast to **parody,** above) or that is made up of selections from several other works (also called a **patchwork**).

**Pastoral**    Literary works that depict rural life, often romanticizing it or at least carrying a strong sense of nostalgia. Contemporary environmental literature attempts to revive the pastoral without idealizing it.

**Poetry slam**    A competition in which poets perform their works before an audience, with judges scoring them.

**Prolepsis**    The announcement or revelation, without explanation, of a key event in a narrative before the event actually occurs. The story will often go on for a good while before the circumstances of the event are described, thereby building the context for understanding the event. In *Beloved* (1987) Toni Morrison makes use of prolepsis in her handling of the central event of the novel: Sethe's murder of her child.

**Short-story cycle**   Also referred to as a **short-story sequence, short-story novel,** or **composite novel.** Occupying a space between the novel and the short-story collection, it lacks a single plotline; the individual stories achieve a unity through a recurrent setting, reappearing characters, or thematic similarities.

**Self-reflexive**   Adjective describing a work that deliberately draws attention to its own fictionality or artifice.

**Simulacrum**   An image of an image, with no stable referent or reality underlying the latter. The literary theorist Jean Baudrillard considers it a key element of Postmodernism. Plural: **simulacra.**

**Spanglish**   The mingling of Spanish and English in speech by people who are fluent in both languages and find themselves moving between the two cultures in their everyday lives (see **code-switching,** above).

**Trickster**   A figure in myth or folklore who is neither good nor evil but may be self-serving. Tricksters tend to wreak havoc, turn the standard order upside down, and use magic or deceit to create situations from which readers or observers within the work may gain new knowledge and insights. Sherman Alexie and Michael Chabon use tricksters in their writings.

# Index